'our future is just our parts away.

lcome to the Becker CPA Exam Review! Congratulations on taking the t step to becoming a CPA. As the industry's leading partner in CPA ım preparation, we know you're not just studying for an exam – you are ›paring for your future. To help you get there, Becker CPA Exam Review ıs close as you can get to the real thing. So let's get started.

cess Becker's CPA Exam Review course

g in to your CPA Exam Review course anytime at **cpa.becker.com**. ıtch our orientation video and download the mobile app to access your ıdies on the go. Your progress will automatically sync among all your vices, so you can pick up where you left off. For more on getting started, ,it **becker.com/cpa-review/getting-started**.

ilize the Becker resources

ıke studying more organized with our study planner. With interactive ols to help you determine your ideal study schedule and to recommend ›ur ideal exam-taking time, it's easy to plan your preparation so you're ady when exam day comes. Here are the added benefits of Becker:

- Take advantage of the personalized review sessions at the end of each unit to identify which topics you need to review and strengthen
- Access 1-on-1 academic support from our experienced CPA instructors
- Watch 400+ SkillMaster videos that coach you through task-based simulations
- Improve upon core concepts with the help of more than 1,300 flashcards
- Test your knowledge with our simulated exams – the closest thing you can get to the actual CPA Exam itself

'ou're not in it alone!

or tips, stories and advice, visit our blog at **becker.com/blog**. 'ou can also collaborate with other Becker students studying AUD on our 'acebook study group at **facebook.com/groups/BeckerAUDStudyGroup/**.

Submit your CPA Exam application

It takes time for your CPA Exam application to be approved – so don't wait til the last minute.

Once your CPA Exam application has been processed, your Notice to Schedule will give you a limited window of time to schedule your exam.

Your state board of accountancy sets the amount of time you have, so be sure to check your state's requirements.

Once you schedule your exam, add it to the study planner so we can share tips, strategies and more as your test date approaches.

Becker™

Join the community!

Becker™

ACADEMIC HELP
Click on Contact Academic Support from within the course software at the top at cpa.becker.com

CUSTOMER SERVICE AND TECHNICAL SUPPORT
Call 1-877-CPA-EXAM (outside the U.S. +1-630-472-2213) or contact us at becker.com/cpa-review/cpa-contact

This textbook contains information that was current at the time of printing. Your course software will be updated on a regular basis as the content that is tested on the CPA Exam evolves and as we improve our materials. Note the version reference below and select your replacement textbook under Replacement Products at **becker.com/cpa-replacement-products** to learn if a newer version of this book is available to be ordered.

CPA Exam Review

Auditing

For Exams Scheduled After December 31, 2020

V 3.5

COURSE DEVELOPMENT TEAM

Timothy F. Gearty, CPA, MBA, JD, CGMA	Editor in Chief, Financial/Regulation (Tax) National Editor
Angeline S. Brown, CPA, CGMA	Sr. Director, Product Management
Valerie Funk Anderson, CPA	Sr. Manager, Curriculum
Stephen Bergens, CPA	Manager, Accounting Curriculum
Cheryl Costello, CPA, CGMA	Sr. Specialist, Curriculum
Tom Cox, CPA, CMA	Financial (GASB & NFP) National Editor
Steven J. Levin, JD	Regulation (Law) National Editor
Danita De Jane	Director, Course Development
Anson Miyashiro	Manager, Course Development
Tim Munson	Project Manager, Course Development

CONTRIBUTING EDITORS

Teresa C. Anderson, CPA, CMA, MPA
Katie Barnette, CPA
Jim DeSimpelare, CPA, MBA
Tara Z. Fisher, CPA
Melisa F. Galasso, CPA
R. Thomas Godwin, CPA, CGMA
Holly Hawk, CPA, CGMA
Liliana Hickman-Riggs, CPA, CMA, CIA, CFE, CITP, CFF, CGMA, FCPA, MS
Patrice W. Johnson, CPA
Julie D. McGinty, CPA
Sandra McGuire, CPA, MBA
Stephanie Morris, CPA, MAcc
Michelle Moshe, CPA, DipIFR
Peter Olinto, JD, CPA
Sandra Owen, JD, MBA, CPA
Michelle M. Pace, CPA
Michael Potenza, CPA, JD
Jennifer J. Rivers, CPA
Josh Rosenberg, MBA, CPA, CFA, CFP
Jonathan R. Rubin, CPA, MBA
Michael Rybak, CPA, CFA
Denise M. Stefano, CPA, CGMA, MBA
Elizabeth Lester Walsh, CPA, CITP

ISBN: 978-1-950713-18-9

Printed in the United States of America.

AUDITING

Table of Contents

AUDITING 4: *Performing Further Procedures, Forming Conclusions, and Communications*

AUDITING 5: *Integrated Audits, Attestation Engagements, Compliance, and Government Audits*

AUDITING 6: *Accounting and Review Service Engagements, Interim Reviews, and Ethics and Professional Responsibilities*

Introduction

AUD

NOTES

Auditing and Attestation (AUD) Overview

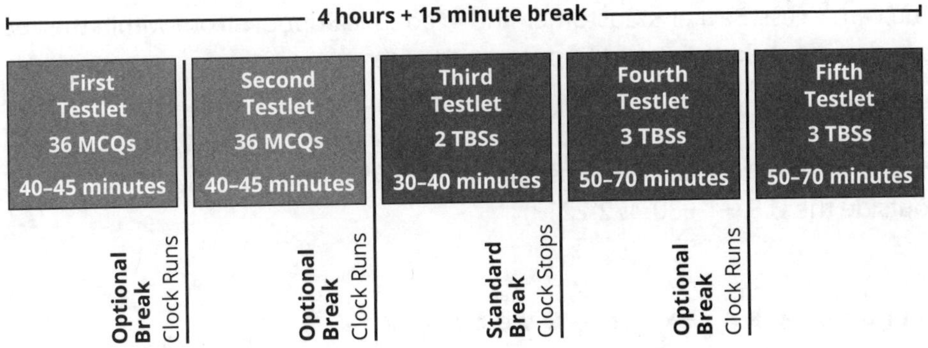

AUD Exam—Summary Blueprint

Content Area Allocation	Weight
Ethics, Professional Responsibilities, and General Principles	15–25%
Assessing Risk and Developing a Planned Response	20–30%
Performing Further Procedures and Obtaining Evidence	30–40%
Forming Conclusions and Reporting	15–25%
Skill Allocation	**Weight**
Evaluation	5–15%
Analysis	15–25%
Application	30–40%
Remembering and Understanding	30–40%

The complete AUD exam blueprint appears in the back of the book.

Becker's CPA Exam Review—Course Introduction

Becker Professional Education's CPA Exam Review products were developed with you, the candidate, in mind. To that end we have developed a series of tools designed to tap all of your learning and retention capabilities. The Becker lectures, comprehensive texts, and course software are designed to be fully integrated to give you the best chance of passing the CPA Exam.

Passing the CPA Exam is difficult, but the professional rewards a CPA enjoys make this a worthwhile challenge. We created our CPA Exam Review after evaluating the needs of CPA candidates and analyzing the CPA Exam over the years. Our course materials comprehensively present topics you must know to pass the examination, teaching you the most effective tactics for learning the material.

Becker Customer and Academic Support

You can access Becker's Customer and Academic Support from within the course software by clicking Contact Support at the top at:

cpa.becker.com

You can also access customer service and technical support by calling 1-877-CPA-EXAM (outside the U.S. +1-630-472-2213).

The Uniform CPA Exam—Overview

Exam Sections

The CPA Examination consists of four sections:

Financial Accounting and Reporting

The *Financial* section consists of a four-hour exam covering financial accounting and reporting for commercial entities under U.S. GAAP, governmental accounting, not-for-profit accounting, and the differences between IFRS and U.S. GAAP.

Auditing and Attestation

The *Auditing* section consists of a four-hour exam. This section covers all topics related to auditing, including audit reports and procedures, generally accepted auditing standards, attestation and other engagements, and government auditing.

Regulation

The *Regulation* section consists of a four-hour exam, combining topics from business law and federal taxation, including the taxation of property transactions, individuals, and entities.

Business Environment and Concepts

The *Business* section consists of a four-hour exam covering general business topics, such as corporate governance, economics, financial management, information technology, and operations management, including managerial accounting.

Question Formats

The chart below illustrates the question format breakdown by exam section.

	Multiple-Choice Questions		Task-Based Simulations or Written Communication Tasks	
Section	*Percentage*	*Number*	*Percentage*	*Number*
Financial	50%	66	50%	8 TBSs
Auditing	50%	72	50%	8 TBSs
Regulation	50%	76	50%	8 TBSs
Business	50%	62	50%	4 TBSs/3 WC

Each exam will contain testlets. A testlet is either a series of multiple-choice questions, a set of task-based simulations, or a set of written communications. For example, the Auditing examination will contain five testlets. The first two testlets will be multiple-choice questions and the third, fourth, and fifth testlets will contain task-based simulations. Each testlet must be finished and submitted before continuing to the next testlet. Candidates cannot go back to view a previously completed testlet or go forward to view a subsequent testlet before closing and submitting the earlier testlet. Our mock exams contain these types of restrictions so that you can familiarize yourself with the functionality of the CPA Exam.

Exam Schedule

Beginning July 1, 2020, in most states and jurisdictions the computer-based CPA Exam moves to continuous testing, which gives candidates the ability to take the exam year-round, without restriction, other than waiting to receive scores from prior attempts of the same section or when there is a major change to the exam. Candidates can schedule an exam date directly with Prometric (www.prometric.com/cpa) after receiving a notice to schedule.

Eligibility and Application Requirements

Each state sets its own rules of eligibility for the examination. Please visit www.becker.com/state as soon as possible to determine your eligibility to sit for the exam.

Application Deadlines

With the computer-based exam format, set application deadlines generally do not exist. You should apply as early as possible to ensure that you are able to schedule your desired exam dates. Each state has different application requirements and procedures, so be sure to gain a thorough understanding of the application process for your state.

Grading System

You must pass all four parts of the examination to earn certification as a CPA. You must score 75 or better on a part to receive a passing grade and you must pass all four exams in 18 months or you will lose credit for the earliest exam that you passed.

NOTES

AUD

1

Audit Reports

Module

NOTES

MODULE

1 Professional Standards

1 Professional Standards

The Auditing and Attestation section tests audits of issuers, nonissuers, governmental entities, not-for-profit entities, and employee benefit plans. In addition to audits, this section also tests other types of engagements that an accountant may be called upon to perform, such as accounting and review service engagements and attestation and assurance engagements. Each engagement requires the accountant to follow the applicable ethical guideline(s) and standard(s) for the engagement. For example, an audit engagement requires the auditor to perform the audit in accordance with generally accepted auditing standards (GAAS). These engagements and applicable standards will be covered in more detail in later modules.

Below is an overview of standards and guidelines that will be tested in this section:

Professional Standards and Guidelines

Standard/ Guideline	*Section Reference*	*Standard-Setting Body*	*Description*	*Applies to:*
Audits				
Statements on Auditing Standards (SAS)	AU-C	AICPA Auditing Standards Board	SAS provide generally accepted auditing standards for the audits of **nonissuers**. In addition, SAS provide guidance for other services, such as review of interim financial information and letters to underwriters.	• Audits of annual historical financial statements: nonissuers • Special reports: nonissuers • Interim financial statements (where the annual financial statements have been audited): nonissuers
Public Company Accounting Oversight Board Auditing Standards (PCAOB AS)	PCAOB AS	Public Company Accounting Oversight Board	PCAOB AS provide generally accepted auditing standards for the audits of **issuers**. In addition, PCAOB AS provide guidance for other services, such as review of interim financial information and letters to underwriters.	• Audits of annual historical financial statements: issuers • Special reports: issuers • Interim financial statements: issuers
Generally Accepted Government Auditing Standards (GAGAS)	GAGAS	Governmental Accountability Office	GAGAS provide guidance for audits of **government** organizations, programs, activities, and of entities that receive government funds.	Financial or performance audits of government organizations, programs, activities, and of entities that receive government funds.

Standard/ Guideline	*Section Reference*	*Standard-Setting Body*	*Description*	*Applies to:*
Other Engagements				
Statements on Standards for Attestation Engagements (SSAE)	AT-C	AICPA	SSAE provide guidance for attestation engagements.	Examination, a review, or agreed-upon procedures report on a subject matter, or an assertion about a subject matter, that is the responsibility of another party.
Statements on Standards for Accounting and Review Services (SSARS)	AR-C	AICPA Accounting and Review Services Committee	SSARS provide guidance for **unaudited** financial statements or unaudited financial information of **nonissuers**.	• Preparation, compilation, and reviews of historical financial statements: nonissuers • Preparation or compilation of pro forma financial information and forecasts: nonissuers
Guidelines				
Code of Professional Conduct	ET	AICPA	The AICPA Code of Professional Conduct provides **members** with guidelines for **behavior** in the conduct of their professional affairs. In addition, it provides assurance to the public that the profession intends to maintain high standards and to enforce compliance with these standards by its members.	Members of the AICPA
Statements on Quality Control Standards (SQCS)	QC	AICPA	SQCS provides guidance to **CPA firms** about a quality control system. A quality control system consists of policies and procedures designed, implemented, and maintained to ensure that the firm complies with professional standards and appropriate legal and regulatory requirements, and that any reports issued are appropriate in the circumstances.	CPA firms providing auditing, attestation, and accounting and review services.

2 Auditing Guidance: The GAAS Hierarchy

There are three levels of audit guidance:

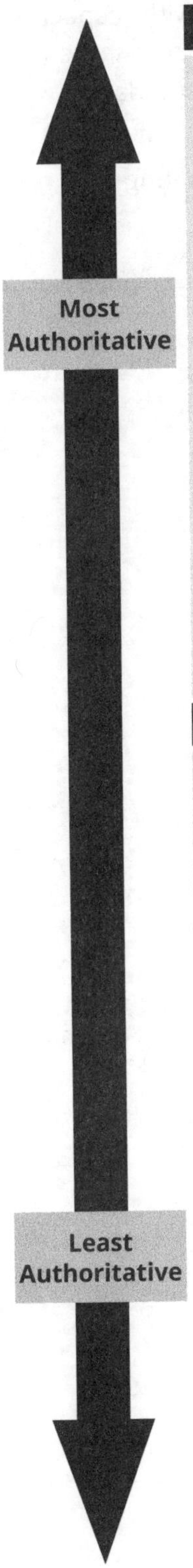

1. SAS (Nonissuers) and PCAOB AS (Issuers)

The auditor should:

- Use professional judgment in applying the SAS or PCAOB AS to a particular engagement.
- Be prepared to justify any departures from presumptively mandatory requirements.

Specific language is used within the standards to clarify the auditor's level of responsibility:

- **"Must"** or **"is required"** indicates an unconditional requirement, which must be followed in all cases in which the requirement is relevant.
- **"Should"** indicates a presumptively mandatory requirement, which must be followed in all cases in which the requirement is relevant, except in rare circumstances when departure from the requirement is permitted if there is appropriate justification, performance of sufficient alternative procedures, and thorough documentation.
- **"May," "might,"** and **"could"** indicate explanatory material that does not impose a professional requirement for performance.

2. Interpretive Publications

Interpretive publications are recommendations regarding how SASs should be applied in specific situations. They are not considered to be auditing standards.

The auditor should:

- Consider the guidance provided by these publications in performing an audit.
- Be able to explain any departures, and how compliance with standards was otherwise achieved.

Examples include: Auditing interpretations of GAAS, exhibits to GAAS, auditing guidance provide in AICPA Audit and Accounting Guides, and AICPA Auditing Statements of Position (SOP).

3. Other Auditing Publications

Other auditing publications have no authoritative status but may be helpful to the auditor.

The auditor should:

- Consider the guidance provided by these publications in performing an audit.
- Be able to explain any departures, and how compliance with standards was otherwise achieved.

Examples include: Auditing articles in the Journal of Accountancy (or other professional journal), auditing articles in the AICPA CPA Letter, continuing professional education materials, textbooks, and other auditing publications.

Question 1 **MCQ-02298**

Which of the following provides the most authoritative guidance for the auditor of a nonissuer?

a. An AICPA audit and accounting guide that provides specific guidance with respect to the accounting practices in the client's industry.

b. A Journal of Accountancy article discussing implementation of a new standard.

c. General guidance provided by a Statement on Auditing Standards.

d. Specific guidance provided by an interpretation of a Statement on Auditing Standards.

MODULE

2 Audit Engagements

1 Audit Process Overview

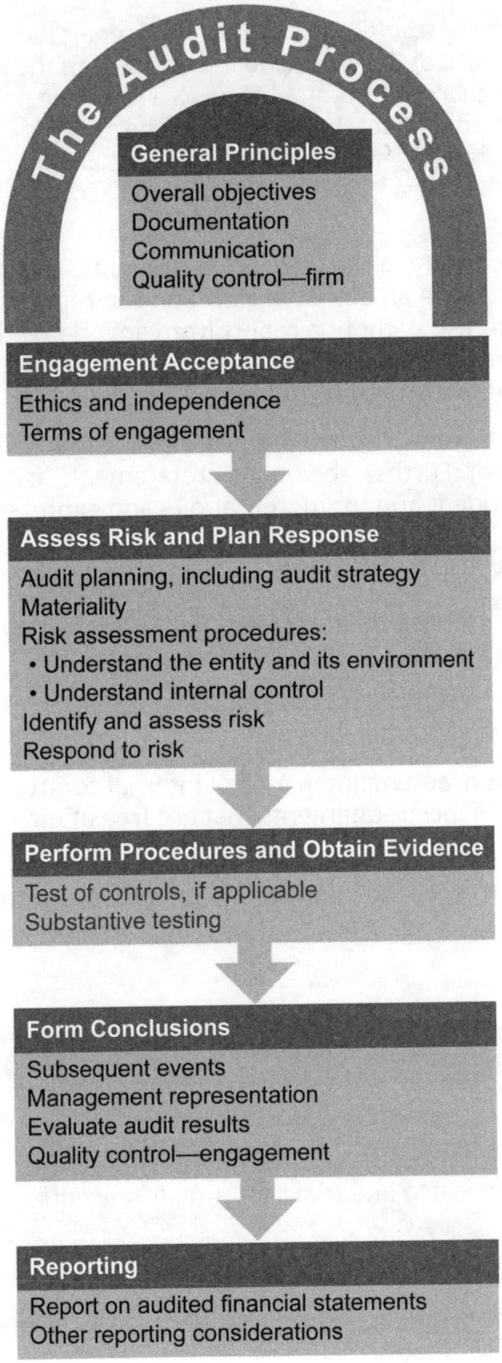

2 The Independent Audit Function: The Basics

The purpose of an audit is to provide financial statement users with an opinion on whether the financial statements are presented fairly, in all material respects, in accordance with the *applicable financial reporting framework*.

Pass Key

The *applicable financial reporting framework* is the financial reporting framework that is acceptable in view of the nature of the entity and the objective of the financial statements, or that is required by law or regulation. Acceptable financial reporting frameworks include general purpose frameworks designed to meet the needs of a wide range of users (e.g., U.S. GAAP and International Financial Reporting Standards [*IFRSs*]), and special purpose frameworks.

The auditor's report gives credibility to the financial statements. The auditors, as a group independent of management, have an objective view and can report on a company's activities without bias or conflict of interest. Without a report from an independent auditor, a company's financial statements would be meaningless, because the public would have little faith in financial statements issued by the inherently biased company.

The financial statements of an enterprise are prepared by the management of the enterprise, not by the independent auditor. Further, the financial statements are the product and property of the enterprise; the independent auditor merely audits and expresses an opinion on them.

2.1 Management Responsibilities

An audit is conducted on the premise that management and, when appropriate, those charged with governance are responsible for:

1. the preparation and fair presentation of the financial statements in accordance with the applicable financial reporting framework;
2. the design, implementation, and maintenance of internal control relevant to the preparation and fair presentation of financial statements that are free of material misstatement due to error or fraud; and
3. providing the auditor with access to information and persons within the entity needed to complete the audit.

Pass Key

The preparation and fair presentation of the financial statements requires:

1. identification of the applicable financial reporting framework;
2. preparation and fair presentation of the financial statements in accordance with the framework; and
3. inclusion of an adequate description of the framework in the financial statements.

2.2 Auditor Responsibilities

The auditor is responsible for expressing an opinion on the financial statements based on the audit. The auditor is also responsible for:

1. maintaining professional skepticism;
2. complying with relevant ethical requirements;
3. exercising professional judgment throughout the planning and performance of the audit;
4. obtaining sufficient appropriate audit evidence; and
5. complying with generally accepted auditing standards (GAAS).

2.2.1 Professional Skepticism

The auditor should plan and perform the audit with professional skepticism. Professional skepticism is the recognition that circumstances may exist that cause the financial statements to be materially misstated. Professional skepticism is necessary to the critical assessment of audit evidence. Auditors should be alert for:

- Audit evidence that contradicts other audit evidence obtained.
- Information that calls into question the reliability of documents and responses to inquiries that may be used as audit evidence.
- Conditions that indicate possible fraud.
- Circumstances that suggest the need for audit procedures in addition to those required by GAAS.

Pass Key

The auditor should neither assume that management is dishonest nor assume unquestioned honesty. A belief that management is honest and has integrity does not relieve the auditor of the need to maintain professional skepticism or allow the auditor to be satisfied with less than persuasive evidence.

2.2.2 Impediments to Acting With Professional Skepticism

An auditor should act with professional skepticism throughout the audit. However, auditors often feel challenged to meet this requirement because of impediments to applying professional skepticism during an audit. Examples of impediments include:

- Unconscious human bias, which may cause the auditor to evaluate and recall information that favors the interest of the client over the interest of the investor. This may be facilitated by incentives and pressures to maintain and build client relationships, provide an unmodified (unqualified) opinion, keep audit costs low, or cross-sell other services.
- Development of an inappropriate level of trust or confidence in management, which may result in the auditor not taking as questioning a stance as needed.
- Pressure to avoid potential negative interactions with, or consequences to, individuals whom auditors know (e.g., management) instead of representing the interest of investors.

- Scheduling and workload demands, which may result in auditors making shortcuts in judgment, such as seeking audit evidence that is easier to obtain rather than evidence that is more reliable and relevant, or giving more weight to supporting evidence without considering contrary evidence.

2.2.3 Ethical Requirements

The auditor should comply with ethical requirements related to financial statement audit engagements, including *independence in both fact and appearance.* Ethical requirements include the AICPA Code of Professional Conduct and the rules of the state boards of accountancy and applicable regulatory agencies that are more restrictive.

Pass Key

The auditor must be independent of an entity when performing an engagement in accordance with GAAS unless: a) GAAS provides otherwise, or b) the auditor is required by law or regulation to accept the engagement and report on the financial statements.

2.2.4 Professional Judgment

The auditor should exercise professional judgment in planning and performing an audit. Professional judgment is necessary because an audit requires interpretation of ethical requirements and GAAS, as well as informed decisions based on the application of knowledge and experience.

In an audit, professional judgment is necessary when making decisions about:

- Materiality
- Audit risk
- The nature, extent, and timing of audit procedures
- Evaluating whether sufficient, appropriate evidence has been obtained
- Evaluating management's judgments in applying the applicable financial reporting framework
- Drawing conclusions based on the audit evidence obtained

2.2.5 Sufficient Appropriate Audit Evidence and Audit Risk

To obtain reasonable assurance, the auditor should obtain sufficient appropriate audit evidence to reduce audit risk to an acceptably low level and thereby enable the auditor to draw reasonable conclusions on which to base the auditor's opinion.

2.2.6 Compliance With GAAS

The auditor should not represent compliance with GAAS in the auditor's report unless the auditor has complied with all GAAS relevant to the audit. If the objective of a relevant GAAS section cannot be achieved, the auditor should consider whether this prevents the auditor from achieving the overall objectives of the auditor and thereby requires the auditor, in accordance with GAAS, to modify the auditor's opinion or withdraw from the engagement.

In certain audit engagements, the auditor may be required to comply with other auditing requirements in addition to GAAS. GAAS do not override laws or regulations that govern an audit of financial statements. The auditor may conduct the audit in accordance with both GAAS and:

- auditing standards issued by the PCAOB;
- International Standards on Auditing (ISAs);
- government auditing standards (GAGAS); or
- auditing standards of a specific jurisdiction or country.

2.3 Reasonable Assurance and Inherent Limitations of an Audit

In order to express an opinion, the auditor obtains reasonable assurance about whether the financial statements are free from material misstatement, whether due to error or fraud.

Reasonable assurance is a high, but not absolute, level of assurance. In order to obtain reasonable assurance, the auditor must:

1. plan the work and properly supervise any assistants;
2. determine and apply appropriate materiality levels;
3. identify and assess risks of material misstatement, whether due to fraud or error; and
4. obtain sufficient appropriate audit evidence.

The auditor is unable to obtain absolute assurance that the financial statements are free from material misstatement because of the following inherent limitations:

- **The Nature of Financial Reporting:** Some financial statement items are subject to an inherent level of variability because they involve judgment by management or because they involve subjective decisions or assessments or a degree of uncertainty (e.g., accounting estimates).
- **The Nature of Audit Procedures:** There are practical and legal limits on an auditor's ability to obtain audit evidence, including:
    - The possibility that management or others may not provide, intentionally or unintentionally, the complete information that is needed for the preparation and presentation of the financial statements or that is requested by the auditor.
    - Fraud may be concealed in such a way that it is difficult to detect with audit procedures.
    - An audit is neither an investigation into a wrongdoing nor does the auditor have specific legal powers.
- **Timeliness of Financial Reporting and the Balance Between Cost and Benefit:** There is an expectation by users of financial statements that the auditor will form an opinion on the financial statements within a reasonable period of time and will achieve a balance between benefit and cost, recognizing that it is impracticable to address all information that may exist. Therefore, it is necessary for the auditor to:
    - plan the audit so that it is performed effectively;
    - direct efforts to areas most expected to contain risks of material misstatement; and
    - use testing and other means of examining populations for misstatement.

3 Determine the Nature and Scope of the Engagement

The following should be considered as the auditor, the audit committee, and management determine the appropriate nature and scope of the engagement:

- An auditor may be hired to perform an audit for a single period or multiple periods.
- An audit may be on the complete financial statement; single financial statement; or specific elements, accounts, or items of a financial statement.
- Many audit firms are hired to perform tax services in addition to audit services.

3.1 Nonissuers

When auditing nonissuers, the auditor must determine if an audit is the most appropriate engagement, or whether a review, compilation, or preparation may be more appropriate. If an audit is needed, nonissuers have the choice of:

- a financial statement audit only (where one opinion is rendered on the fairness of the financial statements); or
- an integrated audit (where two opinions are rendered: one opinion on the fairness of the financial statements and one opinion on the operating effectiveness of internal controls over financial reporting).

3.2 Issuers

When auditing issuers, the auditor must perform an integrated audit of the client's financial statements and internal controls over financial reporting (covered later).

4 Overall Objectives of Audit Engagements

4.1 Objectives of the Financial Statement Audit

The overall objectives of the auditor when conducting a financial statement audit (which apply to audits of issuers, nonissuers, and governmental entities) are:

1. To obtain reasonable assurance about whether the financial statements as a whole are free from material misstatement, whether due to error or fraud, which enables the auditor to express an opinion on whether the financial statements are presented fairly, in all material respects, in accordance with an applicable financial reporting framework; and
2. To report on the financial statements and communicate as required by GAAS based on the auditor's findings.

4.2 Objectives of the Audit of Internal Control Over Financial Reporting

As mentioned previously, issuers are required to have an integrated audit of financial statements and internal control over financial reporting. In some cases, nonissuers and governmental entities may also have an audit of internal control over financial reporting. The overall objectives of the auditor when conducting an audit of internal over financial reporting are:

1. Express an opinion on the effectiveness of the company's internal control over financial reporting; and
2. Plan and perform the audit to obtain appropriate evidence that is sufficient to obtain reasonable assurance about whether material weaknesses exist as of the date specified in management's assessment.

Audits of internal control over financial reporting must be integrated with an audit of the financial statements.

Question 1 **MCQ-02820**

Which of the following is *not* an example of the application of professional skepticism?

- **a.** Designing additional auditing procedures to obtain more reliable evidence in support of a particular financial statement assertion.
- **b.** Obtaining corroboration of management's explanations through consultation with a specialist.
- **c.** Inquiring of prior year engagement personnel regarding their assessment of management's honesty and integrity.
- **d.** Using third-party confirmations to provide support for management's representations.

NOTES

MODULE

3 Forming an Audit Opinion

AUD 1

1 Forming an Opinion on the Financial Statements

The auditor should form an opinion on whether the financial statements are presented fairly, in all material respects, in accordance with the applicable financial reporting framework.

In order to form that opinion, the auditor should take into account the following:

1. Whether sufficient appropriate audit evidence was obtained (as required by GAAS); and
2. Whether the financial statements are prepared, in all material respects, in accordance with the requirements of the applicable financial reporting framework (i.e., GAAP).

Financial statements generally mean a complete set of general-purpose financial statements, including the related notes. The applicable financial reporting framework determines the form and content of a complete set of financial statements. For example, under U.S. GAAP a complete set of financial statements includes a balance sheet, a statement of income (or comprehensive income), a statement of changes in equity, a cash flow statement, and related notes.

When forming the opinion, the auditor should evaluate whether, based on the applicable financial reporting framework:

- The financial statements adequately disclose the significant accounting policies selected and applied, including a description of the applicable financial reporting framework.
- The accounting policies selected and applied are consistent with the applicable financial reporting framework and are appropriate.
- The accounting estimates made by management are reasonable.
- The information presented in the financial statements is relevant, reliable, comparable, and understandable.
- The financial statements provide adequate disclosures to enable the intended users to understand the effect of material transactions and events on the information conveyed in the financial statements.
- The terminology used in the financial statements, including the title of each financial statement, is appropriate.
- The overall structure and content of the financial statements is fairly presented.
- The financial statements, including the related notes, represent the underlying transactions and events in a manner that achieves fair presentation.

Pass Key

The auditor refers to generally acceptable auditing standards (GAAS) for guidelines on how to perform the audit (e.g., inventory count should be observed by the auditor).

The auditor refers to the financial reporting framework (for example, U.S. GAAP) to evaluate whether the transactions are recorded and reported fairly in the financial statements (e.g., land should not be depreciated).

2 Types of Opinions

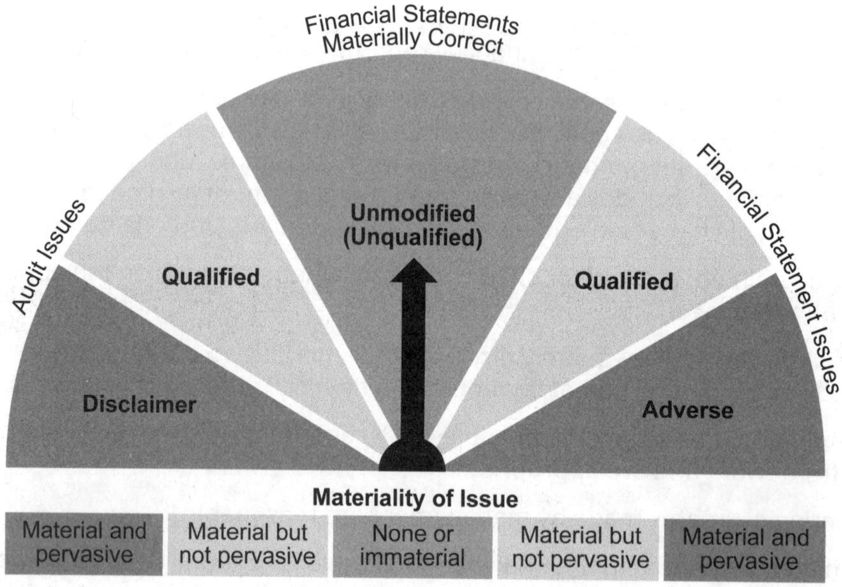

2.1 Unmodified (Unqualified) Opinion

An unmodified (unqualified) opinion states that the financial statements present fairly, in all material respects, the financial position, results of operations, and cash flows of the entity in conformity with the applicable financial reporting framework. Note that *unmodified* is the term used for nonissuers and *unqualified* is the term used for issuers.

In certain circumstances, the auditor may determine that it is necessary to add additional communications to the auditor's report without modifying the auditor's opinion. This is done using emphasis-of-matter, other-matter, and explanatory paragraphs. Nonissuers use the terms *emphasis-of-matter* and *other-matter*, and issuers use the term *explanatory*.

2.2 Modifications to the Auditor's Opinion

The auditor's report should be modified when:

1. the auditor concludes that the financial statements as a whole are materially misstated (financial statement issue); or
2. the auditor is unable to obtain sufficient appropriate audit evidence to conclude that the financial statements as a whole are free from material misstatement (audit issue).

2.2.1 Types of Modified Opinions

There are three types of modified opinions: The qualified opinion, the adverse opinion, and the disclaimer of opinion.

- **Qualified Opinion:** A qualified opinion states that except for the effects of the matter(s) to which the qualification relates, the financial statements present fairly, in all material respects, the financial position, results of operations, and cash flows of the entity in conformity with the applicable financial reporting framework.
- **Adverse Opinion:** An adverse opinion states that the financial statements do not present fairly the financial position, results of operations, or cash flows of the entity in conformity with the applicable financial reporting framework.
- **Disclaimer of Opinion:** A disclaimer of opinion states that the auditor does not express an opinion on the financial statements.

Pass Key

When the auditor expresses an adverse opinion or a disclaimer of opinion on the complete financial statements (i.e., balance sheet, statement of income, statement of changes in equity, statement of cash flows, and the related notes), the auditor's report should not also include an unmodified (unqualified) opinion on a single financial statement (e.g., the statement of cash flows) or one or more specific elements, accounts, or items of a financial statement. Issuing such an unmodified (unqualified) opinion in these circumstances would contradict the adverse opinion or the disclaimer of opinion on the complete financial statements.

2.2.2 Brief Summary of When to Use Different Opinions

The chart below summarizes when to use different opinions.

Materiality of Problem	Financial Statements Are Materially Misstated (Financial Statement Issues)	Inability to Obtain Sufficient Appropriate Audit Evidence (Audit Issues)
None or immaterial	Unmodified (unqualified)	Unmodified (unqualified)
Material but not pervasive	Qualified opinion	Qualified opinion
Material and pervasive	Adverse opinion	Disclaimer of opinion

2.2.3 Definition of Pervasive

Pervasive effects on the financial statements are those which in the auditor's professional judgment:

- are not confined to specific elements, accounts, or items of the financial statements;
- if so confined, represent a substantial proportion of the financial statements; or
- are disclosures fundamental to the users' understanding of the financial statements.

Question 1 **MCQ-02539**

An auditor of a nonissuer concludes that a client's illegal act, which has a material effect on the financial statements, has not been properly accounted for or disclosed. Depending on the pervasiveness of the effect on the financial statements, the auditor should express either a (an):

a. Adverse opinion or a disclaimer of opinion.

b. Qualified opinion or an adverse opinion.

c. Disclaimer of opinion or an unmodified opinion with an emphasis-of-matter paragraph.

d. Unmodified opinion with an other-matter paragraph or a qualified opinion.

MODULE

4 Unmodified (Unqualified) Opinion

AUD 1

1 Unmodified Audit Opinion (Nonissuers)

The auditor of a nonissuer should express an unmodified opinion when the auditor concludes that the financial statements are presented fairly, in all material respects, in accordance with the applicable financial reporting framework. The auditor's report should be in writing. Note that nonissuers use the term *unmodified* and issuers use the term *unqualified*.

1.1 Contents of the Audit Report

The basic elements of the unmodified audit opinion are the following:

Unmodified Opinion: Nonissuer	
Title	"Independent" (auditor's report) should be included in the report title.
Addressee	The report is addressed as required by the circumstances of the engagement.
Introductory Paragraph	The introductory paragraph should: • identify the entity whose financial statements have been audited; • state that the financial statements have been audited; • identify the title of each financial statement; and • specify the date(s) or period(s) covered by each financial statement.
Management's Responsibility Section	The auditor's report should include a section with the heading "**Management's Responsibility** for the Financial Statements" that includes: • an explanation that management is responsible for the preparation and fair presentation of the financial statements in accordance with the applicable financial reporting framework; and • a statement that this responsibility includes the **design**, **implementation**, and **maintenance** of internal control relevant to the preparation and fair presentation of financial statements that are free from material misstatement, whether due to fraud or error.
Auditor's Responsibility Section	The auditor's report should include a section with the heading "Auditor's **Responsibility**" that includes: • A statement that the responsibility of the auditor is to **express** an opinion on the financial statements based on the audit. • A statement that the audit was conducted in accordance with auditing standards generally accepted in the United States of America. • A statement that those standards require that the auditor **plan** and perform the audit to obtain reasonable assurance about whether the financial statements are free from material misstatement. • A description of the audit that states: — An audit involves **performing** procedures to **obtain** audit evidence about the amounts and disclosures in the financial statements. — The procedures selected depend on the auditor's judgment, including the assessment of the **risks** of material misstatement of the financial statements, whether due to fraud or error.

Auditor's Responsibility Section (continued)	— In making those risk assessments, the auditor considers **internal control** relevant to the entity's preparation and fair presentation of the financial **statements** in order to design audit procedures that are appropriate in the circumstances, *but not for the purpose of expressing an opinion on the effectiveness of the entity's internal* ***control****, and accordingly, no such opinion is expressed*. (The italicized portion of this statement should be omitted if the auditor does have a responsibility to express an opinion on the effectiveness of internal control in conjunction with the audit of financial statements.) — An audit includes evaluating the appropriateness of the accounting policies used and the **reasonableness** of significant **accounting** estimates made by **management**, as well as **evaluating** the overall presentation of the financial statements. • A statement whether the auditor believes that the audit evidence obtained is sufficient and appropriate to provide a basis for the auditor's opinion.
Auditor's Opinion	The auditor's report should include a section with the title "Opinion" that includes: • A statement that the financial statements present fairly, in all material respects, the financial position of the entity as of the balance sheet date and the results of operations and its cash flows for the period then ended, in accordance with the applicable financial reporting framework. • Identification of the applicable financial reporting framework and its origin.
Other Reporting Responsibilities	If the auditor addresses other reporting responsibilities in the auditor's report in addition to GAAS, these other reporting responsibilities should be addressed in a separate section of the auditor's report subtitled "Report on Other Legal and Regulatory Responsibilities," or otherwise as appropriate. If the audit report contains a separate section on other reporting responsibilities, the other sections of the audit report already described should be under the subtitle "Report on the Financial Statements."
Signature of the Auditor	The auditor's report should include the manual or printed signature of the auditor's firm.
Auditor's Address	The auditor's report should name the city and state (or country) in which the auditor practices.
Date of the Auditor's Report	The auditor's report should be dated no earlier than the date on which the auditor has obtained sufficient appropriate audit evidence on which to base the auditor's opinion on the financial statements, including evidence that: • the audit documentation has been reviewed; • all the financial statements, including the related notes, have been prepared; and • management has asserted that it has taken responsibility for those financial statements.

Pass Key

The auditor's report date shows the final date of auditor responsibility. For comparative financial statements, the audit report date for the most recent audit should be used.

1.1.1 Sample Report: Unmodified Opinion (Nonissuer)

Independent Auditor's Report

[Appropriate Addressee]

Report on the Financial Statements[1]

We have audited the accompanying financial statements of ABC Company, which comprise the balance sheet as of December 31, 20X1, and the related statements of income, changes in stockholders' equity, and cash flows for the year then ended, and the related notes to the financial statements.

Management's Responsibility for the Financial Statements

Management is **responsible** for the preparation and fair presentation of these financial statements in accordance with accounting principles generally accepted in the United States of America; this includes the **design**, **implementation**, and **maintenance** of internal control relevant to the preparation and fair presentation of financial statements that are free from material misstatement whether due to fraud or error.

Auditor's Responsibility

Our **responsibility** is to **express** an opinion on these financial statements based on our audit. We conducted our audit in accordance with auditing standards generally accepted in the United States of America. Those standards require that we **plan** and perform the audit to obtain reasonable assurance about whether the financial statements are free from material misstatement.

An audit involves **performing** procedures to **obtain** audit evidence about the amounts and disclosures in the financial statements. The procedures selected depend on the auditor's judgment, including the assessment of the **risks** of material misstatement of the financial statements, whether due to fraud or error. In making those risk assessments, the auditor considers **internal control** relevant to the entity's preparation and fair presentation of the financial **statements** in order to design audit procedures that are appropriate in the circumstances, but not for the purpose of expressing an opinion on the effectiveness of the entity's internal **control**. Accordingly, we express no such opinion. An audit also includes evaluating the appropriateness of accounting policies used and the **reasonableness** of significant **accounting** estimates made by **management,** as well as **evaluating** the overall presentation of the financial statements.

We believe that the audit evidence we have obtained is sufficient and appropriate to provide a basis for our audit opinion.

Opinion

In our opinion, the financial statements referred to above present fairly, in all material respects, the financial position of ABC Company as of December 31, 20X1, and the results of its operations and its cash flows for the year then ended in accordance with accounting principles generally accepted in the United States of America.

Report on Other Legal and Regulatory Requirements

[Form and content of this section of the auditor's report will vary depending on the nature of the auditor's other reporting responsibilities.]

[Auditor's signature]
[Auditor's city and state]
[Date of the auditor's report]

[1] "Report on the Financial Statements" is unnecessary in circumstances when the second subtitle, "Report on Legal and Regulatory Requirements," is not used.

1.2 Reference to Auditing Standards in the Auditor's Report

1.2.1 Audits in Accordance With Two Sets of Standards

If the audit was conducted in accordance with two sets of auditing standards in their entirety, the auditor may indicate that the audit was conducted in accordance with another set of auditing standards (e.g., International Standards on Auditing or government auditing standards). Additional language should be added to the Auditor's Responsibility paragraph to describe this situation:

> Our responsibility is to express an opinion on these financial statements based on our audits. We conducted our audits in accordance with auditing standards generally accepted in the United States of America and in accordance with International Standards on Auditing.

1.2.2 Audits in Accordance With GAAS and PCAOB Standards

When conducting an audit of financial statements in accordance with the standards of the PCAOB and the audit is not required to be conducted in accordance with those standards, the auditor is required to also follow GAAS. In addition, the auditor should:

- Use the report required by the PCAOB.
- Amend the PCAOB (issuer) report to state the audit was also conducted in accordance with GAAS.

Pass Key

When the examiners require CPA candidates to respond to questions concerning the unmodified audit opinion (nonissuer), you must remember:

GAAS → Auditor's responsibility paragraph

GAAP (U.S. or other applicable financial reporting framework) → Management's responsibility paragraph and opinion paragraph

2 Unqualified Audit Opinion (Issuers)

The auditor of an issuer should express an unqualified opinion when the auditor concludes that the financial statements are presented fairly, in all material respects, in accordance with the applicable financial reporting framework (e.g., generally accepted accounting principles). The report should be in writing.

2.1 Contents of the Audit Report

The basic elements of the unqualified audit opinion are the following:

Unqualified Opinion: Issuer	
Title	The report must include the title, "Report of Independent Registered Public Accounting Firm."
Addressee	The report must be addressed to the shareholders and the board of directors. It generally is not addressed to management.
Opinion Section	The first section of the auditor's report must include the section title, "Opinion on the Financial Statements," and the following elements. • The name of the company whose financial statements were audited. • A statement identifying each financial statement and any related schedule that has been audited. • The date of, or period covered by, each financial statement and related schedule identified in the report. • A statement indicating that the financial statements were audited. • An opinion that the financial statements present fairly, in all material respects, the financial position of the company as of the balance sheet date and the results of its operations and its cash flows for the period then ended in conformity with the applicable financial reporting framework. The opinion should also include an identification of the applicable financial reporting framework (e.g., GAAP).

Basis for Opinion Section	The Basis for Opinion section contains the following: • A statement that the financial statements are the responsibility of the company's management. • A statement that the auditor's responsibility is to express an opinion on the financial statements based on the audit. • A statement that the auditor is a public accounting firm registered with the PCAOB (United States) and is required to be independent with respect to the company in accordance with the U.S. federal securities laws and the applicable rules and regulations of the SEC and the PCAOB. • A statement that the audit was conducted in accordance with the standards of the PCAOB. • A statement that PCAOB standards require that the auditor plan and perform the audit to obtain reasonable assurance about whether the financial statements are free of material misstatement, whether due to error or fraud. • A statement that the audit included: —performing procedures to assess the risks of material misstatement of the financial statements, whether due to error or fraud, and performing procedures that respond to those risks; —examining, on a test basis, evidence regarding the amounts and disclosures in the financial statements; —evaluating the accounting principles used and significant estimates made by management; and —evaluating the overall presentation of the financial statements. • A statement that the auditor believes the audit provides a reasonable basis for the auditor's opinion.
Critical Audit Matters	The auditor's report must include the section entitled "Critical Audit Matters" and should include discussion of any critical audit matters (CAMs) arising from the current period's audit of the financial statements, or state that the auditor determined that there were no CAMs.
Signature, Tenure, Location	The audit report must include: • The signature of the audit firm. • A statement containing the year the auditor began serving consecutively as the company's auditor. • The city and state (or country) from which the report was issued.
Report Date	The date of the audit report must be included in the report. • The report should be dated on or after the date on which appropriate audit evidence, sufficient to support the opinion, has been obtained. Sufficient appropriate audit evidence includes evidence that: —audit documentation has been reviewed; —financial statements have been prepared; and —management has taken responsibility for the financial statements. • The report date shows the final date of the auditor's responsibility. • For comparative statements, the date appropriate for the most recent audit should be used.

2.1.1 Sample Report: Unqualified Opinion (Issuer)

Report of Independent Registered Public Accounting Firm

To the shareholders and the board of directors of X Company:

Opinion on the Financial Statements

We have audited the accompanying balance sheets of X Company (the "Company") as of December 31, 20X2 and 20X1, the related statements of income, comprehensive income, stockholders equity, and cash flows for each of the years then ended, and the related notes and schedules (collectively referred to as the "financial statements"). In our opinion, the financial statements present fairly, in all material respects, the financial position of the Company as of December 31, 20X2 and 20X1, and the results of its operations and its cash flows for the years then ended, in conformity with accounting principles generally accepted in the United States of America.

Basis for Opinion

These financial statements are the responsibility of the Company's management. Our responsibility is to express an opinion on the Company's financial statements based on our audits. We are a public accounting firm registered with the Public Company Accounting Oversight Board (United States) (PCAOB) and are required to be independent with respect to the Company in accordance with the U.S. federal securities laws and the applicable rules and regulations of the Securities and Exchange Commission and the PCAOB.

We conducted our audits in accordance with the standards of the PCAOB. Those standards require that we plan and perform the audit to obtain reasonable assurance about whether the financial statements are free of material misstatement, whether due to error or fraud. Our audits included performing procedures to assess the risks of material misstatement of the financial statements, whether due to error or fraud, and performing procedures that respond to those risks. Such procedures included examining, on a test basis, evidence regarding the amounts and disclosures in the financial statements. Our audits also included evaluating the accounting principles used and significant estimates made by management, as well as evaluating the overall presentation of the financial statements. We believe that our audits provide a reasonable basis for our opinion.

Critical Audit Matters

The critical audit matters communicated below are matters arising from the current period audit of the financial statements that were communicated or required to be communicated to the audit committee and that: (1) relate to accounts or disclosures that are material to the financial statements and (2) involved our especially challenging, subjective, or complex judgments. The communication of critical audit matters does not alter in any way our opinion on the financial statements, taken as a whole, and we are not, by communicating the critical audit matters below, providing separate opinions on the critical audit matters or on the accounts or disclosures to which they relate.

[*Include critical audit matters*]

[*Signature*]

We have served as the Company's auditor since [*year*].

[*City and state or country*]

[*Date*]

2.1.2 Critical Audit Matters (CAMs): Definition and Identification

The auditor's report must include any critical audit matters (CAMs) arising from the current period's audit of the financial statements, or state that the auditor determined that there were no CAMs. It is expected that, in most audits, the auditor would identify at least one CAM.

A critical audit matter is defined as a matter that was communicated or required to be communicated to the audit committee and that:

1. relates to accounts or disclosures that are material to the financial statements; and
2. involved especially challenging, subjective, or complex auditor judgment.

When determining whether a matter involved especially challenging, subjective, or complex auditor judgment, the auditor takes into account certain factors, including the auditor's assessment of the risks of material misstatement, areas of significant judgment or estimation by management, nature and timing of unusual transactions, the degree of subjectivity in applying audit procedures, and the extent of specialized skill or knowledge regarding a matter.

2.1.3 Reporting Language if CAMs Are Identified

The following language, including the section title "Critical Audit Matters," should precede critical audit matters communicated in the auditor's report:

> **Critical Audit Matters**
>
> The critical audit matters communicated below are matters arising from the current period audit of the financial statements that were communicated or required to be communicated to the audit committee and that: (1) relate to accounts or disclosures that are material to the financial statements and (2) involved our especially challenging, subjective, or complex judgments. The communication of critical audit matters does not alter in any way our opinion on the financial statements, taken as a whole, and we are not, by communicating the critical audit matters below, providing separate opinions on the critical audit matters or on the accounts or disclosures to which they relate.
>
> [*Include critical audit matters*]

For each CAM identified, the audit report should include:

- **identification** of the CAM;
- description of the **principal** considerations that led the auditor to determine that the matter was a CAM;
- description of how the CAM was **addressed** in the audit; and
- reference to the relevant financial statement accounts or **disclosures** .

Pass Key

For each CAM, make sure you **Identify** it on a **PAD** of paper.

2.1.4 Reporting Language if No CAMs Are Identified

In situations in which the auditor determines that there are no critical audit matters, the auditor should include the following language, including the section title "Critical Audit Matters," in the auditor's report:

> **Critical Audit Matters**
>
> Critical audit matters are matters arising from the current period audit of the financial statements that were communicated or required to be communicated to the audit committee and that: (1) relate to accounts or disclosures that are material to the financial statements and (2) involved our especially challenging, subjective, or complex judgments. We determined that there are no critical audit matters.

2.1.5 Other Reporting Requirements for CAMs

- Language that could be viewed as disclaiming, qualifying, restricting, or minimizing the auditor's responsibility for the critical audit matters or the auditor's opinion on the financial statements is not appropriate and may not be used.
- When describing critical audit matters in the auditor's report, the auditor is not expected to provide information about the company that has not been made publicly available by the company unless such information is necessary to describe the principal considerations that led the auditor to determine that a matter is a critical audit matter or how the matter was addressed in the audit.
- When the current period's financial statements are presented on a comparative basis with those of one or more prior periods, the auditor *may* communicate critical audit matters relating to a prior period. This may be appropriate, for example, when (1) the prior period's financial statements are made public for the first time, such as in an initial public offering, or (2) issuing an auditor's report on the prior period's financial statements because the previously issued auditor's report could no longer be relied upon.
- Communication of critical audit matters is not required for audits of (1) brokers and dealers reporting under Exchange Act Rule 17a-5; (2) investment companies registered under the Investment Company Act of 1940 ("Investment Company Act"), other than companies that have elected to be regulated as business development companies; (3) employee stock purchase, savings, and similar plans; and (4) emerging growth companies.

2.1.6 Documentation of CAMs

For each matter arising from the audit of the financial statements that:

1. Was communicated or required to be communicated to the audit committee; and
2. Relates to accounts or disclosures that are material to the financial statements,

the auditor must document whether the matter was determined to be a CAM and the basis for such determination.

2.1.7 Management Reports on Internal Control Over Financial Reporting (Issuer Only)

When management is required to report on the company's internal control over financial reporting but such report is not required to be audited, and the auditor has not been engaged to perform an audit of management's assessment of the effectiveness of internal control over financial reporting, the auditor must include statements in the auditor's report in the Basis for Opinion section that:

- The company is not required to have, nor was the auditor engaged to perform, an audit of its internal control over financial reporting;
- As part of the audit, the auditor is required to obtain an understanding of internal control over financial reporting but not for the purpose of expressing an opinion on the effectiveness of the company's internal control over financial reporting; and
- The auditor expresses no such opinion.

Note: Most issuers are required to have an integrated audit, which means that an additional opinion is rendered on the operating effectiveness of internal control. The auditor's report for the integrated audit of an issuer is described in A5.

Pass Key

When the examiners require CPA candidates to respond to questions concerning the unqualified audit opinion (issuer), you must remember:

PCAOB Auditing Standards	→	Basis for Opinion section
GAAP (U.S. or other applicable financial reporting framework)	→	Opinion on the Financial Statements section

3 Required Auditor Reporting of Certain Audit Participants

3.1 Filing of Form AP

The auditor of an issuer must file Form AP with the PCAOB for each audit report issued. This form includes information about the audit, such as:

- Name of the firm.
- Name of the issuer whose financial statements are audited.
- Date of the audit report.
- The end date of the most recent period's financial statements identified in the audit report.
- The name of the engagement partner on the most recent period's audit and his/her current and prior ID number(s).

- The city and state (or city and country) of the office of the firm issuing the audit report.
- Whether the audit report is dual-dated.
- Whether other accounting firms participated in the audit.
- Whether the firm divided responsibility for the audit.
- Signature of partner or authorized officer.

Form AP must be filed by the 35th day after the audit report is first filed in a document with the SEC or within 10 days if the audit report is included in a registration statement.

3.2 Optional Inclusions

Although not required, the auditor of an issuer may elect to include in the auditor's report information regarding the engagement partner and/or other accounting firms participating in the audit.

If the auditor decides to provide information about the engagement partner, other accounting firms participating in the audit, or both, the auditor must disclose the following:

- The engagement partner's full name; and/or
- For other accounting firms participating in the audit, a statement that the auditor is responsible for the audits or audit procedures performed by the other public accounting firms and has supervised or performed procedures to assume responsibility for their work in accordance with PCAOB standards. In addition, the auditor should include information regarding the percentage of total audit hours the other audit firm participated in the audit.

Question 1 **MCQ-02764**

When financial statements contain a departure from U.S. GAAP because, due to unusual circumstances, the statements would otherwise be misleading, the auditor should express an opinion that is:

a. Unmodified.
b. Qualified.
c. Adverse.
d. Qualified or adverse, depending on pervasiveness.

NOTES

Skills Practice

Nonissuer ⇒ Unmodified

Comparative FS present

Audit partner = Donna Moses

location = Tustin, CA

addressed to BOD

evidence obtained 2/15/Y3

Modified Opinions Due to Financial Statement Issues

1 Financial Statement Issues: Qualified or Adverse Opinion

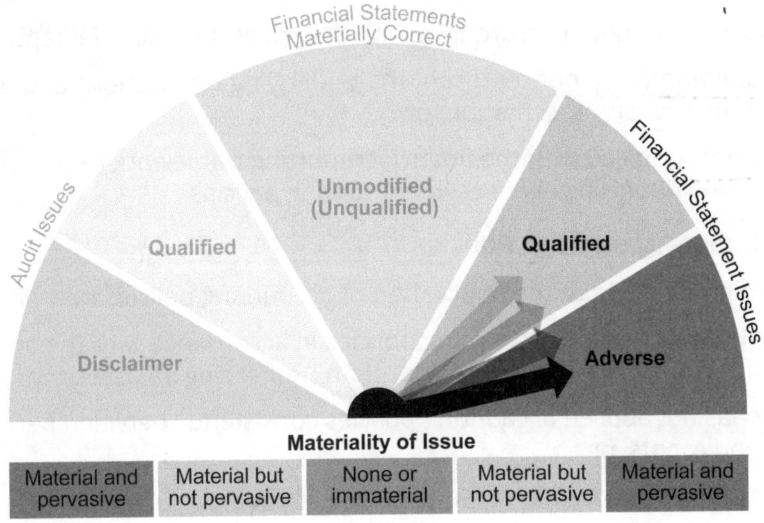

1.1 Qualified Opinion vs. Adverse Opinion

The auditor uses professional judgment to determine whether to issue a qualified opinion or an adverse opinion when audit evidence indicates that there is material misstatement of the financial statements.

Materiality of Problem	Financial Statements Are Materially Misstated (Financial Statement Issues)	Inability to Obtain Sufficient Appropriate Audit Evidence (Audit Issues)
None or immaterial	Unmodified (unqualified)	Unmodified (unqualified)
Material but not pervasive	Qualified opinion	Qualified opinion
Material and pervasive	Adverse opinion	Disclaimer of opinion

A qualified opinion should be expressed when the auditor concludes that misstatements, individually or in the aggregate, are material but not pervasive to the financial statements.

An adverse opinion should be expressed when the auditor concludes that misstatements, individually or in the aggregate, are both material and pervasive to the financial statements.

1.2 Nature of Material Misstatements

A material misstatement of the financial statements may arise in relation to the following:

- The appropriateness of accounting policies.
- The application of accounting policies.
- The appropriateness of the financial statement presentation or the appropriateness or adequacy of disclosures in the financial statements.

1.2.1 Appropriateness of Accounting Policies

Material misstatements related to the appropriateness of accounting policies may arise when:

1. accounting policies are not in accordance with the applicable financial reporting framework;
2. the financial statements do not represent the underlying transactions and events in a manner that achieves fair presentation; or
3. the entity has not complied with the financial reporting framework requirements for accounting for and disclosing changes in accounting policies.

1.2.2 Application of Accounting Policies

Material misstatements related to the application of accounting policies may arise when:

1. management has not applied accounting policies in accordance with the applicable financial reporting framework (e.g., expensing rather than capitalizing an asset);
2. management has not applied accounting policies consistently between periods or to similar transactions and events; or
3. there is an error in the application of an accounting policy.

1.2.3 Appropriateness of Financial Statement Presentation or Disclosures

Material misstatements related to the appropriateness of financial statement presentation or the appropriateness or adequacy of disclosures may arise when:

1. the financial statements do not include all required disclosures;
2. the disclosures are not presented in accordance with the applicable financial reporting framework;
3. the financial statements do not provide the disclosures needed to achieve fair presentation; or
4. information that is required to be presented, such as a statement of cash flows, has not been included or disclosed in the financial statements.

Pass Key

If a company issues financial statements that purport to present financial position and results of operations but omits the related statement of cash flows, the auditor will normally conclude that the omission requires a qualified opinion.

2 Nonissuer Reports

2.1 Form and Content of Auditor's Report (Nonissuers)

When the auditor expresses a qualified or adverse opinion due to material misstatement of the financial statements, the "Auditor's Responsibility" paragraph is modified and the auditor's report will include a "Basis for Modification" paragraph and a "Qualified Opinion" or "Adverse Opinion" paragraph, as appropriate.

2.1.1 Qualified Opinion

Qualified Opinion Due to Material Misstatement of Financial Statements: Nonissuer	
Introductory Paragraph	Same as standard nonissuer audit report.
Management's Responsibility Paragraph	Same as standard nonissuer audit report.
Auditor's Responsibility Paragraph	Modify the paragraph to state: "Auditor believes that the audit evidence obtained is sufficient and appropriate to provide a basis for the *qualified* audit opinion."
Basis for Qualified Opinion Paragraph	This paragraph should be placed immediately before the opinion paragraph and use the heading "Basis for Qualified Opinion." This paragraph should include: • A description and quantification of the financial effects of any misstatement that relates to specific amounts in the financial statements. —If it is not practicable to quantify the financial effects, this should be stated. —If disclosure of the financial effects is made in the notes to the financial statements, the basis for the modification paragraph can be shortened by referring to the disclosure. • An explanation of how disclosures are misstated if there is a material misstatement related to narrative disclosure. • A description of the nature of omitted information and inclusion of the omitted information, when practicable, if there is an omission of information that is required to be presented or disclosed.
Qualified Opinion Paragraph	When the auditor expresses a qualified opinion due to a material misstatement in the financial statements, the opinion paragraph should state that, in the auditor's opinion, *except for* the effects of the matter(s) described in the basis for qualified opinion paragraph, the financial statements are *presented fairly,* in all material respects, in accordance with the applicable financial reporting framework.

Pass Key

Practicable means that the information is reasonably obtainable from management's accounts and records and that providing the information in the auditor's report does not require the auditor to assume the position of a preparer of financial information. For example, the auditor is not expected to prepare a basic financial statement, such as an omitted statement of cash flows, or segment information and include it in the auditor's report when management omits such information.

2.1.2 Sample Report: Qualified Opinion Due to Inadequate Disclosure (Nonissuer)

Independent Auditor's Report

[*Appropriate Addressee*]

[*Introductory paragraph same as standard nonissuer audit report*]

Management's Responsibility for the Financial Statements

[*Same as standard nonissuer audit report*]

Auditor's Responsibility

[*Same as standard nonissuer audit report, except for the final statement below*]

We believe that the audit evidence we have obtained is sufficient and appropriate to provide a basis for our *qualified* audit opinion.

Basis for Qualified Opinion

The Company's financial statements do not disclose [*describe the nature of the omitted information that is not practicable to present in the auditor's report*]. In our opinion, disclosure of this information is required by accounting principles generally accepted in the United States of America.

Qualified Opinion

In our opinion, *except for* the omission of the information described in the Basis for Qualified Opinion paragraph, the financial statements referred to above *present fairly*, in all material respects, the financial position of ABC Company as of December 31, 20X1 and 20X0, and the results of its operations and its cash flows for the years then ended in accordance with accounting principles generally accepted in the United States of America.

[*Auditor's signature*]
[*Auditor's city and state*]
[*Date of the auditor's report*]

2.1.3 Sample Report: Qualified Opinion Due to a Material Misstatement of the Financial Statements (Nonissuer)

Independent Auditor's Report

[*Appropriate Addressee*]

[*Introductory paragraph same as standard nonissuer audit report*]

Management's Responsibility for the Financial Statements

[*Same as standard nonissuer audit report*]

Auditor's Responsibility

[*Same as standard nonissuer audit report, except for the final statement below*]

We believe that the audit evidence we have obtained is sufficient and appropriate to provide a basis for our *qualified* audit opinion.

(continued)

(continued)

Basis for Qualified Opinion

The Company has stated inventories at cost in the accompanying balance sheets. Accounting principles generally accepted in the United States of America require inventories to be stated at the lower of cost or market. If the Company stated inventories at the lower of cost or market, a write down of $XXX and $XXX would have been required as of December 31, 20X1 and 20X0, respectively. Accordingly, costs of sales would have increased by $XXX and $XXX, and net income, income taxes, and stockholders' equity would have been reduced by $XXX, $XXX, and $XXX, and $XXX, $XXX, and $XXX, as of and for the years ended December 31, 20X1 and 20X0, respectively.

Qualified Opinion

In our opinion, *except for* the effects of the matter described in the Basis for Qualified Opinion paragraph, the financial statements referred to above *present fairly*, in all material respects, the financial position of ABC Company as of December 31, 20X1 and 20X0, and the results of its operations and its cash flows for the years then ended in accordance with accounting principles generally accepted in the United States of America.

[*Auditor's signature*]
[*Auditor's city and state*]
[*Date of the auditor's report*]

2.1.4 Adverse Opinion

Adverse Opinion Due to Material Misstatement of Financial Statements: Nonissuer	
Introductory Paragraph	Same as standard nonissuer audit report.
Management's Responsibility Paragraph	Same as standard nonissuer audit report.
Auditor's Responsibility Paragraph	Modify the paragraph to state: "Auditor believes that the audit evidence obtained is sufficient and appropriate to provide a basis for the *adverse* audit opinion."
Basis for Adverse Opinion Paragraph	This paragraph should be placed immediately before the opinion paragraph and use the heading "Basis for Adverse Opinion." This paragraph should include: • A description and quantification of the financial effects of any misstatement that relates to specific amounts in the financial statements. —If it is not practicable to quantify the financial effects, this should be stated. —If disclosure of the financial effects is made in the notes to the financial statements, the basis for the modification paragraph can be shortened by referring to the disclosure. • An explanation of how disclosures are misstated if there is a material misstatement related to narrative disclosure. • A description of the nature of omitted information and inclusion of information, when practicable, if there is an omission that is required to be presented or disclosed.
Adverse Opinion Paragraph	When the auditor expresses an adverse opinion, the opinion paragraph should state that, in the auditor's opinion, *because of* the significance of the matter(s) described in the basis for adverse opinion paragraph, the financial statements *do not present fairly* in accordance with the applicable financial reporting framework.

2.1.5 Sample Report: Adverse Opinion Due to a Material Misstatement of the Financial Statements (Nonissuer)

Independent Auditor's Report

[*Appropriate Addressee*]

[*Introductory paragraph same as standard nonissuer audit report*]

Management's Responsibility for the Financial Statements

[*Same as standard nonissuer audit report*]

Auditor's Responsibility

[*Same as standard nonissuer audit report, except for the final statement below*]

We believe that the audit evidence we have obtained is sufficient and appropriate to provide a basis for our *adverse* audit opinion.

Basis for Adverse Opinion

As described in Note X, the Company has not consolidated the financial statements of subsidiary XYZ Company that it acquired during 20X1 because it has not yet been able to ascertain the fair value of certain of the subsidiary's material assets and liabilities at the acquisition date. This investment is therefore accounted for on a cost basis by the Company. Under accounting principles generally accepted in the United States of America, the subsidiary should have been consolidated because it is controlled by the Company. Had XYZ Company been consolidated, many elements in the accompanying consolidated financial statements would have been materially affected. The effects on the consolidated financial statements of the failure to consolidate have not been determined.

Adverse Opinion

In our opinion, *because of* the significance of the matter discussed in the Basis for Adverse Opinion paragraph, the consolidated financial statements referred to above *do not present fairly* the financial position of ABC Company and its subsidiaries as of December 31, 20X1, or the results of their operations or their cash flows for the year then ended in accordance with accounting principles generally accepted in the United States of America.

[*Auditor's signature*]

[*Auditor's city and state*]

[*Date of the auditor's report*]

3 Issuer Reports

3.1 Form and Content of Auditor's Report (Issuer)

When the auditor expresses a qualified or adverse opinion due to material misstatement of the financial statements, the auditor's report will include an additional paragraph immediately following the opinion paragraph and the opinion paragraph will be modified. The auditor is not required to report critical audit matters in the auditor's report when the auditor expresses an adverse opinion.

3.1.1 Qualified Opinion

Qualified Opinion Due to Material Misstatement of Financial Statements: Issuer	
Opinion Section	The section title and first sentence are the same as the standard issuer audit report. The second sentence is modified to include the appropriate qualifying language (i.e., *except for* or *with the exception of*) and a reference to the paragraph that discloses all of the qualified opinion.
Additional Paragraph(s)	A paragraph should be placed immediately following the opinion paragraph. There is no heading for this paragraph. This paragraph should include: • All of the substantive reasons that lead the auditor to conclude that there has been a departure from generally accepted accounting principles. • Disclosure of the principal effects of the subject matter of the qualification on financial position, results of operations, and cash flows, if practicable. —If the effects are not reasonably determinable, the report should so state. —If such disclosures are made in a note to the financial statements, the explanatory paragraph(s) may be shortened by referring to it.
Basis for Opinion Section	Same as standard issuer audit report.
Critical Audit Matters	Same as standard issuer audit report.

3.1.2 Sample Report: Qualified Opinion Due to a Material Misstatement of the Financial Statements (Issuer)

Report of Independent Registered Public Accounting Firm

To the shareholders and the board of directors of X Company:

Opinion on the Financial Statements

We have audited the accompanying balance sheets of X Company (the "Company") as of December 31, 20X2 and 20X1, the related statements of income, comprehensive income, stockholders equity, and cash flows for each of the years then ended, and the related notes and schedules (collectively referred to as the "financial statements"). In our opinion, *except for* the effects of not capitalizing certain lease obligations *as discussed in the following paragraph,* the financial statements referred to above present fairly, in all material respects, the financial position of the Company as of December 31, 20X2 and 20X1, and the results of its operations and its cash flows for the years then ended in conformity with accounting principles generally accepted in the United States of America.

The Company has excluded, from property and debt in the accompanying balance sheets, certain lease obligations that, in our opinion, should be capitalized in order to conform with accounting principles generally accepted in the United States of America. If these lease obligations were capitalized, property would be increased by $______ and $______, long-term debt by $______ and $______, and retained earnings by $______ and $______ as of December 31, 20X2 and 20X1, respectively. Additionally, net income would be increased (decreased) by $______ and $______ and earnings per share would be increased (decreased) by $______ and $______, respectively, for the years then ended.

Basis for Opinion

[*Basis for Opinion section same as standard issuer audit report*]

Critical Audit Matters

[*Critical Audit Matters section same as standard issuer audit report*]

[*Signature*]

We have served as the Company's auditor since [*year*].

[*City and state or country*]

[*Date*]

3.1.3 Adverse Opinion

Adverse Opinion Due to Material Misstatement of Financial Statements: Issuer	
Opinion Section	When the auditor expresses an adverse opinion, the opinion section should state that, in the auditor's opinion, *because of* the effects of matters discussed in the following paragraph(s), the financial statements *do not present fairly*, in conformity with accounting principles generally accepted in the United States of America, the financial statements.
Additional Paragraph(s)	A paragraph should be placed immediately following the opinion paragraph. There is no heading for this paragraph. This paragraph should include: • All of the substantive reasons that lead the auditor to conclude that there has been a departure from generally accepted accounting principles. • Disclosure of the principal effects of the subject matter of the adverse opinion on financial position, results of operations, and cash flows, if practicable. —If the effects are not reasonably determinable, the report should so state. —If such disclosures are made in a note to the financial statements, the explanatory paragraph(s) may be shortened by referring to it.
Basis for Opinion Section	Same as standard issuer audit report.
Critical Audit Matters	Critical Audit Matters section omitted.

3.1.4 Sample Report: Adverse Opinion Due to a Material Misstatement of the Financial Statements (Issuer)

Report of Independent Registered Public Accounting Firm

To the shareholders and the board of directors of X Company:

Opinion on the Financial Statements

We have audited the accompanying balance sheets of X Company (the "Company") as of December 31, 20X2 and 20X1, the related statements of income, comprehensive income, stockholders' equity, and cash flows for each of the years then ended, and the related notes and schedules (collectively referred to as the "financial statements"). In our opinion, *because of* the effects of the matters discussed in the following paragraphs, the financial statements *do not present fairly,* in conformity with accounting principles generally accepted in the United States of America, the financial position of the Company as of December 31, 20X2 and 20X1, or the results of its operations or its cash flows for the years then ended.

As discussed in Note X to the financial statements, the Company carries its property, plant, and equipment accounts at appraisal values, and provides depreciation on the basis of such values. Further, the Company does not provide for income taxes with respect to differences between financial income and taxable income arising because of the use, for income tax purposes, of the installment method of reporting gross profit from certain types of sales. Accounting principles generally accepted in the United States of America require that property, plant, and equipment be stated at an amount not in excess of cost, reduced by depreciation based on such amount, and that deferred income taxes be provided.

(continued)

(continued)

Because of the departures from accounting principles generally accepted in the United States of America identified above, as of December 31, 20X2 and 20X1, inventories have been increased $______ and $______ by inclusion in manufacturing overhead of depreciation in excess of that based on cost; property, plant, and equipment, less accumulated depreciation, is carried at $______ and $______ in excess of an amount based on the cost to the Company; and deferred income taxes of $______ and $______ have not been recorded; resulting in an increase of $______ and $______ in retained earnings and in appraisal surplus of $______ and $______, respectively. For the years ended December 31, 20X2 and 20X1, cost of goods sold has been increased $______ and $______, respectively, because of the effects of the depreciation accounting referred to above and deferred income taxes of $______ and $______ have not been provided, resulting in an increase in net income of $______ and $______, respectively.

Basis for Opinion

[*Basis for Opinion section same as standard issuer audit report*]

[*Signature*]

We have served as the Company's auditor since [year].

[*City and state or country*]

[*Date*]

Question 1 **MCQ-02469**

Which of the following phrases would an auditor of a nonissuer most likely include in the auditor's report when expressing a qualified opinion due to inadequate disclosure?

a. Subject to the departure from generally accepted accounting principles, as described above.

b. With the foregoing explanation of these omitted disclosures.

c. Except for the omission of the information described in the basis for qualified opinion paragraph.

d. Do not present fairly.

MODULE

6 Modified Opinions Due to Audit Issues

AUD 1

1 Audit Issues: Qualified Opinion or Disclaimer

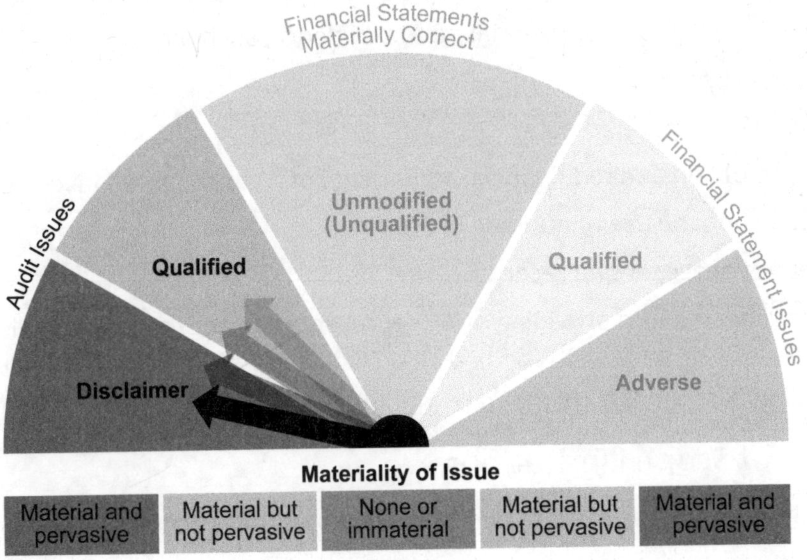

1.1 Qualified Opinion vs. Disclaimer

The auditor uses professional judgment to determine whether to issue a qualified opinion or a disclaimer of opinion.

Materiality of Problem	Financial Statements Are Materially Misstated (Financial Statement Issues)	Inability to Obtain Sufficient Appropriate Audit Evidence (Audit Issues)
None or immaterial	Unmodified (unqualified)	Unmodified (unqualified)
Material but not pervasive	Qualified opinion	Qualified opinion
Material and pervasive	Adverse opinion	Disclaimer of opinion

A qualified opinion due to an audit problem should be expressed when the auditor is unable to obtain sufficient appropriate audit evidence on which to base an opinion and the auditor concludes that the possible effects of any undetected misstatements could be material but not pervasive.

A disclaimer of opinion should be expressed when the auditor is unable to obtain sufficient appropriate audit evidence on which to base an opinion and the auditor concludes that the possible effects of any undetected misstatements could be both material and pervasive. A disclaimer of opinion should also be expressed if the auditor is not independent or if the financial statements are unaudited.

1.2 Examples of Scope Limitations

When the auditor is unable to complete the audit fully, the scope of the audit has been limited. Examples of conditions that restrict scope include the following items.

- Time constraints.
- Inability to obtain sufficient appropriate audit evidence, such as:
  - Inability to observe inventory
  - Inability to confirm receivables
  - Inability to obtain audited financial statements of a consolidated investee
  - Restrictions on the use of auditing procedures
  - Inadequacy of accounting records
- Refusal of management to provide written representation and/or to acknowledge its responsibility for the fair presentation of the financial statements in conformity with GAAP.
- Refusal of client's attorney to respond to inquiry.

1.3 Causes of Scope Limitations

Limitations on the scope of the audit may be imposed by either circumstances or management.

1.3.1 Circumstances

A scope limitation may be caused by circumstances beyond the control of the entity or circumstances relating to the nature or timing of the auditor's work. For example, a scope limitation may exist when an auditor was not engaged at the beginning of the year, when opening inventory should have been observed. When circumstances prevent the auditor from performing a specific procedure, the auditor should determine whether it is possible to perform alternative procedures.

Pass Key

The inability to perform a specific procedure is not a limitation on the scope of the audit if the auditor is able to obtain sufficient appropriate audit evidence by performing alternative procedures. If alternative procedures cannot be performed, the auditor should express a qualified opinion or a disclaimer of opinion.

1.3.2 Management-Imposed Scope Limitation

If the auditor becomes aware that management has imposed a limitation that the auditor believes may result in the need to express a qualified opinion or disclaim an opinion, the auditor should ask management to remove the limitation. If management will not remove the limitation, the auditor should communicate with those charged with governance and determine whether it is possible to perform alternative procedures.

If the auditor is unable to obtain sufficient appropriate audit evidence due to a management-imposed scope limitation and the auditor concludes that the possible effects of any undetected misstatements could be both material and pervasive, then the auditor should either disclaim an opinion or withdraw from the engagement. Withdrawal may not be possible if the auditor has substantially completed the audit, or if the audit is required by law or regulation. The auditor may choose to add an other-matter (explanatory) paragraph to the auditor's report to describe the reasons why the auditor cannot withdraw from an engagement when the auditor is unable to obtain sufficient appropriate audit evidence due to a management-imposed scope limitation and the possible effects on the financial statements of undetected misstatements could be both material and pervasive.

1.4 Unaudited Financial Statements

1.4.1 Association With Financial Statements

Association occurs when an accountant either:

1. consents to the use of his or her name in connection with the financial statements; or
2. has prepared the financial statements, even if the accountant's name is not used.

Pass Key

When the auditor is not independent but is required by law or regulation to report on the financial statements, the auditor should disclaim an opinion and should specifically state that the auditor is not independent. If the auditor chooses to provide the reasons for the lack of independence, the auditor should include all reasons.

1.4.2 Disclaimer on Unaudited Financial Statements

An accountant who is associated with the financial statements of an engagement that is conducted in accordance with PCAOB standards without auditing or reviewing them should issue a disclaimer of opinion. Other requirements for this type of disclaimer on unaudited financial statements include:

- The accountant must read the financial statements for obvious errors.
- The disclaimer may accompany the unaudited financial statements or it may be placed directly on them.
- "Unaudited" should be clearly marked on each page of the financial statements.
- If the client refuses to correct an obvious error, the auditor should add a paragraph modifying the disclaimer to describe, in a separate explanatory paragraph, the nature and effect of the departure from GAAP. If the client refuses to accept the modified disclaimer, the auditor should withdraw from the engagement.

Pass Key

When exam questions indicate that the financial statements are false, fraudulent, deceptive or misleading, that management refuses to correct them, and that modification of the CPA's report is not sufficient to correct the item, the CPA should consider withdrawing from the engagement.

2 Nonissuer Reports

2.1 Form and Content of Auditor's Report (Nonissuer)

When the auditor expresses a qualified opinion or disclaimer of opinion, the "Auditor's Responsibility" paragraph is modified and the auditor's report will include a "Basis for Modification" paragraph and a "Qualified Opinion" or "Disclaimer of Opinion" paragraph, as appropriate. A disclaimer of opinion will also include a modification to the introductory paragraph of the auditor's report.

2.1.1 Qualified Opinion

Qualified Opinion Due to Audit Issues: Nonissuer	
Introductory Paragraph	Same as standard nonissuer audit report.
Management's Responsibility Paragraph	Same as standard nonissuer audit report.
Auditor's Responsibility Paragraph	Modify the paragraph to state: "Auditor believes that the audit evidence obtained is sufficient and appropriate to provide a basis for the *qualified* audit opinion."
Basis for Qualified Opinion Paragraph	This paragraph should be placed immediately before the opinion paragraph and use the heading "Basis for Qualified Opinion." This paragraph should describe the reasons for the inability to obtain sufficient appropriate audit evidence.
Qualified Opinion Paragraph	When the auditor expresses a qualified opinion due to an inability to obtain sufficient appropriate audit evidence, the opinion paragraph should state that, in the auditor's opinion, *except for* the possible effects of the matter(s) described in the basis for qualified opinion paragraph, the financial statements are *presented fairly*, in all material respects, in accordance with the applicable financial reporting framework.

Pass Key

When the auditor expresses a qualified opinion due to a scope limitation, the opinion paragraph states that the qualification relates to the possible effect of the matter on the financial statements and not the scope limitation itself. Wording such as, "In our opinion, except for the above-mentioned limitation on the scope of the audit ... " is not acceptable.

2.1.2 Sample Report: Qualified Opinion Due to the Auditor's Inability to Obtain Sufficient Appropriate Audit Evidence (Nonissuer)

Independent Auditor's Report

[*Appropriate Addressee*]

[*Introductory paragraph same as standard nonissuer audit report*]

Management's Responsibility for the Financial Statements

[*Same as standard nonissuer audit report*]

Auditor's Responsibility

[*Same as standard nonissuer audit report, except for the final statement below*]

We believe that the audit evidence we have obtained is sufficient and appropriate to provide a basis for our *qualified* audit opinion.

Basis for Qualified Opinion

ABC Company's investment in XYZ Company, a foreign affiliate acquired during the year and accounted for under the equity method is carried at $XXX on the balance sheet at December 31, 20X1, and ABC Company's share of XYZ Company's net income of $XXX is included in ABC Company's net income for the year then ended. We were unable to obtain sufficient appropriate audit evidence about the carrying amount of ABC Company's investment in XYZ Company as of December 31, 20X1 and ABC Company's share of XYZ Company's net income for the year then ended because we were denied access to the financial information, management, and the auditors of XYZ Company. Consequently, we were unable to determine whether any adjustments to these amounts were necessary.

Qualified Opinion

In our opinion, *except for* the possible effects of the matter described in the Basis for Qualified Opinion paragraph, the financial statements referred to above *present fairly*, in all material respects, the financial position of ABC Company as of December 31, 20X1, and the results of its operations and its cash flows for the year then ended in accordance with accounting principles generally accepted in the United States of America.

[*Auditor's signature*]

[*Auditor's city and state*]

[*Date of the auditor's report*]

2.1.3 Disclaimer of Opinion

Disclaimer of Opinion Due to Audit Issues: Nonissuer	
Introductory Paragraph	Modify the paragraph to state that the auditor *was engaged to audit* the financial statements.
Management's Responsibility Paragraph	Same as standard nonissuer audit report.
Auditor's Responsibility Paragraph	Modify the description of the auditor's responsibility and the scope of the audit to state only the following: "Our responsibility is to express an opinion on the financial statements based on conducting the audit in accordance with auditing standards generally accepted in the United States of America. Because of the matter(s) described in the basis for disclaimer of opinion paragraph, however, we were not able to obtain sufficient appropriate audit evidence to provide a basis for an audit opinion."
Basis for Disclaimer of Opinion Paragraph	This paragraph should be placed immediately before the opinion paragraph and use the heading "Basis for Disclaimer of Opinion." This paragraph should describe the reasons for the inability to obtain sufficient appropriate audit evidence.
Disclaimer of Opinion Paragraph	When the auditor disclaims an opinion, the auditor should state in the opinion paragraph that: • *Because of* the significance of the matter(s) described in the basis for disclaimer of opinion paragraph, the auditor has not been able to obtain sufficient appropriate audit evidence to provide a basis for an audit opinion; and • Accordingly, the auditor *does not express an opinion* on the financial statements.

2.1.4 Sample Report: Disclaimer of Opinion (Nonissuer)

Independent Auditor's Report

[*Appropriate Addressee*]

We were engaged to audit the accompanying financial statements of ABC Company, which comprise the balance sheets as of December 31, 20X1, and the related statements of income, changes in stockholders' equity, and cash flows for the year then ended, and the related notes to the financial statements.

Management's Responsibility for the Financial Statements

[*Same as standard nonissuer audit report*]

(continued)

(continued)

Auditor's Responsibility

Our responsibility is to express an opinion on these financial statements based on conducting the audit in accordance with auditing standards generally accepted in the United States of America. Because of the matters described in the Basis for Disclaimer of Opinion paragraph, however, we were not able to obtain sufficient appropriate audit evidence to provide a basis for an audit opinion.

Basis for Disclaimer of Opinion

We were not engaged as auditors of the Company until after December 31, 20X1, and, therefore, did not observe the counting of physical inventories at the beginning or end of the year. We were unable to satisfy ourselves by other auditing procedures concerning the inventory held at December 31, 20X1, which is stated in the balance sheet at $XXX. In addition, the introduction of a new computerized accounts receivable system in September 20X1 resulted in numerous misstatements in accounts receivable. As of the date of our audit report, management was still in the process of rectifying the system deficiencies and correcting the misstatements. We were unable to confirm or verify by alternative means accounts receivable included in the balance sheet at a total amount of $XXX at December 31, 20X1. As a result of these matters, we were unable to determine whether any adjustments might have been found necessary in respect of recorded or unrecorded inventories and accounts receivable, and the elements making up the statements of income, changes in stockholder's equity, and cash flows.

Disclaimer of Opinion

Because of the significance of the matters described in the Basis for Disclaimer of Opinion paragraph, we have not been able to obtain sufficient appropriate audit evidence to provide a basis for an audit opinion. Accordingly, we *do not express an opinion* on these financial statements.

[*Auditor's signature*]
[*Auditor's city and state*]
[*Date of the auditor's report*]

3 Issuer Reports

3.1 Form and Content of the Auditor's Report (Issuer)

When the auditor expresses a qualified opinion or disclaimer of opinion, a paragraph immediately following the opinion paragraph is added and the opinion paragraph is modified. A qualified opinion and disclaimer of opinion will include modified language in the Basis for Opinion section. The auditor is not required to report critical audit matters in the auditor's report when the auditor expresses a disclaimer of opinion.

3.1.1 Qualified Opinion

Qualified Opinion Due to Audit Issues: Issuer	
Opinion Section	The section title and first sentence is the same as the standard issuer audit report. The second sentence is modified to include the appropriate qualifying language (i.e., *except for* or *with the exception of*) and a reference to the paragraph that describes the departure from the unqualified opinion.
Additional Paragraph	A paragraph should be placed immediately following the opinion paragraph. There is no heading for this paragraph. This paragraph should describe the reasons for the inability to obtain sufficient appropriate audit evidence.
Basis for Opinion Section	Same as standard issuer audit report, except that the second paragraph in this section should refer to the paragraph that describes the departure from the unqualified opinion.
Critical Audit Matters	Same as standard issuer audit report.

3.1.2 Sample Report: Qualified Opinion Due to a Scope Limitation (Issuer)

Report of Independent Registered Public Accounting Firm

To the shareholders and the board of directors of X Company:

Opinion on the Financial Statements

We have audited the accompanying balance sheets of X Company (the "Company") as of December 31, 20X2 and 20X1, the related statements of income, comprehensive income, stockholders' equity, and cash flows for each of the years then ended, and the related notes and schedules (collectively referred to as the "financial statements"). In our opinion, *except for* the effects of the adjustments, if any, as might have been determined to be necessary had we been able to examine evidence regarding the foreign affiliate investment and earnings, as described below, the financial statements present fairly, in all material respects, the financial position of the Company as of December 31, 20X2 and 20X1, and the results of its operations and its cash flows for the years then ended in conformity with accounting principles generally accepted in the United States of America.

We were unable to obtain audited financial statements supporting the Company's investment in a foreign affiliate stated at $______ and $______ at December 31, 20X2 and 20X1, respectively, or its equity in earnings of that affiliate of $______ and $______, which is included in net income for the years then ended as described in Note X to the financial statements; nor were we able to satisfy ourselves as to the carrying value of the investment in the foreign affiliate or the equity in its earnings by other auditing procedures.

Basis for Opinion

[*Same as standard issuer report, except for the statement below*]

Except as discussed above, we conducted our audits in accordance with the standards of the PCAOB. [*Remainder paragraph the same as standard issuer report.*]

Critical Audit Matters

[*Critical Audit Matters section same as standard issuer audit report*]

[*Signature*]
We have served as the Company's auditor since [*year*].
[*City and state or country*]
[*Date*]

3.1.3 Disclaimer of Opinion

Disclaimer of Opinion Due to Audit Issues: Issuer	
Disclaimer of Opinion Section	Modifications to this section include: • Section title of "Disclaimer of Opinion on the Financial Statements." • Use of the words "*were engaged to audit*" instead of "have audited." • Reference to the paragraph describing the reasons for disclaimer. • A statement that the auditor was *not able to obtain sufficient appropriate audit evidence* to provide a basis for an audit opinion. • A disclaimer of opinion ("*do not express an opinion*") is given on the financial statements as a whole.
Additional Paragraph	An explanatory paragraph should be placed immediately following the opinion paragraph. This paragraph should include: • All of the substantive reasons for the disclaimer. • Disclosure of any reservations regarding fair presentation in conformity with GAAP.
Basis for Disclaimer of Opinion Paragraph	Modification to the Basis of Opinion paragraph includes: • Section title of "Basis for Disclaimer of Opinion." • Elimination of the sentence, "Our responsibility is to express an opinion on the Company's financial statements based on our audits." • Elimination of entire second paragraph in this section, which begins with "We conducted our audits in accordance ... ."
Critical Audit Matters	Critical Audit Matters section omitted.

3.1.4 Sample Report: Disclaimer of Opinion Due to Inability to Obtain Sufficient Appropriate Audit Evidence (Issuer)

Report of Independent Registered Public Accounting Firm

To the shareholders and the board of directors of X Company:

Disclaimer of Opinion on the Financial Statements

We were engaged to audit the accompanying balance sheets of X Company (the "Company") as of December 31, 20X2 and 20X1, and the related statements of income, comprehensive income, stockholders' equity, and cash flows, and the related notes and schedules (collectively referred to as the "financial statements"). As described in the following paragraph, because the Company did not take physical inventories and we were not able to apply other auditing procedures to satisfy ourselves as to inventory quantities and the cost of property and equipment, *we were not able to obtain sufficient appropriate audit evidence* to provide a basis for an audit opinion on the financial statements, and *we do not express* an opinion on these financial statements.

(continued)

(continued)

The Company did not make a count of its physical inventory in 20X2 or 20X1, stated in the accompanying financial statements at $_______ as of December 31, 20X2, and at $________ as of December 31, 20X1. Further, evidence supporting the cost of property and equipment acquired prior to December 31, 20X1, is no longer available. The Company's records do not permit the application of other auditing procedures to inventories or property and equipment.

Basis for Disclaimer of Opinion

These financial statements are the responsibility of the Company's management. We are a public accounting firm registered with the Public Company Accounting Oversight Board (United States) (PCAOB) and are required to be independent with respect to the Company in accordance with the U.S. federal securities laws and the applicable rules and regulations of the Securities and Exchange Commission and the PCAOB.

[*Second paragraph within this section of standard issuer audit report should be omitted*]

[*Signature*]

We have served as the Company's auditor since [*year*].

[*City and state or country*]

[*Date*]

3.1.5 Sample Report: Disclaimer of Opinion Due to Lack of Independence (Issuer)

An accountant who is "associated with" financial statements but is not independent should disclaim an opinion.

We are not independent with respect to XYZ Company, and the accompanying balance sheet as of December 31, 20XX, and the related statements of income, retained earnings, and cash flows for the year then ended were not audited by us and, accordingly, *we do not express an opinion* on them.

Pass Key

A commonly tested area is the concept of uncertainty. The chart below will assist you in mastering this area.

Uncertainty		
No material misstatement and sufficient evidence	**Material misstatement related to the uncertainty**	**Insufficient evidence (scope limitation)**
Unmodified	Qualified or adverse	Qualified or disclaimer

Auditor's Report Summary (Nonissuer)

	Type of Opinion	Intro Paragraph	Management Responsibility Paragraph	Auditor Responsibility Paragraph	Basis for Opinion Paragraph	Opinion Paragraph
Misstatement						
Immaterial	Unmodified	Standard	Standard	Standard	No	Present fairly
Material but not pervasive	Qualified	Standard	Standard	Name type of modified opinion	Yes	Except for
Material and pervasive	Adverse	Standard	Standard	Name type of modified opinion	Yes	Do not present fairly
Scope Limitation						
Immaterial	Unmodified	Standard	Standard	Standard	No	Present fairly
Material but not pervasive	Qualified	Standard	Standard	Name type of modified opinion	Yes	Except for
Material and pervasive	Disclaimer	Engaged to audit	Standard	Not able to obtain...	Yes	Disclaimer

Auditor's Report Summary (Issuer)

	Type of Opinion	Opinion Section	Additional Paragraph	Basis for Opinion Section	Critical Audit Matters
Misstatement					
Immaterial	Unqualified	Standard	No	Standard	Standard
Material but not pervasive	Qualified	Except for	Yes	Standard	Standard
Material and pervasive	Adverse	Do not present fairly	Yes	Standard	Omit
Scope Limitation					
Immaterial	Unqualified	Standard	No	Standard	Standard
Material but not pervasive	Qualified	Except for	Yes	Except as discussed above	Standard
Material and pervasive	Disclaimer	Engaged to audit and Disclaimer	Yes	Omit certain sentences	Omit
Lack of Independence					
	Disclaimer	None	None	Disclaimer	Omit

Question 1 **MCQ-02452**

Under which of the following circumstances would a disclaimer of opinion *not* be appropriate?

a. The auditor is unable to determine the amounts associated with an employee fraud scheme.

b. Management does not provide reasonable justification for a change in accounting principle. FS issue

c. The client refuses to permit the auditor to confirm certain accounts receivable or apply alternative procedures to verify their balances.

d. The chief executive officer is unwilling to sign the management representation letter.

Question 2 **MCQ-02834**

When qualifying an opinion due to an inability to obtain sufficient appropriate audit evidence, an auditor of a nonissuer should include the reasons for that inability to obtain sufficient information in:

	Management's Responsibility paragraph	*Basis for Qualified Opinion paragraph*
a.	No	No
b.	Yes	No
c.	Yes	Yes
d.	No	Yes

MODULE

7 Emphasis-of-Matter, Other-Matter, and Explanatory Paragraphs

AUD 1

1 Emphasis-of-Matter Paragraphs (Nonissuers)

An emphasis-of-matter paragraph is included in the auditor's report when required by GAAS or at the auditor's discretion. An emphasis-of-matter paragraph is used when referring to a matter that is appropriately presented or disclosed in the financial statements and is of such importance that it is fundamental to the users' understanding of the financial statements. The inclusion of an emphasis-of-matter paragraph in the auditor's report does not affect the auditor's opinion.

1.1 Report Requirements

When an emphasis-of-matter paragraph is included in the auditor's report, the auditor should:

1. place the emphasis-of-matter paragraph immediately after the opinion paragraph;
2. use the heading "Emphasis-of-Matter" or other appropriate heading;
3. describe the matter being emphasized and the location of relevant disclosures about the matter in the financial statements; and
4. indicate that the auditor's opinion is not modified with respect to the matter emphasized.

1.2 Use of Emphasis-of-Matter Paragraphs

1.2.1 Use Required

An emphasis-of-matter paragraph is *required* in the following circumstances:

G
- The auditor concludes that there is substantial doubt about the entity's ability to continue as a **going** concern for a reasonable period of time.

A
- To describe a justified change in **accounting** principle that has a material effect on the entity's financial statements.

A
- Subsequently discovered facts lead to a change in **audit** opinion (the auditor may use an emphasis-of-matter or other-matter paragraph, as appropriate).

S P
- The financial statements are prepared in accordance with an applicable **special purpose** framework (other than regulatory basis financial statements intended for general use).

Pass Key

When you hear a **GAASP** during the audit, remember that an emphasis-of-matter paragraph is required.

1.2.2 Use May Be Necessary

At times, the use of an emphasis-of-matter paragraph is not required, but may still be used at the discretion of the auditor. An auditor can use an emphasis-of-matter paragraph when referring to any matter that is appropriately presented or disclosed in the financial statements and is of such importance that it is fundamental to the user's understanding of the financial statements. Examples include:

- An uncertainty related to the outcome of unusually important litigation or regulatory action.
- A major catastrophe having a significant effect on the entity's financial position.
- Significant related party transactions.
- Unusually important subsequent events.

Pass Key

The examiners like to ask questions about uncertainties, such as lawsuits.

Management must analyze the existing conditions surrounding the uncertainties. The decision to accrue and/or disclose is based on the probability of loss and whether the loss can be estimated. The chart below shows the different scenarios.

If Loss Is:	Can Estimate Loss Amount	Cannot Estimate Loss Amount
Probable	Accrue and disclose	Disclose
Reasonably possible	Disclose	Disclose
Remote	Generally ignore	

The auditor will normally not add an emphasis-of-matter paragraph for uncertainties that are appropriately accounted for. However, if a question indicates that the uncertainty (such as the lawsuit) is "unusually important" then an emphasis-of-matter paragraph may be added.

2 Other-Matter Paragraphs (Nonissuers)

An other-matter paragraph is included in the auditor's report when required by GAAS or at the auditor's discretion. Other-matter paragraphs refer to matters other than those presented or disclosed in the financial statements that are relevant to the users' understanding of the audit, the auditor's responsibilities, or the auditor's report.

2.1 Report Requirements

When an other-matter paragraph is included in the auditor's report, the auditor should:

1. place the other-matter paragraph immediately after the opinion paragraph and after any emphasis-of-matter paragraph; and
2. use the heading "Other-Matter" or other appropriate heading.

2.2 Use of Other-Matter Paragraphs

2.2.1 Use Required

An other-matter paragraph is *required* in the following circumstances:

- Anytime the auditor includes an alert in the audit report that restricts the use of the auditor's report.
- Subsequently discovered facts lead to a change in audit opinion (the auditor may use an emphasis-of-matter or other-matter paragraph, as appropriate).
- The financial statements of the prior period were audited by a predecessor auditor and the predecessor's audit report is not reissued.
- Current period financial statements are audited and presented in comparative form with compiled or reviewed financial statements for the prior period, or in comparative form with prior period financial statements that were not audited, reviewed, or compiled.
- Prior to the audit report date, the auditor identifies a material inconsistency in other information that is included in a document containing audited financial statements that requires revision of the other information and management refuses to make the revision.
- When the auditor chooses to report on supplementary information presented with the financial statements in the auditor's report, rather than in a separate report.
- To refer to required supplementary information that a designated accounting standards setter requires to accompany an entity's basic financial statements.
- To restrict the use of the auditor's report when special purpose financial statements are prepared in accordance with a contractual or regulatory basis of accounting (except when regulatory basis financial statements are intended for general use).
- A report on compliance is included in the auditor's report on the financial statements.

2.2.2 Use May Be Necessary

An other-matter paragraph may be necessary in the following circumstances:

- To describe the reasons why the auditor cannot withdraw from an engagement when the auditor is unable to obtain sufficient appropriate audit evidence due to a management-imposed scope limitation and the possible effects on the financial statements of undetected misstatements could be both material and pervasive, but the auditor is unable to withdraw from the engagement.
- Law, regulation, or generally accepted practice require or permit the auditor to provide further explanation of the auditor's responsibilities.
- The auditor has been engaged to report on more than one set of financial statements when each set of financial statements has been prepared in accordance with a different general-purpose framework.

3 Explanatory Paragraph (Issuers)

An explanatory paragraph is included in the auditor's report when required by PCAOB auditing standards or at the auditor's discretion. The inclusion of an explanatory paragraph in the auditor's report does not affect the auditor's opinion.

3.1 Report Requirements

The explanatory paragraph generally should include an appropriate title. The paragraph should describe the matter being emphasized and the location of relevant disclosures about the matter in the financial statements.

The explanatory paragraph will *generally* follow the opinion paragraph when added to an unqualified report.

3.2 Use of Explanatory Paragraphs

3.2.1 Use Required

An explanatory paragraph is required in the following circumstances:

- There is substantial doubt about the entity's ability to continue as a going concern.
- There has been a material change between periods in accounting principles or in the method of their application.
- There has been a change in a reporting entity, unless the change in the reporting entity results from a transaction or event, such as the creation, cessation, or complete or partial purchase or disposition of a subsidiary or other business unit.
- There has been a change in an investee year-end that has a material effect on the company's financial statements.
- A material misstatement in previously issued financial statements has been corrected.
- Other information in a document containing audited financial statements is materially inconsistent with information appearing in the financial statements.
- Selected quarterly financial data required by SEC Regulation S-K has been omitted or has not been reviewed.
- Supplementary information required by an applicable financial reporting framework has been omitted; the presentation of such information departs materially from the applicable financial reporting framework; the auditor is unable to complete prescribed procedures with respect to such information; or the auditor is unable to remove substantial doubts about whether the supplementary information conforms to the requirements of the applicable financial reporting framework.
- The prior year audit report is not presented.*
- The prior year opinion is updated.*
- Management is required to report on the company's internal controls over financial reporting but such report is not required to be audited, and the auditor has not been engaged to perform an audit of management's assessment of the effectiveness of the company's internal control over financial reporting.*

* No title is required for the explanatory paragraph (language) for circumstances notated with the asterisk.

3.2.2 Use May Be Necessary

The auditor may emphasize a matter regarding the financial statements in the auditor's report ("emphasis paragraph"). If the auditor adds an emphasis paragraph in the auditor's report, the auditor should use an appropriate section title.

Pass Key

The circumstances that require an auditor to add an explanatory paragraph in an issuer audit report are very similar to the circumstances that require an auditor to add an emphasis-of-matter or other-matter paragraph to a nonissuer audit report.

4 Other Audit Considerations

4.1 Lack of Consistency

Consistency deals with the comparability of the financial statements from year to year. Unless the auditor's report explicitly states otherwise, the auditor's report implies that the financial statements are comparable between periods. The auditor should evaluate whether the comparability of consistency of the financial statements between periods has been affected by a change in accounting principle or by an adjustment to correct a material misstatement in previously issued financial statements.

4.1.1 Acceptability of a Change in Accounting Principle

When evaluating the acceptability of an accounting change, the auditor should consider whether:

1. the newly adopted accounting principle is in accordance with the applicable financial reporting framework;
2. the method of accounting for the change is acceptable;
3. the disclosures related to the accounting change are appropriate and adequate; and
4. the entity has justified that the alternative accounting principle is preferable.

If the auditor is satisfied that all four criteria are met, the auditor should include an emphasis-of-matter (explanatory) paragraph in the auditors' report. If any of the criteria are not met, the auditor should evaluate whether the accounting change results in a material misstatement and modify the auditor's opinion accordingly.

4.1.2 Examples of Circumstances That Affect Consistency

The following situations require an emphasis-of-matter (explanatory) paragraph:

- A change in accounting estimate that is inseparable from a change in accounting principle (e.g., a change in depreciation method).
- Corrections of an error in accounting principle (e.g., from cash method to accrual method).
- A change in reporting entity that results in financial statements that are, in effect, those of a different reporting entity.
- Correction of a material misstatement in previously issued financial statements.

- If an entity's financial statements include a significant investment accounted for using the equity method, the auditor's evaluation of consistency should include consideration of the investee. If the investee makes a change in accounting principle that is material to the investing entity, the change should be described in an emphasis-of-matter (explanatory) paragraph.

Other changes in accounting estimates or corrections of errors (i.e., mathematical mistakes, oversights, etc.) do not affect the consistency standard and do not affect the auditor's report.

4.1.3 Effect of an Acceptable Change on the Auditor's Report

If the effect of a change in accounting principle is immaterial, no revision to the report is necessary. If the effect is material, an emphasis-of-matter (explanatory) paragraph should be added. The emphasis-of-matter (explanatory) paragraph should describe the change in accounting principle and provide a reference to the entity's disclosure about the change.

The emphasis-of-matter (explanatory) paragraph should be included in the auditor's report in the period of the change in accounting principle and all subsequent periods, until the new accounting principle is applied to all periods presented. If the change in accounting principle is accounted for by retroactive restatement, the emphasis-of-matter (explanatory) paragraph is only needed in the period of the change.

4.2 Alert That Restricts the Use of the Auditor's Written Communication

The auditor may be required by GAAS or may decide that it is necessary to include language in the auditor's report (or other written communication) that restricts the use of the auditor's written communication. In the auditor's report, such language is included in an other-matter (explanatory) paragraph.

4.2.1 Use of the Alert

An auditor's written communication should include an alert that restricts its use when the subject matter of the auditor's written communication is based on:

- measurement or disclosure criteria that are suitable for only a limited number of users who have an adequate understanding of the criteria;
- measurement or disclosure criteria that are available only to specified parties; or
- matters identified during an audit engagement that are not the primary objective of the audit engagement (commonly referred to as a by-product report).

4.2.2 Content of the Alert

Unless otherwise specified by GAAS, the alert that restricts the use of the auditor's written communication should include the following items:

- A statement that the auditor's written communication is intended solely for the information and use of the specified parties.
- Identification of the specified parties for whom use is intended.
- A statement that the auditor's written communication is not intended to be and should not be used by anyone other than the specified parties.

4.2.3 Sample Other-Matter (Explanatory) Paragraph

> This report is intended solely for the information and use of [*list or refer to the specified parties*] and is not intended to be and should not be used by anyone other than these specified parties.

4.2.4 Alert Included in General Use Communications

An auditor's written communication that is required by GAAS to include an alert that restricts its use may be included in a document that also includes an auditor's written communication that is for general use. In such circumstances, the use of the general use communication is not affected by the alert if the two types of communications are clearly differentiated, such as through the use of headers.

5 Summary

Below is a summary of the different circumstances that require an emphasis-of-matter, other-matter, or explanatory paragraph.

Client	**Nonissuer**		**Issuer**
Paragraph Type	*Emphasis-of-Matter*	*Other-Matter*	*Explanatory*
Location Relative to Opinion Paragraph	*After*	*After*	*After*
Going concern	✓		✓
Material justified change in accounting principle	✓		✓
Material misstatement in prior financial statements is corrected	✓		✓
Special purpose framework	✓		✓*
Change in audit opinion	✓ OR	✓	✓
Restrict use of report		✓	✓
Prior financial statements audited by prior auditor and prior auditor's report is not presented		✓	✓
Comparative financial statements where the current year is audited and prior period is not audited		✓	✓*
Material inconsistency in other information		✓	✓*
Report on supplementary information within auditor's report		✓	✓*
Refer to required supplementary information		✓	✓*
Report on compliance included in auditor's report		✓	✓*

*Although PCAOB guidelines do not specify the location for the explanatory paragraph for these circumstances, the explanatory paragraph generally is placed after the opinion paragraph.

Pass Key

Candidates will probably receive questions involving the emphasis-of-matter, other-matter, or explanatory paragraphs. It is important to note that the use of such paragraphs still represents an unmodified (unqualified) opinion. The additional language is used to highlight particular circumstances without modifying the opinion.

Question 1 **MCQ-02787**

Management of a nonissuer believes and the auditor is satisfied that a material loss probably will occur when pending litigation is resolved. Management is unable to make a reasonable estimate of the amount or range of the potential loss, but fully discloses the situation in the notes to the financial statements. If management does not make an accrual in the financial statements, the auditor should express a (an):

- **a.** Qualified opinion due to a scope limitation.
- **b.** Qualified opinion due to a material misstatement of the financial statements.
- **c.** Unmodified opinion with an other-matter paragraph.
- **d.** Unmodified opinion.

Question 2 **MCQ-02417**

For which of the following events would an auditor issue a report that omits any reference to consistency?

- **a.** A change in the method of accounting for inventories.
- **b.** A change from an accounting principle that is not generally accepted to one that is generally accepted.
- **c.** A change in the useful life used to calculate the provision for depreciation expense. prospective, no need to think about consistency
- **d.** Management's lack of reasonable justification for a change in accounting principle.

MODULE

8 Reporting With Different Opinions and Other Auditors

AUD 1

1 Reporting on Comparative Financial Statements

When comparative financial statements are presented, the auditor's report should refer to each period for which financial statements are presented and on which an audit opinion is expressed. Because the report date for the audit of the most recent financial statements is used, the auditor should update the audit reports on financial statements previously issued.

Update can mean reaffirm or it can mean change the original opinion as a result of changed conditions or information coming to the auditor's attention during the current engagement. If comparative information is presented but not covered by the auditor's opinion, the auditor should indicate clearly in the auditor's report the character of the auditor's work, if any, and the degree of responsibility the auditor is taking.

1.1 Reporting With Different Opinions

The auditor's current year report will generally cover all financial statements for all years presented. The auditor may express a qualified or adverse opinion, disclaim an opinion, or include an emphasis-of-matter, other-matter, or explanatory paragraph with respect to one or more financial statements for one or more periods, while expressing a different opinion on one or more financial statements of another period presented. Some examples of varying opinions are included below.

1.1.1 Sample Report: Unmodified Prior Year With Current Year Qualified (Nonissuer)

Independent Auditor's Report

[Appropriate Addressee]

[Introductory paragraph same as standard nonissuer audit report]

Management's Responsibility for the Financial Statements

[Same as standard nonissuer audit report]

Auditor's Responsibility

[Same as standard nonissuer audit report, except for the final statement below.]

We believe that the audit evidence we have obtained is sufficient and appropriate to provide a basis for our *qualified* audit opinion.

(continued)

(continued)

Basis for Qualified Opinion

The company has excluded, from property and debt in the accompanying 20X1 balance sheet, certain capital lease obligations that were entered into in 20X1 which, in our opinion, should be capitalized in accordance with accounting principles generally accepted in the United States of America. If these lease obligations were capitalized, property would be increased by $XXX, long-term debt by $XXX, and retained earnings by $XXX as of December 31, 20X1, and net income and earnings per share would be increased (decreased) by $XXX and $XXX, respectively, for the year then ended.

Qualified Opinion

In our opinion, *except for the effects on the 20X1 financial statements of not capitalizing certain lease obligations as described in the Basis for Qualified Opinion paragraph*, the financial statements referred to above *present fairly*, in all material respects, the financial position of ABC Company as of December 31, 20X1 and 20X0, and the results of its operations and its cash flows for the years then ended in accordance with accounting principles generally accepted in the United States of America.

[*Auditor's signature*]

[*Auditor's city and state*]

[*Date of the auditor's report*]

1.1.2 Sample Report: Unmodified Current Year With Disclaimer on Prior Year Statements of Income, Changes in Stockholders' Equity, and Cash Flows (Nonissuer)

Independent Auditor's Report

[*Appropriate Addressee*]

[*Introductory paragraph same as standard nonissuer audit report*]

Management's Responsibility for the Financial Statements

[*Same as standard nonissuer audit report*]

Auditor's Responsibility

Our responsibility is to express an opinion on these financial statements based on our audits. *Except as explained in the Basis for Disclaimer of Opinion paragraph,* we conducted our audit in accordance with auditing standards generally accepted in the United States of America. Those standards require that we plan and perform the audit to obtain reasonable assurance about whether the financial statements are free from material misstatement.

(continued)

(continued)

An audit involves performing procedures to obtain audit evidence about the amounts and disclosures in the financial statements. The procedures selected depend on the auditor's judgment, including the assessment of the risks of material misstatement of the financial statements, whether due to fraud or error. In making those risk assessments, the auditor considers internal control relevant to the entity's preparation and fair presentation of the financial statements in order to design audit procedures that are appropriate in the circumstances, but not for the purpose of expressing an opinion on the effectiveness of the entity's internal control. Accordingly, we express no such opinion. An audit also includes evaluating the appropriateness of accounting policies used and the reasonableness of significant accounting estimates made by management, as well as evaluating the overall presentation of the financial statements.

We believe that the audit evidence we have obtained is sufficient and appropriate to provide a basis for our audit opinions on the balance sheets as of December 31, 20X2 and 20X1, and the statements of income, changes in stockholders' equity, and cash flows for the year ended December 31, 20X2.

Basis for Disclaimer of Opinion on 20X1 Operations and Cash Flows

We did not observe the taking of the physical inventory as of December 31, 20X0, since that date was prior to our engagement as auditors for the Company, and we were unable to satisfy ourselves regarding inventory quantities by means of other auditing procedures. Inventory amounts as of December 31, 20X0, enter into the determination of net income and cash flows for the year ended December 31, 20X1.

Disclaimer of Opinion

Because of the significance of the matter described in the Basis for Disclaimer of Opinion paragraph, we have not been able to obtain sufficient appropriate audit evidence to provide a basis for an audit opinion on the results of operations and cash flows for the year ended December 31, 20X1. Accordingly, we do not express an opinion on the results of operations and cash flows for the year ended December 31, 20X1.

Opinion

In our opinion, the balance sheets of ABC Company as of December 31, 20X2 and 20X1, and the statements of income, changes in stockholders' equity, and cash flows for the year ended December 31, 20X2, present fairly, in all material respects, the financial position of ABC Company as of December 31, 20X2 and 20X1, and the results of its operations and its cash flows for the year ended December 31, 20X2, in accordance with accounting principles generally accepted in the United States of America.

[*Auditor's signature*]

[*Auditor's city and state*]

[*Date of the auditor's report*]

1.1.3 Sample Report: Unqualified Prior Year Financial Statements With Current Year Qualified (Issuer)

Report of Independent Registered Public Accounting Firm

To the shareholders and the board of directors of X Company:

Opinion on the Financial Statements

We have audited the accompanying balance sheets of X Company (the "Company") as of December 31, 20X2 and 20X1, the related statements of income, comprehensive income, stockholders' equity, and cash flows for each of the years then ended, and the related notes and schedules (collectively referred to as the "financial statements"). In our opinion, *except for* the effects on the 20X2 financial statements of not capitalizing certain lease obligations as described in the following paragraph, the financial statements present fairly, in all material respects, the financial position of the Company as of December 31, 20X2 and 20X1, and the results of its operations and its cash flows for the years then ended in conformity with accounting principles generally accepted in the United States of America.

The Company has excluded, from property and debt in the accompanying 20X2 balance sheet, certain lease obligations that were entered into in 20X2 which, in our opinion, should be capitalized in order to conform with accounting principles generally accepted in the United States of America. If these lease obligations were capitalized, property would be increased by $______, long-term debt by $______, and retained earnings by $______ as of December 31, 20X2, and net income and earnings per share would be increased (decreased) by $______ and $______, respectively, for the year then ended.

Basis for Opinion

[*Basis for Opinion paragraph same as standard issuer audit report*]

Critical Audit Matters

[*Critical Audit Matters section same as standard issuer audit report*]

[*Signature*]

We have served as the Company's auditor since [*year*].

[*City and state or country*]

[*Date*]

1.1.4 Sample Report: Unqualified Current Year With Disclaimer on Prior Year Statements of Income, Changes in Stockholders' Equity, and Cash Flows (Issuer)

Report of Independent Registered Public Accounting Firm

To the shareholders and the board of directors of X Company:

Opinion on the Financial Statements

We have audited the accompanying balance sheets of X Company (the "Company") as of December 31, 20X2 and 20X1, and the related statements of income, comprehensive income, stockholders' equity, and cash flows for the year ended December 31, 20X2, and the related notes and schedules (collectively referred to as the "financial statements").

(continued)

(continued)

In our opinion, the balance sheets of the Company as of December 31, 20X2 and 20X1, and the related statements of income, retained earnings, and cash flows for the year ended December 31, 20X2, present fairly, in all material respects, the financial position of the Company as of December 31, 20X2 and 20X1, and the results of its operations and its cash flows for the year ended December 31, 20X2, in conformity with accounting principles generally accepted in the United States of America. *Because of* the matter discussed in the following paragraph, *we were not able to obtain sufficient appropriate audit evidence* to provide a basis for an audit opinion on the results of operations and cash flows, and *we do not express* an opinion on the results of operations and cash flows for the year ended December 31, 20X1.

We did not observe the taking of the physical inventory as of December 31, 20X0, since that date was prior to our appointment as auditors for the Company, and we were unable to satisfy ourselves regarding inventory quantities by means of other auditing procedures. Inventory amounts as of December 31, 20X0, enter into the determination of net income and cash flows for the year ended December 31, 20X1.

Basis for Opinion

[Same first paragraph under Basis for Opinion as standard issuer audit report]

Except as explained above, we conducted our audits in accordance with the standards of the PCAOB. [*Remainder of paragraph same as standard issuer audit report*]

Critical Audit Matters

[*Critical Audit Matters section same as standard issuer audit report*]

[*Signature*]

We have served as the Company's auditor since [*year*].

[*City and state or country*]

[*Date*]

Pass Key

When the prior year's financial statements were not audited and the current year's financial statements are being audited, the auditor is in essence facing a scope limitation. The beginning balances may not be ascertainable and therefore a disclaimer of opinion on the statements of income, retained earnings, and cash flows may be required.

1.2 Updating (Changing) Prior Opinions

If, during the current examination, the auditor becomes aware of evidence that affects the prior statements and the opinion that was expressed, the auditor should update the opinion in the current year's report. For example, a previous report that was qualified due to a departure from the financial reporting framework would no longer be appropriate in the event of the restatement of the prior year's financial statements.

1.2.1 Format

If the updated opinion differs from the previous opinion, the auditors should disclose the reason(s) in an emphasis-of-matter or other-matter paragraph (nonissuers) or explanatory paragraph (issuers) (following the opinion paragraph). The paragraph should disclose the following:

- **Date** of the auditor's previous report
- **Opinion** type previously issued
- **Reason** for the prior opinion
- **Changes** that have occurred
- **Statement** that the "opinion ... is different."

Pass Key

Remember, only "**DORCS**" change their mind.

1.2.2 Sample Paragraph

In our report dated March 1, 20X1, we expressed an opinion that the 20X0 financial statements did not fairly present the financial position, results of operations, and cash flows of ABC Company in accordance with accounting principles generally accepted in the United States of America because of two departures from such principles: (1) ABC Company carried its property, plant, and equipment at appraisal values, and provided for depreciation on the basis of such values; and (2) ABC Company did not provide for deferred income taxes with respect to differences between income for financial reporting purposes and taxable income. As described in Note X, the Company has changed its method of accounting for these items and restated its 20X0 financial statements to conform accounting principles generally accepted in the United States of America. Accordingly, our present opinion on the restated 20X0 financial statements, as presented herein, is different from that expressed in our previous report.

1.3 Reporting With Predecessor Auditors

1.3.1 Report of the Predecessor Auditor Presented

Predecessor auditors may reissue their report on financial statements as long as the report is still appropriate. However, the current presentation of the prior period statements or the occurrence of subsequent events may make the previous report inappropriate. In deciding whether to reissue their report, the predecessor auditors should:

1. Read the statements for the current period.
2. Compare the statements audited with the current period statements.

3. Obtain a letter of representation from the successor auditor. The representation letter should state whether the successor auditor's audit revealed any matters that, in the successor auditor's opinion, might have a material effect on, or require disclosure in, the statements reported on by the predecessor auditor.
4. Inquire of and obtain a letter of representation from management at or near the date of reissuance. The representation letter should state whether management believes that any of the previous management representations need to be modified and whether there have been any subsequent events requiring adjustment to or disclosure in the reissued financial statements.
5. Date the report as appropriate:
   - **Unrevised:** Use the original report date in any reissue of a previous report, because the predecessor auditor has limited knowledge of the former client's current status.
   - **Revised:** Dual date (covered later) is used in the event that the predecessor auditor revises the report.

1.3.2 Report of the Predecessor Auditor Not Reissued

When the successor auditor does not present the predecessor auditor's report, the successor auditor should express an opinion on the current period financial statements only and indicate in an other-matter paragraph (nonissuer) or explanatory paragraph (issuer):

1. That the financial statements of the prior period were audited by a predecessor auditor. The predecessor auditors should not be named unless the practice of the predecessors was acquired by or merged with that of the successor.
2. The type of opinion expressed by the predecessor auditor and, if the opinion was modified, the reasons for the modification.
3. The nature of any emphasis-of-matter, other-matter, or explanatory paragraph included in the predecessor auditor's report.
4. The date of the predecessor auditor's report.

1.4 Prior Period Financial Statements Not Audited

Whenever unaudited financial statements are presented in comparative form with audited financial statements, the unaudited financial statements should be clearly marked to indicate their status.

1.4.1 Prior Period Statements Reviewed or Compiled

When the current period financial statements are audited and presented in comparative form with prior period financial statements that were reviewed or compiled, and the report of the prior period is not reissued, the auditor should include an other-matter paragraph (nonissuer) or explanatory paragraph (issuer) in the auditor's report that includes:

1. the service (review or compilation) performed in the prior period;
2. the date of the prior period report;
3. a description of any material modifications described in the report; and
4. a statement that the service was less in scope than an audit and does not provide the basis for expressing an opinion on the financial statements as a whole.

The 20X1 financial statements were reviewed by us (other accountants) and our (their) report thereon, dated March 1, 20X2, stated we (they) were not aware of any material modifications that should be made to those statements for them to be in conformity with generally accepted accounting principles. However, a review is substantially less in scope than an audit and does not provide a basis for the expression of an opinion on the financial statements taken as a whole.

1.4.2 Prior Period Statements Not Audited, Reviewed, or Compiled

If the prior period statements were not audited, reviewed, or compiled, the financial statements should be clearly marked, and the auditor's report should include an other-matter paragraph (nonissuer) or explanatory paragraph (issuer) to indicate that the auditor did not audit, review, or compile the prior period financial statements and that the auditor assumes no responsibility for them.

Note: If unaudited financial statements are presented in comparative form with audited financial statements in documents filed with the SEC, such statements should be marked "unaudited," but should not be referred to in the auditor's report.

Question 1 **MCQ-03040**

When reporting on comparative financial statements, an auditor ordinarily should change the previously issued opinion on the prior year's financial statements if the:

a. Prior year's financial statements are restated to conform with generally accepted accounting principles.

b. Auditor is a predecessor auditor who has been requested by a former client to reissue the previously issued report.

c. Prior year's opinion was unmodified and the opinion on the current year's financial statements is modified due to a lack of consistency.

d. Prior year's financial statements are restated following a change in reporting entity in the current year.

Question 2	MCQ-04614

Comparative financial statements include the prior year's statements that were audited by a predecessor auditor whose report is not presented. If the predecessor's report was unmodified, the successor should:

- **a.** Add an emphasis-of-matter paragraph that expresses only limited assurance concerning the fair presentation of the prior year's financial statements.
- **b.** Express an opinion only on the current year's financial statements and make no reference to the prior year's financial statements.
- **c.** Indicate in an other-matter paragraph that the predecessor auditor expressed an unmodified opinion on the prior year's financial statements.
- **d.** Obtain a letter of representation from the predecessor auditor concerning any matters that might affect the successor's opinion.

2 Reporting on Audits of Group Financial Statements

When an auditor acts as the auditor of group financial statements, the auditor must determine whether to make reference to any component auditors in the auditor's report on the group financial statements.

2.1 Definitions

The following definitions will be helpful to understanding audits of group financial statements:

- **Component:** A component is an entity or business activity that prepares financial information that is included in the group financial statements.
- **Component Auditor:** A component auditor is an auditor who performs work on the financial information of a component that will be used as audit evidence for the group audit. A component auditor may be part of the group engagement partner's firm, a network firm, or another firm.
- **Group Engagement Partner:** The group engagement partner (as named by the AICPA)/ principal auditor (as named by the PCAOB auditing standards) is the partner or other person in the firm who is responsible for the group audit engagement and for the auditor's report on the group financial statements.
- **Group Engagement Team:** The group engagement team includes the group engagement partner, other partners, and staff who establish the overall audit strategy, communicate with component auditors, perform work on the consolidation process, and evaluate the conclusions drawn from the audit evidence as the basis for forming an opinion on the group financial statements.
- **Group Financial Statements:** Group financial statements are financial statements that include the financial information of more than one component.

2.2 Understanding the Component Auditor

The group engagement team must understand the following for each component auditor:

- Whether the component auditor is independent and will comply with all relevant ethical requirements.
- The professional competence of the component auditor.
- The extent to which the group engagement team will be involved in the work of the component auditor.
- Whether the group engagement team will be able to get information needed for the consolidation process from the component auditor.
- Whether the component auditor operates in a regulatory environment that actively oversees auditors.

Pass Key

If the component auditor is not independent or the group engagement team has serious concerns about any of the matters listed above, the group engagement team should not use the work of the component auditor or make reference to the component auditor in the auditor's report.

2.3 Determining Whether to Make Reference

The auditor should use the understanding of each component auditor to determine whether to make reference to the component auditor in the auditor's report. The decision is made individually for each component auditor.

When the group engagement team relies on a component auditor to perform a portion of the audit, the group engagement team has two alternatives:

1. Make no reference in the audit report; or
2. Make reference in the audit report.

2.3.1 Option 1: Make No Reference in the Audit Report

When the group engagement partner decides to assume responsibility for the work of a component auditor, no reference to the component auditor should be made in the auditor's report because to do so may cause a reader to misinterpret the degree of responsibility being assumed.

When the group auditor is assuming responsibility for the work of a component auditor, the group engagement team should determine the type of work to be performed on the financial information of the components.

- **Significant Components:** A significant component is a component that is of individual financial significance to the group or is likely to include significant risks of material misstatement of the group financial statements.
  - **Significant Due to Individual Financial Significance:** A component that is significant due to individual financial significance should be audited by the group engagement team or the component auditor.
  - **Significant Due to Significant Risks of Material Misstatement:** If a component that is significant because it is likely to include significant risks of material misstatement to the group financial statements, the group engagement team or a component auditor should perform an audit of the financial information; and/or an audit of the account balances, transactions or disclosures related to the likely significant risk of material misstatement; and/or perform specified procedures related to the likely significant risks of material misstatement.
- **Components That Are Not Significant:** The group engagement team should perform analytical procedures for components that are not significant components.

2.3.2 Option 2: Make Reference in the Audit Report

Reference to the component auditor should not be made unless the following two requirements are met:

1. The component auditor has performed an audit in accordance with the relevant requirements of GAAS, or when required, the PCAOB.
2. The component auditor's report is not restricted use.

When making reference to the component auditor, the auditor's report on the group financial statements should clearly indicate [in the Auditor's Responsibility paragraph (nonissuer) or the Opinion on Financial Statements and Basis for Opinion sections (issuer)]:

- That the component was not audited by the auditor of the group statements but was audited by the component auditor.
- The magnitude of the portion of the financial statements audited by the component auditor.
- When the component's financial statements are prepared using a different financial reporting framework from the group financial statements:
  - the financial reporting framework used by the component; and
  - that the auditor of the group financial statement is taking responsibility for evaluating the appropriateness of the adjustments to convert the component's financial statements to the group financial reporting framework.
- When the component auditor's report on the component's financial statements does not state that the audit was performed in accordance with GAAS or PCAOB standards and the group engagement partner has determined that the component auditor performed additional procedures to meet the relevant requirements of GAAS:
  - the set of auditing standards used by the component auditor; and
  - that additional audit procedures were performed by the component auditor to meet the relevant requirements of GAAS.

2.3.3 Modified Opinion Issued by the Component Auditor

If the opinion of the component auditor is modified or the report includes an emphasis-of-matter or other-matter (explanatory) paragraph, the group auditor should determine the effect on the auditor's report on the group financial statements. When appropriate, the group auditor should modify the opinion on the group financial statements, or include an emphasis-of-matter or other-matter (explanatory) paragraph in the auditor's report.

2.3.4 Sample Report: Referencing the Audit of a Component Auditor (Nonissuer)

Independent Auditor's Report

[*Appropriate Addressee*]

We have audited the accompanying consolidated financial statements of ABC Company and its subsidiaries, which comprise the consolidated balance sheets as of December 31, 20X1 and 20X0, and the related consolidated statements of income, changes in stockholders' equity, and cash flows for the year then ended, and the related notes to the financial statements.

Management's Responsibility for the Financial Statements

[*Same as standard nonissuer audit report*]

Auditor's Responsibility

Our responsibility is to express an opinion on these consolidated financial statements based on our audits. *We did not audit the financial statements of B Company, a wholly owned subsidiary, which statements reflect total assets constituting 20 percent and 22 percent, respectively, of consolidated total assets at December 31, 20X1 and 20X0, and total revenues constituting 18 percent and 20 percent, respectively, of consolidated total revenues for the years then ended. Those statements were audited by other auditors, whose report has been furnished to us, and our opinion, insofar as it relates to the amounts included for B Company, is based solely on the report of the other auditors.* We conducted our audit in accordance with auditing standards generally accepted in the United States of America. Those standards require that we plan and perform the audit to obtain reasonable assurance about whether the financial statements are free from material misstatement.

[*Remainder of auditor's responsibility section same as standard nonissuer audit report*]

Opinion

In our opinion, based on our audit *and the report of the other auditors*, the consolidated financial statements referred to above present fairly, in all material respects, the financial position of ABC Company and its subsidiaries as of December 31, 20X1 and 20X0, and the results of their operations and their cash flows for the year then ended in accordance with accounting principles generally accepted in the United States of America.

2.3.5 Sample Report: Referencing the Audit of a Component Auditor (Issuer)

Report of Independent Registered Public Accounting Firm

To the shareholders and the board of directors of X Company:

Opinion on the Financial Statements

We have audited the accompanying consolidated balance sheets of X Company (the "Company") and subsidiaries as of December 31, 20X2 and 20X1, the related statements of income, comprehensive income, stockholders' equity, and cash flows for each of the years then ended, and the related notes and schedules (collectively referred to as the "financial statements"). In our opinion, *based on our audit and the report of the other auditors,* the consolidated financial statements present fairly, in all material respects, the financial position of the Company as of December 31, 20X2 and 20X1, and the results of its operations and its cash flows for the years then ended in conformity with accounting principles generally accepted in the United States of America.

We did not audit the financial statements of B Company, a wholly owned subsidiary, which statements reflect total assets and revenues constituting 20 percent and 22 percent, respectively, of the related consolidated totals. Those statements were audited by other auditors whose report has been furnished to us, and our opinion, insofar as it relates to the amounts included for B Company, is based solely on the report of the other auditors.

Basis for Opinion

[Same as standard issuer report, except for the statement below]

We believe that our audit and the report of the other auditors provide a reasonable basis for our opinion.

Critical Audit Matters

[*Critical Audit Matters section same as standard issuer audit report*]

[*Signature*]

We have served as the Company's auditor since [*year*].

[*City and state or country*]

[*Date*]

Question 3 **MCQ-02544**

The group auditor decides not to refer to the component auditor who audited a subsidiary of the group auditor's client. In this situation, the group auditor most likely would:

a. Add an emphasis-of-matter paragraph to the auditor's report indicating that the subsidiary's financial statements are not material to the consolidated financial statements.

b. Document in the engagement letter that the group auditor assumes no responsibility for the component auditor's work and opinion.

c. Obtain written permission from the component auditor to omit the reference in the group auditor's report.

d. Determine the type of work to be performed by the group auditor on the financial information of the component.

NOTES

MODULE

9 Reporting on a Single Statement

AUD 1

1 Audits of Single Financial Statements and Specific Elements, Accounts, or Items of a Financial Statement

An auditor may be engaged to audit and express an opinion on a single financial statement or on a specific element, account, or item of a financial statement. An audit of a single financial statement or of specific elements, accounts, or items of a financial statement may be performed as a separate engagement or in conjunction with an audit of an entity's complete set of financial statements.

Examples of single financial statements, each of which would include the related notes, include: balance sheet, statement of income, statement of retained earnings, statement of cash flows, statement of changes in owners' equity, and statement of operations by product line.

The following are examples of specific elements, accounts, or items of a financial statement, each of which would include the related notes:

- Accounts receivable, allowance for doubtful accounts receivable, inventory, or the recorded value of intangible assets.
- A schedule of disbursements regarding a lease property.
- A schedule of profit participation or employee bonuses.

1.1 Acceptability of the Financial Reporting Framework

When auditing a single financial statement or a specific element of a financial statement, the auditor should obtain an understanding of:

1. the purpose for which the single financial statement or specific element of a financial statement is prepared;
2. the intended users; and
3. the steps taken by management to determine that the applicable financial reporting framework is acceptable in the circumstances.

1.2 Audit Procedures

When auditing a single financial statement or a specific element of a financial statement, the auditor should perform procedures on any interrelated items as necessary. Examples of interrelated items include sales and receivables, inventory and payables, and fixed assets and depreciation.

Pass Key

When auditing both a single financial statement or a specific element and an entity's complete set of financial statements, the auditor can use audit evidence obtained during the audit of the complete set of financial statements in the audit of the single financial statement or specific element.

- **Audit of Stockholders' Equity:** When the specific element is, or is based on, stockholders' equity, the auditor should perform procedures necessary to express an opinion about financial position because of the interrelationship between stockholders' equity and the balance sheet accounts.
- **Audit of Net Income:** When the specific element is, or is based on, net income or the equivalent, the auditor should perform procedures necessary to express an opinion about financial position and results of operations because of the interrelationship between net income and the balance sheet and income statement accounts.

1.3 Materiality

- **Audit of a Single Financial Statement:** When auditing a single financial statement, the auditor should determine materiality for the single financial statement rather than for the complete set of financial statements.
- **Audit of a Specific Element:** When auditing a specific element, the auditor should determine materiality separately for each element, rather than for the aggregate of all elements or the complete set of financial statements. As a result, an audit of a specific element is usually more extensive than if the same information is being considered in an audit of the complete set of financial statements.

Pass Key

The only difference between a standard audit report and an audit report on a single financial statement or on a specific element account, or item, is that instead of referring to the financial statements as a whole, the audit report refers only to the single financial statement or specific element, account, or item.

2 Reporting on a Complete Set of Financial Statements and a Single Financial Statement or a Specific Element

When auditing a complete set of financial statements *and* a single financial statement or a specific element of a financial statement, the auditor should:

- Issue a separate auditor's report and express a separate opinion for each engagement. The reports may be published together provided they are sufficiently differentiated and the report on the complete set of financial statements is unmodified (unqualified).
- Indicate in the report on a specific element the date of the auditor's report on the complete set of financial statements and the nature of the opinion expressed on those financial statements under an appropriate heading.

2.1 Modified Opinion on the Complete Set of Financial Statements

2.1.1 Modified Opinion Relevant to the Audit of a Specific Element

If the auditor's modified opinion on the complete set of financial statements is relevant to the audit of a specific element of the financial statements, the auditor should either:

1. express an adverse opinion on the specific element when the modified opinion on the complete set of financial statements is due to a material misstatement of the financial statements; or
2. express a disclaimer of opinion on the specific element when the modified opinion on the complete set of financial statements is due to a scope limitation.

2.1.2 Piecemeal Opinion

When the auditor expresses an adverse opinion or a disclaimer of opinion on the complete set of financial statements, an unmodified (unqualified) opinion on a specific element in the same auditor's report would contradict the adverse opinion or disclaimer of opinion and would be the same as expressing a piecemeal opinion. In this situation, when the auditor considers it appropriate to express an unmodified (unqualified) opinion on the specific element, the auditor should do so only if:

1. the opinion on the specific element is not published with and does not accompany the auditor's report on the complete set of financial statements; and
2. the specific element does not constitute a major portion of the entity's complete set of financial statements or the specific element is not, or is not based on, stockholders' equity or net income.

A single financial statement is considered to be a major portion of a complete set of financial statements. Therefore, an unmodified (unqualified) opinion should not be expressed on a single financial statement if the auditor has expressed an adverse opinion or a disclaimer of opinion on the complete set of financial statements.

2.2 Emphasis-of-Matter, Other-Matter, or Explanatory Paragraphs

If the auditor's report on the complete set of financial statements includes an emphasis-of-matter, other-matter, or explanatory paragraph that is relevant to the audit of the single financial statement or the specific element, the auditor should include a similar emphasis-of-matter, other-matter, or explanatory paragraph in the auditor's report on the single financial statement or specific element.

3 Reporting on an Incomplete Presentation

An incomplete presentation that is otherwise in accordance with GAAP is a type of single financial statement. When the auditor reports on an incomplete presentation that is otherwise in accordance with GAAP, the auditor's report should include an emphasis-of-matter paragraph (following the opinion paragraph) or explanatory paragraph (following the opinion paragraph) for nonissuers and issuers, respectively, that:

1. states the purpose for which the presentation is prepared and refers to the note in the financial statements that describes the basis of the presentation; and
2. indicates that the presentation is not intended to be a complete presentation of the entity's assets, liabilities, revenues, or expenses.

Question 1 **MCQ-02302**

Harris, CPA, has been asked to audit and report on the balance sheet of Fox Co., but not on the statements of income, retained earnings, or cash flows. This audit will not be performed in conjunction with an audit of the complete set of financial statements. Under these circumstances, Harris may:

a. Not accept the engagement because it would constitute a violation of the profession's ethical standards.

b. Not accept the engagement because it would be tantamount to rendering a piecemeal opinion.

c. Accept the engagement because such engagements merely involve special considerations in the application of U.S. GAAS.

d. Accept the engagement but should disclaim an opinion because the complete set of financial statements was not audited.

MODULE

10 Subsequent Events

AUD 1

1 Recognition of Subsequent Events

A subsequent event is an event or transaction that occurs after the balance sheet date but before the financial statements are issued or are available to be issued. Subsequent events can be divided into two categories—recognized subsequent events and nonrecognized subsequent events.

1.1 Recognized Subsequent Events

Subsequent events that provide additional information about conditions that existed at the balance sheet date. Entities must recognize the effects of all recognized subsequent events in the financial statements (for example, by adjusting amounts and/or adding disclosures). Examples of recognized subsequent events include:

- **Settlement of Litigation:** If litigation that arose before the balance sheet date is settled after the balance sheet date but before the date that the financial statements are issued or available to be issued, the settlement amount should be considered when determining the liability to be reported on the balance sheet date.
- **Loss on an Uncollectible Receivable:** The effects of a customer's bankruptcy filing after the balance sheet but before the date that the financial statements are issued or available to be issued should be considered when determining the amount of the uncollectible receivable to be recognized in the financial statements on the balance sheet date.

1.2 Nonrecognized Subsequent Events

Subsequent events that provide information about conditions that occurred after the balance sheet date and did not exist at the balance sheet date. Entities should not recognize nonrecognized subsequent events in the financial statements.

The following subsequent events occurring after the balance sheet date but before the date the financial statements are issued or are available to be issued are considered to be nonrecognized subsequent events:

- Sale of bond or capital stock
- Business combination
- Settlement of litigation, if the litigation arose after the balance sheet date
- Loss of plant or inventory due to fire or natural disaster
- Changes in the fair value of assets or liabilities or foreign exchange rates
- Entering into significant commitments or contingent liabilities

2 Management's Responsibility for Subsequent Events

2.1 Subsequent Event Evaluation Period

Public companies and other entities that intend to widely distribute financial statements must evaluate subsequent events through the date that the financial statements are issued. All other entities must evaluate subsequent events through the date that the financial statements are available to be issued. Financial statements are considered to be issued when they have been widely distributed to financial statement users in a form and format that complies with GAAP. Financial statements are available to be issued when they are in a form and format that complies with GAAP and all approvals for issuance have been obtained.

2.2 Reissuance of Financial Statements

When an entity reissues its financial statements, the entity should not recognize events that occurred between the date the original financial statements were issued or available to be issued and the date that the financial statements were reissued unless an adjustment is required by GAAP or other regulatory requirements.

2.3 Subsequent Event Disclosures

Nonissuers must disclose the date through which subsequent events have been evaluated, including whether that date is the date the financial statements were issued or the date that the financial statements were available to be issued. This disclosure is not required for issuers to avoid potential conflicts with current SEC guidance.

A nonrecognized subsequent event should be disclosed if disclosure is necessary to keep the financial statements from being misleading. Disclosure should include the nature of the subsequent event and an estimate of the financial effect of the event or a statement that no estimate can be made. Pro forma financial statements showing the effect of the subsequent event if it had occurred on the balance sheet date may also be presented.

2.4 Revised Financial Statements

Revised financial statements are financial statements that have been revised to correct an error or to reflect the retrospective application of U.S. GAAP. Revised financial statements are considered reissued financial statements. A nonissuer should disclose in its revised financial statements the dates through which subsequent events have been evaluated in both its issued/available-to-be-issued financial statements and its revised financial statements. This disclosure is not required for issuers.

3 Auditor's Responsibility for Subsequent Events

The period between the date of the financial statements and the date of the auditor's report is called the subsequent period. During this period, the auditor has an active responsibility to investigate certain subsequent events. During the subsequent period, the auditor should obtain an understanding of the procedures management has established to identify subsequent events and should perform the following procedures:

- **Post Balance Sheet Transactions:** The auditor should review post balance sheet transactions for proper cutoff and to better evaluate year-end balances.
- **Representation Letter:** The auditor should obtain a representation letter from management (usually the CEO and CFO) regarding whether any events occurred during the subsequent period that require adjustments to or disclosure in the financial statements.

- **Inquiry:** The auditor should inquire of client's legal counsel concerning litigation, claims, and assessments.

  The auditor should also inquire of management and those charged with governance about whether any subsequent events have occurred that could affect the financial statements. Specific inquiries should be made about the following matters:

  - New commitments, borrowings, or guarantees
  - Sales or acquisitions of assets
  - Increases in capital or issuances of debt
  - Assets appropriated by the government or destroyed
  - Developments regarding contingencies
  - Unusual accounting adjustments
  - Events that call into question the appropriateness of the entity's accounting policies
  - Events relevant to the measurement of estimates or provisions
  - Events relevant to the recoverability of assets

- **Minutes:** The auditor should review the minutes of stockholders, directors, and other committee meetings during the subsequent period.
- **Examine:** The auditor should examine the latest available interim financial statements and compare them with the financial statements under audit.

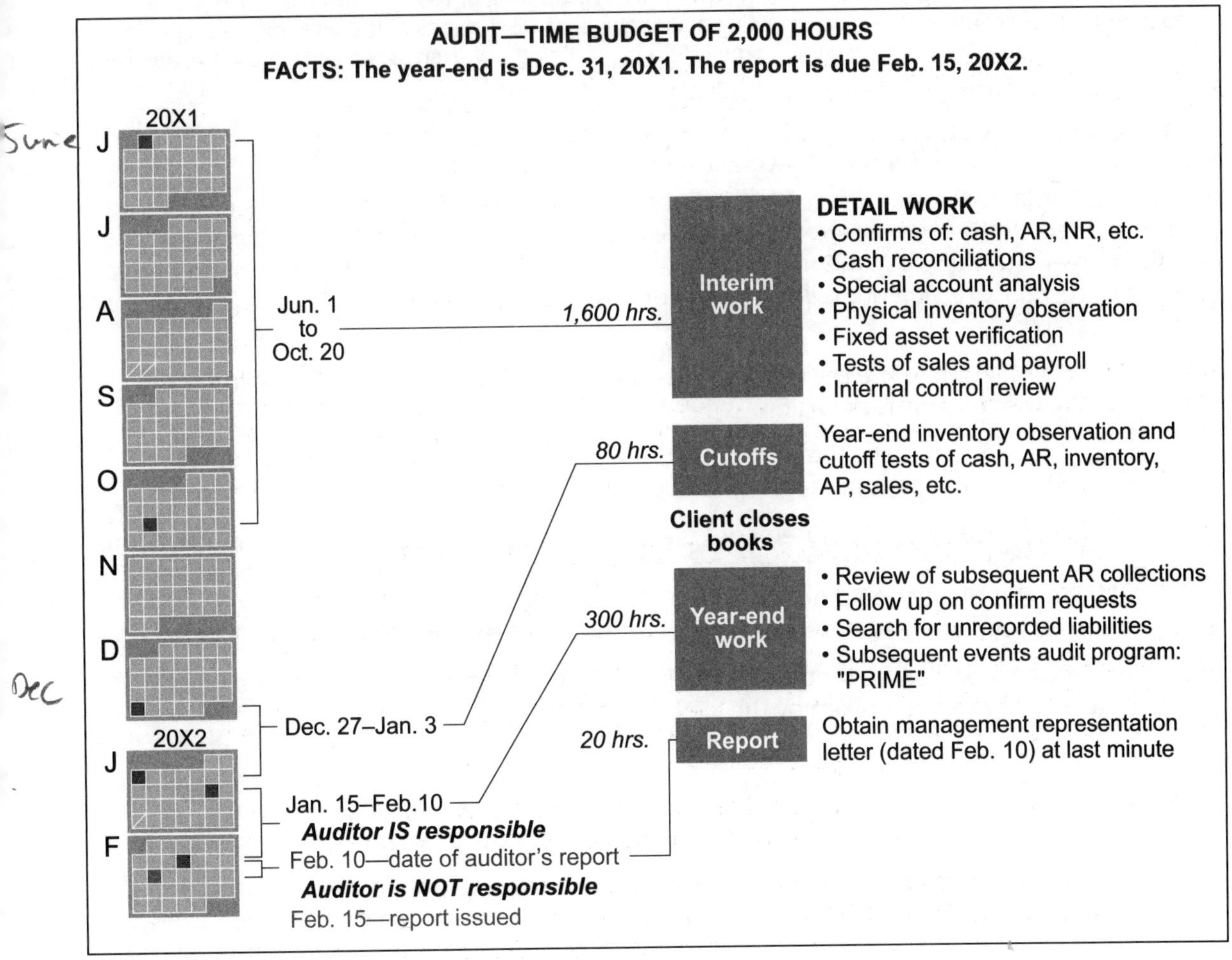

4 Auditor's Responsibility After the Original Date of the Auditor's Report

The auditor has no active responsibility to make any inquiries or to perform any further auditing procedures to discover subsequent events after the original date of the auditor's report except as described in the chart below. However, if the auditor becomes aware of any information relating to subsequent events before the report release date, the auditor should consider whether it is necessary to adjust the financial statements or related disclosures.

The auditor should extend subsequent event procedures beyond the audit report date for the situations identified below. The purpose of these procedures is to identify information that, had it been known to the auditor as of the date of the auditor's report, may have caused the auditor to revise the auditor's report.

Situation	Extend subsequent procedures to:
Auditor's report on financial statements is included in an exempt offering document and the auditor is involved* in the offering.	The date of the distribution, circulation, or submission of the exempt offering document.
Auditor's report is included in a registration statement.	The date of or shortly before the effective date of the registration statement.

* Involvement in the offering includes assisting the entity in preparing or reading information in the document, issuing a comfort letter, participating in due diligence discussions of the offering, issuing an attestation report on information relating to the offering, providing a written agreement to use the auditor's report, or updating an auditor's report for inclusion in that document.

4.1 Auditor Action

If information that materially affects the report and other persons' reliance on it is discovered (and confirmed by the auditor) after issuance of the report, the auditor should advise the client to immediately disclose the new information and its impact on the financial statements to persons currently relying on or likely to rely on the financial statements. This may be accomplished by:

- Advising the client to issue revised financial statements (along with a new audit report) describing the reasons for revision.
- Advising the client to make the necessary disclosures and revisions to any imminent financial statements (accompanied by an auditor's report for a subsequent period); or
- If the effect on the financial statements cannot be determined on a timely basis, providing notification that the financial statements and auditor's report should not be relied upon. In addition, the client should be advised to discuss with the SEC, stock exchanges, and appropriate regulatory agencies (where applicable) the new disclosures or revisions.

Regardless of which disclosure method above is used, the auditor must become satisfied that appropriate steps have been taken by the client.

4.2 Report Date

If adjustments or disclosures are made after the original date of the auditor's report, the auditor may dual date the report to extend responsibility only for the particular subsequent event. The original date of the report is retained for the rest of the financial statements.

- Example of dual dating: "January 21, 20X2, except as to Note 2, which is as of February 3, 20X2."
- For nonissuers, dual dating may occur if adjustments or disclosures are made after the original date of the auditor's report.
- For issuers, dual dating may occur if disclosures are made after the original date of the auditor's report. If adjustments are made to the financial statements without any footnote disclosure, the original date of the report should be used.

Alternatively, a later date may be used for the report, but this extends the auditor's responsibility for all subsequent events to this later date.

4.3 Client Refusal

If the client refuses to proceed as above, the auditor should notify each member of the board of directors of such refusal, and of the fact that the auditor will take additional steps to prevent further reliance on the auditor's report and the financial statements.

Additional steps to prevent further reliance include the following:

- Notify the client that the auditor's report must no longer be associated with the financial statement.
- Notify, if applicable, any regulatory agencies having jurisdiction over the client that the auditor's report should no longer be relied on.
- Notify persons known to be relying or likely to rely on the financial statements that the auditor's report should no longer be relied on.

Any notification to parties other than the client should be as precise and factual as possible, and should contain a description of the effect that the discovered information would have had on the auditor's report on the financial statements.

If the client has refused to cooperate, and as a result the auditors were unable to conduct an adequate investigation of the information, the auditors' disclosure need only state that information has come to their attention and that, if the information is true, their report should no longer be relied upon.

The auditors should use their professional judgment in the circumstances described above, and it may be advisable to consult legal counsel.

Pass Key

If the auditor believes that the financial statements need to be revised to reflect a subsequent event and management does not make the revision, the auditor should express a qualified or adverse opinion.

Question 1 **MCQ-04612**

As of August 13, a CPA had obtained sufficient appropriate audit evidence with respect to fieldwork on an engagement to audit financial statements for the year ended June 30. On August 27, an event came to the CPA's attention that should be disclosed in the notes to the financial statements. The event was properly disclosed by the entity, but the CPA decided not to dual date the auditor's report and dated the report August 27. Under these circumstances, the CPA was taking responsibility for:

a. All subsequent events that occurred through August 27.

b. Only the specific subsequent event disclosed by the entity.

c. All subsequent events that occurred through August 13 and the specific subsequent event disclosed by the entity.

d. Only the subsequent events that occurred through August 13.

MODULE

11 Other Information and Supplementary Information

AUD 1

1 Other Information

Frequently, audited financial statements are incorporated into other documents, such as annual reports to shareholders or reports by charitable organizations to the general public.

Other information includes:

- A report by management or those charged with governance on operations
- Financial summaries or highlights
- Employment data
- Planned capital expenditures
- Financial ratios
- Names of officers and directors
- Selected quarterly data

Other information does not include press releases or cover letters accompanying the document containing the audited financial statements and the auditor's report, information contained in analyst briefings, or information contained on the entity's website.

1.1 Auditor's Responsibility

Generally, an auditor is not responsible for determining whether other information in documents containing the audited financial statements and the auditor's report is properly stated. However, the auditor should read the other information because the credibility of the audited financial statements may be undermined if there are material inconsistencies between the audited financial statements and the other information.

1.2 Material Inconsistency

The document containing the audited financial statements may contain other information that is materially inconsistent with the financial statements. If the auditor identifies a material inconsistency, the auditor should determine whether the audited financial statements or the other information needs to be revised.

Illustration 1 Material Inconsistency

If other information shows revenue for Year 1 at $20,000,000 and the audited financial statements show revenue for Year 1 at $5,000,000, this is a material inconsistency that needs additional attention.

1.2.1 Audited Financial Statements Require Revision

If the audited financial statements require revision for a material inconsistency and management refuses to make the revision, the auditor should modify the audit opinion.

1.2.2 Other Information Requires Revision

If the other information requires revision for a material inconsistency and management refuses to make the revision, the auditor should communicate this matter with those charged with governance and:

- include in the auditor's report an other-matter paragraph (nonissuer) or explanatory paragraph (issuer) describing the material inconsistency;
- withhold the use of the report; or
- withdraw from the engagement and consult with legal counsel.

1.3 Material Misstatement of Fact

Other information may include a material misstatement of fact that is unrelated to financial statement data. If the auditor becomes aware of a material misstatement of fact after reading the other information, the auditor should discuss the matter with management. If management refuses to take corrective action, the auditor should request that management consult with a qualified third party, such as the entity's legal counsel, and the auditor should consider the advice received from the third party in determining whether the matter is a material misstatement of fact. When the auditor concludes that there is a material misstatement of fact that management refuses to correct, the auditor should notify those charged with governance.

1.4 Disclaimer of Opinion on Other Information (Optional)

The auditor is not required to reference the other information in the audit report on the financial statements. However, the auditor may choose to include an other-matter paragraph (nonissuer) or explanatory paragraph (issuer) disclaiming an opinion on the other information:

> Our audit was conducted for the purpose of forming an opinion on the basic financial statements as a whole. The [*identify the other information*] is presented for purposes of additional analysis and is not a required part of the basic financial statements. Such information has not been subjected to the auditing procedures applied in the audit of the basic financial statements and, accordingly, we do not express an opinion or provide any assurance on it.

2 Reporting on Supplementary Information

Supplementary information is information presented outside the basic financial statements that may be presented in a document containing the audited financial statements or separate from the financial statements.

An auditor may be engaged to report on supplementary information in relation to the financial statements as a whole. The auditor has two objectives in such engagements:

1. To evaluate the presentation of the supplementary information in relation to the financial statements as a whole.
2. To report on whether the supplementary information is fairly stated, in all material respects, in relation to the financial statements as a whole.

2.1 Conditions for Reporting

In order to issue an opinion on whether the supplementary information is fairly stated in all material respects in relation to the financial statements as a whole, the auditor must determine that the following five conditions are met:

1. The information was derived from or relates directly to the information used to prepare the financial statements.
2. The information relates to the same period as the financial statements.
3. The financial statements were audited and the auditor issued an auditor's report.
4. Neither an adverse opinion nor a disclaimer of opinion was issued on the financial statements.
5. The supplementary information will accompany the audited financial statements or the audited financial statements will be made readily available by the entity.

2.2 Management Responsibility

The auditor must obtain an agreement of management that it acknowledges and understands its responsibilities to:

1. prepare the information in accordance with applicable criteria;
2. provide the auditor with written representations related to the information;
3. include the auditor's report on the supplementary information in any document that contains the information; and
4. present the information with the audited financial statements or make the audited financial statements readily available to the intended users of the supplementary information by the issuance date of the supplementary information and auditor's report.

2.3 Audit Procedures

In addition to the procedures performed during the audit of the financial statements, the auditor should perform the following audit procedures using the same materiality level used in the financial statement audit:

- Inquire of management regarding the purpose of the supplementary information and the criteria used to prepare the information.
- Determine whether the form and content of the information complies with the applicable criteria.
- Obtain an understanding of the methods used to prepare the information, and any changes from the methods used in the prior periods, including the reasons for the changes.
- Compare and reconcile the information to the audited financial statements and underlying accounting records.
- Inquire regarding any significant assumptions underlying the preparation or presentation of the information.
- Evaluate the appropriateness and completeness of the information.
- Obtain written representations from management regarding the information.

The auditor has no responsibility to consider subsequent events with respect to supplementary information.

PCAOB Standards: Guidance for Issuers

PCAOB standards include the following additional requirements for audit procedures:

- Evaluate the *appropriateness* of methods used to prepare the supplemental information. If the methods have changed, evaluate the *appropriateness* of such changes.
- Determine that the supplemental information reconciles to the underlying accounting and *other records* or to the financial statements, as applicable.
- The auditor generally should use the same materiality considerations as those used in planning and performing the audit of the financial statements, except if an applicable regulatory requirement specifies *a lower materiality level* to be applied to certain supplemental information.

PCAOB standards include the following additional requirements for evaluation of audit results for supplementary information:

- The auditor should evaluate whether the supplemental information, including its form and content, is fairly stated, in all material respects, in relation to the financial statements as a whole, including whether the supplemental information is presented in conformity, in all material respects, with the relevant regulatory requirements or other applicable criteria.
- The auditor should accumulate misstatements on the supplemental information. These misstatements should be communicated to management on a timely basis to provide management with an opportunity to correct them.
- The auditor should evaluate whether uncorrected misstatements related to the supplemental information are material, either individually or in combination with other misstatements, taking into account relevant quantitative and qualitative factors. The auditor should evaluate the effect of uncorrected misstatements related to the supplemental information in evaluating the results of the financial statement audit.

2.4 Reporting for Nonissuers

2.4.1 Presentation of Audit Report

The auditor's report on the supplementary information may either be presented as an other-matter paragraph in the auditor's report on the financial statements or in a separate report.

- **Sample Other-Matter Paragraph**

> Our audit was conducted for the purpose of forming an opinion on the financial statements as a whole. The [*identify accompanying supplementary information*] is presented for purposes of additional analysis and is not a required part of the financial statements. Such information is the responsibility of management and was derived from and relates directly to the underlying accounting and other records used to prepare the financial statements. The information has been subjected to the auditing procedures applied in the audit of the financial statements and certain additional procedures, including comparing and reconciling such information directly to the underlying accounting and other records used to prepare the financial statements or to the financial statements themselves, and other additional procedures in accordance with auditing standards generally accepted in the United States of America. In our opinion, the information is fairly stated in all material respects in relation to the financial statements as a whole.

- **Separate Report**

  When reporting separately, the report should include a reference to the report on the financial statements, the date of that report, the nature of the opinion on the financial statements, and any report modifications. The auditor may also consider including an alert that restricts the use of the separate report solely to the appropriate specified parties to avoid potential misinterpretation or misunderstanding of the supplementary information that is not presented with the financial statements.

  The date of the auditor's report should not be earlier than the date that the required procedures were completed.

2.4.2 Forming an Opinion on Supplementary Information

- **Material Misstatement**

  If the auditor concludes that the supplementary information is materially misstated in relation to the financial statements as a whole and management refuses to revise the information, that auditor should:

  - Modify the opinion on the supplementary information (qualified or adverse) and describe the misstatement.
  - If a separate report is being issued on the supplementary information, withhold the report.

- **Effect of Modifications to the Audit Report on the Financial Statements**

  When the auditor expresses a qualified opinion on the financial statements and the basis for the qualification also applies to the supplemental information, the auditor should describe the effects of the qualification on the supplemental information in the report on supplemental information and should express a qualified opinion on the supplemental information.

  When the auditor's report on the audited financial statements contains an adverse opinion or a disclaimer of opinion and the auditor has been engaged to report on supplementary information, the auditor is prohibited from expressing an opinion on the supplementary information.

2.5 Reporting for Issuers

2.5.1 Presentation of Audit Report

Unless prescribed by regulatory requirements, the auditor may either include the auditor's report on the supplemental information as an explanatory paragraph in the auditor's report on the financial statements, or issue a separate report on the supplemental information. If the auditor issues a separate report on the supplemental information, that report should identify the auditor's report on the financial statements.

> The [*identify supplemental information*] has been subjected to audit procedures performed in conjunction with the audit of [*Company's*] financial statements. The [*supplemental information*] is the responsibility of the Company's management. Our audit procedures included determining whether the [*supplemental information*] reconciles to the financial statements or the underlying accounting and other records, as applicable, and performing procedures to test the completeness and accuracy of the information presented in the [*supplemental information*]. In forming our opinion on the [*supplemental information*], we evaluated whether the [*supplemental information*], including its form and content, is presented in conformity with [*specify the relevant regulatory requirement or other criteria, if any*]. In our opinion, the [*identify supplemental information*] is fairly stated, in all material respects, in relation to the financial statements as a whole.

2.5.2 Report Date

The date of the auditor's report on the supplemental information in relation to the financial statements as a whole should not be earlier than:

1. the date of the auditor's report on the financial statements from which the supplemental information was derived; and
2. the date on which the auditor obtained sufficient appropriate audit evidence to support the auditor's opinion on the supplemental information in relation to the financial statements as a whole.

2.5.3 Forming an Opinion on Supplementary Information

- **Material Misstatements**

  If the auditor determines that the supplemental information is materially misstated in relation to the financial statements as a whole, the auditor should describe the material misstatement in the auditor's report on the supplemental information and express a qualified or adverse opinion on the supplemental information.

- **Inability to Obtain Sufficient Appropriate Audit Evidence**

  If the auditor is unable to obtain sufficient appropriate audit evidence to support an opinion on the supplemental information, the auditor should disclaim an opinion on the supplemental information. In those situations, the auditor's report on the supplemental information should describe the reason for the disclaimer and state that the auditor is unable to and does not express an opinion on the supplemental information.

- **Effect of Modifications to the Audit Report on the Financial Statements**

  When the auditor expresses a qualified opinion on the financial statements and the basis for the qualification also applies to the supplemental information, the auditor should describe the effects of the qualification on the supplemental information in the report on supplemental information and should express a qualified opinion on the supplemental information.

  When the auditor expresses an adverse opinion or disclaims an opinion on the financial statements, the auditor should also express an adverse opinion or disclaim an opinion on the supplemental information, as appropriate.

3 Required Supplementary Information

Certain entities are required by a designated standard setter to prepare specific information that is supplementary to the basic financial statements. In the absence of any separate requirement particular to the engagement, the auditor's opinion on the financial statements does not cover the required supplementary information.

3.1 Required Procedures

The auditor should perform the following procedures on required supplementary information:

1. Inquire of management about the methods used to prepare the required supplementary information, including whether it was prepared in accordance with prescribed guidance, whether there were changes in the methods used from prior years and reasons for those changes, and whether there were any significant assumptions underlying the measurement or presentation of the required information.
2. Determine if the supplementary information is consistent with management's responses, audited financial statements, and other knowledge.
3. Obtain written management representations regarding the required supplementary information.

If the auditor is unable to perform these procedures due to difficulties in dealing with management, the auditor should inform those charged with governance.

3.2 Reporting on Supplementary Information

3.2.1 Other-Matter Paragraph Required (Nonissuer)

The audit report for nonissuers on the financial statements should include an other-matter paragraph with language to explain the following circumstances, as applicable:

- the required supplementary information is included and the auditor has applied the required procedures;
- the required supplementary information is omitted;
- some required supplementary information is missing and some is presented in accordance with the prescribed guidelines;
- the auditor has identified material departures from the prescribed guidelines;
- the auditor is not able to complete the required procedures; or
- there are unresolved doubts about conformance of required supplementary information.

This other-matter paragraph should include a disclaimer of opinion on the required supplementary information. If the auditor determines that the required information has not been presented as prescribed, and management refuses to make revisions, the auditor should describe the departure.

PCAOB Standards: Guidance for Issuers

PCAOB standards do not require the auditor to add an explanatory paragraph to the audited financial statements to refer to the supplementary information or to his or her limited procedures, except if:

- the required information is omitted;
- there are material departures from the prescribed guidelines;
- the auditor is unable to complete prescribed procedures; or
- there are unresolved doubts about conformance of required supplementary information.

3.2.2 Opinion Permitted

An auditor is not required to audit required supplementary information. However, a client may engage the auditor to report on whether required supplementary information is fairly stated, in all material respects, in relation to the financial statements as a whole. This engagement is performed as described earlier in this module.

Question 1 **MCQ-04617**

In the audit of a nonissuer, what is an auditor's responsibility for supplementary information, such as the disclosure of pension information, which is outside the basic financial statements but required by the GASB?

a. The auditor should apply substantive tests of transactions to the supplementary information and verify its conformity with the GASB requirement.

b. The auditor should apply certain limited procedures to the supplementary information and add an other-matter paragraph to the auditor's report.

c. The auditor's only responsibility for the supplementary information is to determine that such information has *not* been omitted.

d. The auditor has *no* responsibility for such supplementary information as long as it is outside the basic financial statements.

MODULE

12 Special Purpose and Other Country Frameworks

AUD 1

1 Special Purpose Frameworks

Normally, financial statements are prepared using a general purpose framework such as U.S. GAAP or IFRS, but special purpose frameworks can also be used by nonissuers (issuers must follow the required general purpose framework).

1.1 Types of Special Purpose Frameworks

A special purpose framework is a financial reporting framework other than GAAP that is one of the following bases of accounting:

- **Cash Basis:** A basis of accounting that the entity uses to record cash receipts and disbursements and modifications of the cash basis having substantial support, such as recording depreciation on fixed assets.
- **Tax Basis:** A basis of accounting that the entity uses to file its income tax return for the period covered by the financial statements.
- **Regulatory Basis:** A basis of accounting used to comply with the requirements or financial reporting provisions of a regulatory agency having jurisdiction over the reporting entity.
- **Contractual Basis:** A basis of accounting that the entity uses to comply with an agreement between the entity and one or more third parties other than the auditor.
- **Other Basis:** A basis of accounting that uses a definite set of logical, reasonable criteria that is applied to all material items appearing in financial statements.

1.2 Additional Requirements for the Auditor

When applying auditing standards to an audit of financial statements prepared in accordance with a special purpose framework, the auditor should:

- Obtain an understanding of:
  - The purpose for which the financial statements are prepared.
  - The intended users.
  - The steps taken by management to determine that the applicable financial reporting framework is acceptable in the circumstances.
- Obtain the agreement of management that it acknowledges and understands its responsibility to include all informative disclosures that are appropriate for the special purpose framework, including:
  - A description of the special purpose framework, including a summary of significant accounting policies and how the framework differs from GAAP.
  - Informative disclosures similar to GAAP when the special purpose framework contains items that are the same as or similar to those in GAAP financial statements.

- A description of any significant interpretations of the contract on which the special purpose financial statements are based, when the financial statements are prepared in accordance with a contractual basis of accounting.
- Additional disclosures beyond those required by the framework, if needed to achieve fair presentation.

- Obtain an understanding of any significant interpretations of the contract that management made in the preparation of the financial statements, when special purpose financial statements are prepared in accordance with a contractual basis of accounting.

2 Auditor's Report on Special Purpose Financial Statements

Special purpose frameworks have additional requirements of elements that must be included in the audit report. These additional elements depend on the particular special purpose framework. Below is a chart that provides an overview of the reporting requirements for special purpose frameworks for nonissuers:

Special Purpose Frameworks: Overview of Reporting Requirements

	Cash Basis	*Tax Basis*	*Regulatory Basis*	*Regulatory Basis (General Use)*	*Contractual Basis*	*Other Basis*
Opinion(s)	Single opinion on special purpose framework	Single opinion on special purpose framework	Single opinion on special purpose framework	Dual opinion on special purpose framework and generally accepted accounting principles	Single opinion on special purpose framework	Single opinion on special purpose framework
Description of purpose for which special purpose financial statements are prepared	No	No	Yes	Yes	Yes	Yes, if the financial statements are restricted
Emphasis-of-matter paragraph alerting readers about the preparation in accordance with a special purpose framework	Yes	Yes	Yes	No	Yes	Yes
Other-matter paragraph restricting the use of the auditor's report	No	No	Yes	No	Yes	Yes, if measurement or disclosure criteria is suitable only for specific users

Pass Key

The cash, tax, and regulatory bases of accounting are commonly referred to as other comprehensive bases of accounting.

2.1 Differences From Standard Auditor's Report

The following items are the significant differences between the standard nonissuer auditor's report and a report on special purpose financial statements.

2.1.1 Describe the Purpose of the Financial Statements

If required (see previous chart), the auditor's report should describe the purpose for which the financial statements were prepared or refer to a note that contains that information.

2.1.2 Non-GAAP Titles

Special purpose statements should be suitably titled. Terms such as balance sheet, statement of financial position, statement of income, statement of operations, and statement of cash flows, or similar unmodified titles, are generally understood to be applicable only to financial statements that are intended to present financial position, results of operations, or cash flows in accordance with GAAP. Examples of suitably titled special purpose financial statements include the following:

- Balance sheet—*cash basis*
- Statement of assets and liabilities arising from cash transactions—*cash basis*
- Statement of assets, liabilities, and stockholders' equity—*income tax basis*
- Statement of revenue collected and expenses paid—*cash basis*
- Statement of revenue and expenses—*income tax basis*
- Statement of income—*regulatory basis*
- Statement of operations—*income tax basis*

2.1.3 Management Responsibility Paragraph

When management has a choice of financial reporting frameworks, the explanation of management's responsibility for the financial statements should also make reference to its responsibility for determining that the applicable financial reporting framework is acceptable in the circumstances.

2.1.4 Emphasis-of-Matter Paragraph

If required (see previous chart), the auditor's report should include an emphasis-of-matter paragraph that:

- Indicates that the financial statements are prepared in accordance with the applicable special purpose framework.
- Refers to the note to the financial statements that describes that framework.
- States that the special purpose framework is a basis of accounting other than GAAP.

2.1.5 Other-Matter Paragraph

If required (see previous chart), the auditor's report should include an other-matter paragraph that restricts the use of the auditor's report to those within the entity, the parties to the contract or agreement, or the regulatory agencies to which the entity is subject.

> Our report is intended solely for the information and use of the board of directors and management of ABC Company and [*name of regulatory agency*] and is not intended to be and should not be used by anyone other than these specified parties.

2.1.6 Regulatory Basis Financial Statements Intended for General Use

If the special purpose financial statements are prepared in accordance with a regulatory basis and intended for general use, the auditor should not include an emphasis-of-matter or other-matter paragraph. Instead, the auditor should express an opinion about whether the financial statements are:

- Fairly presented, in all material respects, in accordance with GAAP.
- Prepared in accordance with the special purpose framework.

2.1.7 Auditor's Report Prescribed by Law or Regulation

If the auditor is required by law or regulation to use a specific layout, form, or wording of the auditor's report, the auditor's report should refer to GAAS only if the auditor's report includes, at a minimum, each of the elements listed below. If the prescribed specific layout, form, or wording of the auditor's report is not acceptable or would cause the auditor to make a statement that the auditor has no basis to make, the auditor should reword the prescribed form of report or attach an appropriately worded separate report.

2.2 Reports on Special Purpose Financial Statements

A report on special purpose financial statements should, at a minimum, include each of the following elements:

- A title.
- An addressee.
- An introductory paragraph that identifies the special purpose financial statements audited.
- A description of the responsibility of management for the preparation and fair presentation of the special purpose financial statements.
- A reference to management's responsibility for determining that the applicable financial reporting framework is acceptable in the circumstances (when management has a choice of frameworks in the preparation of the financial statements).
- A description of the purpose for which the financial statements are prepared when required.

- A description of the auditor's responsibility to express an opinion on the special purpose financial statements and the scope of the audit that includes:
  - A reference to GAAS and, if applicable, the law or regulation.
  - A description of an audit in accordance with those standards.
  - An opinion paragraph that contains an opinion on the special purpose financial statements and a reference to the special purpose framework used to prepare the financial statements.
- If applicable, an opinion on whether the special purpose financial statements are presented fairly, in all material respects, in accordance with GAAP when the special purpose financial statements are prepared in accordance with a regulatory basis and intended for general use.
- An emphasis-of-matter paragraph that indicates that the financial statements are prepared in accordance with a special purpose framework, when required.
- An other-matter paragraph that restricts the use of the auditor's report, when required.
- The auditor's signature.
- The auditor's city and state.
- The date of the auditor's report.

2.2.1 Sample Report: Cash Basis of Accounting (Nonissuer)

The following report would be issued when circumstances include the following:

- The financial statements have been prepared by management of the entity in accordance with the cash basis of accounting.
- Management has a choice of financial reporting frameworks.

Independent Auditor's Report

[*Appropriate Addressee*]

We have audited the accompanying financial statements of ABC Partnership, which comprise *the statement of assets and liabilities arising from cash transactions* as of December 31, 20X1, and the *related statement of revenue collected and expenses paid* for the year then ended, and the related notes to the financial statements.

Management's Responsibility for the Financial Statements

Management is responsible for the preparation and fair presentation of these financial statements in accordance with *the cash basis of accounting described in Note X; this includes determining that the cash basis of accounting is an acceptable basis for the preparation of the financial statements in the circumstances*. Management is also responsible for the design, implementation, and maintenance of internal control relevant to the preparation and fair presentation of financial statements that are free from material misstatement, whether due to fraud or error.

Auditor's Responsibility

[*Same as standard nonissuer audit report*]

(continued)

(continued)

Opinion

In our opinion, the *financial statements* referred to above present fairly, in all material respects, *the assets and liabilities arising from cash transactions of ABC Partnership as of December 31, 20X1, and its revenues collected and expenses paid during the year then ended in accordance with the cash basis of accounting described in Note X.*

Basis of Accounting*

We draw attention to Note X of the financial statements, which describes the basis of accounting. The financial statements are prepared on the cash basis of accounting, which is a basis of accounting other than accounting principles generally accepted in the United States of America. Our opinion is not modified with respect to this matter.

[*Auditor's signature*]
[*Auditor's city and state*]
[*Date of the auditor's report*]

*Another appropriate heading may be used, such as Emphasis-of-Matter.

2.2.2 Sample Report: Regulatory Basis of Accounting (Nonissuer)

The following report would be issued when circumstances include the following:

- The financial statements and auditor's report are intended for general use.
- The financial statements have been prepared by management of the entity in accordance with financial reporting provisions established by a regulatory agency.
- Based on the regulatory requirements, management does not have a choice of financial reporting frameworks.
- The variances between the regulatory basis of accounting and accounting principles generally accepted in the United States of America (U.S. GAAP) are not reasonably determinable and are presumed to be material.

Independent Auditor's Report

[*Appropriate Addressee*]

We have audited the accompanying financial statements of XYZ City, Any State, which comprise *cash and unencumbered cash for each fund as of December 31, 20X1, and the related statements of cash receipts and disbursements and disbursements-budget and actual for the year then ended,* and the related notes to the financial statements.

Management's Responsibility for the Financial Statements

Management is responsible for the preparation and fair presentation of these financial statements in accordance with *the financial reporting provisions of Section Y of Regulation Z of Any State*. Management is also responsible for the design, implementation, and maintenance of internal control relevant to the preparation and fair presentation of financial statements that are free from material misstatement, whether due to fraud or error.

(continued)

(continued)

Auditor's Responsibility

[*Same as standard nonissuer audit report*]

Basis for Adverse Opinion on U.S. Generally Accepted Accounting Principles

As described in Note X of the financial statements, the financial statements are prepared by XYZ City on the basis of the financial reporting provisions of Section Y of Regulation Z of Any State, which is a basis of accounting other than accounting principles generally accepted in the United States of America, to meet the requirements of Any State.

The effects on the financial statements of the variances between the regulatory basis of accounting described in Note X and accounting principles generally accepted in the United States of America, although not reasonably determinable, are presumed to be material.

Adverse Opinion on Generally Accepted Accounting Principles

In our opinion, because of the significance of the matter discussed in the "Basis for Adverse Opinion on U.S. Generally Accepted Accounting Principles" paragraph, the financial statements referred to above do not present fairly, in accordance with accounting principles generally accepted in the United States of America, the financial position of each fund of XYZ City as of December 31, 20X1, or changes in financial position or cash flows thereof for the year then ended.

Opinion on Regulatory Basis of Accounting

In our opinion, the *financial statements* referred to above present fairly, in all material respects, *the cash and unencumbered cash of each fund of XYZ City* as of December 31, 20X1, and their *respective cash receipts and disbursements, and budgetary results* for the year then ended in accordance with the *financial reporting provisions of Section Y of Regulation Z of Any State as described in Note X.*

[*Auditor's signature*]

[*Auditor's city and state*]

[*Date of the auditor's report*]

Question 1 **MCQ-02732**

An auditor's report on financial statements prepared on the cash receipts and disbursements basis of accounting should include all of the following, *except*:

a. A reference to the note to the financial statements that describes the cash receipts and disbursements basis of accounting.

b. A statement that the cash receipts and disbursements basis of accounting is *not* a comprehensive basis of accounting.

c. An opinion as to whether the financial statements are presented fairly in conformity with the cash receipts and disbursements basis of accounting.

d. A statement that the audit was conducted in accordance with auditing standards generally accepted in the United States of America.

3 Other Country Frameworks

An auditor practicing in the United States may be engaged to report on financial statements that have been prepared in accordance with a financial reporting framework generally accepted in another country that has not been adopted by a body designated by the AICPA to establish generally accepted accounting principles, when such audited financial statements are intended for use outside the United States.

Pass Key

Note that the AICPA has designated the International Accounting Standards Board (IASB) as a body that establishes generally accepted accounting principles. Therefore, these rules are not applicable to engagements to report on financial statements prepared in accordance with IFRS. Under AICPA standards, engagements to report on financial statements prepared in accordance with IFRS are conducted in accordance with the same rules that govern engagements to report on financial statements prepared in accordance with U.S. GAAP.

The PCAOB does not include guidance related to reporting on financial statements prepared in accordance with a financial reporting framework generally accepted in another country.

3.1 Engagement Acceptance

In an audit of financial statements prepared in accordance with a financial reporting framework generally accepted in another country, the auditor should obtain an understanding of:

1. the purpose for which the financial statements are prepared;
2. whether the financial reporting framework is a fair presentation framework;
3. the intended users of the financial statements; and
4. the steps taken by management to determine whether the applicable financial reporting framework is acceptable in the circumstances.

The auditor should also obtain an understanding of the applicable legal responsibilities involved if the auditor plans to use the form and content of the auditor's report of another country.

3.2 Engagement Performance

When performing the audit, the auditor should comply with GAAS and should consider whether the application of GAAS requires special consideration in the circumstances of the engagement. If the terms of the engagement require the auditor to apply the auditing standards of the country or the International Standards on Auditing (ISAs), the auditor should obtain an understanding of and apply those standards, as well as GAAS, except for requirements related to the form and content of the auditor's report.

3.3 Reporting: Distribution Outside the United States

For distribution only outside the U.S. (or with limited distribution to specific knowledgeable parties within the U.S.), the auditor may use either of two reporting options:

1. The report of the other country or the report set out in the ISAs, if applicable, provided that:
   - the report would be issued by auditors in the other country in similar circumstances;
   - the auditor has obtained sufficient appropriate audit evidence to support the statements in the report; and
   - the auditor has complied with the reporting standards of that country and identified the other country in the report.
2. A U.S. form of report that reflects that the financial statements being reported on have been prepared in accordance with a financial reporting framework generally accepted in another country, including:
   - all the elements required in a U.S. form report; and
   - a statement that refers to the note in the financial statements that describes the basis of presentation of the financial statements, including the country of origin.

3.3.1 Sample Report: Financial Statements Intended for Use Only Outside the United States (Nonissuer)

Independent Auditor's Report

[*Appropriate Addressee*]

We have audited the accompanying financial statements of ABC Company, which comprise the balance sheet as of December 31, 20X1, and the related statements of income, changes in stockholders' equity, and cash flows for the year then ended, and the related notes to the financial statements, *which, as described by Note X to the financial statements, have been prepared on the basis of* [*specify the financial reporting framework generally accepted*] *in* [*name of country*].

Management's Responsibility for the Financial Statements

Management is responsible for the preparation and fair presentation of these financial statements in accordance with [*specify the financial reporting framework generally accepted*] in [*name of country*]; this includes the design, implementation, and maintenance of internal control relevant to the preparation and fair presentation of financial statements that are free from material misstatement whether due to fraud or error.

Auditor's Responsibility

Our responsibility is to express an opinion on these financial statements based on our audit. We conducted our audit in accordance with auditing standards generally accepted in the United States of America *(and in* [*name of country*]*)*. Those standards require that we plan and perform the audit to obtain reasonable assurance about whether the financial statements are free from material misstatement.

[*Remainder of auditor's responsibility section same as standard nonissuer audit report*]

Opinion

In our opinion, the financial statements referred to above present fairly, in all material respects, the financial position of ABC Company as of December 31, 20X1, and the results of its operations and its cash flows for the year then ended in accordance with [*specify the financial reporting framework generally accepted*] in [*name of country*].

[*Auditor's signature*]

[*Auditor's city and state*]

[*Date of the auditor's report*]

3.4 Reporting: Distribution in the United States

If the financial statements are also intended for use in the United States, the auditor should report using a U.S. form report with an emphasis-of-matter paragraph that:

1. identifies the financial reporting framework;
2. refers to the note in the financial statements that describes the framework; and
3. indicates that the framework differs from accounting principles generally accepted in the United States of America.

3.4.1 Sample Report: Financial Statements That Are Also Intended for Use in the United States (Nonissuer)

Independent Auditor's Report

[*Appropriate Addressee*]

We have audited the accompanying financial statements of ABC Company, which comprise the balance sheet as of December 31, 20X1, and the related statements of income, changes in stockholders' equity, and cash flows for the year then ended, and the related notes to the financial statements, *which, as described by Note X to the financial statements, have been prepared on the basis of* [*specify the financial reporting framework generally accepted*] *in* [*name of country*].

Management's Responsibility for the Financial Statements

Management is responsible for the preparation and fair presentation of these financial statements in accordance with [*specify the financial reporting framework generally accepted*] in [*name of country*]; this includes the design, implementation, and maintenance of internal control relevant to the preparation and fair presentation of financial statements that are free from material misstatement whether due to fraud or error.

Auditor's Responsibility

Our responsibility is to express an opinion on these financial statements based on our audit. We conducted our audit in accordance with auditing standards generally accepted in the United States of America (and in [*name of country*]). Those standards require that we plan and perform the audit to obtain reasonable assurance about whether the financial statements are free from material misstatement.

[*Remainder of auditor's responsibility section same as standard nonissuer audit report*]

Opinion

In our opinion, the financial statements referred to above present fairly, in all material respects, the financial position of ABC Company as of December 31, 20X1, and the results of its operations and its cash flows for the year then ended in accordance with [*specify the financial reporting framework generally accepted*] in [*name of country*].

Emphasis-of-Matter

As discussed in Note X to the financial statements, the Company prepares its financial statements in accordance with [specify the financial reporting framework generally accepted] in [*name of country*], *which differs from accounting principles generally accepted in the United States of America. Our opinion is not modified with respect to this matter.*

[*Auditor's signature*]
[*Auditor's city and state*]
[*Date of the auditor's report*]

4 Reports on Application of the Requirements of an Applicable Financial Reporting Framework

4.1 Reporting Accountant

A reporting accountant is an accountant in public practice, other than the continuing accountant, who prepares a written report (or provides oral advice) on:

- the application of the requirements of an applicable financial reporting framework to a specific transaction; or
- the type of report that may be rendered on a specific entity's financial statements.

The reporting accountant may not report on the application of accounting principles to a hypothetical transaction (a transaction not involving facts or circumstances of a specific entity).

The reporting accountant is not required to be independent of the entity.

4.2 Procedures for Reporting Accountant

The reporting accountant should:

1. obtain an understanding of the form and substance of the specific transaction(s) or the conditions relevant to the type of report that may be issued on a specific entity's financial statements;
2. review the relevant requirements of the applicable financial reporting framework; and
3. if appropriate, consult with other professionals, experts or regulatory authorities, or perform additional research.

4.3 Reporting Accountant and Continuing Accountant

The reporting accountant should request permission from the entity's management to consult with the continuing accountant, and should then consult with the continuing accountant to ascertain all the available facts relevant to forming a professional judgment. If the reporting accountant determines that it is not necessary to consult with the continuing accountant, the reporting accounting should document the rationale for not consulting.

4.4 Reporting Accountant's Report

The accountant's report should be addressed to the requesting party and should include:

- A brief description of the nature of the engagement.
- A statement that the engagement was performed in accordance with AICPA standards or the standards of the PCAOB.
- An identification of the specific entity, a description of the specific transaction(s), a statement of the relevant facts, circumstances, and assumptions, and a statement about the source of the information.
- A statement describing the appropriate application of the requirements of the applicable financial reporting framework (including the country of origin) to the specific transaction or type of report, and if appropriate, a description of the reasons for the reporting accountant's conclusion.

- A statement that the preparers of the financial statements, who should consult with their continuing accountants, are responsible for proper accounting treatment.
- A statement that any difference in the facts, circumstances, or assumptions presented may change the report.
- A separate paragraph at the end of the report restricting its use to specified parties.
- If the reporting accountant is not independent, a statement indicating the lack of independence.

AUD

2

Quality Control, Engagement Acceptance, Planning, and Internal Control

Module

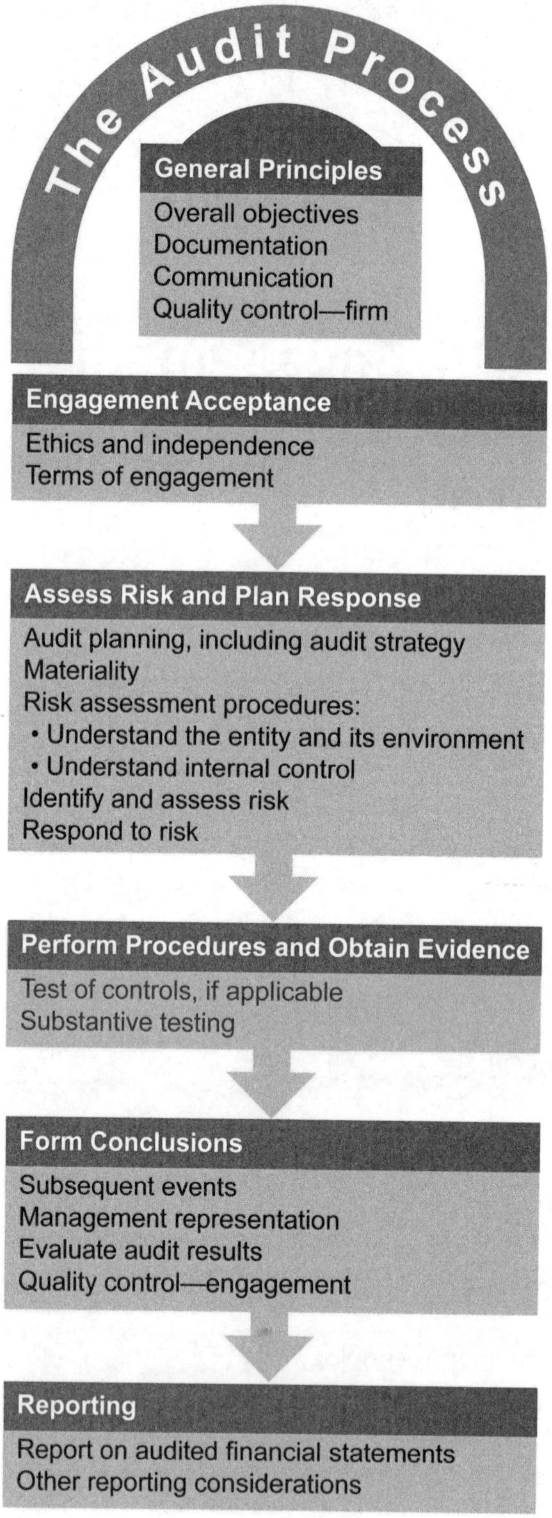
The Audit Process
General Principles
Overall objectives
Documentation
Communication
Quality control—firm
Engagement Acceptance
Ethics and independence
Terms of engagement
Assess Risk and Plan Response
Audit planning, including audit strategy
Materiality
Risk assessment procedures:
• Understand the entity and its environment
• Understand internal control
Identify and assess risk
Respond to risk
Perform Procedures and Obtain Evidence
Test of controls, if applicable
Substantive testing
Form Conclusions
Subsequent events
Management representation
Evaluate audit results
Quality control—engagement
Reporting
Report on audited financial statements
Other reporting considerations

MODULE

1 Quality Control

AUD 2

1 Applicability

The AICPA Code of Professional Conduct requires firms providing auditing, attestation, and accounting and review services to adopt a system of quality control. A quality control system consists of policies and procedures designed, implemented, and maintained to ensure that the firm complies with professional standards and appropriate legal and regulatory requirements, and that any reports issued are appropriate in the circumstances. Statements on Quality Control Standards (SQCS) are issued by the Auditing Standards Board to provide guidance with respect to quality control.

2 Elements of Quality Control

The six interrelated elements of quality control are:

1. **Human resources**
2. **Engagement/client acceptance and continuance**
3. **Leadership responsibilities**
4. **Performance of the engagement**
5. **Monitoring**
6. **Ethical requirements**

Each of these elements of quality control are covered in more detail below.

Pass Key

"HELP ME" maintain good quality in my accounting and auditing practice.

2.1 Human Resources

This element encompasses criteria for recruitment and hiring, determining capabilities and competencies, assigning personnel to engagements, professional development, and performance evaluation, compensation, and advancement.

Personnel management policies and procedures should be established to provide the firm with reasonable assurance that:

- Those hired possess the appropriate characteristics to enable them to perform competently.
- Engagement partners possess the competencies necessary to fulfill engagement responsibilities.

- Work is assigned to personnel having the degree of technical training and proficiency required in the circumstances.
- Personnel participate in continuing professional education and other professional development activities.
- Personnel selected for advancement have the qualifications necessary to fulfill the responsibilities to be assumed, and performance evaluation, compensation, and advancement procedures provide appropriate recognition and reward.

Examples include:

- Requiring timely identification of staffing requirements.
- Planning for the total personnel needs of all the firm's professional engagements.
- Requiring a background check on new personnel.
- Requiring supervisors to prepare performance evaluations.
- Requiring personnel to attend training.
- Consideration of continuity and periodic rotation of personnel.
- Consideration of opportunities for on-the-job training.

2.2 Engagement/Client Acceptance and Continuance

Policies and procedures should be established for deciding whether to accept or continue a client relationship and whether to perform a specific engagement. These policies and procedures should provide the firm with reasonable assurance that the firm:

- Minimizes the likelihood of association with a client whose management lacks integrity.
  - The firm should consider the reputation of the client, its owners, key management, related parties and those charged with governance, the nature of the client's operations, and the client's overall attitude toward matters such as the aggressive application of accounting principles and internal controls.
- Undertakes only those engagements that the firm can reasonably expect to complete with professional competence.
  - The firm must have sufficient personnel with appropriate knowledge and experience, or personnel who can attain appropriate competency levels. Specialists should be available if needed.
  - The firm must be able to perform the engagement within reporting deadlines.
- Can comply with legal and ethical requirements.
  - Potential conflicts of interest should be identified and evaluated.
  - The firm must be able to maintain independence.

The firm should obtain an understanding with the client regarding the nature, scope, and limitations of the services to be provided. The firm should document how any issues with respect to the acceptance and continuance decision were resolved.

The firm should have policies and procedures for withdrawal from an engagement or from an engagement and the client relationship. Policies and procedures should include:

- Documentation of significant issues, consultations, conclusions, and the basis for conclusions.

- Discussion with the client of the appropriate action to be taken by the firm based on the facts and circumstances. The discussion should include the appropriate level of the client's management and those charged with governance.
- Consideration of any professional, legal, or regulatory requirement for the firm to remain in place, or for the firm to report the withdrawal and the reasons for the withdrawal to regulatory authorities.

Examples include:

- Reviewing the financial statements and credit rating of the proposed client.
- Inquiring of third parties as to the reputation of the proposed client.
- Evaluating the firm's ability to service the client properly.
- Periodically reevaluating clients for continuance, including consideration of significant issues that arise during the current or prior engagements.

2.3 Leadership Responsibilities for Quality Within the Firm

The firm's leadership bears ultimate responsibility for the firm's quality control system, and should create a culture that emphasizes quality. The "tone at the top" influences attitudes throughout the firm.

- Quality should be emphasized over commercial considerations.
- Performance evaluation, compensation, and advancement should demonstrate a commitment to quality.
- Sufficient resources should be devoted to developing, communicating, and supporting the quality control system.
- Those with operational responsibility for the quality control system should have appropriate experience, ability, and authority.

2.4 Performance

Policies and procedures should be established to:

- Achieve a consistently high level of performance. This may be accomplished by using written or electronic manuals, software tools, standardized documentation, and/or guidance materials for specific industries or specific types of subject matter.
- Ensure that the engagement is appropriately supervised, and that work is appropriately reviewed.
- Maintain confidentiality, safe custody, integrity, accessibility, retrievability, and retention of engagement documentation. Requirements imposed by specific laws or regulations should be addressed.
- Allow consultation with experts inside or outside the firm with respect to complex, unfamiliar, unusual, difficult, or contentious issues.
- Provide a means to resolve differences of opinion.
- Establish and follow guidelines with respect to determining when an engagement quality control review should be performed.
    - Care should be taken to appoint an appropriate (i.e., independent, technically competent) quality control reviewer.
    - The engagement partner remains responsible for the engagement, despite the involvement of an engagement quality control reviewer.

- Engagement quality control review procedures should include an objective evaluation of judgments, conclusions, reports, and documentation.
- The engagement quality control review should be appropriately documented.
- The review should be completed before the engagement report is released.

Examples include:

- Designating individuals with expertise in matters related to the SEC.
- Referring questions to the appropriate group in the AICPA or state society.
- Developing and using standard audit forms, checklists, and questionnaires.
- Establishing procedures for reviewing engagement documentation and reports.
- Using passwords or other means of restricting access to engagement documentation.

2.5 Monitoring

Policies and procedures should be established to provide the firm with reasonable assurance that its quality control system is relevant, adequate, operating effectively, and complied with in practice.

- Monitoring involves an ongoing consideration and evaluation of the design and effectiveness of the quality control system.
- Monitoring helps the company determine whether:
  - The firm has complied with professional standards and legal/regulatory requirements.
  - The quality control system has been designed appropriately and implemented effectively.
  - The quality control system has operated effectively in ensuring that reports issued are appropriate.
- Monitoring should be performed by qualified individuals.
- A partner (or someone with appropriate experience and authority) should bear responsibility for the monitoring process.

2.5.1 Monitoring Procedures

Monitoring procedures include the performance of engagement quality control reviews, post-issuance reviews of engagement documentation, and inspections (internal or external) of a selection of completed engagements. Specific monitoring procedures include:

- Review of administrative records, working papers, reports, and financial statements.
- Discussions with firm personnel, including communication with management.
- Summarization of findings, and determination of corrective actions to take.
- Assessment of the firm's guidance materials, and compliance with firm guidelines.
- Peer review (covered in more detail below) conducted under AICPA standards, which may substitute for some of a firm's inspection procedures.
- A "wrap-up" or second partner "preissuance" review of the audit documentation by a partner not otherwise involved in the audit. The Sarbanes-Oxley Act requires such review for every public company audit report. The purpose of this review is to focus on the fair presentation of the financial statements in conformity with generally accepted accounting principles.

Monitoring procedures should be documented, including evaluation of deficiencies noted and corrective actions taken. The firm should take appropriate further action to address deficiencies, complaints, and allegations of noncompliance.

2.5.2 Peer Review

The purpose of peer review is to determine and report whether the CPA firm being reviewed has developed adequate policies and procedures for the elements of quality control and is following them in practice.

- Peer review occurs when one CPA firm reviews another CPA firm's compliance with its quality control system.
- A CPA firm that is a member of the AICPA must have a peer review every three years in order to maintain membership in the AICPA.
- The firm being reviewed can select the review firm or may ask the AICPA or state society of CPAs to select a review team.
- Upon completion of the peer review, a report is issued with conclusions and recommendations. A firm that fails to take corrective actions (where necessary to correct deficiencies) is subject to sanctions.

2.6 Ethical Requirements

Policies and procedures should be established to provide the firm with reasonable assurance that personnel maintain independence (in fact and in appearance) in all required circumstances, perform all professional responsibilities with integrity, and maintain objectivity in discharging professional responsibilities.

- Independence encompasses impartiality and freedom from any obligation to or interest in the client.
- Independence requirements should be communicated to firm personnel.
- Threats to independence should be identified and evaluated, and appropriate action should be taken.
- At least annually, all firm personnel subject to independence requirements should confirm their independence in writing (paper or electronic form).
- The firm's quality control system should address requirements for rotation of personnel.

Examples include:

- Maintaining records showing which personnel were previously employed by clients or have relatives holding key positions with clients.
- Notifying personnel as to the names of audit clients publicly held.
- Confirming with staff that prohibited relationships do not exist.
- Emphasizing independence of mental attitude in training and supervision.

3 Other Considerations

3.1 Nature and Extent of Quality Control

The nature and extent of a firm's quality control policies and procedures depend on:

1. the firm's size;
2. its organizational structure;
3. the nature and complexity of its practice;

4. the degree of operating autonomy allowed its personnel and its individual offices; and
5. cost-benefit considerations.

3.2 Communication

Quality control policies and procedures should be communicated to firm personnel. Communication should include procedures and objectives, and should emphasize personal responsibility and the importance of feedback. Written communication is not required, but it can be helpful.

3.3 Documentation

The firm should document its quality control policies and procedures. The extent of documentation may vary based on the size, structure, and nature of the firm. Documentation should be retained for a sufficient period of time.

3.4 Relationship Between Auditing and Quality Control Standards

3.4.1 GAAS vs. Quality Control Standards

Generally accepted auditing standards and quality control standards are not synonymous. GAAS relate to the conduct of each individual audit engagement, whereas quality control standards relate to the conduct of all professional activities of the firm's practice as a whole.

The quality control standards of a firm affect both the performance of each audit and the performance of the audit practice as a whole.

3.4.2 Quality Control Deficiencies

Although an effective system of quality control is conducive to complying with GAAS (or other professional standards), deficiencies in or noncompliance with a firm's quality control standards do not necessarily indicate a lack of compliance with GAAS (or other professional standards) for any one specific engagement.

Deficiencies in quality control for an individual engagement do not necessarily imply that the firm's quality control system overall is insufficient.

4 Reviewing the Work of Others

All work performed on the audit should be reviewed to determine whether the work was adequately performed and documented and to evaluate the results of the work relative to the conclusion to be presented in the audit report. The partner with final responsibility for the audit may delegate some of the review responsibility to other members of the audit team, consistent with the firm's system of quality control. Work should be reviewed by members of the audit team who are senior to those who performed the work.

4.1 Review Considerations

A review consists of consideration of whether:

- The work has been performed in accordance with professional standards and applicable laws and regulations.
- Significant findings or issues need further consideration.
- Appropriate consultations have taken place and have been documented and implemented.
- The nature, extent, and timing of the work performed is appropriate and does not need revision.

- The work performed supports the conclusions reached and is appropriately documented.
- The evidence obtained is sufficient and appropriate to support the auditor's report.
- The objectives of the engagement have been achieved.

4.2 Engagement Partner Review

The engagement partner should review the following significant findings or issues on a timely basis during the audit to allow resolution on or before the date of the auditor's report:

- Critical areas of judgment, especially involving difficult to contentious matters
- Significant risks
- Other areas the engagement partner considers important

4.3 Documentation Requirements

Audit documentation should include:

1. Who performed the work and the date the work was completed.
2. Who reviewed the audit documentation and the date of the review.

5 Quality Control Standards for Nonissuer Engagements

The auditor has specific responsibilities regarding quality control procedures when performing engagements for nonissuers in accordance with U.S. GAAS. Such engagements include nonissuer financial statement audits, reviews of the interim financial statements of nonissuers, and government financial audits performed in accordance with GAAS. As part of a firm's system of quality control, engagement teams have a responsibility to implement quality control procedures that are applicable to the engagement. Engagement teams should also provide the firm with information related to the independence of the engagement team.

5.1 Objective

The objective of the auditor is to implement quality control procedures at the engagement level to provide reasonable assurance that:

1. the audit complies with professional standards and applicable legal and regulatory requirements; and
2. the auditor issues a report that is appropriate.

5.2 Engagement Partner Responsibilities for Quality

The engagement partner is responsible for the overall quality of the engagement, but may delegate responsibility for the performance of certain procedures to other members of the engagement team. The engagement partner may also rely on the firm's system of quality control.

During each engagement, the engagement partner should:

- Remain alert for evidence of noncompliance with relevant ethical requirements by members of the engagement team and take appropriate action when necessary.
- Form a conclusion on compliance with independence requirements.
- Be satisfied that appropriate procedures regarding client acceptance and continuance have been followed.

- Be satisfied that the engagement team and any external specialists have the competence and capabilities needed to perform the engagement and issue an audit report that is appropriate in the circumstances.
- Take responsibility for the direction, supervision, and performance of the engagement and for the report being appropriate in the circumstances.
- Take responsibility for reviews being performed in accordance with the firm's review policies and procedures.
- Be satisfied through review of the audit documentation and discussion with the engagement team that sufficient appropriate audit evidence has been obtained to support the conclusions reached and the report to be issued.
- Take responsibility for the engagement team undertaking appropriate consultation on difficult or contentious matters.

5.3 Engagement Quality Control Review

The engagement quality control review provides an objective evaluation of the significant judgments the engagement team made and the conclusions it reached in formulating the auditor's report. An engagement quality control review is performed only when required by the firm's policies and procedures. The engagement quality control review should be completed before the engagement partner releases the audit report.

The engagement quality control reviewer can be a partner, other person in the firm, suitably qualified external person, or team of such individuals, none of whom is part of the engagement team. The engagement quality control reviewer must have sufficient and appropriate experience and authority to objectively evaluate the engagement team's judgments and conclusions.

The engagement quality reviewer's evaluation of the engagement team's significant judgments and conclusions should include:

- Discussion of significant findings with the engagement partner.
- Reading the financial statements and proposed auditor's report.
- Review of audit documentation related to significant judgments and conclusions.
- Evaluation of the conclusions reached in formulating the auditor's report and consideration of the appropriateness of the proposed auditor's report.

If the engagement quality control review is completed after the date of the auditor's report and identifies instances in which additional evidence or procedures are required, the date of the auditor's report should be changed to the date when the additional evidence has been obtained or the additional procedures have been completed.

6 Quality Control Standards for Issuer Engagements

PCAOB standards require an engagement quality review and concurring approval of audit report issuance for all audits of issuers and for each engagement to review the interim financial statements of an issuer. Many firms also require engagement quality reviews for nonissuer audits.

6.1 Engagement Quality Reviewer

An engagement quality review is performed by a partner who is not otherwise associated with the engagement. The engagement quality reviewer must be competent, independent, objective, and act with integrity.

6.2 Engagement Quality Review Process

Under PCAOB standards, the engagement quality reviewer is required to hold discussions with the engagement partner and other members of the engagement team and review the audit documentation in order to evaluate the significant judgments made by the engagement team and the overall conclusion reached on the engagement. The engagement quality reviewer should do the following:

- Evaluate the significant judgments related to engagement planning, including the firm's prior experience with the client, risks identified related to the client, and judgments about materiality.
- Evaluate the engagement team's assessment of and responses to significant risks, including fraud risk.
- Evaluate significant judgments about materiality, corrected and uncorrected misstatements, and control deficiencies.
- Review the evaluation of the firm's independence in relation to the engagement.
- Review the engagement completion document and confirm that there are no unresolved matters.
- Review the financial statements, management's report on internal control, and the engagement report.
- Read other information to be filed with the SEC and determine whether appropriate action has been taken with respect to material inconsistencies or material misstatements of fact.
- Evaluate the consultations, documentation, and conclusions related to difficult or contentious matters.
- Evaluate communications with management, the audit committee, and regulatory bodies.
- Evaluate whether engagement documentation indicates that the engagement team responded appropriately to significant risks and whether such documentation supports the conclusions reached by the engagement team.
- Evaluate the engagement team's determination, communication, and documentation of critical audit matters.

6.3 Concurring Approval of Issuance

Under PCAOB standards, the firm cannot give the client permission to use the engagement report until the engagement quality reviewer provides concurring approval of issuance. The engagement quality reviewer may provide concurring approval of issuance only if there are no significant engagement deficiencies.

A significant engagement deficiency exists when:

- The engagement team failed to obtain sufficient appropriate evidence.
- The engagement team reached an inappropriate overall conclusion.
- The engagement report is not appropriate for the circumstances.
- The firm is not independent of the client.

Question 1 **MCQ-02432**

Which of the following is an element of a CPA firm's quality control system that should be considered in establishing its quality control policies and procedures?

a. Complying with laws and regulations.

b. Using statistical sampling techniques.

c. Assigning personnel to engagements.

d. Considering audit risk and materiality.

Question 2 **MCQ-02418**

Which of the following is *not* true about the relationship between quality control standards and professional standards such as GAAS?

a. Quality control standards relate to the conduct of a firm's entire practice, whereas professional standards such as GAAS relate to the conduct of an individual engagement.

b. The adoption of quality control standards increases the likelihood of compliance with professional standards on individual engagements.

c. A firm's failure to establish or comply with an appropriate system of quality control implies that the firm has also failed to follow professional standards on individual engagements.

d. A firm that has not adopted an appropriate system of quality control may still be in compliance with professional standards with respect to individual engagements.

MODULE

2 Documentation

1 Overview

Audit documentation (also referred to as "working papers" or "workpapers") is the principal record of audit procedures performed, evidence obtained, and conclusions reached.

Audit documentation should provide:

1. evidence of the basis for the auditor's report and the conclusion about the achievement of the overall objectives of the auditor; and
2. evidence that the audit was conducted in accordance with generally accepted auditing standards and applicable legal and regulatory requirements.

2 Audit Documentation Requirements

2.1 Overall Requirements

Audit documentation should:

- Assist the engagement team in planning, conducting, and supervising the audit.
- Show that the accounting records reconcile with the financial statements.
- Enable the engagement team to show its accountability, emphasizing that the team is responsible for its work.
- Provide a record of accumulated evidence, showing the procedures performed, evidence examined, and conclusions reached.
- Be a record of matters of continuing significance to future audits of the same entity.
- Enable the conduct of quality control reviews and inspections, including external inspections or peer reviews.
- Assist an auditor who reviews a predecessor auditor's documentation.
- Be prepared in enough detail so that an experienced auditor who has no previous connection with the audit can understand:
    1. the nature, extent, and timing of the audit procedures performed;
    2. the results of the procedures performed and the evidence obtained;
    3. the significant findings or issues arising during the audit; and
    4. the conclusions reached, and significant judgments made to reach those conclusions.
- Show who performed the work and the date the work was completed.
- Show who reviewed the work performed and the date and extent of the review.
- Include abstracts or copies of significant contracts or agreements.

- Document discussions of significant findings or issues with management, those charged with governance, and others.
- Document how the auditor addressed any information inconsistent with the auditor's final conclusion regarding a significant finding or issue.
- Document the auditor's justification for a departure from a presumptively mandatory audit requirement and how alternative audit procedures achieved the intent of the requirement.
- Document the performance and review of additional audit procedures or new conclusions after the date of the auditor's report.

2.2 Retention and Completion

Audit documentation should be prepared on a timely basis.

2.2.1 Report Release Date

The "report release date" is defined as the date on which the auditor grants the client permission to use the report. Often, this is the date on which the report is delivered to the client. The auditor should document the report release date.

2.2.2 Document Retention

- **SAS Rules (Nonissuers):** Auditing standards require that audit documentation be retained for at least five years from the report release date.
- **PCAOB Rules (Issuers):** The PCAOB requires auditors of public companies to keep audit documentation for seven years from the report release date.

2.2.3 Documentation Completion Date

The auditor is granted a certain window of time following the report release date in which to assemble the final audit documentation file. The end of this window is referred to as the "documentation completion date." After this date, existing documentation must not be deleted, and additions to the audit documentation must be documented as such.

- **SAS Rules (Nonissuers):** Auditing standards require the final audit documentation file to be assembled within *60 days following the report release date.*
- **PCAOB Rules (Issuers):** The PCAOB defines the documentation completion date as *45 days following the report release date*, and requires preparation of an "engagement completion document" identifying all significant findings and issues. Also, under PCAOB standards, if work is performed by another auditor, the office issuing the report must obtain, review, and retain certain audit documentation from the other auditor.

2.2.4 Safekeeping of Audit Documentation

Reasonable precautions should be established for the safekeeping of audit documentation, as it is the proof that a professional audit was performed. The SOX Act of 2002 imposes tough penalties for failure to retain audit documentation or for the destruction of records.

The auditor should establish appropriate controls for audit documentation to protect its integrity, prevent unauthorized changes, etc.

2.3 Nature and Extent of Audit Documentation

Audit documentation may be in paper form, electronic form, or other media. Oral explanations alone are insufficient, but may be used for clarification of information included in the audit documentation.

The specific quantity, type, and content of audit documentation are based on the auditor's judgment. In determining the nature and extent of documentation for a specific area, the auditor should consider:

1. the size and complexity of the entity;
2. the nature of the specific auditing procedure;
3. the risk of material misstatement;
4. the significance of the evidence obtained;
5. the nature and extent of any exceptions identified;
6. the need to document conclusions that may not be obvious;
7. the audit methodology and tools used; and
8. the extent to which judgment was required in performing the work and evaluating the results.

2.4 Specific Contents

The form and content of audit documentation can vary, but they should be designed to meet the circumstances of the particular engagement. Generally, audit documentation will consist of a *permanent* or *continuous audit file* and a *current file*.

2.4.1 Permanent (Continuous) File

The permanent file includes audit documentation that has a continuing interest from year to year (such as contracts, pension plans, leases, stock options, bylaws, articles of incorporation, minutes of meetings, bond indentures, and internal information).

2.4.2 Current File

The current file contains all audit documentation applicable to the year under audit, and generally includes the following audit documentation:

- The audit plan (audit program).
- Financial statements and the auditor's report.
- Working trial balance, adjusting journal entries, and reclassification entries.
- Letters of confirmation and representation (e.g., letters from attorneys, a management representation letter, and confirmation responses).
- Analyses, worksheets, issues memoranda, and schedules or commentaries prepared or obtained by the auditor. Note that related accounts, such as notes receivable and interest income, are often analyzed together.
- Abstracts or copies of entity documents, such as contracts or agreements, examined to evaluate the accounting for significant transactions.
- Summaries of significant audit findings or issues (see below), actions taken, and conclusions reached.
- Records of tests of controls and substantive tests that include identification of specific items selected for testing (i.e., the source from which the items were selected and specific selection criteria).

2.4.3 Significant Audit Findings

Audit documentation should include significant audit findings, actions taken, and conclusions reached. Significant audit findings include matters that:

- Are related to the selection and application of accounting principles (and the consistency with which they are applied), especially those involving complex or unusual transactions, or estimates and uncertainties.

- Are related to matters that give rise to significant risks.
- Are related to possible material misstatements in the financial statements.
- Suggest a need to revise the auditor's previous risk assessment.
- Cause significant difficulty in applying necessary audit procedures, or indicate the need for significant revision of planned audit procedures.
- May result in modification of the auditor's opinion or the inclusion of an emphasis-of-matter paragraph in the auditor's report.

2.4.4 Other Documentation Requirements

Specific audit documentation may also be required by other auditing standards, such as those related to the consideration of internal control, the consideration of fraud risk factors, etc.

2.4.5 Tickmarks

Auditors often use tickmarks or symbols, indicating the work that has been performed. Audit documentation should include explanations of any tickmarks used.

ABC Company
Bank Reconciliation
December 31, Year X

Cash balance per bank		$275,000 ✓
Add: deposits in transit		
27 – Dec	$8,490 Δ	
29 – Dec	3,000 Δ	
30 – Dec	2,500 Δ	13,990 И
Less: Outstanding checks		
#34582	$2,456 Φ	
#34584	1,300 Φ	
#34585	1,414 Φ	5,170 И
Cash balance per books		$283,820 И X

Tickmark Legend	
✓	Agreed to 12/31 bank statement
Δ	Agreed to deposit ticket
И	Footed
Φ	Agreed to voucher register
X	Agreed to cash balance in general ledger

Question 1 **MCQ-02643**

Audit documentation should:

a. Not be permitted to serve as a reference source for the client.
b. Not contain critical comments concerning management.
c. Show that the accounting records agree or reconcile with the financial statements.
d. Be considered the primary support for the financial statements being audited.

MODULE

3 Terms of Engagement

1 Appointment of the Auditor

1.1 Audit Committees

The audit committee of the client's board of directors is responsible for the selection and appointment of the independent external auditor, and for reviewing the nature and scope of the engagement.

1.1.1 Sarbanes-Oxley Act

Under the Sarbanes-Oxley Act (generally applying to issuers), the auditor reports to and is overseen by the client's audit committee. The audit committee must preapprove all services provided by the auditor. Certain specified non-audit services (covered later) are prohibited.

1.1.2 Those Charged With Governance

The term "those charged with governance" refers to those who bear responsibility to oversee the obligations, financial reporting process, and strategic direction of an entity. This term is broadly interpreted to encompass the terms "board of directors" and "audit committee."

1.1.3 Required Communications

The auditor is required to communicate certain matters to those charged with governance. These communications are further discussed later.

1.2 Timing

Although early appointment of the auditor allows the auditor to plan a more efficient audit, an auditor is permitted to accept an engagement near or after year-end. The auditor should consider whether late appointment will pose limitations on the audit that may lead to a qualified opinion or a disclaimer of opinion, and should discuss such concerns with the client.

2 Client Acceptance and Continuance

As part of the pre-acceptance phase of the engagement, the auditor should consider and document compliance with the firm's quality control policies and procedures related to client acceptance and continuance. Specifically, the auditor should assess the following:

- **Firm's Ability to Meet Reporting Deadlines**

  A firm should not accept or continue a client relationship unless the firm believes that it has the ability to perform the engagement within reporting deadlines. The firm's ability to meet reporting deadlines is affected by many factors, including the timing and complexity of the engagement and the availability of audit staff.

- **Firm's Ability to Staff the Engagement**

  The firm must have personnel with both the experience and availability to meet staffing and supervision requirements. It may be more difficult to staff an engagement during "busy season" than at other times of the year.

- **Independence**

  Independence is required for all audit engagements. Before accepting or continuing a client relationship when independence is required to be maintained, the firm must ensure that it is in fact independent of the client and that it will be able to maintain independence throughout the engagement.

- **Integrity of Client Management**

  The likelihood of financial statement misrepresentation increases when the client's management lacks integrity. The audit firm should minimize the likelihood of association with a client whose management lacks integrity by considering the reputation of the client, its owners, key management, related parties, those charged with governance, the nature of the client's operations, and the client's overall attitude toward matters such as internal controls and the aggressive application of accounting principles.

- **Group Audits**

  The group engagement partner should evaluate whether the group engagement team will be able to obtain sufficient appropriate audit evidence through the group engagement team's work or the work of component auditors to act as the auditor of the group financial statements.

3 Preconditions for an Audit

Before accepting an audit engagement with a new or existing audit client, the auditor should establish that the preconditions for an audit are present. If the preconditions for an audit are not present, the auditor should not accept the proposed engagement, unless the auditor is required by law or regulation to do so.

3.1 Applicable Financial Reporting Framework

The auditor should determine whether the financial reporting framework used by the client is acceptable. Factors related to the acceptability of the financial reporting framework include:

- The nature of the entity (e.g., business, government, or not-for-profit)
- The purpose of the financial statements (e.g., wide or narrow range of users)
- The nature of the financial statements (e.g., complete set or single financial statement)
- Whether law or regulation prescribes the framework

3.2 Management Responsibilities

The auditor should obtain the agreement of management that it acknowledges and understands its responsibility:

1. for the preparation and fair presentation of the financial statements in accordance with the applicable financial reporting framework;
2. for the design, implementation, and maintenance of internal control relevant to the preparation and fair presentation of financial statements that are free from material misstatement, whether due to fraud or error; and

3. to provide the auditor with:
   - access to all information of which management is aware that is relevant to the preparation and fair presentation of the financial statements;
   - additional information that the auditor may request from management for the purpose of the audit; and
   - unrestricted access to persons within the entity from whom the auditor determines it is necessary to obtain audit evidence.

3.3 Management-Imposed Scope Limitation

The auditor should not accept an engagement if, prior to engagement acceptance, management or those charged with governance impose a scope limitation that will result in the auditor disclaiming an opinion on the financial statements as a whole.

3.3.1 Audit Required by Law or Regulation

If the entity is required by law or regulation to have an audit and a disclaimer of opinion is acceptable, such as in the audit of an employee benefit plan, the auditor is permitted, but not required, to accept the engagement when there is a management-imposed scope limitation.

3.3.2 Scope Limitations That Do Not Preclude Engagement Acceptance

If a management-imposed scope limitation will result in a qualified opinion, or if the scope limitation is imposed by circumstances beyond management's control, the auditor may still accept the engagement.

4 Agreement on Audit Engagement Terms

The auditor should agree to the terms of the engagement with management or those charged with governance, as appropriate. This agreement should be documented in an engagement letter or other suitable form of written agreement. If the auditor believes an agreement with the client has not been established, he or she should decline to accept or perform the engagement. The engagement letter should be accepted (signed and dated) by the client and included with the auditor's documentation.

4.1 Reasons for Agreement

A written agreement reduces the risk that either the auditor or the client may misinterpret the needs or expectations of the other party. For example, an agreement reduces the risk that the client may inappropriately rely on the auditor to:

1. protect the entity against certain risks (e.g., defalcations); or
2. perform certain functions that are the client's responsibility (e.g., establishing and maintaining effective internal control over financial reporting).

4.2 Engagement Letter Contents

Engagement letter contents vary for each entity. The agreement may include overall audit strategy, but typically would not include specific audit procedures (unless those procedures were requested by the client).

4.2.1 Required Contents

The engagement letter should include:

- The objective and scope of the audit.
- The responsibilities of the auditor.
- The responsibilities of management.
- A statement that because of the inherent limitations of an audit, together with the inherent limitations of internal control, an unavoidable risk exists that some material misstatements may not be detected, even though the audit is properly planned and performed in accordance with GAAS.
- Identification of the applicable financial reporting framework.
- Reference to the expected form and content of any reports to be issued by the auditor and a statement that circumstances may arise in which a report may differ from its expected form and content.

4.2.2 Other Contents

The engagement letter may also refer to the following:

- Elaboration of the scope of the audit, including reference to applicable legislation, regulations, GAAS, or ethical requirements.
- The form of any other communication of results of the audit engagement.
- Arrangements regarding planning and audit performance, including the composition of the audit team.
- The expectation that management will provide written representations.
- The agreement of management to make information available to the auditor in a timely manner.
- The agreement of management to inform the auditor about subsequent events.
- Fees and billing arrangements.
- Arrangements concerning the involvement of other auditors, specialists, internal auditors, or other staff of the entity.
- Arrangements to be made with the predecessor auditor.
- Any restriction on the auditor's liability (when not prohibited).
- Any obligations of the auditor to provide audit documentation to other parties.
- Additional services to be provided or references to further agreements between the auditor and the entity.

PCAOB Standards: Guidance for Issuers

For audits of issuers, the auditor must agree to the terms of the engagement with the audit committee in an engagement letter. The engagement letter should be provided to the audit committee annually.

5 Recurring Audits

A recurring audit is an audit engagement for an existing audit client for whom the auditor performed the preceding audit.

5.1 Revising the Terms of the Engagement

On recurring audits, the auditor should assess whether circumstances require the terms of the engagement to be revised. The following factors may make it appropriate to revise the terms of the engagement:

- Any indication that management misunderstands the objective or scope of the audit
- Any revised or special engagement terms
- A change in senior management
- A significant change in ownership
- A significant change in the nature or size of the entity's business
- A change in legal or regulatory requirements
- A change in financial reporting framework
- A change in other reporting requirements

5.2 Terms of the Engagement Not Revised

If the auditor concludes that the terms of the engagement do not need to be revised, the auditor should remind management of the terms of the engagement by means of a new engagement letter, or a reminder that the terms of the preceding engagement will govern the current engagement. A reminder can be written or oral and should be documented.

6 Initial Audits

An initial audit is an engagement in which the financial statements for the prior period were not audited or were audited by a predecessor auditor.

6.1 Communication With the Predecessor Auditor

A predecessor auditor is one who was engaged to audit a prior financial statement (even if the audit was not completed). In an initial audit, including a reaudit engagement, it is mandatory to make inquiries of the predecessor auditor. Client permission is needed, however. If the client is unwilling to agree to this procedure, the auditor should consider the implications and decide whether to accept the engagement.

The auditor should make oral or written inquiries of the predecessor auditor before accepting an engagement. Inquiries should be made regarding:

1. information that might bear on management integrity;
2. disagreements with management over accounting principles, auditing procedures, or other similarly significant matters;
3. the predecessor's understanding as to the reasons for the change of auditors; and
4. communication to management, the audit committee, and those charged with governance regarding fraud, noncompliance with laws and regulations, and matters relating to internal control.

PCAOB Standards: Guidance for Issuers

In addition to the above inquiries, auditors of issuers should inquire about the predecessor auditor's understanding of the nature of the company's relationships and transactions with related parties and significant unusual transactions.

7 Change in Engagement

During the course of an engagement, a client may ask the accountant to change an audit to a compilation or review, or a review to a compilation.

7.1 Considerations

Before agreeing to a change, an accountant should consider:

1. the reason for the request, especially if there are scope limitations;
2. the effort required to complete the engagement; and
3. the estimated additional cost to complete the engagement.

If the accountant decides a change in the engagement is justified, he or she must comply with the standards for a compilation or review, and then issue an appropriate report. The report should not refer to the original engagement, any procedures performed as part of the engagement, or any scope limitation.

7.2 Reasons for Change

7.2.1 Acceptable Reasons

An audit may be changed to a compilation or review, or a review may be changed to a compilation, due to a:

- change in client requirements; or
- misunderstanding as to the nature of the service to be rendered.

7.2.2 Unacceptable Reasons

The following are not acceptable reasons for a change:

- The engagement would uncover errors or fraud.
- The client is attempting to create misleading or deceptive financial statements.

7.2.3 Scope Limitations

The auditor must consider the implications of a scope restriction in deciding whether a change in engagement is reasonable. The following are generally considered unacceptable reasons for a change:

- The client refuses to allow correspondence with legal counsel.
- The client refuses to provide a signed representation letter.

7.3 Compilation/Review Report Not Permitted

An accountant is generally precluded from issuing a compilation report or a review report when:

- The accountant has been engaged to audit the entity's financial statements and has been prohibited by the client from corresponding with the entity's legal counsel.
- The accountant has been engaged to audit or review the entity's financial statements and the client does not provide the accountant with a signed representation letter.

Question 1 **MCQ-04620**

A successor auditor should request the new client to authorize the predecessor auditor to allow a review of the predecessor's:

	Engagement Letter	*Working Papers*
a.	Yes	Yes
b.	Yes	No
c.	No	Yes
d.	No	No

Question 2 **MCQ-02673**

Which of the following matters generally is included in an auditor's engagement letter?

a. Management's responsibility for the fair presentation of the financial statements.

b. The factors to be considered in setting preliminary judgments about materiality.

c. Management's vicarious liability for violations of laws and regulations committed by its employees.

d. The auditor's responsibility to search for significant internal control deficiencies.

NOTES

MODULE

4 Planning

1 Overview of Planning

During planning, the auditor is required to:

- Obtain knowledge of the client's business and industry.
- Develop the audit strategy.
- Develop the audit plan.
- Perform risk assessment procedures to obtain an understanding of the entity and its environment, including its internal control, sufficient to assess the risks of material misstatement and design further audit procedures.

The nature and extent of necessary planning activities depend on the size and complexity of the company, the auditor's previous experience with the company, and changes in circumstances that occur during the audit. Factors that indicate less complex operations include fewer business lines, less complex business processes and financial reporting systems, more centralized accounting functions, extensive involvement of senior management in day-to-day operations, and few levels of management.

Pass Key

The auditor plans the audit to be responsive to the initial assessment of the risk of material misstatement, but should be prepared to revise the audit strategy and the audit plan based on the results of audit procedures.

1.1 Involvement of Key Engagement Team Members

The engagement partner and other key members of the engagement team should be involved in planning the audit. The engagement partner is the member of the engagement team with primary responsibility for the audit. The engagement partner is responsible for:

- Planning the audit
- Supervising the work of engagement team members
- Compliance with relevant auditing standards

The engagement partner may seek assistance from appropriate engagement team members in fulfilling these responsibilities.

1.2 Supervision of Assistants

GAAS requires proper supervision of assistants during the course of the audit to ensure that the work performed is adequate to accomplish the objectives of the examination and is consistent with conclusions presented in the report. Guidance should be provided to assistants regarding both technical and personnel aspects of the audit.

1.2.1 Proper Supervision

When assistants are used, proper supervision includes:

- Directing the efforts of assistants.
- Communicating with the audit team regarding the susceptibility of the financial statements to material misstatement due to error or fraud.
- Informing assistants of their responsibilities; the objectives of the procedures they are to perform; the nature, timing, and extent of procedures they are to perform; and any matters that may affect their performance of those procedures.
- Staying informed (e.g., by directing staff to report back) regarding significant accounting and auditing issues, new developments, and difficulties encountered in performing the audit, and evaluating whether appropriate action has been taken in accordance with applicable standards (SAS or PCAOB).
- Reviewing the work performed by assistants to determine whether it was adequately performed and documented, whether the objectives of the audit were accomplished, and whether the work performed is consistent with the conclusions to be presented in the auditor's report.
- Dealing with differences of opinion among members of the audit team.

1.2.2 Nature, Extent, and Timing of Supervision

The nature, extent, and timing of the supervision depend on:

- the size and complexity of the entity.
- the nature of the work assigned.
- the assessed risks of material misstatement.
- the qualifications of the assistants.

1.2.3 Disagreements Among Auditors

A disagreement among members of the audit team regarding certain accounting and auditing issues may exist at the end of the audit. If the differences still exist after consulting with the auditor who has final responsibility for the audit (generally a partner), dissenting staff members should be allowed to disassociate themselves from the resolution by documenting their disagreement. In this event, the basis for the final resolution should also be documented.

2 Knowledge of the Client's Business and Industry

The auditor is not required to have prior experience with a client's business or industry before accepting the engagement. However, once the engagement has been accepted, the auditor must obtain an understanding of the client's industry and business.

2.1 Knowledge of the Client's Industry

Obtaining knowledge about the client's industry helps to highlight practices unique to that industry that may have an effect on the client's financial statements. The most common sources of industry information are:

- AICPA accounting and audit guides;
- trade publications and professional trade associations;
- government publications; and
- AICPA Accounting Trends and Techniques (an annual survey of accounting practices).

2.2 Knowledge of the Client's Business

The auditor should obtain knowledge relating to the client's business before commencing the audit. Understanding the client's business provides information regarding events and transactions that may affect the client's financial statements. The auditor may:

- **Tour Client Facilities**

  A tour of the client's facilities gives the auditor an excellent opportunity to meet the client's personnel and observe the general operation of the company. A well-organized tour can often save the auditor much time and effort during the course of the audit. As a practical matter, this step is most important for new client relationships.

- **Review the Financial History of the Client**

  The auditor should review written documents relating to the current and past financial history of the client. These may include:

  - previous audit reports;
  - annual and permanent audit files;
  - prior year and interim financial statements;
  - minutes of stockholders' and board of directors' meetings;
  - communications with third parties;
  - SEC filings;
  - Dun and Bradstreet reports; and
  - tax returns.

- **Obtain an Understanding of Client Accounting**

  The auditor should obtain an understanding of client accounting methodology because it affects the design of internal control, which in turn affects planned audit procedures. Specifically, the auditor should obtain an understanding of:

  - Methods used to gather and process accounting information, including the extent to which computer processing is used and the use of any outside service organization. Such methods influence the client's design of internal control and the auditor's consideration thereof. Review of the client's policies and procedures manual often provides information about client accounting.
  - Events and transactions that may affect the financial statements or require special audit consideration.
  - Other factors affecting audit risk, such as related party transactions.
  - Applicable accounting and auditing pronouncements.

- **Inquire of Client Personnel**

  The auditor should inquire about current business developments affecting the entity.

3 Developing the Audit Strategy

3.1 Overall Audit Strategy

The audit strategy outlines the scope of the audit engagement, the reporting objectives, timing of the audit, required communications, and the factors that determine the focus of the audit. The audit strategy also includes a preliminary assessment of materiality and tolerable misstatement.

Developing the audit strategy early in the audit process helps the auditor determine the resources needed to complete the audit, including:

- The involvement of other auditors, specialists, and the client's internal auditors.
- The assignment of staff to specific audit areas, including the assignment of more experienced staff to higher risk areas.
- The timing of testing (interim versus year-end) and audit team meetings.
- The budget hours to assign to specific audit areas.
- The extent, location, and timing of reviews of audit work.

3.2 Factors That Determine the Focus of the Audit

The factors that determine the focus of the audit team's efforts include:

- Preliminary evaluations of materiality, audit risk, and internal control.
- Material locations and account balances.
- Areas in which there is a higher risk of material misstatement.
- Significant accounting changes.
- Significant business and industry developments, including any legal or regulatory matters of which the company is aware.
- Management's commitment to the design and operation of internal controls.

3.3 Scope of the Audit

The characteristics that define the scope of the audit include:

- Characteristics of the engagement, including the basis of reporting, reporting currency, and locations of the entity.
- Industry-specific, regulatory, and statutory reporting requirements.
- The size and complexity of the entity to be audited, including parent-subsidiary relationships.
- The effect of information technology on the audit.
- Knowledge gained from prior experience with the entity.
- The use of service organizations by the entity.
- The extent of recent changes in the company, its operations, or internal control over financial reporting.
- The type and extent of evidence related to the effectiveness of internal control over financial reporting.

3.4 Reporting Objectives, Audit Timing, and Required Communications

The following matters should be considered when determining the audit reporting objectives, timing, and required communications:

- Deadlines for interim and final reporting.
- Key dates for meetings with management and those charged with governance.
- The expected type and timing of reports and other communications.
- The nature and timing of audit team communications, including audit team meetings and reviews of audit work.
- Expected or required communications with third parties.

3.5 Other Considerations

3.5.1 Small Entities

For a small entity, establishment of an audit strategy may be a simple and less formal process, such as preparing a brief memorandum at the end of one audit and updating it at the beginning of the next.

3.5.2 Communication With Those Charged With Governance

The auditor is required to communicate the planned scope and timing of the audit with those charged with governance (covered later).

4 Developing the Audit Plan

The audit plan is based on the audit strategy and outlines the nature, extent, and timing of the procedures to be performed during the audit. While creation of an audit plan typically follows development of the audit strategy, the two are closely interrelated and may overlap to some extent.

Pass Key

A written audit plan (i.e., documentation of specific audit procedures) is *required*.

4.1 Audit Procedures

Audit procedures are performed to obtain evidence on which to base the audit opinion. Audit procedures may be categorized as either risk assessment procedures or further audit procedures.

4.1.1 Risk Assessment Procedures

Risk assessment procedures are used to obtain an understanding of the entity and its environment, including its internal control, in order to assess the risks of material misstatement and determine the nature, extent, and timing of further audit procedures.

Risk assessment procedures alone do not provide audit evidence sufficient to support an audit opinion. Specific risk assessment procedures will be discussed later.

4.1.2 Further Audit Procedures

Further audit procedures include tests of the operating effectiveness of internal controls and substantive procedures.

- **Tests of Controls**

  Tests of controls are used to evaluate the operating effectiveness of internal controls in preventing or detecting material misstatements.

  Tests of controls are necessary when:

  - the auditor's risk assessment is based to some extent on the operating effectiveness of internal control.
  - substantive procedures alone are deemed to be insufficient (covered later).

- **Substantive Procedures**

  Substantive procedures are used to detect material misstatements. They include tests of details (as applied to transaction classes, account balances, and disclosures) and substantive analytical procedures.

  - Substantive procedures are performed in response to the planned level of detection risk, which in turn may be based (to some extent) on the results of tests of controls.
  - Because risk assessment is subjective, and because there are inherent limitations of internal control, substantive procedures are required for all relevant assertions related to each material transaction class, account balance, and disclosure item.

- **Other Audit Procedures**

  Other audit procedures (for example, a letter to the client's attorney) may be necessary to comply with GAAS.

4.1.3 Timing of Audit Procedures

- **Testing at an Interim Date**

  During planning, the auditor generally establishes the timing of the audit work, which may include the gathering of audit evidence at interim dates. When audit procedures are performed before year-end, the auditor must assess the incremental risk involved and determine whether sufficient alternative procedures exist to extend the interim conclusions to year-end.

- **Effect of Information Technology**

  The auditor should consider the methods used by the client to process accounting information, and whether those methods affect the availability of data. For example, when computer processing is used, documents may exist only briefly because they are discarded once information is entered into the system. In such situations, the auditor may need to schedule audit procedures to coincide with the availability of information. The auditor should also consider performing tests several times during the year.

5 Consideration of Financial Statement Assertions

Further audit procedures (tests of controls and substantive procedures) are performed at the relevant assertion level for each material account balance, transaction class, and disclosure item in the financial statements.

5.1 What Are Financial Statements?

Financial statements are not statements of facts. They are claims and assertions, made implicitly or explicitly by management, about the recognition, measurement, presentation, and disclosure of information in the financial statements.

5.2 Assertions

There are six main financial statement assertions:

1. **Completeness**
   All account balances, transactions, and disclosures that should have been recorded have been recorded and included in the financial statements.

2. **CutOff**
   Transactions have been recorded in the correct (proper) accounting period.

3. **Valuation, Allocation, and Accuracy**
   Account balances, transactions, and disclosures are recorded fairly and at appropriate amounts, and any resulting valuation or allocation adjustments are appropriately recorded.

4. **Existence and Occurrence**
   Account balances exist, and transactions that have been recorded and disclosed have occurred and pertain to the entity.

5. **Rights and Obligations**
   The entity holds or controls the rights to assets, and liabilities are the obligations of the entity.

6. **Understandability and Classification**
   Transactions have been recorded in the proper accounts. Financial information is appropriately presented and described, and disclosures are clearly expressed.

Pass Key

The mnemonic **COVERU** may be used to aid in your memorization of the financial statement assertions.

5.3 Relevant Assertions

Relevant assertions are assertions that have a meaningful bearing on whether an account, transaction, or disclosure is fairly stated. In determining whether an assertion is relevant to a particular account, transaction, or disclosure, the auditor should consider the nature of the assertion, the volume of activity related to the assertion, and the nature and complexity of the systems used to process information supporting the assertion.

- **Transactions and Events**

  For transactions and events, relevant assertions include completeness, cutoff, accuracy, classification, and occurrence.

- **Account Balances**

  For account balances, relevant assertions include completeness, allocation and valuation, rights and obligations, and existence.

- **Presentation and Disclosure**

  For presentation and disclosure, relevant assertions include completeness, understandability and classification, rights and obligations, and valuation and accuracy.

5.4 Use of Assertions

An auditor uses relevant assertions to form a basis for assessing risk and for the design and performance of further audit procedures. The auditor should identify potential misstatements that may occur and then design audit procedures to address those risks.

The following table provides some examples of the use of relevant assertions in developing audit procedures for inventory.

Relevant Assertion	Potential Misstatement	Audit Procedure
Inventories included in the balance sheet physically exist (existence assertion).	The inventory balance includes amounts that don't physically exist (i.e., inventory is overstated).	Physically examine inventory items.
Inventory balance includes all inventory on hand (completeness assertion).	Inventory items on hand are excluded from the inventory balance (i.e., inventory is understated).	Observe physical inventory counts.
Inventory balance includes all inventory stored at outside locations (completeness assertion).	Inventory items stored at outside locations are excluded from the inventory balance (i.e., inventory is understated).	Obtain confirmation of inventories held at outside locations.

Note the following:

- There may be more than one relevant assertion related to the same transaction class, account balance, or disclosure.
- A given audit procedure may provide evidence supporting more than one assertion. For example, when an auditor obtains confirmation of inventories held at outside locations, evidence is obtained about both the completeness and the existence of inventory.
- More than one procedure may be required to fully support an assertion. For example, in order to be reasonably certain that inventory quantities include all inventory on hand at year-end, the auditor should also inspect receiving reports near year-end for recording in the proper period.

6 Written Audit Plan

6.1 Drafting the Audit Plan

After sufficient planning information has been gathered, an audit plan should be drafted. A written audit plan is *required* for every audit. The audit plan is a listing of audit procedures that the auditor believes are necessary to accomplish the objectives of the audit. It serves as the work plan for the supervising auditor and assistants working on the engagement. Thus, the audit plan should set out procedures in reasonable detail, specifying the nature, extent, and timing of the work to be performed, and include a reference to the assertion under consideration (this reference may be implied as to the objective).

For example:

"Perform a specified procedure (e.g., count/vouch/trace/compare/calculate/confirm/examine)...	***– nature***
"...on [a specified number of records from a specified population]	***– extent***
"...as of [some interim date or year-end, either for the entire period or from the date of interim fieldwork]."	***– timing***

As the audit progresses, the initial audit plan may need to be modified in response to changing conditions or the results of other procedures. Modifications are often made after assessing the risks of material misstatement, or based on the results of audit procedures. The audit plan should be designed so that the audit evidence gathered will support the auditor's conclusions.

6.2 Group Audit Plan

The group audit team should develop a group audit strategy and a group audit plan. The group audit plan should detail the extent to which the group engagement team will use the work of component auditors and whether the auditor's report on the group financial statements will make reference to the audit of a component auditor.

Question 1 **MCQ-02675**

During the initial planning phase of an audit, the auditor most likely would:

a. Identify specific internal control activities that are likely to prevent fraud.

b. Evaluate the reasonableness of the client's accounting estimates.

c. Discuss the timing of the audit procedures with the client's management.

d. Inquire of the client's attorney as to whether any unrecorded claims are probable of assertion.

Question 2 **MCQ-03088**

In developing an overall audit strategy, an auditor should consider:

- **a.** Whether the allowance for sampling risk exceeds the achieved upper precision limit.
- **b.** Findings from substantive tests performed at interim dates.
- **c.** Whether the inquiry of the client's attorney identifies any litigation, claims, or assessments not disclosed in the financial statements.
- **d.** Preliminary evaluations of materiality, audit risk, and internal control.

MODULE

5 Using the Work of Others

1 Client's Internal Auditors

When planning the audit, the auditor should consider the extent of involvement of the client's internal auditors in the performance of the audit. Although internal auditors must maintain objectivity and integrity, they are not independent of the client, their employer. Thus, the independent external auditor cannot share with the internal auditor any of the responsibility for audit decisions, judgments, or assessments made as part of the audit (such as those concerning materiality or accounting estimates), or any of the responsibility for issuing the report.

1.1 Effect of the Internal Auditor's Work

The work of an internal auditor may aid the external auditor in obtaining an understanding of internal control, assessing risk, and performing substantive procedures. In judging the extent of the effect of the internal auditor's work, the CPA should consider the materiality of financial statement amounts, the risks of material misstatement, and the degree of subjectivity involved in evaluating evidence.

For assertions related to material financial statement amounts with a high risk of material misstatement or a high degree of subjectivity, the internal auditor's work alone cannot eliminate direct testing by the CPA (e.g., assertions about the valuation of assets/liabilities involving significant accounting estimates, or assertions about the existence/disclosure of related party transactions, contingencies, uncertainties, and subsequent events).

For assertions related to less material financial statement amounts with a low risk of material misstatement or a low degree of subjectivity, direct testing by the CPA may not be necessary (e.g., assertions about the existence of cash, prepaid assets, or fixed asset additions).

1.2 Direct Assistance Provided by the Internal Auditor

An external auditor may request that the internal auditor perform a specific task to aid in the conduct of the audit. The external auditor should supervise, review, evaluate, and test the work performed, and there should be communication between the auditors regarding responsibilities, objectives, and accounting/auditing issues.

1.3 External Auditor Responsibilities

1.3.1 Obtain an Understanding of the Internal Audit Function

Since internal auditors often review and assess an entity's controls, the internal audit function is considered to be part of the monitoring component of internal control (covered later). The external auditor should therefore obtain an understanding of the internal audit function (scope of activities, procedures used, access to records) and determine whether any internal audit activities are relevant to the audit.

1.3.2 Evaluate the Internal Audit Function

The external auditor may use the internal auditors to provide direct assistance or use the work of the internal audit function in obtaining audit evidence.

- **Direct Assistance:** If the auditor plans to use the internal auditors to provide direct assistance, the internal auditor's competence and objectivity must be assessed.
- **Use of Work of Internal Auditor:** The external auditor may be able to use the work of the internal audit function in obtaining audit evidence depending on the competency of the internal audit function, objectivity of the internal auditors, and whether the internal audit function applies a systematic and disciplined approach, including quality control.
  - Competence is reflected by education, professional certification, experience, performance evaluations, the audit plan, audit procedures, and the quality of internal audit documentation.
  - Objectivity is reflected by the organizational level to which the internal auditor reports, as well as by policies prohibiting audits of areas in which the internal auditor lacks independence.
  - Application of a systematic and disciplined approach is reflected by the existence, adequacy, and use of documented internal audit procedures or guidance covering such areas as risk assessments, work programs, documentation, and reporting. In addition, the internal audit function may demonstrate a systematic and disciplined approach by applying appropriate quality control policies and procedures or quality control requirements in standards set by relevant professional bodies for internal auditors.
- **Supervise and Review:** The external auditor should supervise and review all work performed on the audit.
- **Bear Responsibility:** The external auditor remains solely responsible for the report on the financial statements. Although internal auditors may assist with regard to routine tasks, they may not be utilized to make judgment calls. These remain the responsibility of the independent auditor.

2 Using the Work of a Specialist

An auditor may decide during planning that it is necessary to use the work of a specialist in order to obtain competent audit evidence related to balances, transactions, or disclosures that are material to the fair presentation of financial statements. In addition, the entity may use the work of a specialist to assist the entity in the preparation of the financial statements.

2.1 Who Is a Specialist?

A specialist is a person or firm with special skills in a field other than accounting or auditing (e.g., actuaries, appraisers, attorneys and engineers).

- **Auditor's Specialist:** An auditor's specialist is an individual or organization whose work in a field other than accounting or auditing is used by the auditor to assist in obtaining sufficient appropriate audit evidence. An auditor's specialist may be an internal specialist employed by the auditor's firm or a network firm, or an external specialist.
- **Management's Specialist:** Management's specialist is an individual or organization whose work in a field other than accounting or auditing is used by the entity to assist the entity in preparing the financial statements.

PCAOB Standards: Guidance for Issuers

The guidance for using the work of specialists and supervising specialists is similar under PCAOB and SAS standards. However, the PCAOB standards use terms that are different from the SASs:

SAS	PCAOB
Internal auditor specialist (employed by auditor's firm)	Auditor-employed specialist
External auditor specialist	Auditor-engaged specialist
Management specialist	Company specialist

2.2 Use of an Auditor's Specialist

2.2.1 Determine the Need for an Auditor's Specialist

A auditor's specialist may be engaged whenever the auditor believes that it is desirable or necessary. For example, specialists may be used to:

- Value restricted securities and works of art.
- Determine physical characteristics (e.g., related to mineral reserves or large quantities of fungible goods).
- Determine specialized estimates, such as actuarial calculations used to determine employee benefit obligations.
- Interpret technical standards or legal documents.

2.2.2 Understand the Specialist's Field of Expertise

The auditor should have a sufficient understanding of the specialist's field of expertise to enable the auditor to:

1. determine the nature, scope, and objectives of the work of the auditor's specialist; and
2. evaluate the relevance, reliability, and adequacy of the specialist's work for the auditor's purposes.

2.2.3 Competence, Capabilities, and Objectivity

The auditor must be satisfied as to the professional competence, capabilities, and objectivity of the specialist, including, for an external (auditor-engaged) specialist, the entity employing the specialist. To assess competence and capability, the auditor should obtain an understanding of the specialist's (and when applicable, the employer of the specialist's) professional certification, experience, and reputation. The auditor should evaluate whether the specialist may have a relationship with the entity that may affect the specialist's objectivity (e.g., review engagement contracts between the entity and specialist, responses to questionnaires about business or family relationships).

Generally, a specialist who is unrelated to the client will provide the auditor with greater assurance of reliability, although the auditor should inquire regarding interests and relationships that may create a threat to objectivity. A specialist who is related to the client may be acceptable in some circumstances. The auditor should perform additional procedures when a relationship between the entity and the auditor's specialist might impair the objectivity of the specialist.

2.2.4 Agreement With the Auditor's Specialist

The auditor should agree, in writing when appropriate, with the auditor's specialist (whether internal or external) regarding:

1. the nature, scope, and objectives of the work of the auditor's specialist;
2. the respective roles and responsibilities of the auditor and the auditor's specialist, including the specialist's responsibility for evaluating data, methods, and significant assumptions;
3. the nature, timing, and extent of communication between the auditor and the auditor's specialist; and
4. the need for the auditor's specialist to observe confidentiality requirements.

2.2.5 Evaluate the Adequacy of Work

The auditor should perform specific procedures to evaluate the relevance, reliability, and adequacy of the work of the auditor's specialist, which may include the following:

- Making inquiries of the auditor's specialist.
- Reviewing the working papers, including the data, significant assumptions, and methods used by the specialist.
  - For data based on company-produced data, test the accuracy and completeness of data.
  - For data based on external data, evaluate the relevance and reliability of data.
  - For significant assumptions, determine the consistency of assumptions with relevant information (existing marketing information, assumptions generally accepted in the specialist field, company's objectives, historical experience, economic conditions).
  - For methods, determine whether the method is appropriate for the circumstances, taking into account the requirements of the applicable financial reporting framework.
- Reviewing reports of the auditor's specialist (including considering any limitations in the report).
- Performing procedures, such as:
  - Observing the work of the auditor's specialist.
  - Examining published data, such as statistical reports from reputable, authoritative sources.
  - Confirming relevant matters with third parties.
  - Performing detailed analytical procedures.
  - Reperforming calculations.
- Engaging in discussion with another specialist with relevant expertise when, for example, the findings or conclusions of the auditor's specialist are not consistent with other audit evidence.
- Discussing the report of the auditor's specialist with management.

2.2.6 Extent of Evidence

The necessary extent of evidence from the specialist depends on:

- the significance of the specialist's work to the auditor's conclusion regarding the relevant assertion;
- the risk of material misstatement of the relevant assertion; and
- the knowledge, skill, and ability of the specialist.

2.2.7 Effect on the Auditor's Report

If the specialist's findings indicate that the financial statements are not in conformity with GAAP, a qualified or adverse opinion would be issued. An unresolved difference between the specialist's findings and the financial statements, or an unresolved disagreement between the auditor and the specialist, would lead to a qualified opinion or disclaimer of opinion due to a scope limitation. If, as a result of the work performed by the specialist, the auditor decides to express a modified opinion or add explanatory language, the auditor may refer to the specialist in the report and should indicate that the reference to the specialist does not reduce the auditor's responsibility for the audit opinion. In addition, an auditor of an issuer may reference the specialist if it helps the users understand a critical audit matter. The auditor may need the permission of the auditor's specialist before making reference to the specialist in the report. If the auditor is expressing an unmodified (unqualified) opinion, no reference should be made to the work of the specialist.

2.3 Use of a Management's Specialist

If information to be used as audit evidence is prepared using the work of a management's specialist, the auditor should:

1. evaluate the competence, capabilities, and objectivity of the specialist and the entity that employs the specialist;
2. obtain an understanding of the work of the specialist; and
3. evaluate the appropriateness of the specialist's work as audit evidence for the relevant assertion, including the data, significant assumptions, and methods used by the specialist and the relevance and reliability of the specialist's work and its relationship to the relevant assertion.

Question 1 **MCQ-02682**

For which of the following judgments may an independent auditor share responsibility with an entity's internal auditor who is assessed to be both competent and objective?

	Assessment of Inherent Risk	*Assessment of Control Risk*
a.	Yes	Yes
b.	Yes	No
c.	No	Yes
d.	No	No

NOTES

MODULE

6 Materiality

1 Overview

When establishing the audit strategy, the auditor should determine materiality for the financial statements as a whole, performance materiality, and, when necessary, materiality levels for particular classes of transactions, account balances, or disclosures.

1.1 Materiality for Financial Statements as a Whole

The auditor should determine the materiality level for the financial statements as a whole. Misstatements, including omissions, are considered material if there is a substantial likelihood that, individually or in the aggregate, they would influence the judgment made by a reasonable user based on the financial statements.

Pass Key

The Supreme Court of the United States has held that a fact is material under federal securities laws if there is "a substantial likelihood that the... fact would have been viewed by the reasonable investor as having significantly altered the 'total mix' of information available." The Supreme Court has also noted that determinations of materiality require "delicate assessments of the inferences a 'reasonable shareholder' would draw from a given set of facts and the significance of those inferences to him ... ."

1.1.1 Needs of Users

Materiality is influenced by the auditor's perception of the needs of financial statement users. Users are assumed to:

- Have appropriate knowledge of business, the economy, and accounting.
- Recognize that financial statements inherently include some level of uncertainty.
- Understand how materiality affects both the preparation and audit of the financial statements.
- Have both a willingness and an ability to properly analyze the financial statements, and to make appropriate decisions based on this analysis.

1.1.2 Factors to Be Considered

Materiality is based on professional judgment. Ordinarily it is not practical to design audit procedures to detect misstatements that are material based solely on qualitative factors. Therefore, both qualitative and quantitative factors must be considered when setting materiality for the financial statements as a whole. The materiality level for the financial statements as a whole needs to be expressed as a specified amount. When assessing materiality, the auditor should use the smallest level of misstatement that could be material to any one of the financial statements.

The following factors are used to make the preliminary assessment of materiality:

- The application of a percentage to an appropriate financial statement benchmark. The financial statements used may be the entity's annualized interim financial statements or its prior period annual financial statements.
- When identifying the appropriate benchmark to use to calculate materiality, the auditor should consider:
  - Whether there are financial statement items on which users focus their attention when evaluating the entity's financial position or performance.
  - The nature of the entity and its industry.
  - The size of the entity, the nature of its ownership, and its methods of financing.
  - Examples of materiality benchmarks, including total revenue, gross profit, profit before tax from continuing operations, and net assets.
- Prior period financial results, period-to-date financial results and position, and current period budgets and forecasts.
- Any significant known or expected changes in the entity's circumstances.
- Changes in the conditions of the industry or the economy as a whole.

PCAOB Standards: Guidance for Issuers

PCAOB standards state that separate lower materiality levels should be set for particular accounts or disclosures when there is a substantial likelihood that misstatements of amounts less than the materiality level established for the financial statements as a whole would influence the judgment of a reasonable investor.

1.2 Performance Materiality

Performance materiality is the amount or amounts set by the auditor at less than materiality for the financial statements as a whole to reduce to an appropriately low level the probability that the aggregate of uncorrected and undetected misstatements exceeds materiality for the financial statement as a whole. The auditor should determine performance materiality for purposes of assessing the risks of material misstatement and determining the nature, timing, and extent of further audit procedures.

1.2.1 Tolerable Misstatement

Tolerable misstatement is the maximum error in a population that the auditor is willing to accept. Tolerable misstatement is the application of performance materiality to a particular sampling procedure.

For multilocation audits, the tolerable misstatement for an individual location should be less than the materiality level for the financial statements as a whole.

Example 1 Calculating Materiality

Facts: Evan, senior accountant at Noah CPA firm, is determining the overall financial statement materiality and tolerable misstatement for his client in Year 2. Evan expects that there will be a low likelihood of uncorrected and undetected misstatements.

Noah CPA firm's materiality guidelines are as follows:

- Overall financial statement materiality should be based on the benchmark of either total assets or gross revenue, whichever is larger, and should be calculated by taking the appropriate benchmark and multiplying it by either 1 percent, if the benchmark is total assets, or 0.5 percent, if the benchmark is gross revenue.
- Tolerable misstatement is calculated by multiplying the overall materiality by either 70 percent (for low likelihood of uncorrected and undetected misstatements) or 50 percent (for high likelihood of uncorrected and undetected misstatements).

Selected financial information:

- Revenue: $2,500,000
- Gross profit: $50,000
- Total assets: $1,750,000
- Stockholders' equity: $750,000

Required: Calculate overall financial statement materiality and tolerable misstatement.

Solution:

Overall materiality	=	Applicable benchmark × applicable percentage
Overall materiality	=	$2,500,000 × 0.005
Overall materiality	**=**	**$12,500**
Tolerable misstatement	=	Overall materiality × applicable percentage
Tolerable misstatement	=	$12,500 × 0.7
Tolerable misstatement	**=**	**$8,750**

Note: The applicable percentage and determination of the benchmark vary by CPA firm. Therefore, on the exam, it is important to read the facts to determine the appropriate benchmark, percentage, and formula that should be used.

1.3 Materiality for Particular Classes of Transactions, Account Balances, or Disclosures

In the specific circumstances of an entity, there may be one or more particular classes of transactions, account balances, or disclosures for which misstatements of a lesser amount than materiality for the financial statements as a whole could influence the economic decisions of users. When this is the case, the auditor should determine the separate materiality levels to be applied to those classes of transactions, account balances, or disclosures.

1.4 Materiality in Group Audits

In a group audit, the group engagement team should do the following when making its preliminary assessments of materiality:

1. Assess materiality, including performance materiality, for the group financial statements as a whole.
2. Determine materiality to be applied to particular classes of transactions, account balances, or disclosures in the group financial statements for which misstatements of lesser amounts than materiality for the group financial statements as a whole could influence the economic decisions of users.
3. Determine component materiality for those components on which the group engagement team will perform, or request a component auditor to perform, an audit or review. Component materiality should be determined taking into account all components and should be lower than materiality for the group financial statements as a whole. Component performance materiality should be lower than performance materiality for the group financial statements as a whole.
4. Determine the threshold above which misstatements cannot be regarded as clearly trivial to the group financial statements.

1.5 Revising the Assessment of Materiality

The preliminary assessments of materiality ordinarily will be revised as the audit progresses. The auditor should consider whether the audit plan and the nature, extent, and timing of audit procedures need to be modified in response to any change in the assessments of materiality, and should not assume that a misstatement is an isolated occurrence.

Examples of situations that would require a reevaluation of established materiality levels or tolerable misstatement:

- Materiality levels and tolerable misstatement were originally based on estimated or preliminary financial statement amounts that differ significantly from actual amounts.
- Events or changes (e.g., changes in laws, regulations, the financial reporting framework, or contractual agreements) that occurred after the materiality levels and tolerable misstatement were established are likely to affect investors' perceptions about the company's financial statements.

Question 1 **MCQ-02761**

Which of the following statements is **not** correct about materiality?

a. The concept of materiality recognizes that some matters are important for fair presentation of financial statements in conformity with GAAP, while other matters are not important.

b. An auditor considers materiality for the financial statements as a whole in terms of the largest aggregate level of misstatements that could be material to any one of the financial statements.

c. Materiality judgments are made in light of surrounding circumstances and necessarily involve both quantitative and qualitative judgments.

d. An auditor's consideration of materiality is influenced by the auditor's perception of the needs of a reasonable person who will rely on the financial statements.

MODULE

7 Risk Assessment: Part 1

AUD 2

CPA tests internal control in order to adequately plan the "NET" audit procedures

1 Overview

1.1 Purpose

An auditor should perform risk assessment procedures, which enable the auditor to:

- Identify and assess the risks of material misstatement. → audit planning
- Make informed judgments about other audit matters, including:
  - Materiality and tolerable misstatement.
  - The entity's selection and application of accounting procedures.
  - Areas that require special audit consideration.
  - The development of expectations for analytical procedures.
  - The design and performance of further audit procedures, including tests of controls, when applicable (discussed in more detail later), and substantive procedures.
  - The evaluation of audit evidence.

1.2 Risk Assessment Procedures

The auditor performs the following risk assessment procedures:

- Obtain an understanding of the entity and its environment.
- Obtain an understanding of internal control over financial reporting.
- Inquire of the audit committee, management, and others within the company about the risks of material misstatement.
- Perform analytical procedures to assist with planning.
- Conduct a discussion among engagement team members regarding the risk of material misstatement.
- Perform other procedures.

2 Obtaining an Understanding of the Entity and Its Environment

Obtaining an understanding of the entity and its environment is critical, as it establishes a frame of reference for planning and performing the audit. While the extent of this understanding is left to the auditor's professional judgment, it must be sufficient both to assess the risk of material misstatement and to design and perform further audit procedures. The auditor should obtain an understanding of the following factors, and should also consider whether any of the factors have changed significantly as compared with the prior period.

2.1 Industry, Regulatory, and Other External Factors

The auditor should understand the condition of the entity's industry, the regulatory environment in which the entity operates, and the general economic conditions that affect the entity.

2.1.1 Industry factors

Relevant industry factors include industry conditions, such as the competitive environment, supplier and customer relationships, and technological developments. Examples of matters the auditor may consider include:

- The market and competition, including demand, capacity, and price competition
- Cyclical or seasonal activity
- Product technology relating to the entity's products
- Energy supply and cost

The industry in which the entity operates may give rise to specific risks of material misstatement arising from the nature of the business or the degree of regulation. For example, long-term contracts may involve significant estimates of revenues and expenses that give rise to risks of material misstatement.

2.1.2 Regulatory Factors

Relevant regulatory factors include the regulatory environment. The regulatory environment encompasses, among other matters, the applicable financial reporting framework and the legal and political environment. Examples of matters the auditor may consider include the following:

- Accounting principles and industry-specific practices
- Regulatory framework for a regulated industry, including requirements for disclosures
- Laws and regulations that significantly affect the entity's operations
- Taxation (corporate and other)
- Government policies currently affecting the conduct of the entity's business
- Environmental requirements affecting the industry and the entity's business

2.1.3 Other External Factors

Examples of other external factors affecting the entity that the auditor may consider include the general economic conditions, interest rates and availability of financing, and inflation or currency revaluation.

2.2 Nature of the Entity

The auditor's understanding of the nature of the entity should include an understanding of the entity's operations, ownership, corporate governance, investments, financing methods, and financial reporting practices.

PCAOB Standards: Guidance for Issuers

PCAOB standards state that the auditor should consider performing the following procedures to obtain an understanding of the nature of the entity:

- Read public information about the entity relevant to the evaluation of the likelihood of material financial statement misstatement and the effectiveness of the entity's internal control over financial reporting;
- Observe or read transcripts of earnings calls and other publicly available meetings with investors and ratings agencies;
- Obtain an understanding of compensation arrangements with senior management, including incentive compensation arrangements, changes or adjustments to those arrangements, and special bonuses;
- Obtain information from SEC filings and other sources about trading activity in the entity's securities and holdings of significant shareholders;
- Inquire of the chair of the compensation committee (or its equivalent), and any compensation consultants engaged by either the compensation committee or the company, regarding the structuring of the company's compensation for executive officers; and
- Obtain an understanding of the company's established policies and procedures regarding the authorization and approval of executive officer expense reimbursement.

2.3 Selection and Application of Accounting Policies

The auditor should understand the entity's selection and application of accounting policies, including the reasons for changes. The auditor should evaluate whether the accounting policies are appropriate for the entity's business and consistent with the applicable financial reporting framework and the industry in which the entity operates.

In addition, the auditor should obtain an understanding of the accounts or disclosures for which judgment is used in the application of significant accounting principles, especially in determining management's estimates and assumptions. The auditor should also review the financial reporting competencies of personnel involved in selecting and applying significant new or complex accounting standards.

2.4 Objectives, Strategies, and Business Risks

An entity's objectives are the overall plans for an entity. Its strategies are the means used to achieve objectives. Business risks result from events or circumstances that could adversely affect the entity's ability to achieve its objectives and execute its strategies.

Illustration 1 Business Risks

Examples of matters that may result in a risk of material misstatement of the financial statements include:

Matter	Potential Related Business Risk That May Result in a Risk of Material Misstatement
Industry developments	The entity may not have the personnel or expertise to deal with the changes in the industry. In addition, industry developments may make a particular product obsolete.
New products and services	This may result in an increase in product expense and related liability. Increases in expense may pressure management to fraudulently report those accounts at a lower amount.
Expansion of the business	The demand may not have been accurately estimated, which may result in too much inventory.
New accounting requirements	This may result in incomplete or improper implementation or a cost increase.
Regulatory requirements	Legal exposure may increase.
Current and prospective financing requirements	Financing may be lost due to the entity's inability to meet requirements.
The effects of implementing a strategy, particularly any effects that will lead to new accounting requirements	This may result in incomplete or improper implementation.
Changes in key personnel	The personnel may be unfamiliar with the entity and its policies and procedures.
Deficiencies in internal control, especially those not addressed by management	This may result in transactions being incorrectly recorded on the financial statements.
Pending litigation and contingent liabilities (e.g., sales warranties, financial guarantees, and environmental remediation)	This may result in an increase in expense and related liability.
Past misstatements, history of errors, or a significant amount of adjustments at period-end	A history of errors may indicate that the current financial statements may also have errors.

2.5 Entity's Financial Performance

Management measures and reviews the entity's financial performance to evaluate whether business performance is meeting the desired objectives. The auditor should obtain an understanding of this measurement and review, as it may indicate a risk of misstatement. For example, in situations in which management receives performance-based compensation, unusual growth or profitability may be indicative of management bias in the financial statements.

To obtain an understanding of the entity's performance and the incentives or pressures that may exist to commit fraud, the auditor may consider:

- measures that form the basis for contractual commitments or incentive compensation arrangements;
- measures used by external parties, such as analysts and rating agencies, to review a company's financial performance; and
- indicators of key performance (both financial and nonfinancial).

Pass Key

The auditor's understanding of industry, regulatory, and other factors, as well as the entity's nature, objectives strategies, business risks, and financial performance, aid the auditor in assessing the entity's inherent risk (covered in more detail later).

2.6 Understanding the Group, Its Components, and Their Environment

When obtaining an understanding of the entity and its environment in a group audit, the group engagement team should do the following:

- Enhance its understanding of the group, its components, and their environments, including group-wide controls.
- Obtain an understanding of the consolidation process, including the instructions issued by group management to components.
- Confirm or revise its initial identification of significant components.

2.7 Required Documentation

The auditor should document the key elements of the understanding obtained regarding the entity and its environment, the sources of information used to develop the understanding, and the risk assessment procedures performed.

The key elements that should be documented include:

- Relevant industry, regulatory, and other external factors, including the applicable financial reporting framework.
- The nature of the entity, including:
  - its operations;
  - its ownership and governance structures;
  - the types of investments that the entity is making and plans to make, including investments in entities formed to accomplish specific objectives; and

- the way that the entity is structured and how it is financed.
- The entity's selection and application of accounting policies, including the reasons for changes thereto. Documentation should include the auditor's evaluation of whether the entity's accounting policies are appropriate for its business and consistent with the applicable financial reporting framework and accounting policies used in the relevant industry.
- The entity's objectives and strategies and those related business risks that may result in risks of material misstatement.
- Review of the entity's financial performance.

3 Other Risk Assessment Procedures

The auditor should use the following risk assessment procedures to obtain an understanding of the entity and its environment, including its internal control.

3.1 Inquiries

Inquiries are generally made of management and others within the entity.

Inquiries may also be made of other parties, including the board of directors and audit committee, internal auditors, and parties outside the entity (external legal counsel, valuation experts, etc.).

3.2 Analytical Procedures

Analytical procedures are evaluations of financial information made by a study of plausible relationships among both financial and nonfinancial data.

3.2.1 Analytical Procedures Required to Be Performed During Planning

During planning, analytical procedures consist of a review of data aggregated at a high level, such as comparing financial statements to budgeted or anticipated results.

Generally, financial data are used, although relevant nonfinancial data (e.g., number of employees, square footage of selling space, or volume of goods produced) and their relationships with related financial data may also be considered.

The objective of analytical procedures used during planning is to:

- Enhance the auditor's understanding of the entity and of transactions and events that have occurred since the last audit date.
- Identify unusual transactions and events, and amounts, ratios, or trends that might be significant to the financial statements and may represent specific risks relevant to the audit.

Pass Key

During planning, the auditor is specifically required to perform analytical procedures related to revenue in order to identify unusual or unexpected relationships that might indicate material misstatement, including material misstatement due to fraud. The auditor should also take into account analytical procedures performed during interim reviews (if performed).

3.3 Risk Assessment Discussion

The members of the audit team, including the auditor with final responsibility for the audit, other key members of the audit team, and specialists (as necessary), should discuss the susceptibility of the financial statements to material misstatement.

If the audit involves multiple locations, then there can be multiple discussions. Important matters should be communicated to all engagement members not present for the discussion(s). This discussion:

- Can be held concurrently with the fraud risk discussion.
- Should include areas of significant audit risk, the company's selection and application of accounting principles, including disclosure requirements, areas involving unusual accounting procedures, important control systems, and materiality levels.
- Allows more experienced team members to share their insights with less experienced staff.
- Should emphasize the need to exercise professional skepticism, and to be alert for and rigorously investigate any potential misstatements, whether due to error or fraud.
- Should continue throughout the audit, including when conditions change.

3.4 Audit Data Analytics (ADAs)

An auditor may choose to use audit data analytics (ADAs) when performing risk assessment procedures. ADAs involve analyzing patterns, identifying anomalies, and extracting other useful information in data underlying or related to the subject matter of an audit through analysis, modeling, and visualization. ADAs may also be used in other areas of the audit, such as testing controls, performing substantive procedures, and performing concluding procedures.

3.4.1 Steps for ADAs

Generally, five steps are performed when using ADAs to help with the assessment of the risk of material misstatement:

1. Plan the ADA. This includes determining the objective of the ADA, the data population to be analyzed, selecting the ADA that best meets these objectives, and selecting the tools, graphics, and tables that will be used.
2. Access and prepare the data for purposes of the ADA.
3. Consider the relevance and reliability of the data used.
4. Perform the ADA.
5. Evaluate the results and conclude whether the purpose and specific objectives of performing the ADA have been achieved. If the purpose and objectives have not been achieved, the auditor should redesign and reperform the ADA or select a different procedure that will meet the intended objective.

3.4.2 Notable Items

The application of ADAs may result in the identification of notable items. Notable items include items that may identify a previously unidentified risk, modify or support the assessment of risks of material misstatement, or provide the auditor with information to better plan audit procedures. In situations in which there are a large number of notable items, the auditor may decide to group the data for items that have common characteristics. For each group, the auditor should determine which data include:

- Items that do not identify new or higher risks of material misstatements (also known as false positives).
- Items requiring further consideration because they may represent new or higher risks of material misstatements.

Based on the evaluation of results, the auditor should determine the level of risk of material misstatement and plan audit procedures that appropriately respond to the assessed risk.

Illustration 1 Audit Data Analytics

An auditor is auditing a company that sells commercial copiers for the period of Year 4. During the planning stage, the auditor decides to perform an ADA technique on the number of sold copiers (analyzed at the product level) to evaluate any significant changes in the sales mix of commercial copiers that might identify new or higher risks of material misstatement for revenue. Based on discussion with management and on the prior year audit, the auditor is aware that there was a fire in February Year 3 in the building where Type C copiers are manufactured, which resulted in a significant decrease of Type C copiers available for sale for that year. In addition, Type D copiers were introduced in March Year 2 and the company introduced Copier E, which is very popular with consumers, in January Year 4.

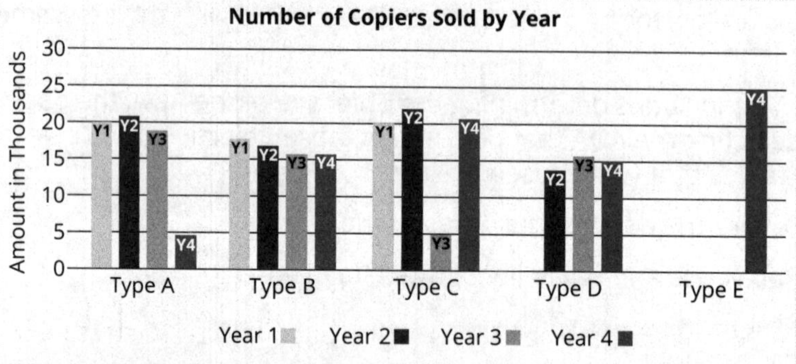

The ADA output (chart) confirmed the following activity that the auditor anticipated:

- The number of copiers sold for Type B and Type D appears to be comparable to prior years.
- The number of Type C copiers sold in Year 4 is comparable to the number sold in Year 1 and Year 2. (Year 3 is lower as a result of the decreased number of Type C copiers available for sale in that year.)
- Copier Type E started selling in Year 4 and appears to be a top seller.

The ADA output also showed a significant decline in Type A copiers that were sold in Year 4 compared with prior years. This leads to a higher risk that the inventory may be overvalued. The auditor plans to respond to this higher risk by obtaining more persuasive evidence regarding the valuation of the inventory.

Note: The auditor may decide to perform additional ADAs related to sales, such as creating a line chart that shows sales by year, by month, etc.

3.5 Other Procedures

The auditor should also consider:

- Reviewing external information (e.g., trade journals and analysts' reports).
- The results of the fraud risk assessment.
- Information obtained during the client acceptance or continuance process.
- Information obtained on other engagements performed for the entity.
- Prior period evidence, to the extent that it is still relevant.

3.6 Risk Assessment Procedures and Audit Evidence

Risk assessment procedures sometimes provide audit evidence about transactions, balances, disclosures, or controls, even if they were not designed to provide such evidence.

The auditor may also choose to perform substantive procedures or tests of controls concurrently with risk assessment procedures, if it is efficient to do so.

3.7 Ongoing Assessment

Obtaining an understanding of the entity and its environment is a process that continues and evolves throughout the audit, and the auditor's assessment of risk may change as additional audit evidence is obtained. For example, the initial risk assessment may presume effective operation of controls, but:

1. tests of controls may indicate that controls are not operating effectively; or
2. the auditor may detect more or less frequent misstatements than would have been expected given the initial risk assessment.

In such situations, the auditor should revise the assessment and modify planned audit procedures.

Question 1 **MCQ-02426**

The primary objective of procedures performed to obtain an understanding of the entity and its environment is to provide an auditor with:

a. Knowledge necessary for risk assessment and audit planning.
b. Audit evidence to use in assessing inherent risk.
c. A basis for issuing an opinion on the financial statements.
d. An evaluation of the consistency of application of management's policies.

Question 2 **MCQ-02799**

The objective of performing analytical procedures in planning an audit is to identify the existence of:

a. Unusual transactions and events.
b. Acts of noncompliance with laws and regulations that went undetected because of internal control weaknesses.
c. Related party transactions.
d. Recorded transactions that were not properly authorized.

NOTES

MODULE

8 Risk Assessment: Part 2

AUD 2

1 Overview of Internal Control

Another key component of risk assessment procedures is obtaining an understanding of internal control. Even if an auditor does not test or rely on internal controls, the auditor must obtain an understanding of internal control.

Internal control is a process—effected by those charged with governance, by management, and other personnel—designed to provide reasonable assurance about the achievement of the entity's objectives.

An entity's objectives may be divided into three categories:

1. Reliability of financial reporting
2. Effectiveness and efficiency of operations
3. Compliance with applicable laws and regulations

Pass Key

The reliability of the financial reporting objective is most relevant to the audit. Controls relating to the operations and compliance objectives may occasionally be relevant to the audit, for example, if they relate to nonfinancial data used in analytical procedures, or if they relate to noncompliance with laws or regulations that have a direct and material effect on the financial statements.

2 Components of Internal Control

Pass Key

An auditor must obtain an understanding of the design and implementation of internal control during the planning stage of the audit. In order for the auditor to understand the design and implementation of internal control, the auditor should understand the components of internal control.

2.1 Five Components of Internal Control

Internal control consists of five interrelated components. The components represent means used by an entity to help it achieve its objectives.

1. **Control Environment:** The overall tone of the organization.
2. **Risk Assessment:** Management's identification of risk.
3. **Information and Communication Systems:** A means of recording transactions and communicating responsibilities.
4. **Monitoring:** Assessment of internal control performance over time.
5. **Existing Control Activities:** Control policies and procedures.

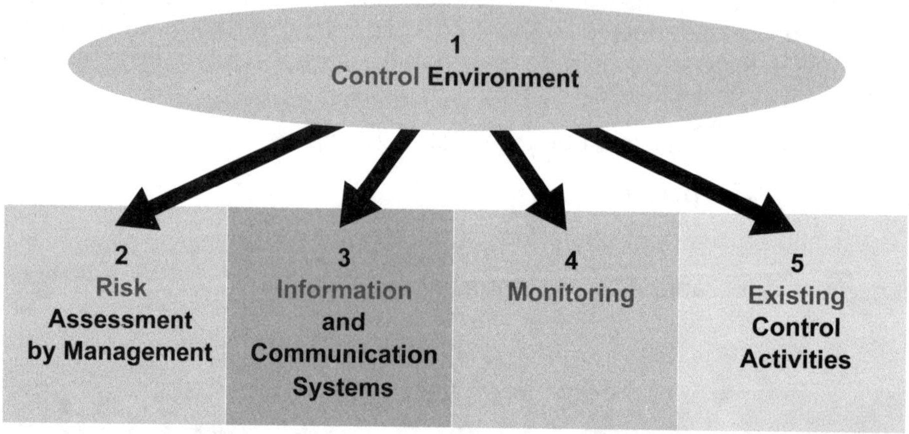

Pass Key

The examiners' questions focus on the control environment and on an entity's existing control activities.

2.2 Control Environment

The control environment:

- Sets the tone of an organization, influencing the control consciousness of its employees.
- Provides discipline and structure as the foundation for all other components of internal control.
- Originates with, and is generated by, management and those charged with governance.

The control environment includes such factors as the following:

- Communication and enforcement of integrity and ethical values of the people who create, administer, and monitor internal controls. The control environment is affected by the collective effect of control environment factors, such as written policy statements and codes of conduct, management's actions to reduce occurrence of unethical acts, and management's reaction to violations.

- Commitment to competence as reflected in management's consideration of the knowledge and skills required for particular jobs.
- Participation of those charged with governance, including an assessment of their knowledge, experience, stature, and independence from management, the extent of their scrutiny of activities and willingness to raise difficult questions, and their interaction with internal and external auditors.
- Management's philosophy and operating style, particularly with respect to its approach to risk-taking, its attitudes and actions toward financial reporting, and its attitudes toward information processing, accounting functions, and personnel.

Pass Key

The following circumstances would raise concerns regarding management's philosophy and operating style:

- Management consumed with meeting the budget.
- Management dominated by one person.
- Management compensation contingent upon the entity's financial performance.

- Organizational structure, which is the framework within which the entity plans, executes, controls, and monitors its activities, including establishment of key areas of authority and responsibility and lines of reporting.
- Assignment of authority, responsibility, and accountability.
- Human resource policies and practices related to recruitment, orientation, training, evaluating, counseling, promoting, compensating, and remedial activities.

The auditor's focus must be on the substance of the control environment rather than the form, because appropriate procedures may be established but not enforced.

2.2.1 Those Charged With Governance

The auditor should understand the attitudes, awareness, and actions of those charged with governance, with respect to internal control. The responsibilities of those charged with governance include:

- Overseeing the financial reporting and disclosure process.
- Balancing the conflicting pressures that may be placed on management (i.e., fair financial reporting versus positive operating results).
- Bearing responsibility, together with management, for the prevention and detection of error and fraud.
- Overseeing "whistle-blower" procedures.
- Overseeing the process for reviewing the effectiveness of the entity's internal control.

2.2.2 Pervasive Effect of Control Environment

The control environment has a pervasive effect on the auditor's risk assessment, and preliminary judgments about its effectiveness may influence the nature, extent, and timing of further audit procedures to be performed.

- **Weak Control Environment:** When there is a weak control environment, the auditor may perform more substantive procedures as of the balance sheet date rather than at interim; may modify the nature of tests to obtain more persuasive evidence; or may increase the extent of testing (e.g., include more items and locations).
- **Strong Control Environment:** When there is a strong control environment, the auditor may perform tests at an interim date rather than at the balance sheet date; may use tests that provide somewhat less persuasive evidence; or may reduce the extent of testing.

2.3 Risk Assessment

Risk assessment is an entity's identification and analysis of risks to the achievement of its objectives. (Note that this component concerns the assessment by management of risk facing the entity, not the auditor's assessment of control risk.)

The entity's risk assessment for financial reporting purposes involves the identification, analysis, and management of business risks relevant to the preparation of fairly presented GAAP financial statements. Relevant accounting risks include, for example, the occurrence of external and internal events and circumstances that may adversely affect the entity's ability to initiate, authorize, record, process, and report financial data.

Circumstances from which risks may arise include:

- Change in the regulatory or operating environment
- New personnel
- New or revamped information systems
- Rapid expansion of operations
- Incorporation of new technology
- New business models, products, or activities
- Corporate restructuring
- Expansion or acquisition of foreign operations
- Adoption of new or different accounting principles or pronouncements

Management may take action to address risk, or may decide to accept a risk based on cost or other considerations. The auditor should consider whether business risks identified by management may result in material misstatement. If management fails to identify a significant risk, the auditor should consider why the entity's risk assessment process failed.

2.4 Information and Communication Systems

Information and communication systems support the identification, capture, and exchange of information in a timely and useful manner.

2.4.1 Information Systems

The information system relevant to financial reporting objectives consists of the procedures (both automated and manual) and records established to initiate, authorize, record, process, and report entity transactions, events, and conditions, and to maintain accountability for the related assets, liabilities, and equity. It encompasses the accounting system as well as any other methods and records designed and established to:

- Identify and record all valid transactions.
- Process and account for system overrides or bypasses to controls.

- Describe transactions in a timely manner and in sufficient detail to allow proper classification.
- Measure and record the proper monetary value of transactions.
- Determine and ensure proper recording of transactions and events in the appropriate time period.
- Present transactions and related disclosures properly in the financial statements.

2.4.2 Accounting Information System

The auditor is especially interested in the business processes relevant to financial reporting, and should obtain an understanding of:

- The classes of transactions that are significant to the financial statements.
- Accounting processing (both automated and manual), from initiation of a transaction to inclusion in the financial statements.
- The accounting records (both electronic and manual), supporting information, and specific accounts involved in initiating, authorizing, recording, processing, and reporting transactions.
- The way in which other significant events and conditions are captured by the system.
- The financial reporting process, including the development of significant accounting estimates and the inclusion of appropriate disclosures.
- The controls surrounding journal entries.
- Whether related accounts involve accounting estimates and, if so, the processes used to develop accounting estimates, including the methods, data, assumptions, and use of third parties to develop estimates.

2.4.3 Communication Systems

Communication involves providing an understanding of individual roles and responsibilities pertaining to internal control over financial reporting. Communication may be written (policy and procedure manuals, financial reporting manuals, and memoranda), oral, or by example (through the actions of management). The auditor should obtain an understanding of:

- The methods used to communicate roles, responsibilities, and significant matters related to financial reporting.
- Communications between management and those charged with governance (particularly the audit committee), and between management and external parties, such as regulatory authorities.

2.5 Monitoring

Monitoring is the process that assesses the quality of internal control performance over time, by assessing the design and operation of controls on a timely basis and taking the necessary corrective actions.

Establishing and maintaining internal control is a responsibility of management. Management must monitor controls to determine whether they are operating as intended and whether they have been modified appropriately for changes in conditions.

The monitoring process may include:

- Ongoing monitoring activities built into normal recurring activities, including regular management and supervisory activities.
- Separate evaluations of internal control performance.

- An internal audit function that provides both an evaluation of internal control (including its strengths and weaknesses) and recommendations for improvement.
- Evaluation of communications from external parties, such as customers (through the payment or questioning of invoices), regulatory agencies, and independent external auditors.

The auditor should obtain an understanding of the activities used by the entity to monitor internal control and to initiate corrective actions.

2.6 Existing Control Activities

Existing control activities are the policies and procedures that help ensure that management directives are carried out and that necessary steps to address risks are taken.

Pass Key

The mnemonic "**PAID TIPS**" will help you remember the control activities in a strong system of internal control.

Control activities relevant to an audit include the following procedures.

- **Prenumbering of Documents**

  Prenumbering helps to assure that:

  - All transactions are recorded (completeness).
  - No transactions are recorded more than once (existence).

- **Authorization of Transactions**

  Authorization should occur before commitment of resources.

- **Independent Checks to Maintain Asset Accountability**

  Independent checks involve the verification of work previously performed by others. Examples include:

  - Review of bank reconciliations.
  - Comparison of subsidiary records to control accounts.
  - Comparison of physical counts of inventory to perpetual records.

- **Documentation**

  Documentation provides evidence of the underlying transactions and is a basis for establishing responsibility for the execution and recording of transactions.

- **Timely and Appropriate Financial Performance Reviews**

  - Comparison of actual performance to budgets, forecasts, and prior periods.
  - Comparison of financial and nonfinancial information (for example, the management of a sports team might use attendance data to ascertain the reasonableness of ticket sales).
  - Review and evaluation of functions or activities (for example, sales reports and receivable reports may be used to analyze performance and to identify errors).

- **Information Processing Controls**

  Information processing controls include general and application controls. These controls ensure that transactions are valid, properly authorized, and completely and accurately recorded.

  - Application controls apply to the processing of individual transactions.
  - General controls apply to information processing throughout the company.

- **Physical Controls for Safeguarding Assets**

  Physical controls for safeguarding assets involve security devices and limited access to programs and restricted areas, including computer facilities. Physical controls include:

  - Physical segregation and security of assets, protective devices, and bonded or independent custodians (e.g., banks, safe deposit boxes, lock boxes, and independent warehouses).
  - Authorized access to assets and records (such as through the use of computer access codes, prenumbered forms, and required signatures on documents for the removal or disposition of assets).
  - Periodic counting and comparison of actual assets with amounts shown in accounting records (e.g., physical counts and inspections of assets, reconciliations, and user review of computer-generated reports).

- **Segregation of Duties**

  Segregation of duties involves ensuring that individuals do not perform incompatible duties. Duties should be segregated such that the work of one individual provides a cross-check on the work of another individual. Generally, assigning different people the responsibilities of authorizing transactions, recording transactions, and maintaining custody of the related assets reduces the opportunities for any individual to both perpetrate and conceal errors or fraud in the normal course of duties.

Pass Key

The examiners frequently test segregation of duties. To help you remember the functions that should not be combined: "Segregation of duties" is your **ARC** to protect against a flood of troubles:

- **Authorization**
- **Record** keeping
- **Custody** of related assets

The auditor often obtains knowledge about control activities while studying the other components of internal control, and uses judgment to determine whether additional knowledge must be obtained.

An audit does not require an understanding of all control activities. The auditor's primary consideration should be whether, and how, a control prevents, or detects and corrects, material misstatements.

Summary of the Five Components of Internal Control		
Component	*Description*	*Key Points*
Control Environment	Sets the tone of the organization.	• Integrity • Competence • Participation of those charged with governance • Management philosophy • Organizational structure • Assignment of responsibility • Human resource policies
Risk Assessment	Identification by management of the risks relevant to the preparation of the financial statements.	• Risks are generally related to changes.
Information and Communications Systems	Methods used to classify and report transactions, and to communicate roles and responsibilities.	• Initiating, authorizing, recording, processing, and reporting entity transactions, conditions, and events • Communicating roles and responsibilities
Monitoring	Procedures established to assess the quality of internal control performance over time.	• Internal audit function • Regular management and supervisory activities • Other procedures such as mailing customer statements
Existing Control Activities	Policies and procedures established to ensure that management objectives are carried out.	• Authorization • Segregation of duties • Safeguarding of assets • Asset accountability

3 Auditor's Consideration of Internal Control

3.1 Consideration of the Components of Internal Control

Although the five components of internal control provide a useful framework for identifying and evaluating controls, an auditor should be more concerned with whether and how a specific control prevents, detects, and corrects material misstatements than with the classification of controls into categories.

3.1.1 Relevance to the Audit

- Internal control is relevant to the entire entity or to any of the entity's operating units or business functions.
- The five components of internal control are applicable to the audit of every entity.
- Each of the five components of internal control may affect any of the three entity objectives.

3.1.2 Factors Affecting the Application of Framework

The applicability and importance of internal control components are affected by the entity's size, organization, complexity, information processing methodology, and ownership-management characteristics. The auditor does not need to understand each component with the same degree of detail in every case.

3.1.3 Acceptable Internal Control Frameworks

Management can elect to use the COSO framework or another recognized internal control framework when establishing and evaluating internal control. If management uses an acceptable internal control framework other than the COSO framework, the auditor may use that other framework or the COSO framework when evaluating the design and implementation of controls when performing an audit of financial statements only. However, for integrated audits, the auditor should use the framework used by management in its annual evaluation of the effectiveness of internal control over financial reporting.

3.2 Identifying Controls Relevant to Reliable Financial Reporting

Relevant internal controls are internal controls that prevent, detect, and correct material misstatements. Internal controls can impact the financial statements as a whole or a specific class of transactions, account balances, or disclosures.

3.2.1 Preventive Controls

Preventive controls are designed to provide reasonable assurance that only valid transactions are recognized, approved, and submitted for processing. Most preventive controls are applied before the processing activity occurs.

3.2.2 Detective Controls

Detective controls are designed to provide reasonable assurance that errors or irregularities are discovered and corrected on a timely basis. Detective controls are normally performed after processing has been completed.

Pass Key

It is not necessary for the auditor to assess all of an entity's internal controls over financial reporting. The auditor must use judgment to determine which controls should be assessed during the audit. The auditor should focus the assessment of control risk on the entity's relevant controls.

3.3 Evaluate the Design and Implementation of Internal Control

The auditor should obtain an understanding of the five components of internal control sufficient to evaluate the design and implementation of relevant controls; assess the risks of material misstatement; and design the nature, extent, and timing of further audit procedures.

3.3.1 Evaluate the Design and Implementation of Relevant Controls

- **Design:** Evaluating the design of a control involves determining whether it is capable, individually or in combination with other controls, of preventing or detecting and correcting material misstatements.

- **Implementation:** A control has been implemented if it exists and is being used. To determine whether internal controls have been implemented, the auditor must obtain evidence about whether the individuals responsible for performing the controls have:
  - an awareness of the existence of the procedure and their responsibility for its performance; and
  - a working knowledge of how the procedures should be performed.
- **Procedures:** Procedures used to obtain evidence about the design and implementation of internal controls include:
  - Inquiry of entity personnel (inquiry alone is not sufficient)
  - Observation of the application of controls
  - Inspection of documents and reports
  - Observation of the entity's premises and plant facilities
  - Walk-throughs (described further below)

3.3.2 Assess the Risks of Material Misstatement

An understanding of the design and implementation of an entity's relevant controls is *required* to complete the assessment of the risks of material misstatement, even when the audit strategy contemplates performing only substantive procedures with no planned reliance on the entity's internal controls.

The auditor's understanding of the entity's internal control allows the auditor to make a preliminary assessment of the entity's control risk.

3.3.3 Design the Nature, Extent, and Timing of Further Audit Procedures

The nature, timing, and extent of procedures needed to obtain an understanding of internal control depend on the size and complexity of the company, the auditor's existing knowledge of the company's internal control over financial reporting, the nature of the controls, the company's use of IT, the nature and extent of changes in systems and operations, and the nature of the company's internal control documentation.

3.4 Walk-Throughs

Walk-throughs trace transactions relevant to financial reporting through the accounting system from inception through recording in the general ledger and presentation in the financial statements.

The purpose of a walk-through is to:

- Confirm the auditor's understanding of key elements of the entity's information processing system and internal controls.
- Evaluate the design of the relevant internal controls.
- Determine whether certain controls have been implemented.

A walk-through can be performed by:

- Selecting a single transaction and tracing it through the entity's information processing system from inception to financial reporting.
- Identifying the key steps in the processing of a class of transactions from inception to financial reporting and then performing risk assessment procedures for each step. At each step, the auditor should perform procedures for a specific transaction, but not necessarily the same transaction at each step.

Walk-through procedures include inquiry and additional procedures.

- **Inquiry:** To perform walk-throughs, the auditor should make inquiries of those who actually perform the information processing and internal control procedures. Inquiries should include:
  - The individual's understanding of the entity's procedures and controls.
  - Whether the processing and controls are performed as required and on a timely basis.
  - Situations in which the individual and others do not perform the required control procedures.
  - The individual's understanding of the processing and controls performed on the information before and after the information is handled by the individual.
- **Other Procedures:** Inquiry alone is not sufficient. The auditor should corroborate inquiry responses by performing additional procedures:
  - Observe individuals performing their information processing and control procedures.
  - Re-perform the information processing or control procedures.
  - Inspect the relevant documents and accounting records.
  - Corroborate inquiry responses with others knowledgeable about the information processing and control procedures.

3.5 Document the Understanding of Internal Control

The auditor must document the understanding of the design and implementation of the entity's internal controls. This documentation should include key elements of understanding each of the internal control components as well as the sources of information from which the understanding was obtained.

Pass Key

Documentation may include any item the auditor can **FIND**:

- **Flowchart**
- **Internal** Control Questionnaire or Checklists
- **Narrative**
- **Documentation** from the client, including copies of the entity's procedures manuals and organizational charts.

3.5.1 Flowcharts

A flowchart is a symbolic diagram representing the sequential flow of authority, processes, and documents. It can be an essential aid in understanding and evaluating internal control.

Flowcharting is of use to the auditor in two ways. First, flowcharts of systems are prepared in order to evaluate internal control. Second, IT flowcharts, used as documentation tools in programming, are useful to the auditor in evaluating the internal control in an automated accounting environment.

- **System Flowcharts:** An adequate flowchart shows the origin of each document in the system, its subsequent processing, and its final disposition. Flowcharts are useful to the auditor in evaluating internal control because they document the steps in a process and the practices in use. The use of standard symbols makes flowcharts easy to understand. Sample flowcharts for the major transaction cycles appear in A4.
- **Program Flowcharts:** IT flowcharts are initially created to document the logic and existing flow of a computer program. The auditor can use these flowcharts to evaluate both the flow of the program and the internal controls related to the IT function in general.
- **Flowchart Organization**

  Flowcharts should:

  - Show the general flow of documents and data.
  - Start at the top of the page and move from top to bottom and from left to right.
  - Use descriptive wording familiar to the reader.
  - Avoid intersecting flow lines by using off-page/on-page connectors.
- **Flowcharting Symbols:** The symbols shown below and used in the flowcharts in A4 represent the most commonly used symbols.

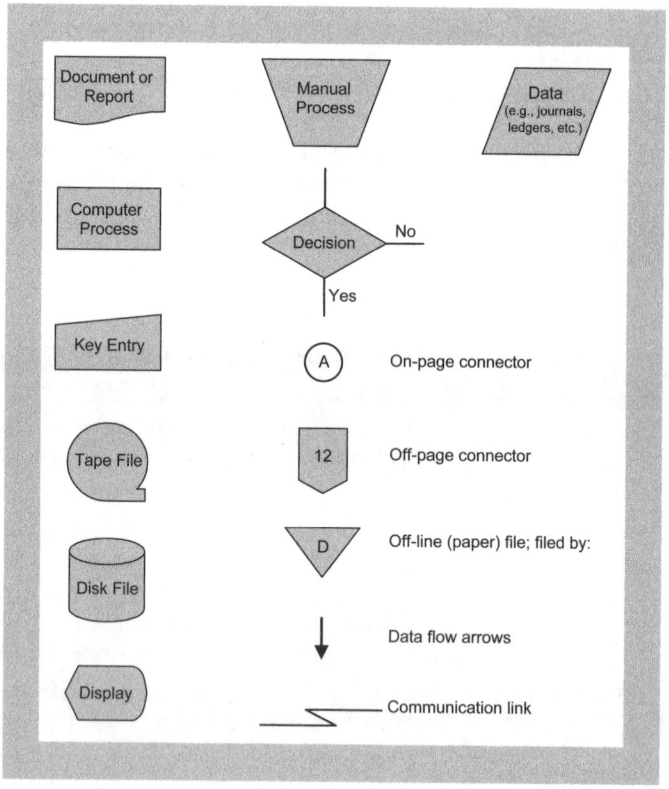

3.5.2 Internal Control Questionnaires

An internal control questionnaire generally consists of a list of questions to be answered by "yes" or "no" responses. A negative response is designed to draw attention to a possible weakness in internal control. Written explanations are required for "no" answers. The questionnaire format can also be open-ended, requiring explanation by the employee being interviewed.

The questions address internal controls over an element, account, or process. Specifically, questions should address each of the relevant control procedures.

3.5.3 Narratives

A narrative is a written version of a flowchart. It is a description of the auditor's understanding of the system of internal control. A narrative is prepared by following a sequence of events for a transaction. Note that flowcharts are more appropriate for documenting complex control structures, and written narratives are more appropriate for less complex structures.

Illustration 1 Sales Processing System Written Narrative

Customer purchase orders are received, and a sales order is prepared in duplicate. New customers' orders are approved for credit, and any orders received from old customers are automatically granted credit. The finished goods department fills the order and sends the sales order to the shipping department, where a bill of lading is prepared. A copy of the bill of lading is then sent to the billing department, where a sales invoice is prepared. A copy of the sales invoice is sent to the accounts receivable department for posting to the accounts receivable ledger.

3.5.4 **Documentation** From the Client

An entity's procedures manuals may include documentation of the entity's accounting system and related controls. The entity's organizational chart outlines designated lines of authority and responsibility. Both documents can assist the auditor in understanding the entity's system of internal control.

3.6 Consider the Limitations of Internal Control

Internal control provides only reasonable (not absolute) assurance regarding the achievement of objectives due to the following three inherent limitations of internal control:

1. Management override of internal control.
2. Human error, which may include errors in the design or use of automated controls.
3. Deliberate circumvention of controls by collusion of two or more people.

4 Other Audit Considerations

4.1 Effect of Information Technology on Internal Control

An entity's use of information technology may affect any of the five components of internal control:

- Management's failure to appropriately address IT risks may negatively impact the *control environment*.
- The use of IT may enhance an entity's *risk assessment* by providing more timely information.
- Many *information and communication systems* make extensive use of IT, and the way in which IT is used often affects an entity's internal control.
- Much of the information used in *monitoring* is provided by IT, and therefore, the accuracy of the IT system is crucial.
- The use of IT may affect the way in which *existing control activities* are implemented. Also, the effectiveness of user controls may depend on the accuracy of information provided to the user by IT systems.

4.1.1 Manual vs. Automated Controls

Controls in most IT systems include a combination of manual controls and automated controls.

- **Manual Controls:** Manual controls are internal controls performed by people and are more suitable when judgment and discretion are required, such as when there are:
  - Large, unusual, or nonrecurring transactions
  - Potential misstatements are difficult to define or predict
  - Changes in circumstances that require changes in controls

  Manual controls are also used to monitor automated controls. Manual controls, however, may pose additional risks because they can be more easily ignored or overridden, they are subject to human error, and they are less consistent than automated controls.

- **Automated Controls:** Automated controls are internal controls performed using IT and are more suitable for:
  - High volume or recurring transactions
  - Control activities that can be adequately designed and automated

4.1.2 General and Application Controls

IT specific controls include IT general controls and IT application controls:

- **IT General Controls:** General controls are policies and procedures that relate to many applications and support the effective functioning and proper operation of the information system. General controls can be categorized as:
  - Controls over data center and network operations
  - System software acquisition; change and maintenance controls
  - Access security controls
  - Application system acquisition; development and maintenance controls

  Examples of general controls include passwords, change management procedures, backup/recovery systems, and administrative rights to the network.

- **IT Application Controls:** Application controls apply to the processing of individual transactions and help to ensure that transactions occurred, are authorized, and are completely and accurately processed and reported. Application controls are controls over input, processing, and output, including:
  - Administrative access rights
  - Controls over interfaces, integrations, and e-commerce
  - Checking the mathematical accuracy of records
  - Maintaining and reviewing accounts and trial balances
  - Automated edit checks of input data
  - Manual follow-ups of exception reports

4.1.3 IT Benefits

IT is used by an entity to improve the efficiency and effectiveness of its internal control. The auditor should consider the effect of such benefits as part of assessing internal control. Benefits may include:

- The ability to process large volumes of transactions and data accurately and consistently.
- Improved timeliness and availability of information.
- Facilitation of data analysis.
- Reduction in the risk that controls will be circumvented.
- Enhanced segregation of duties through effective implementation of security controls.
- Enhanced ability to monitor the performance of the entity's activities and its policies and procedures.

4.1.4 IT Risks

The use of IT may also create additional internal control risks. The auditor must evaluate the entity's use of IT to determine whether and to what extent the following risks exist:

- Potential reliance on inaccurate systems.
- Unauthorized access to data, which may result in loss of data and/or data inaccuracies.
- Unauthorized changes to data, systems, or programs.
- Failure to make required changes or updates to systems or programs.
- Inappropriate manual intervention.
- Potential loss of data.

4.2 Small and Midsized Entities

Small and midsized entities often use less formal means to achieve internal control objectives. For example, while a small or midsized entity may not have written or extensive policies and procedures manuals or an independent party charged with governance, its management may be more actively involved in financial reporting, or may establish a corporate culture emphasizing integrity. The auditor must use his or her judgment to apply the components of internal control and to make an overall assessment of control risk.

Question 1	**MCQ-02374**

In obtaining an understanding of the entity and its environment, including its internal control, an auditor is required to obtain knowledge about the:

a. Design of relevant internal controls pertaining to financial reporting in each of the five internal control components.
b. Effectiveness of the internal controls that have been placed in operation.
c. Consistency with which the internal controls are currently being applied.
d. Controls related to each principal transaction class and account balance.

Question 2 **MCQ-02348**

In planning an audit, the auditor's knowledge about the design of relevant internal controls should be used to:

a. Identify the types of potential misstatements that could occur.
b. Assess the operational efficiency of internal control.
c. Determine whether controls have been circumvented by collusion.
d. Document the assessed level of control risk.

Question 3 **MCQ-02372**

Which of the following types of evidence would an auditor most likely examine to determine whether internal controls are operating as designed?

a. Gross margin information regarding the client's industry.
b. Confirmations of receivables verifying account balances.
c. Client records documenting the use of EDP programs.
d. Anticipated results documented in budgets or forecasts.

MODULE

9 The Effect of Information Technology on the Audit

AUD 2

1 Overview

Information technology (IT) encompasses automated means of originating, processing, storing, and communicating information. The use of information technology affects the manner in which transactions are initiated, recorded, processed, and reported. An entity's use of information technology affects both the evaluation of internal control and the procedures used to gather evidence. Note, however, that the audit objectives are the same in a computerized environment as they are in a manual environment.

2 Differences Between Manual and Computerized (IT) Environments

The differences between manual and computerized (IT) environments in an audit include the following:

- **Segregation of Duties**
  - In a computerized environment, transaction processing often results in a combination of functions that are normally separated in a manual environment.
  - The additional risk associated with this (possibly incompatible) concentration of functions may be mitigated by the implementation of compensating controls.
- **Disappearing Audit Trail**
  - Paper audit trails are substantially reduced in a computerized environment (particularly in on-line, real-time systems). If a client processes most of its financial data in electronic form, without any paper documentation, audit tests should be performed on a continuous basis.
  - Computer systems should be designed to supply electronic audit trails, which are often as effective as paper trails.
  - Use of IT may make it more difficult to use physical inspection to identify nonstandard or unusual transactions or adjustments.
- **Uniform Transaction Processing**
  - Processing consistency is improved in a computerized environment because clerical errors (e.g., random arithmetic errors, missed postings, etc.) are virtually eliminated.
  - In a computerized environment, however, there is an increased potential for systematic errors, such as errors in programming logic (e.g., using the incorrect tax rate).
- **Computer-Initiated Transactions**
  - Automated transactions are not subject to the same types of authorization as are used for manual transactions and may not be as well-documented.

- When information is automatically transferred from transaction processing systems to financial reporting systems, inadvertent errors are reduced, but unauthorized interventions may not be evident.

- **Potential for Increased Errors and Irregularities**

  Several characteristics of computerized processing act to increase the likelihood that fraud may occur and may remain undetected for long periods of time.

  - The opportunity for remote access to data in networked environments increases the likelihood of unauthorized access. Therefore, specific controls should exist to ensure that users can only access and update authorized data elements.
  - Concentration of information in computerized systems means that, if system security is breached, the potential for damage is much greater than in manual systems.
  - Decreased human involvement in transaction processing results in decreased opportunities for observation.
  - Errors or fraud may occur in the design or maintenance of application programs.
  - Computer disruptions may cause errors or delays in recording transactions.

- **Potential for Increased Supervision and Review**

  - Computer systems provide more opportunities for data analysis and review, including integration of audit procedures in the application programs themselves.
  - Utilization of these opportunities can help mitigate the additional risks associated with a lack of segregation of duties.
  - In a computerized environment, the increased availability of raw data and management reports affords greater opportunity for both the client and the auditor to perform analytical procedures.

- **Dependence on IT General Controls Over Computer Processing**

  Controls for specific applications are only as effective as the general controls in place in the information technology department, which processes the transactions and produces the reports.

3 Effect of Information Technology on Evidence Gathering

An auditor can use manual audit procedures (called *auditing around the computer*), computer-assisted audit techniques (CAATs, commonly called *auditing through the computer*), or a combination of both. In either event, because the reliability of automated systems is highly dependent on the adequacy of control design and execution, it is crucial that the auditor gain a thorough understanding of the structure and usage of the control system through inquiry and observation.

3.1 Factors to Consider

In selecting the appropriate audit procedures in a computerized environment, the auditor should consider:

1. the extent of computer utilization in each accounting application;
2. the complexity of the entity's computer operations;
3. the organizational structure of the information technology department;
4. the availability of an audit trail; and
5. the use of computer-assisted audit techniques (covered below).

3.2 Use of an IT Professional

Because some systems depend so heavily on computerized processing, it may be difficult or impossible for the auditor to access certain information without assistance. If specialized IT skills are needed, the auditor should seek the help of an IT professional from the staff or from the outside.

- The auditor should have enough IT-related knowledge to:
  1. communicate audit objectives to the IT professional;
  2. evaluate the sufficiency of the procedures performed; and
  3. evaluate the results of the procedures performed.
- The CPA's responsibility to guide IT professionals is the same as that of other accounting specialists.
- The auditor need not personally possess the required level of IT skills.

3.3 Auditing Around the Computer

- When auditing around the computer, the auditor does not directly test the application program. The auditor tests the input data, processes the data independently, and then compares the independently determined results to the program results. Emphasis is on the input and output stages of transaction processing.
- Auditing around the computer is often appropriate for simple batch systems with a good audit trail, and will result in the same level of confidence as would auditing through the computer.
- Risks of auditing around the computer include insufficient, paper-based evidence and insufficient audit procedures.

3.4 Computer Assisted Audit Techniques (CAATs)

When using CAATs, emphasis is on the input and processing stages of transaction processing. In highly automated systems, complex audit trails and the elimination of physical source documents may mean that CAATs are the only feasible way to complete the audit in a timely manner. CAATs include:

- **Transaction Tagging**

  Transaction tagging is a technique the auditor uses to electronically mark (or "tag") specific transactions and follow them through the client's system.

  - Tagging allows the auditor to test both the computerized processing and the manual handling of transactions.
- **Embedded Audit Modules**

  Embedded audit modules are sections of the application program code that collect transaction data for the auditor.

  - For example, an auditor might want to examine all transactions affecting a specific account code that are greater than $500.
  - Embedded audit modules are most often built into the application program when the program is developed. They are used to ensure that controls operate effectively.

- **Test Data**

  Test data refers to a technique that uses the application program to process a set of test data, the results of which are already known. (The client's system is used to process the auditor's data, off-line, while still under the auditor's control.)

  - The test data contains the types of invalid conditions in which the auditor is interested (it is not necessary to test all combinations of invalid conditions).
  - An advantage of the test data technique is that the live computer files are not affected in any way.

- **Integrated Test Facility**

  An *integrated test facility* (ITF) is similar to the test data approach, except that the test data is commingled with live data. (The client's system is used to process the auditor's data, online.)

  - The test data must be separated from the live data before the reports are created. This is usually accomplished by processing the test data to dummy accounts (e.g., a fictitious customer, branch, vendor, etc.).
  - Client personnel are not informed that the test is being run.

- **Parallel Simulation**

  Parallel simulation (reperformance test) is a technique in which the auditor reprocesses some or all of the client's live data (using software provided by the auditor) and then compares the results with the client's files. (The auditor's system is used to process the client's data.)

  - With controlled processing, the auditor observes an actual processing run and compares the actual results with the expected results (based on the auditor's program).
  - With controlled reprocessing, the auditor uses an archived copy of the program in question (generally the auditor's control copy) to reprocess transactions. The results are then compared with the results from the normal processing run. (Differences indicate that there have been changes to the program.)
    - —Source code comparison programs are programs that compare two versions of software to determine whether they match. This type of software can be used to look for unauthorized program changes.
  - Programs to accomplish parallel processing can be specifically developed for the application, bought as a packaged program or utility, or produced by a generalized audit software package.

3.5 Generalized Audit Software Packages (GASPs)

Generalized audit software packages (GASPs) allow the auditor to perform tests of controls and substantive tests directly on the client's system. The auditor first defines the client's system (to the GASP) and then specifies the tests and selections that should be made. The GASP generates the programs necessary to interrogate the files and extract and analyze the data.

Tasks Typically Performed by GASPs include:

- Examining transactions for control compliance.
- Selecting items meeting specified criteria.
- Recalculating amounts and totals.
- Reconciling data from two separate files.
- Performing statistical analysis on transactions.

Advantages of Using GASPs include:

- GASPs allow the auditor to sample and test a much higher percentage of transactions, which should result in a more reliable audit.
- GASPs require little technical knowledge.
- After the initial use, GASPs can significantly reduce audit time without sacrificing quality.

Question 1 **MCQ-02927**

Which of the following computer-assisted auditing techniques allows fictitious and real transactions to be processed together without client operating personnel being aware of the testing process?

a. Integrated test facility.
b. Input controls matrix.
c. Parallel simulation.
d. Data entry monitor.

Question 2 **MCQ-02920**

Which of the following computer-assisted auditing techniques processes client input data on a controlled program under the auditor's control to test controls in the computer system?

a. Test data.
b. Review of program logic.
c. Integrated test facility.
d. Parallel simulation.

Question 3 **MCQ-02924**

A primary advantage of using generalized audit software packages to audit the financial statements of a client that uses an EDP system is that the auditor may:

a. Access information stored on computer files while having a limited understanding of the client's hardware and software features.
b. Consider increasing the use of substantive tests of transactions in place of analytical procedures.
c. Substantiate the accuracy of data through self-checking digits and hash totals.
d. Reduce the level of required tests of controls to a relatively small amount.

NOTES

AUD

3

Risk, Evidence, and Sampling

Module

The Audit Process

General Principles

Overall objectives
Documentation
Communication
Quality control—firm

Engagement Acceptance

Ethics and independence
Terms of engagement

↓

Assess Risk and Plan Response

Audit planning, including audit strategy
Materiality
Risk assessment procedures:
- Understand the entity and its environment
- Understand internal control

Identify and assess risk
Respond to risk

↓

Perform Procedures and Obtain Evidence

Test of controls, if applicable
Substantive testing

↓

Form Conclusions

Subsequent events
Management representation
Evaluate audit results
Quality control—engagement

↓

Reporting

Report on audited financial statements
Other reporting considerations

MODULE

1 Fraud Risk

AUD 3

1 Overview of Fraud

1.1 Fraud vs. Error

- **Error:** Errors are unintentional misstatements or omissions of amounts or disclosures in the financial statements. They include mistakes in gathering or processing accounting data, inaccurate accounting estimates, and misunderstanding or unintentional misapplication of accounting principles.
- **Fraud:** Fraud is an intentional act by one or more individuals among management, those charged with governance, employees, or third parties involving the use of deception that results in a misstatement of the financial statements.

1.2 Types of Fraud

Frauds can be categorized as either fraudulent financial reporting or misappropriation of assets.

1.2.1 Fraudulent Financial Reporting

Fraudulent financial reporting involves intentional misstatements or omissions of amounts or disclosures in the financial statements that are designed to deceive financial statement users. These are usually acts of management and may involve:

- manipulation, falsification, or alteration of accounting records or supporting documents from which financial statements are prepared;
- misrepresentation in, or intentional omission from, the financial statements of events, transactions, or other significant information; or
- intentional misapplication of accounting principles relating to amounts, classification, manner of presentation, or disclosures.

1.2.2 Misappropriation of Assets

Misappropriation of assets, or defalcation, involves theft of an entity's assets when the effect of the theft causes the financial statements not to be presented in conformity with GAAP. These acts usually involve one or more individuals among management, employees, or third parties, and may involve stealing assets or causing an entity to pay for something that has not been received.

1.3 Fraud Risk Factors

Three conditions generally are present when fraud occurs. These conditions are referred to as "fraud risk factors," and the auditor considers such factors when assessing fraud risk.

1. **Incentives/Pressures:** a reason to commit fraud.
2. **Opportunity:** a lack of effective controls.
3. **Rationalization/Attitude:** an attempt to justify fraudulent behavior.

2 Consideration of Fraud During an Audit

2.1 Reasonable Assurance

Because of the concealment aspects of fraud and the need to apply judgment in evaluating fraud risk, even a properly planned and executed audit may fail to detect fraud. In expressing an audit opinion, the auditor provides only reasonable (not absolute) assurance that the financial statements are free of material misstatements resulting from errors or fraud.

- The risk of not detecting a material misstatement that results from fraud is higher than the risk of not detecting one that results from error.
- The risk of not detecting a material misstatement resulting from management fraud is greater than that for employee fraud because management is in a position to manipulate accounting records, present fraudulent financial information, or override controls.
- Fraud is often difficult to detect because those engaged in fraud generally will try to conceal it. Collusion among various parties also can make it difficult to detect fraud.
- The auditor's ability to detect fraud depends on the skillfulness of the perpetrator, the frequency and extent of manipulation, the degree of collusion involved, the relative size of the individual amounts manipulated, and the seniority of the individuals involved.

2.2 Responsibility

2.2.1 Management's Responsibility

Management is responsible for designing and implementing programs and controls to prevent, deter, and detect fraud.

2.2.2 Auditor's Responsibility

The auditor has a responsibility to plan and perform the audit to obtain reasonable assurance about whether the financial statements are free of material misstatement, whether caused by error or fraud. As part of audit planning, the auditor must specifically assess the risk of material misstatement of the financial statements due to fraud and should consider this assessment in designing the audit procedures to be performed. This fraud risk assessment is an ongoing process and should be considered in every phase of the audit.

2.3 Audit Requirements

2.3.1 Professional Skepticism

The auditor should maintain an attitude of professional skepticism, which includes a questioning mind and a critical assessment of audit evidence.

The auditor should consider that fraud can occur regardless of any past experience with the entity or any belief about management's honesty and integrity. The auditor should not rationalize or dismiss information that may be indicative of fraud.

2.3.2 Audit Procedures

The auditor should perform the following procedures:

1. Discuss fraud risk with engagement personnel.
2. Obtain information to identify specific fraud risks.
3. Assess fraud risk and develop an appropriate response.

4. Evaluate audit evidence regarding fraud.
5. Make appropriate communications about fraud.
6. Document the auditor's consideration of fraud.

2.4 Required Discussion Among Engagement Personnel

A discussion of the potential for material misstatement as the result of fraud is required as part of planning.

The discussion should include:

- Brainstorming regarding:
  - How and where the financial statements might be susceptible to material misstatement due to fraud, including consideration of material misstatements through related party transactions.
  - How management could perpetuate and conceal fraudulent financial reporting, including perpetuating and concealing material misstatements by omitting or presenting incomplete or inaccurate disclosures.
  - How assets could be misappropriated.
  - How the financial statements could be manipulated through management bias in accounting estimates in significant accounts and disclosures.
- An emphasis on the importance of professional skepticism.
- Consideration of factors that create incentives or pressures to commit fraud and provide an opportunity for fraud to be perpetrated, or that indicate a culture or environment that enables management to rationalize committing fraud.
- Consideration of the risk of management override of controls.
- How the auditor might respond to identified fraud risks.

The discussions should involve all key members of the audit team, including the engagement partner; may include specialists; and may occur in multiple locations. Communication should continue throughout the audit.

2.5 Obtaining Information

The auditor should perform the following procedures to obtain information useful in identifying potential fraud risks.

1. **Inquire of Entity Personnel Regarding Their Views of Fraud Risk**

   The auditor should direct inquiries to management, employees involved in financial reporting, operating personnel, internal auditors, in-house legal counsel, those charged with governance, etc.

   Inquiries should be made regarding:

   - The overall risk of fraud.
   - Identified or suspected instances of fraud.
   - The process for identifying and responding to fraud risk and controls established to address fraud risk.
   - The extent of oversight of distant locations and whether there are particular locations or business segments for which a fraud risk might be more likely to exist.
   - Communication of management's code of ethics.

- Whether management has reported to those charged with governance regarding internal control and how it functions to prevent, deter, or detect material misstatement due to fraud.
- What type of oversight the audit committee provides.
- Whether management or those charged with governance received and responded to tips or complaints regarding the company's financial reporting.
- The internal auditors' procedures performed to identify or detect fraud and whether management responded appropriately to any findings from those procedures.
- Whether the company has entered into any significant unusual transactions.

Inconsistent responses or responses that are otherwise unsatisfactory (e.g., vague or implausible responses) indicate a need for additional evidence.

2. **Consider the Results of Analytical Procedures**
   - The auditor is required to perform analytical procedures in planning the audit, and should consider the implications of any unusual or unexpected relationships identified.
   - During planning, the auditor is specifically required to perform analytical procedures relating to *revenue*, in order to identify unusual relationships that might be indicative of fraud.
   - Analytical procedures performed during planning often use data aggregated at a high level, and therefore such procedures may provide only a broad indication regarding fraud risk.

3. **Evaluate Fraud Risk Factors**

   As discussed previously, three conditions (incentives/pressures, opportunity, and rationalization/attitude) generally are present when fraud occurs. The auditor should use professional judgment to determine whether and to what extent such conditions are present.
   - The risk of material misstatement due to fraud is greatest when all three risk factors are present, but the existence of all three fraud risk factors is not an absolute indication that fraud has occurred.
   - Lack of observation of any or all of the three fraud risk factors does not imply that there is no fraud risk. One condition may be significant enough on its own to cause a risk of material misstatement due to fraud.

2.6 Identifying Risks

The auditor should use the information gathered to identify risks that may result in a material misstatement (at either the financial statement or relevant assertion level) due to fraud.

2.6.1 Attributes of Risk

In analyzing risk, the following four attributes should be considered.

- **Type of Risk:** Does it involve fraudulent financial reporting or misappropriation of assets?
- **Significance of the Risk:** Can it lead to a *material* misstatement?
- **Likelihood of the Risk:** How likely is this to happen?
- **Pervasiveness of the Risk:** Does it affect the financial statements as a whole or only specific accounts, transactions, or assertions?

2.6.2 Presumption of Risk

There is a presumption in every audit that the following two risks exist:

1. Improper revenue recognition
2. Management override of controls

These risks should be addressed by the auditor in evaluating the overall fraud risk.

2.6.3 Additional Considerations

The auditor should also consider the following factors.

- Whether and to what extent the three fraud risk factors are present.
- The size, complexity, and ownership characteristics of the entity.
  - Large entities may have an audit committee, an internal audit function, or a formal code of conduct, all of which may serve to deter fraud.
  - A smaller entity may lack such features; however, it may exhibit a strong corporate culture that discourages fraud.
- The susceptibility of items to manipulation. Items are more susceptible to manipulation when they involve:
  - a high degree of management judgment and subjectivity; or
  - highly complex accounting principles.
- How fraud can be perpetrated or concealed by presenting incomplete or inaccurate disclosures, or by omitting required disclosures.

2.6.4 Assessing Risks

The auditor evaluates the identified fraud risks after considering the effect of the entity's programs and controls.

- The auditor is required to obtain an understanding of the entity and its environment, including its internal control, as part of planning the audit.
- Specific controls may mitigate specific risks; broader controls (such as those promoting a culture of honesty) may mitigate overall risk.
- An identified control deficiency may increase the fraud risk assessment.

2.7 Responding to Assessed Fraud Risk

2.7.1 Required Response

The auditor is required to respond to the results of the fraud risk assessment on three levels.

1. **Overall, General Response**

   The auditor should consider the overall fraud risk when:

   - Assigning personnel to the engagement.
   - Determining the appropriate level of supervision of engagement personnel.
   - Evaluating management's selection and application of accounting principles.
   - Incorporating an appropriate level of unpredictability in the selection of auditing procedures from one year to the next. The auditor should incorporate an element of unpredictability into every audit.

2. **Response Encompassing Specific Audit Procedures**

   The auditor should respond to specifically identified fraud risks by altering the nature, extent, or timing of audit procedures. Although the auditor's response may include both substantive tests and tests of controls, tests of controls alone generally are insufficient because of the risk of management override.

3. **Response Addressing Risks Related to Management Override**

   The following procedures should be performed to address the risk of management override of controls.

   - Examine journal entries and other adjustments for evidence of possible material misstatement due to fraud. For example, the auditor might focus on nonstandard or unusual entries.
   - Review accounting estimates for biases that could result in material misstatement due to fraud. The auditor should also perform a retrospective review (comparing prior period estimates to actual subsequent events) to provide insight regarding management bias.
   - Evaluate the business purpose for significant unusual transactions. For instance, the auditor might consider transactions that are overly complex or those where the accounting does not reflect the underlying substance of the transaction.

2.7.2 Significant Risks

The auditor should treat the assessed risks of material misstatement due to fraud as significant risks and should obtain an understanding of the entity's related controls, including whether the controls have been suitably designed and implemented to mitigate fraud risks.

2.8 Evaluating Audit Evidence

The auditor is required to assess fraud risk throughout the audit and to evaluate, at the completion of the audit, whether accumulated audit results affect this assessment.

2.8.1 Conditions Identified During Fieldwork

Certain conditions noted during fieldwork may affect the auditor's assessment of fraud risk. Although such conditions suggest the possibility of fraud, they are not absolute evidence that fraud has occurred. These conditions may include:

- Discrepancies in the accounting records
- Conflicting or missing evidential matter
- Problematic relationships between the auditor and management
- Objections by management to the auditor meeting privately with the audit committee
- Accounting policies that appear inconsistent with industry practices that are widely recognized and prevalent
- Frequent changes in accounting estimates that do not appear to result from changing circumstances
- Tolerance of violations of the company's code of conduct

2.8.2 Analytical Procedures

The results of analytical procedures performed by the auditor during or at the completion of the audit may indicate a fraud risk that was not previously identified. The auditor should pay careful attention to unusual relationships relating to year-end revenue and income.

2.8.3 Misstatements Due to Fraud

The auditor should consider whether any misstatements identified during the audit are indicative of fraud, and should evaluate the related implications. Misstatement caused by fraud (even immaterial misstatements) may be indicative of an underlying problem with management integrity.

The auditor may need to reevaluate the assessment of fraud risk, the assessed effectiveness of controls, and the appropriateness of the audit procedures applied.

2.8.4 Final Evaluation

A final evaluation (at or near the completion of fieldwork) should be made regarding the assessment of the risks of material misstatement due to fraud. Such evaluation should include communication among engagement personnel and may indicate the need to perform additional audit procedures. In situations in which significant risk of material misstatement because of fraud remains, the auditor should consider withdrawing from the engagement.

3 Communications

3.1 Management and Those Charged With Governance

Generally, any indication of fraud (even immaterial fraud) should be discussed with an appropriate level of management at least one level above those involved.

- Fraud that causes a material misstatement of the financial statements should be discussed with senior management and reported directly to those charged with governance.
- Any fraud involving senior management, regardless of the effect on the financial statements, should be reported directly to those charged with governance.
- The auditor should consider whether any identified risk factors represent significant deficiencies or material weaknesses relating to the entity's internal control. Such items should be communicated to senior management and those charged with governance.
- The auditor may also choose to discuss identified fraud risks in other communications to those charged with governance.

3.2 Parties Outside the Entity

Ordinarily, the disclosure of fraud to parties outside of senior management and those charged with governance is not part of the auditor's responsibility. However, in certain circumstances, a duty to disclose outside the entity may exist, such as:

- to comply with certain legal and regulatory requirements, such as on Form 8-K and on reports required by the Private Securities Litigation Reform Act of 1995.
- to a successor auditor when the successor makes inquiries of the predecessor auditor, with specific permission of the client.
- in response to a subpoena.
- to a funding agency or other specified agency in accordance with requirements for the auditors of entities that receive governmental financial assistance.
- in some circumstances, to authorities when management and those charged with governance fail to take corrective action.

3.3 Documentation Requirements

Complete documentation of the auditor's fraud risk assessment and response is required. The auditor should document the following items.

- The planning discussion among engagement personnel regarding fraud risk, including how and when the discussion occurred, the participants, and the subject matter discussed.
- The procedures performed to obtain information related to fraud risk.
- Specific identified risks of material misstatement due to fraud.
- If the auditor has not identified improper revenue recognition as a fraud risk, support for this conclusion.
- The results of procedures performed to address the risk of management override of controls.
- Other conditions and analytical relationships that warranted further audit work.
- The nature of communications made about fraud.

3.3.1 Sarbanes-Oxley Act

Under the Sarbanes-Oxley Act, severe penalties apply to those who destroy records (or willfully fail to maintain them for at least seven years), commit securities fraud, or fail to report fraud. The statute of limitations for the discovery of fraud has also been extended by this act, and protections have been provided for corporate whistle-blowers.

Question 1 **MCQ-02903**

Which of the following statements best describes an auditor's responsibility to detect errors and fraud?

a. An auditor should design an audit to provide reasonable assurance of detecting errors and fraud that are material to the financial statements.

b. An auditor has a responsibility to detect material errors, but has no responsibility to detect fraud that is concealed through employee collusion or management override of internal control.

c. An auditor has no responsibility to detect errors and fraud unless analytical procedures or tests of transactions identify conditions causing a reasonably prudent auditor to suspect that the financial statements were materially misstated.

d. An auditor has no responsibility to detect errors and fraud because an auditor is not an insurer and an audit does not constitute a guarantee.

MODULE

2 Audit Risk

AUD 3

1 Overview

1.1 What Is Audit Risk?

Audit risk is the risk that the auditor may unknowingly fail to appropriately modify the opinion on financial statements that are materially misstated.

- Audit risk arises because the auditor obtains only reasonable (and not absolute) assurance about whether the financial statements are free of material misstatement.
- Audit risk should be reduced to an appropriately low level before an opinion on the financial statements is expressed.

1.2 What Is Material Misstatement?

A material misstatement is defined as an omission or misstatement of accounting information that, in light of surrounding circumstances, makes it probable that the judgment of a reasonable person relying on the information would have been changed or influenced by the omission or misstatement.

Misstatements can result from errors, which are unintentional, or fraud, which is intentional. Misstatements include:

- Inaccuracies in the collection or processing of data
- Departures from generally accepted accounting principles
- Omissions
- Incorrect estimates or judgments
- Inappropriate selection or application of accounting policies
- Inappropriate classification, aggregation, or disaggregation of information

The auditor should consider what level of misstatement would be material, either alone or when aggregated with other misstatements.

1.2.1 Types of Misstatements

Misstatements may be described as factual misstatements, judgmental misstatements, or projected misstatements.

- **Factual Misstatements:** Factual misstatements are misstatements about which there is no doubt.
- **Judgmental Misstatements:** Judgmental misstatements are differences arising from the judgments of management concerning accounting estimates that the auditor considers unreasonable or the selection or application of accounting policies that the auditor considers inappropriate.
- **Projected Misstatements:** Projected misstatements are the auditor's best estimate of misstatements in populations, involving the projection of misstatements identified in audit samples to the entire population from which the samples were drawn.

2 Audit Risk Model

Audit risk comprises the risk that the financial statements are materially misstated (risk of material misstatement, or RMM) and the risk that the auditor will not detect such misstatements (detection risk, or DR).

AR		RMM		DR
Audit risk	=	Risk of material misstatement	×	Detection risk
(should be low)		(assessed by auditor)		(controlled by auditor)

The components of audit risk may be assessed either quantitatively (e.g., as a percentage), or nonquantitatively (e.g., high, medium, low, etc.).

2.1 Risk of Material Misstatement (RMM = IR × CR)

The auditor makes an assessment of the risks of material misstatement by performing risk assessment procedures and, where appropriate, tests of controls.

The assessment of the risks of material misstatement includes the assessment of the entity's inherent risk (IR) and control risk (CR).

The auditor can either:

1. make a single overall assessment of the risks of material misstatement; or
2. separately assess inherent risk and control risk and then combine these risk assessments to determine an overall risk of material misstatement.

2.2 Inherent Risk (IR)

Inherent risk is the susceptibility of a relevant assertion to a material misstatement, assuming that there are no related controls.

An auditor assesses inherent risk as high if the account is more likely to contain a material misstatement. Assertions involving the following factors generally have a *high* inherent risk:

- high-volume transactions
- complex calculations
- amounts derived from estimates
- cash

Other factors specific to the entity and its environment may also tend to increase inherent risk, such as:

- technology that renders a product obsolete;
- a lack of working capital; or
- a decline in the overall industry or economy.

Business risk factors identified when the auditor obtained an understanding of the entity may also increase inherent risk. Examples of business risk factors are provided in A2.

An auditor assesses inherent risk as low if the account is not likely to contain a material misstatement.

2.3 Control Risk (CR)

Control risk is the risk that a material misstatement that could occur in a relevant assertion will not be prevented or detected (and corrected) on a timely basis by the entity's internal control. Control risk is a function of the effectiveness of the design and operation of internal control. Some amount of control risk will always exist due to inherent limitations of any system of internal control.

An auditor assesses control risk as *high* if:

- there are no effective controls relative to the specific assertion;
- the implemented controls are not operating effectively; or
- it would not be efficient to test the operating effectiveness of controls.

Pass Key

Inherent risk and control risk exist independently of the audit, and the auditor generally cannot change these risks. However the auditor can change his or her *assessment* of these risks as the audit progresses. Many exam questions present a change in the auditor's assessed level of risk and require the candidate to determine the effect of this change.

2.4 Detection Risk (DR)

Detection risk is the risk that the auditor will not detect a material misstatement that exists in a relevant assertion. Detection risk is a function of the effectiveness of audit procedures and of the manner in which they are applied.

- Some amount of detection risk will always exist because the auditor does not typically examine 100 percent of an account balance or transaction class, and because the auditor may make mistakes in applying audit procedures or in interpreting results.
- Detection risk can be subdivided into tests of details risk and substantive analytical procedures risk.

2.5 Effect on the Audit

The auditor's overall judgment about the level of risk in an engagement will affect the staffing, level of supervision, and scope of the audit. Auditors use professional judgment to assess each aspect of audit risk, but they only can control the level of detection risk. The auditor uses his or her assessment of the risks of material misstatement as a basis for determining an appropriate level of detection risk.

2.5.1 Inverse Relationship of RMM to DR

When the auditor determines that the risk of material misstatement is high, detection risk should be set at a low level. Conversely, when the risk of material misstatement is low, the auditor can justify a higher detection risk.

2.5.2 The Auditor Controls Detection Risk

The auditor's determination of detection risk will have a direct effect on the nature, extent, and timing of audit procedures performed. For example, as the acceptable level of detection risk decreases, the assurance provided from substantive procedures should increase. To ensure a low level of detection risk, the auditor may:

1. Change the nature of substantive tests from a less effective to a more effective procedure (e.g., direct test toward independent parties outside the entity rather than toward parties or documentation inside the entity).
2. Change the extent of substantive tests (e.g., use a larger sample size).
3. Change the timing of substantive tests (e.g., perform substantive tests at year-end rather than at interim).

Alternatively, if the acceptable level of detection risk is higher, the assurance that must be obtained from substantive tests decreases, allowing for somewhat less persuasive evidence to be used, for a reduction in the extent of testing, or for more testing to be performed on an interim basis.

2.5.3 Substantive Procedures Required

Note that even when the assessed risk of material misstatement is low, substantive procedures will always be necessary for all relevant assertions related to material transaction classes, account balances, and disclosures.

2.6 Summary of Audit Risk

The audit risk equation is:

$$AR = RMM \times DR = IR \times CR \times DR$$

The equation may be rewritten as follows:

$$DR = \frac{AR}{IR \times CR}$$

The steps required in assessing audit risk during engagement planning are as follows:

- **Step 1:** Determine audit risk. Audit risk is typically determined by the audit firm and is set at a low level to ensure that the auditor does not render an incorrect opinion.
  - Note: Some exam questions related to determining detection risk may not discuss the level of audit risk. This is because audit risk is generally assumed to be assessed low.
- **Step 2:** Assess inherent risk. This determination is based on the auditor's understanding of the client. A high inherent risk means the accounts are likely to contain a material misstatement, and a low inherent risk means the accounts are less likely to be materially misstated.

- **Step 3:** Assess control risk. This determination is based on the auditor's understanding of internal control, specifically the design and implementation of internal controls, and, if applicable, the operating effectiveness of controls.
  - Note: If control risk is assessed below high, then the auditor needs to test internal controls to prove that the controls are operating effectively.
- **Step 4:** Determine detection risk based on the assessed levels of inherent risk and control risk. There is an inverse relationship between risk of material misstatement (IR × CR) and detection risk.

Example 1 Audit Risk Assessment

Facts: Katie is auditing Sweet Strawberries' investment account. Sweet Strawberries engages in several complex transactions, including derivative transactions. Katie has tested Sweet Strawberries' internal controls related to its derivative transactions and has determined that they are not operating effectively.

Required: Determine the level of detection risk that Katie should set for the investment account.

Solution:

The acceptable level of detection risk is low because inherent risk and control risk are high.

- Inherent risk is high because derivative transactions are complex and are more likely to result in material misstatements.
- Control risk is high because tests of controls indicate that controls are not operating effectively.
- There is an inverse relationship between risk of material misstatement and detection risk. A high risk of material misstatement (due to the high inherent risk and high control risk) results in a low detection risk.
- Because the account is likely to contain misstatements (complex transactions and ineffective controls), Katie must obtain more persuasive evidence (e.g., testing closer to year-end, increasing sample size, and/or obtaining more reliable evidence).

Pass Key

Many exam questions deal with the relationship between the risk of material misstatement (RMM) and detection risk, or between RMM and substantive procedures. Although there is an inverse relationship between RMM and detection risk, there is a direct relationship between RMM and the assurance required from substantive procedures. In other words, greater risk requires more persuasive evidence, a larger sample size, and/or a shift from interim to year-end testing.

3 Audit Risk and Materiality

3.1 Overall Considerations

Audit risk and materiality should be considered together in designing the nature, extent, and timing of audit procedures and in evaluating the results of those procedures.

Considerations of audit risk and materiality are affected by the size and complexity of the entity, as well as the auditor's experience with and knowledge of the entity, its environment, and its internal control.

Audit risk and materiality must be considered at both the financial statement level and the account balance, individual transaction class, or disclosure item level.

3.2 Inverse Relationship Between Audit Risk and Materiality

There is an inverse relationship between audit risk and materiality. The risk of a very large misstatement may be low, whereas the risk of a small misstatement may be high. Also, the more material a misstatement is, the *less likely* it is that the auditor will *not* detect it.

Question 1 **MCQ-02754**

Inherent risk and control risk differ from detection risk in that they:

- **a.** Arise from the misapplication of auditing procedures.
- **b.** May be assessed in either quantitative or nonquantitative terms. AR
- **c.** Exist independently of the financial statement audit.
- **d.** Can be changed at the auditor's discretion.

Question 2 **MCQ-02759**

On the basis of audit evidence gathered and evaluated, an auditor decides to increase the assessed risk of material misstatement from that originally planned. To achieve an overall audit risk level that is substantially the same as the planned audit risk level, the auditor would:

- **a.** Decrease substantive testing.
- **b.** Decrease detection risk.
- **c.** Increase inherent risk.
- **d.** Increase materiality levels.

RMM ↑ DR ↓

MODULE

3 Identifying, Assessing, and Responding to Risk

AUD 3

1 Identifying and Assessing the Risks of Material Misstatement

The auditor uses the understanding of the entity and its environment, including its internal controls, to identify and assess the risks of material misstatement at the financial statement level and at the relevant assertion level and to identify any significant risks.

1.1 Financial Statement Level Risks

Financial statement level risks are risks that relate pervasively to the financial statements as a whole and potentially impact many relevant assertions. The risk of material misstatement at the financial statement level may be especially relevant to the auditor's consideration of the risk of material misstatement due to fraud. Financial statement level risks include weaknesses related to:

- The process used to prepare the financial statements, including the development of significant accounting estimates and the preparation of financial statement footnotes.
- The overall control environment.
- Lack of qualified personnel in financial reporting roles.
- The selection and application of significant accounting policies.

1.2 Assertion Level Risks

Assertion level risks are risks that relate to specific transactions, account balances, or disclosures at the relevant assertion level. When assessing the risk of material misstatement at the assertion level, the auditor should identify controls that have been properly designed and implemented such that the controls are capable of effectively preventing or detecting and correcting material misstatements that could arise from the risks.

1.3 Identifying Significant Risks

Significant risks are risks that require special audit consideration. The auditor uses professional judgment to determine whether a given risk of material misstatement is a significant risk. The auditor's judgment should be based on the nature of the risk and the magnitude and likelihood of the potential misstatement.

Pass Key

The determination of whether a risk is a significant risk should ignore the effects of controls related to the risk and should be based entirely on inherent risk. A significant risk exists when inherent risk is exceptionally high.

Factors that may be indicative of significant risks include:

- Risk of fraud
- Significant recent economic, accounting, or other developments
- Related parties and related party transactions
- Improper revenue recognition
- Nonroutine, unusual, or complex transactions
- Accounting estimates or other subjective measurements of financial information
- Noncompliance with laws and regulations
- Accounting principles that are subject to different interpretations

1.4 Assessing Specific Risks

For each identified risk, the auditor should consider:

- What could go wrong at the relevant assertion level.
- The significance and likelihood of potential material misstatements.
- Whether the risk is significant enough to require special audit consideration.
- Whether tests of controls are required because substantive tests alone are insufficient to reduce detection risk to an acceptably low level.
- Whether the risk relates to a specific relevant assertion or whether it has a more pervasive effect on the financial statements.

PCAOB Standards: Guidance for Issuers

PCAOB standards state that the auditor should identify significant accounts and disclosures and their relevant assertions when assessing the risk of material misstatement. The determination of significant accounts and disclosures and their relevant assertions is made based on inherent risk, without regard for the effect of controls. The auditor should evaluate both qualitative and quantitative risk factors. When a company has multiple locations and business units, the auditor should identify significant accounts and disclosures and their relevant assertions based on the consolidated financial statements. Significant accounts and disclosures and their relevant assertions are the same in the audit of internal control over financial reporting and the audit of the financial statements.

1.5 Required Documentation

The auditor should document:

- The discussion among the audit team regarding risk assessment, including how and when it occurred, the participants, the subject matter discussed, and significant decisions reached.
- Key elements of the understanding of the entity and its environment (including each of the components of internal control), the sources of information used to develop the understanding, and the risk assessment procedures performed.
- The assessment of the risks of material misstatement (at both the financial statement and relevant assertion level) and the basis for the assessment.
- The identified risks and related controls evaluated by the auditor.

A more complex entity/environment results in more extensive audit procedures, which in turn should result in more extensive audit documentation.

PCAOB Standards: Guidance for Issuers

PCAOB standards require that in an audit of the financial statements of a company with operations in multiple locations or business units, the auditor should determine the extent to which audit procedures should be performed at selected locations or business units. The amount of audit attention devoted to a location or business unit should be correlated with the assessment of the risk of material misstatement associated with that location or business unit.

Factors that are relevant to the assessment of the risks of material misstatement associated with a particular location or business unit and the determination of the necessary audit procedures include:

- the nature and amount of assets, liabilities, and transactions executed at the location or business unit, including any significant transactions that are outside the normal course of business for the company or that otherwise appear to be unusual due to their timing, size, or nature ("significant unusual transactions");
- the materiality of the location or business unit;
- the specific risks associated with the location or business unit that present a reasonable possibility of material misstatement to the company's consolidated financial statements;
- whether the risks of material misstatement associated with the location or business unit apply to other locations or business units such that, in combination, they present a reasonable possibility of material misstatement to the company's consolidated financial statements;
- the degree of centralization of records or information processing;
- the effectiveness of the control environment, particularly with respect to management's control over the exercise of authority delegated to others and its ability to effectively supervise activities at the location or business unit; and
- the frequency, timing, and scope of monitoring activities by the company, or others at the location or business unit.

2 Responding to the Assessed Risks of Material Misstatement

In order to reduce audit risk to an acceptably low level, the auditor should develop the following responses to the assessed risks of material misstatement:

1. An overall response to address financial statement level risks.
2. A response at the relevant assertion level, whereby the nature, extent, and timing of audit procedures are designed to address risks related to specific assertions.
3. A response to significant risks.

2.1 Overall Response to Financial Statement Level Risk

In response to risk assessed at the financial statement level, the auditor may:

- Communicate to the audit team an increased need for professional skepticism.
- Assign staff with more experience or specialized skills.
- Increase the level of supervision.
- Incorporate a greater level of unpredictability into the audit.
- Make pervasive changes to the nature, extent, or timing of tests, such as shifting substantive procedures closer to period end.

PCAOB Standards: Guidance for Issuers

PCAOB standards state that the overall response to financial statement level risk should include an evaluation of the company's selection and application of significant accounting principles.

2.2 Response to Risks at the Relevant Assertion Level

The auditor should design audit procedures that address the risks of material misstatement for each relevant assertion of each significant account, balance, or disclosure. The linkage should be clear between the assessed level of risk at the relevant assertion level and the nature, extent, and timing of further audit procedures, including tests of controls and substantive procedures.

Pass Key

Three elements of further audit procedures can be varied by the auditor. An easy way to remember these elements is: We cast our "**NET**" over the audit.

- **Nature:** The nature of an audit procedure includes both its purpose (test of control vs. substantive procedure) and its type (inspection, observation, inquiry, confirmation, recalculation, reperformance, or analytical procedure).
  - The higher the assessed risks of material misstatement, the more reliable and relevant audit evidence must be. The auditor varies the nature of audit procedures in order to achieve the desired level of reliability and relevancy.
  - If the auditor uses information provided by the entity's information system, the accuracy and completeness of that system must be tested.
  - In responding to assessed risks, the nature of selected audit procedures is of primary importance.
- **Extent:** The extent of an audit procedure refers to the quantity to be performed, such as the number of observations to be made or the sample size to be used.
  - The higher the assessed risks of material misstatement, the greater the extent of audit procedures should be.
  - The auditor should also consider the tolerable misstatement and the degree of assurance the auditor plans to obtain.
- **Timing:** Audit tests may be performed at an interim date or at period end.
  - The higher the assessed risks of material misstatement, the closer to period-end substantive procedures should be performed.
  - Performing audit procedures before period end allows earlier identification of significant matters; however, additional evidence is necessary for the remaining period.
  - In considering the timing of audit tests, the auditor should consider when relevant information is available. Some procedures occur only at certain times and electronic data may not be retained indefinitely.

In designing further audit procedures that are responsive to the assessed risks, the auditor should consider:

- the significance and likelihood of the risk;
- the characteristics of the transaction, balance, or disclosure;
- the nature of controls used (especially whether they are manual or automated); and
- whether the auditor expects to test the operating effectiveness of the controls.

2.2.1 Audit Approach

The auditor's specific approach to identified risks at the relevant assertion level may consist of either a substantive approach only or a combined approach.

- **Substantive Approach**

  For certain relevant assertions and risks, only substantive procedures will be performed. This occurs when control risk is assessed at maximum because:
  - there are no effective controls relative to the specific assertion;
  - the implemented controls are assessed as ineffective; or
  - it would not be efficient to test the operating effectiveness of controls.

- **Combined Approach**

  A combined approach uses both tests of the operating effectiveness of controls and substantive procedures. Typically, if controls are operating effectively, less assurance will be required from substantive procedures.

- **Tests of Controls May Be Required**

  In situations in which a significant amount of information is initiated, authorized, recorded, processed, or reported electronically, substantive procedures alone may not be sufficient. Tests of controls are generally required when:

  - An entity conducts its business using information technology (IT) and no documentation of transactions is produced or maintained, other than through the IT system.
  - Audit assertions are related to routine day-to-day business transactions that permit highly automated processing with little or no manual intervention.
  - Audit evidence is obtained in electronic form. The sufficiency and appropriateness of such evidence is dependent on the effectiveness of controls over the accuracy and completeness of the information.

- **Dual-Purpose Tests**

  A dual-purpose test is a test of controls that is performed concurrently with a test of details on the same transaction. The purpose of a test of controls is to evaluate the operating effectiveness of a control, whereas the purpose of a test of details is to support relevant assertions or to detect material misstatements. A dual-purpose test should be designed to accomplish both objectives.

Pass Key

Audit Approach			
Status of Internal Control	*Control Risk Assessment*	*Perform Control Tests*	*Perform Substantive Procedures*
None or Weak	High	No (unless heavy use of IT)	Yes: Maximum
Some	Medium	Yes	↕
Strong	Low	Yes	Minimal (but never eliminate for material balances, transaction classes, or disclosures)

2.3 Response to Significant Risks

For all significant risks, the auditor should:

- Evaluate the design of the entity's related controls and determine whether the controls have been implemented.
- If relying on the operating effectiveness of internal controls intended to mitigate significant risk, tests of controls must be performed in the current period. The auditor cannot rely on tests of controls performed in prior periods.

- Perform substantive procedures that are clearly linked and responsive to the risk. For areas of significant risk, substantive procedures can consist of:
  - tests of details only; or
  - a combination of tests of details and substantive analytical procedures.

3 Responding to RMM: Tests of Controls

3.1 When to Perform Tests of Controls

In making risk assessments, the auditor should identify those controls that are likely to prevent or detect and correct material misstatements in specific relevant assertions. Obtaining an understanding of a control is not sufficient to determine whether the control is operating effectively.

Tests of controls are performed when:

1. the auditor's risk assessment is based on the assumption that controls are operating effectively; or
2. when substantive procedures alone are insufficient (i.e., when the entity makes extensive use of information technology).

Only those controls that are suitably designed to prevent or detect material misstatements are subject to tests of operating effectiveness.

3.2 Operating Effectiveness of Controls

Some risk assessment procedures performed to obtain an understanding of internal control may provide evidence about operating effectiveness, even if they were not intended for that purpose.

For example, as long as there are adequate controls surrounding computer security and program changes, the consistent nature of IT processing may allow procedures performed to determine whether an automated control has been implemented to also serve as a test of that control's operating effectiveness.

If it is efficient to do so, the auditor may choose to test the operating effectiveness of controls concurrently with obtaining an understanding of internal control.

Pass Key

In a financial statement audit, the auditor is required to obtain an understanding of the design and implementation of internal control as part of understanding the entity and its environment. The auditor is not required to evaluate operating effectiveness as part of obtaining an understanding of the design and implementation of internal control.

3.3 Tests of Design and Operating Effectiveness

When performing tests of controls, the auditor must obtain evidence that the controls selected for testing were both designed effectively and operated effectively during the period of reliance. Testing the design and operating effectiveness of controls includes obtaining evidence regarding:

1. Whether the controls were applied at relevant times.
2. How controls were applied.
3. The consistency with which controls were applied.
4. By whom or by what means controls were applied.

Auditor judgment is used to determine the nature, extent, and timing (NET) of tests of controls.

3.3.1 Nature of Tests of Controls

Tests of the operating effectiveness of controls, presented in the order of the evidence that they would ordinarily produce, from least to most, include the following: inquiries, observation, inspection, and reperformance. The auditor should use a combination of procedures to obtain sufficient evidence of operating effectiveness.

- Inquiry alone is not sufficient.
- Observation generally is pertinent only at the time the observation is made, so observation should be supplemented with other procedures, such as inquiry, inspection, and reperformance.

For some controls, operating effectiveness may be evidenced by documentation; for other controls (such as the assignment of responsibility or segregation of duties), documentation may not be available or relevant. To test such controls, the auditor would likely rely on inquiry and observation.

Pass Key

Procedures to test design effectiveness include a mix of inquiry, observation, and inspection. Walk-throughs that include these procedures are sufficient to test design effectiveness.

Procedures the auditor performs to test operating effectiveness include a mix of inquiry of appropriate personnel, observation of the company's operations, inspection of relevant documentation, and reperformance of the control.

3.3.2 Extent of Tests of Controls

The more extensively a control is tested, the greater the evidence obtained from that test. The auditor should consider the following factors in determining the appropriate extent of testing controls:

- The frequency of the performance of the control during the period.
- The length of time during which the auditor wishes to rely on the control.
- The relevance and reliability of the evidence to be obtained.
- The extent to which other tests provide audit evidence about the same assertion.
- The extent to which the auditor wishes to rely on the operating effectiveness of the control to reduce substantive procedures.
- The expected deviation rate from the control.

- Additional considerations:
  - If a control is applied on a transaction basis throughout the period, the auditor should use sampling to test the control.
  - IT processing is inherently consistent, so it is possible to test only a few instances of the operation of an automated control. Once the auditor has determined that an automated control is functioning as expected, the auditor should determine that it continues to function effectively.

3.3.3 Timing of Tests of Controls

- **Testing at a Particular Time vs. Testing Throughout a Period**
  - When tests of controls are performed at one particular time, they provide evidence that controls operated effectively only at that time. Controls tested throughout the period provide evidence of operating effectiveness during that period.
  - The auditor may choose to test the operating effectiveness of a control only at one particular time, but then supplement this test with other tests that provide evidence for the remainder of the period. For example, tests relating to the modification and use of computer programs may provide evidence that a control operated consistently throughout the period.
  - Tests related to period-end controls, such as tests of controls over the counting of physical inventory at period end, may be performed at only one time, if the auditor only intends to rely on the control at that one time.
  - Controls that are tested only during an interim period should be supplemented by additional evidence for the remaining period.
- **Evidence Obtained in Prior Audits**

  Evidence obtained in a prior audit about the operating effectiveness of controls may be used in the current audit, as long as the auditor obtains evidence about whether changes in those controls have occurred.
  - If controls have changed since they were last tested, operating effectiveness must be retested in the current period.
  - Even if controls have not changed, operating effectiveness must be tested at least once every third year.
    - —Care should be taken to avoid the possibility that all controls are tested in the same period, with no controls tested in the intervening two periods.
  - The auditor may also choose, based on the circumstances, to retest operating effectiveness more often than once every third year.
    - —Generally, the higher the assessed risk, or the greater the intended reliance on controls, the more frequently the auditor will choose to test operating effectiveness.
    - —A weak control environment or a significant manual component to relevant controls may also result in more frequent testing, or in choosing not to rely on prior period evidence at all.
  - The auditor may not rely on audit evidence obtained in prior audits for controls that mitigate a significant risk.

3.4 Results of Tests of Controls

After performing tests of controls, the auditor may conclude that audit evidence indicates that controls are either:

1. Operating effectively and can be relied upon. The auditor then proceeds to substantive procedures based on the assessed risks of material misstatement.
2. Not operating effectively, in which case the auditor can:
   - test alternative controls; or
   - reassess control risk (i.e. reassess from low to high), thereby resulting in the need for more reliable and extensive substantive procedures.

4 Responding to RMM: Substantive Procedures

4.1 Overview

- Substantive procedures are used to detect material misstatements at the relevant assertion level.
- The nature, extent, and timing (**NET**) of substantive procedures should be responsive to the assessed risks of material misstatement, including the results of tests of controls and the planned level of detection risk.
- Regardless of the assessed risks of material misstatement, substantive procedures are required for each material transaction class, account balance, or disclosure.
- The fact that a substantive procedure does not identify any material misstatements does not necessarily imply that the related control is operating effectively.
- Substantive procedures should include:
  - Agreement of the financial statements to the underlying accounting records.
  - Examination of material journal entries or adjustments made while preparing the financial statements.
  - Evaluation of the overall presentation of the financial statements in accordance with the applicable financial reporting framework, including disclosures.

4.2 Nature of Substantive Procedures

4.2.1 Types of Substantive Procedures

There are two types of substantive procedures:

1. Tests of details applied to transaction classes, account balances, and disclosures.

   Tests of details consist of audit procedures used to gather evidence to support the account balances as reflected in the financial statements. Tests of details are performed on ending balances, the details of transactions, or a combination of the two.

2. Substantive analytical procedures.

   Analytical procedures are evaluations of financial information made by a study of plausible relationships among both financial and nonfinancial data, and they generally involve comparisons of recorded amounts to independent expectations developed by the auditor.

4.2.2 Selection of Substantive Procedures

The auditor may use only substantive analytical procedures, only tests of details, or a combination of both.

- Substantive analytical procedures are often used when there is a large volume of predictable transactions.
- Tests of details are generally more appropriate when obtaining evidence regarding the existence and valuation of account balances.
- If tests of controls indicate that controls are operating effectively, then substantive analytical procedures may be sufficient to reduce detection risk to an acceptably low level.
- If tests of controls indicate that controls are not operating effectively or tests of controls were not performed, then the auditor may perform tests of details only.

4.3 Extent of Substantive Procedures

- The more extensively a substantive procedure is performed, the greater the evidence obtained from the procedure. The extent of substantive procedures is affected by:
  - The overall risks of material misstatement: The greater these risks, the less detection risk that can be accepted, and the greater the extent of substantive procedures.
  - Control risk: If controls are operating effectively, the extent of substantive procedures may be reduced.
- In designing tests of details, the extent of substantive procedures generally refers to sample size (sampling will be discussed in more detail later).

4.4 Timing of Substantive Procedures

Substantive procedures can be performed during an interim period, at period end, or after period end.

- If substantive procedures are performed at an interim date, the auditor should perform further substantive procedures, or substantive procedures combined with tests of controls, to provide a reasonable basis for extending audit conclusions to period end.
- Performing substantive procedures at an interim date increases the risk that the auditor will not detect material misstatements in the financial statements. The longer the period between the interim date and period end, the greater the risk.
- In certain situations, such as those in which there is an identified fraud risk or high risk of material misstatement, the auditor may choose to perform substantive procedures at or near period end.
- If substantive analytical procedures are to be used to extend audit conclusions from interim testing to period end, the auditor should consider whether:
  - Period-end balances are reasonably predictable with respect to amount, relative significance, and composition.
  - The entity's accounting procedures are appropriate.
  - The entity's information system will provide sufficient information to allow investigation of unusual or unexpected transactions or balances.
- If misstatements are discovered at an interim date, the auditor should modify the related risk assessment and the procedures to be performed for the remaining period, or should consider repeating audit procedures at period end.
- Evidence obtained from substantive tests performed in a prior audit generally is not sufficient for the current period.

Question 1 **MCQ-05603**

Which of the following is always necessary in a financial statement audit?

I. Tests of the operating effectiveness of controls.
II. Analytical procedures.
III. Risk assessment procedures.

a. I, II, and III.
b. I and III.
c. I and II.
d. II and III.

Question 2 **MCQ-02888**

After performing risk assessment procedures, an auditor decided not to perform tests of controls. The auditor most likely decided that:

a. The available evidence obtained through tests of controls would not support an increased level of control risk.
b. A reduction in the assessed level of control risk is justified for certain financial statement assertions.
c. It would be inefficient to perform tests of controls that would result in a reduction in planned substantive tests.
d. The assessed level of inherent risk exceeded the assessed level of control risk.

MODULE

4 Specific Areas of Engagement Risk

AUD 3

1 Overview

This module expands on the auditor's responsibility and appropriate response for the following specific areas of engagement risk:

- An entity's compliance with laws and regulations, including possible legal acts
- Accounting estimates (including fair value estimates)
- Evaluating contingencies
- Related parties and related party transactions

2 Compliance With Laws and Regulations

The effects of laws and regulations on financial statements vary considerably. Some laws and regulations have a direct effect on the financial statements because they determine the amounts reported and the disclosures in the financial statements. Other laws and regulations do not have a direct effect on the financial statements.

2.1 Noncompliance

Noncompliance is an act of omission or commission by an entity, whether intentional or unintentional, which is contrary to prevailing laws and regulations. Such acts may be committed by, or in the name of, the entity or on its behalf by those charged with governance, management, or employees. Noncompliance does not include personal misconduct unrelated to the business activities of the entity.

Noncompliance with laws and regulations can result in fines, litigation, or other consequences to the entity that may have a material effect on the financial statements.

2.2 Responsibility for Compliance

2.2.1 Management's Responsibility

Management and those charged with governance are responsible for ensuring that the entity's operations are conducted in accordance with applicable laws and regulations, including laws and regulations that determine the reported amounts and disclosures in the financial statements.

2.2.2 Auditor's Responsibility

The auditor is responsible for obtaining reasonable assurance that the financial statements are free of material misstatement due to noncompliance with laws and regulations. However, the auditor is not responsible for preventing noncompliance and cannot be expected to detect noncompliance with all laws and regulations. The further removed that noncompliance is from the financial statements, the less likely that the auditor is to recognize the noncompliance.

2.2.3 Inherent Limitations

The potential effects of inherent limitations on an auditor's ability to detect material misstatements are greater for material misstatements due to laws and regulations because:

- Many laws and regulations relating to an entity's operations do not affect the financial statements and are not captured by information systems relevant to financial reporting.
- Noncompliance may be concealed by collusion, forgery, deliberate failure to record transactions, management override of controls, or intentional misrepresentations to the auditor.
- Whether an act constitutes noncompliance is a matter for legal determination.

2.3 Auditor Procedures Related to Noncompliance

2.3.1 The Auditor's Consideration of Noncompliance

When obtaining an understanding of the entity and its environment, the auditor should obtain an understanding of:

- the legal and regulatory framework applicable to the entity and the industry or sector in which it operates; and
- how the entity is complying with that framework.

The auditor should obtain sufficient appropriate audit evidence regarding material amounts and disclosures in the financial statements that are determined by the provisions of laws and regulations that have a *direct effect* on the financial statements.

For the provisions of laws and regulations that have an *indirect effect* on the financial statements but have a fundamental effect on the entity's operations, the auditor should perform the following procedures to identify instances of noncompliance that may have a material effect on the financial statements:

- Inquire of management and those charged with governance about whether the entity is in compliance with such laws and regulations.
- Inspect correspondence with relevant licensing and regulatory authorities.

The auditor should consider the evidence gathered in other audit procedures that may reveal instances of noncompliance or suspected noncompliance.

2.3.2 Procedures When Noncompliance Is Identified or Suspected

If the auditor suspects that noncompliance may exist, the auditor should discuss the matter with management at least one level above those suspected of noncompliance and, when appropriate, those charged with governance. If management or those charged with governance cannot provide sufficient information that shows the entity is in compliance with laws and regulations and the effects of the noncompliance may be material, the auditor may consider it necessary to consult with the entity's in-house or external legal counsel or with the auditor's own legal counsel.

The auditor may also withdraw from the engagement, if withdrawal is possible under applicable law or regulation.

Illustration 1 Compliance With Laws and Regulations

James is auditing Healthy Healthcare, which is an entity that provides health care for children. Healthy Healthcare must follow the Health Insurance Portability and Accountability Act (HIPAA), which includes requirements for protecting the privacy of patient information.

Maintaining the privacy of patient information (i.e., age and health background of patients) does not directly affect the recording and disclosure of the financial statements. However, unauthorized disclosure of this confidential information can result in a need to disclose a contingent liability because of the allegation of suspected noncompliance with HIPAA.

Therefore, James should inquire of management and those charged with governance about the entity's compliance with HIPAA and he may inspect any correspondence with the regulatory agency.

2.4 Reporting Noncompliance

2.4.1 Reporting to Those Charged With Governance

If those charged with governance are not involved in management of the entity, the auditor should communicate with those charged with governance matters involving noncompliance, other than matters that are clearly inconsequential. If the noncompliance appears to be intentional and material, the auditor should communicate the matter to those charged with governance as soon as practicable.

If management or those charged with governance are involved in noncompliance, the auditor should communicate the matter to the next higher level of authority at the entity. If there is no higher level of authority, the auditor may need to obtain legal advice.

2.4.2 Reporting to Regulatory and Enforcement Authorities

Ordinarily, the disclosure of noncompliance to parties other than management and those charged with governance is not part of the auditor's responsibility because of the auditor's professional duty of confidentiality. In the following circumstances, a duty to disclose outside the entity may exist:

- In response to inquiries from an auditor to a predecessor auditor.
- In response to a court order.
- In compliance with requirements for the audits of entities that receive federal financial assistance from a government agency.

2.4.3 Reporting Noncompliance in the Auditor's Report

- **Material Effect on the Financial Statements**

  If the noncompliance has a material effect on the financial statements and has not been adequately reflected in the financial statements, a qualified opinion or adverse opinion should be issued.

- **Insufficient Evidence**

  If the auditor is unable to obtain sufficient appropriate audit evidence about the noncompliance or suspected noncompliance, a qualified opinion or a disclaimer of opinion should be expressed.

- **Client Response**

  If the client refuses to accept the auditor's report as modified, the auditor should withdraw from the engagement and notify those charged with governance in writing.

3 Accounting Estimates

3.1 Nature of Accounting Estimates

Accounting estimates are imprecise and can be influenced by management judgment. These judgments may involve unintentional or intentional management bias. The susceptibility of an accounting estimate to management bias increases with the subjectivity involved in making it. The degree of estimation uncertainty affects, in turn, the risks of material misstatement of accounting estimates, including their susceptibility to unintentional or intentional management bias.

3.2 Identify and Assess Risk of Material Misstatement

The auditor should evaluate the degree of estimation uncertainty associated with an accounting estimate. Estimation uncertainty is the susceptibility of an accounting estimate to an inherent lack of precision in its measurement.

Examples of accounting estimates involving relatively low estimation uncertainty include:

- accounting estimates arising in entities that engage in business activities that are not complex.
- accounting estimates that are frequently made and updated because they relate to routine transactions.
- accounting estimates derived from data that is readily available, such as published interest rate data or exchange-traded prices of securities.
- fair value accounting estimates in which the method of measurement prescribed by the applicable financial reporting framework is simple and applied easily to the asset or liability requiring measurement at fair value.
- fair value accounting estimates in which the model used to measure the accounting estimate is well-known or generally accepted, provided that the assumptions or inputs to the model are observable.

Examples of accounting estimates involving relatively high estimation uncertainty include:

- accounting estimates relating to the outcome of litigation.
- fair value accounting estimates for derivative financial instruments not publicly traded.
- fair value accounting estimates for which a highly specialized, entity-developed model is used or for which there are assumptions or inputs that cannot be observed in the marketplace.

3.3 Audit Procedures

The auditor should determine whether accounting estimates with high estimation uncertainty give risk to significant risks. Significant risks require special audit consideration (i.e., more detailed review of documents).

The auditor should review the judgments and decisions made by management in the making of accounting estimates to identify whether indicators of possible management bias exist. Indicators of possible management bias do not, themselves, constitute misstatements for the purposes of drawing conclusions on the reasonableness of individual accounting estimates.

Examples of indicators of possible management bias with respect to accounting estimates include the following:

- Changes in an accounting estimate, or the method for making it, when management has made a subjective assessment that there has been a change in circumstances.

- The use of an entity's own assumptions for fair value accounting estimates when they are inconsistent with observable market assumptions.
- The selection or construction of significant assumptions that yield a point estimate favorable for management objectives.
- The selection of a point estimate that may indicate a pattern of optimism or pessimism.

3.4 Impact of Estimates on Risk of Material Misstatement

3.4.1 Low Estimation Uncertainty

Estimates with low estimation uncertainty typically result in a lower assessed risk of material misstatement. A lower assessed risk of material misstatement results in less persuasive evidenced needed.

3.4.2 High Estimation Uncertainty and Indicators of Management Bias

Accounting estimates that have a high estimation uncertainty and have an indicator of management bias found may lead to an increase in the assessed risk of material misstatement. An increase in risk of material misstatement will result in an increase in persuasive evidence needed.

4 Evaluating Contingencies

In performing an audit in accordance with generally accepted auditing standards, the independent auditor must obtain appropriate evidence regarding contingent liabilities. Contingent liabilities may arise from many sources, including:

- Pending and threatened litigation
- Actual or possible claims and assessments
- Guarantees of the indebtedness of others
- Product warranties
- Income tax disputes

Under GAAP, contingent liabilities that are probable and can be reasonably estimated must be accrued and disclosed.

4.1 Identifying Contingencies

The auditor should ask management about contingent liabilities, including pending litigation or possible future litigation and about controls adopted to identify, evaluate, and account for such items. In conjunction with these inquiries, the auditor should perform the following procedures:

- Review the minutes of meetings of stockholders, board of directors, and other executive committees.
- Review correspondence and invoices from lawyers.
- Review contracts, loan agreements, loan guarantees, leases, and correspondence from taxing authorities.
- Review bank confirmations for hidden bank loans, discounted drafts, guarantee of notes, etc.
- Discuss long-term purchase commitments with the purchasing agent.
- Review the status of long-term leases.

- Discuss sales contracts with the sales manager.
- Review the interim financial statements after year-end.
- Obtain a client representation letter.
- Send an inquiry letter to the client's attorneys.

4.2 Specific Inquiry Into Litigation, Claims, and Assessments

For actual or potential litigation, claims, and assessments, the auditor should obtain audit evidence relevant to:

- the period in which the underlying cause for legal action occurred;
- the degree of probability of an unfavorable outcome; and
- the amount or range of potential loss.

Note: It is management's responsibility to identify and account for contingent liabilities, including litigation, claims, and assessments, through the policies adopted by management for such purposes. The management representation letter should indicate that management has disclosed to the independent auditor all such relevant information.

5 Related Party Transactions

5.1 Accounting for Related Party Transactions

Except for very routine transactions, it is virtually impossible to determine whether a transaction would have taken place in exactly the same manner if the parties weren't related. Therefore, a related party transaction is not considered to be an arm's-length transaction. For this reason, the substance of a related party transaction may be very different from its form, and GAAP requires that such transactions be disclosed.

5.2 Auditor's Responsibility

When auditors are performing an audit of financial statements, they are responsible for identifying any related party transactions encountered during the course of the audit and for determining whether the transactions have been properly accounted for and disclosed in the financial statements. An understanding of related party transactions and relationships is also relevant to the auditor's evaluation of fraud risk because fraud is more easily committed through related parties. *Related parties may include the reporting entity's affiliates, principal owners, management, and members of their immediate families.*

5.2.1 Audit Objectives

The auditor should obtain an understanding of related party relationships and transactions sufficient to:

- Recognize fraud risk factors, if any, arising from related party relationships and transactions that are relevant to the assessment of the risk of material misstatement due to fraud.
- Conclude whether the financial statements achieve fair presentation, insofar as they are affected by related party relationships.
- Obtain sufficient appropriate audit evidence about whether related party transactions and relationships have been appropriately identified, accounted for, and disclosed.

5.2.2 Audit Procedures

Application of specific procedures regarding material transactions with related parties should include:

- Obtaining an understanding and evaluating the company's process (including controls) for identifying related parties, authorizing and approving transactions with related parties, and accounting for and disclosing relationships and transactions. The auditor should obtain a conflict-of-interest statement from the client.
- Requesting that management provide the names of all related parties, including changes from the prior period, background information concerning related parties (e.g., physical location, industry), the nature of the relationships between the entity and related parties, whether the entity entered into, modified, or terminated any transactions with related parties, and the types and purposes of any related party transactions.
- Inquiring about any unauthorized or unapproved related party transactions and any related party transactions for which exceptions were granted and the reasons for granting those exceptions.
- Inquiring of those charged with governance their understanding of any significant relationships and transactions with related parties and whether they have any concerns regarding relationships or transactions with related parties.
- Reviewing the reporting entity's filings with the SEC and other regulatory agencies concerning the names of officers and directors who occupy management or directorship positions in other businesses.
- Reviewing material transactions (especially investment transactions) for related party evidence, including bank and legal confirmations, minutes, and other appropriate records and documents.
- Reviewing prior years' audit documentation or inquiring of the predecessor auditor.

5.2.3 Risk-Based Approach

The auditor should identify and assess the risks of material misstatement associated with related party transactions and determine whether any of those risks are significant risks. If the auditor identifies any fraud risk factors in connection with related parties, the auditor should consider this information when assessing the risks of material misstatement due to fraud. The auditor should design and perform further audit procedures to obtain sufficient appropriate audit evidence about the assessed risk of material misstatement associated with related party transactions.

5.2.4 Impact on the Auditor's Report

If management indicates in the financial statements that the transaction was consummated on arm's-length terms and the auditor believes that this statement is unsubstantiated, the auditor should express a qualified or adverse opinion.

5.2.5 Documentation

The auditor should include the names of all identified related parties and the nature of the related party relationships in the audit documentation.

5.3 Identifying and Examining Related Party Transactions

5.3.1 Identifying Related Party Transactions

The auditor should discuss the entity's relationships and transactions with related parties with the engagement team and provide the names of known related parties to the audit staff. The auditor should remain alert for the following items, which may be indicative of a related party transaction:

- Compensating balance arrangements (which may be maintained by or for related parties)
- Loan guarantees
- Unusual, nonrecurring transactions near year-end
- Transactions based on terms that differ significantly from market terms
- Nonmonetary exchanges

5.3.2 Identified Significant Related Party Transactions

When the auditor identifies significant related party transactions outside of the normal course of the entity's business, the auditor should:

- Inspect the underlying contracts or agreements, if any, and evaluate whether:
  - The business rationale of the transactions suggests that they may have been entered into to engage in fraud.
  - The terms of the transactions are consistent with management's explanations.
  - The transactions have been appropriately accounted for and disclosed.
- Obtain audit evidence that the transactions have been appropriately authorized and approved.

Illustration 2 Related Party Transaction

Doug owns 60 percent of ABC Company. ABC Company purchased a building from Doug for $15 million, although its fair market value is $40 million.

The auditor should verify that this related party transaction is recorded at $15 million and disclosed in the financial statement notes.

5.3.3 Identification of Previously Unidentified or Undisclosed Related Parties or Significant Related Party Transactions

If the auditor identifies related parties or significant related party transactions that management has not previously identified or disclosed to the auditor, the auditor should:

1. Communicate the information to the other members of the engagement team.
2. Request management to identify all transactions with the newly identified related parties.
3. Inquire why the entity's controls failed to enable the identification and disclosure of the related party relationships or transactions.
4. Perform appropriate substantive procedures.
5. Reconsider the risk that other related parties or related party transactions may not have been identified or disclosed.
6. Evaluate the audit implications if management's nondisclosure appears intentional.

PCAOB Standards: Guidance for Issuers

PCAOB guidance provides additional procedures that should be performed for each related party transaction that is either required to be disclosed in the financial statements or determined to be a significant risk:

- Determine whether any exceptions to the company's established policies or procedures were granted.
- Evaluate the financial capability of the related parties with respect to significant uncollected balances, loan commitments, supply arrangements, guarantees, and other obligations, if any.
- Perform procedures on intercompany account balances as of concurrent dates, even if fiscal years of the respective companies differ.

Question 1 **MCQ-02536**

Which of the following auditing procedures most likely would assist an auditor in identifying related party transactions?

a. Inspecting correspondence with lawyers for evidence of unreported contingent liabilities.

b. Vouching accounting records for recurring transactions recorded just after the balance sheet date.

c. Reviewing confirmations of loans receivable and payable for indications of guarantees.

d. Performing analytical procedures for indications of possible financial difficulties.

NOTES

MODULE

5 Sufficient Appropriate Evidence

AUD 3

1 Audit Evidence Overview

Audit evidence is all the information the auditor uses to arrive at the conclusions on which the audit opinion is based. It includes information in written or electronic form as well as observable assets or activities, and it must be obtained to support auditor conclusions. The use of sampling to collect audit evidence will be discussed in a later module. Audit evidence is gathered throughout the audit when performing:

- Risk assessment procedures
- Tests of controls
- Substantive procedures
- Other audit procedures

Audit evidence may also come from other sources, such as previous audits or a firm's quality control procedures for client acceptance and continuance.

2 Types of Audit Evidence

Audit evidence consists of underlying accounting records and corroborating evidence. The auditor should have access to all pertinent accounting data and corroborating audit evidence.

2.1 Accounting Records

Accounting records consist of records of initial entries and any supporting records. For example, accounting records include checks, records of electronic fund transfers, invoices, contracts, ledgers, journal entries, and worksheets. The auditor tests the accounting records through analytical procedures and substantive procedures, such as retracing procedural steps, recalculation, and reconciliation. Note that accounting records alone do not provide sufficient support for the audit opinion. However, internal consistency among the accounting records provides some evidence that the financial statements are presented fairly.

2.2 Corroborating Evidence

Corroborating evidence includes minutes of meetings, confirmations, industry analysts' reports, data about competitors, and information obtained through observation, inquiry, and inspection. Corroborating evidence provides additional support and gives validity to the recorded accounting data.

2.3 Evidence in Electronic Form

In certain entities, some of the accounting records or corroborating evidence may be available only in electronic form. Source documents may be replaced by electronic messages, or business may be transacted electronically. Although electronic evidence may be initially available, it may not be retrievable indefinitely. The auditor should therefore consider the time during which information exists or is available in determining the nature, extent, and timing of auditing procedures.

3 Obtaining Sufficient Appropriate Audit Evidence

3.1 Reasonable Basis for an Opinion

The audit evidence must persuade the auditor that the ending balances in the financial statements are fairly presented. The audit provides *reasonable assurance* regarding the fairness of the financial statements. The auditor is not a guarantor, and, in most cases, cost-benefit considerations prohibit an examination of 100 percent of the accounting data. Therefore, it is generally not practical or possible to obtain assurance beyond all doubt, and the auditor usually must rely on evidence that is *persuasive*, rather than *conclusive*. Persuasiveness is a subjective concept and relates uniquely to each audit.

Note that although the cost-benefit relationship may be a valid reason for performing only certain procedures, cost alone or difficulty in obtaining evidence is *not* a valid basis for omitting a procedure for which there is no appropriate alternative. Thus, the auditor must exercise professional judgment in determining the procedures to be performed and the sufficiency and appropriateness of the evidence gathered.

3.2 Sufficiency of Audit Evidence

Sufficiency refers to the quantity of audit evidence. The auditor must use professional judgment in determining the amount and kinds of evidence sufficient to support an opinion. As mentioned previously, judgments about materiality and audit risk underlie this determination. The amount of evidence gathered directly affects the level of detection risk, which is the risk that the auditor's evidence-gathering procedures will not be sufficient to support the financial statement assertions.

The auditor's decision regarding the sufficiency of evidence is influenced by:

- **The Risk of Material Misstatement:** Greater risk implies more evidence will be required.
- **The Quality of Audit Evidence:** Less audit evidence may be required when that evidence is of higher quality.

Note that even if it is conclusive, evidence regarding a small portion of a balance or a single transaction is generally insufficient to support the entire balance. For instance, overwhelming evidence of the existence of a $500 account receivable is not sufficient to substantiate a total accounts receivable balance of $1,000,000.

3.3 Appropriateness of Audit Evidence

Appropriate audit evidence must be reliable and relevant. The appropriateness of evidence depends on it being pertinent, objective, timely, and corroborated by other evidence.

3.3.1 Reliability of Evidence

Reliability of audit evidence is dependent on the circumstances under which it is gathered. Reliability of evidence is also influenced by its source and nature.

- **Auditor's Direct Personal Knowledge**

  Any evidence obtained directly by the auditor (i.e., through observation, physical examination, inspection, or recalculation) provides more persuasive evidence than evidence obtained indirectly.

- **External Evidence**

  External evidence obtained from independent sources outside the enterprise provides greater assurance of reliability than internally generated evidence.

  The two types of external evidence are:

  1. evidence sent directly to an independent auditor; and
  2. evidence received and held by the client.

  Evidence sent directly to the auditor (e.g., a bank confirmation) is more valid than evidence received and held by the client.

- **Importance of Effective Controls**

  Internal evidence generated within the enterprise is not as reliable as external evidence, but strong, effective internal controls improve reliability. Internal evidence includes purchase orders, sales orders, general ledgers, and management reports.

- **Documentary Evidence**

  Audit evidence in documentary form is more reliable than oral evidence, and original documentation is more reliable than photocopies, faxes, or documents that have been converted to electronic form. Oral evidence consists of statements made by clients concerning the procedures involved in a given transaction, often resulting in the explanation of an account balance. Oral evidence is the least reliable form of evidence.

- **Consistency of Evidence**

  When audit evidence obtained from different sources is consistent, a greater degree of assurance is provided.

- **Information Produced by the Client**

  If the auditor intends to use information produced by the client, the auditor should determine whether the information is sufficiently reliable for the auditor's purposes by:

  - Obtaining evidence about the accuracy and completeness of the information.
  - Evaluating whether the information is sufficiently precise and detailed for the auditor's purposes.

Pass Key

Memorize the following hierarchy of audit evidence (from most reliable to least reliable):

1. Auditor's direct personal knowledge
2. External evidence
3. Internal evidence
4. Oral evidence

3.3.2 Relevance of Evidence

Evidence must relate to the financial statement assertion(s) under consideration. For example, accounts receivable confirmations are relevant to the existence of receivables, not to their valuation, because a customer can confirm that a receivable exists, but this does not necessarily imply that the customer has the intent or the ability to pay.

PCAOB Standards: Guidance for Issuers

PCAOB standards state that the relevance of audit evidence depends on:

- the design of the audit procedure, in particular whether it is designed to test the assertion directly and whether it is designed to test for understatement or overstatement; and
- the timing of the audit procedure.

4 Evaluating the Sufficiency and Appropriateness of Audit Evidence

4.1 Results of Further Audit Procedures

The results of further audit procedures may lead the auditor to:

- Reassess the risks of material misstatement.
- Identify control deficiencies as a result of tests of controls or substantive procedures. Control deficiencies will be discussed further in A4.
- Identify misstatements as a result of substantive procedures. The evaluation of misstatements will be discussed further in A4.

4.2 Revising the Assessed Risks of Material Misstatement

The results of further audit procedures should be used to determine whether the assessed risks of material misstatement at the relevant assertion level is still appropriate. Audit evidence obtained may cause the auditor to modify the initial risk assessment. When there is a change in the assessed level of risk, the auditor should modify planned audit procedures accordingly.

- The results of tests of controls may indicate that controls are not functioning effectively, which will result in a higher assessment of the risks of material misstatement and more extensive and reliable substantive procedures.
- Material misstatements discovered while performing substantive procedures that were not detected by the entity's controls are considered a significant deficiency or material weakness that will cause the auditor to change the judgment regarding the effectiveness of internal control and revise the assessed risks of material misstatement.
- If fraud is discovered, the auditor should not assume that an identified instance of fraud or error is an isolated occurrence, but instead should consider whether such an instance affects the assessed risks of material misstatement.
- All relevant audit evidence should be considered, regardless of whether it is consistent with or contradicts relevant assertions in the financial statements.

4.3 Sufficiency and Appropriateness of Evidence

The auditor uses judgment to evaluate the sufficiency and appropriateness of audit evidence, but should consider:

- The achievement of audit objectives.
- The auditor's risk assessment.
- The significance of uncorrected misstatements and the likelihood of their having a material effect on the financial statements, individually or in aggregate, considering the possibility of further undetected misstatements.
- The effectiveness of management's responses and controls.
- Experience gained during previous audits.
- The results of audit procedures performed in the financial statement audit and in the audit of internal control over financial reporting (if the audit is an integrated audit).
- The appropriateness of audit evidence obtained.
- Understanding of the entity and its environment.

4.3.1 Contradictory and Supporting Information

Auditors should take into account all relevant audit evidence, regardless of whether the evidence corroborates or contradicts the assertions in the financial statements, when determining whether sufficient and appropriate audit evidence has been obtained. Auditors should be attentive when weighing audit evidence and should reduce instances in which they fail to consider contradictory evidence. Contradictory evidence should be documented. Often the discovery of contradictory evidence results in the need for additional procedures and obtaining more persuasive evidence.

4.4 Documentation Requirements

The auditor should document:

- The overall response addressing assessed risk at the financial statement level.
- The nature, extent, and timing of further audit procedures.
- The linkage of those audit procedures with assessed risks at the relevant assertion level.
- The results of audit procedures.
- The conclusions reached regarding the use of prior period audit evidence in evaluating the current operating effectiveness of controls.

Question 1	**MCQ-02342**

Which of the following types of audit evidence is the most persuasive?

- **a.** Prenumbered client purchase order forms.
- **b.** Client work sheets supporting cost allocations.
- **c.** Bank statements obtained from the client.
- **d.** Client representation letter.

NOTES

MODULE

6 Procedures to Obtain Evidence

AUD 3

1 Standard Auditing Procedures

In performing an audit, the auditor gathers evidence using a variety of procedures to accomplish specific objectives. Sampling, which will be covered in a later module, is an aspect of the performance of most audit procedures. The specifics for the sampling plan (objective, population, sample size, method of selection) are included in the audit plan for each procedure and are documented along with the results and evaluation of the results.

The following standard procedures are used in audits as risk assessment procedures, tests of controls, or substantive tests.

Pass Key

C the **FIVE CARROT WARS** identifies the procedures used in an audit to be victorious!

- **Confirmation**

  Confirmation is a specific type of inquiry that involves obtaining representations from independent external third parties about account balances and transactions or events. Examples include bank confirmations of the amount on deposit or of a loan outstanding, or a confirmation from a customer regarding the existence of a receivable balance at a certain date.

- **Footing, Cross-Footing, and Recalculation**

  An auditor may verify the mathematical accuracy of statements and schedules by adding down (footing), adding across (cross-footing), or recalculating amounts. For example, the auditor may substantiate the valuation of financial accounts and the allocation of items such as depreciation, amortization, and accruals by recalculating those items.

- **Inquiry**

  Inquiry consists of requesting information from knowledgeable parties both internally (e.g., managers and supervisors) and externally (e.g., attorneys and bankers). Examples include inquiries about pending litigation or pledged or obsolete inventories.

  Inquiry is used extensively throughout most audits. However, inquiry of company personnel alone is generally considered insufficient and therefore should be used in conjunction with other audit procedures. In using inquiry, the auditor should:

  - Consider the specific characteristics (knowledge, objectivity, qualifications, etc.) of the person to whom the inquiry is directed.
  - Ask appropriate questions.
  - Evaluate the response and take appropriate action (e.g., following up with additional inquiry, modifying planned audit procedures, etc.)

- **Vouching**

  Vouching is directional testing in which the auditor examines support for what has been recorded in the records and statements, going from the financial statements back to supporting documents. The objective of vouching is to gather evidence regarding possible overstatement errors (the existence or occurrence assertions).

- **Examination / Inspection**

  The auditor may inspect or examine records, documents, or tangible assets. Records or documents may be internal or external, and may be in paper or electronic form.

  Inspection or examination generally provides evidence about the existence assertion, rather than about ownership, rights, obligations, or valuation. Examination may also provide evidence of the terms of contracts, loans, and commitments. The procedure of inspecting documents is often referred to as examination of evidence, and includes the activities of scanning, scrutinizing, and reading. For example, the auditor may *scan* or *scrutinize* entries in general ledger accounts for a period, looking for evidence of unusual amounts or unusual sources of input, which, if found, would be investigated further. The auditors should read the minutes of the board of directors' meetings, shareholder meetings, and management committee meetings.

- **Cutoff Review**

  The auditor should perform a cutoff review of year-end transactions, especially inventory, cash, purchases, sales, and accruals.

- **Analytical Procedures**

  Analytical procedures consist of evaluations of financial information made by a study of meaningful relationships among data, to help highlight unusual fluctuations that could be the result of errors or fraudulent omissions or overstatements.

  Analytical procedures also include comparisons within the current year's financial statements for internal consistency. For example, net income on the income statement should agree with the increase in retained earnings on the statement of retained earnings.

  Scanning also may be considered an analytical procedure, as the auditor uses professional judgment to search for large, significant, or unusual items in the accounting records.

- **Reperformance**

  Reperformance occurs when an auditor independently performs procedures or controls that were originally performed as part of an entity's internal control.

- **Reconciliation**

  Reconciliation substantiates the existence and valuation of accounts. It involves comparing financial amounts from two independent sources for agreement, such as reconciling the physical inventory count with the perpetual inventory records. Other examples include reconciling the cash balance per the books with the balance per bank, and reconciling lead schedules to general ledger amounts.

- **Observation**

  Observation occurs when an auditor looks at a process or procedure performed by others. For example, at the beginning of an audit, the auditor may tour the client's facilities to gain an understanding of the client's business, or the auditor may observe the client's employees taking a physical inventory to obtain firsthand knowledge regarding ending inventory.

  Note that although observation provides the auditor with direct personal knowledge, the evidence provided applies only to the point in time during which the observation occurred. The auditor should also be aware that a process or procedure may be performed differently when the client is aware that the auditor is observing.

- **Tracing**

  As with vouching, tracing is directional testing. However, tracing is looking for coverage in the opposite direction from vouching. Tracing starts with the source documents and traces *forward* to provide assurance that the event is being given proper recognition in the books and records. The objective of tracing is to gather evidence regarding possible understatement errors (the completeness assertion).

- **Walk-through**

  A walk-through includes questioning an entity's personnel about their understanding of what is required by the entity's prescribed procedures and controls at the points at which important processing procedures occur. Walk-through procedures may include a combination of inquiry, observation, inspection of relevant documentation, recalculation, and control reperformance.

- **Auditing Related Accounts Simultaneously**

  Certain accounts can be audited simultaneously, such as:

  - Long-term liabilities and interest expense
  - Capital additions to plant and equipment, and repairs and maintenance expense
  - Investments and dividend and interest income

- **Representation Letter**

  At the conclusion of fieldwork, the independent auditor must obtain a management representation letter from the client.

- **Subsequent Events Review**

  The auditor is required to perform certain procedures for the period after the balance sheet date through the date of the auditor's report. Evidence not available at the close of the period often becomes available before the auditors complete their fieldwork and write their report. For example, the bankruptcy of the auditor's client's customer shortly after the balance sheet date indicates that the financial strength of the customer had probably deteriorated before year-end.

  The settlement of a pending lawsuit constitutes evidence that a real (rather than a contingent) liability may have existed at year-end. Decreases in long-term debt occurring after year-end may indicate that such debt should be reported as a current liability on the balance sheet. Evidence becoming available after the balance sheet date should be used in making judgments about the valuation of assets and liabilities on the balance sheet date.

2 Types of Audit Procedures

2.1 Substantive Procedures

Substantive procedures are designed to detect material misstatements at the assertion level. They consist of:

1. tests of details applied to transactions, balances, and disclosures; and
2. substantive analytical procedures.

2.1.1 Tests of Details

Tests of details consist of audit procedures used to gather evidence to support the account balances as reflected in the financial statements. Tests of details are performed on ending balances, the details of transactions, or a combination of the two.

- If an account has a high turnover rate with many transactions occurring during the year, the auditor generally will concentrate testing on the ending balance. When this approach is used, the auditor must be satisfied that internal control is strong.
- An alternative approach is to test the details of transactions. This approach is employed when the account being substantiated has relatively few transactions occurring during the year (e.g., an account for land or treasury stock).
- One approach need not be used exclusively, and a combination of the two might be appropriate. For example, during an audit of the sales revenue account, the auditor uses procedures to substantiate the ending balance while also performing extensive procedures on samples of transactions and related accounts (e.g., cash receipts and accounts receivable).

The auditor may test the details supporting transactions, balances, and disclosures through inspection, observation, inquiry, confirmation, recalculation, reperformance, etc.

2.1.2 Analytical Procedures

Analytical procedures are evaluations of financial information made by a study of plausible relationships among both financial and nonfinancial data, and they generally involve comparisons of recorded amounts to independent expectations developed by the auditor. As discussed previously, the auditor must use analytical procedures for planning and overall review in all audits, and also may decide to use analytical procedures as substantive tests.

The following chart summarizes the use of analytical procedures:

Phase	Requirement	Purpose
Planning	Required	To assist the auditor in understanding the entity and its environment. Used during risk assessment to alert the auditor to problem areas requiring attention. This serves a vital planning function.
Substantive procedures	Not required	As a substantive test to obtain audit evidence about specific management assertions related to account balances or transactions. The evidence is circumstantial and generally additional corroborating evidence (such as documentation) must be obtained.
Final review	Required	To assist the auditor in the final review of the overall reasonableness of account balances.

2.2 Substantive Analytical Procedures

In certain situations, analytical procedures are a more effective and efficient means of gathering evidence than tests of details, and in those cases, analytical procedures may be used as substantive tests.

2.2.1 Designing and Performing Substantive Analytical Procedures

When designing and performing analytical procedures as substantive procedures, the auditor should do the following:

1. Determine the analytical procedures that are suitable for testing the assertion(s), taking into account the assessed risks of material misstatement and tests of details.

   If using audit data analytics (ADAs), the auditor should select an ADA procedure that best fits the intended purpose and objectives of the procedure as well as determine the techniques, tools, graphics, and tables that may be used.

2. Evaluate the reliability of the data from which the auditor's expectation is to be developed. The following factors are relevant when determining whether the data is reliable:
   - The source and comparability of the information
   - The nature and relevance of the information
   - Controls over the preparation of the information

3. Develop an expectation of recorded amounts or ratios and evaluate whether the expectation is sufficiently precise to identify material misstatement. Expectations may be developed based on:
   - financial information for comparable prior periods;
   - anticipated results from budgets and forecasts;
   - relationships among data within the current period;
   - industry norms; and
   - relationships of financial data with nonfinancial information.

   Ratios are discussed in more detail in the next module.

4. Perform the analytical procedures and compare the results of the analytical procedures with the expectations.
5. Investigate any significant differences by:
   - inquiring of management and obtaining appropriate evidence relevant to management's responses; and
   - performing other audit procedures as necessary.

2.2.2 Efficiency and Effectiveness of Analytical Procedures

The efficiency and effectiveness of analytical procedures in detecting potential misstatements depends, among other things, on the following four factors.

1. **Nature of the Assertion Being Tested**

   Analytical procedures are most effective and efficient for assertions in which potential misstatements are not apparent from an examination of the detailed evidence or when such detail is unavailable.

2. **Plausibility and Predictability of the Data Relationship**

   In order to use analytical procedures as a substantive test, the auditor must have a clear understanding of the relationships among data. It is possible that data may appear to be related when in fact they are not, and failure to properly understand such situations may lead to erroneous conclusions.

   In order to provide an appropriate level of assurance, analytical procedures should be based on predictable relationships. More predictable relationships are provided by data generated in a stable, rather than dynamic, environment; involve income statements, rather than just balance sheet accounts; and involve transactions that are less subject to management discretion.

3. **Availability and Reliability of Data Used to Develop the Expectation**

   Data used by the auditor to develop expectations should be both readily available and reliable. Reliability of data is enhanced if it is obtained from external rather than internal sources, obtained from independent internal sources (i.e., unrelated to those who are responsible for the amount being audited), generated under effective internal controls, audited previously, and obtained from a variety of sources.

4. **Precision of the Expectation**

   More precise expectations are more effective in detecting misstatements. An expectation is more precise when it is developed at a sufficiently detailed level, and when there is effective identification and consideration of factors that significantly influence the relationship.

5. Methods Used to Develop the Auditor's Expectation

Below are some examples of methods that the auditor may use to develop the auditor's expectation:

Method	Description	Best Used When:	Level of Assurance
Trend analysis	Compare financial statement item or account balance for the current period with prior periods.	Amount/relationship is fairly predictable and operations are stable.	Trend analysis is often used with other audit procedures, as trend analysis results in a relatively imprecise auditor's expectation that provides only a low level of assurance.
Ratio analysis	Ratios are calculated based on known relationships among accounts or nonfinancial information and compared with the same ratio for prior periods or with comparable entities.	Analyzing data at a disaggregated level (e.g., by segment, product, location).	Ratio analysis is often used with other audit procedures, as ratio analysis results in a relatively imprecise auditor's expectation that provides only a low level of assurance.
Nonstatistical predictive modeling	Uses predictive model to estimate financial statement amount.	Creating expectation based on simple variables.	May provide a very high level of precision and may be used as the principal substantive procedure.
Regression analysis	Advanced statistical technique that often uses data from prior period(s) to develop a model to predict future periods.	Creating expectation based on several independent variables.	May provide a very high level of precision and may be used as the principal substantive procedure.

Regression analysis has several advantages over the other methods discussed in this chart because it:

- Provides an explicit, mathematically objective, and precise method for forming an expectation.
- Allows inclusion of a large number of independent variables.
- Provides direct and quantitative measures of the precision of the expectation.

2.2.3 Documentation Requirements

When an analytical procedure is used as the principal substantive test of a significant financial statement assertion, the auditor is required to document:

- The auditor's expectation.
- Factors considered in the development of the expectation.
- The results of the comparison of the expectation to recorded amounts.
- Additional audit procedures performed in response to significant unexplained differences.
- The results of such additional procedures.

2.2.4 Limitations of Analytical Procedures

Analytical review comparisons are based on expected plausible relationships among data. Differences do not necessarily indicate errors or fraud, but simply indicate the need for further investigation. Changes in an account, changes in accounting principle, and inherent differences between industry norms and the client all contribute to fluctuations in expected amounts.

2.2.5 Analytical Procedures Used as an Overall Review

Analytical procedures are *required* during the overall review stage of an audit. Generally, a manager or partner who has a comprehensive knowledge of the client's business and industry reads the financial statements and disclosures and performs this review.

The purpose of applying analytical procedures during the overall review stage of an audit is to evaluate the overall financial statement presentation, to assess the conclusions reached, and to assist in forming an opinion on whether the financial statements as a whole are free of material misstatement. The auditor should determine whether adequate evidence has been gathered in response to unusual or unexpected balances identified during the audit. The auditor may also discover additional unusual or unexpected balances, transactions, events, or relationships, including fraud risks, during this overall review, and should consider whether additional audit procedures are warranted.

The nature and extent of the analytical procedures performed during the overall review may be similar to the analytical procedures performed as risk assessment procedures, including the use of audit data analytics. In addition, the auditor may consider updating ratios and data analytics used as risk assessment procedures to include the most recent financial statement numbers, especially if management has made significant adjustments to the financial statements. The auditor should perform analytical procedures relating to revenue through the end of the reporting period.

2.3 Directional Testing: Existence and Completeness

Directional testing refers to testing either forward or backward.

1. Tracing forward from source documents to journal entries provides evidence of *completeness*.
2. Vouching backward from journal entries to source documents provides evidence of *existence*.

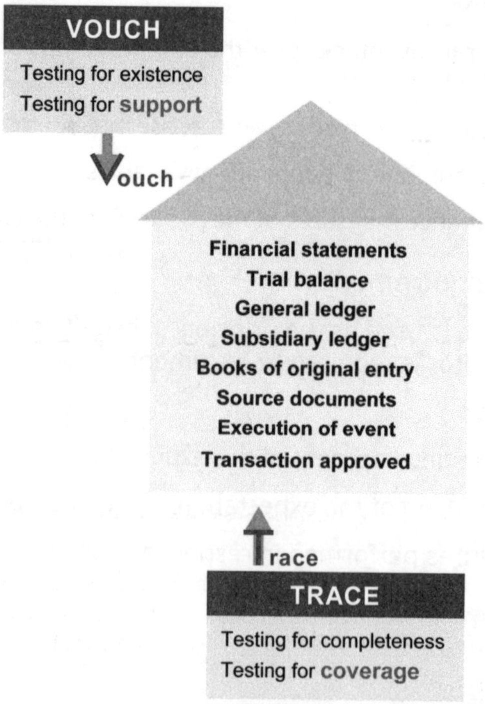

Pass Key

Many exam questions require the candidate to determine which assertion is being tested by a specific audit procedure. Remember that if a test starts with items in the financial statements, the proper assertion is most likely to be existence—the auditor searches for evidence indicating that the item truly exists and has not been created by management. If a test starts with source documents, however, it is most likely related to the completeness assertion, because the goal probably is to make sure all transactions (as identified by the source documents) have been included in the financial statements.

Accounting Records

Balance Sheet [Excerpt]
As of December 31, Year 2

Assets	
Cash	$60
Accounts receivable, less allowance of $15	80
Inventory	30

The auditor starts with the accounts receivable (a/r) balance from the balance sheet.

Trial Balance [Excerpt]
December 31, Year 2

	Debit	Credit
Cash	$60	
Accounts receivable	95 ✓	
Allowance for doubtful accounts		15

The auditor verifies that the total from the balance sheet agrees to the trial balance (net a/r of $80 = $95 gross a/r − $15 allowance).

General Ledger
December 31, Year 2

Date	Explanation	Debit	Credit	Balance
01/01/X2	Beg. Balance	$10		$ 10
05/10/X2	See JE No. 1	90		100
08/10/X2	See JE No. 2	40		140
	See JE No. 3		$55	85
	See JE No. 4	10		95 ✓

The auditor verifies that the total from the trial balance agrees with the ending general ledger (g/l) balance.

Subsidiary Ledger-Accounts Receivable
As of December 31, Year 2

Evan Grocery	$20
Jacob Grocery	40
Noah's Fruit Store	35
Total	$95 ✓

The auditor agrees the g/l balance to the subsidiary ledger and then examines the source documents (sales order, shipping documentation and sales invoice) for a sample of customers from the subsidiary ledger.

Existence Testing

Note: If the existence assertion is being tested, then the direction of testing is backward (downward). On the exam, the existence assertion does not always have to be from the financial statements all the way to the source documents. For example, it may be from the financial statements to the general ledger.

2.4 External Confirmation

External confirmation is a form of audit evidence obtained as a direct written response to the auditor from a third party, either in paper form or by electronic or other medium. *An oral response to a confirmation request does not meet the definition of an external confirmation.* Confirmations usually involve obtaining representations about account balances and transactions or events. Confirmations also can be used to confirm the terms of agreements, contracts, or transactions between an entity and other parties, or to confirm the absence of certain conditions, such as side agreements.

Pass Key

The auditor's direct access to information held by a third party meets the definition of an external confirmation if the auditor is provided by the third party with electronic access codes or information necessary to access a secure website where data is held that addresses the subject matter of the confirmation. When access is provided to the auditor by management, the evidence obtained by the auditor does not meet the definition of an external confirmation.

2.4.1 Positive Confirmation vs. Negative Confirmation

A positive confirmation is a request that the confirming party respond directly to the auditor by providing the requested information or by stating that the party agrees or disagrees with the information in the request. A negative confirmation is a request that the confirming party respond directly to the auditor only if the confirming party disagrees with the information in the request.

2.4.2 External Confirmation Procedures

The auditor should maintain control over external confirmation requests, including:

- Determining the information to be confirmed or requested.
- Selecting the appropriate confirming party or parties.
- Designing the confirmation requests. Factors to be considered when designing confirmation requests include:
  - The assertion(s) being addressed
  - Identified risks of material misstatement, including fraud
  - The layout and presentation of the request (e.g. positive or negative)
  - Prior experience on the audit
  - The method of communication (e.g., paper or electronic)
  - Management's authorization or encouragement to the confirming parties to respond to the auditor
  - The ability of the confirming party to provide the requested information
- Sending the requests, including follow-up requests when necessary, to the confirming party or parties.

2.4.3 Management's Refusal to Allow External Confirmation Procedures

If management refuses to allow the auditor to perform external confirmation procedures, the auditor should evaluate the validity and reasonableness of management's refusal; evaluate the effect of the refusal on the risks of material misstatement, including the risk of fraud, and on the nature, extent, and timing of other audit procedures; and perform alternative procedures. If the auditor determines that management's refusal is unreasonable or the auditor is unable to obtain sufficient appropriate evidence from alternative procedures, the auditor should communicate with those charged with governance and determine the implications for the auditor's opinion.

2.4.4 Results of External Confirmation Procedures

- **Reliability of Responses to Confirmation Requests**

  All confirmation responses carry some risk of interception, alteration, or fraud. If the auditor determines that a response to a confirmation request is not reliable, the auditor should evaluate the implications on the assessment of the risks of material misstatement, including fraud, and on the related nature, extent, and timing of other audit procedures.

  When responses are received electronically, the auditor may address the reliability of the responses by directly contacting the confirming party to validate the identity of the sender and the accuracy of the information received. An electronic confirmation system or a process that creates a secure confirmation environment may mitigate the risks of interception or alteration.

- **Confirmation Nonresponses**

  A nonresponse is a confirmation request returned undelivered or a failure of the confirming party to respond, or fully respond, to a positive confirmation request. The auditor may send additional confirmation requests when a previous request has not been received within a reasonable time. For each confirmation nonresponse, the auditor should perform alternative procedures.

  A nonresponse to a confirmation request may indicate a previously unidentified risk of material misstatement. For example, a greater number of nonresponses than expected may indicate a previously unidentified fraud risk factor.

- **Oral Responses**

  An oral response to a confirmation request does not meet the definition of an external confirmation because it is not a direct written response. If the auditor has not concluded that a direct written response to a positive confirmation is necessary to obtain sufficient appropriate audit evidence, the auditor may take an oral response into consideration when designing the alternative audit procedures required to be performed for nonresponses.

- **Exceptions**

  An exception is a response that indicates a difference between the information in the entity's records and the information provided by the confirming party. All exceptions should be investigated to determine whether they are indicative of material misstatement, fraud, or deficiencies in internal control over financial reporting. Exceptions that result from timing or measurement differences, or clerical errors, do not represent material misstatements.

3 Review of Relevant Assertions

As described previously, the main assertions relevant to the audit of account balances, transactions, and presentation and disclosure are outlined below.

3.1 Account Balances (CVER)

When audit procedures relate to asset, liability, and equity account balances, the most relevant assertions are:

- **Completeness**

  All assets, liabilities, and equity interests that should have been recorded have been recorded.

- **Valuation, Allocation, and Accuracy**

  Assets, liabilities, and equity interests are recorded fairly and at appropriate amounts, and any resulting valuation or allocation adjustments are appropriately recorded.

- **Existence and Occurrence**

  Assets, liabilities, and equity interests exist.

- **Rights and Obligations**

  The entity holds or controls the rights to assets, and liabilities are the obligations of the entity.

Pass Key

When auditing asset balances, the auditor generally focuses on testing the existence assertion (rather than the completeness assertion) because assets are more likely to be overstated (existence) than understated (completeness). The auditor generally focuses on testing the completeness assertion for liability balances, because liabilities are more likely to be understated than overstated.

3.2 Transactions and Events (COVEU)

When testing transactions, the most relevant assertions are:

- **Completeness**

  All transactions and events that should have been recorded have been recorded.

- **Cutoff**

  Transactions and events have been recorded in the correct accounting period.

- **Valuation, Allocation, and Accuracy**

  Amounts and other data relating to recorded transactions and events have been recorded appropriately.

- **Existence and Occurrence**

  Transactions and events that have been recorded have occurred and pertain to the entity.

- **Understandability and Classification**

  Transactions and events have been recorded in the proper accounts.

Pass Key

When auditing revenue transactions, the auditor generally focuses on testing the existence/occurrence assertion (rather than the completeness assertion) because revenues are more likely to be overstated (existence) than understated (completeness). The auditor generally focuses on testing the completeness assertion for expense transactions, because expenses are more likely to be understated than overstated.

3.3 Presentation and Disclosure (CVRU)

When testing financial statement disclosures, the most relevant assertions are:

- **Completeness**
  All disclosures that should have been included in the financial statements have been included.
- **Valuation, Allocation, and Accuracy**
  Financial information and other information are disclosed fairly and at appropriate amounts.
- **Rights and Obligations, and Occurrence**
  Disclosed events and transactions have occurred and pertain to the entity.
- **Understandability and Classification**
  Financial information is appropriately presented and described and disclosures are clearly expressed.

	C	O	V	E	R	U
Account balances	C		V	E	R	
Transactions and events	C	O	V	E		U
Presentation and disclosure	C		V		R	U

3.4 Matching Auditing Procedures to Specific Assertions

A workable outline for developing an audit plan uses the financial statement assertions approach. Although audit procedures for each account balance, transaction, and disclosure vary significantly, a generic framework can be developed using the financial statement assertions. Certain audit procedures relate specifically to the six main financial statement assertions (**COVERU**):

Assertion	Auditing Procedure
Completeness	1. **Tracing** of transactions forward, starting from source documents through their accounting recognition and ultimately to the financial statements. Note that this directional test is the opposite of vouching (the directional test for the existence/occurrence assertion). 2. **Analytical review** procedures. The auditor should consider how certain items might be omitted from the account balance, such as unrecorded liabilities or omissions of pledged assets. 3. **Observation** of processes and procedures.
Cutoff	1. **Cutoff procedures** to analyze transactions before and after year-end for proper accounting period recognition.
Valuation, Allocation, and Accuracy	1. **Inspection** of documentation supporting transactions. 2. **Footing** and cross-footing of schedules. 3. **Independent recalculation.** Examples would be aging of accounts receivable to substantiate the value of the allowance account, or the recalculation of depreciation charges. A prime area for recalculation are estimates made by the client. 4. **Reconciliation** of supporting schedules to general ledger line items.
Existence and Occurrence	1. **Confirmation** of accounts with third parties. 2. **Observation, inspection, and examination** of assets, processes, and procedures. (These provide very persuasive forms of evidence.) 3. **Vouching** of transactions from financial statements back to supporting documents.
Rights and Obligations	1. **Inspection** of documentation supporting transactions, inspection of contracts, etc.
Understandability and Classification	1. **Inspection** of documentation supporting transactions. 2. **Review** of all related disclosures for compliance with GAAP. 3. **Inquiry of management** regarding disclosures for the account and for related accounts.

This basic financial statement assertion outline is by no means a complete audit plan, but it provides a good starting point when addressing audit plans for a given account.

Question 1	MCQ-02334

The objective of tests of details of transactions performed as substantive tests is to:

a. Comply with generally accepted auditing standards.

b. Attain assurance about the reliability of the information system relevant to financial reporting.

c. Detect material misstatements in the financial statements.

d. Evaluate whether management's controls operated effectively.

Question 2	MCQ-02373

Auditors try to identify predictable relationships when using analytical procedures. Relationships involving transactions from which of the following accounts most likely would yield the highest level of evidence?

a. Accounts receivable

b. Interest expense

c. Accounts payable

d. Travel and entertainment expense

Question 3	MCQ-02354

In determining whether transactions have been recorded, the direction of the audit testing should be from the:

a. General ledger balances.

b. Adjusted trial balance.

c. Original source documents.

d. General journal entries.

STUDY THIS

NOTES

Skills Practice

Tolerable misstatement = 25,200

	Yr 1	Yr 2
Salary	300,000	397,000
Insurance	50,000	76,000

1) Salary ↑ 4% on April Yr 2

Head count 12 -> 15 on 4/1/Yr 2

Yr 2 Jan -> Mar

300,000
X 1/4 = 75,000

April -> Dec

300,000 / 12 ppl
= 25,000 per person
X 15 ppl
375,000 X 1.04 X 9/12
= 292,500

75,000 + 292,500
= 367,500 guess
397,000 real
29,500 > 25,200
significant difference

2) 40 emp -> 55 emp Yr 2
↑ 8%

50,000/40 = 1250 X 55 = 68,750
X 1.08
= 74,250 guess
76,000 real
1,750 < 25,200
no significant difference

assets and rev overst
Vouching
↓ Vouch

↑ ?
tracing
understate
expense
liability

#5

Simulation

Tolerable misstatement = 10,000

new hire 83,000 x 6/12 = 41,500

79,000 x 6/12 = 39,500 } 120,500

79,000 x 6/12 = 39,500

549,000 x 2/12 = 91,500 Jan-Feb

83,000	1	1.07 =	88,810
			82,950
79,000	2	1.05 =	
79,000	3	1.03 =	81,370
83,000	3	1.03 =	85,490
73,000	3	1.03 =	75,190
79,000	3	1.03 =	81,370
73,000	4	1 =	73,000
			568,180

x 10/12 = 473,483.33

+91,500

564,983.33

+120,500

685,483.33

720,000 − 683,483.33

= 34,516.67 > 10,000

significant difference

Bonus expense

7,900,000 x 5% = 395,000

−361,500

33,500 > 10,000

significant differe

Health insurance expense

↑10%

40,000 / 7 emp = 5,714/emp

x 1.10

= 6286

x 7

= 44,000

6286 x 3 x 6/12

= 9429

= 53,429

55,000

1k < 10k

no sig diff

Payroll tax expense

549,000 + 240,000 = 789,000

120,700 / 789,000 = 0.153

720,000

+361,500

1,081,500 x 0.153 = 165,469.5

166,750

−165,469.5

1,280 < 10,000

no significant diff

MODULE

7 Financial Ratios

AUD 3

1 Overview

Auditors often use ratio analysis when performing analytical procedures.

Ratios are financial indicators that distill relevant information about a business entity by quantifying the relationships among selected items on the financial statements. An entity's ratios may be compared with ratios of a different period and with industry ratios. These comparative analyses identify trends that may be important to investors, lenders, and other interested parties.

Pass Key

Ratio questions on the auditing exam may require a simple ratio calculation, an interpretation of what the ratio means, or an analysis of the effects of a change.

When asked to analyze whether a ratio is likely to increase or decrease, you can gain efficiency by knowing the following:

- The numerator has a direct relationship with the ratio. For example, an increase in the numerator results in an increase in the ratio.

$$\frac{\uparrow \text{Numerator}}{\text{Denominator}} = \text{Resulting ratio} \uparrow$$

- The denominator has an inverse relationship with the ratio. For example, an increase in the denominator results in a decrease in the ratio.

$$\frac{\text{Numerator}}{\uparrow \text{Denominator}} = \text{Resulting ratio} \downarrow$$

Sometimes, when both the numerator and denominator are affected by a given change, the final result (increase or decrease) is not easy to determine. The best way to answer questions such as these is to make up numbers and plug them into the ratio formula.

2 Basic Financial Analysis Ratios

Key financial ratios may be classified as:

- **Liquidity Ratios:** Liquidity ratios are measures of a firm's short-term ability to pay maturing obligations.
- **Activity Ratios:** Activity ratios are measures of how effectively an enterprise is using its assets.
- **Profitability Ratios:** Profitability ratios measure the financial performance of an enterprise for a given time period.
- **Investor Ratios:** Investor ratios are measures that are of interest to investors.
- **Long-Term Debt-Paying Ability Ratios (Coverage Ratios):** Coverage ratios are measures of security for long-term creditors/investors.

3 Limitations of Ratios

Although ratios are easy to compute, they depend entirely on the reliability of the data on which they are based (e.g., on estimates and on historical costs).

Other limitations include:

- There are few industry benchmarks for comparison.
- Dissimilar business units may make analysis difficult.
- Inflation can reduce comparability of balance sheet items.
- Manipulation of ratios by management can occur.
- The choice of different generally accepted accounting principles can affect ratios and reduce comparability.
- Generalizations are difficult to make.
- Ratios may use accounting data (e.g., fixed assets) that do not reflect fair values.

4 Other Analyses

Additional analyses, such as common size analysis (vertical and horizontal), analysis of industry statistics, and trend analysis, may also be valuable.

- **Common Size Analysis:** Common size financial statements are used to compare a company's performance with the performance of other smaller or larger companies, or with its own performance over time. To draft a common size balance sheet, simply divide each balance by the total assets. The result is that each balance sheet component is expressed as a percentage of the whole, with total assets representing 100 percent. Similarly, to draft a common size income statement, simply divide each income statement amount by the total revenue. Common size financial statements can be compared with industry norms or with those of competitors.
- **Analysis of Industry Statistics:** Ratio analysis is useful when comparing against norms in an industry. Benchmarking may be performed against competitors or industry averages.
- **Trend Analysis:** Ratio analysis can be used to analyze trends over time.

5 Comprehensive Example

The following pages provide a comprehensive example illustrating how a variety of ratios can be computed based on given financial information.

Gi Company
Balance Sheet

	December 31 Year 2	Year 1
Current Assets:		
Cash and cash equivalents	$ 50,000	$ 35,000
Trading securities (at fair value)	75,000	65,000
Accounts receivable	300,000	390,000
Inventory (at lower of cost or market)	290,000	275,000
Total current assets	715,000	765,000
Investments available-for-sale (at fair value)	350,000	300,000
Fixed assets:		
Property, plant, and equipment (at cost)	1,900,000	1,800,000
Less: accumulated depreciation	(180,000)	(150,000)
	1,720,000	1,650,000
Goodwill	30,000	35,000
Total assets	$2,815,000	$2,750,000
Current Liabilities:		
Accounts payable	$ 150,000	$ 125,000
Notes payable	325,000	375,000
Accrued and other liabilities	220,000	200,000
Total current liabilities	695,000	700,000
Long-Term Debt:		
Bonds and notes payable	650,000	700,000
Total liabilities	1,345,000	1,400,000
Stockholders' Equity:		
Common stock (100,000 shares outstanding)	500,000	500,000
Additional paid-in capital	670,000	670,000
Retained earnings	300,000	180,000
Total equity	1,470,000	1,350,000
Total liabilities and equity	$2,815,000	$2,750,000

In addition, assume the following information for Gi Company for the year ended December 31, Year 2:

Sales	$1,800,000
Cost of goods sold	(1,000,000)
Gross profit	800,000
Operating expenses	(486,970)
Interest expense	(10,000)
Net income before income taxes	303,030
Income taxes (34%)	(103,030)
Net income after income taxes	$ 200,000
Earnings per share	$2
Operating cash flows	$275,000
Dividends for the year	$0.80 per share
Market price per share	$12

5.1 Liquidity Ratios

1. Current ratio $= \dfrac{\text{Current assets}}{\text{Current liabilities}}$

$$\text{Year 2} = \frac{\$715{,}000}{\$695{,}000} = 1.03$$

$$\text{Year 1} = \frac{\$765{,}000}{\$700{,}000} = 1.09$$

(Industry average = 1.5)

The ratio, and therefore Gi's ability to meet its short-term obligations, has declined, and it is low compared with the industry average.

2. Quick ratio $= \dfrac{\text{Cash and cash equivalents + Short-term marketable securities + Receivables (net)}}{\text{Current liabilities}}$

$$\text{Year 2} = \frac{\$50{,}000 + \$75{,}000 + \$300{,}000}{\$695{,}000} = 0.61$$

$$\text{Year 1} = \frac{\$35{,}000 + \$65{,}000 + \$390{,}000}{\$700{,}000} = 0.70$$

(Industry average = 0.80)

The industry average of 0.80 is higher than Gi's ratio, which indicates that Gi may have trouble meeting short-term needs.

5.2 Activity Ratios

Pass Key

Turnover ratios generally use average balances [i.e., (beginning balance + ending balance) / 2] for balance sheet components. However, on some recent CPA Exam questions, candidates have been instructed to use year-end balances instead. Please be sure to read the question carefully to determine the appropriate method to use.

The ratios given in this module match the most recent ratios provided by the AICPA as an exhibit on task-based simulations requiring ratio calculations.

1. **Accounts receivable turnover**

$$= \frac{\text{Sales (net)}}{\text{Average accounts receivable (net)}}$$

$$= \frac{\$1{,}800{,}000}{(\$300{,}000 + \$390{,}000) / 2}$$

$$= \frac{\$1{,}800{,}000}{\$345{,}000}$$

$$= 5.22 \text{ times}$$

This ratio indicates the receivables' quality and indicates the success of the firm in collecting outstanding receivables. Faster turnover gives credibility to the current and acid-test ratios.

2. **Days sales in accounts receivable**

$$= \frac{\text{Ending accounts receivable (net)}}{\text{Sales (net) / 365}}$$

$$= \frac{\$300{,}000}{\$1{,}800{,}000 / 365}$$

$$= 60.83 \text{ days}$$

This ratio indicates the average number of days required to collect accounts receivable.

3. **Inventory turnover**

$$= \frac{\text{Cost of goods sold}}{\text{Average inventory}}$$

$$= \frac{\$1{,}000{,}000}{(\$290{,}000 + \$275{,}000) / 2}$$

$$= \frac{\$1{,}000{,}000}{\$282{,}500}$$

$$= 3.54 \text{ times}$$

This measure of how quickly inventory is sold is an indicator of enterprise performance. The higher the turnover, in general, the better the performance.

4. **Days in inventory**

$$= \frac{\text{Ending inventory}}{\text{Cost of goods sold / 365}}$$

$$= \frac{\$290{,}000}{\$1{,}000{,}000 / 365}$$

$$= 105.85 \text{ days}$$

This ratio indicates the average number of days required to sell inventory.

5. **Accounts payable turnover**

$$= \frac{\text{Cost of goods sold}}{\text{Average accounts payable}}$$

$$= \frac{\$1{,}000{,}000}{(\$150{,}000 + \$125{,}000) / 2}$$

$$= 7.27 \text{ times}$$

This ratio indicates the number of times trade payables turn over during the year. A low turnover may indicate a delay in payment, such as from a shortage of cash.

6. **Days of payables outstanding** $= \dfrac{\text{Ending accounts payable}}{\text{Cost of goods sold / 365}}$

$$= \frac{\$150{,}000}{\$1{,}000{,}000 / 365}$$

$$= 54.75 \text{ days}$$

This ratio indicates the average length of time trade payables are outstanding before they are paid.

7. **Cash conversion cycle** = Days sales in accounts receivable + Days in inventory − Days of payables outstanding

$$= 60.83 \text{ days} + 105.85 \text{ days} - 54.75 \text{ days}$$

$$= 111.93 \text{ days}$$

This ratio indicates the average length of time it takes from when the company pays cash for an inventory purchase to when the company receives cash from a sale.

8. **Asset turnover** $= \dfrac{\text{Sales (net)}}{\text{Average total assets}}$

$$= \frac{\$1{,}800{,}000}{(\$2{,}815{,}000 + \$2{,}750{,}000) / 2}$$

$$= \frac{\$1{,}800{,}000}{\$2{,}782{,}500}$$

$$= 0.65 \text{ times}$$

This ratio is an indicator of how Gi makes effective use of its assets. A high ratio indicates effective asset use to generate sales.

5.3 Profitability Ratios

1. **Profit margin** $= \dfrac{\text{Net income}}{\text{Sales (net)}}$

$$= \frac{\$200{,}000}{\$1{,}800{,}000}$$

$$= 11.11\%$$

2. **Return on assets** $= \dfrac{\text{Net income}}{\text{Average total assets}}$

$$= \frac{\$200{,}000}{\$2{,}782{,}500}$$

$$= 7.19\%$$

3. **Return on sales** $= \dfrac{\text{Income before interest income, interest expense, and taxes}}{\text{Sales (net)}}$

$$= \frac{\$303{,}030 + \$10{,}000}{\$1{,}800{,}000}$$

$$= 17.39\%$$

4. **Return on equity** $= \dfrac{\text{Net income}}{\text{Average total equity}}$

$= \dfrac{\$200{,}000}{(\$1{,}470{,}000 + \$1{,}350{,}000) / 2}$

$= 14.18\%$

5. **Gross (profit) margin** $= \dfrac{\text{Sales (net)} - \text{Cost of goods sold}}{\text{Sales (net)}}$

$= \dfrac{\$800{,}000}{\$1{,}800{,}000}$

$= 44.44\%$

6. **Operating cash flow ratio** $= \dfrac{\text{Cash flow from operations}}{\text{Ending current liabilities}}$

$= \dfrac{\$275{,}000}{\$695{,}000}$

$= 0.396$

5.4 Investor Ratios

1. **Basic earnings per share** $= \dfrac{\text{Income available to common shareholders}}{\text{Weighted average common shares outstanding}}$

$= \dfrac{\$200{,}000}{100{,}000 \text{ shares}}$

$= \$2\text{/share}$

2. **Price earnings ratio** $= \dfrac{\text{Price per share}}{\text{Basic earnings per share}}$

$= \dfrac{\$12}{\$2}$

$= 6$

This statistic indicates the investment potential of an enterprise; a rise in this ratio indicates that investors are pleased with the firm's opportunity for growth.

3. **Dividend payout** $= \dfrac{\text{Cash dividends}}{\text{Net income}}$

$= \dfrac{\$0.80 \text{ dividend per share} \times 100{,}000 \text{ shares outstanding}}{\$200{,}000}$

$= 40\%$

This ratio indicates the portion of current earnings being paid out in dividends.

5.5 Long-Term Debt Paying Ability Ratios

1. **Debt to equity** $= \dfrac{\text{Total liabilities}}{\text{Total equity}}$

Year 2 = \$1,345,000 / \$1,470,000 = 0.91

Year 1 = \$1,400,000 / \$1,350,000 = 1.04

This ratio indicates the degree of protection to creditors in case of insolvency. The lower this ratio, the better the company's position. In Gi's case, the ratio is very high, indicating that a large portion of funds come from creditors. However, the ratio is improving.

2. **Total debt ratio** $= \dfrac{\text{Total liabilities}}{\text{Total assets}}$

Year 2 = \$1,345,000 / \$2,815,000 = 47.78%

Year 1 = \$1,400,000 / \$2,750,000 = 50.91%

This debt ratio indicates the percentage of a company's assets that are financed by creditors.

3. **Equity multiplier** $= \dfrac{\text{Total assets}}{\text{Total equity}}$

Year 2 = \$2,815,000 / \$1,470,000 = 1.91

Year 1 = \$2,750,000 / \$1,350,000 = 2.01

This ratio measures a company's leverage. A higher ratio indicates a company has a greater proportion of its assets financed by debt rather than equity.

4. **Times interest earned** $= \dfrac{\text{Income before interest expense and taxes}}{\text{Interest expense}}$

Or

$$\dfrac{\text{Earnings before interest and taxes}}{\text{Interest expense}}$$

$$= \dfrac{\$303{,}030 + \$10{,}000}{\$10{,}000}$$

= 31.30 times

This ratio reflects the ability of a company to cover interest charges. It uses income before interest and taxes to reflect the amount of income available to cover interest expense.

Question 1 **MCQ-04769**

The accounts receivable turnover ratio increased significantly over a two-year period. This trend could indicate that:

a. The accounts receivable aging has deteriorated.

b. The company has eliminated its discount policy.

c. The company is more aggressively collecting customer accounts.

d. Customer sales have substantially decreased.

MODULE

8 Sampling: Part 1

AUD 3

1 Introduction

Concept of risk

1.1 Selecting Items for Testing

Designing substantive procedures and tests of controls includes determining the means of selecting items for testing. The following methods can be used:

1.1.1 Selecting All Items

Selecting all items in an account or all occurrences of a control may be done when the population consists of a small number of high-dollar-value items, the audit procedure can be automated and applied to the entire population, or the audit procedure is designed to respond to a significant risk and other means of selecting items for testing do not provide sufficient appropriate evidence.

1.1.2 Selecting Specific Items

Selecting specific items refers to the testing of all items in a population that have a specific characteristic, such as testing key items that are important for accomplishing the objective of the procedure or exhibit some other characteristic, or testing all items over a certain amount. When specific items are selected for testing, the results of the audit procedure cannot be projected to the population.

1.1.3 Audit Sampling

Audit sampling is the application of an audit procedure to less than 100 percent of the items in the account balance or class of transactions for the purpose of evaluating some characteristic of the balance or class. Audit sampling is especially useful in cases in which an auditor has no special knowledge about likely misstatements contained in account balances and transactions.

1.2 Audit Sampling Overview

When auditors sample from a population (universe), the assumption is that the sample is representative of the population (i.e., the characteristics of the sample are comparable to the characteristics of the population).

Inherent in audit sampling is the concept of *sampling risk*. This is the risk that the sample is not representative of the population and that the auditor's conclusion will be different from the conclusion had the auditor examined 100 percent of the population.

Pass Key

Rule 1: Always assume that the population being sampled is normally distributed, that is, it can be described by a "normal," or "bell-shaped," curve.

Rule 2: For the estimates that the CPA makes about the population to have mathematical validity, the samples have to be unrestricted and randomly selected, which means that:

- Every item in a population must have an absolutely equal chance of being selected.
- The CPA cannot use "bias" in deciding which items will be selected. No substitute items may be used.

Rule 3: If the sample is large enough and is randomly selected, the sample will likely have the same statistical characteristics (mean and standard deviation) as the underlying population; that is, it will be representative of the population.

Rule 4: Standard deviation is a measure of "variability," which refers to the range of values within the population.

1.3 Sampling Methods

Audit *sampling methods* can be either statistical or nonstatistical. Both approaches require the use of professional judgment.

1. **Statistical Sampling**

   In *statistical sampling,* auditors specify the sampling risk they are willing to accept and then calculate the sample size that provides that degree of reliability. Results are evaluated quantitatively.

2. **Nonstatistical Sampling**

   In *nonstatistical sampling,* the sample size is not determined mathematically. Auditors use their judgment in determining sample size, and sample results are evaluated using auditor judgment.

1.4 Sufficient Audit Evidence

Either a statistical or a nonstatistical approach is acceptable under generally accepted auditing standards. When properly applied, either method should result in a sample size that provides *sufficient audit evidence.*

- The sufficiency of audit evidence is related to the design and size of the sample.
- The size of a sample depends on the objectives and the design of the sample. Careful design generally produces a more efficient sample (i.e., one that achieves its objectives with a smaller sample size).

1.5 Professional Judgment

Although statistical sampling aids the auditor in quantitative ways, it is not a substitute for *professional judgment.* The auditor must exercise professional judgment in both statistical and nonstatistical sampling to:

1. define the population and the sampling unit;
2. select the appropriate sampling method;

3. evaluate the appropriateness of audit evidence;
4. evaluate the nature of deviations or errors;
5. consider sampling risk; and
6. evaluate the results obtained from the sample and project those results to the population.

Pass Key

Many questions try to trick the candidate into thinking that statistical sampling eliminates the need for auditing judgment. This is completely false. Although statistical sampling is a quantitative approach, judgment is required to set many of the parameters and to evaluate the overall results.

1.6 Statistical Sampling

1.6.1 Advantages of Statistical Sampling

Statistical sampling enables the auditor to:

- Measure the sufficiency of the audit evidence obtained.
- Provide an objective basis for quantitatively evaluating sample results.
- Design an efficient sample.
- Quantify sampling risk to limit risk to an acceptable level.

1.6.2 Random Sample Selection

Random sample selection methods should be used in statistical sampling. Such methods give all items in the population an equal chance to be included in the sample to be audited.

1.7 Use of Sampling

1.7.1 Types of Sampling

Auditors may use sampling procedures to estimate many different characteristics of populations, but generally estimates are either of a rate of occurrence (attribute sampling) or of a numerical quantity (variables sampling or probability-proportional-to-size [PPS] sampling).

- Attribute sampling is primarily used for testing internal controls.
- Variables sampling and PPS sampling are typically used in substantive testing of account balances.

Pass Key

Remember that attribute sampling is more likely to deal with tests of controls, and variables sampling generally deals with dollar values. Often the attribute sampling application can be identified by finding the option that deals with yes-or-no questions (e.g., is the invoice properly approved?).

1.7.2 Situations in Which Sampling May Not Apply

Sampling concepts generally do not apply to:

- Risk assessment procedures performed to obtain an understanding of internal control.
- Tests of automated application controls when effective general controls are present. (Generally, such controls would only be tested once or a few times.)
- Analyses of security and access controls, or other controls that do not provide documentary evidence of performance (e.g., controls related to segregation of duties).
- Some tests related to the operation of the control environment or the accounting system (e.g., examination of the effectiveness of activities performed by those charged with governance).

2 Uncertainty and Audit Sampling

2.1 Audit Risk

Audit risk is the uncertainty inherent in applying audit procedures. Audit risk includes both:

1. uncertainties due to sampling; and
2. uncertainties due to factors other than sampling.

2.2 Sampling Risk

Sampling risk arises from the possibility that, when a test of controls or a substantive test is restricted to a sample, the auditor's conclusions may be different from the conclusions that would have been reached had the tests been applied to all items in the account balance or class of transactions.

2.2.1 Sampling Risks in Substantive Testing

In performing substantive tests of details, the auditor is concerned with two aspects of sampling risk.

1. **Risk of Incorrect Acceptance:** The *risk of incorrect acceptance* is the risk that the sample supports the conclusion that the recorded account balance is not materially misstated when in fact it is materially misstated (i.e., sample results fail to identify an existing material misstatement).

2. **Risk of Incorrect Rejection:** The *risk of incorrect rejection* is the risk that the sample supports the conclusion that the recorded account balance is materially misstated when in fact it is not materially misstated (i.e., sample results *mistakenly* indicate a material misstatement).

Illustration 1 Risk of Incorrect Acceptance

An auditor was testing the existence accounts receivable through confirmation. Based on the results of the confirmations received, the auditor concluded that the accounts receivable balance was materially correct and issued an unmodified opinion.

However, if the auditor tested the entire accounts receivable balance, the auditor would have concluded that the balance was materially misstated.

This scenario represents *risk of incorrect acceptance*. When an auditor samples a population, there is always the risk that the sample may not represent the population. This is what occurred. The sample showed that the accounts receivable balance was not misstated. However, the actual account balance of accounts receivable was misstated.

2.2.2 Sampling Risks in Tests of Controls

In performing tests of controls, the auditor is also concerned with two aspects of sampling risk:

1. **Risk of Assessing Control Risk Too Low**

   The *risk of assessing control risk too low* is the risk that the assessed level of control risk based on the sample is less than the true risk based on the actual operating effectiveness of the control (i.e., sample results indicate a lower deviation rate than actually exists in the population).

2. **Risk of Assessing Control Risk Too High**

   The *risk of assessing control risk too high* is the risk that the assessed level of control risk based on the sample is greater than the true risk based on the actual operating effectiveness of the control (i.e., sample results indicate a greater deviation rate than actually exists in the population).

Illustration 2 Risk of Assessing Control Risk Too Low

An auditor is sampling controls for cash disbursements for Year 2. The auditor decides to test the operating effectiveness of a control that requires checks greater than $10,000 to have a signature from both the chief executive officer and the treasury manager.

One hundred checks written in Year 2 had an amount greater than $10,000. The auditor selected 10 of those checks. All 10 of those checks had the required signatures. Therefore, the auditor concluded that the control was operating effectively and assessed the control risk as low. The auditor then planned to obtain less persuasive evidence for substantive testing (e.g., decrease sample size.)

However, if the auditor had reviewed the remaining 90 checks, the auditor would have seen that 89 of the 90 checks had only one signature. The auditor would have concluded that the control was not operating effectively and assessed control risk as high.

This scenario represents *risk of assessing control risk too low.* The sample showed that the control was operating effectively when, in fact, it was not. In other words, the sample indicated a lower deviation rate (0 percent) than the actual deviation rate (89 percent) in the population.

Pass Key

Sampling risk can be thought of as the chance that, based on the results of a sample, the auditor will make a mistake. There are two primary mistakes the auditor can make: the auditor may fail to identify an existing problem (incorrect acceptance and assessing control risk too low), or the auditor may falsely identify a problem where none actually exists (incorrect rejection or assessing control risk too high).

2.2.3 Efficiency

The risk of incorrect rejection and the risk of assessing control risk too high relate to the *efficiency* of the audit (the auditor does more audit work than is necessary). When the auditor's evaluation of an audit sample leads the auditor to this erroneous conclusion, the application of additional audit procedures and consideration of other audit evidence ordinarily leads the auditor to the correct conclusion.

2.2.4 Effectiveness

The risk of incorrect acceptance and the risk of assessing control risk too low relate to the *effectiveness* of an audit in (possibly not) detecting an existing material misstatement. Auditors usually accept a risk of 5 or 10 percent. A related concept is that of confidence level (also called reliability). The auditor is 95 percent (or 90 percent) confident that the sample is representative of the population. (**Note:** Risk [of being ineffective] + Confidence level = 100 percent.)

2.2.5 Summary Charts

The following two charts summarize the possible outcomes.

Substantive Tests of Details			
		The recorded value of the population is:	
		OK	Not OK
The sample indicates that the population is:	OK	• Correct decision	• Incorrect decision • **Risk of incorrect acceptance** • Not effective
	Not OK	• Incorrect decision • **Risk of incorrect rejection** • Not efficient	• Correct decision

Tests of Controls			
		The true operation of the control is:	
		OK	Not OK
The sample indicates that the control's operation is:	OK	• Correct decision	• Incorrect decision • **Risk of assessing control risk too low** • Not effective
	Not OK	• Incorrect decision • **Risk of assessing control risk too high** • Not efficient	• Correct decision

2.3 Nonsampling Risk

Nonsampling risk includes all aspects of audit risk that are not due to sampling. Nonsampling risk is always present and cannot be measured; the auditor can only attempt to reduce this risk to a very low level through adequate planning and supervision of the audit engagement and quality control of all firm practices. Examples of nonsampling risk are selecting audit procedures that are not appropriate to achieve a specific objective, and failure by the auditor to recognize misstatements in documents examined.

3 Sampling in Tests of Controls: Attribute Sampling

3.1 Purpose

Attribute sampling is a statistical sampling method used to estimate the rate (percentage) of occurrence (exception) of a specific characteristic (attribute). Samples taken to test the operating effectiveness of controls are intended to provide a basis for the auditor to conclude whether the controls are being applied as prescribed. Attribute sampling generally deals with yes-or-no questions. For example, "Are time cards properly authorized (i.e., to assure recorded hours were worked)?" or, "Are invoices properly voided (e.g., stamped "paid") to prevent duplicate payments?"

3.2 Planning Considerations

When planning a particular audit sample for tests of controls, the auditor applies professional judgment in considering:

- The relationship of the sample to the objective of the test of controls.
- The tolerable deviation rate.
  - The *tolerable deviation* rate is the maximum rate of deviation from a prescribed procedure the auditor will tolerate without modifying planned reliance on internal control.
  - In assessing the tolerable rate of deviation, the auditor should consider that although deviations from pertinent controls increase the risk of material misstatements in the accounting records, such deviations do not necessarily result in misstatements.
- The auditor's allowable risk of assessing control risk too low.
- Characteristics of the population (i.e., the expected or likely rate of deviation).

3.3 Deviation Rate vs. Tolerable Rate

3.3.1 Deviation Rate

The *deviation rate* in the sample is the auditor's best estimate of the deviation rate in the population from which it was selected.

Pass Key

Students often mistakenly assume that the sample deviation rate also should be used as the estimated error rate in the total population. Consider the following example: Assume a population of 1,000 items, a sample of 100 items, and 7 deviations identified within the sample of 100 (a 7 percent sample deviation rate). While our best guess would be that there are 70 deviations in the entire population (also a 7 percent rate), it is unlikely that, if we were to individually examine each of those 1,000 items, we would find exactly 70 deviations. More likely, we might find 68, 69, 71, or 72 deviations. There are statistical formulae that determine whether the actual range is 68 to 72, 60 to 80, or something different, and there are tables available that provide the top end of the range. (As conservative auditors, we are concerned with the worst-case scenario, so we generally do not bother with the low end of the range.) The top end of the range is formally known as the "upper deviation rate."

3.3.2 Evaluation

If the estimated deviation rate is less than the tolerable rate for the population, the auditor should consider the risk that such a result might be obtained even though the true deviation rate for the population exceeds the tolerable rate for the population.

For example, assume that the tolerable rate for a population is 5 percent and the sample consists of 60 items:

- If no deviations are found in the sample of 60 items, the auditor may conclude that there is an acceptably low sampling risk that the true deviation rate in the population exceeds the tolerable rate of 5 percent. (This is because the sample deviation rate is much less than the tolerable rate.)
- If the sample includes two or more deviations (2 in 60 = 3.33 percent), the auditor may conclude that there is an unacceptably high sampling risk that the rate of deviations in the population exceeds the tolerable rate of 5 percent. (This is because the sample deviation rate is close to the tolerable rate.)
- The auditor applies professional judgment in making such evaluations.

3.3.3 Conclusion

If the auditor concludes that the sample results do not support the planned assessed level of control risk for an assertion, the nature, extent, and timing of substantive procedures should be reevaluated based on a revised consideration of the assessed level of control risk for the relevant financial statement assertions.

3.4 Attribute Sampling Example

The auditor performs the following steps when conducting an attribute sampling application.

1. **Define the Objective of the Test**

   Assume that the auditor wants to determine the percentage of sales orders that are missing credit approval.

2. **Define the Population**

The population must be appropriate for the objective. The period covered by the test should also be defined.

- In this example, the population would consist of all sales orders used during the year.
- If tests of controls are performed at an interim date, the auditor must perform such additional procedures as are necessary to obtain reasonable assurance regarding the remaining period.

3. **Define the Sampling Unit**

Consider the completeness of the population in defining the *sampling unit*.

- Each sales order is a sampling unit.
- The "population" must agree with the "physical representation." Completeness would be more assured by a register of prenumbered sales orders than by the physical file. For example, sales orders may be removed from the file, but the sales order number will be in the register. Note that the size of a population of consecutively numbered documents is the difference between the beginning and ending numbers plus one.

4. **Define the Attributes of Interest**

Deviations are situations in which the control was not properly applied, such as:

- Missing credit approval
- Missing sales order (items that cannot be located are generally considered deviations)

5. **Determine the Sample Size**

The auditor must specify the following factors.

- **Risk of Assessing Control Risk Too Low**

  This is the risk that the assessed level of control risk based on the sample is less than the true level of control risk based on the actual operating effectiveness of the control. There is an inverse relationship to sample size: As the auditor is willing to accept greater risk, a smaller sample size can be used.

- **Tolerable Deviation Rate**

  This is the maximum rate of error the auditor is willing to accept without changing control risk assessment or planned reliance on internal control. There is an inverse relationship to sample size: As the auditor is willing to accept a greater deviation rate, a smaller sample size can be used.

- **Expected Deviation Rate**

  This is the auditor's best estimate of the rate of deviation from a prescribed control procedure. There is a direct relationship to sample size: As the auditor expects fewer deviations, a smaller sample size would be needed.

- **Population Size**

  Population size is not an issue provided the population is large (i.e., greater than 5,000 items).

Example 1 Calculating Sample Size

Facts: Assume that an auditor is testing the sales orders for credit approval deviations. Also assume that the auditor is willing to accept a 5 percent risk of assessing control risk too low. The auditor expects a deviation rate of 1 percent, and the tolerable deviation rate is 6 percent.

Required:

1. Determine the sample size using Table 1, which follows.
2. Would the sample size increase or decrease if the expected deviation rate decreased to 0 percent?
3. Would the sample size increase or decrease if the tolerable deviation rate increased to 7 percent?
4. Would the sample size increase or decrease if the risk of assessing control risk too low increased to 10 percent?

Table 1: Attribute Sample Size Table
5% Risk of Assessing Control Risk Too Low

Expected Deviation Rate	*Tolerable Rate*										
	2%	3%	4%	5%	6%	7%	8%	9%	10%	15%	20%
0.00%	149	99	74	59	49	42	36	32	29	19	14
0.50	*	157	117	93	78	66	58	51	46	30	22
1.00	*	*	156	93	78	66	58	51	46	30	22
1.50	*	*	192	124	103	66	58	51	46	30	22
2.00	*	*	*	181	127	88	77	68	46	30	22
3.00	*	*	*	*	195	129	95	84	61	30	22
4.00	*	*	*	*	*	*	146	100	89	40	22

Solution:

1. The sample size is 78.
2. The sample size would decrease.
3. The sample size would decrease.
4. The sample size would decrease.

6. **Select the Sample**
   - The most common technique is random selection, whereby each item in the population has an equal opportunity to be included in the sample.
   - Systematic selection (i.e., every "nth" item) is also acceptable, but a disadvantage is that results may be skewed if errors occur in a systematic pattern.
   - Block (cluster) sampling, where groups of adjacent items are selected, is not acceptable.

7. **Evaluate the Sample Results**

   The auditor calculates the sample deviation rate and projects the results to the population. Table 2, which follows, is used to determine the upper deviation rate, which is based on the deviation rate in the sample plus an allowance for sampling risk.
   - Be sure to use a table that corresponds to the appropriate risk of assessing control risk too low (in this case, 5 percent).
   - Locate the sample size and the number of deviations found in the sample. The number at this intersection is the auditor's estimate of the maximum deviation rate in the population, or the upper deviation rate.
   - The upper (maximum) deviation rate is the sum of the sample deviation rate and the allowance for sampling risk. This allowance is a "cushion" for protection against undetected deviations.

Sample deviation rate + Allowance for sampling risk = Upper deviation rate

Pass Key

Students often have trouble with the concepts of upper deviation rate and allowance for sampling risk, both of which have been tested on the exam. The allowance for sampling risk recognizes that it is likely that what we found in the sample isn't exactly what we would find in the population. Assume a population of 1,000 items, a sample of 100 items, and a sample deviation rate of 4 percent (4 deviations out of 100). If the upper deviation rate (from a table) is 8.5 percent, this implies a 4.5 percent allowance for sampling risk. Conversely, should the examiners provide the allowance for sampling risk (say, 3.6 percent), it would be added to the sample deviation rate (4 percent) to find an upper deviation rate of 7.6 percent.

Example 2 Evaluation of Sample Results

Facts: Assume that the auditor finds one sales order that is missing the proper credit approval in a sample of 100 sales orders (i.e., one deviation).

Required:

1. Calculate the sample deviation rate.
2. Determine the upper deviation rate using Table 2, which follows.
3. What is the allowance for sampling risk?
4. Conclusion: The auditor is ____% sure the deviation rate does not exceed ____%.

Table 2: Attribute Sample Evaluation Table—Upper Deviation Rate 5% Risk of Assessing Control Risk Too Low

Sample Size	*Actual Number of Deviations Found*										
	0	1	2	3	4	5	6	7	8	9	10
25	11.3	17.6	*	*	*	*	*	*	*	*	*
50	5.9	9.2	12.1	14.8	17.4	19.9	*	*	*	*	*
60	4.9	7.7	10.2	12.5	14.7	16.8	18.8	*	*	*	*
70	4.2	6.6	8.8	10.8	12.6	14.5	16.3	18.0	19.7	*	*
75	3.9	6.2	8.2	10.1	11.8	13.6	15.2	16.9	18.5	20.0	*
100	3.0	4.7	6.2	7.6	9.0	10.3	11.5	12.8	14.0	15.2	16.4
125	2.4	3.8	5.0	6.1	7.2	8.3	9.3	10.3	11.3	12.3	13.2
150	2.0	3.2	4.2	5.1	6.0	6.9	7.8	8.6	9.5	10.3	11.1

Solution:

1. The sample deviation rate is 1%.
2. The upper deviation rate is 4.7%
3. The allowance for sample risk is 3.7% (4.7% – 1%).
4. The auditor is 95% sure the deviation rate does not exceed 4.7%.

8. Form Conclusions About the Internal Control Tested

- If the upper deviation rate is less than or equal to the auditor's tolerable deviation rate, the auditor may rely on the control (assuming the results of other audit tests do not contradict such results).
- If the upper deviation rate exceeds the auditor's tolerable deviation rate, the auditor would not rely on the control. Instead, the auditor would either:
  1. select and test compliance with some other internal accounting control; or
  2. modify the nature, extent, or timing of related substantive tests to reflect the reduced reliance.
- If the sample is representative of the population, the auditor will generally make a correct decision regarding whether or not the control is operating effectively.
- If the sample is not representative of the population, the auditor will make an incorrect decision, either relying on a control that is not reliable, or not relying on a control that is reliable.

Example 3 Forming Conclusions on a Control

Facts: Assume that the upper deviation rate has been determined to be 4.7 percent.

Required:

1. If the tolerable rate is 3 percent, would the auditor rely on the control?
2. If the tolerable rate is 6 percent would the auditor rely on the control?

Solution:

1. No. 4.7 > 3
2. Yes. 4.7 < 6

Pass Key

The examiners sometimes try to trick candidates into using the sample deviation rate (instead of the upper deviation rate) in drawing conclusions about a population. In keeping with the concept of conservatism, auditors must consider the worst-case scenario, or the high end of the range, in evaluating a population. It is therefore the upper deviation rate (and not the rate found in the sample) that is compared with the tolerable rate in developing conclusions.

9. Document the Sampling Procedure

Remember that as with all audit procedures, the auditor must document each step in audit sampling, starting with planning and including the rationale for the auditor's parameters, the performance of procedures, the observed results, and the evaluation and interpretation of those results.

4 Other Attribute Sampling Models

4.1 Discovery Sampling

Discovery sampling is a special type of attribute sampling appropriate when the auditor believes that the population deviation rate is zero or near zero. It is used when the auditor is looking for a very critical characteristic (e.g., fraud). The auditor predetermines the desired reliability (confidence) level (e.g., 95 percent) and the maximum acceptable tolerable rate (e.g., 1 percent), and a table is then used to determine sample size.

If no deviations are found in the sample, the auditor can be 95 percent certain that the rate of deviation in the population does not exceed 1 percent. If deviations are found, a regular attribute sampling table may be used to estimate the deviation rate in the population, and audit procedures may need to be expanded.

4.2 Stop-or-Go Sampling

Stop-or-go sampling (sequential sampling) is designed to avoid oversampling for attributes by allowing the auditor to stop an audit test before completing all steps. It is used when few errors are expected in the population.

Question 1	**MCQ-02588**

For which of the following audit tests would an auditor most likely use attribute sampling?

a. Selecting accounts receivable for confirmation of account balances.
b. Inspecting employee time cards for proper approval by supervisors.
c. Making an independent estimate of the amount of a LIFO inventory.
d. Examining invoices in support of the valuation of fixed asset additions.

Question 2	**MCQ-02602**

As a result of tests of controls, an auditor assessed control risk too low and decreased substantive testing. This assessment occurred because the true deviation rate in the population was:

a. Less than the risk of assessing control risk too low, based on the auditor's sample.
b. Less than the deviation rate in the auditor's sample.
c. More than the risk of assessing control risk too low, based on the auditor's sample.
d. More than the deviation rate in the auditor's sample.

Question 3	**MCQ-02620**

While performing a test of details during an audit, an auditor determined that the sample results supported the conclusion that the recorded account balance was materially misstated. It was, in fact, not materially misstated. This situation illustrates the risk of:

a. Assessing control risk too high.
b. Assessing control risk too low.
c. Incorrect rejection. it is
d. Incorrect acceptance.

Question 4	**MCQ-02594**

An auditor who uses statistical sampling for attributes in testing internal controls should reduce the planned reliance on a prescribed control when the:

- **a.** Sample rate of deviation plus the allowance for sampling risk equals the tolerable rate.
- **b.** Sample rate of deviation is less than the expected rate of deviation used in planning the sample.
- **c.** Tolerable rate less the allowance for sampling risk exceeds the sample rate of deviation.
- **d.** Sample rate of deviation plus the allowance for sampling risk exceeds the tolerable rate.

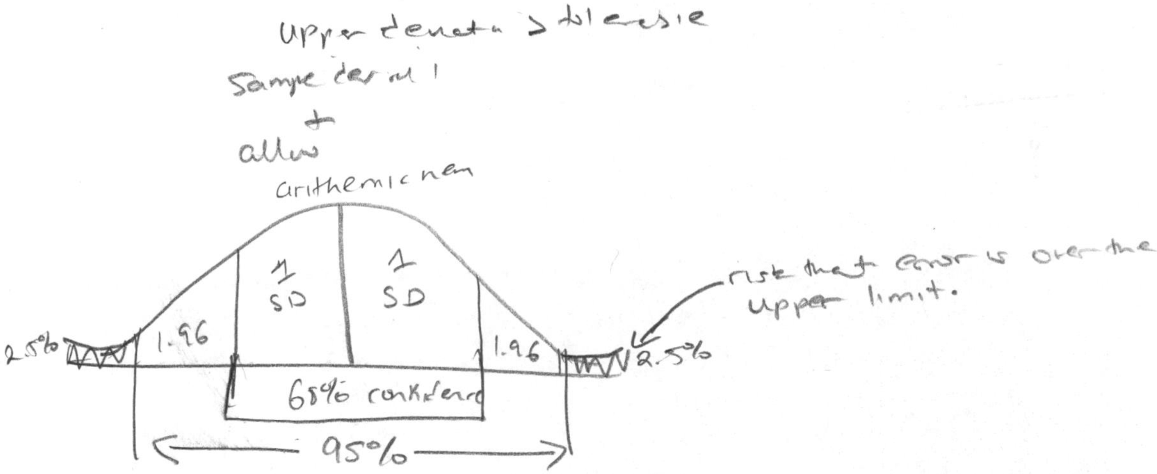

NOTES

200,000

CR 1.5:1 CA/CL ↓/↓ no effect

QR 0.5:1 Cash + Sec + AR / CL ↓ ↓

CA↓ / CL↓

400 / 600 = 0.66

200 / 400 = 0.5

5% or expected

40,000

41,667

4.8 52,000

960,000

540,000

1,500,000

MODULE

9 Sampling: Part 2

1 Sampling in Substantive Tests: Variables Sampling

1.1 Purpose

Variables sampling is a statistical sampling method used to estimate the numerical measurement of a population, such as a dollar value (e.g., accounts receivable balance). This sampling method is used primarily in substantive testing. The objective of variables sampling is to obtain evidence about the reasonableness of monetary amounts. The auditor estimates the true value of the population by computing a point estimate of the population and computing a precision interval around this point estimate.

1.2 Planning Considerations

When planning a particular sample for a substantive test of details, the auditor should consider:

1. The relationship of the sample to the relevant audit objective.
2. Preliminary estimates of materiality levels.

   Tolerable misstatement is the maximum monetary misstatement in the related account balance or class of transactions that the auditor is willing to accept.

Pass Key

Tolerable misstatement is the application of performance materiality to a particular sampling procedure. Tolerable misstatement may be the same as performance materiality, or it may be an amount smaller than performance materiality if, for example, the population from which the sample is selected is smaller than the total account balance.

3. The auditor's allowable risk of incorrect acceptance.

   The audit risk model may be useful in establishing the allowable risk of incorrect acceptance.
4. Characteristics of the population.

1.3 Sample Selection Considerations

The auditor uses professional judgment to determine which items should be subject to sampling. Certain items may be individually examined, such as those for which potential misstatements could individually exceed tolerable misstatement. All (100 percent) of such items are examined and they are not considered to be part of the sample.

Items subject to sampling may also be separated into relatively homogeneous groups. Each group is treated as a separate population. This technique, known as stratification, generally results in a reduced sample size. Stratification is commonly used when a population has highly variable recorded amounts.

Pass Key

When stratification is used, each group is treated as a separate population. For example, assume that 1,000 items are stratified into two groups: The 100 largest items will all be examined individually, but sampling techniques will be applied to the remaining 900 items. In this case, the population size for the sampling application would be 900, not 1,000.

1.4 Projected Misstatement vs. Tolerable Misstatement

1.4.1 Projected Misstatement

Upon completion of the sampling procedures, the auditor projects the misstatement results of the sample to the items in the population.

1.4.2 Evaluation

- If the total projected misstatement is less than the tolerable misstatement for the account balance or class of transactions, the auditor should consider the risk that such a result might be obtained even though the true monetary misstatement for the population exceeds tolerable misstatement.
- For example, assume that the tolerable misstatement in an account balance of $1 million is $50,000:
  - If the total projected misstatement (based on the sample) is $10,000, the auditor may be reasonably assured that there is an acceptably low sampling risk that the true monetary misstatement for the population exceeds the tolerable misstatement of $50,000. (This is because $10,000 is significantly less than $50,000.)
  - If the total projected misstatement is close to the tolerable misstatement, the auditor may conclude that there is an unacceptably high risk that the actual error in the population exceeds the tolerable misstatement.
  - The auditor uses professional judgment in making such evaluations.

1.4.3 Conclusion

Projected misstatement results for all audit sampling applications and all known misstatements from nonsampling applications should be considered in the aggregate along with other relevant audit evidence when the auditor evaluates whether the financial statements taken as a whole may be materially misstated.

1.5 Variables Sampling Plans

Classical variables sampling measures sampling risk by using the variation of the underlying characteristic of interest. There are three commonly used classical variables sampling plans.

1.5.1 Mean-per-Unit Estimation

Mean-per-unit (MPU) estimation is a sampling plan that uses the average value of the items in the sample to estimate the true population value (i.e., Estimate = Average sample value × Number of items in population). MPU does not require the book value of the population to estimate true population value.

1.5.2 Ratio Estimation

Ratio estimation is a sampling plan that uses the ratio of the audited (correct) values of items to their book values to project the true population value. Ratio estimation is a highly efficient technique when the calculated audit amounts are approximately proportional to the client's book amounts.

1.5.3 Difference Estimation

Difference estimation is a sampling plan that uses the average difference between the audited (correct) values of items and their book values to project the actual population value. Difference estimation is used instead of ratio estimation when the differences are not nearly proportional to book values.

1.5.4 Comparison of Methods

- MPU is very sensitive to the variability of the population. For that reason, when using MPU, auditors normally stratify (or divide) the population into relatively similar groups. The purpose of such stratification is to reduce sample size.
- The ratio and difference methods usually require smaller sample sizes than the MPU method; however, they are only effective when the auditor expects large numbers of over- and understatements.
- All three methods use the same sample size formulas and evaluation formulas. The sample size for the three methods varies because the standard deviations of the populations are calculated differently for each of the three methods.

1.6 Variables Sampling Example

The auditor must perform the following steps when conducting a variables sampling application.

1. **Define the Objective of the Test**

   Assume that the auditor wishes to estimate the value of an account balance (e.g., the client's accounts receivable balance).

2. **Define the Population**

   It must be appropriate for the objective. Individually significant items should be identified for possible stratification.

   - In this example, the population might consist of 5,000 accounts with a recorded book value of $4,500,000.
   - The auditor would examine 100 percent of accounts for which potential errors could equal or exceed the tolerable error and would exclude those accounts from the population to be sampled.

3. **Define the Sampling Unit**

   Consider the completeness of the population in defining the sampling unit.

   - In this case, each of the 5,000 accounts is a sampling unit.

4. **Determine the Sample Size**

   - The auditor uses the following parameters, in conjunction with tables or formulas, to determine sample size.

     —Tolerable misstatement

     —Expected misstatement (size, frequency, etc.)

     —Acceptable level of risk: audit risk, risk of incorrect acceptance, and risk of incorrect rejection

- —Characteristics of the population (e.g., an estimate of the standard deviation, or variability, of the population)
- —Assessed risk: assessed risk of material misstatement (inherent risk and control risk) and assessed risk for other substantive procedures related to the same assertion

- Sample size will increase as the following increase (direct relationship):
  - —Expected misstatement
  - —Standard deviation (population variability)
  - —Assessed level of risk
- Sample size will decrease as the following increase (inverse relationship):
  - —Tolerable misstatement
  - —Acceptable level of risk

5. Select the Sample

- Sample items should be selected in such a way that the sample can be expected to be representative of the population (e.g., random sampling).
- In this example, an appropriate sample would consist of individual account balances. Confirmations could then be used to determine the audited values for sample items.

6. Evaluate the Sample Results

The auditor projects the misstatements found in the sample to the population using one of several methods (e.g., MPU, ratio, difference, etc.). The projected misstatement is applied to the recorded balance to obtain a "point estimate" of the true balance. As shown below, the different methods result in different projected misstatements.

The auditor must then add an allowance for sampling risk (sometimes called a "precision interval") to the point estimate.

Example 1 Sample Evaluation

Facts: Assume that from the population of 5,000 accounts with a total value of $4,500,000, the auditor selects a sample of 200 accounts with a book value of $184,200. The audited value of these accounts based on confirmation results is $175,000, with an average value of $875 ($175,000 / 200) per account.

Required: Determine the point estimate using mean-per-unit estimation, ratio estimation, and difference estimation.

Solution:

Mean-per-unit estimation:

$$\text{\$875 average value} \times \text{5,000 accounts} = \text{\$4,375,000 point estimate}$$

Ratio estimation:

$$\frac{\text{\$175,000 audited value}}{\text{\$184,200 book value}} \times \text{\$4,500,000} = \text{\$4,275,244 point estimate}$$

Difference estimation:

$$\frac{\text{\$184,200 book value} - \text{\$175,000 audited value}}{200} \times \text{5,000} = \text{\$230,000 projected error}$$

$$\text{\$4,500,000} - \text{\$230,000} = \text{\$4,270,000 point estimate}$$

7. Form Conclusions About the Balances (or Transactions) Tested

- In deciding whether to accept the client's book value, the auditor determines whether the recorded book value falls within the acceptable range (i.e., the point estimate +/− the allowance for sampling risk). If so, the book value is fairly stated.
- The auditor's treatment of items selected for sampling that cannot be located (e.g., are "lost") will depend on their effect on the auditor's evaluation of the sample.
  - —If considering the missing items to be misstated would not alter the auditor's evaluation of the sample results, it is not necessary to examine the items.
  - —If considering the missing items to be misstated would lead to the conclusion that the balance or class contains a material misstatement, the auditor should consider alternative procedures.
- If the sample is representative of the population, the auditor generally will make a correct decision regarding whether the account balance is fairly stated.
- If the sample is not representative of the population, the auditor will make an incorrect decision, either accepting a materially misstated balance, or rejecting a fairly stated balance.

8. Document the Sampling Procedure

Remember that as with all audit procedures, the auditor must document each step in audit sampling, starting with planning and including the rationale for the auditor's parameters, the performance of procedures, the observed results, and the evaluation and interpretation of those results.

9. Additional Considerations When Using Audit Data Analytics (ADAs)

When an auditor uses an ADA technique when performing tests of details, the auditor should select an ADA technique that best fits the intended purpose and objectives of the procedure as well as select the techniques, tools, graphics, and tables that will be used to evaluate the results.

After performing the ADA procedure, the auditor should group the data for items that have common characteristics (when appropriate). For each group, the auditor should determine which data:

- Do not contain misstatements (also known as false positives)
- Contain possible misstatements that are clearly inconsequential (in aggregate)
- Contain possible misstatements that are not clearly inconsequential (in aggregate)

For groups that contain possible misstatements that are not clearly inconsequential (in aggregate), the auditor should perform further analysis to determine whether these items represent actual misstatements.

2 Sampling in Substantive Tests: Probability-Proportional-to-Size (PPS) Sampling

2.1 PPS Sampling

PPS sampling is a technique in which the sampling unit is defined as an individual dollar in a population. Once a dollar is selected, the entire account (containing that dollar) is audited. PPS sampling is considered to be a hybrid method, because it uses attribute sampling theory to express a conclusion in dollar amounts rather than as a rate of occurrence.

2.1.1 Advantages of PPS Sampling

- PPS automatically emphasizes larger items by stratifying the sample. The chance of an item being selected is proportionate to its dollar amount.
- If no errors are expected, PPS sampling generally requires a smaller sample than other methods.

2.1.2 Disadvantages of PPS Sampling

A disadvantage of PPS sampling is that zero balances, negative balances, and understated balances generally require special design considerations.

2.2 PPS Sample Size Determination

The auditor selects a PPS sample by dividing the total number of dollars in the population (book value) into uniform groups of dollars or intervals. The auditor then selects a logical unit (the balance that includes the selected dollar) from each sampling interval.

The sampling interval is determined as follows:

$$\text{Sampling interval} = \frac{\text{Tolerable misstatement}}{\text{Reliability factor}}$$

The sample size is determined as follows:

$$\text{Sample size} = \frac{\text{Recorded amount of the population}}{\text{Sampling interval}}$$

- Tolerable misstatement is the maximum dollar error that may exist in the account without causing the financial statements to be materially misstated.
- Reliability factors correspond to the risk of incorrect acceptance and are generally obtained from a table.
- The above formula assumes that the auditor's expected misstatement is zero. Otherwise, a more complex version of the formula is required.

Illustration 1 PPS Sample Size Determination

With zero expected errors, the reliability factors are as follows:

Risk of Incorrect Acceptance	Reliability Factor
1%	4.6
5%	3.0
10%	2.3

Assume that the auditor assesses tolerable misstatement at $15,000 and the risk of incorrect acceptance at 5 percent. The recorded amount (book value) of the population is $500,000.

Sampling interval = $15,000/3 = $5,000

Sample size = $500,000/$5,000 = 100

2.3 Sample Selection

A random number between 1 and the sampling interval (inclusive) is selected. This number is the random start, and it will also determine the first item selected. Systematic selection is then used to select the remainder of the sample. The recorded amounts of the logical units (e.g., account balances) throughout the population are added and individual dollars are selected based on the interval. Once a dollar in an account is selected, that entire account will be audited.

Illustration 2 PPS Sample Selection

Assume that the random start is 300 and the sampling interval is 5,000. Every 5,000th dollar will be selected, so the auditor will select the accounts that contain dollars 300; 5,300; 10,300; 15,300; 20,300; 25,300; etc.

Customer Account	Book Value	Cumulative Total
1	$ 150	$ 150
2	800	950*
3	1,400	2,350
4	4,350	6,700*
5	2,300	9,000
6	4,900	13,900*
7	8,500	22,400*
8	990	23,390
9	1,000	24,390
10	1,500	25,890*
	etc.	etc.
900	$1,000	$500,000

* Accounts including the selected dollars would be included in the sample.

Note: Using this methodology, all account balances greater than the interval are automatically selected.

2.4 Evaluation of Sample Results

If no errors are found in the sample, the error projection is zero and the allowance for sampling risk would not exceed the auditor's tolerable error. As a result, the auditor would generally conclude that the recorded balance is fairly stated.

If, on the other hand, errors are found in an account, the errors need to be projected to the interval as illustrated below.

If the account selected has a balance greater than the interval, the actual dollar amount of the error should be used.

Illustration 3 PPS Evaluation of Sample Results

"A" Recorded Amount	"B" Audit Amount	Tainting					Sample Interval	Projected Error
		A-B	/	A	=	%		
$ 800	$ 600	$ 200		$ 800		25%	$5,000	$1,250
4,350	4,350			4,350		0%	5,000	0
4,900	0	4,900		4,900		100%	5,000	5,000
8,500	6,900	1,600					N/A	1,600
1,500	1,200	300		1,500		20%	5,000	1,000
Projected Error								$8,850

Note that as with other variables sampling plans, an allowance for sampling risk would be calculated and added to the projected error, and the result would be compared with the tolerable misstatement.

3 Qualitative Considerations

For all types of sampling, the auditor should consider qualitative aspects of deviations. These include:

- **Nature and Cause of Deviations:** Deviations may be caused by errors, which are unintentional, or fraud, which is intentional.
- **Possible Relationship of Deviations to Other Phases of the Audit:** The discovery of fraud ordinarily requires a broader consideration of possible implications than does the discovery of an error.

4 Dual-Purpose Samples

In some instances, the auditor may use the same sample to perform both tests of controls and tests of details. *Dual-purpose samples* are generally used only when the auditor believes that there is an acceptably low risk that the deviation rate in the population exceeds the tolerable rate. The size of a sample designed for dual purposes should be the larger of the samples that would otherwise have been designed for the two separate purposes.

In evaluating dual-purpose samples, deviations from the control and monetary misstatements should be evaluated separately using the appropriate risk levels. The auditor should consider whether the existence of misstatements is indicative of a control failure; however, the absence of monetary misstatements does not necessarily imply that controls are operating effectively.

Question 1	MCQ-02584

In a probability-proportional-to-size sample with a sampling interval of $10,000, an auditor discovered that a selected account receivable with a recorded amount of $5,000 had an audited amount of $4,000. If this were the only misstatement discovered by the auditor, the projected misstatement of this sample would be:

- **a.** $1,000
- **b.** $2,000
- **c.** $5,000
- **d.** $10,000

Question 2	MCQ-02607

In statistical sampling methods used in substantive testing, an auditor most likely would stratify a population into meaningful groups if:

- **a.** Probability-proportional-to-size (PPS) sampling is used.
- **b.** The population has highly variable recorded amounts.
- **c.** The auditor's estimated tolerable misstatement is extremely small.
- **d.** The standard deviation of recorded amounts is relatively small.

Question 3	MCQ-02596

In addition to evaluating the frequency of deviations in tests of controls, an auditor should also consider certain qualitative aspects of the deviations. The auditor most likely would give broader consideration to the implications of a deviation if it was:

- **a.** The only deviation discovered in the sample.
- **b.** Identical to a deviation discovered during the prior year's audit.
- **c.** Caused by an employee's misunderstanding of instructions.
- **d.** Initially concealed by a forged document.

NOTES

Skills Practice

Call or the question

Sampling interval = tolerable misstatement / reliability factor

= 105,000 / 3 = 35,000

(BV)

Sample size = recorded amount / sampling interval

4,500,000 / 35,000 = 129 rounded up

1,000 accounts

PPS sampling → random start 873

BV = 4,500,000

873 + 35,000 = 35,873

35873 + 35,000 = 70,873

70,873 + 35,000 = 105,873

105,873 + 35,000 = 140,873

Year 2 sampling interval = 40,000

Tainting % = (BV − AV) / BV

Projected error = tainting % × 40,000

AUD

4

Performing Further Procedures, Forming Conclusions, and Communications

Module

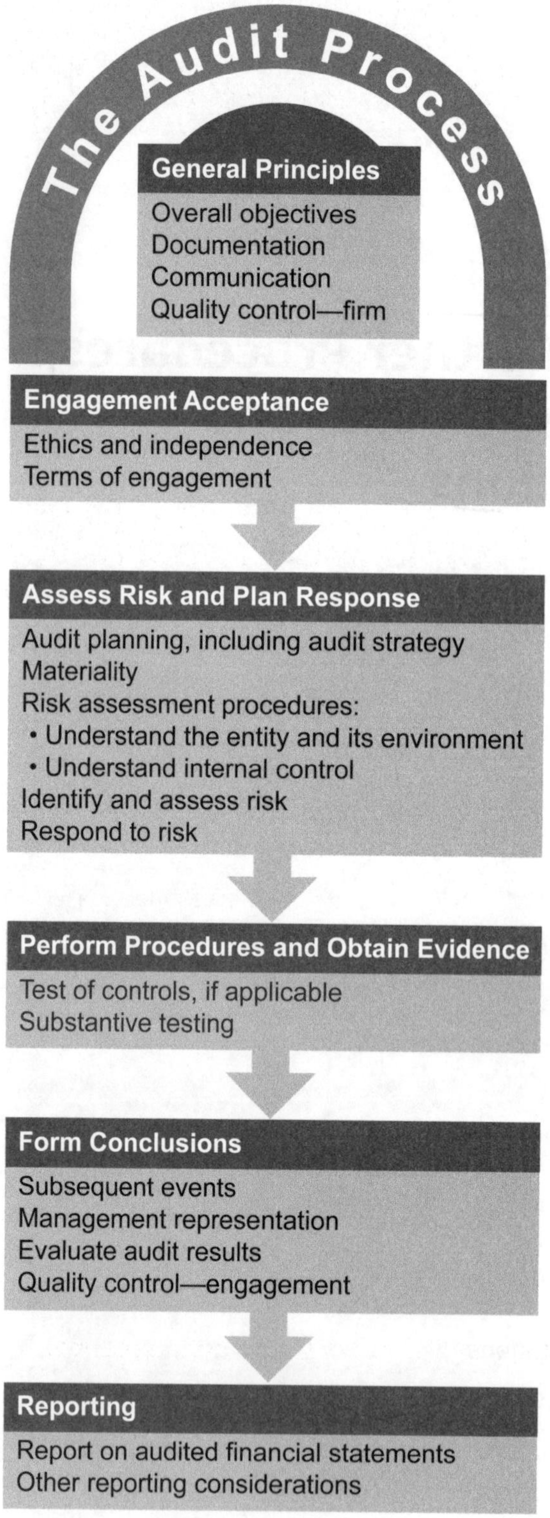
The Audit Process
General Principles
Overall objectives
Documentation
Communication
Quality control—firm
Engagement Acceptance
Ethics and independence
Terms of engagement
Assess Risk and Plan Response
Audit planning, including audit strategy
Materiality
Risk assessment procedures:
• Understand the entity and its environment
• Understand internal control
Identify and assess risk
Respond to risk
Perform Procedures and Obtain Evidence
Test of controls, if applicable
Substantive testing
Form Conclusions
Subsequent events
Management representation
Evaluate audit results
Quality control—engagement
Reporting
Report on audited financial statements
Other reporting considerations

MODULE

1 Revenue Cycle

1 Transaction Cycles

Audits are generally performed by transaction cycle. The most common transaction cycles are listed in the chart below and will be covered in the first six modules of this unit. Auditing by transaction cycle enables the auditor to gather evidence for related accounts, transactions, and disclosures simultaneously. This makes the audit process more efficient.

Module	Cycle	Description
1	Revenue	Includes sales revenues, receivables, and cash receipts
2	Expenditure	Includes purchases, payables, and cash disbursements
3	Cash	Includes cash receipts and cash disbursements
4	Inventory	Includes perpetual inventory, physical counts, and manufacturing costs
5	Investments	Includes investments in debt and equity and the income received from investments
6	Other Transaction Cycles	Includes cycles for property, plant, and equipment; payroll and personnel; and financing

2 Fraud Risk Related to the Revenue Cycle

There should be a presumption in every audit that there is the risk of material misstatement due to revenue recognition fraud. Common revenue cycle frauds include:

- Early revenue recognition.
- Holding the books open past the close of the accounting period.
- Fictitious sales.
- Failure to record sales returns.
- Side agreements used to alter sales terms and conditions to induce customers to accept goods and services they otherwise do not need.
- Channel stuffing achieved by convincing distributors to purchase more inventory than they can sell in the near term.
- Overstatement of receivables, achieved by overstating balances, reporting fictitious balances, or understating the allowance for uncollectible accounts.

3 Internal Controls Related to the Revenue Cycle

3.1 Sales

Under strong internal control, segregation of the functions in a sales transaction should exist as follows:

1. **Preparation of the Sales Order**

   The sales function begins with the receipt of a customer purchase order by the sales department. If it is determined that the order can be filled, a serially numbered sales order is prepared and sent to the credit department for approval.

2. **Credit Approval**

   The credit department determines whether or not the customer may receive goods on credit. If the order is approved, a copy of the approved sales order is sent to the shipping department, the billing department, and the accounting department.

3. **Shipment**

   In the shipping department, a serially numbered bill of lading is prepared and a copy is sent to the customer. The goods are shipped, and at this point a receivable is created based on invoice shipping terms.

4. **Billing**

   The billing department prepares a serially numbered sales invoice. Shipping documents, sales orders, and invoices are compared to assure that all shipments were based on valid customer orders and were properly billed. Prices and discounts are applied to the invoice, and necessary extensions and footings are computed. The invoice is then sent to the customer and to the accounts receivable department.

5. **Accounting**

   The sale is entered into the sales journal, and a receivable is recorded.

3.2 Accounts Receivable

Under strong internal control, segregation of the functions in an accounts receivable transaction should exist as follows:

1. **Sales**

   A receivable is recorded in the accounts receivable control account in the general ledger and in the accounts receivable subsidiary ledger. Periodically, an independent person should reconcile these two records.

2. **Collection of Cash Receipts**

   When payment is received from the customer, the receivable is eliminated.

3. **Uncollectible Receivables**

   An aging schedule is prepared and sent to the credit department for use in carrying out its collection program. At some point, receivables deemed uncollectible should be written off. Controls for writing off receivables include proper authorization (by the treasurer) and record keeping. Without proper control, amounts subsequently collected easily could be misappropriated by employees.

4. Sales Returns

Returned goods must be examined to ensure that they correspond with the reason for return before credit is given. A serially numbered receiving report may be used as a sales return slip. Once the return is approved, the sales return is recorded and the related outstanding receivable is eliminated.

Credit memos should not be prepared by individuals who collect or receive cash payments on accounts receivable; to do so would be an inadequate segregation of duties.

5. Sales Discounts

Sales discount procedures and records should be reviewed to ensure that discounts are properly given and recorded based on the selected method (gross versus net). This ensures that receivables are not overstated.

3.3 Cash Receipts

Incoming mail must be opened by a person who does not have access to the accounts receivable ledger. The receipts should be listed in detail and three copies distributed to the following personnel:

1. **Cashier:** Receives actual receipts and prepares bank deposit.
2. **Accounts Receivable Department:** Enters receipts into the accounts receivable subsidiary records.
3. **Accounting Department:** Enters receipts into accounts receivable control account.

The accounts receivable department should match the details from the bank deposit ticket with the details from the remittance advices. This will reveal any discrepancies. Cash collections should be restrictively endorsed upon receipt and deposited daily. Devices such as cash registers or lock boxes should be used as safeguards.

3.4 Sales Flowchart

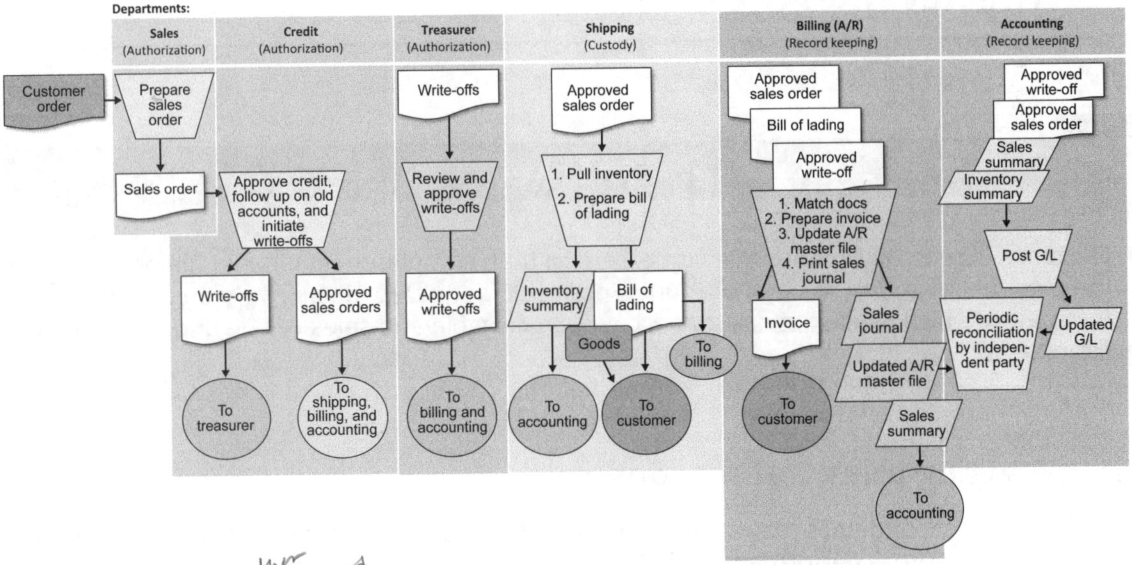

other ears
A R C

3.5 Collections Flowchart

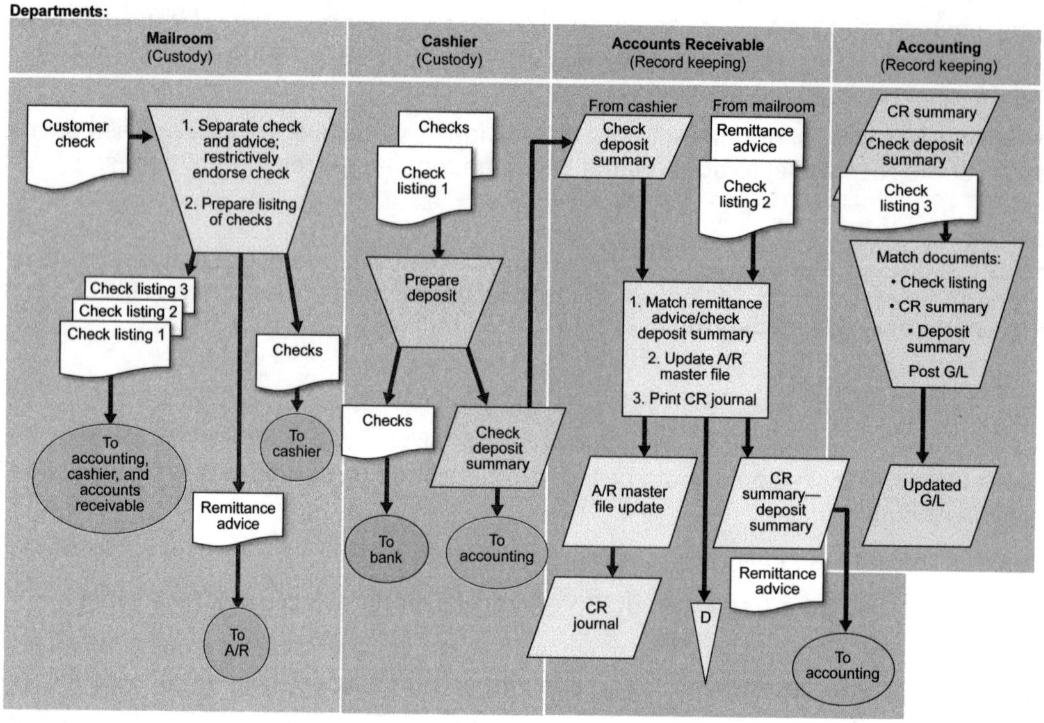

Note: The Appendix: Control Procedures and Tests of Controls contains information on revenue cycle control procedures and tests of controls.

4 Performing Specific Procedures to Obtain Evidence: The Revenue Cycle

Pass Key

Existence is generally a more relevant assertion than completeness when auditing the revenue cycle. The risk that accounts receivable and sales will be overstated (existence) is high, while the risk that accounts receivable and sales will be understated (completeness) is low.

4.1 Auditing Sales Transactions

The following tests of details may also be performed as tests of controls or dual-purpose tests. The cutoff procedure is performed most often as a substantive procedure.

- **Completeness:** The auditor should trace a sample of shipping documents to the corresponding sales invoices, and to the sales journal and accounts receivable subsidiary ledger.

- **Cutoff:** To ensure that sales were recorded in the proper period, the auditor should compare a sample of sales invoices from shortly before and after year-end with the shipment dates and with the dates the sales were recorded in the sales journal. To ensure that significant returns were not made following year-end, the auditor should analyze the record of sales returns following year-end.
- **Valuation, Allocation, and Accuracy:** The auditor should compare prices and terms on a sample of sales invoices with authorized price lists and terms of trade to determine whether sales are recorded at the appropriate amount.
- **Existence and Occurrence:** The auditor should vouch a sample of sales transactions from the sales journal to the sales invoice back to the customer order and shipping documents.
- **Understandability and Classification:** The auditor should examine a sample of sales invoices for proper classification into the appropriate revenue accounts.

4.2 Auditing Accounts Receivable

- **Completeness:** The auditor should obtain an aged trial balance of accounts receivable and trace the total to the general ledger control account.
- **Valuation, Allocation, and Accuracy:** The auditor should examine the results of confirmations (a test of accuracy) and test the adequacy of the allowance for doubtful accounts (a test of valuation). Procedures used to test the adequacy of the allowance for doubtful accounts are outlined in the discussion of accounting estimates presented later in this lecture.
- **Existence and Occurrence**: The auditor should confirm a sample of accounts receivable.
- **Rights and Obligations:** The auditor should review bank confirmations and debt agreements for liens on receivables. The auditor should also inquire of management and review debt agreements and board minutes for evidence that accounts receivable have been factored or sold.

4.3 Accounts Receivable Confirmations

The auditor should review the accounts receivable schedule for accuracy and collectibility. Confirmation of accounts receivable is a required generally accepted auditing procedure unless: (i) receivables are immaterial; (ii) confirmation would be ineffective; or (iii) inherent and control risks are very low and evidence provided by other procedures is sufficient to reduce audit risk to an acceptably low level. If confirmations are not sent, the auditor must document how omission of this procedure was alternatively tested.

4.3.1 Positive Confirmations

Auditors send confirmations to their client's customers stating the amount of receivables owed by the customer at fiscal year-end. The customers are requested to return a statement to the auditor indicating whether they agree with the amount and to provide information about any exceptions. This type of confirmation is known as a positive confirmation. Positive confirmations should be used to confirm accounts receivable when:

1. there are large individual accounts;
2. there are expected errors or items in dispute; and
3. when internal control is weak.

Note that positive confirmations may also be "blank," which means that the recipient is requested to fill in the balance. Blank forms provide a greater degree of assurance (since the recipient cannot simply sign off without actually checking the balance) but may also result in lower response rates because a greater effort is required by the recipient.

Confirmation responses received electronically (e.g., faxes, e-mails) should be verified by calling the sender. The sender should also be requested to mail the original confirmation directly to the auditor.

The auditor should consider the types of information respondents will be readily able to confirm. For instance, some accounting systems facilitate the confirmation of single transactions rather than entire balances. In such cases, the auditor would either confirm individual invoices, or would include a client-prepared statement of account showing details of the customer's account balance being confirmed.

Note that confirmations generally provide evidence regarding existence and rights and obligations. They do not provide reliable evidence regarding valuation (e.g., customers may confirm a balance owed despite an inability to pay) or completeness (e.g., customers may not report understatement errors).

4.3.2 Negative Confirmations

Negative confirmations differ from positive confirmations in that customers are requested to respond to the auditor only if they disagree with the stated amount owed. Negative confirmations may be used to confirm accounts receivable when:

1. the combined assessed level of inherent and control risk is low;
2. a large number of small account balances are being confirmed; and
3. there is no reason to expect that recipients of the requests will ignore them.

Negative confirmations are less effective than positive confirmations because lack of a response does not provide explicit verification of the existence of the receivable.

4.3.3 Confirmation Exceptions

Accounts receivable confirmation exceptions occur when there is a disparity between the amount of the receivable recorded in the client's accounting records and the amount of the receivable confirmed by the client's customer. For confirmation exceptions, the auditor should determine whether the exception is due to a timing difference or a misstatement.

1. **Timing Differences**

   Timing differences occur when there is a delay in the recording of the transaction by the client or their customer. For example, an entity may correctly record a receivable on December 31 when the goods are shipped to the customer, but the customer may not record the payable until the goods are received on January 5. This is not a misstatement.

2. **Misstatements**

   A confirmation exception would be indicative of misstatement if the exception is due to any of the following errors or frauds:

   - Fictitious sale
   - Goods sent to the wrong customer
   - Invoice sent to the wrong customer
   - Incorrect price or quantity charged to the customer
   - Misappropriation of cash received from customer
   - Payment applied to the wrong customer account

Additionally, a confirmation exception could be due to a dispute between the client and the customer because the customer claims that the goods do not meet their specifications, that the goods were damaged in transit, or that the price of the goods is in dispute.

4.3.4 Confirmation Nonresponses

Nonresponses should be followed up with second and even third confirmation requests if necessary. The client may be asked to intervene. When confirmation responses are not received, the auditor should perform alternative procedures, such as inspecting shipping documents or reviewing subsequent cash receipts. If a 100 percent overstatement of the accounts receivable from the nonresponding customers would be immaterial, alternative procedures may not be necessary. This assumes that there is no unusual pattern to the nonresponses.

4.4 Auditing Presentation and Disclosure

- **Completeness:** The auditor should ensure that all required disclosures related to accounts receivable and sales have been included in the notes to the financial statements. Revenue cycle disclosures include:
  - Revenue recognition method(s).
  - Revenue by reportable segment.
  - Related party revenues and receivables.
  - Receivables by type (trade, officer/employee, affiliates) and term (short term and long term).
  - Pledged or discounted receivables.
  - Allowance for doubtful accounts related to the receivables and a discussion of the analysis to assess credit risk.
  - Inclusion in receivables of amounts related to long-term contracts.
- **Valuation, Allocation, and Accuracy:** The auditor should read the footnotes and other information related to accounts receivable and sales to determine whether the information is accurate and presented at the appropriate amounts.
- **Rights and Obligations, and Occurrence:** The auditor should determine whether any receivables have been pledged, assigned, or discounted and, if so, determine whether disclosure is required. The auditor should compare disclosures to other audit evidence to ensure that all disclosed information related to accounts receivable and sales has occurred.
- **Understandability and Classification:** The auditor should read all accounts receivable and sales related disclosures to ensure that they are understandable.

Question 1 **MCQ-04627**

An auditor is confirming accounts receivable using positive confirmations. The auditor decides to leave the accounts receivable amount blank rather than stating the amount owed. The auditor should be aware that the blank form may be less efficient because:

a. Subsequent cash receipts need to be verified.

b. Statistical sampling may not be used.

c. A higher assessed level of detection risk is required.

d. More nonresponses are likely to occur.

NOTES

MODULE

2 Expenditure Cycle

1 Internal Controls Related to the Expenditure Cycle

1.1 Purchases

The following three functions in a purchase transaction should be segregated:

1. **Purchase Requisition**

   The purchase requisition begins the purchasing cycle. The department in need of the asset or services sends a properly approved, serially numbered requisition to the purchasing department. The requisitioning department should not have the authority to actually place the purchase order. This would indicate a weakness in internal control.

2. **Purchase Orders**

   Prior to placing the order, the purchasing department should request bids from various suppliers to make sure that the best price is obtained. Once properly approved, the purchasing department should create the purchase order, which will indicate the description, quantity, and related information for the goods and services that are being requested. For internal control purposes, it is best that prenumbered purchase orders be used. There should be multiple copies that will be sent to: (i) the requisitioning department; (ii) the vendor; (iii) the receiving department; and (iv) the accounting department. If the purchase order is canceled, all copies should be recalled and filed so that every purchase order number is accounted for.

3. **Receipt of Goods or Services**

   The copy of the purchase order sent to the receiving department serves as an authorization to accept the goods or services when they arrive. It is preferable that the copy not indicate the quantity ordered so that the receiving department is forced to count the goods upon arrival. In addition, the description of the goods should be matched to the purchase order and the condition of the goods should be examined. A receiving report is prepared by the receiving department and forwarded to the accounting department. The goods are forwarded to the requisitioning department.

1.2 Accounts Payable

Once the accounting department obtains the receiving report, it will record the payable, approve the invoice for payment, and record the payment after it is paid by the treasurer.

1. **Recording the Payable**

   The copy of the purchase order sent to the accounting department notifies it that there will be a future cash disbursement. The receiving report is compared with the purchase order and the vendor's invoice to confirm quantity and to prevent payment of charges for goods in excess of those ordered and received. The accounting department records the goods as received in inventory, and records a payable.

2. **Approving Invoice for Payment and Recording Payment**

   When the invoice arrives, the accounting department approves it by matching the invoice, purchase order, receiving report, and (sometimes) the requisition. When payment is made, the payable is reversed. The accounting department should ensure that the invoice amount is correct, and that it accurately reflects any purchase discounts or returns, before approving it for payment.

1.3 Cash Disbursements

Ideally invoices should be paid by check. For effective internal control, the functions of approving the payment and signing the checks should be segregated. Approved voucher packets (matched invoice, purchase order, receiving report, and requisition) prepared by the accounting department (accounts payable) are received by the treasurer, who prepares, signs, and mails the checks and cancels all supporting documents after payment. Paid vouchers are returned to the accounting department for posting of the payment and filing of the documents.

Note: The Appendix: Control Procedures and Tests of Controls contains information on expenditure cycle control procedures and tests of controls.

1.4 Expenditures Flowchart

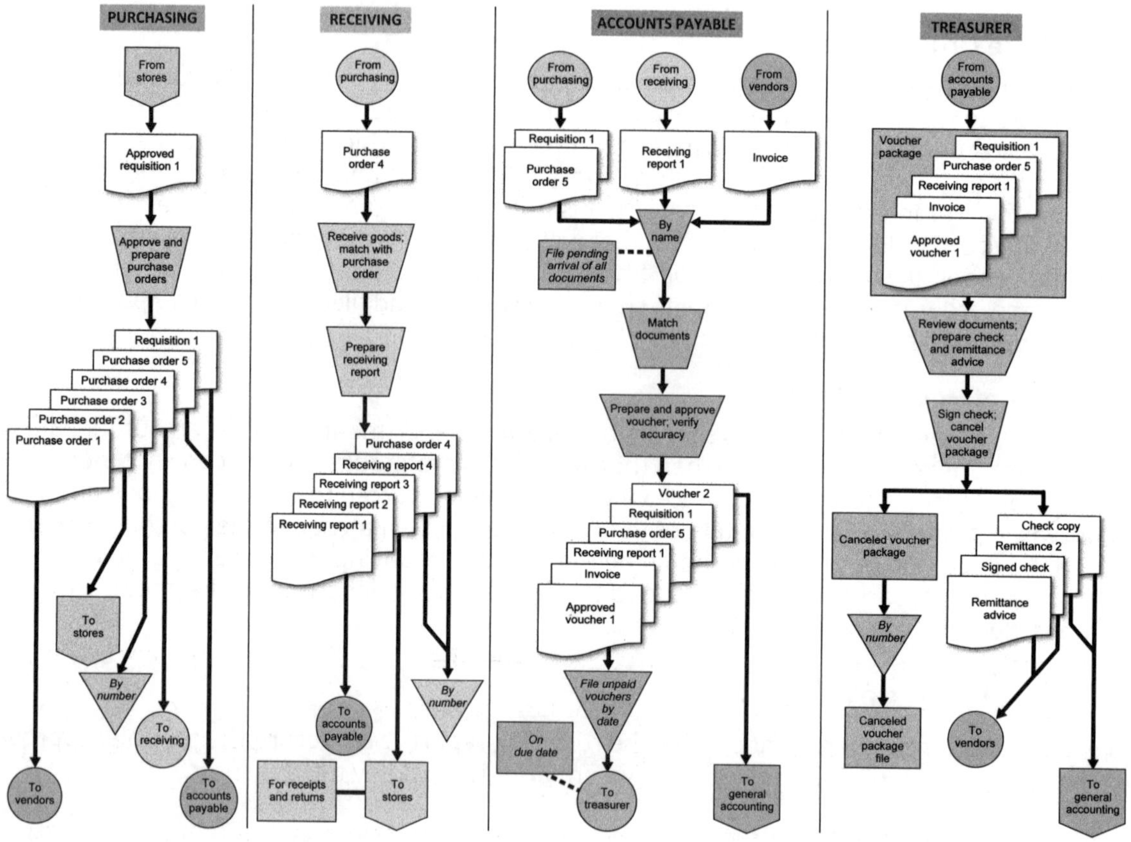

2 Performing Specific Procedures to Obtain Evidence: The Expenditure Cycle

2.1 Auditing Accounts Payable

Pass Key

For accounts payable, the completeness and accuracy assertions are generally more relevant than the existence and rights and obligations assertions, because the risk of understatement is greater than the risk of overstatement.

- **Completeness:** The auditor should perform the following procedures to ensure completeness of accounts payable:
  1. Agree the accounts payable listing to the general ledger.
  2. Obtain a sample of vendor statements and agree to the vendor accounts.
  3. Perform a search for unrecorded liabilities.
     - —The auditor should select cash disbursements made subsequent to year-end and examine the supporting documentation (e.g., receiving reports, vendor invoices, etc.). The auditor looks for items that should have been recorded at the balance sheet date, but were not.
     - —Note that cash disbursements made subsequent to year-end may be identified by reviewing the cash disbursements journal, subsequent bank statements, or the voucher register.
     - —The auditor should also examine open vouchers, receiving reports, vendors' invoices, and statements received for a period after year-end as part of the search for unrecorded liabilities.
- **Valuation, Allocation, and Accuracy:** The auditor should perform the following procedures:
  1. Obtain the accounts payable listing, foot the listing, and agree the listing to the general ledger.
  2. Obtain a sample of vendor statements and agree the amounts to the vendor accounts.
  3. Review the results of accounts payable confirmations (see below).
- **Existence and Occurrence:** The auditor should vouch selected amounts from the accounts payable listing to the voucher packages. The auditor may also confirm accounts payable.
  - Accounts payable confirmations are not required because strong external evidence to support accounts payable is generally available. However, confirmations of accounts payable may be sent when internal control is weak, when there are disputed amounts, or when monthly vendor statements are not available. Typically, vendors with small or zero balances would be selected for confirmation. Note that although confirmations are generally used to test existence, the accounts payable confirmation is primarily a test of completeness that also provides evidence of existence.

- Accounts payable confirmations are similar to those used for accounts receivable. Accounts payable confirmations are positive and generally "blank" (i.e., they do not state a balance). The objective is to determine whether accounts payable are understated at the balance sheet date.
- The major limitation of accounts payable confirmations is that they may only be sent to vendors of record. If a material error were present in accounts payable, it would most likely involve unrecorded liabilities; therefore, no record would exist. Although accounts payable confirmations may have limitations, evidence of unrecorded liabilities eventually will surface when unpaid vendors stop delivering goods.

- **Rights and Obligations:** The auditor should review a sample of voucher packages for the presence of the purchase requisition, purchase order, receiving report, and vendor invoice to verify that the accounts payable are owed by the entity.

2.2 Auditing Purchase Transactions

The following substantive tests may also be performed as tests of controls or dual-purpose tests.

- **Completeness:** The auditor should trace a sample of vouchers to the purchase journal. The auditor should also account for the prenumbered sequencing of purchase orders, receiving reports, and vouchers.
- **Cutoff:** The auditor should compare dates on a sample of vouchers with the dates the transactions were recorded in the purchase journal. The auditor should also examine purchases before and after year-end to determine if they were recorded in the proper period.
- **Valuation, Allocation, and Accuracy:** The auditor should recompute the mathematical accuracy of a sample of vendor invoices.
- **Existence and Occurrence:** The auditor should test a sample of vouchers to confirm proper authorization and the presence of the receiving report.
- **Understandability and Classification:** The auditor should verify the account classification of a sample of purchases.

2.3 Auditing Presentation and Disclosure

- **Completeness:** The auditor should ensure that all required disclosures related to accounts payable and purchases have been included in the notes to the financial statements. Required disclosures include:
  - Payables by type (trade, officer/employee, affiliates) and term (short term and long term)
  - Purchase contracts and purchase commitments
  - Related party purchases and payables
  - Expenses by segment
- **Valuation, Allocation, and Accuracy:** The auditor should read the footnotes and other information related to accounts payable and purchases to determine whether the information is accurate and presented at the appropriate amounts.
- **Rights and Obligations, and Occurrence:** The auditor should compare disclosures to other audit evidence to ensure that all disclosed information related to accounts payable and purchases has occurred.

- **Understandability and Classification:** The auditor should read all accounts payable and purchase related disclosures to ensure that they are understandable. The auditor should determine whether material long-term payables or nontrade payables require separate disclosure.

Question 1	**MCQ-02314**

An auditor suspects that certain client employees are ordering merchandise for themselves over the Internet without recording the purchase or receipt of the merchandise. When vendors' invoices arrive, one of the employees approves the invoices for payment. After the invoices are paid, the employee destroys the invoices and the related vouchers. In gathering evidence regarding the fraud, the auditor most likely would select items for testing from the file of all:

a. Cash disbursements
b. Approved vouchers
c. Receiving reports
d. Vendors' invoices

Simulation

Materialty = 75,000
Performance materiality = 50,000
GL is tied to AP ⇒ 386,154

NOTES

MODULE

3 Cash Cycle

AUD 4

1 Fraud Risk Related to the Cash Cycle

Cash is an area with high fraud risk, especially when internal control is weak. Lapping and kiting are two common cash fraud schemes.

1.1 Lapping

The theft of cash is often concealed by failing to account for cash receipts. The most common of these methods is known as lapping. Lapping occurs when an employee withholds funds received by a customer for personal use and fails to apply these receipts of cash or checks to the customer's receivable balance. The unrecorded receipt is covered by applying a subsequent receipt to the previously unrecorded account.

Safeguards against lapping include the following:

- Independent comparison of recorded cash receipts with funds actually deposited.
- Separation of incoming receipts from subsidiary accounts receivable remittance advices.
- Comparison of the details of bank deposits and the details of remittance credits.
- Provision of timely statements.
- Confirmation of customer balances.

One of the best methods to guard against lapping is use of a "lock box" system. In this system, customers send their payments directly to the bank, which prevents company employees from having access to payments received. A statement is then sent by the bank to the company so the cash can be applied in the general ledger to the outstanding receivable balance.

1.2 Kiting

Kiting occurs when a check drawn on one bank is deposited in another bank and no record is made of the disbursement in the balance of the first bank until after year-end. Kiting may be used to cover a cash shortage or to pad a company's cash position. Kiting results in an intentional overstatement of cash in the financial statements as the cash is simultaneously reflected in two different bank accounts.

To detect kiting effectively, a bank transfer schedule should be prepared. For any bank-to-bank transfers that occur near year-end, the disbursement date on the check and in the ledger for the disbursing account should precede the receipt date noted by the bank and in the ledger for the receiving account.

To ensure that kiting has not occurred, evidence should exist that all deposits in transit and outstanding checks listed on the bank reconciliation at year-end cleared in the next period. This information can be confirmed by using a bank cutoff statement, which is discussed later.

2 Internal Controls Related to the Cash Cycle

Control procedures and tests of controls related to cash receipts and cash disbursements were covered previously in the discussions of the revenue cycle and the expenditure cycle.

Segregation of duties is a key control over cash. Proper segregation of duties demands that close consideration be given to check-writing authority. Separation of cash handling, record keeping, and reconciliation of bank statements should exist, as well as separation of petty cash activities. Good internal control for cash would also include the use of a voucher system for cash disbursements.

3 Performing Specific Procedures to Obtain Evidence: The Cash Cycle

3.1 Auditing the Cash Balance

- **Completeness, Valuation and Allocation, Existence:** The primary audit procedures performed to test the completeness, valuation and allocation, and existence of the ending cash balance are the bank confirmation and the audit of the year-end bank reconciliation.
  - **Bank Confirmation:** The standard bank confirmation should be sent to all banks with which the client has done business during the year, regardless of whether there is a year-end balance to confirm. This is done because the bank confirmation, in addition to verifying year-end balances, also provides evidence about actual loans, contingent liabilities, discounted notes, pledged collateral, and guarantee or security agreements. A sample bank confirmation is shown here.

STANDARD FORM TO CONFIRM ACCOUNT BALANCE INFORMATION WITH FINANCIAL INSTITUTIONS

ORIGINAL
To be mailed to accountant

CUSTOMER NAME

Financial Institution's Name and Address [ ] [ ]

We have provided to our accountants the following information as of the close of business on ________, 20____, regarding our deposit and loan balances. Please confirm the accuracy of the information, noting any exceptions to the information provided. If the balances have been left blank, please complete this form by furnishing the balance in the appropriate space below.* Although we do not request nor expect you to conduct a comprehensive, detailed search of your records, if during the process of completing this confirmation additional information about other deposit and loan accounts we may have with you comes to your attention, please include such information below. Please use the enclosed envelope to return the form directly to our accountants.

1. At the close of business on the date listed above, our records indicated the following deposit balance(s):

ACCOUNT NAME	ACCOUNT NO.	INTEREST RATE	BALANCE*

2. We were directly liable to the financial institution for loans at the close of business on the date listed above as follows:

ACCOUNT NO./ DESCRIPTION	BALANCE*	DATE DUE	INTEREST RATE	DATE THROUGH WHICH INTEREST IS PAID	DESCRIPTION OF COLLATERAL

(Customer's Authorized Signature) (Date)

The information presented above by the customer is in agreement with our records. Although we have not conducted a comprehensive, detailed search of our records, no other deposit or loan accounts have come to our attention except as noted below.

(Financial Institution Authorized Signature) (Date)

(Title)

EXCEPTIONS AND/OR COMMENTS

Please return this form directly to our accountants: [ ] [ ]

* Ordinarily, balances are intentionally left blank if they are not available at the time the form is prepared.

Approved 1990 by American Bankers Association, American Institute of Certified Public Accountants, and Bank Administration Institute. Additional forms available from: AICPA – Order Department, P.O. Box 1003, NY, NY 10108-1003 D 451 5951

- **Bank Reconciliation:** The year-end bank reconciliation for every account should be tested by:
  1. Footing the bank reconciliation and the list of outstanding checks.
  2. Agreeing the balance per the books on the year-end bank reconciliation to the general ledger.
  3. Agreeing the balance per the bank on the year-end bank reconciliation to the balance per the bank confirmation.
  4. Agreeing deposits in transit and outstanding checks to the cutoff bank statement. The cutoff bank statement is obtained by the auditor from the bank and covers the first 10 to 15 days of the period after year-end. Reconciling items should generally clear during the 10- to 15-day period. Any item that does not clear should be investigated by the auditor and resolved with the client if necessary.

3.2 Auditing Cash Receipts and Cash Disbursements

The following tests of details are generally performed as dual-purpose tests.

- **Completeness:** For cash receipts, the auditor should trace a sample of remittance advices to the cash receipts journal and deposit slips. For cash disbursements, the auditor should trace a sample of canceled checks to the cash disbursements journal.
- **Cutoff:** The auditor should verify the cutoff of cash receipts and cash disbursements shortly before and after year-end for recording in the proper period. The auditor should also compare the dates for recording a sample of cash receipts with the dates the cash was deposited in the bank, and the dates for recording a sample of checks with the dates the checks cleared the bank, noting any significant delays.
- **Valuation, Allocation, and Accuracy:** For cash receipts, from a sample of daily deposits, the auditor should foot the remittance advices and entries on the deposit slip and agree to the cash receipts journal and bank statement. For cash disbursements, from a sample of voucher packages, the auditor should agree the purchase order, receiving report, invoice, cancelled check, and disbursement journal.
- **Existence and Occurrence:** For cash receipts, the auditor should vouch a sample of entries in the cash receipts journal to remittance advices, deposit slips, and the bank statement. For cash disbursements, the auditor should vouch a sample of entries from the cash disbursements journal to canceled checks, the voucher package, and the bank statement.
- **Understandability and Classification:** The auditor should examine a sample of remittance advices and canceled checks for recording in the proper account.

3.3 Auditing Presentation and Disclosure

- **Completeness:** The auditor should ensure that all required disclosures related to cash have been included in the notes to the financial statements. Required disclosures related to cash include:
  - Policy defining cash and cash equivalents.
  - Restrictions on cash, including sinking fund requirements.
  - Compensating balance requirements.

- **Valuation, Allocation, and Accuracy:** The auditor should read the footnotes and other information related to cash to determine whether the information is accurate and presented at the appropriate amounts.
- **Rights and Obligations, and Occurrence:** The auditor should compare disclosures to other audit evidence to ensure that all disclosed information related to cash has occurred.
- **Understandability and Classification:** The auditor should read all cash-related disclosures to ensure that they are understandable.

Question 1 **MCQ-02574**

On receiving a client's bank cutoff statement, an auditor most likely would trace:

a. Prior-year checks listed in the cutoff statement to the year-end outstanding checklist.

b. Deposits in transit listed in the cutoff statement to the year-end bank reconciliation.

c. Checks dated after year-end listed in the cutoff statement to the year-end outstanding checklist.

d. Deposits recorded in the cash receipts journal after year-end to the cutoff statement.

MODULE

4 Inventory Cycle

1 Internal Controls Related to the Inventory Cycle

Internal control over inventory purchases and sales was covered in the sections on the revenue cycle and the expenditure cycle. For inventory held by the entity, proper internal control includes adequate safeguarding of inventory and proper segregation of duties.

The following duties should be segregated:

1. **Purchasing**
   Serially numbered, properly approved purchase orders should be prepared and issued to the accounting and receiving departments.
2. **Receiving**
   The receiving department is solely responsible for the receipt of goods. This department is responsible for verification of quantities received, detection of damaged goods, preparation of a receiving report, and delivery of goods received to the warehouse department. The receiving department should receive a copy of the purchase order that does not indicate the quantity ordered so the receiving department is forced to count the goods upon arrival.
3. **Warehouse**
   The warehouse department acts as custodian for the verified quantity of goods received.
4. **Shipping**
   The shipping department is responsible for shipment of goods after authorization (in the form of an approved sales order from the credit department).

2 Performing Specific Procedures to Obtain Evidence: The Inventory Cycle

2.1 Auditing the Inventory Balance

The observation of the beginning and ending physical inventory counts is a required generally accepted auditing procedure. Attendance by the auditor at the physical inventory count involves the following dual-purpose tests:

1. evaluating management's instructions and procedures for the inventory count;
2. observing the performance of management's count procedures;
3. inspecting the inventory to ascertain its existence and condition; and
4. performing test counts.

An auditor who is not present to observe the physical inventory must use alternative procedures to justify any opinion expressed. This is acceptable when it is impractical or impossible to observe physical inventory, or when inventories are not material.

If the company maintains a well-kept perpetual inventory system and performs physical cycle counts throughout the year to ensure accuracy, the auditor may observe the inventory before or after year-end if necessary. If inventory counting is done at a date other than the date of the financial statements, the auditor should obtain evidence about whether changes in inventory between the count date and the financial statement date are recorded properly. If the assessed level of control risk is high, the observation procedures should be performed at year-end.

The auditor should observe the physical inventory count of goods held off-site in public warehouses or on consignment if the inventory held therein is significant; otherwise, confirmation of such inventory is sufficient.

Pass Key

Candidates sometimes believe that "inventory observation" implies that the auditor counts the client's inventory. This is not the case—the client counts the inventory, and the auditor simply observes. The auditor may make test counts of certain items, but generally the auditor would not count the client's entire inventory.

Auditing the Inventory Cycle

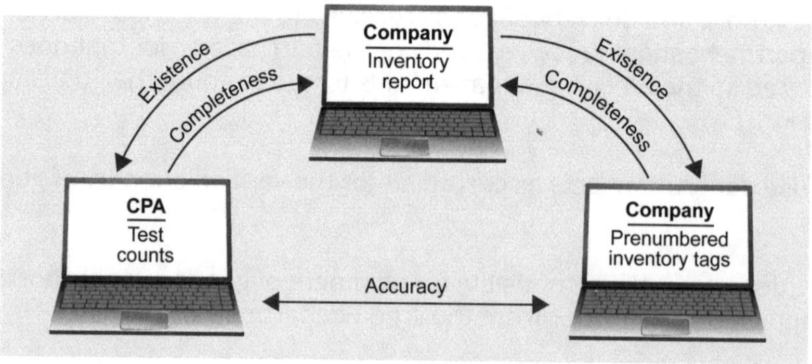

- **Completeness:** In conjunction with the inventory observation, the auditor should test the physical inventory report by tracing test counts to the report, thereby verifying its completeness. The auditor should also select from a sample of prenumbered inventory tags and trace to the physical inventory report sheets to test their completeness.
- **Valuation, Allocation, and Accuracy:** The auditor should perform the following procedures:
  1. Test the mathematical accuracy of the inventory report and reconcile it to the general ledger inventory accounts.
  2. Inquire about obsolete or damaged goods, scan the perpetual records for slow-moving items, and be alert during the inventory observation for damaged goods or signs of obsolescence.
  3. Examine vendor invoices, review direct labor rates, test the computation of standard overhead rates, and examine standard cost variance analyses. These prices and rates can then be applied to a sample of inventory items to determine whether the inventory is valued appropriately.

- **Existence and Occurrence:** The primary purpose of the observation of the client's inventory count is to establish the existence of inventory. During the observation, the auditor should verify the existence of a sample of items in the physical inventory report by locating and performing test counts of the items. The auditor should also test the existence of the items on the client's inventory report sheets by vouching a sample of items from the inventory report sheet to the corresponding prenumbered inventory tags.
- **Rights and Obligations:** The auditor should ascertain that consigned inventory on hand is excluded from the physical inventory count, whereas consigned goods in the hands of consignees are included in inventory balances. The auditor should also confirm that any inventory held off-site is properly accounted for at year-end. In addition, inventory in transit at year-end should be properly accounted for based on shipping terms.

2.2 Auditing Inventory Transactions

Inventory sales and purchases should be audited as part of the audits of the revenue cycle and the expenditure cycle, as described previously.

2.3 Auditing Presentation and Disclosure

- **Completeness:** The auditor should ensure that all required disclosures related to inventory have been included in the notes to the financial statements. Inventory disclosures include:
  - Cost method (LIFO, FIFO, weighted average) and valuation method (net realizable value or lower of cost or market).
  - Raw materials, work-in-process, and finished goods inventory balances.
  - Consigned inventory.
  - Pledged or assigned inventory.
  - Significant losses from inventory write-downs or purchase commitments.
  - Warranty obligations.
- **Valuation, Allocation, and Accuracy:** The auditor should read the footnotes and other information related to inventory to determine whether the information is accurate and presented at the appropriate amounts.
- **Rights and Obligations, and Occurrence:** The auditor should determine that inventory-related obligations have been properly disclosed by inquiring of management and reviewing loan agreements and minutes for evidence that inventory has been pledged or assigned. The auditor should also inquire about warranty obligations. The auditor should compare disclosures to other audit evidence to ensure that all disclosed information related to inventory has occurred.
- **Understandability and Classification:** The auditor should read all inventory-related disclosures to ensure that they are understandable. The auditor should review inventory records for proper classification between raw materials, work in process, and finished goods.

Question 1 **MCQ-02443**

To gain assurance that all inventory items in a client's inventory listing schedule are valid, an auditor most likely would trace:

- **a.** Inventory tags noted during the auditor's observation to items listed in the inventory-listing schedule.
- **b.** Inventory tags noted during the auditor's observation to items listed in receiving reports and vendors' invoices.
- **c.** Items listed in the inventory-listing schedule to inventory tags and the auditor's recorded count sheets.
- **d.** Items listed in receiving reports and vendors' invoices to the inventory-listing schedule.

MODULE

5 Investment Cycle

AUD 4

1 Internal Controls Related to the Investment Cycle

Internal control over investments requires strong segregation of the following duties:

- **Authorization of Purchase or Sale of Investments:** Ideally, the board of directors should authorize the purchase or sale of investments.
- **Custody of Investments:** An independent, third-party custodian is recommended but, at minimum, custody should take the form of joint control by two company officials with the investments kept in a safe-deposit box. If held by the company, the investments should be periodically counted and reconciled with the investment subsidiary ledger by a party not associated with the investments.
- **Record Keeping:** A separate party from those mentioned above must keep detailed records of the investments.

Internal controls should also exist regarding processing and fair value measurement. The initial classification of investments as trading, available-for-sale, or held to maturity significantly impacts subsequent reporting. Controls surrounding fair value estimates, whether inside the company or outside the company (should a third party be used to assess fair value), also must be understood.

2 Performing Specific Procedures to Obtain Evidence: The Investment Cycle

Sufficient audit evidence must be obtained by the auditor for investments which may be in the form of debt and equity investments, derivative investments, and loan and advance accounts.

Substantive tests of details related to the investment cycle generally focus on the ending balance in the investment accounts and presentation and disclosure. Analytical procedures are used to test the reasonableness of related gains and losses and investment income.

2.1 Auditing the Investment Balance

- **Completeness:** The auditor should obtain evidence of completeness of the ending investment balance through the following procedures:

  1. If the entity has a high volume of material investment transactions, the auditor should search for unrecorded purchases of securities by examining transactions for a few days after year-end.

     One of the characteristics of derivatives is that they may involve only a commitment to perform under a contract and not an initial exchange of tangible consideration. Therefore, auditors designing tests related to the completeness assertion should not focus exclusively on evidence relating to cash receipts and disbursements.

  2. The auditor should confirm securities held by the third-party custodian or count securities on hand to determine that all securities have been recorded, although these are primarily tests of existence.

3. The auditor should request information from the counterparty to the derivative or the holder of a security to determine whether any side agreements or agreements to repurchase securities exist. Even if the entity states that no derivatives exist with a frequently used counterparty or holder, the auditor may want to confirm that this information is true.

4. If there is a difference between the expectation of interest earned, determined from the underlying agreement, and actual interest earned, this may indicate the existence of an interest rate swap agreement.

- **Valuation and Allocation:** The auditor should perform the following procedures:

  1. Obtain and foot a listing of investments by category (trading, available for sale, held-to-maturity, derivative, and equity method) and agree the totals to the general ledger.

  2. Review the schedule of investment activity and obtain evidence of any additions and subtractions that occurred during the year.

  3. Obtain evidence corroborating the quoted year-end fair value by comparing assigned values to prices published by various sources (exchanges registered with the SEC or other reliable sources of financial information) or obtained from a third party, such as an independent broker-dealer or appraiser.

  4. Recalculate the ending values of investments not reported at fair value. Investments classified as held-to-maturity should be valued at amortized cost at year-end. Investments in another entity where significant influence exists and ownership is between 20 percent and 50 percent should be accounted for using the equity method.

  5. Determine whether there has been any permanent impairment in the value of individual securities.

  6. Assess the reasonableness and appropriateness of assumptions, market variables, and valuation models, and of any decline in fair value.

- **Existence:** The two primary tests of existence of investments are confirmations of securities held by third parties and examination of securities on hand. A third test of existence is analytical procedures over interest earned.

  1. Confirmations should be requested from the custodian for securities that are in the possession of third parties. It is also advisable to send confirmations to the broker-dealer and to counterparties concerning any unsettled transactions.

  2. An examination of the securities on hand should be made to coincide with the examinations of other liquid assets, such as cash. This procedure prevents the concealment of theft by making it impossible for one asset to serve as a substitute for another (e.g., to conceal a stolen asset). The face of the instrument should be examined to determine if ownership is correctly recorded. The auditor should record the details of the security count on a worksheet, which should also include an acknowledgement by the client that the securities were returned intact. If a safe-deposit box is used, the securities should be counted on the balance sheet date, or the bank should be requested to seal the box until the count is later completed.

  3. There is an expectation that interest earned on an investment in a debt security will agree to the effective interest rate when the security was purchased. The auditor may perform analytical procedures to obtain evidence that the interest earned does not materially differ from the expectation as evidence of existence of the security.

- **Rights and Obligations:** The confirmation of securities and the count of securities on hand provide evidence of the entity's ownership of investments. Additionally, the auditor may examine broker's advices for a sample of securities purchased during the year to verify the entity's ownership.

2.2 Auditing Investment Transactions

- **Completeness:** The auditor should perform analytical procedures testing the reasonableness of dividend and interest income to determine that all investment income has been recorded.
- **Cutoff:** A cutoff review should be performed to ensure that purchases, sales, and investment income were recorded in the proper period.
- **Valuation, Allocation, and Accuracy:** Independent calculations should be made to determine the validity of recorded gains or losses from security sales and of discount and premium amortization. In addition, a recalculation should be made to determine the accuracy of recorded dividend and interest income. Investment income from dividends may be recalculated by comparing recorded income with dividend records produced by investment advisory services such as Moody's.
- **Existence and Occurrence:** The analytical procedures performed to test the reasonableness of dividend and interest income provide evidence of the existence of investment income.
- **Understandability and Classification:** The auditor should examine a sample of investment transactions to determine that the transactions were recorded in the proper accounts. For example, unrealized gains and losses on available-for-sale securities should be recorded in other comprehensive income, and unrealized gains and losses on trading securities should be recorded in earnings.

2.3 Auditing Presentation and Disclosure

- **Completeness:** The auditor should ensure that all required disclosures related to investments have been included in the notes to the financial statements. Specifically, the auditor should determine whether all required marketable security and derivative disclosures have been made.
- **Valuation, Allocation, and Accuracy:** The auditor should read the footnotes and other information related to investments to determine whether the information is accurate and presented at the appropriate amounts.
- **Rights and Obligations, and Occurrence:** The auditor should inquire of management and review loan agreements, minutes, and other documents to determine whether investments have been pledged as collateral. The auditor should compare disclosures to other audit evidence to ensure that all disclosed information related to investments has occurred.
- **Understandability and Classification:** The auditor should read required disclosures for understandability, and review and evaluate the methods used to account for, classify, and value securities.

3 Auditing Particular Types of Investments

3.1 Marketable Securities

Trading and available-for-sale securities over which the investor has no significant influence should be carried at fair value, and classification of Level 1, 2, or 3 should be disclosed in the footnotes. Held-to-maturity debt securities should be carried at amortized cost.

Trading securities are always reported as current assets with unrealized gains and losses reported in net income. Available-for-sale securities and held-to-maturity securities are reported as current or long-term based on management's intent to hold versus sell. Unrealized gains and losses on available-for-sale securities are reported in other comprehensive income.

The auditor should inquire of management and obtain written representation concerning management's intent and ability with respect to holding versus selling securities in the near term.

3.2 Derivatives

An entity may invest in derivatives to hedge against risks, such as the risk associated with fluctuating prices. Under these circumstances, generally accepted accounting principles specify that, in order to qualify for hedge treatment, the entity must demonstrate and disclose a number of transaction features, including risk exposure. The auditor would therefore need to examine the contracts to evaluate the character of the hedge and the degree to which losses should be recognized in the determination of income, as well as to determine the appropriate character of any disclosures.

3.2.1 Considerations Regarding Hedging Activities

If management accounts for a derivative as a hedge, the auditor must ensure that the following has occurred:

- The derivative was designated as a hedge at its inception by management.
- Management has documented the hedging relationship, risk management objective, and strategy for undertaking the hedge.
- Management has established an expectation that the hedge will be effective in achieving the hedging strategy and is periodically assessing its effectiveness.

The auditor also should gather audit evidence supporting the adjustment in the carrying amount of the hedged items for the change in the hedged item's fair value that is attributable to the hedged risk.

3.2.2 Cash Flow Hedge of a Forecasted Transaction

The auditor must assess management's determination that the forecasted transaction is probable of occurring. The transaction's probability should be supported by observable facts and the attendant circumstances, such as the following:

- The frequency of similar past transactions.
- The financial and operational ability of the entity to carry out the transaction.
- The extent of loss that could result if the transaction does not occur.
- The likelihood that transactions with substantially different characteristics might be used to achieve the same business purpose.

3.3 Investments in Securities When Valuations Are Based on the Investee's Financial Results

When investments in securities are valued based on an investee's financial statements, such as equity method investments, the auditor should perform the following procedures to obtain sufficient appropriate audit evidence in support of the investee's financial results:

1. Obtain and read the financial statements and audit report of the investee.
2. If the financial statements are not audited or the audit report is not satisfactory, request that the entity arrange with the investee to have the financial statements audited.
3. If the carrying amount of the investment reflects factors that are not recognized in the investee's financial statements or fair values that are materially different from the investee's carrying amounts, obtain sufficient appropriate evidence in support of such amounts.
4. If the difference between the financial statement periods of the entity and the investee could have a material effect on the entity's financial statements, determine whether management has considered the lack of comparability and determine the effect, if any, on the auditor's report.

For equity method investments, the auditor should inquire of management regarding the entity's ability to exercise significant influence over investments to determine whether investments have been properly classified.

4 Investments Measured at Fair Value

4.1 Measuring Fair Value

Certain financial assets and liabilities, such as marketable securities and derivatives, are presented or disclosed at fair value in the financial statements.

Fair value is defined as the amount at which an asset could be sold (or the amount at which a liability could be settled) in a current transaction between willing parties at the measurement date. A three-level hierarchy is used to measure fair value.

- **Level 1:** Observable quoted prices in active markets for identical assets or liabilities.

  Quoted prices from national exchanges or over-the-counter markets are available from national publications and the exchanges, and generally are considered to provide sufficient evidence of the fair value of the derivatives and securities. If a quoted market price is available, this should be the method used to determine the fair value of the investment.

- **Level 2:** Observable inputs other than quoted market prices for identical assets or liabilities.

  When quoted prices for identical assets or liabilities are not available, the next consideration is whether there are other directly or indirectly observable inputs. The most common of these observable inputs are quoted prices for similar assets or liabilities in active markets and quoted prices for identical or similar assets in markets that are not active.

- **Level 3:** Unobservable inputs using estimates and valuation methods, such as discounted cash flow, determined based on management's judgments.

  If quoted prices are not available, estimates of fair value may be available from broker-dealers or other third-party sources based on proprietary valuation models or from the entity based on an internal valuation model. The auditor should ensure that the pricing source does not have a relationship that would impair objectivity in determining fair value. The auditor should also consider obtaining further estimates if subjective information was used in the valuation process.

Fair value measurements may arise from both the initial recording of a transaction and later changes in value. Changes in fair value measurement may be treated in different ways under GAAP (e.g., included in net income, reflected in other comprehensive income and equity, etc.).

4.2 Management's Responsibility

Management is responsible for making fair value measurements and disclosures in accordance with GAAP.

When a Level 3 valuation is used to estimate fair value, an appropriate valuation method should be used. The method should incorporate assumptions that a market participant would use. These assumptions must be identified and supported in the fair value disclosures included in the financial statements.

4.3 Auditor's Responsibilities

The auditor should obtain sufficient appropriate audit evidence to provide reasonable assurance that fair value measurements and disclosures are in conformity with GAAP. The auditor should:

- Understand the entity's process for determining fair value measurements and disclosures.
- Understand relevant controls.
- Assess the risk of material misstatement of fair value measurements.
- Evaluate whether the method used is in conformity with GAAP.
- Consider the need for a specialist.
- Test fair value measurements and disclosures (covered further below).
- Evaluate whether fair value disclosures are in conformity with GAAP.
- Evaluate the sufficiency, competency, and consistency of evidence obtained with respect to fair value measurements and disclosures.
- Obtain relevant management representations (e.g., relating to the reasonableness of significant assumptions, management's intent and ability to carry out planned courses of action, completeness and adequacy of disclosure, the effect of subsequent events, etc.).
- Communicate relevant matters to those charged with governance (e.g., matters related to particularly sensitive fair value estimates).

The auditor bases his or her evaluation on information available at the time of the audit, and is not responsible for predicting future conditions that, if known at the time of the audit, might have affected fair value measurements and disclosures.

4.4 Testing Fair Value Measurements and Disclosures

In testing an entity's fair value measurements and disclosures, the auditor may:

- Verify quoted market prices.
- Determine whether management's significant assumptions provide a reasonable basis for fair value measurements.
- Consider management's intent and ability to carry out courses of action that may affect fair values.
- Determine whether modifications made to observable information reflect assumptions that market participants would use when pricing the instrument.
- Evaluate whether the valuation model is appropriate given the entity's circumstances.
- Test the underlying data for accuracy, completeness, relevancy, and consistency.
- Develop independent fair value estimates for corroborative purposes.
- Review subsequent events and transactions (occurring before the date of the auditor's report) for evidence regarding fair value measurements at the balance sheet date.
- Consider the use of a specialist. If a specialist is used, the auditor must understand the methods used to determine fair values.

4.5 Using Pricing Information From Third Parties as Evidence

Auditors may obtain evidence about the fair value of instruments by obtaining pricing information from organizations that routinely provide uniform pricing information to users ("pricing services") or broker-dealers.

4.5.1 Pricing Services

The reliability of pricing information depends on the nature and source of the evidence and the circumstances under which it is obtained. Reliability of pricing services is affected by the experience and expertise of the pricing service, methodology used, and whether the pricing service has a relationship with the entity.

Relevance of pricing information refers to its relationship with the assertion or the objective of the control being tested. Relevance of pricing information is affected by the basis of fair value measurement (i.e., based on identical, similar, or no recent transactions). When the fair value measurement is based on an identical instrument, this provides more persuasive evidence than if the instrument has no recent transactions and is based on assumptions of the pricing service.

When using information from multiple pricing services, less information is needed about the particular methods and inputs used by the individual pricing services.

4.5.2 Broker-Dealers

When a fair value measurement is based on a quote from a broker or dealer, the relevance and reliability is based on whether the broker or dealer is a market maker for similar instruments (i.e., creates a market to help facilitate buying or selling of instrument); whether the broker or dealer has a relationship with the entity; whether the quote is binding on the broker or dealer; and whether there are limitations in the quote.

4.6 Impairment Indications

Regardless of the valuation method used, an impairment loss resulting from a decline in fair value that is other than temporary may need to be recorded. If an impairment loss has been recorded, the auditor should evaluate management's basis for the decision. If an impairment loss has not been recorded the auditor should consider whether the following situations exist that could indicate the need for an impairment loss:

- Fair value is significantly below cost and:
  - The decline is attributable to adverse conditions specifically related to the security or to specific conditions in an industry or in a geographic area.
  - The decline has existed for an extended period of time.
  - Management does not possess both the intent and the ability to hold the security for a period of time sufficient to allow for any anticipated recovery in fair value.
- The security has been downgraded by a rating agency.
- The financial condition of the issuer has deteriorated.
- Dividends have been reduced or eliminated, or scheduled interest payments have not been made.
- The entity recorded losses from the security subsequent to the end of the reporting period.

Question 1 **MCQ-02500**

Which of the following would an auditor *least* likely consider with respect to fair values?

a. Segregation of duties between those committing the entity to certain transactions and those responsible for undertaking the valuations related to those transactions.

b. The effect on fair value measurement and disclosures of information available subsequent to the audit.

c. The role of information technology in determining fair value measurements and disclosures.

d. Whether the valuation methods used are appropriate in relation to the industry in which the entity operates.

MODULE

6 Other Transaction Cycles

AUD 4

1 Property, Plant, and Equipment Cycle

Property, plant, and equipment (PP&E) includes all tangible assets with service lives greater than one year that are used in the operation of a business and are not acquired for resale. The major transactions associated with these assets are purchases, repairs and maintenance, depreciation, disposal, and leasing.

1.1 Internal Controls Related to the PP&E Cycle

The internal control for property, plant, and equipment includes the controls in both the revenue and expenditure cycles as well as the following special controls:

- **Acquisition:** A special requisition form is generated for acquisitions. This form includes a description, reason for acquisition, amount to be charged, and probable cost, and it should be approved by top management. Acquisitions are tied to the capital budget, which the board of directors usually approves. Variances from this budget should be promptly investigated. The board of directors should also approve acquisitions of assets over a certain amount, regardless of whether these assets are purchased or constructed.

  The auditor should ascertain that company policy was followed and that fixed asset purchases were properly authorized.

- **Subsidiary Ledgers:** Detailed information concerning each asset is kept in the subsidiary ledger. Usually information including the asset's description, identification number, location, acquisition date, cost, depreciation method, and amount of depreciation can be found in this ledger.

- **Physical Security:** Fixed assets should have identification plates. The serial number on the plate should be listed in the control account. Physical controls to safeguard assets from theft, destruction, or unauthorized disposition should also be in place, including periodic physical inspection of plant and equipment.

  Comparison of the serial number on the identification plate to that listed in the control account should be made. The auditor should also determine whether there are appropriate controls in place to safeguard fixed assets and prevent theft or destruction.

- **Written Policies:** Written depreciation policies and records should be maintained. Specific capitalization policies are also necessary to prevent misstatement of revenues and expenses.

- **Disposition:** Retirements of assets should be documented on a sequentially numbered work order containing evidence of proper authorization and the reason for retirement. This asset retirement order form is the basis for recording any cash received and for removing the asset and its accumulated depreciation from the subsidiary ledger. There should be a proper segregation of duties between authorization and custody (e.g., those who authorize a disposal should not be permitted to actually dispose of the asset).

1.2 Performing Specific Procedures to Obtain Audit Evidence: Property, Plant, and Equipment

1.2.1 Auditing the Property, Plant, and Equipment Balance

- **Completeness:** The auditor should obtain and foot the fixed asset schedule and agree the total to the general ledger, obtain and foot a schedule of additions and dispositions of fixed assets and agree amounts to the fixed asset schedule, and select a sample of actual fixed assets and trace to the fixed asset subsidiary ledger.
- **Valuation and Allocation:** The auditor should recalculate accumulated depreciation for reasonableness. The auditor should also evaluate fixed assets for impairment by examining the entity's documented impairment analysis, identifying circumstances that could indicate that the book value of fixed assets is not recoverable, and reperforming the entity's impairment analysis to determine whether recorded impairment losses are reasonable. If the entity uses IFRS, the auditor should verify the reasonableness of any fixed asset revaluations.
- **Existence:** The auditor should vouch additions to the fixed asset accounts by examining internal documents (such as the asset requisition form), by examining external evidence (such as invoices), and by inspecting the actual asset. The auditor should also consider selecting older fixed assets from the subsidiary ledgers and then locating those assets, as a means of testing for unrecorded retirements.
- **Rights and Obligations:** The auditor should examine invoices, deeds, and title documents to confirm ownership of fixed assets.

1.2.2 Auditing Property, Plant, and Equipment Transactions

The following tests of details can be performed as dual-purpose tests.

- **Completeness:** The auditor should trace a sample of fixed asset purchase requisitions to receiving reports and the fixed asset subsidiary ledger. The auditor should also review the related repair and maintenance expense accounts to test for completeness of asset additions. The auditor is looking for items recorded as repairs that should have been capitalized. The auditor also should review lease and rental agreements to ensure that finance leases are properly recorded and that operating leases are excluded.

Pass Key

The examiners sometimes try to trick candidates with questions about the repairs and maintenance account. Keep in mind that the auditor often reviews this account in order to locate items that should have been capitalized.

- **Cutoff:** The auditor should review fixed asset purchases and dispositions from shortly before and after year-end for recording in the proper period.
- **Valuation, Allocation, and Accuracy:** Depreciation expense should be recalculated for reasonableness and conformity with GAAP. Gains and losses and the removal of accumulated depreciation for fixed assets sold or retired should be tested for reasonableness.
- **Existence and Occurrence:** The auditor should vouch a sample of purchases to the receiving report and vendor invoice and a sample of dispositions to the asset retirement form and other supporting documentation.

- **Understandability and Classification:** The auditor should examine a sample of significant charges to repairs and maintenance expense for items that should have been capitalized (also a completeness test) and should review lease transactions for proper classification as operating or finance.

1.2.3 Auditing Presentation and Disclosure

- **Completeness:** The auditor should ensure that all required disclosures related to fixed assets have been included in the notes to the financial statements. Required disclosures include:
  - Depreciation methods and useful lives.
  - Depreciation expense for the period.
  - Balance of each class of capital assets by nature or function.
  - Accumulated depreciation allowances by class or in total.
  - Liens and mortgages.
  - Finance and operating lease information.
- **Valuation, Allocation, and Accuracy:** The auditor should read the footnotes and other information related to fixed assets to determine whether the information is accurate and presented at the appropriate amounts.
- **Rights and Obligations, and Occurrence:** The auditor should inquire of management and review loan agreements, minutes, and other documents to determine whether fixed assets have been pledged as collateral. The auditor should compare disclosures with other audit evidence to ensure that all disclosed information related to fixed assets has occurred.
- **Understandability and Classification:** The auditor should also read required disclosures for understandability.

Question 1 **MCQ-02447**

In performing a search for unrecorded retirements of fixed assets, an auditor most likely would:

a. Inspect the property ledger and the insurance and tax records, and then tour the client's facilities.

b. Tour the client's facilities, and then inspect the property ledger and the insurance and tax records.

c. Analyze the repair and maintenance account, and then tour the client's facilities.

d. Tour the client's facilities, and then analyze the repair and maintenance account.

Vouch - existence

2 Payroll and Personnel Cycle

2.1 Internal Controls Related to the Payroll and Personnel Cycle

The most significant payroll and personnel cycle risks are the creation of fictitious employees and the falsification of hours worked.

2.1.1 Service Organizations

Many entities use service organizations to process payroll transactions. The service organization's services are considered to be part of a user entity's information system when those services affect the initiation, execution, processing, or reporting of the user company's transactions. In such cases, the controls placed in operation by the service organization are considered to be part of the user organization's information system.

2.1.2 Segregation of Duties

Even when a service organization is used, there should be a proper segregation of duties, as follows:

- **Authorization to Employ and Pay:** It is the function of the human resources department to hire new employees (on the basis of requisitions from user departments) and to maintain the personnel records containing hire date, department, salary, and position.
- **Supervision:** All pay base data (hours, absences, time off, etc.) should be approved by an employee's immediate supervisor.
- **Timekeeping and Cost Accounting:** Data on which pay is based, such as hours worked or jobs completed, should be accumulated independent of any other function.

  Where there are employees who are paid by the hour, it is advisable to use time clocks. Each department supervisor should compare the job time tickets with employee clock cards that have been signed by the employee. Salaried employees do not usually complete time sheets, although they may be required to submit reports for vacation, sick leave, and overtime.
- **Payroll Check Preparation:** The payroll department computes salary based on information received; for example, total hours worked for hourly employees. If a service organization is not used, this department is responsible for issuing the unsigned payroll checks that are later signed by the treasurer or the CFO. If a check signature plate is used to sign the payroll checks, the treasurer or CFO should supervise this process. There should be controls over access to blank checks and check signature plates.

Pass Key

Remember that the payroll department is a record-keeping department, not a custodial department. Although employees in this department compute salaries, create the payroll register, and prepare unsigned checks, they should have neither the authority to initiate changes in hours or rates, nor the ability to sign checks.

- **Check Distribution:** In many companies, payroll checks are deposited directly into employees' bank accounts. If paychecks are manually distributed, then the payroll checks should be distributed by a person who has no other payroll function. In larger corporations, this individual is often referred to as the paymaster.

Employees should be required to show some form of identification before receiving their paychecks. Unclaimed payroll checks should be investigated by an independent party.

The internal auditing department periodically compares the personnel files with the payroll files. This is to help ensure that only authorized payments have been made in the proper amounts to appropriate personnel.

2.1.3 Internal Control Evaluation

The auditor should evaluate whether internal controls provide reasonable assurance that only valid employees are being paid, that payment is for the actual hours worked, and that the correct rate of pay is used. The following procedures should be performed:

- Observe segregation of duties between human resource responsibilities and payroll distribution.
- Compare the personnel records for each department with the actual time cards and the employees actually working in each department.
- Observe payroll distribution on an unannounced basis to ensure that all personnel being paid are actually employed by the company.
- Observe the use of time clocks and investigate time cards not used.
- Test transfers and underlying employee authorizations if direct deposit is used.
- Test general and application controls to ensure that payroll transactions are valid, properly authorized, and completely and accurately recorded. For example, hours worked should be compared to predetermined minimums and maximums (a range test), or to prior periods (a reasonableness test).
- Test to ensure that only employees existing in the computer data files are accepted when entered.

2.2 Performing Specific Procedures to Obtain Evidence: The Payroll and Personnel Cycle

2.2.1 Auditing the Payroll Accrual

When internal control over payroll is effective, the auditor generally focuses substantive procedures on analytical procedures and the recalculation of payroll accruals (valuation assertion). Tests related to completeness, existence, and rights and obligations are generally performed only when the entity's internal control over payroll cannot be relied upon.

- **Completeness:** The auditor should test the completeness of the payroll accrual when performing the search for unrecorded liabilities.
- **Valuation and Allocation:** The auditor should recalculate any year-end payroll accrual and compare the calculated amount to the reported accrual.
- **Existence:** The auditor should vouch amounts from the client's calculation of the payroll accrual to supporting documentation.
- **Rights and Obligations:** The auditor should examine supporting documentation to verify that the payroll accrual is an obligation of the entity.

2.2.2 Auditing Payroll Transactions

The following tests of details can be performed as dual-purpose tests.

- **Completeness:** The auditor should trace a sample of time cards to the payroll register.
- **Cutoff:** The auditor should examine a sample of time cards from before and after year-end and compare with the payroll report to determine whether the transactions were recorded in the proper period.

- **Valuation, Allocation, and Accuracy:** The auditor should test the accuracy and valuation of payroll expense by performing the following procedures:
  1. Compare total recorded payroll with total payroll checks issued.
  2. Test extensions and footings of payroll.
  3. Verify pay rates and payroll deductions with employee records from personnel.
  4. Recalculate gross and net pay on a test basis.
  5. Compare payroll costs with standards or budgets.
  6. Recompute the mathematical accuracy of a sample of paychecks.
- **Existence and Occurrence:** The auditor should vouch time on payroll summaries by selecting a sample of payroll register entries and comparing with time cards and approved time reports. From a sample of payroll transactions, the auditor should find the related employee to verify existence and current employment status.
- **Understandability and Classification:** The auditor should examine a sample of paychecks for classification into the proper expense accounts.

2.2.3 Auditing Presentation and Disclosure

- **Completeness:** The auditor should ensure that all required disclosures related to payroll have been included in the notes to the financial statements. Required disclosures include:
  - Pension and postretirement benefit disclosures
  - Stock-based compensation disclosures
  - Deferred compensation and profit-sharing plans
- **Valuation, Allocation, and Accuracy:** The auditor should read the footnotes and other information related to payroll to determine whether the information is accurate and presented at the appropriate amounts.
- **Rights and Obligations, and Occurrence:** The auditor should inquire about accruals for proper disclosure. The auditor should compare disclosures to other audit evidence to ensure that all disclosed information related to payroll has occurred.
- **Understandability and Classification:** The auditor should read required disclosures for understandability.

Question 2 **MCQ-02416**

An auditor vouched data for a sample of employees in a payroll register to approved clock card data to provide assurance that:

a. Payments to employees are computed at authorized rates.

b. Employees work the number of hours for which they are paid.

c. Segregation of duties exists between the preparation and distribution of the payroll.

d. Internal controls relating to unclaimed payroll checks are operating effectively.

3 Financing Cycle

The financing cycle includes an entity's debt and equity.

3.1 Internal Controls Related to the Financing Cycle

3.1.1 Internal Control Over Debt

An entity's internal control over debt should include the following:

- Adequate documentation of all financing agreements.
- Authorization of new debt financing by the board of directors or management.
- Detailed records of long-term debt and periodic independent verification of amounts between the ledger, details of debt, and the note holders' records.
- Adequate controls over interest and principal payments and the recording of bond premium and discount amortization amounts.

3.1.2 Internal Control Over Equity

All stock issuances, dividend declarations, and treasury stock purchases must be authorized by the board of directors. Evidence of these events should be duly recorded in the minutes of board meetings.

Many large entities use a stock transfer agent, who ensures that stock issuances comply with the articles of incorporation, prepares stock certificates, and maintains records of shares authorized, issued, and outstanding. If a stock transfer agent is not used, then the entity should implement the following controls:

- An officer of the entity should be responsible for ensuring that stock transactions comply with the articles of incorporation and regulatory requirements and should maintain the stock certificate book. To ensure proper segregation of duties, the individual who maintains the stock certificate book should have no accounting responsibilities.
- There should be a periodic independent reconciliation of the stock certificate book with the number of shares outstanding.

3.2 Performing Specific Procedures to Obtain Evidence: The Financing Cycle

3.2.1 Auditing the Debt Balance

- **Completeness:** The auditor should review board minutes for evidence of new debt, obtain new debt agreements, and trace all new debt contracts to the financial statements. The auditor should obtain a listing of all debt and agree the total to the general ledger. Any debt disclosed on the standard bank confirmation should be traced to the debt agreements and the financial statements. Notes and bonds should be confirmed directly with creditors. The auditor should inquire of management regarding new debt and any off-balance sheet financing transactions.
- **Valuation and Allocation:** The auditor should examine new debt agreements to determine whether they were recorded at the proper amount. The auditor should recompute any interest payable and recompute the amortization of premiums or discounts.
- **Existence:** The auditor should confirm notes or bonds directly with creditors.
- **Rights and Obligations:** The auditor should examine note and bond agreements to verify that they are the obligations of the entity.

3.2.2 Auditing Debt Transactions

The following tests of details can be performed as dual-purpose tests.

- **Completeness:** The auditor should examine new debt agreements and the board minutes for evidence of new agreements. The auditor should review interest expense for payments to debt holders not included in the debt listing. The auditor should examine lease agreements for proper classification as operating or finance.
- **Cutoff:** The auditor should review debt activity shortly before and after year-end to ensure that transactions were reported in the proper period.
- **Valuation, Allocation, and Accuracy:** The auditor should test a sample of debt receipts and payments and should compare interest expense to the debt balance for reasonableness.
- **Existence and Occurrence:** The auditor should verify the existence of new debt by reviewing the board minutes for evidence of new agreements and then inspecting the agreements.
- **Understandability and Classification:** The auditor should examine the due dates of notes and bonds to determine whether the debt should be classified as short term or long term.

3.2.3 Auditing Presentation and Disclosure Related to Debt

- **Completeness:** The auditor should ensure that all required disclosures related to debt have been included in the notes to the financial statements. Required disclosures include:
  - Details of maturity dates, interest rates, call and conversion privileges, and assets pledged as collateral.
  - Future sinking fund payments and maturities for each of the next five years.
  - Restrictive loan covenants.
- **Valuation, Allocation, and Accuracy:** The auditor should read the footnotes and other information related to debt to determine whether the information is accurate and presented at the appropriate amounts.
- **Rights and Obligations, and Occurrence:** The auditor should compare disclosures with other audit evidence to ensure that all disclosed information related to debt has occurred.
- **Understandability and Classification:** The auditor should read required disclosures for understandability.

3.2.4 Auditing the Equity Balance and Transactions

When auditing equity, the auditor is primarily concerned about completeness, valuation, and existence and occurrence. The auditor should also focus on evaluating classification and understandability.

- **Completeness:** If the client uses a stock transfer agent, third-party confirmations should be used to provide evidence of the completeness of shares authorized, issued, and outstanding, as well as to provide evidence of the individual transactions.

  If a client does not use a stock transfer agent, the primary source of evidence of completeness is the stock certificate book. The auditor should examine the stock certificate stubs for proper recording, for any canceled certificates, and for the existence of the remaining unissued certificates. The auditor should foot the shares outstanding in the stock certificate book and agree the total to the general ledger. The auditor should examine all shares of treasury stock and agree the total to the general ledger.

The auditor should ensure that all required disclosures related to equity have been included in the notes to the financial statements. Required equity disclosures include:

- Number of shares authorized, issued, and outstanding.
- Rights and privileges of securities, including dividend and liquidation preferences, participation rights, call prices and dates, conversion or exercise prices or rates and pertinent dates, sinking-fund requirements, unusual voting rights, and significant contracts to issue additional shares.
- Stock option plans.
- Appropriations of retained earnings and restrictions on dividends.

- **Valuation:** The auditor may recompute the value assigned to stock transactions during the period. The auditor should also analyze the retained earnings account from inception (or since the last audit) and should review the propriety of any direct entries to retained earnings.
- **Existence and Occurrence:** Existence and occurrence can be tested by vouching transactions recorded during the current period to board minutes. The stock transfer agent confirmation and the inspection of the stock certificate book also provide evidence of existence.
- **Understandability and Classification:** The auditor should determine whether there are restrictions on retained earnings resulting from loans, agreements, or state laws. The auditor should also inquire of management regarding any appropriations of retained earnings. Restrictions and appropriations must be properly disclosed.

Question 3 **MCQ-02478**

In auditing long-term bonds payable, an auditor most likely would:

a. Perform analytical procedures on the bond premium and discount accounts.

b. Examine documentation of assets purchased with bond proceeds for liens.

c. Compare interest expense with the bond payable amount for reasonableness.

d. Confirm the existence of individual bondholders at year-end.

NOTES

MODULE

7 Matters That Require Special Consideration

AUD 4

1 Opening Balances

1.1 Auditor's Responsibility

In initial audits and reaudit engagements, the auditor should obtain sufficient appropriate audit evidence about whether:

1. Opening balances contain misstatements that could materially affect the current period financial statements; and
2. Accounting policies reflected in the opening balances have been consistently applied in the current period financial statements and whether any changes in accounting policies have been properly accounted for, presented, and disclosed in accordance with the applicable financial reporting framework.

1.2 Audit Procedures

In order to obtain sufficient appropriate evidence regarding opening balances, the auditor should:

1. Read the most recent financial statements, if any, and the predecessor auditor's report.
   - If a modification was made to the predecessor auditor's opinion, the auditor should consider the effect of the matter giving rise to the modification on the current period assessment of the risks of material misstatement. If the modification of the predecessor auditor's opinion is relevant to the current period's financial statements, the auditor should modify the auditor's opinion on the current period's financial statements.
2. Request that management authorize the predecessor auditor to allow a review of the predecessor auditor's audit documentation related to the most recently completed audit.
   - The predecessor auditor ordinarily permits the auditor to review documentation of planning, risk assessment procedures, further audit procedures, audit results, and other matters of continuing accounting and audit significance. Examples include the schedule of uncorrected misstatements, working paper analysis of balance sheet accounts, and those related to contingencies, related parties, and significant unusual transactions.
3. Perform audit procedures on current period transactions that provide evidence about the opening balances or consistency. Examples may include:
   - Tracing cash collections (payments) during the period, which will provide evidence of the accounts receivable (payable) opening balance.
   - Observing current physical inventory counts and reconciling to the opening balance.
   - Considering confirmation with third parties regarding investments and debt.

1.3 Auditor Remains Responsible

Although the current period auditor may consider information obtained from the review of the predecessor's audit documentation, the auditor remains solely responsible for the audit work performed and the conclusions reached during the current audit. The auditor should not make reference to the report or work of the predecessor auditor as the basis for the auditor's opinion.

1.4 Discovery of Material Misstatements in Opening Balances

If the auditor obtains audit evidence that opening balances contain misstatements, the auditor should determine the effect on the current period financial statements. If the auditor believes that the financial statements reported on by the predecessor auditor require revision, the auditor should ask the client to arrange a meeting (involving both auditors and the client) to resolve the matter. If the client's management refuses to inform the predecessor auditor, or if the auditor is not satisfied with the resolution, the auditor should consider the implications on the current audit and whether to resign from the engagement.

1.5 Effect on the Auditor's Report

1.5.1 Qualified or Disclaimer

The inability of the auditor to obtain sufficient appropriate audit evidence regarding opening balances may result in one of the following report modifications:

1. A qualified opinion or a disclaimer of opinion, as appropriate; or
2. An opinion that is qualified or disclaimed, as appropriate, regarding the results of operations and cash flows, and unmodified regarding financial position.

1.5.2 Qualified or Adverse

A qualified or adverse opinion should be expressed if one or more of the following conditions exist:

1. The opening balances contain a misstatement that materially affects the current period financial statements, and the effect of the misstatement is not appropriately accounted for or adequately presented or disclosed.
2. The current period's accounting policies are not consistently applied regarding opening balances.
3. A change in accounting policy is not properly accounted for or adequately presented or disclosed.

2 Litigation, Claims, and Assessments

For actual or potential litigation, claims, and assessments, the auditor should obtain audit evidence relevant to:

1. the period in which the underlying cause for legal action occurred;
2. the degree of probability of an unfavorable outcome; and
3. the amount or range of potential loss.

Potential litigation, claims, and assessments can be discovered by conducting the following audit procedures:

- Inquiring of management about unrecorded contingencies related to litigation.
- Reviewing IRS reports and tax returns for unsettled disagreements.
- Reviewing minutes of board and stockholder meetings.
- Obtaining a letter from the client's attorney.

Pass Key

It is management's responsibility to identify and account for contingent liabilities, including litigation, claims, and assessments, through the policies adopted by management for such purposes. The management representation letter should indicate that management has disclosed to the independent auditor all such relevant information.

2.1 Letter of Inquiry to Client's Attorneys

When audit procedures indicate that there are actual or potential litigation, claims, or assessments, the auditor should seek direct communication with the entity's external legal counsel through a letter of inquiry regarding litigation, claims, and assessments. This letter is prepared by management and sent by the auditors to the attorneys. When in-house legal counsel has responsibility for litigation, claims, and assessments, the auditor should also seek direct communication with the in-house legal counsel through a letter of inquiry.

The auditor should document the basis for any decision not to seek direct communication with legal counsel.

A client's refusal to permit inquiry of the attorneys generally will result in a disclaimer of opinion or withdrawal from the audit.

2.1.1 Response by Attorneys

The attorneys in turn send their replies directly to the independent auditor. In these replies, attorneys give their evaluation concerning litigation, claims, and assessments within their knowledge or control. The date of the attorney's response should be as close as possible to the date of the auditor's report.

The lawyer's response to the letter of inquiry should include a professional opinion on the expected outcome of any lawsuit and the likely outcome of any liability, including court costs.

- **Substantial Attention Limitation:** Lawyers may limit their replies to matters to which they have given substantial attention. Responses may also be limited to material matters if an understanding has been reached between the lawyer and the auditor as to what amount would be considered material.
- **Confidentiality Limitation:** In some cases, it may be unwise for an attorney to disclose certain confidential information. An example of this may be knowledge of a patent violation, if the disclosure of the violation in the financial statements could bring about a lawsuit.

2.1.2 Refusal to Respond by Attorneys

An attorney's refusal to respond to a letter of inquiry where the attorney has devoted substantial attention to litigation matters is a limitation in the scope of an independent auditor's examination, sufficient to preclude an unmodified opinion.

2.1.3 Inherent Uncertainties

In some cases, inherent uncertainties may make it difficult for an attorney to form conclusions regarding pending litigation. If the auditor is satisfied that financial statement disclosure is adequate, no modification to the opinion would be required.

Pass Key

Note that management is the primary source of information regarding contingencies, including litigation, claims, and assessments. The letter sent to the client's attorney is simply a means of corroborating information provided by management.

2.1.4 Concluding Procedures

Once the auditor has reviewed audit evidence regarding potential claims and assessments and has received the letter of inquiry from the client's attorney, the information should be analyzed to determine if management has adequately accounted for and recorded any amounts that are considered probable and are reasonably estimable. The auditor should also verify that amounts that are probable but not reasonably estimable, or that are reasonably possible, are adequately disclosed in the footnotes.

2.1.5 Sample Letter of Audit Inquiry

[*Company Letterhead*]

[*Appropriate Addressee*]

In connection with an audit of our financial statements at (balance sheet date) and for the (period) then ended, management of the Company has prepared, and furnished to our auditors (name and address of auditors), a description and evaluation of certain contingencies, including those set forth below involving matters with respect to which you have been engaged and to which you have devoted substantive attention on behalf of the Company in the form of legal consultation or representation. These contingencies are regarded by management of the Company as material for this purpose *(management may indicate a materiality limit if an understanding has been reached with the auditor)*. Your response should include matters that existed at (balance sheet date) and during the period from that date to the date of your response.

Pending or Threatened Litigation

[*Ordinarily management's information would include (i) the nature of the litigation, (ii) the progress of the case to date, (iii) how management is responding or intends to respond to the litigation, and (iv) an evaluation of the likelihood of an unfavorable outcome and an estimate, if one can be made, of the amount or range of potential loss.*]

This letter will serve as our consent for you to furnish to our auditor all the information requested therein. Accordingly, please furnish to our auditors such explanation, if any, that you consider necessary to supplement the foregoing information, including an explanation of those matters as to which your views may differ from those stated and an identification of the omission of any pending or threatened litigation, claims, and assessments or a statement that the list of such matters is complete.

(continued)

(continued)

Unasserted Claims and Assessments

[*Ordinarily management's information would include (i) the nature of the matter, (ii) how management intends to respond if the claim is asserted, and (iii) an evaluation of the likelihood of an unfavorable outcome and an estimate, if one can be made, of the amount or range of potential loss.*]

Please furnish to our auditors such explanation, if any, that you consider necessary to supplement the foregoing information, including an explanation of those matters as to which your views may differ from those stated.

We understand that whenever, in the course of performing legal services for us with respect to a matter recognized to involve an unasserted possible claim or assessment that may call for financial statement disclosure, if you have formed a professional conclusion that we should disclose or consider disclosure concerning such possible claim or assessment, as a matter of professional responsibility to us, you will so advise us and will consult with us concerning the question of such disclosure and the applicable requirements of Financial Accounting Standards Board (FASB) *Accounting Standards Codification* (ASC) 450, *Contingencies*. Please specifically confirm to our auditors that our understanding is correct.

Please specifically identify the nature of and reasons for any limitations on your response.

Very truly yours,

[*Name*]

Question 1 **MCQ-02529**

Which of the following is an audit procedure that an auditor would most likely perform concerning litigation, claims, and assessments?

a. Request the client's lawyer to evaluate whether the client's pending litigation, claims, and assessments indicate a going concern problem.

b. Examine the legal documents in the client's lawyer's possession concerning litigation, claims, and assessments to which the lawyer has devoted substantial attention.

c. Discuss with management the controls adopted for evaluating and accounting for litigation, claims, and assessments.

d. Confirm directly with the client's lawyer that all litigation, claims, and assessments have been recorded or disclosed in the financial statements.

3 An Entity's Ability to Continue as a Going Concern

On every audit engagement, the auditor is responsible for evaluating audit evidence to determine whether there is substantial doubt about the entity's ability to continue as a going concern for a reasonable period of time. "Reasonable period of time" depends on the financial reporting framework used:

- FASB: one year after the date the financial statements are issued (or available to be issued, as applicable)
- GASB: one year beyond the date of the financial statements. GASB further requires that, if a governmental entity currently knows information that may raise substantial doubt shortly thereafter (for example, within an additional three months), such information should also be considered.

If the going concern basis is not applicable to the financial reporting framework (e.g., cash basis, tax basis), the auditor should use one year after the date the financial statements are issued (or available to be issued).

If there are conditions or events, considered in the aggregate, that raise substantial doubt, the auditor should:

- Obtain sufficient appropriate audit evidence by performing additional audit procedures, including consideration of mitigating factors.
- Evaluate management's plans to alleviate substantial doubt.
- Conclude on whether there is substantial doubt and the appropriateness of going concern basis of accounting (as opposed to the liquidation basis of accounting).
- Include an emphasis-of-matter or explanatory paragraph in the auditor's report for a nonissuer or issuer, respectively, to reflect this conclusion.

3.1 Audit Procedures

The auditor examines evidence obtained during the audit to determine whether there is information that is contrary to the basic principle of going concern. The auditor should examine the evidence obtained from the following procedures:

- **Analytical procedures**
- **Debt compliance:** The auditor should review the terms of debt and loan agreements
- **Minutes:** The auditor should review minutes from stockholder and board of director meetings
- **Inquiry** of client's legal counsel
- **Third parties:** The auditor should obtain audit evidence about the ability and intent of third parties to provide necessary financial support, including written evidence of such intent.
- **Subsequent events** review

Pass Key

An auditor should examine evidence from certain audit procedures before the auditor **ADMITS** there may be a going concern uncertainty.

3.2 Factors That May Indicate Substantial Doubt

Based on the procedures performed, the auditor identifies conditions and events that may be indicative of substantial doubt.

- **Financial difficulties:** Loan defaults, dividend arrearages, denial of usual trade credit, debt restructuring, noncompliance with capital requirements, new financing sources or methods, disposal of substantial assets
- **Internal matters:** Work stoppages, labor difficulties, substantial dependence on a particular project, uneconomic long-term commitments, significant revision of operations
- **Negative trends:** Recurrent losses, working capital deficiencies, negative cash flows, adverse financial ratios
- **External matters:** Legal proceedings; new legislation; loss of a key franchise, license, or patent; loss of a principal customer or supplier; natural disasters

Pass Key

Remember, if the auditor identifies conditions or events that may be indicative of substantial doubt, everything is not **FINE**.

3.3 Mitigating Factors

When an auditor believes that there is substantial doubt about an entity's ability to continue as a going concern, the auditor is required to consider management's plans for dealing with the conditions or events that led to the auditor's belief, including:

- Plans to borrow money or restructure debt
- Plans to sell assets
- Plans to delay or reduce expenditures
- Plans to increase ownership equity

Note: Mitigating factors must include both intent and the ability to carry out the planned procedures.

After considering management's plans, the auditor may decide that substantial doubt about the entity's ability to continue as a going concern for a reasonable period of time has been alleviated. In such cases, the auditor should still consider the need for disclosure of the conditions and events that initially gave rise to the substantial doubt.

3.4 Reporting for Nonissuers

The determination of wording depends on whether or not substantial doubt has been alleviated by management's plans.

- If the going concern basis of accounting is appropriate and substantial doubt has been alleviated based on management's plans, the auditor may, but is not required to, include an emphasis-of-matter paragraph. The emphasis-of-matter paragraph should draw attention to the disclosures of the conditions and management's plans to alleviate going concern doubts.
- If the going concern basis of accounting is appropriate and substantial doubt remains, the accountant should include an emphasis-of-matter paragraph that includes the terms "substantial doubt" and "going concern."

Emphasis of Matter Regarding Going Concern

The accompanying financial statements have been prepared assuming that the Company will continue as a going concern. As discussed in Note X to the financial statements, the Company has suffered recurring losses from operations and has a net capital deficiency, and has stated that *substantial doubt* exists about the Company's ability to continue as a *going concern.* Management's evaluation of the events and conditions and management's plans regarding these matters are also described in Note X. The financial statements do not include any adjustments that might result from the outcome of this uncertainty. Our opinion is not modified with respect to this matter.

3.5 Reporting for Issuers

An explanatory paragraph should be added when there is a going concern uncertainty. The wording of the explanatory paragraph must include the terms "substantial doubt" and "going concern."

Although the general rule in going concern cases is to add an explanatory paragraph to the unqualified opinion, the auditor is not precluded from choosing to disclaim an opinion due to a going concern uncertainty. The decision between an unqualified opinion with an explanatory paragraph and a disclaimer of opinion is based on the auditor's judgment.

3.6 Documentation Requirements

When the auditor believes that there is substantial doubt about the ability of the entity to continue as a going concern for a reasonable period of time, the following items should all be included in the audit documentation:

1. The conditions or events that gave rise to the substantial doubt.
2. Any mitigating factors that the auditor considers significant.
3. Audit work performed to evaluate management's plans, including written representation from management (1) describing its plans to mitigate substantial doubt and the probability that those plans can be effectively implemented; and (2) that the financial statements disclose all matters relevant to an entity's ability to continue as a going concern.
4. The auditor's conclusion about whether substantial doubt remains or is alleviated.
5. The effect of the auditor's conclusion on the evaluation of the financial statements and related disclosures, and on the resulting auditor's report.

3.7 Other Going Concern Considerations

- If, in the auditor's judgment, the entity's going concern disclosures are inadequate, a departure from GAAP exists. This may result in either a qualified or adverse opinion.
- If management is unwilling to perform or extend its evaluation to meet the period of time required by the applicable financial reporting framework when requested to do so by the auditor, the auditor should issue a qualified or adverse opinion.
- If the financial statements have been prepared using the going concern basis of accounting but, in the auditor's judgment, management's use of the going concern basis of accounting in the preparation of the financial statements is inappropriate, the auditor should express an adverse opinion.
- If the auditor's doubts about the entity's ability to continue as a going concern are removed in a subsequent period, the emphasis-of-matter (explanatory) paragraph of the prior period need not be repeated.
- The auditor should communicate going concern issues to those charged with governance.

Question 2 **MCQ-02389**

An auditor concludes that there is substantial doubt about an entity's ability to continue as a going concern for a reasonable period of time and management's plans do not alleviate the substantial doubt. If the entity's financial statements adequately disclose its financial difficulties, the auditor's report is required to include an emphasis-of-matter paragraph that specifically uses the phrase(s):

	"Reasonable period of time, not to exceed one year"	*"Going concern"*
a.	Yes	Yes
b.	Yes	No
c.	No	Yes
d.	No	No

4 Accounting Estimates Including Fair Value Estimates

An accounting estimate is a measurement or recognition in the financial statements of (or a decision to not recognize) an account, disclosure, transaction, or event that generally involves subjective assumptions and measurement uncertainty. Estimates are used because either data about past events cannot be accumulated in a timely, cost-effective manner or because measurement of some accounts depends on the outcome of future events. It is the responsibility of management to make reasonable estimates and include them in the financial statements.

Examples of estimates include:

- Net realizable values of inventory and accounts receivable
- Compensation in stock option plans
- Future pension and warranty expenses
- Probability of loss and related amounts due to litigation
- Fair value amounts

4.1 Auditor's Responsibilities

The auditor has the following responsibilities when evaluating estimates:

1. Evaluate the degree of estimation uncertainty associated with an accounting estimate.
   - Estimation uncertainty is the susceptibility of an accounting estimate to an inherent lack of precision in its measurement.
   - The auditor should determine whether accounting estimates with high estimation uncertainty give rise to significant risks.
2. Assess management's written policies and practices regarding the development and use of estimates.
3. Verify that all material estimates have been developed.
4. Determine that the accounting estimates are reasonable. In evaluating reasonableness, the auditor should apply professional skepticism and focus on significant assumptions. Examples of assumptions that would be considered significant assumptions include those that are:
   - significant to the estimate;
   - sensitive to variations;
   - deviations from historical patterns;
   - based on unobservable data;
   - depend on the company's intent and ability to carry out specific courses of action; or
   - subjective and susceptible to misstatement or management bias.
5. Ensure that the accounting estimates are properly accounted for and disclosed in conformity with GAAP.

4.2 Audit Procedures

In evaluating the reasonableness of an estimate, the auditor must first obtain an understanding of how management developed its estimate. The auditor would then perform one or a combination of the following procedures:

- Review and test the procedures used by management to develop the estimate, including performing procedures to test and evaluate the methods, data, and significant assumptions used in developing the estimate.
  - **Methods:** Determine whether the method used by the company is in conformance with the framework and is appropriate based on the auditor's understanding of the company. If the company has changed its method for determining the accounting estimate, the auditor should determine the reason for the change and evaluate the appropriateness of the change.
  - **Data:** Test the accuracy and completeness of company-produced data, and evaluate the reliability and relevance of data the company used that was obtained from an external source.
  - **Significant Assumptions:** Evaluate the reasonableness of assumptions, including based on economic conditions, company objectives, historical experience, and the entity's ability to carry out a particular action.
- For critical accounting estimates, the auditor should obtain an understanding of how management analyzed the sensitivity to change of its significant assumptions, based on reasonably likely outcomes that would have a material effect on financial condition or operating performance.

- Develop an independent estimate of the item for comparative purposes.
- Evaluate subsequent events and transactions (occurring prior to the date of the auditor's report) for comparison with the value of the estimate. For complex estimates, including fair value estimates, the auditor may need to consider using a specialist to assist in the audit process, especially if a Level 3 valuation is performed by management.

Pass Key

When an auditor determines that the amount of an accounting estimate included in the financial statements is unreasonable or was not determined in conformity with the requirements of the applicable financial reporting framework, then the auditor should treat as a misstatement the difference between the recorded estimate and the best estimate supported by the audit evidence. If the auditor determines a range of reasonable estimates, then the auditor should treat as a misstatement the difference between the recorded estimate and the closest reasonable estimate supported by the audit evidence.

Illustration 1 Evaluating the Estimate of Allowance for Doubtful Accounts

The allowance for doubtful accounts related to accounts receivable is a required estimate to ensure that the receivables are recorded at net realizable value. In order for an auditor to evaluate the reasonableness of the estimate, procedures similar to the following may occur:

- Based on discussions with the client, the auditor will determine the approach taken to estimate the allowance balance, either percentage of sales or percentage of receivables.
- For each approach the auditor will discuss percentages used in the analysis and relevant factors that must be considered in the estimation process.
- Based on the approach used by the client, the auditor will obtain information about sales and receivables provided in the trial balance.
- In addition, receivable aging reports may be obtained at year-end to determine whether the estimates have been calculated appropriately.
  - If different percentages are applied to receivable aging buckets, the percentages used will be assessed for reasonableness.
  - It is important for the auditor to obtain an explanation of customer balances that are noted as significantly past due on the aging detail. These balances may significantly affect the allowance estimate if the accounts will not be written off by year-end.
- As the allowance balance provides an estimate for potential write-offs, the auditor will obtain information regarding accounts written off during the current year and the adequacy of the previous year's allowance balance. Historical write-offs can also be reviewed as these are typically a basis for percentages used to estimate the allowance balance. Based on this information, the auditor can begin to assess whether the balance is too low or too high.

The auditor must always be aware that the allowance account in the balance sheet is tied to an expense on the income statement and will affect net income. Therefore, management's estimates regarding the allowance account are susceptible to bias.

Pass Key

The auditor should also evaluate whether the difference between the reported estimate and the best estimate supported by the audit evidence indicates possible management bias.

MODULE

8 Misstatements and Internal Control Deficiencies

AUD 4

1 Forming Conclusions

The auditor's evaluation of audit results should include evaluation of the following:

- The results of the analytical procedures performed during the overall review of the financial statements.
- Misstatements found during the audit, including uncorrected misstatements.
- The qualitative aspects of the company's accounting practices.
- Conditions identified during the audit that relate to fraud risk.
- The presentation of the financial statements, including disclosures.
- The sufficiency and appropriateness of the audit evidence obtained.

2 Addressing Misstatements Discovered in the Audit

The auditor must evaluate the audit evidence gathered to determine whether the financial statements are free of material misstatement due to error or fraud.

2.1 Identification of Misstatements

The auditor should accumulate misstatements identified during the audit, other than those that are clearly trivial.

"Clearly trivial" is not the same as "not material." Matters that are clearly trivial are inconsequential, both individually and in aggregate, and when judged by any criteria of size, nature, or circumstance. If there is uncertainty about whether an item is clearly trivial, then it cannot be considered trivial.

The auditor may designate an amount below which misstatements are clearly trivial and do not need to be accumulated. The amount should be set so that any misstatement below the amount would not be material to the financial statements, individually or in aggregate, considering the possibility of undetected misstatement.

2.2 Evaluation of Misstatements

The auditor must evaluate the materiality of all misstatements found during the audit.

- The size of a misstatement is often evaluated in comparison to a relevant financial base, such as net income, gross sales, gross margin, total assets, or total liabilities.
- The auditor must consider the effects, both individually and in the aggregate, of uncorrected misstatements. The misstatements should be evaluated in relation to the specific accounts or disclosures involved and the financial statements as a whole, considering all quantitative and qualitative factors.

- As the aggregate misstatements accumulated during the audit approach the materiality level, the auditor should consider the risk that the addition of undetected misstatements could cause materiality levels to be exceeded.
- Prior period misstatements may affect the financial statements of the current period.
- Whether or not a misstatement is considered material is ultimately a matter of professional judgment.
- Qualitative considerations sometimes may cause an otherwise immaterial misstatement to be deemed material.
  - The specific circumstances surrounding an entity may lead to situations in which misstatements that do not exceed materiality limits are still likely to influence the economic decisions of users.
  - Misstatements are more likely to be considered material if they:
    —Affect trends in profitability or mask a change in a trend, or change a loss into income (or vice versa).
    —Affect the entity's compliance with loan covenants, contracts, or regulatory requirements.
    —Increase management compensation, indicate a pattern of management bias, or involve fraud or an illegal act.
    —Affect significant financial statement elements, such as those involving recurring earnings (as opposed to those involving nonrecurring items).
    —Can be objectively determined, as opposed to including an element of subjectivity.
    —Affect segment information presented in the financial statements.
    —Misclassify between certain account balances, for example, between operating and nonoperating income or recurring and nonrecurring items.
    —Are significant relative to the needs of users.
    —Offset effects of individually significant but different misstatements.
    —Are currently immaterial, but will have a material effect in the future.
    —Are costly to correct.
    —Represent a risk that possible additional undetected misstatements could affect the auditor's evaluation.

Pass Key

When evaluating audit findings, the auditor should consider any potential bias in management's judgments about the amounts and disclosures in the financial statements. Examples of management bias include:

- Selective correction of misstatements brought to management's attention during the audit.
- The identification by management of additional adjusting entries that offset misstatements accumulated by the auditor.
- Bias in the selection and application of accounting principles.
- Bias in accounting estimates.

If the auditor identifies bias in management's judgments, the auditor should evaluate whether this bias, together with the effect of uncorrected misstatements, results in material misstatement in the financial statements.

2.3 Communication and Correction of Misstatements

The auditor should communicate on a timely basis with the appropriate level of management all misstatements accumulated during the audit. The auditor should request that management correct those misstatements.

- If, at the auditor's request, management has examined a class of transactions, account balance, or disclosure and corrected misstatements that were detected, the auditor should perform additional audit procedures to determine whether misstatements remain.
- The auditor may request that management examine and perform procedures to determine the amount of the actual misstatement in the class of transactions, account balance, or disclosure, and to make appropriate adjustments to the financial statements. This may occur when the misstatement is based on the auditor's projection of misstatements.
- The auditor may request that management record an adjustment needed to correct all factual misstatements, including the effect of prior period misstatements other than those that the auditor believes are clearly trivial.
- When the auditor has identified a judgmental misstatement involving differences in estimates, such as a difference in a fair value estimate, the auditor may request that management review the assumptions and methods used in developing management's estimate.
- If management refuses to correct some or all of the misstatements communicated by the auditor, the auditor should obtain an understanding of management's reasons for not making the corrections, and should take that understanding into account when evaluating whether the financial statements as a whole are free from material misstatement.

Below is a sample communication that the auditors might submit to management regarding discovered misstatements.

Illustration 1 Summary of Possible Misstatements

ABC Company
Summary of Possible Misstatements
12/31/XX

Possible Misstatement: Overstatement/(Understatement)

Type of misstatement	Total Amount	Assets	Liabilities	Income Before Tax
Unrecorded liabilities	$ 80,000		$(80,000)	$80,000
Overstated allowance for uncollectible accounts	45,000	$(45,000)		(45,000)
Difference between inventory count and ledger	60,000	60,000		60,000
Total	$185,000	$ 15,000	$(80,000)	$95,000

Net effect of misstatements

Assets	15,000
Liabilities	(80,000)
Income before taxes	95,000

Pass Key

Based on the results of substantive audit procedures, the auditor will propose adjusting journal entries to the client. The client may or may not book these proposed entries. Management is responsible for the financial statements and has the final decision on whether or not to book the recommended entries. The examiners may ask for basic adjusting journal entries on the audit exam. Adjusting journal entries are discussed below.

If management does not make the recommended entries and the auditor determines that the uncorrected errors are not material in the aggregate, the auditor should document the errors in the summary of uncorrected errors and document the conclusion that the errors do not cause the financial statements to be misstated.

2.4 Documentation Requirements

The auditor should document the following items:

- The amount below which misstatements are clearly trivial.
- All misstatements accumulated during the audit and whether they have been corrected.
- The auditor's conclusion about whether uncorrected misstatements are material, individually or in the aggregate, and the basis for that conclusion.

Documentation of uncorrected misstatements should include:

- The aggregate effect on the financial statements.
- The evaluation of whether the materiality level or levels for particular classes of transactions, account balances, or disclosures, if any, have been exceeded.
- The effect of uncorrected misstatements on key ratios or trends and compliance with legal, regulatory, and contractual requirements (e.g., debt covenants).

Question 1 **MCQ-02310**

Which of the following circumstances most likely would cause an auditor to suspect that material misstatements exist in a client's financial statements?

a. The assumptions used in developing the prior year's accounting estimates have changed.

b. Differences between reconciliations of control accounts and subsidiary records are not investigated.

c. Negative confirmation requests yield fewer responses than in the prior year's audit.

d. Management consults with another CPA firm about complex accounting matters.

2.5 Effect of Identified Misstatements on Assessment of Control Risk

A material weakness is a deficiency, or a combination of deficiencies, in internal control over financial reporting, such that there is a reasonable possibility that a material misstatement of the entity's financial statements will not be prevented, or detected and corrected on a timely basis.

Identification by the auditor of a material misstatement that would not have been detected by the entity's internal control is an indicator of material weakness. However, the reverse is not necessarily true. The existence of a material weakness does not necessarily mean that the financial statements are materially misstated.

It is essential for the auditor to evaluate the type and cause of misstatements discovered during audit testing. In order to decide whether the misstatements are consistent with the assessment of control risk, the auditor should consider:

1. the frequency with which the misstatement occurred;
2. the effect on other audit areas; and
3. the financial statement implications.

If inconsistent, the audit risk model should be reassessed, and implications on the entire audit (including sample size) must be considered. All misstatements should be evaluated, even misstatements of small dollar amounts, as they could be an indication of a more serious internal control problem.

2.6 Internal Control Deficiencies and the Risk of Material Misstatement

Once tests of controls have been performed, the auditor will assess control risk. If evidence indicates that controls are operating effectively, the auditor will rely on those controls during the audit testing. If evidence indicates that the controls are not operating effectively, further testing will be required.

Control deficiencies may be noted in the design of controls or in the failure of the effectively designed control. Examples include the following:

- Deficiencies in the design of controls:
  - Inadequate documentation and design of internal control over the preparation of financial statements or over a significant account or process.
  - Lack of appropriate controls over segregation of duties or safeguarding of assets.
  - Inadequate design of IT controls.
  - Lack of appropriate qualifications or training of client personnel.
  - Inadequate design of monitoring controls or the absence of an appropriate process to report control deficiencies.
- Failure in effectively designed controls:
  - Failure of control over a significant account or process (for example: failure to obtain appropriate authorization, to perform reconciliations, or to safeguard assets).
  - Undue bias or lack of objectivity.
  - Misrepresentation by client personnel to the auditor.
  - Management override of controls.
  - An observed deviation rate that exceeds the auditor's expected rate.
  - Failure of the information and communication component of internal control to provide complete, accurate, and timely information.

If these deficiencies are noted, further testing is required and may take the form of additional internal controls testing or more extensive substantive procedures.

When control deficiencies are noted, the auditor should:

1. Consider compensating controls.
2. Decide whether there is a significant deficiency or material weakness.
3. Determine potential misstatements that could occur.
4. Design substantive tests related to the deficiency to provide evidence that the financial statements are free from material misstatement with regard to that audit objective and area.

3 Adjusting Journal Entries

Misstatements can be corrected using adjusting journal entries. Adjusting journal entries may affect any account that appears in the financial statements. These questions often require basic knowledge of journal entries. (For example, revenue related to Year 2 should not be included in Year 1 revenue.) Some methods the examiners may use to test adjusting entries can be found below (this is not meant to be a comprehensive list, however).

3.1 Correct Accounts That Are Overstated or Understated

For questions related to adjusting accounts that are overstated or understated, it is important to be familiar with the natural debit or credit balance of an account. With the exception of contra-accounts, the general rule is:

- Assets have a natural debit balance.
- Liabilities and stockholder equity have a natural credit balance.
- Sales have a natural credit balance.
- Expenses have a natural debit balance.

Knowing the natural balance of accounts will help you understand how to adjust journal entries. For example, if sales made "on account" are overstated, this means that the auditor thinks sales and the related receivable are too large and need to be smaller. To decrease these accounts, the auditor would propose:

DR	Sales	$XXX	
CR	Accounts receivable		$XXX

(To adjust sales and accounts receivable to correct amounts.)

Rationale: Sales has a natural credit balance, so sales should be debited to decrease it. Accounts receivable has a natural debit balance, so accounts receivable should be credited to decrease it.

3.2 Purchases

Questions related to purchases may require knowledge of free on board (FOB) shipping point and FOB destination. It is important to note whether the client is the buyer or seller to help determine whether purchases (such as inventory) should be included or excluded from a balance.

3.2.1 If the Client Is the Buyer

- **FOB Shipping Point:** An item shipped FOB shipping point should be included in the client's inventory as soon as the item is with the carrier (e.g., in a delivery truck).
- **FOB Destination:** An item shipped FOB destination should be included in the client's inventory as soon as the item has reached the destination (e.g., the client's place of business).

3.2.2 If the Client Is the Seller

- **FOB Shipping Point:** An item shipped FOB shipping point should be excluded from the client's inventory as soon as the item is with the carrier (e.g., in a delivery truck).
- **FOB Destination:** An item shipped FOB destination should be excluded from the client's inventory as soon as the item has reached the destination (e.g., the buyer's place of business).

3.3 Inventory

3.3.1 Perpetual Inventory

In a perpetual inventory system the journal entries to record the sale of inventory are:

DR	Cash or accounts receivable	$XXX	
CR	Sales		$XXX

(To record the sale of an item.)

And:

DR	Cost of goods sold	$XXX	
CR	Inventory		$XXX

(To record the relief of inventory.)

3.3.2 Periodic Inventory System

In a periodic inventory system, sales are recorded after every sale is made, and inventory is adjusted at the end of the period through a periodic count. The formula to calculate cost of goods sold is:

	Beginning inventory
+	**Purchases**
	Cost of goods sold available for sale
–	**Ending inventory (based on physical inventory count)**
	Cost of goods sold

The journal entry to record a sale under the periodic method is:

DR	Cash or accounts receivable	$XXX	
CR	Sales		$XXX

(To record the sale of inventory.)

Cost of goods sold are recorded at period end. The journal entry at the end of the period (based on the formula above) would be:

DR	Cost of goods sold	$XXX	
CR	Inventory		$XXX

(To record the relief of inventory.)

Example 1 Inventory Adjusting Entry

Facts: The auditor is auditing ABC Company, which utilizes a periodic inventory system. The auditor discovers that inventory stored at a distribution center on December 31, Year 2, was inadvertently omitted during the Year 2 physical inventory count. This inventory was valued at $20,000.

Required: What should the adjusting journal entry be?

Solution:

DR	Inventory	$20,000	
CR	Cost of goods sold		$20,000

(*To correct inventory and cost of goods sold for inventory held at off-site location.*)

The company needs to increase inventory by $20,000. In addition, when the company computed cost of goods sold, the ending inventory was lower by $20,000, which resulted in a higher cost of goods sold of $20,000. To decrease cost of goods sold, the auditor would propose a credit to cost of goods sold for $20,000.

3.3.3 Consignment

- **Audit Client Is the Consignee (Holding Another Company's Goods):** This inventory should be excluded from the client's financial statements.
- **Audit Client Is the Consignor (Goods Are Held at Consignee's Place of Business):** This inventory should be included in the client's financial statements.

Question 2 **MCQ-06812**

According to PCAOB standards, which one of the following statements does not reflect a qualitative standard that should be considered when evaluating the materiality of an uncorrected misstatement?

- **a.** The effects of misclassifications, for example, between operating and nonoperating.
- **b.** The significance of the misstatement relative to the needs of users.
- **c.** The cost of the correction.
- **d.** The dollar amount of the error.

Question 3	**MCQ-06701**

An auditor finds several errors in the financial statements that the client prefers not to correct. The auditor determines that the errors are not material in the aggregate. Which of the following actions by the auditor is most appropriate?

a. Document the errors in the summary of uncorrected errors, and document the conclusion that the errors do *not* cause the financial statements to be misstated.

b. Document the conclusion that the errors do *not* cause the financial statements to be misstated, but do *not* summarize uncorrected errors in the working papers.

c. Summarize the uncorrected errors in the working papers, but do *not* document whether the errors cause the financial statements to be misstated.

d. Do *not* summarize the uncorrected errors in the working papers, and do *not* document a conclusion about whether the uncorrected errors cause the financial statements to be misstated.

NOTES

MODULE

9 Written Representations

AUD 4

1 Management Representation Letter

At the conclusion of fieldwork, the independent auditor must obtain a management representation letter from the client. The auditor prepares the text of the representation letter, which is then printed on client letterhead and signed by the client.

1.1 Purposes of Representation Letter

The three primary purposes for obtaining written representations from management are:

1. To confirm representations explicitly or implicitly given to the auditor.
2. To indicate and document the continuing appropriateness of such representations.
3. To reduce the possibility of misunderstanding concerning matters that are the subject of the representations.

1.2 Requirements

In the management representation letter, the client asserts that all material matters have been adequately disclosed to the independent auditor.

- **Final Piece of Evidential Matter:** The representation letter is obtained at the end of the auditor's fieldwork and covers the period up to the date of the auditor's report. It should address all financial statements and periods covered by the report, even if current management was not present during all such periods.
- **Letter Is Mandatory:** The auditor must receive the letter in order to render an unmodified opinion. Management's refusal to furnish a written representation letter generally results in a disclaimer of opinion or in withdrawal from the engagement.
- **Dated Same Date as Audit Report:** The client representation letter should be dated as of the date of the auditor's report.
  - Occasionally, circumstances may prevent management from signing the representation letter and returning it to the auditor on the date of the auditor's report. When this happens, the auditor may accept management's oral confirmation, on or before the date of the auditor's report, that management has reviewed the final representation letter and will sign the representation letter without exception as of the date of the auditor's report.
  - Possession of the signed representation letter is necessary before releasing the auditor's report.
- **Signed by CEO and CFO:** The members of management with overall responsibility for financial and operating matters who are responsible for and knowledgeable about the items contained in the letter (usually the CEO and CFO) should sign the letter. Other officers and employees also may be asked to sign the letter.

- **Representations:** In the representation letter, management provides information on the financial statements, the completeness of information, recognition, measurement, and disclosure, and subsequent events.
- **Materiality:** Representations may be limited to items that management and the auditor agree are material. Materiality considerations do not apply to items not directly related to financial statement amounts (e.g., all minutes and all financial records should be made available to the auditor).
- **Doubt About the Reliability of Written Representations:** If the auditor concludes that written representations are not reliable due to concerns about the competence, integrity, ethical values, or diligence of management, or because of unresolved inconsistencies between the written representations and other audit evidence, the auditor should consider the possible effect on the audit opinion. When the auditor concludes that there is sufficient doubt about the integrity of management, the auditor should disclaim an opinion or withdraw from the engagement.

1.3 Contents of Management Representation Letter

The management representation letter should include the following representations by management.

- **Financial Statements:** Management is responsible for:
  - the fair presentation of the financial statements in accordance with the applicable financial reporting framework; and
  - the design, implementation, and maintenance of internal control relevant to the preparation and fair presentation of financial statements that are free from material misstatement, whether due to fraud or error.
- **Completeness of Information:** Management has provided the auditor with all relevant information and access, as agreed on in the terms of the engagement. All transactions have been recorded and are reflected in the financial statements.
- **Fraud**
  - Acknowledgment of management's responsibility for the design, implementation, and maintenance of internal control to prevent and detect fraud.
  - Management has disclosed to the auditor the results of its assessment of the risk that the financial statements may be materially misstated as a result of fraud.
  - Management has disclosed to the auditor its knowledge of fraud or suspected fraud affecting the entity involving:

    —management;

    —employees who have significant roles in internal control; or

    —others, when the fraud could have a material effect on the financial statements.
  - Management has disclosed to the auditor its knowledge of any allegations of fraud or suspected fraud affecting the entity's financial statements communicated by employees, former employees, analysts, regulators, or others.
- **Laws and Regulations:** All instances of identified or suspected noncompliance with laws and regulations whose effects should be considered by management when preparing financial statements have been disclosed to the auditor.

- **Uncorrected Misstatements:** Management believes that the effects of uncorrected misstatements are immaterial, individually or in the aggregate, to the financial statements as a whole. A summary of these items should be included in or attached to the written representation.
- **Litigation and Claims:** All known actual or possible litigation and claims whose effects should be considered by management when preparing the financial statements have been disclosed to the auditor and accounted for and disclosed in accordance with the applicable financial reporting framework.
- **Estimates:** Management believes that significant assumptions used when making accounting estimates are reasonable.
- **Related Party Transactions**
  - Disclosure of the identity of all the entity's related parties and all related party relationships and transactions of which it is aware.
  - Management has appropriately accounted for and disclosed such relationships and transactions.
- **Subsequent Events:** All events occurring subsequent to the date of the financial statements and for which the applicable financial reporting framework requires adjustment or disclosure have been adjusted or disclosed.
- **Additional Representations:** The auditor should obtain additional representations from management regarding issues specific to the entity's financial statements. Possible topics include the impact of a new accounting principle, impairment of assets, intent to hold debt securities to maturity, obsolescence of inventory, restrictions on cash, plans to discontinue a line of business, etc.

1.3.1 Sample Management Representation Letter

[*Entity Letterhead*]

To [*Auditor*] [*Date*]

This letter is provided in connection with your audit of the financial statements of ABC Company, which comprise the balance sheet as of December 31, 20XX, and the related statements of income, changes in stockholders' equity, and cash flows for the year then ended, and the related notes to the financial statements, for the purpose of expressing an opinion on whether the financial statements are presented fairly, in all material respects, in accordance with accounting principles generally accepted in the United States (U.S. GAAP).

Certain representations in this letter are described as being limited to matters that are material. Items are considered material, regardless of size, if they involve an omission or misstatement of accounting information that, in the light of surrounding circumstances, makes it probable that the judgment of a reasonable person relying on the information would be changed or influenced by the omission or misstatement.

(continued)

(continued)

Except where otherwise stated below, immaterial matters less than $[*insert amount*] collectively are not considered to be exceptions that require disclosure for the purpose of the following representations. This amount is not necessarily indicative of amounts that would require adjustment to or disclosure in the financial statements.

We confirm that, [*to the best of our knowledge and belief, having made such inquiries as we considered necessary for the purpose of appropriately informing ourselves*] [*as of (date of auditor's report)*]:

Financial Statements

1. We have fulfilled our responsibilities, as set out in the terms of the audit engagement dated [*insert date*], for the preparation and fair presentation of the financial statements in accordance with U.S. GAAP.
2. We acknowledge our responsibility for the design, implementation, and maintenance of internal control relevant to the preparation and fair presentation of financial statements that are free from material misstatement, whether due to fraud or error.
3. We acknowledge our responsibility for the design, implementation, and maintenance of internal control to prevent and detect fraud.
4. Significant assumptions used by us in making accounting estimates, including those measured at fair value, are reasonable.
5. Related party relationships and transactions have been appropriately accounted for and disclosed in accordance with the requirements of U.S. GAAP.
6. All events subsequent to the date of the financial statements and for which U.S. GAAP requires adjustment or disclosure have been adjusted or disclosed.
7. The effects of uncorrected misstatements are immaterial, both individually and in the aggregate, to the financial statements as a whole. A list of the uncorrected misstatements is attached to the representation letter.
8. The effects of all known or possible litigation and claims have been accounted for and disclosed in accordance with U.S. GAAP.

[*Any other matters that the auditor may consider appropriate.*]

Information Provided

9. We have provided you with:
    a. Access to all information, of which we are aware that is relevant to the preparation and fair presentation of the financial statements such as records, documentation, and other matters;
    b. Additional information that you have requested from us for the purpose of the audit; and
    c. Unrestricted access to persons within the entity from whom you determined it necessary to obtain audit evidence.

(continued)

(continued)

10. All transactions have been recorded in the accounting records and are reflected in the financial statements.

11. We have disclosed to you the results of our assessment of the risk that the financial statements may be materially misstated as a result of fraud.

12. We have [*no knowledge of any*] [*disclosed to you all information that we are aware of regarding*] fraud or suspected fraud affecting the entity and involves:

- **a.** Management;
- **b.** Employees who have significant roles in internal control; or
- **c.** Others where the fraud could have a material effect on the financial statements.

13. We have [*no knowledge of any*] [*disclosed to you all information that we are aware of regarding*] allegations of fraud, or suspected fraud, affecting the entity's financial statements communicated by employees, former employees, analysts, regulators, or others.

14. We disclosed to you all known instances of noncompliance or suspected noncompliance with laws and regulations whose effects should be considered when preparing financial statements.

15. We [*have disclosed to you all known actual or possible*][*are not aware of any pending or threatened*] litigation and claims whose effects should be considered when preparing financial statements [*and we have not consulted legal counsel concerning litigation or claims*].

16. We have disclosed to you the identity of the entity's related parties and all the related party relationships and transactions of which we are aware.

[*Any other matters that the auditor may consider necessary.*]

____

[*Name of Chief Executive Officer and Title*]

____

[*Name of Chief Financial Officer and Title*]

Pass Key

Remember that the management representation letter is required. Management's refusal to furnish written representations generally will result either in a disclaimer of opinion or in withdrawal from the engagement.

1.3.2 Written Representation Regarding Internal Control

When performing an integrated audit, which includes an audit of internal controls over financial reporting, the auditor should obtain additional written representations from management about its responsibility for internal control over financial reporting, in which management:

- Acknowledges its responsibility for establishing and maintaining effective internal control, and states that management has performed an evaluation of the effectiveness of the entity's internal control.
- States the assertion and specifies the criteria used to evaluate the assertion.
- Affirms that management did not rely on the auditor's procedures as the basis for the assertion.
- Confirms that all significant deficiencies and material weaknesses have been disclosed to the auditor, and indicates whether any such deficiencies identified in previous engagements remain unresolved.
- Describes fraud resulting in material misstatement or fraud involving senior management or key employees.
- States whether there were any significant changes to internal control after the "as of" date of the report.

Failure to obtain such written representations is a scope limitation that generally will result in the auditor's withdrawal from the engagement or in a disclaimer of opinion.

Question 1 **MCQ-02533**

Which of the following matters would an auditor most likely include in a management representation letter?

a. Communications with those charged with governance concerning weaknesses in internal control.

b. The reasonableness of significant assumptions used in making accounting estimates.

c. Plans to acquire or merge with other entities in the subsequent year.

d. Management's acknowledgment of its responsibility for the detection of employee fraud.

MODULE

10 Communication With Management and Those Charged With Governance

AUD 4

1 Those Charged With Governance

The term "those charged with governance" refers to those who bear responsibility to oversee the obligations and strategic direction of an entity, including the financial reporting process. This term is broadly interpreted to encompass the terms "board of directors" and "audit committee."

1.1 Governance Structure

Those charged with governance may include:

- Members of the entity's legal structure, such as company directors.
- Parties external to the entity, such as certain government agencies.
- A collective group of people such as a board of directors or audit committee, or a single person, such as an owner-manager.
- Personnel who also have management responsibilities.

1.2 Audit Committees

An audit committee is a committee of the board of directors, generally made up of three to five members of the board who are "outside directors." Outside directors are individuals who are neither employees nor part of management and who do not have a material financial interest in the company. An audit committee is generally a subgroup of those charged with governance.

1.2.1 Purpose of an Audit Committee

Many companies have established audit committees because:

- The SEC has strongly recommended this action, and the New York Stock Exchange requires all companies listed on the exchange to have audit committees.
- Many large accounting firms and leading accountants in the country have strongly supported the formation of audit committees.
- The use of audit committees tends to strengthen the public's sense of the independence of the public accountant.

1.2.2 Specific Functions of Audit Committees

The main function of an audit committee is to enhance internal control by creating a means of direct communication between the "outside directors" and the independent auditor. An audit committee is considered to be part of the internal control structure. The audit committee typically:

- Selects and appoints the independent auditor and sets the audit fee.
- Assures that the auditor is independent of the company.
- Reviews the nature and details of the audit engagement.

- Reviews the quality of the auditor's work.
- Reviews the scope of the audit.
- Ensures that any recommendations made by the auditor are given proper attention.
- Maintains lines of communication between the auditor and the board of directors.
- Helps solve any disagreements related to the accounting treatment of any material items in the financial statements.
- Evaluates the internal control of the company with the help of the independent auditor.
- Makes reports to the board of directors and the stockholders when necessary.

1.2.3 Communication With the Audit Committee

Communication with the audit committee is a key element in the auditor's communication with those charged with governance. The auditor should:

- Have appropriate access to the audit committee periodically.
- Meet with the audit committee without management present at least once each year.
- Consider whether communication with the audit committee is sufficient or whether there is also a need to communicate with others charged with governance.

1.2.4 Sarbanes-Oxley Requirements

The Sarbanes-Oxley Act, which applies to issuers, requires the audit committee to approve the engagement of the auditor, to preapprove the services to be performed, and to have ongoing communications with the auditor. In effect, auditors of issuers report to and are overseen by the audit committee, not by management.

2 Required Communications

An auditor conducting an audit of financial statements has a responsibility to communicate certain matters to those charged with governance.

2.1 Matters Related to the Auditor's Responsibility

An auditor is required to communicate to those charged with governance the auditor's responsibilities with regard to a financial statement audit, including that:

- The auditor is responsible for forming and expressing an opinion about whether the financial statements are prepared, in all material respects, in conformity with the applicable financial reporting framework.
- The audit does not relieve management or those charged with governance of their responsibilities.
- The auditor is responsible for performing the audit in accordance with GAAS.
- The audit is designed to provide reasonable, rather than absolute, assurance about whether the financial statements are free from material misstatement.
- The audit of financial statements includes consideration of internal control over financial reporting as a basis for designing audit procedures that are appropriate in the circumstances, but not for the purpose of expressing an opinion on the effectiveness of the entity's internal control over financial reporting (nonissuers only).

- The auditor is responsible for communicating significant matters related to the financial statement audit.
- When applicable, the auditor is responsible for communicating particular matters required by law or regulation, by agreement with the entity, or by additional requirements applicable to the engagement.
- In certain situations, the auditor may determine that it is appropriate to communicate circumstances or relationships that, in the auditor's professional judgment, may reasonably be thought to bear on independence, and to which the auditor gave significant consideration, in reaching the conclusion that independence has not been impaired.

These responsibilities may be communicated through the engagement letter (required for issuers), or other form of contract that records the terms of the engagement, if the letter or contract is given to those charged with governance.

2.2 Planned Scope and Timing of the Audit Engagement

The auditor should communicate with those charged with governance regarding the planned scope and timing of the audit. The purpose of communicating this information is to provide insight to those charged with governance regarding the auditor's activities, as well as to improve the auditor's understanding of the entity. The auditor should consider the following when communicating the planned scope and timing:

- The auditor may communicate how significant risks of material misstatement will be addressed, the planned approach toward internal control, factors affecting materiality, and any potential use of internal audit staff or specialist.
- The auditor should be careful not to compromise the effectiveness of audit procedures, for example by making them too predictable.
- The auditor also may solicit information from those charged with governance. For example, the auditor may inquire as to the party with whom the auditor should communicate; the allocation of responsibility between management and those charged with governance; the entity's objectives, strategies, and risks, matters to which the auditor should pay particular attention; and significant communications with regulators.
- The communication also may include discussion of the attitudes, awareness, and actions of those charged with governance with respect to internal control, fraud, relevant changes (e.g., changes to financial reporting, accounting standards, laws, etc.), and matters previously communicated by the auditor.

2.3 Significant Audit Findings

The auditor should communicate:

- The auditor's views about qualitative aspects of the entity's accounting practices, including:
  - the initial selection of, changes in, and appropriateness of significant accounting policies;
  - the process used by management in formulating significant accounting estimates and the basis for the auditor's conclusions regarding the reasonableness of the estimates;
  - significant management judgments; and
  - the adequacy of financial statement disclosures.
- Significant difficulties encountered in performing the audit (e.g., delays, unreasonable timetables, lack of cooperation).
- Disagreements with management, whether or not resolved.

- Uncorrected, nontrivial misstatements and their possible effect on the audit opinion, including the effect of uncorrected misstatements related to prior periods.
  - Material uncorrected misstatements should be identified individually and should be corrected at the request of the auditor.
  - The auditor should request the correction of uncorrected material misstatements.
  - The auditor may also communicate uncorrected immaterial misstatements, such as frequently occurring misstatements that could indicate bias in the preparation of financial statements.
- Any circumstances that may appear to impair independence (although presumably the auditor has concluded that independence has not been impaired).
- Evaluation of the company's identification of, accounting for, and disclosure of its relationships and transactions with related parties.
- Other issues that the auditor judges to be significant.

If all of those charged with governance are not involved with managing the entity, the auditor should also communicate:

- Significant issues or findings arising during the audit that were discussed with management.
- Material, corrected misstatements brought to management's attention as a result of the audit. (The auditor may also choose to communicate corrected misstatements that are immaterial but frequently recurring.)
- Management representations requested by the auditor.
- Management's consultation with other accountants.

3 Other Communication Considerations

3.1 Two-Way Communication

Communication should be two-way. The auditor should communicate the purpose, form, timing, and expected general content of further communications as a means of establishing effective two-way communication, but those charged with governance should also communicate relevant matters to the auditor.

The auditor may request additional information from those charged with governance as a means of obtaining further audit evidence. There should be an established process for each party to take action and report back to the other.

Inadequate two-way communication may be indicative of an unsatisfactory control environment, which may affect the auditor's assessment of the risk of material misstatement.

3.2 Communication With Management

Generally, the auditor may discuss matters with management prior to communicating those matters to those charged with governance. Certain matters communicated to those charged with governance, such as those related to the competence and integrity of management, might not be appropriate for discussion with management.

3.3 Other Standards

3.3.1 Other Auditing Standards

Other auditing standards may also require communication with those charged with governance. For example, communication may be required with respect to internal control-related matters, fraud, illegal acts, compliance-related matters in government audits, going concern issues, and matters related to a review of interim financial information.

3.3.2 Additional Requirements for Issuers

Auditors of issuers are required to report (to the audit committee) all critical accounting policies, all material alternative GAAP accounting treatments, and other material communications between the auditor and management (e.g., management letters, schedules of unadjusted differences, etc.). In addition, auditors of issuers should discuss and provide a draft of the auditor's report to the audit committee. If no formal audit committee exists, communications should be made to the full board of directors.

4 Form and Timing of Communication

4.1 Form of Communication

In general, communications may be oral or in writing.

- Significant audit findings should be communicated in writing when, in the auditor's judgment, oral communication would be inadequate. Matters communicated during the audit that were appropriately resolved need not be included in the written communication.
- The auditor may also choose to communicate other matters in writing based on the specific circumstances involved.
- Written communications should include a limitation on the use of the communication indicating for whom it is intended, and warning that it should not be used by others.
- Oral communications should be documented; copies of written communications should be retained.

4.2 Timing of Communication

Timing of the communications may vary according to circumstance, but should occur on a timely basis in a manner that allows appropriate action to be taken.

For audits of issuers, communications are required to be made before issuance of the auditor's report.

PCAOB Standards: Guidance for Issuers

In addition to the items already covered, the PCAOB's audit committee communication requirements for issuers include the following:

- Additional information related to the planned scope and timing of the audit, including:
  - The nature and extent of specialized skill or knowledge needed to complete the engagement.
  - The extent to which the auditor will use the work of the company's internal auditors when performing the financial statement audit.
  - The extent to which the auditor will use the work of internal auditors, company personnel, and third parties when performing the internal control audit.
  - The names, locations, and responsibilities of other public accounting firms that will perform audit procedures.
  - The basis for the determination that the auditor is the principal auditor, if other auditors will perform significant work in the engagement.
- Additional matters related to significant audit findings, including:
  - The effect on the financial statements or disclosures of significant accounting policies in controversial areas or areas in which there is a lack of authoritative guidance.
  - Critical accounting policies and practices (defined as the company's accounting policies and practices that are most important to the portrayal of financial position and require significant management judgment, including the need to make estimates).
  - Critical accounting estimates.
  - Significant unusual transactions.
  - Situations in which the auditor identified bias in management's judgments.
  - The auditor's views on matters about which management consulted with other accountants.

(continued)

(continued)

- Matters related to going concern, when there is substantial doubt about the company's ability to continue as a going concern, including:
  - The conditions and events that the auditor identified that indicate that there is substantial doubt.
  - The effect of the substantial doubt on the financial statements and adequacy of disclosure.
  - The effect of the substantial doubt on the auditor's report.
  - If the auditor concludes that substantial doubt about the company's ability to continue as a going concern is alleviated by management's plans, the basis for this conclusion.
- The reasons for modification of the auditor's opinion.
- The reasons for and wording of explanatory language added to the auditor's report.

5 Internal Control Communications

5.1 Applicability

An accountant communicates internal control-related matters in the following situations:

5.1.1 Financial Statement Audit (Nonissuers)

- Although the purpose of an audit of a nonissuer is to express an opinion on the financial statements and not to express an opinion on the effectiveness of internal control, certain deficiencies related to internal control may be noticed by the auditor during the audit. Such deficiencies create a reporting responsibility for the auditor, which is covered in this section.
- This situation is governed by Statements on Auditing Standards (SAS).

5.1.2 Integrated Audits (Nonissuers and Issuers)

- **Audit of Internal Control (Nonissuers)**
  - An auditor may be hired to perform an audit of a nonissuer's internal control. If so, the audit of internal control should be integrated with an audit of the entity's financial statements.
  - This situation is governed by Statements on Auditing Standards (SAS).
- **Audit of Internal Control (Issuers)**
  - All issuers are required to have an audit of internal control over financial reporting that is integrated with an audit of the financial statements.
  - This situation is governed by Public Company Accounting Oversight Board (PCAOB) auditing standards.

Integrated audits and communications related to integrated audits will be covered in more detail in A5.

5.2 Definitions

Certain definitions are virtually the same for all three types of engagements. Where slight differences exist, wording used for nonissuers is shown first; wording for issuers is shown in (parentheses).

5.2.1 Control Deficiency

A control deficiency exists when the design or operation of a control does not allow management or employees, in the normal course of performing their assigned functions, to prevent, or detect and correct (prevent or detect) misstatements on a timely basis.

- A deficiency in design occurs when a necessary control is missing or when an existing control does not achieve the desired objective.
- A deficiency in operation occurs when a properly designed control does not operate as designed, or is performed by an inappropriate person.

5.2.2 Material Weakness

A material weakness is a deficiency, or a combination of deficiencies, in internal control (over financial reporting), such that there is a reasonable possibility that a material misstatement of the entity's (company's annual or interim) financial statements will not be prevented, or detected and corrected (prevented or detected) on a timely basis.

"Reasonable possibility" implies that the likelihood of an event is either "reasonably possible" or "probable."

5.2.3 Significant Deficiency

A significant deficiency is a deficiency, or a combination of deficiencies, in internal control (over financial reporting) that is less severe than a material weakness, yet important enough to merit attention by those charged with governance (responsible for oversight of the company's financial reporting).

5.2.4 Indicators of Material Weakness

Although there are three distinct sets of standards with respect to internal control communications, they all provide the same guidance with respect to evaluation of control weaknesses. The following situations are considered indicators of a material weakness in internal control.

- Identification of any level of fraud (even immaterial fraud) perpetrated by senior management.
- Restatement of previously issued financial statements to correct a material misstatement.
- Identification by the auditor of a material misstatement that would not have been detected by the entity's internal control.
- Ineffective oversight by those charged with governance (the company's audit committee).

5.3 Detection of Control Deficiencies

An auditor of financial statements (nonissuer) is not required to perform procedures to identify deficiencies in internal control, or to express an opinion on the effectiveness of internal control. The auditor may, however, become aware of control deficiencies while performing the audit. The auditor has a responsibility to evaluate control deficiencies identified during the audit and, in some cases, to report those deficiencies.

Pass Key

The auditor may discuss relevant facts and circumstances with management when determining whether the auditor has identified internal control deficiencies. The level of management with whom it is appropriate to discuss the findings is one that is familiar with the internal control area concerned and that has authority to take remedial action. However, when findings call into question management's integrity or competence, it may not be appropriate to discuss the findings directly with management.

5.4 Evaluation of Control Deficiencies

The auditor must evaluate control deficiencies (both individually and in combination) to determine whether they represent significant deficiencies or material weaknesses.

The severity of a deficiency, or a combination of deficiencies, depends on not only whether a misstatement has actually occurred, but also on:

1. the magnitude of the potential misstatement; and
2. whether there is a reasonable possibility that the entity's controls will fail to prevent, or detect and correct, a misstatement of an account balance or disclosure.

Pass Key

Significant deficiencies and material weaknesses may exist even though the auditor has not identified misstatements during the audit.

The auditor should consider both the likelihood and the magnitude of potential misstatements.

- **Likelihood:** Is there a reasonable possibility that the entity's controls will fail to prevent, or detect and correct, the misstatement? Consider the nature of the related accounts (e.g., susceptibility to fraud, subjectivity, complexity, etc.).
- **Magnitude:** Consider both the dollar amount and the volume of activity in accounts exposed to the deficiency.

If more than one control deficiency affects the same account balance or disclosure, individually insignificant deficiencies may, in combination, constitute a significant deficiency or material weakness.

The auditor should consider whether any controls tend to compensate for the identified deficiency. A compensating control is one that limits the severity of a control deficiency and may prevent it from being identified as a significant deficiency or material weakness.

Indicators of material weaknesses include senior management fraud; restatement of previous financial statements to correct a material error; identification by the auditor of a material misstatement that the entity's controls would not have detected; and ineffective oversight by those charged with governance.

5.5 Communication of Control Deficiencies

Significant deficiencies and material weaknesses, even those that were corrected during the audit, must be communicated on a timely basis in writing to management and those charged with governance.

5.5.1 Previously Existing Deficiencies

Previously communicated significant deficiencies and material weaknesses that have not been corrected should be communicated again, in writing, during the current audit by referring to the previously issued written communication and the date of that communication.

5.5.2 Timing

Although it is recommended that the written communication be made by the report release date, a window extending 60 days beyond this date is acceptable. Earlier communication (i.e., during the audit) is also acceptable. While such early communication need not be in writing, it does not negate the requirement for eventual written communication of all significant deficiencies and material weaknesses.

5.5.3 Management's Evaluation

It is management's responsibility to evaluate and address control deficiencies. Management may decide to accept certain significant deficiencies or material weaknesses based on the costs that would be incurred to correct them. Even in such situations, the auditor is still required to communicate such deficiencies in writing.

5.5.4 Communication of Other Deficiencies

The auditor should communicate to management only, in writing or orally, other deficiencies in internal control identified during the audit that are of sufficient importance to merit management's attention but are not significant deficiencies or material weaknesses. If other deficiencies are communicated orally, the communication should be documented.

- If the auditor has communicated other deficiencies in a prior period and management has chosen not to correct the deficiencies for cost or other reasons, the auditor need not repeat the communication in the current period.
- The auditor is not required to repeat information about other deficiencies if the information has already been communicated to management by other parties, such as internal auditors or regulators.
- The auditor may communicate the details of other deficiencies to those charged with governance, either orally or in writing, if those charged with governance wish to be made aware of the details or if the auditor chooses to inform them.

Communication of Deficiencies in Internal Control
(Financial Statement Audit Only: Nonissuer)

	*Communicate the deficiency **to management only**, either orally or in writing.*	*Communicate the deficiency **to management**, in writing.*	*Communicate the deficiency **to those charged with governance**, in writing.*	*Communication should be made **within 60 days of the report release date.***
Control deficiency	✓			✓
Significant deficiency		✓	✓	✓
Material weakness		✓	✓	✓

5.6 Communication Requirements

The written communication of significant deficiencies and material weaknesses should include the following:

1. The definition of the term material weakness and, when relevant, the definition of the term significant deficiency.
2. A description of the significant deficiencies and material weaknesses, including an explanation of their potential effects.
   - The auditor does not need to quantify the potential effects.
   - Potential effects can be described in terms of the control objectives and types of errors the control was designed to prevent, or detect and correct, or in terms of the risks of misstatement the control was designed to address.
3. Sufficient information to enable those charged with governance and management to understand the context of the communication, including statements that:
   - The purpose of the audit was for the auditor to express an opinion on the financial statements.
   - The auditor is not expressing an opinion on the effectiveness of internal control.
   - The audit included consideration of internal control over financial reporting in order to design audit procedures that are appropriate in the circumstances but not for the purpose of expressing an opinion on the effectiveness of internal control.
   - The auditor's consideration of internal control was not designed to identify all deficiencies in internal control that might be material weaknesses or significant deficiencies, and therefore, material weaknesses and significant deficiencies may exist that were not identified.
4. A restriction regarding the use of the communication to management, those charged with governance, others within the organization, and any governmental authority to which the auditor is required to report.

5.6.1 Optional Communication Content

The auditor may also include the following information in the communication when appropriate:

- A description of the inherent limitations of internal control.
- The specific nature and extent of the auditor's consideration of internal control during the audit.
- The auditor may not report the absence of significant deficiencies, because there is too great a potential for misinterpretation of the very limited degree of assurance the auditor would be providing in such instances.
- The auditor may issue a communication indicating that no material weaknesses were identified during the audit, typically for the client to submit to governmental authorities.

Management may prepare a written response to the auditor's communication regarding significant deficiencies and material weaknesses identified during the audit. Management's response may describe corrective actions taken or planned for the future, or indicate that the cost of correcting the identified deficiencies would exceed the benefits to be derived.

If such response is included in a document containing the auditor's written communication, the auditor may add a paragraph disclaiming an opinion on management's response.

5.6.2 Sample Written Communication on Internal Control (Nonissuer)

To Management and [*identify the body or individuals charged with governance*] of ABC Company:

In planning and performing our audit of the financial statements of ABC Company (the "Company") as of and for the year ended December 31, 20XX, in accordance with auditing standards generally accepted in the United States of America, we considered the Company's internal control over financial reporting (internal control) as a basis for designing audit procedures that are appropriate in the circumstances for the purpose of expressing our opinion on the financial statements, but not for the purpose of expressing an opinion on the effectiveness of the Company's internal control. Accordingly, we do not express an opinion on the effectiveness of the Company's internal control.

Our consideration of internal control was for the limited purpose described in the preceding paragraph and was not designed to identify all deficiencies in internal control that might be material weaknesses or significant deficiencies and therefore, material weaknesses or significant deficiencies may exist that were not identified. However, as discussed below, we identified certain deficiencies in internal control that we consider to be material weaknesses and significant deficiencies.

A deficiency in internal control exists when the design or operation of a control does not allow management or employees, in the normal course of performing their assigned functions, to prevent, or detect and correct, misstatements on a timely basis. A material weakness is a deficiency, or a combination of deficiencies, in internal control, such that there is a reasonable possibility that a material misstatement of the entity's financial statements will not be prevented, or detected and corrected, on a timely basis. We consider the following deficiencies in the Company's internal control to be material weaknesses:

[*Describe the material weaknesses that were identified and an explanation of their potential effects.*]

A significant deficiency is a deficiency, or combination of deficiencies, in internal control that is less severe than a material weakness, yet important enough to merit attention by those charged with governance. We consider the following deficiencies in the Company's internal control to be significant deficiencies:

[*Describe the significant deficiencies that were identified and an explanation of their potential effects.*]

[*If the auditor is communicating significant deficiencies and did not identify any material weaknesses, the auditor may state that none of the identified deficiencies are considered to be material weaknesses.*]

This communication is intended solely for the information and use of management, [*identify the body or individuals charged with governance*], others within the organization, and [*identify any specified governmental authorities to which the auditor is required to report*] and is not intended to be, and should not be, used by anyone other than these specified parties.

[*Auditor's Signature*]

[*Date*]

Question 1 **MCQ-02540**

Which of the following statements is correct about an auditor's required communication with those charged with governance? Assume those charged with governance are not involved in managing the entity.

a. Any matters communicated to those charged with governance also are required to be communicated to the entity's management.

b. The auditor is required to inform those charged with governance about significant errors discovered by the auditor and subsequently corrected by management.

c. Disagreements with management about the application of accounting principles are not required to be communicated to those charged with governance if they have been appropriately resolved.

d. Significant deficiencies in internal control previously reported to those charged with governance that have not been corrected need not be communicated again.

Question 2 **MCQ-02542**

An auditor's letter issued on significant deficiencies relating to a nonissuer's internal control observed during a financial statement audit should:

a. Include a brief description of the tests of controls performed in searching for significant deficiencies and material weaknesses.

b. Indicate that the significant deficiencies should be disclosed in the annual report to the entity's shareholders.

c. Include a paragraph describing management's assessment concerning the effectiveness of internal control.

d. Indicate that the audit's purpose was to report on the financial statements and not to provide an opinion on internal control.

NOTES

MODULE

11 Other Communications

AUD 4

1 Communications With Component Auditors

When an auditor acts as the auditor of group financial statements, the group auditor must communicate its requirements to the component auditor on a timely basis. This communication should include:

- Explanation of how the group engagement team will use the work of the component auditor, and a request for confirmation that the component auditor will cooperate with the group engagement team.
- Ethical requirements, including independence requirements, that are relevant to the group audit.
- List of related parties prepared by the group management, and a request that the component auditor communicate on a timely basis any related parties not previously identified by the group engagement team.
- Identified significant risks of material misstatement of the group financial statements that are relevant to the work of the component auditor.

At the conclusion of the audit, the group engagement team should request that the component auditor communicate back to them all matters relevant to the group engagement team's conclusion. This communication should include:

- Whether the component auditor has complied with ethical requirements relevant to the group audit, including independence and professional competence.
- Identification of the financial information of the component being audited.
- The component auditor's overall findings, conclusions, or opinion.

1.1 Assuming Responsibility for the Work of the Component Auditor

When the group engagement team is assuming responsibility for the work of the component auditor, in addition to the requirements noted previously, the content of the communication to the component auditor should be detailed and include the work to be performed by the component auditor, the component materiality levels, and the threshold above which misstatements cannot be regarded as clearly trivial to the group financial statements. The communication requested from the component auditor should also include the following:

- The component auditor's compliance with the group engagement team's requirements.
- Instances of noncompliance at the component that could give rise to a material misstatement of the group financial statements.
- Significant risks of material misstatement of the group financial statements, due to fraud or error, and the component auditor's responses to such risks. These significant risks should be communicated on a timely basis.

- A list of corrected and uncorrected misstatements of the financial information of the component.
- Indicators of possible management bias regarding accounting estimates and the application of accounting principles.
- Identified material weaknesses and significant deficiencies in internal control.
- Other significant findings including fraud or suspected fraud involving component management or employees, or others that resulted in a material misstatement of the financial information of the component.

2 Communications Regarding Noncompliance

2.1 Reporting to Those Charged With Governance

If those charged with governance are not involved in management of the entity, the auditor should communicate with those charged with governance matters involving noncompliance. Matters that are clearly inconsequential need not be communicated. If the noncompliance appears to be intentional and material, the auditor should communicate the matter to those charged with governance as soon as practicable.

If management or those charged with governance are involved in noncompliance, the auditor should communicate the matter to the next higher level of authority at the entity. If there is no higher level of authority, the auditor may need to obtain legal advice.

2.2 Reporting to Regulatory and Enforcement Authorities

Ordinarily, the disclosure of noncompliance to parties other than management and those charged with governance is not part of the auditor's responsibility because of the auditor's professional duty of confidentiality. In the following circumstances, a duty to disclose outside the entity may exist:

- In response to inquiries from an auditor to a predecessor auditor.
- In response to a court order.
- In compliance with requirements for the audits of entities that receive federal financial assistance from a government agency.

2.3 Reporting Noncompliance in the Auditor's Report

- **Material Effect on the Financial Statements:** If the noncompliance has a material effect on the financial statements and has not been adequately reflected in the financial statements, a qualified opinion or adverse opinion should be issued.
- **Insufficient Evidence:** If the auditor is unable to obtain sufficient appropriate audit evidence about the noncompliance or suspected noncompliance, a qualified opinion or a disclaimer of opinion should be expressed.
- **Client Response:** If the client refuses to accept the auditor's report as modified, the auditor should withdraw from the engagement and notify those charged with governance in writing.

3 Communications Regarding Confidential Client Information

Under most circumstances, a member of the AICPA in public practice shall not disclose any confidential client information without the specific consent of the client.

3.1 Exceptions

A member is obligated to disclose confidential information even without the consent of the client in the following circumstances:

1. A member must disclose confidential client information if necessary to comply with a validly issued subpoena or summons.
   - The member is not required to notify the client that its records have been subpoenaed or that a summons related to the client's records has been issued. The member may wish to consult with legal counsel to determine the validity and enforceability of the subpoena or summons and the specific client information required to be provided. The member may also wish to consult with his or her state board of accountancy.
2. A member must disclose confidential information as a part of a quality review of the member's professional practices authorized by the AICPA (e.g., a request for confidential information by a state CPA society voluntary quality-control review panel).
3. A member must disclose confidential client information in response to any inquiry either made by the ethics division or the trial board of the AICPA or by a duly constituted investigative or disciplinary body of a state CPA society, or under authority of state statutes.

Pass Key

The examiners often ask to whom a CPA may disclose client audit documentation without consent of the client. Memorize the above three paragraphs and you will have no problem with such a question on your exam.

Question 1 **MCQ-06712**

During the audit of a new client, the auditor determined that management had given illegal bribes to municipal officials during the year under audit and for several prior years. The auditor notified the client's board of this act of noncompliance with laws and regulations, but the board decided to take no action because the amounts involved were immaterial to the financial statements. Under these circumstances, the auditor should:

a. Add an explanatory paragraph emphasizing that certain matters, while not affecting the unmodified opinion, require disclosure.

b. Report the illegal bribes to the municipal official at least one level above those persons who received the bribes.

c. Consider withdrawing from the audit engagement and disassociating from future relationships with the client.

d. Issue an "except for" qualified opinion or an adverse opinion with a separate paragraph that explains the circumstances.

NOTES

MODULE

12 Appendix: Control Procedures and Tests of Control

AUD 4

1 Testing Controls: Sales

Department	Control Procedure	Sample Test of Control Procedure
Order and Credit	**1.** Prepare prenumbered sales order. **2.** Perform credit check (authorization). **3.** Approve credit for returns. **4.** Follow up on old or past-due accounts. **5.** Initiate write-offs, which should be approved by the treasurer.	• Inquire about credit procedure for new customers (valuation). • From a population of approved sales orders (and returns), select a sample and examine documents for evidence of credit check (valuation).
Warehouse and Shipping	**1.** Receive approved sales order from credit dept. (must have approved sales order before release of goods from warehouse). **2.** Pull inventory from warehouse and release to shipping. **3.** Perform independent check of goods received from warehouse and approved sales orders in shipping department. **4.** Prepare bill of lading.	• Observe warehouse personnel filling sales orders (existence). • Observe physical controls over inventory. • Observe evidence of independent checks (existence). • Inspect a sample of prenumbered shipping documents and: —Agree to sales order (existence). —Account for prenumbering (completeness).
Billing/Accounts Receivable (continued)	**1.** Match shipping documents and sales orders before preparing invoice. **2.** Periodically account for all prenumbered shipping documents. **3.** Perform independent check of sales order pricing. **4.** Prepare prenumbered sales invoice. **5.** Batch and total invoices. **6.** Update A/R master file. Agree input to invoice batch totals.	• Vouch a sample of sales invoices (select approved sales orders from the sales journal) to shipping documents and approved sales orders (existence). • Trace a sample of shipping documents (selection from prenumbered shipping documents) to sales invoice, sales journal, and A/R master file (completeness). • Observe matching of shipping documents and sales orders Reperform procedures for a sample period (completeness). • Reperform pricing check: From a sample of sales invoices, check pricing with master price list (valuation).

(continued) *Billing/Accounts Receivable*	**7.** Print sales journal. **8.** Print sales summary. Agree to invoice batch totals (independent check). **9.** Mail monthly customer statements.	• Observe periodic counts and independent checks and reperform (valuation). • Observe mailing (existence, completeness, valuation).
Accounting	**1.** Receive sales summary. **2.** Perform independent check of invoice batch totals and sales summary. **3.** Review sales account classifications. **4.** Post to G/L. **5.** Follow-up customer exceptions (independent check).	• Observe and reperform independent checks (valuation, existence, completeness). • Observe and reperform review of sales account classifications (report presentation). • Inspect customer exception file and disposition (existence, completeness, rights, valuation).

Note: A formal audit program can be prepared and organized by assertion and sample population.

Segregation of Duties:

Authorization: Sales order and credit, treasurer

Record keeping: Billing/accounts receivable/accounting

Custody: Warehouse and shipping

2 Testing Controls: Cash Receipts

Department	Control Procedure	Sample Test of Control Procedure
Mail Room	**1.** Separate checks and remittance advices. **2.** Stamp restrictive endorsement on checks. **3.** Prepare prelisting of checks received. **4.** Forward checks to cashier. Forward remittance advices to A/R. Forward prelisting to accounting, cashier, and accounts receivable.	• Inspect checks prior to deposit for endorsement (completeness). • Observe preparation of prelisting (existence, completeness, valuation).
Cashier	**1.** Receive checks and prepare deposit. **2.** Prepare daily cash summary (copy to A/R and accounting). **3.** Deliver checks to bank. **4.** File validated deposit slip.	• Observe preparation of cash summary (existence, completeness, valuation). • Inspect deposit slip and compare to cash summary (existence, completeness, valuation).

Accounts Receivable	**1.** Match remittance advices and check deposit summary. **2.** Update A/R master file. **3.** Print CR journal/updated A/R master file. **4.** Print CR summary (copy to accounting).	• Observe matching of remittance advices and check deposit summary (completeness).
Accounting	**1.** Independent check: compare the cash summary (cashier), the prelisting of checks (mail room), and the CR summary (A/R). **2.** Post G/L. **3.** Prepare bank reconciliation.	• Inspect evidence of independent check (existence, completeness, valuation). • Reperform independent check for selected dates (existence, completeness, valuation). • Inspect bank reconciliation (existence, completeness, valuation).

Segregation of Duties:

Record keeping: Accounts receivable/accounting

Custody: Mail room and cashier (treasurer)

3 Testing Controls: Purchases

Department	Control Procedure	Sample Test of Control Procedure
Requisitioner	**1.** Prepare prenumbered requisition. **2.** Obtain approvals needed (authorization). **3.** Send original copy to purchasing. **4.** Inspect goods when received from receiving dept. Sign receiving report upon receipt of goods (independent check).	• Inspect requisitions for proper approval. • Observe procedures to account for prenumbering.
Purchasing	**1.** Receive approved requisition. **2.** Contact approved vendors. **3.** Issued prenumbered purchase order (PO): • Original to vendor • Blind copy to receiving • Copy to A/P • File copy	• Inspect purchase orders for approved requisition. • Observe procedures to account for prenumbering.

Receiving	**1.** Receive goods from vendor. **2.** Inspect goods. All shipments received must have a PO. **3.** Prepare receiving report (RR). **4.** Match details of order received with blind copy of PO and indicate quantity received. **5.** Send goods to requisitioning department. Obtain signature on receiving report that requisitioner received goods. **6.** Distribute receiving report: • Original to A/P • Copy to purchasing • File copy	• Inspect receiving report and matching PO. • Observe performance of procedures by receiving clerk. • Inspect receiving report for signed receipt (existence). • Trace a sample of receiving reports (selection made from prenumbered documents) to PO, requisition, invoice, and entry in the purchase journal and A/P master file (completeness).
Accounts Payable	**1.** Receive vendor's invoice. **2.** Match documents: vendor's invoice, RR, PO, requisition. **3.** Check mathematical accuracy, approvals, G/L account coding (independent check). **4.** Prepare prenumbered voucher. **5.** Account for the numerical sequence of vouchers. **6.** Data entry: • Prepare purchase journal • Update A/P master file • Daily purchase summary **7.** Reconcile daily purchase summary totals and daily entries to purchases journal.	• Inspect vouchers for supporting documents and evidence of independent checks (existence). • Observe and reperform accounting for numerical sequence of vouchers (completeness). • Vouch a sample of vouchers (selection made from the purchases journal) to all required supporting documents (existence). • Observe evidence of independent check; reperform (valuation).
Accounting	**1.** Receive purchase summary. **2.** Post to G/L. **3.** Reconcile G/L and A/P file. **4.** Reconcile vendor's monthly statements and A/P master file (independent check).	• Observe evidence of independent check; reperform. • Observe evidence of independent check; reperform (valuation, existence, completeness).

Segregation of Duties:

Authorization: Purchasing/requisitioning dept.
Record keeping: Accounts payable/accounting
Custody: Receiving

4 Testing Controls: Payables and Cash Disbursements

Department	Control Procedure	Sample Test of Control Procedure
Accounts Payable	**1.** Pull voucher at due date and send to treasurer for payment. **2.** Receive cancelled voucher and supporting documents from treasurer. **3.** Receive check summary from treasurer for data entry. **4.** Data entry: • Update A/P master file. • Print cash disbursements journal.	• Compare debits to accounts payable to properly cancelled voucher packages (existence). • Trace from cancelled voucher packages to cash disbursement journal entries (completeness). • Vouch cash disbursement journal entries back to cancelled voucher packages (existence).
Treasurer	**1.** Receive voucher for payment. **2.** Review document for completeness and approvals. **3.** Prepare prenumbered checks. **4.** Prepare check summary. **5.** Sign checks (authorized signatory) and cancel voucher and supporting documents. **6.** Mail check to vendor. **7.** Forward cancelled voucher/ supporting documents to Accounts payable. **8.** Send copy of check summary: • Accounts payable • Accounting	• Observe performance of independent check. • Observe accounting for sequence (completeness). • Inquire about procedures performed; observe. Select checks for testing and inspect signatures. • Observe cancellation of vouchers by check signer. • Inquire about procedure. Observe performance.
Accounting	**1.** Receive check summary. **2.** Post to G/L. **3.** Perform independent check of totals per check summary and amounts journalized and posted by A/P. **4.** Perform periodic independent bank reconciliation.	• Observe procedures of posting and performing independent check and reperform. • Inspect bank reconciliation.

Segregation of Duties:

Authorization:	Purchasing/requisitioning dept.
Record keeping:	Accounts payable/accounting
Custody:	Receiving (purchased item) and treasurer (cash)

NOTES

AUD

5

Integrated Audits, Attestation Engagements, Compliance, and Government Audits

Module

NOTES

Integrated Audit = FS & IC
Issues = must
nonissues = may

1 Integrated Audit Procedures

1 Overview of Integrated Audits (Issuers and Nonissuers)

Under PCAOB standards, auditors of issuers are required to perform an integrated audit, auditing both the financial statements and management's assessment of the effectiveness of internal control over financial reporting (ICFR). The audit of management's assessment is commonly referred to as an "audit of internal control over financial reporting."

Impact of the Dodd-Frank Act on the Issuer Integrated Audit Requirement
The Dodd-Frank Act amended Rule 404 of the Sarbanes-Oxley Act to provide that an audit of an issuer's internal control over financial reporting is only required for issuers that are large accelerated filers or accelerated filers. A large accelerated filer is defined by the U.S. Securities and Exchange Commission (SEC) as an issuer with a worldwide market value of outstanding common equity held by nonaffiliates of $700 million or more. An accelerated filer is defined as an issuer with a worldwide market value of outstanding common equity held by nonaffiliates of $75 million or more, but less than $700 million. Smaller reporting companies, which are entities with annual revenues of less than $100 million, are excluded from the definition of large accelerated filers or accelerated filers.

For nonissuers, SAS 130 governs the audit and report on a nonissuer's internal control over financial reporting that is integrated with a financial statement audit. The rules regarding the conduct of issuer and nonissuer integrated audits are very similar. The similarities and differences between the two sets of integrated audit standards are highlighted below.

1.1 Objective of the Engagement (Issuers and Nonissuers)

The auditor's objective in an audit of internal control is to express an opinion on the effectiveness of the entity's internal control over financial reporting. Because an entity's internal control cannot be considered effective if one or more material weaknesses exist, the auditor should plan and perform the engagement to obtain sufficient appropriate evidence to obtain reasonable assurance about whether material weaknesses exist as of the date specified in management's assessment, which should correspond to the balance sheet date for the financial statement audit.

2 Conditions for Engagement Performance

2.1 Auditor Requirements (Issuers and Nonissuers)

The audit of internal control should be integrated with an audit of the financial statements. The auditor should plan and perform the integrated audit to achieve the objectives of both engagements.

The auditor should use the same control criteria to perform the audit of internal control as management uses for its evaluation of the effectiveness of the entity's internal control.

2nd opinion

Tests of controls should be designed to provide sufficient appropriate evidence to support both the opinion on internal control and the control risk assessment needed for the financial statement audit.

2.2 Management Requirements (Issuers Only)

Section 404 of the *Sarbanes-Oxley Act of 2002* requires each issuer's annual report to contain an internal control report that:

1. states management's responsibility for establishing and maintaining an adequate internal control structure and procedures for financial reporting; and
2. contains an assessment, as of the end of the most recent fiscal year of the issuer, of the effectiveness of the internal control structure and procedures of issuer for financial reporting.

Note: The American Institute of Certified Public Accountants (AICPA) standards use the term "management's assessment" while the Public Company Accounting Oversight Board (PCAOB) uses the term "management's assertion." The term "assessment" is being used in this text for consistency.

2.3 Management Requirements (Nonissuers Only)

An audit of internal control can only be performed if management:

- Accepts responsibility for the effectiveness of internal control.
- Evaluates the effectiveness of the entity's internal control using suitable and available criteria, such as criteria issued by the AICPA or by regulatory agencies.
- Supports its assessment about the effectiveness of internal control with sufficient appropriate evidence.
  - Management is responsible for identifying and documenting control objectives and the controls that meet those objectives.
  - Management's monitoring activities may provide evidence supporting its assertion.
- Provides a written assessment about the effectiveness of the entity's internal control in a report that accompanies the auditor's report.
  - The "as of" date in management's assertion should coincide with the date of the financial statements.
  - If management refuses to furnish a written assessment, the auditor should withdraw from the engagement. In rare instances, in which the auditor is not permitted by law or regulation to withdraw, a disclaimer of opinion on ICFR should be issued and the auditor should consider the impact on the financial statement audit. Management's refusal to provide a written assessment would be treated as a scope limitation.

mgmt also assess and report on IC

2.4 Written Representations (Issuers and Nonissuers)

The auditor should obtain a written representation letter from management in which management:

1. Acknowledges its responsibility for establishing and maintaining effective internal control, and states that management has performed an assessment of the effectiveness of the entity's internal control.
2. States management's assessment as of a specified date and specifies the criteria used.
3. Affirms that management did not rely on the auditor's procedures as the basis for the assessment.
4. States that management has disclosed all deficiencies in design and operation. Confirms that all significant deficiencies and material weaknesses have been disclosed to the auditor, and indicates whether any such deficiencies identified in previous engagements remain unresolved.
5. Describes fraud resulting in material misstatement or fraud involving senior management or other employees who have a significant role in ICFR.
6. States whether there were any significant changes to internal control after the "as of" date of the report, including any corrective action taken by management regarding significant deficiencies and material weaknesses identified. → subsequent event

Failure to obtain such written representations is a scope limitation that will generally result in the auditor's withdrawal from the engagement or in a disclaimer of opinion.

3 Planning the Engagement (Issuers and Nonissuers)

3.1 Overall Planning

Planning involves developing an overall strategy for the scope and performance of the engagement. The auditor should consider:

- Matters affecting the industry of the entity—financial reporting practices, economic conditions, laws and regulations, and technological change.
- Prior knowledge of the entity's internal control (obtained during other professional engagements or by reviewing a predecessor's working papers).
- Matters concerning the entity and its business—organization, operations, and capital structure.
- The relative complexity of entity operations, as well as the extent of any recent changes in the entity, its operations, or its internal control.
- Management's method of evaluating control effectiveness.
- Judgments about materiality and risk, including risks evaluated as part of the auditor's acceptance and retention decision and preliminary judgments about the effectiveness of internal control.
  - The same level of materiality and the same risk assessment process should be used for both the financial statement audit and the audit of internal control.
  - More attention should be focused on areas of higher risk.

- The results of the fraud risk assessment performed in the financial statement audit should be considered in the audit of internal control, and the auditor should evaluate whether controls sufficiently address fraud risk.

- Previously communicated deficiencies, legal or regulatory matters, and public information about the entity.
- The nature and extent of available evidence.
- Scaling the audit: Smaller or less complex companies might achieve their control objectives differently from more complex companies, so the audit should be scaled appropriately.

3.2 Fraud Risk Assessment

The auditor's fraud risk assessment (required in the financial statement audit) should be integrated into the audit of internal control, and the auditor should consider management fraud and management override of controls as areas of high risk. Controls that might address these risks include controls over:

- Significant or unusual transactions
- Period-end journal entries and adjustments
- Related party transactions
- Significant management estimates

The auditor should also consider controls that mitigate incentives and pressures that may lead management to falsify or inappropriately manage financial results.

3.3 Using the Work of Others

The auditor may use the work of others (internal auditors, other company personnel, and certain third parties) who are sufficiently competent and objective, in evaluating the effectiveness of internal control.

The auditor should consider the risk associated with a particular control, in determining whether and to what extent to use the work of others. As risk increases, a greater degree of competence and objectivity is required. For high-risk areas, use of the work of others might be reduced or eliminated.

4 Top-Down Approach (Issuers and Nonissuers)

A *top-down approach* is used in selecting controls to test. The auditor evaluates overall risks at the financial statement level, considers controls at the entity level, and then focuses on accounts, disclosures, and assertions for which there is a reasonable possibility of material misstatement.

4.1 Entity-Level Controls

The auditor should identify and test entity-level controls that are important to the auditor's overall opinion about internal control. Entity-level controls include controls related to:

- The control environment
- Management override
- The company's risk assessment process
- Centralized processing

- Monitoring the results of operations
- Monitoring other controls
- Period-end financial reporting
- Policies that address significant business control and risk management practices

The auditor's evaluation of entity-level controls can result in increasing or decreasing the testing that the auditor otherwise would have performed on other controls. Entity-level controls that are working effectively may allow the auditor to reduce the testing of lower-level controls, or might affect the nature, extent, or timing of the auditor's tests of lower-level controls.

4.2 Identifying Significant Classes of Transactions, Account Balances, Disclosures, and Assertions

The auditor should evaluate qualitative and quantitative risk factors to identify significant classes of transactions, account balances and disclosures, and their relevant assertions. Risk factors include:

- Account size and composition
- Susceptibility to misstatement
- Volume of activity, complexity, and homogeneity of transactions
- The nature of the account, class of transactions, or disclosure
- Accounting and reporting complexities
- Exposure to loss, or to the possibility of significant contingent liabilities
- The existence of related party transactions
- Changes from the prior period

In determining what amount of audit attention should be applied to a particular class of transactions, account balance, disclosure, or assertion, the auditor should assess the risk that a material weakness in that area may exist, as well as the risk that such weakness will lead to a material misstatement in the financial statements.

- A greater risk implies that more audit attention should be applied, more evidence should be obtained, etc.
- The evaluation of risk factors is the same for both an audit of the financial statements and an audit of internal control.
- A *walk-through* (in which a transaction is followed from origination through financial recording) is one of the most effective ways to identify likely sources of potential misstatement.

4.3 Selecting Controls to Test

The auditor should test those controls that are important in addressing the risk of material misstatement.

5 Testing Controls (Issuers and Nonissuers)

Pass Key

AICPA Standards

In an integrated audit, the auditor should evaluate the components of ICFR and determine whether the components are:

1. present and functioning in design, implementation and operation; and
2. operating together in an integrated manner.

Components of ICFR: Recall that the components of internal control over financial reporting (ICFR) are:

- **Control** environment
- **Risk** assessment
- **Information** and communication systems
- **Monitoring**
- **Existing** control activities

5.1 Tests of Controls

In testing controls, the auditor should:

- Evaluate the *design* effectiveness of the controls to determine whether the controls, if applied as prescribed, satisfy the company's control objectives and can effectively prevent or detect (and correct) material misstatements.
  - Walk-throughs, which include inquiry, observation, and inspection of documentation, are often used to evaluate design effectiveness.
- Test and evaluate the *operating* effectiveness of the controls to determine whether the controls are operating as designed, and whether the persons implementing the controls are qualified to implement them effectively.
  - Operating effectiveness is typically tested through inquiry, inspection of documentation, observation, recalculation, and reperformance.
  - Inquiry alone is not sufficient to support a conclusion about operating effectiveness.
- Obtain relatively more evidence for controls that are subject to a greater risk of failure.
- Obtain sufficient appropriate evidence to support the opinion about the overall effectiveness of the entity's internal control.
  - The auditor is not responsible for obtaining sufficient evidence to support an opinion about the effectiveness of each individual control, but rather the effectiveness of the entity's internal control overall.

- Determine the effect of any identified control deviations on the assessment of risk associated with the control, the amount of evidence to be obtained, and the operating effectiveness of the control.
  - An individual control does not have to operate without any deviation to be considered effective.
- Determine the appropriate timing for tests of controls.
  - Tests performed over a longer period of time provide more evidence of effectiveness than tests performed over a shorter period.
  - Tests performed closer to the date of management's assertion provide more evidence than testing performed earlier in the year. (Tests performed earlier in the year should be supplemented with additional evidence for the remainder of the year.)
  - The auditor should use judgment in balancing the timing of tests.
- Consider knowledge obtained during past audits.
- Incorporate an element of unpredictability into the testing.

5.2 Use of Service Organizations

A service organization may be part of an entity's internal control. In such cases, the auditor should:

- Obtain an understanding of relevant controls.
- Obtain evidence that the controls at the service organization are operating effectively by performing one or more of the following: Obtaining a service auditor's report (covered in more detail in a later module), testing the entity's controls over the activities of the service organization, and/or performing tests of controls at the service organization.
  - If the date specified in management's assertion is significantly beyond the time period covered by the service auditor's report, the auditor should perform additional procedures.
  - No reference should be made to the service auditor's report in the auditor's report on internal control.

5.3 Benchmarking of Automated Controls

Automated application controls are not particularly susceptible to human error. If general controls with respect to program modifications, access, and operations are tested and continue to be effective, and if the automated controls have not changed from one year to the next, the auditor may not need to repeat specific testing performed in the previous year (but would need to verify that the control has not changed). This "benchmarking" strategy is most appropriate in low-risk situations.

6 Evaluating Control Deficiencies (Issuers and Nonissuers)

The auditor should determine whether identified deficiencies represent significant deficiencies or material weaknesses (either alone or in combination). This determination should be based on:

1. the magnitude of the potential misstatement resulting from the deficiency; and
2. whether there is a reasonable possibility that the control will fail to prevent, or detect and correct, a material misstatement.

As indicated previously, indicators of material weaknesses include senior management fraud, restatement of previous financial statements to correct a material error, identification by the auditor of a material misstatement that the entity's controls would not have detected, and ineffective oversight by those charged with governance. A control weakness may be a material weakness even if no misstatement actually occurred.

Compensating controls, if tested and found to be operating effectively, may limit the severity of an identified deficiency and prevent it from being a material weakness.

7 Forming an Opinion (Issuers and Nonissuers)

The auditor should form an opinion about the effectiveness of internal control. The auditor should base this opinion on all available evidence, including both evidence obtained from the financial statement audit and evidence obtained during the audit of internal control.

After forming an opinion on the effectiveness of the entity's internal control over financial reporting, the auditor should evaluate management's report on internal control.

Management's report should:

- Indicate that management is responsible for internal control.
- Describe the subject matter (e.g., controls over financial statement preparation).
- Identify the criteria used by management to measure the effectiveness of the entity's internal control.
- Include a statement of management's assessment about the effectiveness of internal control, including an "as of" date. The "as of" date should be the end of the entity's most recent fiscal year.
- Describe any material weaknesses identified by management.
- If the auditor determines that the required disclosures for one or more material weaknesses have not been included in management's report, this should be stated in the auditor's report. The auditor's report should include a description of each material weakness not included in management's report.
- If management's report is incomplete or improperly presented, the auditor should modify his or her own report to discuss the situation. If management refuses to supply a report, the auditor should withdraw from the engagement.
- If management's report contains additional information beyond that noted above, the auditor should disclaim an opinion on such information. For example, if the report states that management believes the cost of correcting a weakness would exceed the benefits to be derived from implementing new policies and procedures, the auditor should disclaim an opinion on management's "cost-benefit statement":

  We do not express an opinion or any other form of assurance on management's cost-benefit statement.

8 Financial Statement Audit vs. Audit of Internal Control (Nonissuers)

8.1 Differences Between the Two Engagements

8.1.1 Purpose

The purpose of an audit of the effectiveness of an entity's internal control is to express an opinion about whether the entity maintained, in all material respects, effective internal control as of a point in time based on the control criteria. The purpose of an auditor's consideration of internal control in an audit of financial statements conducted in accordance with GAAS is to enable the auditor to plan the audit and determine the nature, extent, and timing of tests to be performed.

8.1.2 Relevant Period

An audit of internal control results in an opinion on internal control as of a point in time, and an opinion on financial statements relates to a longer period, such as a year.

8.1.3 Extent of Testing

An auditor's consideration of internal control in a financial statement audit is more limited than that of an auditor engaged to audit the effectiveness of the entity's internal control. In order to render an opinion on internal control, the auditor should obtain evidence about the effectiveness of selected controls over *all* relevant assertions. In a financial statement audit, the auditor is not required to test controls over *all* relevant assertions (for example, if a substantive approach is to be used instead).

8.1.4 Communication of Control Deficiencies

In a financial statement audit, the communication of significant deficiencies and material weaknesses must be made within 60 days of the report release date, whereas in an audit of internal control, the communication must be made by the report release date.

In a financial statement audit, the communication of significant deficiencies and material weaknesses should include restricted-use language, but in an audit of internal control, no restriction on the use of the report is required.

8.2 Interrelationships Between the Two Engagements

The results from one type of engagement should be considered in performing the other type of engagement.

- In forming an opinion on internal control, the auditor should consider the results of tests of controls performed as part of the financial statement audit.
- In concluding on the effectiveness of controls as part of the financial statement audit, the auditor should consider the results of tests performed as part of the internal control audit.
- If during the audit of internal control a deficiency is noted, the auditor should consider this deficiency in determining the nature, timing, and extent of substantive tests in the financial statement audit.
- The auditor should consider whether any observations made during the financial statement audit impact the auditor's opinion on internal control. For example, identified misstatements might imply that controls are not functioning effectively.
  - Note that the absence of misstatements does not imply operating effectiveness, although it may affect the auditor's assessment of risk.

Question 1 **MCQ-05389**

In an audit of an issuer, the auditor must provide an opinion on which of the following?

I. The financial statements.

II. The audit committee's oversight of financial reporting and internal control.

III. The effectiveness of internal control.

a. I and III only.

b. I, II, and III.

c. I and II only.

d. I only.

Communication and Reporting in an Integrated Audit

1 Communications With Management and Those Charged With Governance (Nonissuers Only)

1.1 Significant Deficiencies and Material Weaknesses

The auditor should *communicate to management and those charged with governance, in writing, all significant deficiencies and material weaknesses* found during the audit of the internal controls of a nonissuer (including those remediated during the integrated audit and those that were previously communicated in writing, but which have not been corrected).

- Such communication generally should be made by the report release date.
- Significant deficiencies and material weaknesses that were previously communicated in writing, but which have not been corrected, may be communicated by referring to the previously issued written communication and the date of the communication.
- The auditor may choose to communicate significant matters earlier, during the course of the integrated audit, but this does not negate the requirement for a written communication, even if the deficiencies were corrected during the audit.

1.1.1 Sample Communication: To Management and Those Charged With Governance

To Management and [*identify the body or individuals charged with governance, such as the entity's board of directors*] of ABC Company:

In connection with our audit of ABC Company's (the Company) financial statements as of December 31, 20XX, and for the year then ended, and our audit of the Company's internal control over financial reporting as of December 31, 20XX (integrated audit), auditing standards generally accepted in the United States of America require that we advise you of the following matters relating to internal control over financial reporting (internal control) identified during our integrated audit.

Our responsibility is to plan and perform our integrated audit to obtain reasonable assurance about whether the financial statements are free from material misstatement, whether due to fraud or error, and whether effective internal control was maintained in all material respects (that is, whether material weaknesses exist as of the date specified in management's assessment). The integrated audit is not designed to detect deficiencies that, individually or in combination, are less severe than a material weakness.

(continued)

(continued)

A deficiency in internal control exists when the design or operation of a control does not allow management or employees, in the normal course of performing their assigned functions, to prevent, or detect and correct, misstatements on a timely basis. A material weakness is a deficiency, or a combination of deficiencies, in internal control, such that there is a reasonable possibility that a material misstatement of the entity's financial statements will not be prevented, or detected and corrected, on a timely basis. [*We consider the following deficiencies in the Company's internal control to be material weaknesses:*]

[*Describe the material weaknesses that were identified during the integrated audit and provide an explanation of their potential effects. The auditor may separately identify those material weaknesses that exist as of the date specified in management's assessment about ICFR by referring to the auditor's report.*]

[*A significant deficiency is a deficiency, or a combination of deficiencies, in internal control that is less severe than a material weakness, yet important enough to merit attention by those charged with governance. We consider the following deficiencies in the Company's internal control over financial reporting to be significant deficiencies:*]

[*Describe the significant deficiencies that were identified during the integrated audit and provide an explanation of their potential effects.*]

This communication is intended solely for the information and use of management [*identify the body or individuals charged with governance*], others within the organization, and [*identify any governmental authorities to which the auditor is required to report*], and is not intended to be and should not be used by anyone other than these specified parties.

[*Auditor's signature*]

[*Auditor's city and state*]

[*Date of the auditor's report*]

1.2 All Deficiencies

The auditor should *communicate to management, in writing, all deficiencies* identified during the integrated audit (i.e., even those that do not rise to the level of being significant deficiencies or material weaknesses).

- This written communication should be made *no later than 60 days following the report release date*. The auditor should also *inform those charged with governance* when such a communication has been made. Deficiencies previously communicated in writing need not be repeated.
- If the auditor concludes that the oversight of financial reporting and internal control by the company's audit committee (or similar body) is ineffective, the auditor must communicate that conclusion in writing to the board of directors.
- The auditor is not required to search for control deficiencies that are less severe than a material weakness, but those that are identified should be reported.

- An audit does not provide assurance that all deficiencies less severe than a material weakness have been identified, so the auditor should not issue a report stating that no such deficiencies were noted. The auditor also should not issue a report stating that no material weaknesses were identified.

Communication of Deficiencies in Internal Control (Nonissuer)				
	Communicate *the deficiency* ***to management,*** *in writing.*	***Communicate*** *the deficiency* ***to those charged with governance,*** *in writing.*	***Communication*** *should be made* ***by the report release date.***	***Communication*** *should be made* ***within 60 days of the report release date.***
Control deficiency	✓			✓
Significant deficiency	✓	✓	✓	
Material weakness	✓	✓	✓	

2 Communications With Management and the Audit Committee (Issuers Only)

The auditor *must communicate, in writing, to management and the audit committee, all material weaknesses* identified during the audit. The written communication should be made *prior to the issuance of the auditor's report on internal control* over financial reporting.

- The auditor is required to *communicate any identified significant deficiencies, in writing, to the audit committee.*
- The auditor should *communicate to management, in writing, all deficiencies in internal control* over financial reporting (i.e., those deficiencies in internal control over financial reporting that are of a lesser magnitude than material weaknesses) identified during the audit *and inform the audit committee* when such a communication has been made.
- If the auditor concludes that the oversight of financial reporting and internal control by the company's audit committee is ineffective, the auditor must communicate that conclusion in writing to the board of directors.
- The auditor is not required to search for control deficiencies or significant deficiencies, but those that are identified should be communicated.
- An audit does not provide assurance that all control deficiencies or all significant deficiencies have been identified, so the auditor should not issue a report stating that no such deficiencies were noted.
- The PCAOB has not provided sample communications to management or the audit committee.

Communication of Deficiencies in Internal Control (Issuer)			
	Communicate *the deficiency to* ***management,*** *in writing, and inform the audit committee that this communication has been made.*	***Communicate*** *the deficiency* ***to the audit committee,*** *in writing.*	***Communication*** *(to management and the audit committee) should be made* ***prior to the issuance of the auditor's report*** *on internal control.*
Control deficiency	✓		
Significant deficiency	✓	✓	
Material weakness	✓	✓	✓

3 Reporting on Internal Control (Nonissuers)

The auditor must report directly on the effectiveness of the entity's internal control.

3.1 Separate or Combined Reports

The auditor is required to report on both the company's financial statements and on its internal control over financial reporting. Two separate reports, or one combined report (that is, one report containing both an opinion on the financial statements and an opinion on internal control), may be issued.

3.1.1 Separate Reports

If separate reports are issued, each report should contain an other-matter paragraph making reference to the other report and indicating the nature of the opinion expressed.

3.1.2 Sample Report: Separate Report on Internal Control Over Financial Reporting (Nonissuer)

Independent Auditor's Report

[*Appropriate Addressee*]

Report on Internal Control Over Financial Reporting

We have audited ABC Company's internal control over financial reporting as of December 31, 20XX, based on [*identify criteria*].*

Management's Responsibility for Internal Control Over Financial Reporting

Management is responsible for designing, implementing, and maintaining effective internal control over financial reporting, and for its assessment about the effectiveness of internal control over financial reporting, included in the accompanying [*title of management's report*].

(continued)

(continued)

Auditor's Responsibility

Our responsibility is to express an opinion on the entity's internal control over financial reporting based on our audit. We conducted our audit in accordance with auditing standards generally accepted in the United States of America. Those standards require that we plan and perform the audit to obtain reasonable assurance about whether effective internal control over financial reporting was maintained in all material respects.

An audit of internal control over financial reporting involves performing procedures to obtain audit evidence about whether a material weakness exists. The procedures selected depend on the auditor's judgment, including the assessment of the risks that a material weakness exists. An audit includes obtaining an understanding of internal control over financial reporting and testing and evaluating the design and operating effectiveness of internal control over financial reporting based on the assessed risk.

We believe that the audit evidence we have obtained is sufficient and appropriate to provide a basis for our audit opinion.

Definition and Inherent Limitations of Internal Control Over Financial Reporting

An entity's internal control over financial reporting is a process effected by those charged with governance, management, and other personnel, designed to provide reasonable assurance regarding the preparation of reliable financial statements in accordance with [*applicable financial reporting framework, such as accounting principles generally accepted in the United States of America*].

An entity's internal control over financial reporting includes those policies and procedures that (1) pertain to the maintenance of records that, in reasonable detail, accurately and fairly reflect the transactions and dispositions of the assets of the entity; (2) provide reasonable assurance that transactions are recorded as necessary to permit preparation of financial statements in accordance with [*applicable financial reporting framework, such as accounting principles generally accepted in the United States of America*], and that receipts and expenditures of the entity are being made only in accordance with authorizations of management and those charged with governance; and (3) provide reasonable assurance regarding prevention, or timely detection and correction of unauthorized acquisition, use, or disposition of the entity's assets that could have a material effect on the financial statements.

Because of its inherent limitations, internal control over financial reporting may not prevent, or detect and correct, misstatements. Also, projections of any assessment of effectiveness to future periods are subject to the risk that controls may become inadequate because of changes in conditions, or that the degree of compliance with the policies or procedures may deteriorate.

(continued)

(continued)

Opinion

In our opinion, ABC Company maintained, in all material respects, effective internal control over financial reporting as of December 31, 20XX, based on [*identify criteria*].

Report on Financial Statements

We also have audited, in accordance with auditing standards generally accepted in the United States of America, the [*identify financial statements*] of ABC Company, and our report dated [*date of report, which should be the same as the date of the report on the audit of ICFR]* expressed *[include nature of opinion*].

[*Auditor's signature*]

[*Auditor's city and state*]

[*Date of the auditor's report*]

*For example, the following may be used to identify the criteria: "criteria established in the *Internal Control—Integrated Framework* (2013), issued by the Committee of Sponsoring Organizations of the Treadway Commission (COSO)."

Pass Key

The examiners have focused many questions in prior exams on the "inherent limitations paragraph."

The following paragraph should be added to the separate report on the financial statements (nonissuer):

Report on Audit of ICFR

We also have audited, in accordance with auditing standards generally accepted in the United States of America, [*entity name*]'s internal control over financial reporting as of December 31, 20X8, based on [*identify criteria*] and our report dated [*date of report, which should be the same as the date of the report on the financial statements*] expressed [*include nature of opinion*].

3.1.3 Sample Report: Combined Report on Internal Control Over Financial Statements and on the Financial Statements (Nonissuer)

Independent Auditor's Report

[*Appropriate Addressee*]

Report on the Financial Statements and Internal Control

We have audited the accompanying financial statements of ABC Company, which comprise the balance sheet as of December 31, 20XX, and the related statements of income, changes in stockholders' equity, and cash flows for the year then ended, and the related notes to the financial statements. We also have audited ABC Company's internal control over financial reporting as of December 31, 20XX, based on [*identify criteria*].

Management's Responsibility for the Financial Statements and Internal Control Over Financial Reporting

Management is responsible for the preparation and fair presentation of these financial statements in accordance with accounting principles generally accepted in the United States of America; this includes the design, implementation, and maintenance of effective internal control over financial reporting relevant to the preparation and fair presentation of financial statements that are free from material misstatement, whether due to fraud or error. Management is also responsible for its assessment about the effectiveness of internal control over financial reporting, included in the accompanying [*title of management's report*].

Auditor's Responsibility

Our responsibility is to express an opinion on these financial statements and an opinion on the entity's internal control over financial reporting based on our audits. We conducted our audits in accordance with auditing standards generally accepted in the United States of America. Those standards require that we plan and perform the audits to obtain reasonable assurance about whether the financial statements are free from material misstatement and whether effective internal control over financial reporting was maintained in all material respects.

An audit of financial statements involves performing procedures to obtain audit evidence about the amounts and disclosures in the financial statements. The procedures selected depend on the auditor's judgment, including the assessment of the risks of material misstatement of the financial statements, whether due to fraud or error. In making those risk assessments, the auditor considers internal control relevant to the entity's preparation and fair presentation of the financial statements in order to design audit procedures that are appropriate in the circumstances. An audit of financial statements also includes evaluating the appropriateness of accounting policies used and the reasonableness of significant accounting estimates made by management, as well as evaluating the overall presentation of the financial statements.

(continued)

(continued)

An audit of internal control over financial reporting involves performing procedures to obtain evidence about whether a material weakness exists. The procedures selected depend on the auditor's judgment, including the assessment of the risk that a material weakness exists. An audit of internal control over financial reporting also involves obtaining an understanding of internal control over financial reporting and testing and evaluating the design and operating effectiveness of internal control over financial reporting based on the assessed risk.

We believe that the audit evidence we have obtained is sufficient and appropriate to provide a basis for our audit opinions.

Definition and Inherent Limitations of Internal Control Over Financial Reporting

An entity's internal control over financial reporting is a process effected by those charged with governance, management, and other personnel, designed to provide reasonable assurance regarding the preparation of reliable financial statements in accordance with accounting principles generally accepted in the United States of America. An entity's internal control over financial reporting includes those policies and procedures that (1) pertain to the maintenance of records that, in reasonable detail, accurately and fairly reflect the transactions and dispositions of the assets of the entity; (2) provide reasonable assurance that transactions are recorded as necessary to permit preparation of financial statements in accordance with accounting principles generally accepted in the United States of America, and that receipts and expenditures of the entity are being made only in accordance with authorizations of management and those charged with governance; and (3) provide reasonable assurance regarding prevention, or timely detection and correction of unauthorized acquisition, use, or disposition of the entity's assets that could have a material effect on the financial statements.

Because of its inherent limitations, internal control over financial reporting may not prevent, or detect and correct, misstatements. Also, projections of any assessment of effectiveness to future periods are subject to the risk that controls may become inadequate because of changes in conditions, or that the degree of compliance with the policies or procedures may deteriorate.

Opinions

In our opinion, the financial statements referred to above present fairly, in all material respects, the financial position of ABC Company as of December 31, 20XX, and the results of its operations and its cash flows for the year then ended in accordance with accounting principles generally accepted in the United States of America. Also, in our opinion, ABC Company maintained, in all material respects, effective internal control over financial reporting as of December 31, 20XX, based on [*identify criteria*].

[*Auditor's signature*]

[*Auditor's city and state*]

[*Date of the auditor's report*]

3.2 Report Date

The report should be dated no earlier than the date on which sufficient appropriate evidence has been obtained.

The date of the report on internal control should coincide with the date of the audit report on the financial statements.

3.3 Material Weakness in Internal Control

3.3.1 Adverse Opinion

The presence of a material weakness in internal control results in an adverse opinion. The auditor's report should include a paragraph defining the term "material weakness," stating that one or more material weaknesses were noted, and referring to the material weakness described in management's assertion. Preceding the opinion paragraph, the report should include a basis for opinion paragraph:

> **Basis for Adverse Opinion**
>
> A material weakness is a deficiency, or a combination of deficiencies, in internal control over financial reporting, such that there is a reasonable possibility that a material misstatement of the entity's financial statements will not be prevented, or detected and corrected, on a timely basis. The following material weakness has been identified and included in the accompanying [*title of management's report*].
>
> **Adverse Opinion**
>
> In our opinion, because of the effect of the material weakness described in the basis for adverse opinion paragraph on the achievement of the objectives of [*identify criteria*], ABC Company has not maintained effective internal control over financial reporting as of December 31, 20XX, based on [*identify criteria*].

3.3.2 Other Considerations

- If management's report fails to include one or more material weaknesses identified by the auditor, the auditor's report should state this, and should describe the omitted weaknesses. The auditor also should communicate this situation, in writing, to those charged with governance.
- If management's report includes a material weakness but does not fairly present the weakness, the auditor's report should indicate this situation and should fairly describe the material weakness.
- The auditor should consider the effect of this adverse opinion on the financial statement opinion, and should indicate whether the opinion on the financial statements was affected by the material weaknesses.

4 Reporting on Internal Control (Issuers)

The auditor is required to report on both the company's financial statements and on its internal control over financial reporting. Two separate reports, or one combined report (that is, one report containing both an opinion on the financial statements and an opinion on internal control), may be issued.

4.1 Separate or Combined Reports

If separate reports are issued, each report should contain an explanatory paragraph making reference to the other report and indicating the nature of the opinion expressed.

4.1.1 Sample Report: Separate Report on Internal Control Over Financial Statements (Issuer)

Report of Independent Registered Public Accounting Firm

To the shareholders and the board of directors of W Company:

Opinion on the Internal Control Over Financial Reporting

We have audited the Company's internal control over financial reporting as of December 31, 20X8, based on [*identify control criteria, for example, "criteria established in Internal Control-Integrated Framework: (20XX) issued by the Committee of Sponsoring Organizations of the Treadway Commission (COSO)"*]. In our opinion, the Company maintained, in all material respects, effective internal control over financial reporting as of December 31, 20X8, based on [*identify control criteria, for example, "criteria established in Internal Control-Integrated Framework: (20XX) issued by COSO"*].

We also have audited, in accordance with the standards of the Public Company Accounting Oversight Board (United States) (PCAOB), the [*identify financial statements*] of W Company and our report dated [*date of report, which should be the same as the date of the report on the effectiveness of internal control over financial reporting*] expressed [*include nature of opinion*].

Basis for Opinion

The Company's management is responsible for these financial statements, for maintaining effective internal control over financial reporting, and for its assessment of the effectiveness of internal control over financial reporting, included in the accompanying [*title of management's report*]. Our responsibility is to express an opinion on the company's internal control over financial reporting based on our audits. We are a public accounting firm registered with the Public Company Accounting Oversight Board (United States) (PCAOB) and are required to be independent with respect to the Company in accordance with the U.S. federal securities laws and the applicable rules and regulations of the Securities and Exchange Commission and the PCAOB.

(continued)

(continued)

We conducted our audit in accordance with the standards of the PCAOB. Those standards require that we plan and perform the audits to obtain reasonable assurance about whether effective internal control over financial reporting was maintained in all material respects.

Our audit of internal control over financial reporting included obtaining an understanding of internal control over financial reporting, assessing the risk that a material weakness exists, and testing and evaluating the design and operating effectiveness of internal control based on the assessed risk. Our audit also included performing such other procedures as we considered necessary in the circumstances. We believe that our audit provides a reasonable basis for our opinion.

Definition and Limitations of Internal Control Over Financial Reporting

A company's internal control over financial reporting is a process designed to provide reasonable assurance regarding the reliability of financial reporting and the preparation of financial statements for external purposes in accordance with generally accepted accounting principles. A company's internal control over financial reporting includes those policies and procedures that (1) pertain to the maintenance of records that, in reasonable detail, accurately and fairly reflect the transactions and dispositions of the assets of the company; (2) provide reasonable assurance that transactions are recorded as necessary to permit preparation of financial statements in accordance with generally accepted accounting principles, and that receipts and expenditures of the company are being made only in accordance with authorizations of management and directors of the company; and (3) provide reasonable assurance regarding prevention or timely detection of unauthorized acquisition, use, or disposition of the company's assets that could have a material effect on the financial statements.

Because of its inherent limitations, internal control over financial reporting may not prevent or detect misstatements. Also, projections of any evaluation of effectiveness to future periods are subject to the risk that controls may become inadequate because of changes in conditions, or that the degree of compliance with the policies or procedures may deteriorate.

[*Signature*]
We have served as the Company's auditor since [*year*].

[*City and state or country*]

[*Date*]

The following paragraph (no title for this paragraph) should be added immediately following the opinion paragraph in the separate report on the financial statements.

> We also have audited, in accordance with the standards of the Public Company Accounting Oversight Board (United States) (PCAOB), the effectiveness of X Company's internal control over financial reporting as of December 31, 20X3, based on [*identify control criteria*] and our report dated [*date of report, which should be the same as the date of the report on the financial statements]* expressed *[include nature of opinions*].

4.1.2 Sample Report: Combined Report on Internal Control Over Financial Statements and on the Financial Statements (Issuer)

> **Report of Independent Registered Public Accounting Firm**
>
> To the shareholders and the board of directors of W Company:
>
> **Opinions on the Financial Statements and Internal Control Over Financial Reporting**
>
> We have audited the accompanying balance sheets of W Company (the "Company") as of December 31, 20X8 and 20X7, and the related statements of income, comprehensive income, stockholders' equity, and cash flows for each of the years in the two-year period ended December 31, 20X8, and the related notes [*and schedules*] (collectively referred to as the "financial statements"). We also have audited the Company's internal control over financial reporting as of December 31, 20X8, based on [*identify control criteria, for example, "criteria established in Internal Control-Integrated Framework: (20XX) issued by the Committee of Sponsoring Organizations of the Treadway Commission (COSO)"*].
>
> In our opinion, the financial statements referred to above present fairly, in all material respects, the financial position of the Company as of December 31, 20X8 and 20X7, and the results of its operations and its cash flows for each of the years in the two-year period ended December 31, 20X8, in conformity with accounting principles generally accepted in the United States of America. Also in our opinion, the Company maintained, in all material respects, effective internal control over financial reporting as of December 31, 20X8, based on [*identify control criteria, for example, "criteria established in Internal Control-Integrated Framework: (20XX) issued by COSO"*].
>
> **Basis for Opinion**
>
> The Company's management is responsible for these financial statements, for maintaining effective internal control over financial reporting, and for its assessment of the effectiveness of internal control over financial reporting, included in the accompanying [*title of management's report*]. Our responsibility is to express an opinion on the Company's financial statements and an opinion on the Company's internal control over financial reporting based on our audits. We are a public accounting firm registered with the Public Company Accounting Oversight Board (United States) (PCAOB) and are required to be independent with respect to the Company in accordance with the U.S. federal securities laws and the applicable rules and regulations of the Securities and Exchange Commission and the PCAOB.
>
> (continued)

(continued)

We conducted our audits in accordance with the standards of the PCAOB. Those standards require that we plan and perform the audits to obtain reasonable assurance about whether the financial statements are free of material misstatement, whether due to error or fraud, and whether effective internal control over financial reporting was maintained in all material respects.

Our audits of the financial statements included performing procedures to assess the risks of material misstatement of the financial statements, whether due to error or fraud, and performing procedures that respond to those risks. Such procedures included examining, on a test basis, evidence regarding the amounts and disclosures in the financial statements. Our audits also included evaluating the accounting principles used and significant estimates made by management, as well as evaluating the overall presentation of the financial statements. Our audit of internal control over financial reporting included obtaining an understanding of internal control over financial reporting, assessing the risk that a material weakness exists, and testing and evaluating the design and operating effectiveness of internal control based on the assessed risk. Our audits also included performing such other procedures as we considered necessary in the circumstances. We believe that our audits provide a reasonable basis for our opinions.

Definition and Limitations of Internal Control Over Financial Reporting

A company's internal control over financial reporting is a process designed to provide reasonable assurance regarding the reliability of financial reporting and the preparation of financial statements for external purposes in accordance with generally accepted accounting principles. A company's internal control over financial reporting includes those policies and procedures that (1) pertain to the maintenance of records that, in reasonable detail, accurately and fairly reflect the transactions and dispositions of the assets of the company; (2) provide reasonable assurance that transactions are recorded as necessary to permit preparation of financial statements in accordance with generally accepted accounting principles, and that receipts and expenditures of the company are being made only in accordance with authorizations of management and directors of the company; and (3) provide reasonable assurance regarding prevention or timely detection of unauthorized acquisition, use, or disposition of the company's assets that could have a material effect on the financial statements.

Because of its inherent limitations, internal control over financial reporting may not prevent or detect misstatements. Also, projections of any evaluation of effectiveness to future periods are subject to the risk that controls may become inadequate because of changes in conditions, or that the degree of compliance with the policies or procedures may deteriorate.

Critical Audit Matters

[*Include critical audit matters*]

[*Signature*]

We have served as the Company's auditor since [*year*].

[*City and state or country*]

[*Date*]

4.2 Report Date

The report should be dated no earlier than the date on which sufficient appropriate evidence has been obtained.

The date of the report on internal control should coincide with the date of the audit report on the financial statements.

4.3 Material Weakness in Internal Control

A material weakness requires the auditor to issue an adverse opinion. The auditor's report must include the definition of a material weakness, a statement that a material weakness has been identified, and an identification of the material weakness described in management's assessment.

- If management's report fails to include one or more material weaknesses identified by the auditor, the auditor's report should state this, and should describe the omitted weaknesses. The auditor should also communicate this situation, in writing, to those charged with governance.
- If management's report includes a material weakness but does not fairly present the weakness, the auditor's report should indicate this situation and should fairly describe the material weakness.
- The auditor should consider the effect of this adverse opinion on the financial statement opinion, and should indicate whether the opinion on the financial statements was affected by the material weaknesses.

4.4 Reporting on a Previously Reported Internal Control Weakness

In some cases, management's assessment of the company's internal control over financial reporting may reveal that the company has one or more material weaknesses.

If the material weaknesses are subsequently eliminated, management may wish to communicate this fact to the investing public, and may also wish to have an independent auditor attest to the improvements in internal control.

- An engagement to report on whether a previously reported internal control weakness continues to exist is a voluntary engagement, not required by professional standards. The engagement may be performed at any time during the year.
- The auditor's objective is to express an opinion on whether a previously reported material weakness has been eliminated.
- The auditor may perform such an engagement only if:
  - He or she has sufficient overall knowledge of both the company and its internal control over financial reporting.
  - Management accepts responsibility for the effectiveness of internal control, evaluates its effectiveness, asserts that internal control is effective, provides support for this assertion, and presents a written report that will accompany the auditor's report.
- The auditor's testing is limited to the controls specifically identified by management as eliminating the material weakness.
- To issue an unmodified opinion, the auditor must obtain evidence about the design and operating effectiveness of the specifically identified controls, determine that the material weakness has been eliminated, and determine that no scope limitations were placed on the auditor's work.

5 Other Reporting Issues (Issuers and Nonissuers)

5.1 Scope Limitations

The auditor should withdraw from the engagement or issue a disclaimer of opinion if the scope of the audit is restricted.

When disclaiming an opinion because of a scope limitation, the auditor should state that an opinion is not being expressed and, in a separate paragraph or paragraphs, the substantive reasons for the disclaimer. In a disclaimer of opinion, the auditor should:

1. Modify the first sentence of the introductory paragraph slightly ("We were engaged to examine ... ") and omit the last sentence.
2. Omit the scope paragraph (issuer) or amend the auditor's responsibility paragraph (nonissuer) to state, "Our responsibility is to express an opinion on ABC Company's internal control over financial reporting based on conducting the audit in accordance with auditing standards generally accepted in the United States of America. Because of the matter described in the basis for disclaimer of opinion paragraph, however, we were not able to obtain sufficient appropriate audit evidence to provide a basis for an audit opinion."
3. Include an explanatory paragraph (issuer) or basis for disclaimer of opinion paragraph (nonissuer) describing the reason for the disclaimer.
4. Revise the opinion paragraph, as shown below.

5.1.1 Sample Opinion Paragraph: Disclaimer Due to Scope Limitation (Issuer)

Because of the limitation on the scope of our audit described in the second paragraph, the scope of our work was not sufficient to enable us to express, and we do not express, an opinion on the effectiveness of W Company's internal control over financial reporting.

5.1.2 Sample Opinion Paragraph: Disclaimer Due to Scope Limitation (Nonissuer)

Disclaimer of Opinion

Because of the significance of the matter described in the basis for disclaimer of opinion paragraph, we have not been able to obtain sufficient appropriate audit evidence to provide a basis for an audit opinion. Accordingly, we do not express an opinion on the effectiveness of ABC Company's internal control over financial reporting.

The auditor should also consider the following:

- Language that might overshadow the disclaimer (e.g., a list of procedures performed or commonly performed) should not be used.
- Any material weaknesses identified should be described, and the definition of a material weakness should be included, in the disclaimer.
- If the auditor cannot express an opinion due to a scope limitation, management and those charged with governance should be informed, in writing.
- The auditor may issue a report disclaiming an opinion on internal controls as soon as the auditor concludes that a scope limitation will prevent the auditor from obtaining the assurance necessary to express an opinion.

5.2 Use of Component Auditor (Other Auditor)

As is the case with a financial statement audit, a component auditor (other auditor) may be involved in the audit of an entity's internal control. The group engagement partner (principal auditor) decides whether the involvement of the other auditor warrants reference in the auditor's report.

The decision about whether to make reference to another auditor in the report on internal control is independent of the similar decision made with respect to the financial statement audit. The two decisions may differ.

5.3 Subsequent Events

As is the case with a financial statement audit, *subsequent events* (in this case, changes in internal control) may occur after the "as of" date of the report, but prior to the date of the auditor's report.

- The auditor should:
  - Inquire of management.
  - Obtain written representations from management.
  - Inquire about and examine documentation for the subsequent period.
- If, before the date of the auditor's report, the auditor obtains information about a matter that existed on the "as of" date of the report, appropriate action should be taken (for example, an adverse opinion would be issued if a material weakness were discovered).
- If the auditor obtains information about conditions that arose subsequent to the "as of" date of the auditor's report, this information should be included in an explanatory paragraph of the report.
- The auditor has no responsibility to keep informed with respect to events occurring after the date of the report, but if the auditor becomes aware of conditions that existed at the report date, appropriate action should be taken.

Question 1 **MCQ-05391**

Which of the following best describes the responsibility of the auditor with respect to significant deficiencies and material weaknesses in an audit of an issuer?

	Must be Communicated to Management and the Audit Committee	*Results in an Adverse Opinion of the Effectiveness of Internal Control*
a.	Both significant deficiencies and material weaknesses	Both significant deficiencies and material weaknesses
b.	Both significant deficiencies and material weaknesses	Material weaknesses but not significant deficiencies
c.	Material weaknesses but not significant deficiencies	Both significant deficiencies and material weaknesses
d.	Material weaknesses but not significant deficiencies	Material weaknesses but not significant deficiencies

MODULE

3 Attestation Engagements and Standards

AUD 5

1 Introduction

Attestation services are a type of engagement gaining in importance. Attest engagements have grown out of the need for independent expression of assurance on subject matters *other than basic financial statements*.

1.1 Definition

Attest engagements are defined as those in which a practitioner (CPA) is engaged to issue or does issue an examination, a review, or an agreed-upon procedures report on subject matter, or on an assertion about the subject matter, that is the responsibility of another party (usually management). An attest engagement may be part of a larger engagement, such as a feasibility study or a business acquisition study.

1.2 Attestation Engagements

Statements on Standards for Attestation Engagements (SSAE) established by the AICPA provide information addressing attestation services for the following subject matters:

- Agreed-upon procedures
- Financial forecasts and projections
- Pro forma financial statements
- Compliance
- Management's discussion and analysis (MD&A)
- Reporting on controls at a service organization

Each type of attestation service allows a different combination of reporting options:

	Report Type		
Attestation Service	*Examination*	*Review*	*Agreed-Upon Procedures*
Agreed-upon procedures			✓
Prospective financial statements	✓		✓
Pro forma financial statements	✓	✓	
Compliance	✓		✓
MD&A	✓	✓	
Service organizations	✓		

Note that preparations and compilations are also allowed for prospective financial statements. However, with the issuance of SSAE 18, preparations and compilations of prospective financial statements are no longer addressed in the attestation standards and are instead governed by the SSARS standards. Prospective financial statements will be covered later in this unit. SSARS will be covered in more detail in A6.

Pass Key

The following standards apply to services a CPA may provide:

- **Audit Engagements:** SAS (Statements on Auditing Standards); PCAOB standards for issuers
- **Preparation, Compilation, and Review Engagements:** SSARS (Statements on Standards for Accounting and Review Services)
- **Attest Engagements:** SSAE (Statements on Standards for Attestation Engagements)

Statements on Standards for Attestation Engagements (SSAE) do not apply to:

- Audits
- Preparation, compilations, and reviews of the financial statements of nonissuers under SSARS
- Return preparation (income tax, franchise, other)
- Advocating for the client (litigation services)
- Providing consulting/advisory services
- Audits of internal controls over financial reporting

2 Attestation Standards

2.1 Overview

Attestation standards are intended to provide guidance and set boundaries around the increasingly broad variety of attestation services rendered by a CPA (also referred to as a practitioner). Attestation standards provide a measure of quality and describe the objectives to be achieved in an attestation engagement.

Attestation standards are much broader in scope than GAAS and apply specifically to attestation engagements. They do not supersede any existing standards (SAS, SSARS) for other engagements.

Attestation standards are a natural extension of GAAS but differ conceptually from GAAS in two ways:

1. No reference is made to historical financial statements.
2. No reference is made to generally accepted accounting principles.

In addition, attestation standards provide for services tailored to the needs of the user, who may directly participate in specifying either the nature and scope of the engagement or the criteria against which the assertions are measured. (In such engagements, a limited use report is provided.)

Attestation standards include a hierarchy similar to the GAAS hierarchy covered previously:

- Departures from presumptively mandatory requirements must be justified.
- Interpretive publications should be considered (with departures explained).
- Other attestation publications have no authoritative status but may be helpful.

2.2 Common Concepts

The attestation standards include guidance on concepts that are common to all attestation engagements. An easy way to remember these common concepts is with the mnemonic "**CAPE CORP.**"

- **Compliance** with all attestation standards relevant to the engagement.
  - In rare circumstances when the practitioner judges it necessary to depart from a relevant presumptively mandatory requirement, alternative procedures should be performed to achieve the intent of that requirement.
- **Acceptance** and continuance are satisfactorily performed for client relationships and attestation engagements.
- **Preconditions** for an attestation engagement are present, including:
  - The practitioner must be independent, except when required by law or regulation to accept the engagement.
  - The responsible party takes responsibility for the subject matter.
  - The subject matter is appropriate, the criteria to be applied against the subject matter are appropriate, and the practitioner expects to be able to obtain the evidence needed, and the opinion, conclusion, or findings will be issued in a written report.
- **Engagement** documentation standards for timeliness, retention, ownership, and confidentiality apply.
- Acceptance of a **change** in the terms of the engagement as reasonable, when applicable.
- Using the work of an **other** practitioner is allowed.
  - The practitioner should perform appropriate due diligence on the other practitioner's independence, professional competence, willingness to comply with ethical requirements, and adequate performance of work.
- **Responsibility** for quality control, including:
  - The engagement partner should take responsibility for the overall quality of the attestation engagement.
  - The engagement team and any specialists have the appropriate competence and capabilities and are informed of their responsibilities, the objectives of procedures, and matters that may affect the nature, extent, and timing of procedures.
  - If an engagement quality control review is required for an engagement, the engagement partner is responsible for discussing with the reviewer significant findings or issues and should not release the practitioner's report until completion of the engagement quality control review.
- **Professional** skepticism and professional judgment are required in the planning and performance of an attestation engagement.

2.3 Attestation Risk

In an examination or review engagement, attestation risk is the risk that the practitioner expresses an inappropriate opinion or conclusion, as applicable, when the subject matter or assertion is materially misstated. Attestation risk is very similar to the audit risk model covered previously.

Note that attestation risk does not apply to agreed-upon procedures engagements, as such engagements involve performing specific procedures and reporting findings without providing an opinion or conclusion.

In general, attestation risk can be represented by the following three components, although not all of these components will necessarily be present or significant for all engagements:

1. **Inherent Risk**

   The susceptibility of the subject matter to a material misstatement before consideration of any related controls. Inherent risk exists independent of the engagement. The practitioner cannot change this risk, but can change the assessment of the risk.

2. **Control Risk**

   The risk that a material misstatement that could occur in the subject matter will not be prevented, or detected and corrected, on a timely basis by the appropriate party's internal control. Control risk exists independent of the engagement. The practitioner cannot change this risk, but can change the assessment of the risk.

   The stronger the system of controls, the greater the reliance that may be placed on the controls, and the fewer the tests of details (or the lower the quality of evidence) required.

3. **Detection Risk**

   The risk that the practitioner will not detect material misstatement that exists. Detection risk relates to the practitioner's procedures. The practitioner can change this risk by varying the nature, extent, or timing of procedures.

   As the acceptable level of detection risk decreases, the assurance provided by tests of details should increase.

Attestation risk (should be low)	=	**Inherent risk (assessed by practitioner)**	×	**Control risk (assessed by practitioner)**	×	**Detection risk (controlled by practitioner)**

2.4 Additional Reporting Requirements

The following reporting requirements also should be considered.

- The report may be issued on the assertion itself (e.g., "We have examined management's assertion that the accompanying schedule ...") or on the subject matter to which the assertion relates (e.g., "We have examined the accompanying schedule ... ").
  - In either case, a written assertion is generally obtained in examination, review, and agreed-upon procedure engagements.
  - When there are material misstatements or deviations from the criteria, the report should be modified and the conclusion should be expressed directly on the subject matter.

- If reporting on the assertion, it should accompany the practitioner's report or the assertion should be clearly stated in the report.
- Concerns about the assertion, conformity with the criteria, or the adequacy of disclosure can result in a qualified or adverse opinion for an examination engagement, or in a modified conclusion for a review engagement.

2.4.1 Scope Restrictions

- **Examination:** Restrictions on the scope of an examination engagement may result in a qualified opinion, disclaimer of opinion, or in the practitioner's withdrawal from the engagement.
- **Review:** Restrictions on the scope of a review engagement that prevent necessary procedures from being performed result in the practitioner's withdrawal from the engagement.

Question 1 **MCQ-02445**

A CPA is required to comply with the provisions of *Statements on Standards for Attestation Engagements* (SSAE) when engaged to:

a. Report on financial statements that the CPA generated through the use of computer software.

b. Review management's discussion and analysis (MD&A) prepared pursuant to rules and regulations adopted by the SEC.

c. Provide the client with a financial statement format that does not include dollar amounts.

d. Audit financial statements that the client prepared for use in another country.

3 Reporting

The conclusions expressed by the practitioner fall into three groups:

3.1 Examination

An examination provides a positive opinion, high level of assurance, generally based on a variety of procedures, including search, verification, inquiry, and analysis.

3.1.1 Sample Report: Examination Report on a Subject Matter

Independent Accountant's Report

[*Appropriate Addressee*]

We have examined [*identify the subject matter, for example, the accompanying schedule of investment returns of XYZ Company for the year ended December 31, 20XX*]. XYZ Company's management is responsible for [*identify the subject matter, for example, presenting the schedule of investment returns*] in accordance with (or based on) [*identify the criteria, for example, the ABC criteria set forth in Note 1*]. Our responsibility is to express an opinion on [*identify the subject matter, for example, the schedule of investment returns*] based on our examination.

Our examination was conducted in accordance with attestation standards established by the American Institute of Certified Public Accountants. Those standards require that we plan and perform the examination to obtain reasonable assurance about whether [*identify the subject matter, for example, the schedule of investment returns*] is in accordance with (or based on) the criteria, in all material respects. An examination involves performing procedures to obtain evidence about [*identify the subject matter, for example, the schedule of investment returns*]. The nature, timing, and extent of the procedures selected depend on our judgment, including an assessment of the risks of material misstatement of [*identify the subject matter, for example, the schedule of investment returns*], whether due to fraud or error. We believe that the evidence we obtained is sufficient and appropriate to provide a reasonable basis for our opinion.

[*Include a description of significant inherent limitations, if any, associated with the measurement or evaluation of the subject matter against the criteria.*]

[*Additional paragraph(s) may be added to emphasize certain matters relating to the attestation engagement or the subject matter.*]

In our opinion, [*identify the subject matter, for example, the schedule of investment returns of XYZ Company for the year ended December 31, 20XX, or the schedule of investment returns referred to above*] is presented in accordance with (or based on) [*identify the criteria, for example, the ABC criteria set forth in Note 1*], in all material respects.

[*Practitioner's signature*]

[*Practitioner's city and state*]

[*Date of the practitioner's report*]

3.1.2 Sample Report: Examination Report on an Assertion About a Subject Matter

Independent Accountant's Report

[*Appropriate Addressee*]

We have examined management of XYZ Company's assertion that [*identify the assertion, including the subject matter and the criteria, for example, the accompanying schedule of investment returns of XYZ Company for the year ended December 31, 20XX, is presented in accordance with (or based on) the ABC criteria set forth in Note 1*]. XYZ Company's management is responsible for its assertion. Our responsibility is to express an opinion on management's assertion based on our examination.

Our examination was conducted in accordance with attestation standards established by the American Institute of Certified Public Accountants. Those standards require that we plan and perform the examination to obtain reasonable assurance about whether management's assertion is fairly stated, in all material respects. An examination involves performing procedures to obtain evidence about management's assertion. The nature, timing, and extent of the procedures selected depend on our judgment, including an assessment of the risks of material misstatement of management's assertion, whether due to fraud or error. We believe that the evidence we obtained is sufficient and appropriate to provide a reasonable basis for our opinion.

[*Include a description of significant inherent limitations, if any, associated with the measurement or evaluation of the subject matter against the criteria.*]

[*Additional paragraph(s) may be added to emphasize certain matters relating to the attestation engagement or the subject matter.*]

In our opinion, management's assertion that [*identify the assertion, including the subject matter and the criteria, for example, the accompanying schedule of investment returns of XYZ Company for the year ended December 31, 20XX, is presented in accordance with (or based on) the ABC criteria set forth in Note 1*] is fairly stated, in all material respects.

[*Practitioner's signature*]
[*Practitioner's city and state*]
[*Date of the practitioner's report*]

3.2 Review (Limited Assurance)

A review results in a conclusion, which provides a moderate level of assurance, generally based on inquiry and analytical procedures.

3.2.1 Sample Report: Review Report on a Subject Matter

Independent Accountant's Review Report

[*Appropriate Addressee*]

We have reviewed [*identify the subject matter, for example, the accompanying schedule of investment returns of XYZ Company for the year ended December 31, 20XX*]. XYZ Company's management is responsible for [*identify the subject matter, for example, presenting the schedule of investment returns*] in accordance with (or based on) [*identify the criteria, for example, the ABC criteria set forth in Note 1*]. Our responsibility is to express a conclusion on [*identify the subject matter, for example, the schedule of investment returns*] based on our review.

Our review was conducted in accordance with attestation standards established by the American Institute of Certified Public Accountants. Those standards require that we plan and perform the review to obtain limited assurance about whether any material modifications should be made to [*identify the subject matter, for example, the schedule of investment returns*] in order for it to be in accordance with (or based on) the criteria. A review is substantially less in scope than an examination, the objective of which is to obtain reasonable assurance about whether [*identify the subject matter, for example, the schedule of investment returns*] is in accordance with (or based on) the criteria, in all material respects, in order to express an opinion. Accordingly, we do not express such an opinion. We believe that our review provides a reasonable basis for our conclusion.

[*Include a description of significant inherent limitations, if any, associated with the measurement or evaluation of the subject matter against the criteria.*]

[*Additional paragraph(s) may be added to emphasize certain matters relating to the attestation engagement or the subject matter.*]

Based on our review, we are not aware of any material modifications that should be made to [*identify the subject matter, for example, the accompanying schedule of investment returns of XYZ Company for the year ended December 31, 20XX*], in order for it be in accordance with (or based on) [*identify the criteria, for example, the ABC criteria set forth in Note 1*].

[*Practitioner's signature*]

[*Practitioner's city and state*]

[*Date of the practitioner's report*]

3.2.2 Sample Report: Review Report on an Assertion About a Subject Matter

Independent Accountant's Review Report

[*Appropriate Addressee*]

We have reviewed management of XYZ Company's assertion that [*identify the assertion, including the subject matter and the criteria, for example, the accompanying schedule of investment returns of XYZ Company for the year ended December 31, 20XX, is presented in accordance with (or based on) the ABC criteria set forth in Note 1*]. XYZ Company's management is responsible for its assertion. Our responsibility is to express a conclusion on management's assertion based on our review.

Our review was conducted in accordance with attestation standards established by the American Institute of Certified Public Accountants. Those standards require that we plan and perform the review to obtain limited assurance about whether any material modifications should be made to management's assertion in order for it to be fairly stated. A review is substantially less in scope than an examination, the objective of which is to obtain reasonable assurance about whether management's assertion is fairly stated, in all material respects, in order to express an opinion. Accordingly, we do not express such an opinion. We believe that our review provides a reasonable basis for our conclusion.

[*Include a description of significant inherent limitations, if any, associated with the measurement or evaluation of the subject matter against the criteria.*]

[*Additional paragraph(s) may be added to emphasize certain matters relating to the attestation engagement or the subject matter.*]

Based on our review, we are not aware of any material modifications that should be made to management of XYZ Company's assertion in order for it to be fairly stated.

This report is intended solely for the information and use of [*identify the specified parties, for example, ABC Company and XYZ Company*], and is not intended to be, and should not be, used by anyone other than the specified parties.

[*Practitioner's signature*]

[*Practitioner's city and state*]

[*Date of the practitioner's report*]

Note: The above report is restricted as to use. The last paragraph demonstrates how to indicate this restricted use, and a similar paragraph could be added to any of the other sample reports.

3.3 Agreed-Upon Procedures

Agreed-upon procedures provide no assurance, but procedures and findings are listed. A sample agreed-upon procedures report will be shown later in the text.

Type of Engagement	Amount of Assurance	Result	Similar To
Examination	Reasonable (positive)	Opinion	Audit (SAS)
Review	Limited (negative)	Conclusion	Review (SSARS)
Agreed-upon procedures	None	List of findings	N/A

3.4 Written Assertion

A written assertion is generally obtained in examination, review, and agreed-upon procedures engagements. If no written assertion is provided by management, the outcome depends on whether the client is also the responsible party.

If the client is the responsible party, failure to provide a written assertion constitutes a scope limitation.

- In an examination engagement, the report should be modified based on the scope limitation, and its use should be restricted.
- A review engagement subject to such a scope limitation is incomplete and the practitioner should withdraw. When withdrawal is not possible under applicable law or regulation, the practitioner may report on the subject matter but should modify the report and restrict the use of the report.
- In an agreed-upon procedures engagement, the practitioner should modify the report based on the scope limitation.

If the client is not the responsible party, a report may be issued as long as appropriate procedures are performed and sufficient evidence is obtained. However, the form of the report may vary, and its use should be restricted.

3.5 Other Requirements

- Documentation requirements for attestation engagements are similar to those for any other audit or review engagement.
- An understanding with the client should be established, preferably through a written communication.
- A representation letter from the responsible party should be obtained for examination and review engagements.
- Inquiry should be made regarding subsequent events.

MODULE

4 Agreed-Upon Procedures and Prospective Financial Statements

AUD 5

1 Agreed-Upon Procedures Engagements

An agreed-upon procedures engagement is one in which the practitioner is engaged by a client to issue a report of findings based on specific agreed-upon procedures. It may be performed on the designated subject matter of a wide variety of assertions as a result of a need of specific parties. The client and the practitioner agree to the procedures the practitioner will perform that the client believes are appropriate. Because the needs of the specified parties may vary widely, the client assumes responsibility for whether the procedures are sufficient, since the client best understands its own needs. The practitioner has no responsibility for the sufficiency of the procedures.

Attestation standards apply to all agreed-upon procedures engagements, including those related to items from a financial statement. The practitioner does not provide an opinion or negative assurance.

1.1 Conditions

Agreed-upon procedures attestation engagements may be performed provided that the following conditions exist:

1. **Independence of the Practitioner**
2. **Agreement of the Parties**

   The practitioner and the specified parties agree regarding the procedures to be performed, the criteria to be used in the determination of the findings, and any materiality limits to be used for reporting purposes.
3. **Measurability and Consistency**

   The subject matter should be capable of reasonably consistent measurement, procedures should be expected to result in reasonably consistent findings, and evidential matter to support the report should be expected to exist.
4. **Sufficiency of the Procedures**

   The specified parties take responsibility for the sufficiency of the procedures for their purposes.
5. **Use of the Report Is Restricted to the Specified Parties**
6. **Responsibility for the Subject Matter**
   - The client is responsible for (or has a reasonable basis for providing an assertion about) the subject matter; or
   - The client is able to provide evidence that a third party is responsible for the subject matter.
7. **Engagements to Perform Agreed-Upon Procedures on Prospective Financial Statements**

   Prospective financial statements must include a summary of significant assumptions.

Pass Key

"I-AM-SURE" you can perform these agreed-upon procedures.

1.2 Reporting (Required Elements)

The practitioner's report on agreed-upon procedures should be in the form of procedures and findings. The practitioner's report should contain the following elements:

- A title (including the word *independent*), a signature, city and state where the practitioner practices, and a date.
- Identification of the specified parties, the subject matter (or related assertion), the nature of the engagement, and the responsible party.
- A statement that the subject matter is the responsibility of the responsible party.
- A statement that the procedures performed were those agreed to by the specified parties identified in the report, and a description of any agreed-upon materiality limits.
- A statement that the sufficiency of the procedures is solely the responsibility of the specified parties and a disclaimer of responsibility for the sufficiency of those procedures.
- A statement that the engagement was conducted in accordance with attestation standards established by the American Institute of Certified Public Accountants.
- A list of the procedures performed (or reference thereto) and related findings (the practitioner should not provide an opinion or conclusion).
- A statement that the practitioner was not engaged to, and did not, conduct an examination or review, the objective of which would be the expression of an opinion or conclusion, respectively, on the subject matter; a statement that the practitioner does not express an opinion or conclusion; and a statement that if the practitioner had performed additional procedures, other matters might have come to his or her attention that would have been reported.
- A statement of restrictions on the use of the report because it is intended to be used solely by the specified parties.
- Where applicable, reservations or restrictions concerning procedures or findings.
- Certain additional items for agreed-upon procedures for attestation engagements on prospective financial information.
- Where applicable, a description of the nature of the assistance provided by a specialist.

Exam => + assurance
Review => - assu
Agreed => no assurance

1.2.1 Sample Report: Agreed-Upon Procedures Report

Independent Accountant's Report on Applying Agreed-Upon Procedures

[*Appropriate Addressee*]

We have performed the procedures enumerated below, which were agreed to by [*identify the specified party(ies), for example, the audit committees and managements of ABC Inc. and XYZ Fund*], on [*identify the subject matter, for example, the accompanying Statement of Investment Performance Statistics of XYZ Fund for the year ended December 31, 20X1*]. XYZ Fund's management is responsible for [*identify the subject matter, for example, the Statement of Investment Performance Statistics for the year ended December 31, 20X1*]. The sufficiency of these procedures is solely the responsibility of the parties specified in this report. Consequently, we make no representation regarding the sufficiency of the procedures enumerated below either for the purpose for which this report has been requested or for any other purpose.

[*Include paragraphs to enumerate procedures and findings.*]

This agreed-upon procedures engagement was conducted in accordance with attestation standards established by the American Institute of Certified Public Accountants. We were not engaged to and did not conduct an examination or review, the objective of which would be the expression of an opinion or conclusion, respectively, on [*identify the subject matter, for example, the accompanying Statement of Investment Performance Statistics of XYZ Fund for the year ended December 31, 20X1*]. Accordingly, we do not express such an opinion or conclusion. Had we performed additional procedures, other matters might have come to our attention that would have been reported to you.

[*Additional paragraph(s) may be added to describe other matters.*]

This report is intended solely for the information and use of [*identify the specified party(ies), for example, the audit committees and managements of ABC Inc. and XYZ Fund*], and is not intended to be, and should not be, used by anyone other than the specified parties.

[*Practitioner's signature*]
[*Practitioner's city and state*]
[*Date of the practitioner's report*]

1.3 Explanatory Language

The practitioner may include explanatory language regarding matters such as:

- Disclosure of stipulated facts, assumptions, or interpretations (including the source thereof) used in the application of agreed-upon procedures.
- Description of the condition of records, controls, or data to which the procedures were applied.
- Explanation that the practitioner has no responsibility to update his or her report.
- Explanation of sampling risk.

2 Prospective Financial Statements

In contrast to historical financial statements, which are the subject of audit engagements, prospective financial statements are forward-looking and based on projections rather than past events.

- Prospective financial statements may cover a period that has partially expired.
- Statements for periods that have completely expired are not considered to be prospective.
- Pro forma financial statements and partial presentations are not prospective financial statements.

2.1 Types of Prospective Financial Statements

Financial forecasts and projections are two types of prospective financial statements that attempt to reflect a company's expected financial position and expected results of operations.

1. **Financial Forecast**

   A financial forecast reflects, to the best of the responsible party's knowledge, the expected financial results of a future period. It is based on *expected* conditions and *expected* courses of action.

   Note: In almost all situations, the party responsible for the prospective financial statements is the management of the company.

2. **Financial Projection**

   A financial projection is different from a forecast in that it is based on *hypothetical* assumptions. A projection reflects the financial position and results of operations based on a *"what-if"* type of scenario.

2.2 Uses of Prospective Financial Statements

The uses of prospective financial statements can be categorized as:

- **General Use** — no restrictions

  General use means that the statements issued will be used by parties not negotiating directly with the responsible party (the issuing company). Only a financial forecast is appropriate for general use.

- **Limited Use** — restricted

  Limited use means that the financial statements will only be used by the responsible party alone or by parties negotiating directly with the responsible party (the issuing company). Both financial forecasts and financial projections are appropriate for limited use.

  Examples include use in negotiations for a bank loan, submission to a regulatory agency, and use solely within the entity.

2.3 Engagement Types

A practitioner is associated with prospective financial statements primarily in one of four ways:

1. Preparation engagement
2. Compilation engagement
3. Examination engagement
4. Agreed-upon procedures engagement

Note that a review of prospective financial statements is not allowed.

2.4 Preparation of Prospective Financial Statements

SSARS provides guidance for preparation of prospective financial statements. The requirements for a preparation of prospective financial statements are very similar to the requirements for a preparation of historical financial statements (i.e., agree on engagement terms, understand the entity's financial reporting framework, prepare financial statements, include a legend on each page). Preparation engagements of historical financial statements will be covered in more detail in A6.

A practitioner should not prepare prospective financial information that:

1. excludes the summary of significant assumptions; or
2. in the case of a financial projection, excludes either an identification of the hypothetical assumptions or a description of the limitations on the usefulness of the presentation.

2.5 Compilation of Prospective Financial Statements

SSARS provides guidance for compilations of prospective financial statements.

2.5.1 Purpose

The purpose of a compilation of prospective financial statements is the proper assembling of the financial data based on the responsible party's assumptions.

- There is no assurance of any kind given that the statements have been prepared in accordance with AICPA guidelines or that the assumptions used are reasonable.
- The accountant should read the prospective financial statements with the summaries of significant assumptions and accounting policies, and consider whether they appear to be presented in conformity with AICPA presentations.
- The practitioner is not required to gather supporting evidence, but should be aware of obvious inappropriate assumptions used to construct the statements. Independence is not required, but lack of independence should be disclosed in a separate paragraph in the compilation report. The practitioner is permitted, but not required, to disclose the reason(s) for the lack of independence in the report. All reasons must be included in the disclosure.

2.5.2 Contents of Compilation Report

The following items would appear in the practitioner's compilation report:

- Identification of the entity, the prospective financial information that has been subjected to the compilation engagement, and the date or period covered by the prospective financial information;
- A statement that management is responsible for the prospective financial information;
- A statement that the practitioner has performed the compilation engagement in accordance with Statements on Standards for Accounting and Review Services (SSARSs) promulgated by the Accounting and Review Services Committee of the AICPA;
- A statement that the practitioner did not examine or review the prospective financial information nor was the practitioner required to perform any procedures to verify the accuracy or completeness of the assumptions made by management, and, accordingly, does not express an opinion, a conclusion, nor provide any assurance on the prospective financial information;
- A caveat that the prospective results *may not be achieved*;
- A statement that the practitioner assumes *no responsibility to update* the report for events and circumstances occurring after the date of the report; and
- The signature of the practitioner's firm, the date of the report, and the city and state where the practitioner practices.

2.5.3 Sample Report: Compilation of a Financial Forecast*

[*The responsible party*] is responsible for the accompanying financial forecast of XYZ Company, which comprises the forecasted balance sheet as of December 31, 20X2, and the related forecasted statements of income, changes in stockholders' equity, and cash flows for the year then ending, and the related summaries of significant assumptions and accounting policies in accordance with guidelines for the presentation of a financial forecast established by the American Institute of Certified Public Accountants (AICPA). We have performed a compilation engagement in accordance with Statements on Standards for Accounting and Review Services promulgated by the Accounting and Review Services Committee of the AICPA. We did not examine or review the financial forecast nor were we required to perform any procedures to verify the accuracy or completeness of the information provided by management. Accordingly, we do not express an opinion, a conclusion, nor provide any form of assurance on this financial forecast.

The forecasted results may not be achieved as there will usually be differences between the forecasted and actual results, because events and circumstances frequently do no occur as expected, and these differences may be material. We have no responsibility to update this report for events and circumstances occurring after the date of this report.

[*Signature of practitioner's firm or practitioner, as appropriate*]

[*Practitioner's city and state*]

[*Date of the practitioner's report*]

*With the issuance of SSAE 18, compilations of prospective financial statements are no longer addressed in the attestation standards and are instead governed by AR-C section 80 of the SSARS standards.

2.5.4 Compilation of a Financial Projection

The standard report above would be changed slightly to refer to a "financial projection" rather than a "financial forecast."

2.6 Examination of Prospective Financial Statements

An examination of prospective financial statements is more substantial in scope and responsibility than a compilation or an engagement utilizing agreed-upon procedures.

2.6.1 Purpose

The purpose of an examination of prospective financial statements is to express an opinion as to whether:

1. the statements are presented in conformity with AICPA guidelines; and
2. the underlying assumptions provide a reasonable basis for the prospective statements.

2.6.2 Independence Required

Independence is required for examination engagements.

2.6.3 Evidence Required

In order for the accountant to make such a claim, sufficient evidence must be obtained. The accountant must evaluate the preparation, support, and presentation of the statements.

2.6.4 Content of Report Based on Examination

The standard examination report issued by the accountant would contain the following:

- A title that includes the word *independent*, the signature of the practitioner's firm, the city and state of the practitioner's firm, and the date of the report;
- Identification of the prospective financial statements presented;
- An indication that the criteria against which the prospective financial information was measured or evaluated are the guidelines for the presentation of a forecast (or projection) established by the AICPA.
- An identification of the responsible party and a statement that the prospective financial statements are the responsibility of the responsible party;
- A statement that the practitioner's responsibility is to express an opinion on the prospective financial statements based on his or her examination;
- A statement that the examination was conducted in accordance with attestation standards established by the AICPA;
- A statement that those standards require that the practitioner plan and perform the examination to obtain reasonable assurance about whether the forecast (or projection) is presented in accordance with the guidelines for the presentation of a forecast (or projection) established by the AICPA, in all material respects;

- A statement that the practitioner believes that the examination provides a reasonable basis for his or her opinion;
- A description of the nature of an examination engagement;
- An opinion that the prospective financial statements are presented in conformity with AICPA guidelines and that the underlying assumptions provide a reasonable basis for the forecast or the projection given the hypothetical assumptions;
- A statement indicating that the prospective results may not be achieved and describing other significant inherent limitations, if any; and
- A statement that the practitioner assumes no responsibility to update the report due to subsequent events.

For a projection, the report should also include identification of the hypothetical assumptions, a description of the projection's purpose, and a restrictive use paragraph.

2.6.5 Modifications to the Opinion

The following issues would require the practitioner to modify the opinion:

- AICPA presentation guidelines are not followed (qualified "except for" or adverse opinion).
- Significant assumptions are not disclosed (adverse opinion).
- Basis not reasonable: One or more of the significant assumptions do not provide a reasonable basis for the financial statements (adverse opinion).
- Scope limitation (disclaimer).

2.6.6 Sample Report: Examination of a Financial Forecast

Independent Accountant's Report

[Appropriate Addressee]

We have examined the accompanying forecast of XYZ Company, which comprises the forecasted balance sheet as of December 31, 20XX, and the related forecasted statements of income, stockholders' equity, and cash flows for the year then ending, based on the guidelines for the presentation of a forecast established by the American Institute of Certified Public Accountants. XYZ Company's management is responsible for preparing and presenting the forecast in accordance with the guidelines for the presentation of a forecast established by the American Institute of Certified Public Accountants. Our responsibility is to express an opinion on the forecast based on our examination.

(continued)

(continued)

Our examination was conducted in accordance with attestation standards established by the American Institute of Certified Public Accountants. Those standards require that we plan and perform the examination to obtain reasonable assurance about whether the forecast is presented in accordance with the guidelines for the presentation of a forecast established by the American Institute of Certified Public Accountants, in all material respects. An examination involves performing procedures to obtain evidence about the forecast. The nature, timing, and extent of the procedures selected depend on our judgment, including an assessment of the risks of material misstatement of the forecast, whether due to fraud or error. We believe that the evidence we obtained is sufficient and appropriate to provide a reasonable basis for our opinion.

In our opinion, the accompanying forecast is presented, in all material respects, in accordance with the guidelines for the presentation of a forecast established by the American Institute of Certified Public Accountants, and the underlying assumptions are suitably supported and provide a reasonable basis for management's forecast.

There will usually be differences between the forecasted and actual results because events and circumstances frequently do not occur as expected, and those differences may be material. We have no responsibility to update this report for events and circumstances occurring after the date of this report.

[*Practitioner's signature*]
[*Practitioner's city and state*]
[*Date of the practitioner's report*]

2.6.7 Examination of a Financial Projection

The standard report above would be changed slightly to include:

- A description of the hypothetical assumption used in the first paragraph (" ... management is responsible for preparing and presenting the projection based on [*identify the hypothetical assumption, for example, the granting of the requested loan as described in the summary of significant assumptions*] ... ").
- A description of the purpose of the projection in the first paragraph (" ... The projection was prepared for [*describe the special purpose, for example, the purpose of negotiating a loan to expand XYZ Company's plant*] ... ").
- A reference to the hypothetical assumption in the third and fourth paragraphs.
- A paragraph restricting the use of the report.

2.7 Agreed-Upon Procedures Applied to Prospective Financial Statements

The preceding discussion regarding conditions and required elements for agreed-upon procedures engagements ("**I-AM-SURE**" mnemonic, presented earlier in this module) also applies when such engagements are related to prospective financial statements. An additional condition is that the prospective financial statements must include a summary of significant assumptions.

Additional reporting elements include a reference to the prospective financial statements, a disclaimer on whether the statements are presented in conformity with AICPA guidelines and on whether the underlying assumptions provide a reasonable basis for the statements, a caveat that prospective results may not be achieved, and a statement that the accountant assumes no responsibility to update the report for events occurring after the date of the report.

2.8 Partial Presentations

A presentation of prospective financial information that excludes certain essential elements is considered to be a partial presentation that generally is not appropriate for general use. Partial presentations are those that omit one of the following essential elements: Sales, gross profit (or cost of sales), unusual or infrequent items, income tax expense, discontinued operations, income from continuing operations, net income, earnings per share, and significant changes in financial position.

Because partial presentations are generally appropriate only for limited use, reports on partial presentations of both forecasted and projected information should include a description of any limitations on the usefulness of the presentation.

2.9 Prospective Financial Statement Summary

General Procedures	Compilation Report*	Examination Report	Agreed-Upon Procedures
Prospective financial statements	Assemble	Evaluate	Apply specific procedures
Responsible party's assumptions	Assemble	Evaluate	Should be included in PFS
Are financial statements and significant assumptions in conformance with AICPA guidelines?	Look for obvious errors	Opinion	Disclaimer
Obtain agreed-upon scope from specified users	N/A	N/A	Yes

*With the issuance of SSAE 18, preparations and compilations of prospective financial statements are no longer addressed in the attestation standards and are instead governed by AR-C section 80 of the SSARS standards.

Reports Include a Statement Regarding:	Compilation Report*	Examination Report	Agreed-Upon Procedures
Identification of prospective financial statements	Yes	**Yes**	Yes
Compliance with AICPA standards	Yes	Yes	Yes
Limitation of scope	Yes	No	Yes
An enumeration of procedures performed	No	No	Yes
A caveat that prospective results may not be achieved	Yes	Yes	Yes
CPA has no responsibility for updating report	Yes	Yes	Yes
Opinion on PFS accordance with AICPA presentation guidelines	No	Yes	No
Limited use of report	Only required for projection	Only required for projection	Yes

*With the issuance of SSAE 18, preparations and compilations of prospective financial statements are no longer addressed in the attestation standards and are instead governed by AR-C section 80 of the SSARS standards.

2.10 Pro Forma Financial Statements

Pro forma financial statements are not prospective financial statements, but they may be used to demonstrate the effect of a future or hypothetical event by showing how it might have affected the historical financial statements if it had occurred during the period covered by those financial statements.

- Pro forma adjustments should be based on management's assumptions and include all material effects directly attributable to the transaction (or event).
- Pro forma financial information should be labeled accordingly to prevent confusion with historical financial information.
- Pro forma financial statements may be examined or reviewed.
- The practitioner should obtain an understanding of the event and evaluate the pro forma adjustments, including any assumptions on which the adjustments are based. The practitioner should also obtain written representations from management.
- A practitioner's report should make reference to the financial statements from which the historical financial information is derived, and state whether such financial statements were audited or reviewed.

2.10.1 Sample Report: Examination of Pro Forma Financial Statements

Independent Accountant's Report

We have examined the pro forma adjustments giving effect to the underlying transaction (or event) described in Note 1 and the application of those adjustments to the historical amounts in the accompanying pro forma condensed balance sheet of X Company as of December 31, 20X1, and the related pro forma condensed statement of income for the year then ended (pro forma financial information), based on the criteria in Note 1. The historical condensed financial statements are derived from the historical financial statements of X Company, which were audited by us, and of Y Company, which were audited by other accountants, appearing elsewhere herein [*or "and are readily available"*]. The pro forma adjustments are based on management's assumptions described in Note 1. X Company's management is responsible for the pro forma financial information. Our responsibility is to express an opinion on the pro forma financial information based on our examination.

Our examination was conducted in accordance with attestation standards established by the American Institute of Certified Public Accountants. Those standards require that we plan and perform the examination to obtain reasonable assurance about whether, based on the criteria in Note 1, management's assumptions provide a reasonable basis for presenting the significant effects directly attributable to the underlying transaction (or event), and, in all material respects, the related pro forma adjustments give appropriate effect to those assumptions, and the pro forma amounts reflect the proper application of those adjustments to the historical financial statement amounts. An examination involves performing procedures to obtain evidence about management's assumptions, the related pro forma adjustments, and the pro forma amounts in the pro forma condensed balance sheet of X Company as of December 31, 20X1, and the related pro forma condensed statement of income for the year then ended. The nature, timing, and extent of the procedures selected depend on our judgment, including an assessment of the risks of material misstatement of the pro forma financial information, whether due to fraud or error. We believe that the evidence we obtained is sufficient and appropriate to provide a reasonable basis for our opinion.

The objective of this pro forma financial information is to show what the significant effects on the historical financial information might have been had the underlying transaction (or event) occurred at an earlier date. However, the pro forma condensed financial statements are not necessarily indicative of the results of operations or related effects on financial position that would have been attained had the above-mentioned transaction (or event) actually occurred at such earlier date.

In our opinion, based on the criteria in Note 1, management's assumptions provide a reasonable basis for presenting the significant effects directly attributable to the above-mentioned transaction (or event) described in Note 1, and, in all material respects, the related pro forma adjustments give appropriate effect to those assumptions, and the pro forma amounts reflect the proper application of those adjustments to the historical financial statement amounts in the pro forma condensed balance sheet of X Company as of December 31, 20X1, and the related pro forma condensed statement of income for the year then ended.

[*Practitioner's signature*]

[*Practitioner's city and state*]

[*Date of the practitioner's report*]

2.10.2 Sample Report: Review of Pro Forma Financial Statements

Independent Accountant's Report

We have reviewed the pro forma adjustments giving effect to the transaction (or event) described in Note 1 and the application of those adjustments to the historical amounts in the accompanying pro forma condensed balance sheet of X Company as of March 31, 20X2, and the related pro forma condensed statement of income for the three months then ended (pro forma financial information), based on the criteria in Note 1. These historical condensed financial statements are derived from the historical unaudited financial statements of X Company, which were reviewed by us, and of Y Company, which were reviewed by other accountants, appearing elsewhere herein [*or "and are readily available"*]. The pro forma adjustments are based on management's assumptions as described in Note 1. X Company's management is responsible for the pro forma financial information. Our responsibility is to express a conclusion based on our review.

Our review was conducted in accordance with attestation standards established by the American Institute of Certified Public Accountants. Those standards require that we plan and perform our review to obtain limited assurance about whether, based on the criteria in Note 1, any material modifications should be made to management's assumptions in order for them to provide a reasonable basis for presenting the significant effects directly attributable to the underlying transaction (or event); the related pro forma adjustments, in order for them to give appropriate effect to those assumptions; or the pro forma amounts, in order for them to reflect the proper application of those adjustments to the historical financial statement amounts. A review is substantially less in scope than an examination, the objective of which is to obtain reasonable assurance about whether, based on the criteria, management's assumptions provide a reasonable basis for presenting the significant effects directly attributable to the underlying transaction (or event), and, in all material respects, the related pro forma adjustments give appropriate effect to those assumptions, and the pro forma amounts reflect the proper application of those adjustments to the historical financial statement amounts, in order to express an opinion. Accordingly, we do not express such an opinion. We believe that our review provides a reasonable basis for our conclusion.

The objective of this pro forma financial information is to show what the significant effects on the historical financial information might have been had the underlying transaction (or event) occurred at an earlier date. However, the pro forma condensed financial statements are not necessarily indicative of the results of operations or related effects on financial position that would have been attained had the above-mentioned transaction (or event) actually occurred at such earlier date.

Based on our review, we are not aware of any material modifications that should be made to management's assumptions in order for them to provide a reasonable basis for presenting the significant effects directly attributable to the above-mentioned transaction (or event) described in Note 1, the related pro forma adjustments in order for them to give appropriate effect to those assumptions, or the pro forma amounts, in order for them to reflect the proper application of those adjustments to the historical financial statement amounts in the pro forma condensed balance sheet of X Company as of March 31, 20X2, and the related pro forma condensed statement of income for the three months then ended, based on the criteria in Note 1.

[*Practitioner's signature*]

[*Practitioner's city and state*]

[*Date of the practitioner's report*]

For both examinations and reviews, nothing precludes the CPA from restricting the use of the report.

Question 1	MCQ-02450

Mill, CPA, was engaged by a group of royalty recipients to apply agreed-upon procedures to financial data supplied by Modern Co. regarding Modern's written assertion about its compliance with contractual requirements to pay royalties. Mill's report on these agreed-upon procedures should contain a (an):

- **a.** Disclaimer of opinion about the fair presentation of Modern's financial statements.
- **b.** List of the procedures performed (or reference thereto) and Mill's findings.
- **c.** Opinion about the effectiveness of Modern's internal control activities concerning royalty payments.
- **d.** Acknowledgment that the sufficiency of the procedures is solely Mill's responsibility.

Question 2	MCQ-02514

Accepting an engagement to examine an entity's financial projection most likely would be appropriate if the projection were to be distributed to:

hypo

- **a.** All employees who work for the entity.
- **b.** Potential stockholders who request a prospectus or a registration statement.
- **c.** A bank with which the entity is negotiating for a loan.
- **d.** All stockholders of record as of the report date.

Question 3	MCQ-02436

When a CPA examines a client's projected financial statements, the CPA's report should:

- **a.** Explain the principal differences between historical and projected financial statements.
- **b.** State that the CPA performed procedures to evaluate management's assumptions.
- **c.** Refer to the CPA's auditor's report on the historical financial statements.
- **d.** Include the CPA's opinion on the client's ability to continue as a going concern.

MODULE

5 Reporting on Controls at a Service Organization

AUD 5

1 Reporting on Controls at a Service Organization

Many entities use outside organizations to process some portion of their accounting transactions (e.g., ADP and Paychex are service organizations that provide processing for payroll checks and reports).

1.1 Relationship Between the Entity and the Service Organization

A service organization's services are considered to be part of a user entity's information system when those services affect the initiation, execution, processing, or reporting of the user company's transactions. In such cases, the controls placed in operation by the service organization are considered to be part of the user organization's information system. Service organizations often have an auditor perform an attestation examination engagement to report on the controls of the service organization that are relevant to the user entities' internal control over financial reporting.

Illustration 1 Service Organization

ABC Firm audits Party Solutions. Party Solutions uses Quick Payroll to process its payroll transactions. XYZ Firm audits Quick Payroll:

- Party Solutions is the user entity or user organization (Party Solutions is using the service of Quick Payroll).
- ABC Firm is the user auditor.
- Quick Payroll is the service organization.
- XYZ Firm is the service auditor.

1.2 Objectives

The objectives of the service auditor are to:

1. Obtain reasonable assurance about whether, in all material respects, based on suitable criteria:
   - Management's description of the service organization's system fairly presents the system that was designed and implemented throughout the specified period (or in the case of a Type 1 Report, as of a specified date).
   - The controls related to the control objectives stated in management's description of the service organization's system were suitably designed throughout the specified period (or in the case of a Type 1 Report, as of a specified date).
   - When included in the scope of the engagement, the controls operated effectively to provide reasonable assurance that the control objectives stated in management's description of the service organization's system were achieved throughout the specified period.
2. Report in accordance with the service auditor's findings.

1.3 Procedures

The service auditor should perform the following procedures:

- Assess the suitability of the criteria
- Obtain an understanding of the service organization's system
- Obtain evidence regarding management's description of the service organization's system
- Obtain evidence regarding the design of controls
- Obtain evidence regarding the operating effectiveness of controls (Type 2 Report only)
- Obtain written representations from management
- Consider subsequent events

1.4 Service Auditor Reports

There are two types of reports a service auditor may provide:

1.4.1 Type 1 Report

A "Type 1 Report" is a report on the design and implementation of a service organization's controls. It does not provide assurance on the operating effectiveness of the controls. A Type 1 Report contains the following:

1. Management's description of the service organization's system.
2. A written assertion by management of the service organization about whether, in all material respects, and based on suitable criteria:
   - Management's description of the service organization's system *fairly presents the design and implementation* of the system as of a specified date.
   - The controls related to the control objectives outlined in management's description were *suitably designed* to achieve the control objectives *as of a specified date*.
3. The auditor's opinion on management's assertion.

1.4.2 Sample Report: Type 1 Service Auditor's Report

Independent Service Auditor's Report on XYZ Service Organization's Description of Its System and the Suitability of the Design of Controls

To: XYZ Service Organization

Scope

We have examined XYZ Service Organization's description of its [*type or name of*] system entitled, "XYZ Service Organization's Description of Its [*type or name of*] System," for processing user entities' transactions [*or identification of the function performed by the system*] as of [*date*] (description) and the suitability of the design of the controls included in the description to achieve the related control objectives stated in the description, based on the criteria identified in "XYZ Service Organization's Assertion" (assertion).

(continued)

(continued)

The controls and control objectives included in the description are those that management of XYZ Service Organization believes are likely to be relevant to user entities' internal control over financial reporting, and the description does not include those aspects of the [*type or name of*] system that are not likely to be relevant to user entities' internal control over financial reporting.

Service Organization's Responsibilities

In [*section number where assertion is presented*], XYZ Service Organization has provided an assertion about the fairness of the presentation of the description and suitability of the design of the controls to achieve the related control objectives stated in the description. XYZ Service Organization is responsible for preparing the description and its assertion, including the completeness, accuracy, and method of presentation of the description and assertion, providing the services covered by the description, specifying the control objectives and stating them in the description, identifying the risks that threaten the achievement of the control objectives, selecting the criteria stated in the assertion, and designing, implementing, and documenting controls that are suitably designed and operating effectively to achieve the related control objectives stated in the description.

Service Auditor's Responsibilities

Our responsibility is to express an opinion on the fairness of the presentation of the description and on the suitability of the design of the controls to achieve the related control objectives stated in the description, based on our examination.

Our examination was conducted in accordance with attestation standards established by the American Institute of Certified Public Accountants. Those standards require that we plan and perform the examination to obtain reasonable assurance about whether, in all material respects, based on the criteria in management's assertion, the description is fairly presented and the controls were suitably designed to achieve the related control objectives stated in the description as of [*date*]. We believe that the evidence we obtained is sufficient and appropriate to provide a reasonable basis for our opinion.

An examination of a description of a service organization's system and the suitability of the design of controls involves:

- performing procedures to obtain evidence about the fairness of the presentation of the description and the suitability of the design of the controls to achieve the related control objectives stated in the description, based on the criteria in management's assertion.
- assessing the risks that the description is not fairly presented and that the controls were not suitably designed to achieve the related control objectives stated in the description.
- evaluating the overall presentation of the description, suitability of the control objectives stated in the description, and suitability of the criteria specified by the service organization in its assertion.

(continued)

(continued)

Inherent Limitations

The description is prepared to meet the common needs of a broad range of user entities and their auditors who audit and report on user entities' financial statements and may not, therefore, include every aspect of the system that each individual user entity may consider important in its own particular environment. Because of their nature, controls at a service organization may not prevent, or detect and correct, all misstatements in processing or reporting transactions [*or identification of the function performed by the system*]. Also, the projection to the future of any evaluation of the fairness of the presentation of the description, or conclusions about the suitability of the design of the controls to achieve the related control objectives, is subject to the risk that controls at a service organization may become ineffective.

Other Matter

We did not perform any procedures regarding the operating effectiveness of controls stated in the description and, accordingly, do not express an opinion thereon.

Opinion

In our opinion, in all material respects, based on the criteria described in XYZ Service Organization's assertion:

a. the description fairly presents the [*type or name of*] system that was designed and implemented as of [*date*].

b. the controls related to the control objectives stated in the description were suitably designed to provide reasonable assurance that the control objectives would be achieved if the controls operated effectively as of [*date*].

Restricted Use

This report is intended solely for the information and use of management of XYZ Service Organization, user entities of XYZ Service Organization's [*type or name of*] system as of [*date*], and their auditors who audit and report on such user entities' financial statements or internal control over financial reporting and have a sufficient understanding to consider it, along with other information, including information about controls implemented by user entities themselves, when assessing the risks of material misstatements of user entities' financial statements. This report is not intended to be, and should not be, used by anyone other than the specified parties.

[*Service auditor's signature*]

[*Service auditor's city and state*]

[*Date of the service auditor's report*]

1.4.3 Type 2 Report

A "Type 2 Report" is a report on the design, implementation, and operating effectiveness of a service organization's controls. A Type 2 Report contains the following:

1. Management's description of the service organization's system.
2. A written assertion by management of the service organization about whether, in all material respects, and based on suitable criteria:
   - Management's description of the service organization's system *fairly presents the design and implementation* of the system *throughout a specified period.*
   - The controls related to the control objectives outlined in management's description were *suitably designed* to achieve the control objectives *throughout a specified period.*
   - The controls related to the control objectives outlined in management's description *operated effectively* to achieve the control objectives *throughout a specified period.*
3. The auditor's opinion on management's assertion and a description of the service auditor's tests of controls and the results of those tests.

1.4.4 Sample Report: Type 2 Service Auditor's Report

Independent Service Auditor's Report on XYZ Service Organization's Description of Its System and the Suitability of the Design and Operating Effectiveness of Controls

To: XYZ Service Organization

Scope

We have examined XYZ Service Organization's description of its [*type or name of*] system entitled "XYZ Service Organization's Description of Its [*type or name of*] System" for processing user entities' transactions [*or identification of the function performed by the system*] throughout the period [*date*] to [*date*] (description) and the suitability of the design and operating effectiveness of the controls included in the description to achieve the related control objectives stated in the description, based on the criteria identified in "XYZ Service Organization's Assertion" (assertion). The controls and control objectives included in the description are those that management of XYZ Service Organization believes are likely to be relevant to user entities' internal control over financial reporting, and the description does not include those aspects of the [*type or name of*] system that are not likely to be relevant to user entities' internal control over financial reporting.

Service Organization's Responsibilities

In [*section number where the assertion is presented*], XYZ Service Organization has provided an assertion about the fairness of the presentation of the description and suitability of the design and operating effectiveness of the controls to achieve the related control objectives stated in the description. XYZ Service Organization is responsible for preparing the description and assertion, including the completeness, accuracy, and method of presentation of the description and assertion, providing the services covered by the description, specifying the control objectives and stating them in the description, identifying the risks that threaten the achievement of the control objectives, selecting the criteria stated in the assertion, and designing, implementing, and documenting controls that are suitably designed and operating effectively to achieve the related control objectives stated in the description.

(continued)

(continued)

Service Auditor's Responsibilities

Our responsibility is to express an opinion on the fairness of the presentation of the description and on the suitability of the design and operating effectiveness of the controls to achieve the related control objectives stated in the description, based on our examination.

Our examination was conducted in accordance with attestation standards established by the American Institute of Certified Public Accountants. Those standards require that we plan and perform the examination to obtain reasonable assurance about whether, in all material respects, based on the criteria in management's assertion, the description is fairly presented and the controls were suitably designed and operating effectively to achieve the related control objectives stated in the description throughout the period [*date*] to [*date*]. We believe that the evidence we obtained is sufficient and appropriate to provide a reasonable basis for our opinion.

An examination of a description of a service organization's system and the suitability of the design and operating effectiveness of controls involves:

- performing procedures to obtain evidence about the fairness of the presentation of the description and the suitability of the design and operating effectiveness of the controls to achieve the related control objectives stated in the description, based on the criteria in management's assertion.
- assessing the risks that the description is not fairly presented and that the controls were not suitably designed or operating effectively to achieve the related control objectives stated in the description.
- testing the operating effectiveness of those controls that management considers necessary to provide reasonable assurance that the related control objectives stated in the description were achieved.
- evaluating the overall presentation of the description, suitability of the control objectives stated in the description, and suitability of the criteria specified by the service organization in its assertion.

Inherent Limitations

The description is prepared to meet the common needs of a broad range of user entities and their auditors who audit and report on user entities' financial statements and may not, therefore, include every aspect of the system that each individual user entity may consider important in its own particular environment. Because of their nature, controls at a service organization may not prevent, or detect and correct, all misstatements in processing or reporting transactions [*or identification of the function performed by the system*]. Also, the projection to the future of any evaluation of the fairness of the presentation of the description, or conclusions about the suitability of the design or operating effectiveness of the controls to achieve the related control objectives, is subject to the risk that controls at a service organization may become ineffective.

Description of Tests of Controls

The specific controls tested and the nature, timing, and results of those tests are listed in [*section number where the description of tests of controls is presented*].

(continued)

(continued)

Opinion

In our opinion, in all material respects, based on the criteria described in XYZ Service Organization's assertion:

a. the description fairly presents the [*type or name of*] system that was designed and implemented throughout the period [*date*] to [*date*].

b. the controls related to the control objectives stated in the description were suitably designed to provide reasonable assurance that the control objectives would be achieved if the controls operated effectively throughout the period [*date*] to [*date*].

c. the controls operated effectively to provide reasonable assurance that the control objectives stated in the description were achieved throughout the period [*date*] to [*date*].

Restricted Use

This report, including the description of tests of controls and results thereof in [section number where the description of tests of controls is presented], is intended solely for the information and use of management of XYZ Service Organization, user entities of XYZ Service Organization's [*type or name of*] system during some or all of the period [*date*] to [*date*], and their auditors who audit and report on such user entities' financial statements or internal control over financial reporting and have a sufficient understanding to consider it, along with other information, including information about controls implemented by user entities themselves, when assessing the risks of material misstatement of user entities' financial statements. This report is not intended to be, and should not be, used by anyone other than the specified parties.

[*Service auditor's signature*]

[*Service auditor's city and state*]

[*Date of the service auditor's report*]

2 User Auditor Considerations

2.1 User Auditor Responsibilities

The user auditor should obtain an understanding of the nature and significance of the services provided by the service organization and the effect on the user entity's internal control, sufficient to identify and assess the risks of material misstatement and design and perform audit procedures responsible to those risks.

When a service auditor's report is available, the user auditor may utilize the report in its assessment of the user entity's internal controls.

- **Type 1 Report:** A Type 1 Report may aid the user auditor in obtaining an understanding of controls. However, a Type 1 Report is provided when tests of the operating effectiveness of the service organization's controls were not performed, and therefore it does not provide the user auditor with a basis for reducing the assessment of control risk below maximum for areas of the entity's accounting that are affected by the service organization.
- **Type 2 Report:** A Type 2 Report provides the user auditor with assurance about the design, implementation, and operating effectiveness of the service organization's internal controls and therefore may provide evidence that would allow a reduction in the assessed level of control risk for areas of the entity's accounting that are affected by the service organization.

Alternatively, such evidence (to allow reduction in assessed risk) can be obtained directly by the user auditor, either by testing the user organization's controls over the service organization's activities, or by performing tests of controls at the service organization.

The user auditor should be satisfied regarding:

1. the service auditor's competence and independence; and
2. the adequacy of the standards under which the Type 1 or Type 2 report were issued.

2.2 Reporting by the User Auditor

The user auditor should issue a qualified opinion or a disclaimer of opinion if the user auditor is unable to obtain sufficient appropriate audit evidence regarding the services provided by a service organization relevant to the audit.

The user auditor should not make reference to the report of the service auditor in an unmodified opinion issued by the user auditor.

The user auditor is permitted to make reference to the work of a service auditor in the user auditor's report to explain a modification of the user auditor's opinion.

Question 1 **MCQ-04739**

When an auditor is to conduct an audit of a service organization, what considerations should the auditor make in the planning stages regarding internal controls of the organization?

a. The auditor should assess the control risk before obtaining an understanding of internal controls.

b. The auditor should obtain an understanding of the entity's internal controls after performing substantive procedures.

c. The auditor should obtain an understanding of the effect of the user organization upon the service organization. → complimentary controls

d. The auditor should be engaged to perform agreed-upon procedures.

MODULE

6 Reporting on Compliance

AUD 5

1 Compliance Reporting

Reporting on compliance may be done in several situations:

- An auditor may be asked to report on compliance with contractual agreements or regulatory requirements in connection with a financial statement audit (covered below).
- A practitioner may be asked to report on an attestation engagement regarding an entity's compliance with requirements of specific laws and regulations or on internal control over compliance (covered later in this module).
- An auditor may report on compliance and internal control over compliance as part of a single audit engagement when auditing a recipient of federal financial assistance (covered in Module 8).

2 Compliance Reports in Connection With Audited Financial Statements

Often an auditor is asked to issue a report on a client's compliance with contractual agreements or regulatory requirements in connection with a financial statement audit. The auditor must have audited the client's financial statements and may only issue negative assurance on compliance.

This engagement is neither a compliance audit nor an attestation engagement, both of which may also be performed in relation to an entity's compliance with contractual agreements or regulatory requirements.

2.1 Negative Assurance

2.1.1 No Identified Instances of Noncompliance

Negative assurance, in the form of a statement that nothing came to the auditor's attention that caused the auditor to believe that the entity failed to comply with the specified aspects of the contractual agreement or regulatory requirement, may be given when:

1. there are no identified instances of noncompliance;
2. the auditor has expressed an unmodified opinion or qualified opinion on the financial statements; and
3. the applicable covenants or regulatory requirements have been subjected to audit procedures as part of the financial statement audit.

2.1.2 Identified Instances of Noncompliance

When the auditor identifies one or more instances of noncompliance, the report on compliance should describe the noncompliance. If an adverse opinion or a disclaimer of opinion is expressed on the financial statements, a report on compliance can only be issued when there are identified instances of noncompliance.

2.2 Report on Compliance

The report on compliance should be in writing and may either be a separate report or provided in one or more paragraphs in the auditor's report on the financial statements.

2.2.1 Separate Report on Compliance

When the auditor issues a separate report on compliance, the report should include the following:

- A title that includes the word "independent."
- An appropriate addressee.
- A paragraph that states that the financial statements were audited in accordance with U.S. GAAS and the date of the auditor's report on the financial statements.
- If the auditor expressed a modified opinion, a description of the nature of the modification.
- A reference to the specific covenants or paragraphs of the contractual agreement or regulatory requirement.
- When there are no identified instances of noncompliance, a statement that nothing came to the auditor's attention that caused the auditor to believe that the entity failed to comply with the specified aspects of the contractual agreement or regulatory requirements, insofar as they relate to accounting matters.
- When instances of noncompliance are identified, a description of the instances of noncompliance. When the entity has obtained a waiver for such noncompliance, the auditor may include a statement in the report on compliance that a waiver has been obtained.
- A statement that the report is provided in connection with the audit of the financial statements.
- A statement that the audit was not directed primarily toward obtaining knowledge regarding compliance and, accordingly, had the auditor performed additional procedures, other matters may have come to the auditor's attention regarding noncompliance with the specific covenants or paragraphs of the contractual agreement or regulatory requirement, insofar as they relate to accounting matters.
- A paragraph that includes a description and the source of the significant interpretations, if any, made by management relating to the provisions of the relevant contractual agreement or regulatory requirement.
- A paragraph that restricts the use of the report to management, those charged with governance, others within the organization, the regulatory agency, or other parties to the contract or agreement.
- Signature of the firm.
- City and state in which the auditor practices.
- Date of the report, which should be the same as the date of the auditor's report.

2.2.2 Sample Report: Separate Report on Compliance

Independent Auditor's Report

[*Appropriate Addressee*]

We have audited, in accordance with auditing standards generally accepted in the United States of America, the financial statements of XYZ Company, which comprise the balance sheet as of December 31, 20X2, and the related statements of income, changes in stockholders' equity, and cash flows for the year then ended, and the related notes to the financial statements, and have issued our report thereon dated February 16, 20X3.

In connection with our audit, nothing came to our attention that caused us to believe that XYZ Company failed to comply with the terms, covenants, provisions, or conditions of sections XX to YY inclusive, of the Indenture dated July 21, 20X0, with ABC Bank, insofar as they relate to accounting matters. However, our audit was not directed primarily toward obtaining knowledge of such noncompliance. Accordingly, had we performed additional procedures, other matters may have come to our attention regarding the Company's noncompliance with the above-referenced terms, covenants, provisions, or conditions of the Indenture, insofar as they relate to accounting matters.

This report is *intended solely* for the information and use of the boards of directors and management of XYZ Company and ABC Bank and is not intended to be and should not be used by anyone other than these specified parties.

[*Auditor's signature*]

[*Auditor's city and state*]

[*Date of the auditor's report*]

2.2.3 Report on Compliance Included in Auditor's Report

The report on compliance is included in the auditor's report in an *other-matter paragraph* that includes the following:

- A reference to the specific covenants or paragraphs of the contractual agreement or regulatory requirement.
- When there are no identified instances of noncompliance, a statement that nothing came to the auditor's attention that caused the auditor to believe that the entity failed to comply with the specified aspects of the contractual agreement or regulatory requirements, insofar as they relate to accounting matters.
- When instances of noncompliance are identified, a description of the instances of noncompliance. When the entity has obtained a waiver for such noncompliance, the auditor may include a statement in the report on compliance that a waiver has been obtained.
- A statement that the communication is provided in connection with the audit of the financial statements.

- A statement that the audit was not directed primarily toward obtaining knowledge regarding compliance, and, accordingly, had the auditor performed additional procedures, other matters may have come to the auditor's attention regarding noncompliance with the specific covenants or paragraphs of the contractual agreement or regulatory requirement, insofar as they relate to accounting matters.
- A paragraph that includes a description and the source of the significant interpretations, if any, made by management relating to the provisions of the relevant contractual agreement or regulatory requirement.
- A paragraph that restricts the use of the report to management, those charged with governance, others within the organization, the regulatory agency, or other parties to the contract or agreement.

Other Matter

In connection with our audit, nothing came to our attention that caused us to believe that ABC Company failed to comply with the terms, covenants, provisions, or conditions of sections XX to YY, inclusive, of the Indenture dated July 21, 20X0, with XYZ Bank, insofar as they relate to accounting matters. However, our audit was not directed primarily toward obtaining knowledge of such noncompliance. Accordingly, had we performed additional procedures, other matters may have come to our attention regarding the Company's noncompliance with the above-referenced terms, covenants, provisions, or conditions of the Indenture, insofar as they relate to accounting matters.

Restricted Use Relating to the Other Matter

The communication related to compliance with the aforementioned Indenture described in the other-matter paragraph is intended solely for the information and use of the boards of directors and management of ABC Company and XYZ Bank and is not intended to be and should not be used by anyone other than these specified parties.

Pass Key

When the auditor's report on compliance is included in the auditor's report on the financial statements, the restriction on the use of the report applies to the entire audit report. If a separate report is issued, then only the report on compliance needs to be restricted as to use.

3 Attestation Standards: Compliance Attestation

The attestation standards address two types of engagements:

1. **Compliance With Specified Requirements:** An entity's compliance with requirements of specified laws, regulations, rules, contracts, or grants.

2. **Internal Control Over Compliance:** An entity's internal control over compliance with specified requirements.

An SSAE report does not provide a legal determination of an entity's compliance with specified requirements. However, such a report may be useful to legal counsel or others in making such determinations.

Practitioners may be engaged to perform agreed-upon procedures or examination engagements on an entity's compliance. A practitioner should not accept an engagement to perform a review.

3.1 Agreed-Upon Procedures Engagements

The practitioner may be engaged to perform agreed-upon procedures to assist users in evaluating the following subject matter (or assertions):

- The entity's compliance with specified requirements.
- The entity's internal control over compliance with specified requirements.
- Both the entity's compliance with specified requirements and the entity's internal control over compliance with specified requirements.

A practitioner may perform an agreed-upon procedures engagement related to an entity's compliance with specified requirements or the entity's internal control over compliance if the following conditions are met:

- The responsible party accepts responsibility for the entity's compliance with specified requirements and the entity's internal control over compliance with specified requirements.
- The responsible party evaluates the entity's compliance with specified requirements or the entity's internal control over compliance with specified requirements.

The objective of the practitioner's agreed-upon procedures is to present specific findings to assist users in evaluating an entity's compliance with specified requirements or the entity's internal control over compliance based on procedures agreed upon by the users of the report.

In agreed-upon procedures engagements on an entity's compliance with specified requirements or about the entity's internal control over compliance, the practitioner is required to perform only the procedures that have been agreed to by users. The practitioner has no obligation to perform procedures beyond the agreed-upon procedures.

3.2 Reporting

An agreed-upon procedures over compliance report uses the same elements as a standard agreed-upon procedures report.

3.2.1 Sample Report: Agreed-Upon Procedures Report on an Entity's Compliance With Specified Requirements

Independent Accountant's Report on Applying Agreed-Upon Procedures

[*Appropriate Addressee*]

We have performed the procedures enumerated below, which were agreed to by [*identify the specified parties, for example, the management and board of directors of XYZ Company*], related to XYZ Company's compliance with [*identify the specified requirements, for example, the requirements listed in Attachment 1*] during the period January 1, 20X1, to December 31, 20X1. XYZ Company's management is responsible for its compliance with those requirements. The sufficiency of these procedures is solely the responsibility of those parties specified in this report. Consequently, we make no representations regarding the sufficiency of the procedures enumerated below either for the purpose for which this report has been requested or for any other purpose.

[*Include paragraphs to enumerate procedures and findings.*]

This agreed-upon procedures engagement was conducted in accordance with attestation standards established by the American Institute of Certified Public Accountants. We were not engaged to and did not conduct an examination or review, the objective of which would be the expression of an opinion or conclusion, respectively, on compliance with specified requirements. Accordingly, we do not express such an opinion or conclusion. Had we performed additional procedures, other matters might have come to our attention that would have been reported to you.

This report is intended solely for the information and use of [*identify the specified parties, for example, the management and board of directors of XYZ Company*] and is not intended to be, and should not be, used by anyone other than the specified parties.

[*Practitioner's signature*]

[*Practitioner's city and state*]

[*Date of the practitioner's report*]

3.2.2 Sample Report: Agreed-Upon Procedures Report Related to an Entity's Internal Control Over Compliance

Independent Accountant's Report on Applying Agreed-Upon Procedures

[*Appropriate Addressee*]

We have performed the procedures enumerated below, which were agreed to by [*identify the specified parties, for example, the management and board of directors of XYZ Company*], related to XYZ Company's internal control over compliance with [*identify the specified requirements, for example, the requirements listed in Attachment 1*], as of December 31, 20X1. XYZ Company's management is responsible for its internal control over compliance with those requirements. The sufficiency of these procedures is solely the responsibility of the parties specified in this report. Consequently, we make no representations regarding the sufficiency of the procedures enumerated below either for the purpose for which this report has been requested or for any other purpose.

[*Include paragraphs to enumerate procedures and findings.*]

This agreed-upon procedures engagement was conducted in accordance with attestation standards established by the American Institute of Certified Public Accountants. We were not engaged to and did not conduct an examination or review, the objective of which would be the expression of an opinion or conclusion, respectively, on internal control over compliance with specified requirements. Accordingly, we do not express such an opinion or conclusion. Had we performed additional procedures, other matters might have come to our attention that would have been reported to you.

This report is intended solely for the information and use of [*identify the specified parties, for example, the management and board of directors of XYZ Company*] and is not intended to be, and should not be, used by anyone other than the specified parties.

[*Practitioner's signature*]

[*Practitioner's city and state*]

[*Date of the practitioner's report*]

In some agreed-upon procedures engagements, procedures may relate to both compliance with specified requirements and the entity's internal control over compliance. In these engagements, the practitioner may issue one report that addresses both.

3.3 Examination Engagements

The practitioner may be engaged to examine the entity's compliance with requirements of specified laws, regulations, rules, contracts or grants (specified requirements), or a written assertion about compliance with specified requirements.

A practitioner may perform an examination engagement related to an entity's compliance with specified requirements if the following conditions are met:

1. The responsible party accepts responsibility for the entity's compliance with specified requirements and the effectiveness of the entity's internal control over compliance;
2. The responsible party evaluates the entity's compliance with specified requirements; and
3. Sufficient evidential matter exists or could be developed to support management's evaluation.

The objective of the practitioner's examination procedures applied to an entity's compliance with specified requirements is to express an opinion on an entity's compliance (or assertion related thereto), based on the specified criteria. To express such an opinion, the practitioner accumulates sufficient evidence about the entity's compliance with specified requirements, thereby restricting attestation risk to an appropriately low level.

3.4 Materiality

In an examination of an entity's compliance with specified requirements, the practitioner's consideration of materiality is affected by (a) the nature of the compliance requirements, which may or may not be quantifiable in monetary terms; (b) the nature and frequency of noncompliance identified with appropriate consideration of sampling risk; and (c) qualitative considerations, including the needs and expectations of the report's users.

3.5 Overall Requirements for Compliance Examination

Practitioners are expected to perform the following in relation to a compliance examination:

1. Perform a risk assessment.
2. Design responses to the risk assessment.
3. Determine if supplementary audit requirements exist.
4. Obtain written representations from management.
5. Prepare reports.
6. Prepare required documentation.

3.6 Required Documentation

Required documentation includes the following:

- The assessed risk of material noncompliance, including:
  - The procedures performed.
  - Documentation of internal control (narratives, flowcharts, etc.).
- Responses to the risk assessment, including:
  - The procedures performed to test compliance and results of procedures.
  - Tests of controls.
- The basis or rationale for materiality levels.
- Compliance with supplemental requirements.

3.7 Reporting

An examination of compliance uses the same elements as a standard examination report.

3.7.1 Sample Report: Examination Report on an Entity's Compliance With Specified Requirements

Independent Accountant's Report

We have examined XYZ Company's compliance with [*identify the specified requirements, for example, the requirements listed in Attachment 1*] during the period January 1, 20X1, to December 31, 20X1. Management of XYZ Company is responsible for XYZ Company's compliance with the specified requirements. Our responsibility is to express an opinion on XYZ Company's compliance with the specified requirements based on our examination.

Our examination was conducted in accordance with attestation standards established by the American Institute of Certified Public Accountants. Those standards require that we plan and perform the examination to obtain reasonable assurance about whether XYZ Company complied, in all material respects, with the specified requirements referenced above. An examination involves performing procedures to obtain evidence about whether XYZ Company complied with the specified requirements. The nature, timing, and extent of the procedures selected depend on our judgment, including an assessment of the risks of material noncompliance, whether due to fraud or error. We believe that the evidence we obtained is sufficient and appropriate to provide a reasonable basis for our opinion.

Our examination does not provide a legal determination on XYZ Company's compliance with specified requirements.

In our opinion, XYZ Company complied, in all material respects, with [*identify the specified requirements, for example, the requirements listed in Attachment 1*] during the period January 1, 20X1 to December 31, 20X1.

[*Practitioner's signature*]

[*Practitioner's city and state*]

[*Date of the practitioner's report*]

3.7.2 Sample Report: Examination Report on Management's Assertion About Compliance With Specified Requirements

Independent Accountant's Report

We have examined management of XYZ Company's assertion that XYZ Company complied with [*identify the specified requirements, for example, the requirements listed in Attachment 1*] during the period January 1, 20X1, to December 31, 20X1. XYZ Company's management is responsible for its assertion. Our responsibility is to express an opinion on management's assertion about XYZ Company's compliance with the specified requirements based on our examination.

Our examination was conducted in accordance with attestation standards established by the American Institute of Certified Public Accountants. Those standards require that we plan and perform the examination to obtain reasonable assurance about whether management's assertion about compliance with the specified requirements is fairly stated, in all material respects. An examination involves performing procedures to obtain evidence about whether management's assertion is fairly stated, in all material respects. The nature, timing, and extent of the procedures selected depend on our judgment, including an assessment of the risks of material misstatement of management's assertion, whether due to fraud or error. We believe that the evidence we obtained is sufficient and appropriate to provide a reasonable basis for our opinion.

Our examination does not provide a legal determination on XYZ Company's compliance with the specified requirements.

In our opinion, management's assertion that XYZ Company complied with [*identify the specified requirements, for example, the requirements listed in Attachment 1*], is fairly stated, in all material respects.

[*Practitioner's signature*]

[*Practitioner's city and state*]

[*Date of the practitioner's report*]

Pass Key

Type of Engagement	Standards	Assurance Provided
Compliance report in connection with audited financial statements	Auditing standards (SAS)	Negative assurance
Agreed-upon procedures	Attestation standards (SSAE)	No assurance
Examination	Attestation standards (SSAE)	Reasonable assurance

3.8 Representation Letter

In an examination engagement or an agreed-upon procedures engagement, the practitioner should obtain written representations from the responsible party (management), which includes the following statements:

- Management takes responsibility for complying with the specified requirements.
- Management takes responsibility for establishing and maintaining effective internal control over compliance.
- Management has performed an evaluation of:
  - the entity's compliance with specified requirements; or
  - the entity's controls for ensuring compliance and detecting noncompliance with requirements, as applicable.
- Management has disclosed to the practitioner all known noncompliance.
- Management has made available all documentation related to compliance.
- Management's interpretation of any compliance requirements that have varying interpretations.
- Management has disclosed any communications from regulatory agencies, internal auditors, and other practitioners concerning possible noncompliance.
- Management has disclosed any known noncompliance occurring subsequent to the period for which, or date as of which, they made their assertion.

4 Attestation Risk of Noncompliance

Attestation risk is the risk that the practitioner may unknowingly fail to modify appropriately his or her opinion. Similar to a financial statement audit, it is composed of inherent risk (assessed by auditor), control risk (assessed by auditor), and detection risk (controlled by auditor). The audit risk of noncompliance model adapts the terminology and relationships of the audit risk model.

Audit risk of noncompliance (should be low)	=	Risk of material noncompliance (assessed by auditor)	×	Detection risk (controlled by auditor)

4.1 Risk of Material Noncompliance

The *risk of material noncompliance* is composed of two elements:

1. **Inherent Risk of Noncompliance**

   The susceptibility of a compliance requirement to noncompliance that could be material, assuming that there are no related controls. Inherent risk exists independent of the audit. The *auditor cannot change* this risk, but *can* change the *assessment* of the risk based on evidence gathered during the audit.

2. Control Risk of Noncompliance

The risk that noncompliance with a compliance requirement that could be material will not be prevented or detected on a timely basis by an entity's internal control. Control risk exists independent of the audit. The *auditor cannot change* this risk, but *can* change the *assessment* of the risk based on evidence gathered during the audit.

The stronger the system of controls over compliance, the greater the reliance that may be placed on the controls, and the fewer the tests of details (or the lower the quality of evidence) required.

4.2 Detection Risk of Noncompliance

The risk that the auditor will not detect material noncompliance that exists. Detection risk relates to the auditor's procedures. The *auditor can change* this risk by varying the nature, extent, or timing of audit procedures.

As the acceptable level of detection risk decreases, the assurance provided by tests of details (including tests of implementation of corrective actions from previous audits) should increase.

Question 1 **MCQ-02499**

A CPA's report on agreed-upon procedures related to management's assertion about an entity's compliance with specified requirements should contain:

a. A statement of limitations on the use of the report.
b. An opinion about whether management's assertion is fairly stated.
c. Negative assurance that control risk has not been assessed.
d. An acknowledgment of responsibility for the sufficiency of the procedures.

MODULE

7 Government Audits

AUD 5

1 Sources of Government Auditing Standards

GAAS and GAGAS are the sources of standards for governmental audits.

1.1 GAAS: Generally Accepted Auditing Standards

Generally accepted auditing standards (*GAAS*) for the audits of nonissuers are issued by the AICPA's Auditing Standards Board (ASB) in the form of Statements on Auditing Standards (SAS). The ASB's Statements on Auditing Standards are outlined in Section AU-C of the AICPA Professional Standards and have been described previously. GAAS are applicable to all audits.

1.2 GAGAS: Government Auditing Standards (Yellow Book)

Generally accepted government auditing standards (*GAGAS*) are organized as foundations and ethical principles, general standards, standards for financial audits and attestation engagements, and field work and reporting standards for performance audits. GAAS are incorporated by reference and additional standards applicable to government expand the auditors' requirements.

GAGAS contain standards for audits of:

- Government organizations, programs, activities, and functions.
- Government assistance received by contractors, not-for-profit organizations, and other nongovernmental organizations.

Pass Key

GAGAS define "unconditional requirements" with which the auditor "must" comply and "presumptively mandatory requirements" with which the auditor "should" comply. The reason for not observing presumptively mandatory requirements that are not observed must be documented.

2 Purposes and Types of Government Audits

2.1 Financial Audits

2.1.1 GAAP Basis Financial Statements

Financial statement audits performed according to *Government Auditing Standards* (the Yellow Book) incorporate GAAS and determine whether the financial statements present fairly the financial position, results of operations, and, where applicable, cash flows in accordance with generally accepted accounting principles.

2.1.2 Financial Statements in Conformity With Special Purpose Frameworks

Engagements can also include audits of financial statements prepared in conformity with a special purpose framework or other comprehensive basis of accounting (OCBOA). Government regulators generally specify the OCBOA to be used in relation to financial assistance provided to organizations. Government audit standards can be used in connection with audits of nonissuers for audits otherwise conducted using AICPA standards, and audits of issuers otherwise conducted using PCAOB standards.

2.2 Attestation Engagements

Attestation engagements performed in conformity with *Government Auditing Standards* (the Yellow Book) incorporate the AICPA's standards for examinations, reviews, and agreed-upon procedures by reference and include expanded requirements. Subjects of attestation agreements could include:

1. Compliance with specified laws, regulations, rules, contracts, or grants.
2. Effectiveness of internal control over compliance with specified requirements (e.g., bidding etc.).
3. Presentation of management's discussion and analysis (MD&A).
4. Reliability of performance measures.

2.3 Performance Audits

Performance audits provide objective analysis, findings, and conclusions to assist management and those charged with governance and oversight to, among other things, improve program performance and operations, reduce costs, facilitate decision making by parties with responsibility to oversee or initiate corrective action, and contribute to public accountability.

Performance audits under GAGAS include a range of engagements governed by specific standards and can have varying objectives. Some objectives may overlap with each other and with the objectives of attestation engagements. Because of this, some engagements can be satisfied by following the standards applicable to either an attestation engagement or performance audit.

Key categories of performance audit objectives include:

1. **Effectiveness, Economy, and Efficiency**

   Audit objectives that focus on program effectiveness and results to evaluate whether programs are meeting their goals and objectives, and which address the costs and resources used to execute program initiatives. Examples include:

   - Achievement of legislative, regulatory, or organizational goals.
   - Evaluation of cost benefit or cost effectiveness.
   - Validity or reliability of performance measures.

2. **Internal Control**

   Audit objectives that relate to evaluating internal control over effective and efficient operations, reliable reporting, or compliance with laws and regulations. Examples include:

   - Organizational missions, goals, and objectives are achieved efficiently and effectively.
   - Resources are used in compliance with laws, rules, and regulations.
   - Security over computerized systems is effective. IT security
   - Disaster plans for computerized systems are adequate.

3. **Compliance**

   Audit objectives that relate to evaluating compliance with criteria established by provisions of laws, regulations, contracts, and grant agreements, or other requirements that could affect the acquisition, protection, use, and disposition of resources and the quantity, quality, timeliness, and cost of services provided in connection with programs. Compliance requirements can be either financial or nonfinancial. Examples include:

   - Compliance criteria established by laws, regulations, contract, etc., have been met.
   - Appropriate target population has been served.

4. **Prospective Analysis**

   Audit objectives to evaluate events that may occur in the future or to suggest actions an entity may take in response to future needs.

   - Provide analysis or conclusions about information that is based on assumptions about events that may occur in the future, along with possible actions that the entity may take in response to the future events.

In the 2018 Revision of Yellow Book, the GAO added guidance that auditors should consider whether internal controls are significant to the audit objectives and, if so, should determine which of the five COSO components are significant. Similar to a financial statement audit, the auditors would then assess the design and implementation of internal controls and potentially test the operating effectiveness of internal controls. Any deficiencies should be assessed and used in the evaluation of identified findings.

2.4 Determine if Supplementary Audit Requirements Exist

The entity may have audit requirements that go beyond GAAS and GAGAS. The auditor must make that determination.

A common example of supplementary audit requirements is the Single Audit requirements related to federal financial assistance (covered later).

3 Government Auditing Standards (GAGAS)

Generally accepted government auditing standards (GAGAS) include the following standards for financial audits.

3.1 Standards for Financial Audits: Performing Financial Audits

GAGAS include a number of requirements for performing financial audits in addition to the standard GAAS requirements.

3.1.1 Previous Audits and Attestation Engagements

The auditor should evaluate whether appropriate corrective actions to address findings and recommendations from previous audit and attestation engagements have been addressed. Planning procedures should include inquiry of management about the status of previous audits and recommendations. Management's response should be included in the auditor's risk evaluation.

3.1.2 Fraud, Noncompliance, and Abuse

Audits in accordance with GAGAS require additional attention to fraud, noncompliance with laws and regulations, and abuse. The auditor should:

- Consider compliance with contracts or grant agreements in addition to laws and regulations.
- Consider the occurrence of abuse:
    - Abuse involves deficient or improper behavior, including the misuse of authority or position for gain. It does not necessarily involve fraud or noncompliance
    - Auditors are not required to detect abuse because abuse is subjective.
    - Awareness of abuse that is quantitatively or qualitatively material to the audit obligates the auditor to perform further testing.
- Auditors should avoid interference with investigations or legal proceedings when pursuing indications of fraud or noncompliance.

3.1.3 Developing a Finding

GAGAS define the specific requirements associated with developing a finding to be reported to both the audited entity and others. Auditors should plan and perform procedures to develop the elements of a finding that are relevant and necessary to achieve audit objectives. The elements of a finding include criteria, conditions, cause, and effect or potential effect.

- **Criteria:** Criteria define expectations of a program or operation. Criteria are often laws, regulations, contracts, or grant agreements. Criteria may also be standards or benchmarks.
- **Condition:** The condition is the situation or status that exists.
- **Cause:** The cause is the reason for the condition or the deviation from the criteria. Examples include poorly designed policies, inconsistent implementation of policies, etc.
- **Effect or Potential Effect:** The effect or potential effect is a clear logical link between the condition and the deviation from criteria. It describes the outcomes or consequences of the condition. Effect demonstrates the need for corrective action.

3.1.4 Audit Documentation

Under GAGAS, auditors also should document, before the audit report is issued, evidence of supervisory review of the work performed that supports findings, conclusions, and recommendations contained in the audit report.

Auditors should also document departures from GAGAS and the impact on the audit due to noncompliance caused by law, regulation, scope limitations, etc.

3.1.5 Auditor Communication

In addition to the AICPA requirements for auditor communication, auditors should communicate pertinent information that in the auditors' professional judgment needs to be communicated to individuals contracting for or requesting the audit, and to cognizant legislative committees when auditors perform the audit pursuant to a law or regulation, or they conduct the work for the legislative committee that has oversight of the audited entity.

This requirement does not apply if the law or regulation requiring an audit of the financial statements does not specifically identify the entities to be audited, (i.e., single audits).

3.2 Standards for Financial Audits: Reporting on Financial Audits

GAGAS also include a number of requirements for reporting on financial audits in addition to the standard GAAS requirements. Auditors should include a statement in the audit report that they complied with GAGAS.

3.2.1 Report on Internal Control and Compliance With Provisions of Laws, Regulations, Contracts, and Grant Agreements

When providing an opinion or a disclaimer on financial statements, auditors should also report on internal control over financial reporting and on compliance with provisions of laws, regulations, contracts, or grant agreements that have a material effect on the financial statements.

Auditors should include in the same or separate reports a description of the scope of the auditors' testing of internal control over financial reporting and compliance with laws, regulations, contracts, and grant agreements. Auditors should state whether the tests the auditor performed provide sufficient appropriate evidence to support an opinion on the effectiveness of internal control over compliance.

- Reports should be made regardless of whether there are internal control deficiencies.
- The objective of the GAGAS requirement for reporting on internal control over financial reporting differs from the objective of an audit of internal control in accordance with AICPA standards. GAGAS does not require that the auditor express an opinion on internal controls.
  - GAGAS only require a report on internal control and compliance that describes the scope of the auditor's testing and any findings. However, the auditor may elect to increase testing to a level that provides sufficient appropriate evidence to support an opinion on the effectiveness of internal control over compliance.
  - In an audit of internal control in accordance with AICPA standards, the standards require the auditor to provide a high level of assurance about internal control over financial reporting in the form of an opinion.
- The report on financial statements should reference the existence of a separate report on internal control and compliance if separate reports are used (including separate reports bound in the same document).

3.2.2 Communicate Deficiencies in Internal Control, Fraud, and Noncompliance

- **Deficiencies in Internal Control:** Auditors should communicate in the report on internal control over financial reporting and compliance, based upon the work performed, significant deficiencies and material weaknesses in internal control.
- **Instances of Fraud and Noncompliance:** The auditor should report to the appropriate members of the audited organization:
  - Fraud and noncompliance with laws or regulations that have a material effect on the financial statements;
  - Noncompliance with provisions of contracts or grant agreements that have a material effect on the financial statements; and
  - Abuse that is material either quantitatively or qualitatively. Examples of abuse include creating unneeded overtime, requesting staff to perform personal errands for a supervisor or manager, making expensive or extravagant travel arrangements, and making vendor selections contrary to policy.
- **Less Than Material Findings:** Less than material findings should be communicated in writing to appropriate officials.
- **Presenting Findings in the Auditors' Reports:** A listing of findings and management responses is included in the report on internal control and compliance, or may be separately presented in a schedule of findings. The presentation of findings should:
  - Comply with the guidance for elements of a finding.
  - Be placed in perspective by describing the nature and extent of the issues reported and the extent of the work performed.
- **Reporting Findings to Outside Parties:** Findings may be communicated to parties outside the audited organization when management fails to:
  - Satisfy legal or regulatory requirements to report.
  - Take time and appropriate steps to respond to known or likely fraud, noncompliance, or abuse.

3.2.3 Report Views of Responsible Officials

Auditors must report their findings and also solicit and report the views of responsible officials along with any planned corrective actions. Providing a draft report with findings to appropriate members of the audited organization promotes the development of fair, complete, and objective reports. Responses of the audited organization should be in writing, but oral comments are acceptable.

- Written responses by the audited organization are included in the auditor's report.
- Oral responses will be confirmed in writing by the auditor, but not published in the report.
- Responses from the audited organization that either contradict or fail to fully address the auditor's comments should prompt the following actions:
  - Evaluate the validity of the audited organization's comments; and
  - Explain the basis for the disagreement in the report or modify the comment.
- Auditors may issue their reports without responses if the audited entity refuses to make comments or is unable to make comments. The audit report should disclose that the audited entity did not provide comments.

3.2.4 Reporting Confidential or Sensitive Information

Audit reports should disclose the exclusion of confidential or sensitive information from an audit report by:

- reporting the omission of information, and
- stating the reason or other circumstances that made the omission necessary.

Auditors may issue separate, classified, or limited use reports that are distributed to only the persons authorized by law or regulation to receive the confidential information.

Auditors should evaluate whether the omission of confidential or sensitive information could distort audit results or conceal improper or illegal practices.

3.2.5 Distribution of Reports

Audit organizations should distribute auditor's reports to:

- those charged with governance;
- audited entity officials;
- oversight bodies or those who require or arrange for the audits;
- officials with oversight authority or who may be responsible for acting on audit findings and recommendations; and
- all others authorized to receive reports.

Other distribution considerations include:

- Internal audit organizations in government entities must follow Institute of Internal Auditors (IIA) International Standards for the Professional Practice of Internal Auditing.
  - The head of the internal audit organization must consider the risks to the audited organization prior to release of reports outside of the organization.
  - The head of the internal audit organization should consult with senior management and control dissemination of reports to intended users.
- Independent external auditors should clarify report distribution responsibilities with the party contracting for the audit.
- Auditors should document any limitation on report distribution.

3.2.6 Additional GAGAS Considerations for Financial Audits

- **Materiality Thresholds**

  GAGAS auditors should consider reducing materiality thresholds in response to:

  - public accountability issues;
  - various legal and regulatory requirements; and
  - visibility and sensitivity of government programs.
- **Early Communication of Deficiencies**

  Deficiencies may be reported early when:

  - Urgency or significance of findings may require faster corrective actions or follow-up.
  - Ongoing noncompliance undetected by management should be stopped.

3.2.7 Sample Report: GAGAS (Yellow Book) Report on Internal Control and Compliance

Independent Auditor's Report

[*Appropriate Addressee*]

We have audited, in accordance with the auditing standards generally accepted in the United States of America and the standards applicable to financial audits contained in *Government Auditing Standards* issued by the Comptroller General of the United States, the financial statements of the governmental activities, the business-type activities, the aggregate discretely presented component units, each major fund, and the aggregate remaining fund information of the [*name of entity*], as of and for the year ended June 30, 20X1, and the related notes to the financial statements, which collectively comprise the [*name of entity*]'s basic financial statements, and have issued our report thereon dated August 15, 20X1.

Internal Control Over Financial Reporting

In planning and performing our audit of the financial statements, we considered the [*name of entity*]'s internal control over financial reporting (*internal control*) to determine the audit procedures that are appropriate in the circumstances for the purpose of expressing our opinions on the financial statements, but not for the purpose of expressing an opinion on the effectiveness of the [*name of entity*]'s internal control. Accordingly, we do not express an opinion on the effectiveness of the [*name of entity*]'s internal control.

A *deficiency in internal control* exists when the design or operation of a control does not allow management or employees, in the normal course of performing their assigned functions, to prevent, or detect and correct, misstatements on a timely basis. A *material weakness* is a deficiency, or a combination of deficiencies, in internal control, such that there is a reasonable possibility that a material misstatement of the entity's financial statements will not be prevented, or detected and corrected on a timely basis. A *significant deficiency* is a deficiency, or a combination of deficiencies, in internal control that is less severe than a material weakness, yet important enough to merit attention by those charged with governance.

Our consideration of internal control was for the limited purpose described in the first paragraph of this section and was not designed to identify all deficiencies in internal control that might be material weaknesses or significant deficiencies. Given these limitations, during our audit we did not identify any deficiencies in internal control that we consider to be material weaknesses. However, material weaknesses may exist that have not been identified.

Compliance and Other Matters

As part of obtaining reasonable assurance about whether the [*name of entity*]'s financial statements are free from material misstatement, we performed tests of its compliance with certain provisions of laws, regulations, contracts, and grant agreements, noncompliance with which could have a direct and material effect on the determination of financial statement amounts. However, providing an opinion on compliance with those provisions was not an objective of our audit, and, accordingly, we do not express such an opinion. The results of our tests disclosed no instances of noncompliance or other matters that are required to be reported under *Government Auditing Standards*.

(continued)

(continued)

Purpose of this Report

The purpose of this report is solely to describe the scope of our testing of internal control and compliance and the results of that testing, and not to provide an opinion on the effectiveness of the entity's internal control or on compliance. This report is an integral part of an audit performed in accordance with *Government Auditing Standards* in considering the entity's internal control and compliance. Accordingly, this communication is not suitable for any other purpose.

[*Auditor's signature*]

[*Auditor's city and state*]

[*Date of the auditor's report*]

Pass Key

The "Yellow Book" report is an additional report required under GAGAS.

For the financial statement audit, the audit report is the same as a standard nonissuer report, except for the following changes:

- The auditor's responsibility paragraph should state that the audit was conducted in accordance with both U.S. GAAS and *Government Auditing Standards*.
- An other-matter paragraph should be added to the end of the report referencing the GAGAS (Yellow Book) report.

3.3 Written Representations From Management (GAGAS)

GAAS guidance with respect to client representations should be followed. The following representations, consistent with or in addition to GAAS, should be included:

- There are no violations or possible violations of laws or regulations whose effects should be considered for disclosure in the financial statements or as a basis for recording a loss contingency (same as GAAS).
- Management is responsible for the entity's compliance with laws and regulations applicable to it.
- Management has identified and disclosed in writing to the auditor all the laws and regulations that have a direct and material effect on its financial statements.

Compliance
strong control
deficiency or not

3.4 Reporting: Internal Control

The auditor should report all significant deficiencies and material weaknesses in internal control.

GAGAS (like GAAS) require the auditor to:

- Obtain an understanding of the design of relevant controls and determine whether they have been implemented.
- Communicate all significant deficiencies (reportable conditions) noted during the audit, even those that are not material weaknesses.

GAGAS require a written report on the auditor's understanding of internal control and the assessment of control risk in all audits. This is different from GAAS, which require written communication only when significant deficiencies (reportable conditions) are noted.

Significant deficiencies should be reported to specific legislative and regulatory bodies.

Pass Key

One of the most tested features related to government audits is the requirement that a written report on internal control be prepared. The content of that report is also frequently tested, and it includes:

- The assertion that evaluating compliance with laws, rules, and regulations with a direct and material effect on the financial statements is part of developing an opinion on financial statements.
- The assertion that specific controls relating to financial reporting are considered.
- An indication that either no weaknesses were found or that significant deficiencies (reportable conditions) were found, and an indication whether those deficiencies were material.

In a financial statement audit, GAGAS require a report on internal controls over financial reporting, *not* a report on internal controls over compliance.

Question 1 **MCQ-03542**

Which of the following statements is a standard applicable to financial statement audits in accordance with *Government Auditing Standards*?

a. An auditor should assess whether the entity has reportable measures of economy and efficiency that are valid and reliable.

b. An auditor should report on the scope of the auditor's testing of internal controls.

c. An auditor should briefly describe in the auditor's report the method of statistical sampling used in performing tests of controls and substantive tests.

d. An auditor should determine the extent to which the entity's programs achieve the desired level of results.

MODULE

8 Single Audits

1 Overview of Single Audits

1.1 Audit Requirements for Federal Financial Assistance

Audits of recipients of federal financial assistance should be conducted in accordance with both GAAS and GAGAS. The following requirements also apply:

- Expanded internal control documentation and testing requirements.
- Expanded reporting to include formal written reports on the consideration of internal control and the assessment of control risk.
- Expanded reporting to include whether the federal financial assistance has been administered in accordance with applicable laws and regulations (i.e., compliance requirements).
- Application of *single audit standards* to federal financial assistance.

Pass Key

The examiners focus on expanded audit and reporting requirements related to audits of organizations that receive government assistance, particularly federal financial assistance. Fact patterns often focus on either the additional requirements associated with GAGAS and 2 CFR 200 single audits or on the differences between government and commercial auditing.

1.2 Responsibilities Under the Single Audit Act

1.2.1 Entities Subject to the Single Audit Act

The *Single Audit Act* is governed by provisions of federal regulations in Title 2 of the Code of Federal Regulations, 200.500–521, part of regulations included in what is commonly known as the "Uniform Grant Guidance." It requires entities that expend total federal assistance equal to or in excess of $750,000 in a fiscal year to have an audit performed in accordance with the act.

The act allows for either a single or program-specific audit. The program-specific audit election is only available to certain grant recipients who meet highly restrictive criteria, including:

- Awards are expended under a single federal program.
- No financial statement audit is required.

Nonfederal entities that expend less than $750,000 a year in federal awards are exempt from federal audit requirements for that year.

1.2.2 Objectives of the Single Audit

A single audit has two main objectives:

1. Audit of the entity's financial statements and reporting on a separate schedule of expenditures of federal awards in relation to those financial statements.
2. Compliance audit of federal awards expended during the year as a basis for issuing additional reports on compliance related to major programs and on internal control over compliance.

1.2.3 Materiality Determinations

The Single Audit Act requires that the materiality of the transaction or other compliance finding be considered separately in relation to each major program, not simply in relation to the financial statements taken as a whole.

Major programs are determined in accordance with formulas prescribed by 2 CFR 200 single audit requirements. Generally, programs classified as major are those that expend $750,000 or more in federal financial assistance, but smaller programs may be deemed major if they are classified as "high risk," even if they do not meet the monetary threshold. The Uniform Grant Guidance provides guidance on applying this "risk-based approach" to program selection.

Pass Key

The *audit threshold* for federal audit requirements is *expenditure of $750,000* of federal financial assistance.

Single audits are *generally required* unless the restrictive requirements of a program-specific audit are met.

Program-specific audits are used when the expenditures are made under only *one program* and the terms of the award *do not require a financial statement audit.*

Under both GAAS and GAGAS, materiality is considered in relation to the financial statements being audited taken as a whole.

Pass Key

Remember, a single audit includes a separate evaluation of materiality for each major program selected.

1.2.4 Audit Requirements Apply to Recipients and Subrecipients

Audit requirements apply to recipients and subrecipients of federal financial assistance. Contractors have more limited requirements.

Pass Key

Federal award recipients (e.g., a city expending funds received directly from the U.S. Department of Housing and Urban Development, or HUD) or a *subrecipient* (e.g., a city expending funds received from a state that received the funds from HUD) are subject to audit requirements associated with federal financial assistance.

Contractors (e.g., those who are paid by recipients or subrecipients of federal financial assistance, such as an electrician performing service upgrades to a public housing authority) are not subject to the same audit requirements as recipients and subrecipients.

1.3 Program-Specific Audits

Under certain circumstances, recipients are permitted to have a program-specific audit instead of a single audit. Entities not covered by the Single Audit Act are also eligible.

The auditor must contact the Inspector General of the applicable federal agency and obtain a current program-specific audit guide. The auditor must follow GAGAS and the guide when performing a program-specific audit. If a program-specific audit guide is not available, the auditor has basically the same responsibilities as in an audit of a major program for a single audit.

Pass Key

All governmental audits carried out under the Single Audit Act are not the same:

- Audits of an entire organization that include additional audit procedures on specific programs are called "single audits." These audits include a report on the financial statements of the whole organization and audit reports on the specific programs.
- Audits of specific programs are called "program-specific audits" and do not include reports on the financial statements of the organization taken as a whole.

Question 1 **MCQ-05604**

In auditing compliance with requirements governing major federal financial assistance programs under the Single Audit Act, the auditor's consideration of materiality differs from materiality under generally accepted auditing standards. Under the Single Audit Act, materiality is:

a. Calculated in relation to the financial statements taken as a whole.
b. Determined separately for each major federal financial assistance program.
c. Decided in conjunction with the auditor's risk assessment.
d. Ignored, because all account balances, regardless of size, are fully tested.

2 Auditee Responsibilities

2.1 Auditor Selection

Auditors must be selected using procurement standards established by federal guidelines. Procurement standards preclude limitations on competition, including:

- The use of a single or sole source vendor (only considering one firm).
- Providing preferences to local firms (giving advantages to firms based on geographic location).

Proposals made by auditors must be evaluated for:

- Responsiveness to the request for proposal.
- Relevant experience.
- The availability of professionally qualified staff.
- The results of peer reviews.
- Auditees must request a copy of the audit organization's peer review report. In selecting an auditor, the use of small and minority-owned businesses is encouraged.
- Consultants engaged to develop indirect cost plans may not be engaged as the auditor when the indirect costs recovered by the auditee during the prior year exceed $1 million.

Pass Key

Auditor selection is made by the auditee, subject to federal guidelines that seek to ensure the appointment of an auditor possessing the necessary expertise through an open and competitive proposal process.

2.2 Report Submission

The audit report must be submitted within the earlier of:

1. Thirty calendar days of receipt of the auditor's report; or
2. Nine months after the end of the audit period.

Reports must be retained for three years from the date of submission. Copies must be made available for public inspection (unless restricted by federal statute or regulation).

The audit report must be submitted in the following format:

- The report must be transmitted using a Data Collection Form that follows a specific data set required by the Office of Management and Budget (OMB).
- The form must be signed by a responsible official.
- The reporting package must include:
  - Financial statements
  - A summary schedule of prior audit findings
  - Auditor's reports
  - Corrective action plans
- The report must be submitted electronically.

Pass Key

The organization subject to audit is responsible for the production of financial statements and a schedule of federal expenditures, along with corrective actions, in response to audit findings. Auditee reports, along with auditor reports and findings, must be submitted by the auditee within 30 days of receipt or nine months after the end of the audit period.

3 Auditor Responsibilities

3.1 The Scope of the Audit

The auditor should express an opinion regarding the fair presentation of the financial statements and related schedules. In addition, the auditor should consider internal control, compliance, and previous audit findings.

3.1.1 Internal Control

The auditor should consider internal controls over compliance using major programs as a basis for both testing and reporting. Auditors have no responsibility to obtain an understanding of internal control over compliance or perform related tests of compliance for any federal program deemed to be nonmajor.

Internal control guidance is taken from both the U.S. Office of the Comptroller General and the Committee of Sponsoring Organizations (COSO) Internal Control Framework as best practices for frameworks of internal controls.

The audit must be planned to support a low assessed level of control risk of noncompliance for major programs. The auditor must plan and perform tests of controls over compliance for major programs, keeping in mind the following:

- The auditor is not required to test controls that are ineffective.
- Significant deficiencies and material weaknesses must be reported.
- When controls are deemed ineffective, additional tests of compliance must be considered.

3.1.2 Compliance

The auditor should express an opinion regarding major program compliance with statutes, regulations, and terms and conditions of the related federal award. The compliance testing must include tests of transactions and any other procedures necessary to provide sufficient appropriate audit evidence to support an opinion on compliance.

Compliance requirements are typically found in the Compliance Supplement. Otherwise, the auditor should look to the sources of compliance requirements (e.g., laws, regulations, or terms and conditions of the award).

3.1.3 Previous Audit Findings

The auditor is required to follow up on audit findings from previous audits. The auditor must perform procedures to assess the reasonableness of the summary schedule of prior audit findings prepared by the auditee.

3.2 Audit Reporting

The auditor should:

1. Express an opinion regarding the fair presentation of the financial statements, in accordance with GAAP (Financial Statement Report).
2. Express an opinion regarding the fair presentation of the Schedule of Expenditures of Federal Awards (SEFA) in relation to the financial statements (SEFA Report).
3. Report on internal control over financial reporting and compliance with federal statutes, regulations, and the terms and conditions for the federal award (Yellow Book Report required by GAGAS), including:
   - The scope of testing of internal control and compliance.
   - The results of tests.
   - Reference to a separate Schedule of Findings and Questioned Costs.
4. Report on compliance for each major program and report on internal control over compliance (Single Audit Report) including:
   - The scope of testing of internal control over compliance.
   - An opinion with regard to compliance with federal statues, regulations, and the terms and conditions of the federal award.
     - —For reportable instances of noncompliance with the requirements governing a major federal financial assistance program, reports should be qualified ("except for") or adverse, depending on materiality.
     - —Immaterial instances of noncompliance should be reported, but need not be specifically identified.
   - Reference to a separate Schedule of Findings and Questioned Costs.
5. Provide a Schedule of Findings and Questioned Costs that includes:
   - A summary of the auditor's results:
     - —The type of report issued by the auditor over the financial statements (e.g. unmodified, qualified, etc.).
     - —A statement regarding whether significant deficiencies or material weaknesses in internal control were found during the financial statement audit.
     - —A statement regarding whether significant deficiencies or material weaknesses in internal control over major programs were disclosed by the Single Audit.
     - —Discovery of any material noncompliance.
     - —The type of report the auditor issued on compliance for major programs (e.g. unmodified, adverse, etc.).
     - —A statement regarding whether the audit disclosed any audit findings the auditor is required to report (significant deficiencies, material weaknesses, material noncompliance, known or likely questioned cost, known or likely fraud).
     - —Identification of the major programs (a list of the major programs).
     - —The dollar threshold used to distinguish between type A and type B programs
     - —A statement as to whether the auditee qualified as a low-risk auditee
   - GAGAS findings.
   - Findings and questioned costs for federal awards.

Pass Key

Because single audits require that the financial statements also be audited, the Uniform Grant Guidance requires the use of both GAAS and GAGAS.

Five reports are issued:

1. Financial Statement Report (GAAS)
2. SEFA Report (in relation to)
3. GAGAS (Yellow Book) Report
4. Single Audit Report
5. Schedule of Findings and Questioned Costs

3.3 Audit Findings

The auditor must report the following audit findings:

- Significant deficiencies and material weaknesses in internal control over major programs and significant instances of abuse related to major programs.
- Material noncompliance with provisions of federal statutes, regulations, or the terms and conditions of federal awards related to major programs.
- Questioned costs of a given type of compliance requirement if those costs exceed $25,000.

Illustration 1 Questioned Costs

An auditor is performing compliance testing on a rental assistance program, a major program administered by a federally funded public housing authority. A compliance requirement for this major program is that tenants must meet eligibility requirements, including income limitations. The auditor finds that a number of tenants for whom rent subsidies have been claimed earned income in excess of the tenant income limitations. The auditor accumulates the amounts associated with the noncompliance and questions $36,000 of the public housing authority's rent subsidies. Because the questioned costs are greater than $25,000, the auditor is required to report them.

- The circumstances concerning why the auditor's report on compliance for each major program is other than an unmodified opinion, as applicable.
- Known or likely fraud affecting a federal award.
- Instances in which the results of audit follow-up procedures disclosed that the summary schedule of prior audit findings prepared by the auditee was materially misrepresented.

Findings must be stated clearly and in a manner that defines the deficiency and the implications of the deficiency.

3.4 Audit Documentation

Audit documentation must be maintained for three years after the date of issuance.

Contested audit findings or requests by the awarding or cognizant agency may extend the retention period. The cognizant agency is generally the lead agency that provides the most funding to the recipient and the one that receives and distributes the reports.

Pass Key

Both the auditor and the auditee must retain audit documentation for three years after issuance and receipt.

3.5 Major Program Determination

3.5.1 Risk-Based Approach

The determination of major programs uses a risk-based approach and a four-step process.

The risk-based approach includes the consideration of:

- Current and prior audit experience
- Oversight by federal agencies
- Inherent risk

Audit workpapers should include documentation of the risk analysis defined in the federal guidance. Major programs determined in accordance with federal guidance will not be challenged by federal agencies.

The four-step process is as follows:

Step 1 Identify type A (under most circumstances, $750,000 or more) and type B programs (those not meeting the requirements of type A).

Step 2 Identify type A programs that are low risk.

For a type A program to be considered low risk, it must have been audited as a major program in at least one of the two most recent audit periods. Type A programs cannot be low risk if they had:

- material weaknesses in internal control for major programs;
- a modified opinion on the program; or
- known or likely questioned costs that exceed 5 percent of the total federal awards expended for the program.

Step 3 Identify type B programs that are high risk, using professional judgment.

Step 4 At a minimum, major programs include all type A programs not identified as low risk and all type B programs identified as high risk that meet the coverage requirements described below.

3.5.2 Percentage of Coverage

For low-risk auditees, the auditor must test 20 percent of the total federal awards expended. For other auditees, the auditor must test 40 percent of the total federal awards expended. If the percentage of coverage requirements are not met after selecting all high-risk type A and high-risk type B programs, continuing selecting other programs until the threshold is met.

Pass Key

Auditors select major programs for audit using a risk-based approach that follows a specific methodology, but the process ultimately relies on auditor judgment.

3.5.3 Criteria for Federal Program Risk

Current and prior audit experience could indicate higher risk:

- Multiple internal control structures
- Weak monitoring systems for subrecipients
- Programs not recently audited as major

Oversight exercised by federal agencies and pass-through entities can be used to assess risk.

The inherent risk of a federal program is increased by:

- The complexity of the program (e.g., complex eligibility requirements).
- Being in the early phase of a program's life cycle (with new or untested requirements).

3.5.4 Criteria for a Low-Risk Auditee

- Single audits have been performed on an annual basis for two years.
- The financial statements received an unmodified opinion.
- No material weaknesses in internal control were identified under GAGAS.
- No going concern contingencies were reported.
- Type A programs, that had:
  - No material weaknesses in the auditor's report on internal controls over compliance.
  - No questioned costs in excess of 5 percent of the award expended.
  - No modified opinion on major programs.

4 Reporting Requirements

The following chart summarizes when each of four reports is required.

Recommended Reporting

Report	*REQUIRED BY*		
	GAAS	*Government Auditing Standards*	*Single Audits*
Opinion (or disclaimer) on financial statements and supplementary schedule of expenditures of federal awards.	✓	✓	✓
Report on internal control and compliance with provisions of laws, regulations, contracts, and grant agreements.		✓	✓
Report on compliance and internal control over compliance applicable to each major program. This report must include an opinion (or disclaimer) on compliance.			✓
Schedule of findings and questioned costs.			✓

Pass Key

Remember that government audits and single audits require more work and responsibility for the auditor. The examiners usually focus on the additional audit report requirements.

Pass Key

Government audit and single audit reports focus the reader on compliance with laws, rules, and regulations; the internal controls associated with maintaining compliance; and any findings of noncompliance.

Question 2	MCQ-03517

In auditing a not-for-profit entity that receives governmental financial assistance, the auditor has a responsibility to:

a. Issue a separate report that describes the expected benefits and related costs of the auditor's suggested changes to the entity's internal control.

b. Assess whether management has identified laws and regulations that have a direct and material effect on the entity's financial statements.

c. Notify the governmental agency providing the financial assistance that the audit is not designed to provide any assurance of detecting errors and fraud.

d. Render an opinion concerning the entity's continued eligibility for the governmental financial assistance.

Question 3	MCQ-03514

Although the scope of audits of recipients of federal financial assistance in accordance with federal audit regulations varies, these audits generally have which of the following elements in common?

a. The auditor is to determine whether the federal financial assistance has been administered in accordance with applicable laws and regulations.

b. The materiality levels are lower and are determined by the government entities that provided the federal financial assistance to the recipient.

c. The auditor should obtain written management representations that the recipient's internal auditors will report their findings objectively.

d. The auditor is required to express both positive and negative assurance that illegal acts that could have a material effect on the recipient's financial statements are disclosed to the inspector general.

NOTES

AUD

6

Accounting and Review Service Engagements, Interim Reviews, and Ethics and Professional Responsibilities

Module

NOTES

MODULE

1 SSARS Engagements

AUD 6

1 Levels of Service

CPAs can perform three levels of service with respect to unaudited financial statements of a nonissuer.

1.1 Preparation

The objective of a preparation engagement is to prepare financial statements in accordance with a specified financial reporting framework. The CPA does not perform any audit or review procedures. A preparation provides no assurance and is considered a non-attest service. Therefore, it does not require a determination of whether the accountant is independent of the entity.

1.2 Compilation

In a compilation engagement, the objective is to present in the form of financial statements information that is the representation of management without undertaking to express any assurance on the financial statements. The CPA does not perform any audit or review procedures. A compilation does not provide assurance, but because a report is required, it is an attest engagement. Although independence is not required, a determination of whether the accountant is independent of the entity is required.

1.3 Review

A CPA may express limited (negative) assurance on financial statements that have not been audited. The objective of a review engagement is to express limited assurance that there are no material modifications that should be made to the financial statements in order for the statements to be in conformity with the applicable financial reporting framework. A review is based on inquiry and analytical procedures performed by the CPA. A review is both an assurance engagement and an attest engagement. Independence is required.

1.4 Performance of More Than One Service

When an accountant performs more than one service (for example, a compilation and an audit), the accountant generally should issue the report that is appropriate for the highest level of service rendered.

Pass Key

- Attest—report
- Non-attest—no report
- Assurance—opinion (reasonable)/conclusion (limited)
- No assurance—no opinion/conclusion

2 Professional Standards

2.1 Statements on Standards for Accounting and Review Services (SSARS)

The Accounting and Review Services Committee of the AICPA is the authoritative body designated to issue pronouncements in connection with the unaudited financial statements of nonissuers. The pronouncements issued are known as Statements on Standards for Accounting and Review Services, or SSARS.

An accountant should:

1. have sufficient knowledge to identify applicable SSARS;
2. exercise professional judgment in applying SSARS; and
3. be able to justify departures from SSARS.

Specific language is used within SSARS to clarify the accountant's level of responsibility. The terms "must" and "should" are defined as described in A1.

2.2 SSARS Applicability

SSARS provide standards with respect to preparations, compilations, and reviews of financial statements. An accountant who is engaged to prepare, compile, or review unaudited financial statements of a nonissuer should comply with SSARS.

- **Nonissuer:** A nonissuer is an entity (i) for which securities are not registered with the SEC; (ii) that is not required to file reports with the SEC; and (iii) that has not filed a registration statement (that is still pending) with the SEC.

SSARS also apply to engagements in which the accountant is engaged to prepare, compile or review specified elements, accounts, or items of a nonissuer's financial statements, or engaged to prepare or compile pro forma financial information of a nonissuer.

2.3 SSARS Do Not Apply

2.3.1 Other Accounting Services

SSARS do not apply to other accounting services provided by accountants, such as preparing one or a few adjusting or correcting entries, consulting on financial matters, preparing tax returns, rendering manual or automated bookkeeping or data processing services, and processing financial data for clients of other accounting firms.

- Note that if the accountant prepares many adjusting or correcting entries, this could be considered preparation of financial statements, and SSARS would apply. The accountant must exercise judgment in making this determination.

2.3.2 Reviews of Interim Financial Statements

SSARS are not applicable to reviews of interim financial information of nonissuers whose annual financial statements are audited. Statements on Auditing Standards (SAS) apply to these engagements, which will be covered later.

3 Elements of SSARS Engagements

Preparation, compilation, and review engagements include the following elements.

3.1 Three-Party Relationship

Preparation, compilation, and review engagements involve three parties: management (the responsible party), an accountant in the practice of public accounting, and the intended users of the financial statements or financial information.

3.1.1 Management

The responsibilities of management—and when appropriate, those charged with governance—are:

- The identification of an applicable financial reporting framework and individual accounting policies when alternatives are provided by the financial reporting framework;
- The preparation and fair presentation of the financial statements in accordance with that framework;
- The design, implementation, and maintenance of internal control;
- Preventing and detecting fraud;
- Ensuring that the entity complies with laws and regulations;
- The accuracy and completeness of the records, documents, explanations, and other information, including significant judgments provided by management for the preparation of financial statements; and
- Providing the accountant with access to all information and access to persons within the entity of which the accountant determines it necessary to make inquiries.

The accountant should not accept an engagement to be performed in accordance with SSARS when management is unwilling to accept these responsibilities. In addition, an accountant should not accept an engagement if the accountant has reason to believe that information needed to perform the engagement is unavailable or unreliable or if the accountant doubts management's integrity.

3.1.2 Accountant in the Practice of Public Accounting

The accountant should possess knowledge of the accounting principles and practices of the industry in which the entity operates that will enable the accountant to prepare, compile, or review the financial statements. An accountant should not accept an engagement if preliminary understanding of the engagement circumstances indicates that ethical requirements regarding quality control cannot be satisfied.

- The accountant should comply with relevant ethical requirements, including the AICPA Code of Professional Conduct, together with rules of state boards of accountancy and applicable regulatory agencies.
- The accountant should exercise professional judgment in the performance of an engagement in accordance with SSARS.
- SSARS also require the accountant maintain appropriate engagement level quality control.

3.1.3 Intended Users

The intended users are the person(s) or class of persons who understand the limitations of the engagement and the financial statements. Management and the intended users may be the same. Intended users may be from the same entity or from different entities. The accountant has no responsibility to identify the intended users.

3.2 Establish an Understanding With the Client

All SSARS engagements require a written agreement with management, and, when appropriate, those charged with governance, regarding the terms of the engagement.

3.3 Compilations or Reviews Conducted in Accordance With SSARS and Another Set of Standards

When the accountant performs a compilation or review in accordance with SSARS and another set of standards, the accountant's compilation or review report should identify the other set of compilation or review standards, as well as its origin in the compilation or review report.

3.4 Other Frameworks

Financial statements may be prepared in accordance with a financial reporting framework other than GAAP or IFRS. For example, financial statements may be prepared in accordance with a special purpose framework or a framework generally accepted in another country.

3.4.1 Special Purpose Framework

Financial statements prepared in accordance with a special purpose framework are not considered appropriate in form unless the financial statements include:

1. a description of the special purpose framework, including a summary of significant accounting policies and a description of the material differences from GAAP; and
2. disclosures similar to those required by GAAP if the financial statements contain items that are similar to those included in financial statements prepared in accordance with GAAP.

3.4.2 Financial Reporting Framework Generally Accepted in Another Country

When performing a compilation or review on financial statements prepared in accordance with a financial reporting framework generally accepted in another country, the accountant should obtain an understanding of such framework and follow the appropriate reporting requirements depending on the distribution of the report:

- **Distribution Outside the United States**

  If the accountant is issuing an accountant's compilation or review report on financial statements and the financial statements are intended for use only outside the United States, the accountant should use either of the following:

  - A report in accordance with SSARS that includes a statement that refers to the note of the financial statements that describes the basis of presentation, including identification of the country of origin of the accounting principles.
  - A report in accordance with another set of compilation or review standards.

- **Distribution in the United States**

  If the financial statements will be used in the United States, the accountant should report in accordance with SSARS, including the requirements related to financial statements prepared in accordance with a special purpose framework.

3.5 Financial Statements or Financial Information

The financial reporting framework determines what constitutes a complete set of financial statements. An accountant may be engaged to prepare, compile, or review a complete set of financial statements or an individual financial statement. Financial statements may be for an annual period, or for a shorter or longer period.

4 Subsequent Events and Subsequently Discovered Facts

4.1 Subsequent Events

When evidence or information about subsequent events that require adjustment of, or disclosure in, the financial statements comes to the accountant's attention, the accountant should request that management consider whether each such event is appropriately reflected in the financial statements in accordance with the applicable financial reporting framework. If the accountant determines that the subsequent event is not adequately accounted for in the financial statements or disclosed in the notes, the accountant should treat as a departure from GAAP or applicable financial reporting framework.

4.2 Subsequently Discovered Facts That Become Known to the Accountant Before the Report Release Date

The accountant is not required to perform any review procedures regarding the financial statements after the date of the review report. However, if a subsequently discovered fact becomes known to the accountant after the date of the review report but before the report release date, the accountant should:

1. discuss the matter with management and, when appropriate, those charged with governance; and
2. determine whether the financial statements need revision and, if so, inquire how management intends to address the matter in the financial statements.

If management updates the financial statements, the accountant should perform the additional review procedures. The accountant should also either:

1. date the accountant's review report as of a later date; or
2. dual date the review report.

If management does not revise the financial statements and the accountant believes they need to be revised, the accountant should modify the review report.

4.3 Subsequently Discovered Facts That Become Known to the Accountant After the Report Release Date

Usually, an accountant has no obligation to make continuing inquiries after the date of the report. However, if an accountant becomes aware of material information that existed as of the date of his or her report that would have affected the report and that persons are currently relying or are likely to rely on the financial statements covered by the report, the accountant should take appropriate action.

4.3.1 Accountant Action

Upon discovering, after issuance of the report, information (confirmed by the accountant) that materially affects the report and other persons' reliance on it, the accountant should advise the client to immediately disclose the new information and its impact on the financial statements to persons currently relying or likely to rely on the financial statements.

The accountant should discuss the matter with management and, when appropriate, those charged with governance and determine whether the financial statements need revision and, if so, inquire how management intends to address the matter in the financial statements.

If management revises the financial statements, the accountant should perform the review procedures necessary in the circumstances on the revision.

The accountant also should either:

1. date the accountant's review report as of a later date; or
2. Include an additional date in the accountant's review report on the revised financial statements that is limited to the revision (that is, dual-date the accountant's review report for that revision), thereby indicating that the accountant's review procedures subsequent to the original date of the accountant's review report are limited solely to the revision of the financial statements described in the relevant note to the financial statements.

If the reviewed financial statements (before revision) have been made available to third parties, assess whether the steps taken by management are timely and appropriate to ensure that anyone in receipt of those financial statements is informed of the situation, including that the reviewed financial statements are not to be used.

If the accountant's conclusion on the revised financial statements differs from the accountant's conclusion on the original financial statements, disclose in an emphasis-of-matter paragraph the date of the accountant's previous report, a description of the revisions, and the substantive reasons for the revisions. The accountant must become satisfied that appropriate steps have been taken by the client.

4.3.2 Management's Action

Management's steps may include the following:

- Notify anyone who is known to be using, or who is likely to use, the financial statements and the accountant's review report that they are not to be used and that revised financial statements, together with a new accountant's review report, will be issued. This may be necessary when the issuance of revised financial statements and a new accountant's review report is not imminent.
- Issue, as soon as practicable, revised financial statements with appropriate disclosure of the matter.
- Issue the subsequent period's financial statements with appropriate disclosure of the matter. This may be appropriate when issuance of the subsequent period's reviewed or audited financial statements is imminent.

4.3.3 Client Refuses to Follow Procedures

If the client refuses to proceed as above, the accountant should notify the appropriate entity personnel, such as the manager (owner) or board of directors, of such refusal and of the fact the accountant will take additional steps to prevent further reliance on the accountant's report and the financial statements, such as the following:

- Notify the client that the accountant's report must no longer be associated with the financial statements.
- Notify, if applicable, any regulatory agencies having jurisdiction over the client that the accountant's report should no longer be relied on.
- Notify persons known to be relying or likely to rely on the financial statements that the accountant's report should no longer be relied on.

Any notification to parties other than the client should be as precise and factual as possible, and should contain a description of the effect the discovered information would have had on the accountant's report on the financial statements.

If the client has refused to cooperate, and as a result the accountants were unable to conduct an adequate investigation of the information, the accountants' disclosure need only state that information has come to their attention and that, if the information is true, their report should no longer be relied on or be associated with the financial statements.

The accountants should use their professional judgment in the circumstances described above, and it may be advisable to consult legal counsel.

5 Reporting Fraud and Noncompliance With Laws and Regulations

In a SSARS (Statements on Standards for Accounting and Review Services) engagement, if an accountant becomes aware that fraud or noncompliance with laws and regulations may have occurred, such matters should be communicated to an appropriate level of management. Management should be asked to consider the effect of the fraud or noncompliance with laws and regulations on the financial statements. The accountant should consider the impact of the matter on the compilation or review report. When the accountant believes that the financial statements are materially misstated, the accountant should obtain additional or revised information. If the entity will not provide additional or revised information, the accountant should withdraw from the engagement.

- **Inconsequential Matters:** Inconsequential matters need not be communicated.
- **Documentation:** Communication may be made in writing or orally, but oral communications should be documented.
- **Other Options:** The accountant should consider withdrawing or consulting legal counsel if fraud or noncompliance with laws and regulations involve an owner of the business.
- **Confidentiality:** Obligations of confidentiality preclude disclosure outside the entity, except in certain limited circumstances (e.g., legal/regulatory requirements, successor accountant, subpoena).

Question 1 **MCQ-06300**

An accountant is most likely required to follow Statements on Standards for Accounting and Review Services (SSARS) when the accountant has:

a. Typed client-prepared financial statements, without modification, as an accommodation to the client.

b. Provided a client with a financial statement format that does not include dollar amounts, to be used by the client in preparing financial statements.

c. Proposed correcting journal entries to be recorded by the client that change client-prepared financial statements.

d. Used the information in a general ledger to prepare financial statements outside of an accounting software system.

NOTES

MODULE

2 Preparation Engagements

1 Preparation of Financial Statements

The objective of the accountant in a preparation engagement is to prepare financial statements in accordance with a specified financial reporting framework.

Accountants should follow SSARS standards on preparation engagements when they are engaged to prepare financial statements. Preparation standards do not apply when an accountant prepares financial statements and:

- is engaged to perform an audit, review, or compilation of those financial statements;
- solely for submission to taxing authorities;
- for inclusion in written personal financial plans prepared by the accountant;
- in conjunction with litigation services that involve pending or potential legal or regulatory proceedings; or
- in conjunction with business valuation services.

Pass Key

An engagement to prepare financial statements is a non-attest service and does not require a determination about whether the accountant is independent of the entity.

1.1 Establishing an Understanding With the Client

The accountant should establish an understanding with management and, when appropriate, those charged with governance, regarding the services to be performed for the preparation engagement and should document the understanding in an engagement letter.

The understanding with management should include:

- The objectives of the engagement.
- Management's responsibilities.
- The agreement of management that each page of the financial statements will include a statement indicating that no assurance is provided on the financial statements or the accountant will be required to issue a disclaimer that makes clear that no assurance is provided on the financial statements.
- The accountant's responsibilities.
- The limitations of the engagement.

- Identification of the applicable financial reporting framework.
- Whether the financial statements are to contain a known departure or departures from the applicable financial reporting framework (including inadequate disclosure) or omit substantially all disclosures required by the applicable financial reporting framework.

The engagement letter or other suitable form of written agreement should be signed by the accountant or the accountant's firm *and* management or those charged with governance, as appropriate.

1.1.1 Sample: Preparation Engagement Letter

[Appropriate representative of management of ABC Company]

You have requested that we prepare the financial statements of ABC Company, which comprise the balance sheet as of December 31, 20XX, and the related statements of income, changes in stockholders' equity, and cash flows for the year then ended and the related notes to the financial statements. We are pleased to confirm our acceptance and our understanding of this engagement to prepare the financial statements of ABC Company by means of this letter.

Our Responsibilities

The objective of our engagement is to prepare financial statements in accordance with accounting principles generally accepted in the United States of America based on information provided by you. We will conduct our engagement in accordance with Statements on Standards for Accounting and Review Services (SSARS) promulgated by the Accounting and Review Services Committee of the AICPA and comply with the AICPA's Code of Professional Conduct, including the ethical principles of integrity, objectivity, professional competence, and due care.

We are not required to, and will not, verify the accuracy or completeness of the information you will provide to us for the engagement or otherwise gather evidence for the purpose of expressing an opinion or a conclusion. Accordingly, we will not express an opinion or a conclusion or provide any assurance on the financial statements.

Our engagement cannot be relied upon to identify or disclose any financial statement misstatements, including those caused by fraud or error, or to identify or disclose any wrongdoing within the entity or noncompliance with laws and regulations.

Management Responsibilities

The engagement to be performed is conducted on the basis that management acknowledges and understands that our role is the preparation of the financial statements in accordance with the accounting principles generally accepted in the United States of America. Management has the following overall responsibilities that are fundamental to our undertaking this engagement, in accordance with SSARS, to prepare your financial statements:

a. The selection of accounting principles generally accepted in the United States of America as the financial reporting framework to be applied in the preparation of the financial statements.

b. The prevention and detection of fraud.

(continued)

(continued)

c. To ensure that the entity complies with the laws and regulations applicable to its activities.

d. The accuracy and completeness of the records, documents, explanations, and other information, including significant judgments, you provide to us for the engagement to prepare financial statements.

e. To provide us with:

1. Documentation, and other related information that is relevant to the preparation and presentation of the financial statement;
2. Additional information that may be requested for the purpose of the preparation of the financial statements; and
3. Unrestricted access to persons within ABC Company to whom we determine necessary to communicate.

The financial statements will not be accompanied by a report. However, you agree that the financial statements will clearly indicate that no assurance is provided on them.

[*If the accountant expects to issue a disclaimer, instead of the preceding paragraph, the following may be added: As part of our engagement, we will issue a disclaimer that will state that the financial statements were not subjected to an audit, review, or compilation engagement by us, and accordingly, we do not express an opinion, a conclusion, nor provide any assurance on them.*]

Other Relevant Information

Our fees for these services … .

[*The accountant may include language, such as the following, regarding limitation of, or other arrangements regarding, the liability of the accountant or the entity, such as indemnification to the accountant for liability arising from knowing misrepresentations to the accountant by management (regulators may restrict or prohibit such liability limitation arrangements):*

You agree to hold us harmless and to release, indemnify, and defend us from any liability or costs, including attorney's fees, resulting from management's knowing misrepresentations to us.]

Please sign and return the attached copy of this letter to indicate your acknowledgment of, and agreement with, the arrangements for our engagement to prepare the financial statements described herein, and our respective responsibilities.

Sincerely yours,

____

[*Signature of accountant or accountant's firm*]

Acknowledged and agreed on behalf of ABC Company by:

____

[*Name, title, and date*]

2 Preparation Requirements

The following performance requirements are applicable to a preparation.

2.1 Possess Knowledge of and Understanding of the Entity's Financial Reporting Framework

The accountant should obtain an understanding of the financial reporting framework and the significant accounting policies intended to be used in the preparation of the financial statements. This does not prevent accountants from accepting engagements in an industry in which the accountants have no previous experience. However, the accountants are responsible for gaining the required level of knowledge.

2.2 Prepare the Financial Statements

The accountant should prepare the financial statements using the records, documents, explanations, and other information provided by management.

If, during the preparation of the financial statements, the accountant assists management with significant judgments regarding amounts or disclosures to be reflected in the financial statements, the accountant should discuss those judgments with management so that management understands and accepts responsibility for those judgments.

The accountant should ensure that a statement is included on each page of the financial statements indicating that "no assurance is provided" on the financial statements. The accountant or accountant's firm name is not required to be included in prepared financial statements. Examples of statements that would be placed on each page of the financial statement include:

- No assurance is provided on these financial statements.
- These financial statements have not been subjected to an audit, review, or compilation engagement, and no assurance is provided on them.

Other statements that convey that no assurance is provided on the financial statements are also acceptable.

If the accountant is unable to include a statement on each page of the financial statements, the accountant should:

- issue a disclaimer that makes clear that no assurance is provided on the financial statements; or
- perform a compilation engagement.

2.2.1 Sample Report: Disclaimer on Preparation of Financial Statements

> The accompanying financial statements of XYZ Company as of and for the year ended December 31, 20XX, were not subjected to an audit, review, or compilation engagement by us, and accordingly, we do not express an opinion, a conclusion, nor provide any assurance on them.
>
> [*Signature of accounting firm or accountant, as appropriate*]
> [*Accountant's city and state*]
> [*Date*]

3 Other Preparation Considerations

3.1 Financial Statements Prepared With a Special Purpose Framework

The accountant should include a description of the financial reporting framework on the face of the financial statements or in a note to the financial statements when preparing financial statements in accordance with a special purpose framework.

3.2 Inaccurate or Incomplete Financial Statements

Accountants are *not required to*, but may, make inquiries or perform other procedures to verify, corroborate, or review the information supplied by the client. However, if they discover the information is incorrect, incomplete, or unsatisfactory, they should obtain additional or revised information from the client.

If, after discussion with management, the accountant prepares financial statements that contain a known departure or departures from the applicable financial reporting framework, the accountant should disclose the material misstatement or misstatements in the financial statements.

3.3 Financial Statements That Omit Substantially All Disclosures

If requested by the client, an accountant may prepare financial statements that omit substantially all disclosures required by the applicable financial reporting framework (but are otherwise in conformity with the financial reporting framework). The accountant may prepare these statements provided:

- The accountant discloses such omission in the financial statements.
- To the accountant's knowledge, the omission is not intended to mislead any person who might be expected to use such financial statements.

If the accountant concludes that limited disclosure is acceptable and if the financial statements include only limited notes, the notes may be labeled as follows:

> Selected Information—Substantially All Disclosures Required by [the applicable financial reporting framework] Are Not Included.

4 Documentation in a Preparation Engagement

Documentation provides the support that the accountant complied with SSARS when performing the preparation engagement. Documentation should provide clear detail of the work performed. The form and content of the documentation depends on the engagement, the methodology and tools, and the accountant's professional judgment.

Documentation should include:

- The engagement letter.
- A copy of the financial statements prepared by the accountant.
- Any significant findings or issues.

Other Information that may be included in documentation includes:

- Oral or written communications with management regarding fraud or noncompliance with laws and regulations that came to the accountant's attention.
- If, in rare circumstances, the accountant judges it necessary to depart from a relevant presumptively mandatory requirement, the justification for the departure and how the alternative procedures performed in the circumstances were sufficient to achieve the intent of that requirement.

NOTES

MODULE

3 Compilation Engagements

1 Compilation of Financial Statements

A compilation of financial statements is a service, the objective of which is to apply accounting and financial reporting expertise to assist management in the presentation of financial statements without undertaking to obtain or provide any assurance on the financial statements.

Because a compilation engagement is not an assurance engagement, a compilation engagement does not require the accountant to verify the accuracy or completeness of the information provided by management or otherwise gather evidence to express an opinion or a conclusion on the financial statements.

1.1 Establishing an Understanding With the Client

The accountant should establish an understanding with management and, when appropriate, those charged with governance, regarding the services to be performed for the compilation engagement and should document the understanding in an engagement letter.

The understanding with management should include:

- The objectives of the engagement.
- Management's responsibilities.
- The accountant's responsibilities.
- The limitations of the engagement, including a statement that the engagement cannot be relied upon to disclose errors, fraud, or noncompliance with laws and regulations.
- Identification of the applicable financial reporting framework.
- The expected form and content of the accountant's compilation report, and a statement that there may be circumstances in which the report may differ from its expected form and content.

The engagement letter or other suitable form of written agreement should be signed by the accountant or the accountant's firm and management or those charged with governance, as appropriate.

1.1.1 Sample: Compilation Engagement Letter

[Appropriate representative of management of ABC Company]

You have requested that we prepare the financial statements of ABC Company, which comprise the balance sheet as of December 31, 20XX, and the related statements of income, changes in stockholder's equity, and cash flows for the year then ended and the related notes to the financial statements. We are pleased to confirm our acceptance and our understanding of this engagement by means of this letter.

(continued)

(continued)

Our Responsibilities

The objective of our engagement is to:

a. prepare financial statements in accordance with accounting principles generally accepted in the United States of America based on information provided by you; and

b. apply accounting and financial reporting expertise to assist you in the presentation of financial statements without undertaking to obtain or provide any assurance that there are no material modifications that should be made to the financial statements in order for them to be in accordance with accounting principles generally accepted in the United States of America.

We will conduct our engagement in accordance with Statements on Standards for Accounting and Review Services (SSARS) promulgated by the Accounting and Review Services Committee of the AICPA and comply with the AICPA's Code of Professional Conduct, including the ethical principles of integrity, objectivity, professional competence, and due care.

We are not required to, and will not, verify the accuracy or completeness of the information you will provide to us for the engagement or otherwise gather evidence for the purpose of expressing an opinion or a conclusion. Accordingly, we will not express an opinion or a conclusion or provide any assurance on the financial statements.

Our engagement cannot be relied upon to identify or disclose any financial statement misstatements, including those caused by fraud or error, or to identify or disclose any wrongdoing within the entity or noncompliance with laws and regulations.

Management Responsibilities

The engagement to be performed is conducted on the basis that management acknowledges and understands that our role is to prepare financial statements in accordance with the accounting principles generally accepted in the United States of America and assist you in the presentation of the financial statements in accordance with accounting principles generally accepted in the United States of America. Management has the following overall responsibilities that are fundamental to our undertaking the engagement in accordance with SSARS:

a. The selection of accounting principles generally accepted in the United States of America as the financial reporting framework to be applied in the preparation of the financial statements.

b. The preparation and fair presentation of financial statements in accordance with accounting principles generally accepted in the United States of America.

c. The design, implementation, and maintenance of internal control relevant to the preparation and fair presentation of the financial statements.

d. The prevention and detection of fraud.

e. To ensure that the entity complies with the laws and regulations applicable to its activities.

(continued)

(continued)

f. To make all financial records and related information available to us.

g. The accuracy and completeness of the records, documents, explanations, and other information, including significant judgments, you provide to us for the engagement to prepare financial statements.

Management is also responsible for all management decisions and responsibilities and for designating an individual with suitable skills, knowledge, and experience to oversee our preparation of your financial statements. You are responsible for evaluating the adequacy and results of services performed and accepting responsibility for such services.

Our Report

As part of our engagement, we will issue a report that will state that we did not audit or review the financial statements and, that, accordingly, we do not express an opinion, a conclusion, nor provide any assurance on them.

You agree to include our accountant's compilation report in any document containing financial statements that indicates that we have performed a compilation engagement on such financial statements and, prior to inclusion of the report, to ask our permission to do so.

Other Relevant Information

Our fees for these services ... .

[*The accountant may include language, such as the following, regarding limitation of or other arrangements regarding the liability of the accountant or the entity, such as indemnification to the accountant for liability arising from knowing misrepresentations to the accountant by management (regulators may restrict or prohibit such liability limitation arrangements):*

You agree to hold us harmless and to release, indemnify, and defend us from any liability or costs, including attorney's fees, resulting from management's knowing misrepresentations to us.]

Please sign and return the attached copy of this letter to indicate your acknowledgment of, and agreement with, the arrangements for our engagement to prepare the financial statements described herein and to perform a compilation engagement with respect to those financial statements, and our respective responsibilities.

Sincerely yours,

____

[*Signature of accountant or accountant's firm*]

Acknowledged and agreed on behalf of ABC Company by:

____

[*Name, title, and date*]

2 Compilation Requirements

The following performance requirements are applicable to a compilation.

2.1 Knowledge of Industry Accounting Principles and Practices

Accountants should possess adequate knowledge of the accounting principles and practices of a client's industry to enable them to compile financial statements in an appropriate form. This does not prevent accountants from accepting engagements in an industry in which the accountants have no previous experience. However, the accountants are responsible for gaining the required level of knowledge.

2.2 Understanding of Client's Business

An accountant performing a compilation is required to have a general understanding of the client's business and the accounting principles and practices used by the client, including:

- **Staff** qualifications
- **Transaction** types and frequency
- **Accounting** basis used to prepare the financial statements
- **Form** of the accounting records
- **Financial** statements' form and content

2.3 Reading the Financial Statements

Before issuing a report, accountants should read the compiled financial statements and consider whether they are appropriate in form and free from obvious material errors. The term "error" refers to arithmetical and clerical mistakes, as well as to mistakes related to the applicable financial reporting framework.

2.4 Noncompliance With Laws and Regulations, Going Concern, and Subsequent Events

If an accountant becomes aware that noncompliance with laws and regulations may have occurred, that there is a going concern uncertainty, or that a subsequent event has occurred, he or she should request management to consider the effect on the financial statements, evaluate management conclusions, and consider the effect of the matter on the compilation report.

2.5 Financial Statements That May Be Inaccurate or Incomplete

Accountants are not required to, but may, make inquiries or perform other procedures to verify, corroborate, or review the information supplied by the client. However, if they discover the information is incorrect, incomplete, or unsatisfactory, they should obtain additional or revised information from the client. If the client refuses to provide such information, the accountants should withdraw from the compilation engagement.

If, in the course of the engagement, the accountant becomes aware that the records, documents, explanations, or other information, including significant judgments, provided by management are incomplete, inaccurate, or otherwise unsatisfactory, the accountant should bring that to the attention of management and request additional or corrected information.

The accountant should withdraw from the engagement and inform management of the reasons for withdrawing if the accountant is unable to complete the engagement because management has failed to provide records, documents, explanations, or other information, including significant judgments, as requested, or management does not make appropriate revisions that are proposed by the accountant or does not disclose such departures in the financial statements, and the accountant determines to not disclose such departures in the accountant's compilation report.

2.6 Documentation in a Compilation Engagement

Documentation provides the support that the accountant complied with SSARS when performing the compilation engagement. Documentation should include:

- The engagement letter.
- A copy of the financial statements.
- A copy of the accountant's report.

Other information that may be included in the documentation includes:

- Any significant findings or issues, including the following:
  - Results of compilation procedures indicating that the financial statements could be materially misstated and the actions taken to address these findings.
  - The resolution of questions and concerns raised during compilation procedures.
- Oral or written communications with management regarding fraud or noncompliance with laws and regulations that came to the accountant's attention.

3 Reporting on a Compilation

3.1 Overview

The report is the method by which the accountant communicates the extent of the responsibility assumed for the financial statements. An accountant may issue a compilation report when the accountant has complied with the standards for a compilation.

The accountant's report in a compilation engagement should be in writing and:

- Include a statement that management is responsible for the financial statements.
- Identify the financial statements that have been subjected to the compilation engagement.
- Identify the entity for which financial statements have been subjected to the compilation engagement.
- Specify the date or period covered by the financial statements.
- Include a statement that the accountant performed the compilation engagement in accordance with SSARS promulgated by the Accounting and Review Services Committee of the AICPA.
- Include a statement that the accountant did not audit or review the financial statements nor was the accountant required to perform any procedures to verify the accuracy or completeness of the information provided by management, and, accordingly, does not express an opinion, a conclusion, nor provide any assurance on financial statements.

- Include the signature of the accountant or the accountant's firm.
- Include the city and state where the accountant practices (this may be indicated in the letterhead).
- Include the date of the report.

Additional paragraphs are required when:

- Financial statements are prepared in accordance with a special purpose framework.
- Disclosures are omitted.
- The accountant is not independent.
- There are known departures from the applicable financial reporting framework.
- The financial statements include supplementary information.

3.2 Additional Requirements

Each page of the statements should be marked "see Accountant's Compilation Report" or "see Independent Accountant's Compilation Report."

SSARS do not require that the compilation report be printed on the accountant's letterhead. The signature of the accountant or the accountant's firm may be manual, printed, or digital.

At the accountant's discretion, a separate paragraph of the report may be used to emphasize any matter already disclosed in the financial statements, such as going concern issues or subsequent events.

3.2.1 Sample Report: Standard Compilation Report

> Management is responsible for the accompanying financial statements of XYZ Company, which comprise the balance sheets as of December 31, 20X2 and 20X1, and the related statements of income, changes in stockholders' equity, and cash flows for the years then ended, and the related notes to the financial statements in accordance with accounting principles generally accepted in the United States of America. We have performed compilation engagements in accordance with Statements on Standards for Accounting and Review Services promulgated by the Accounting and Review Services Committee of the AICPA. We did not audit or review the financial statements nor were we required to perform any procedures to verify the accuracy or completeness of the information provided by management. Accordingly, we do not express an opinion, a conclusion, nor provide any form of assurance on these financial statements.
>
> [*Signature of accounting firm or accountant*]
>
> [*Accountant's city and state*]
>
> [*Date*]

3.3 Reporting on Financial Statements That Are Prepared in Accordance With a Special Purpose Framework

A compilation report prepared in accordance with a special purpose framework should include an additional paragraph that:

- references management's responsibility for determining the applicable financial reporting framework is acceptable.
- indicates that the financial statements are prepared in accordance with the applicable special purpose framework, refers to the note to the financial statements that describes the framework (if notes are included), and states that the special purpose framework is a basis of accounting other than GAAP.
- *if prepared in accordance with regulatory or contractual basis,* describes the purpose for which the financial statements are prepared or refer to the appropriate note in the financial statements.

3.4 Reporting on Financial Statements That Omit Substantially All Disclosures

Similar to a preparation, if requested by the client, an accountant may compile financial statements that omit substantially all disclosures required by the applicable financial reporting framework (but are otherwise in conformity with the financial reporting framework). The accountant may compile these statements provided:

- The accountant's report clearly indicates the omission by including an additional paragraph disclosing such omissions. This paragraph should state that if the disclosures were included, they might influence the user's conclusions, and should indicate that the financial statements are not designed for those who are uninformed about the omitted disclosures.
- To the accountant's knowledge, the omission is not intended to mislead any person who might be expected to use such financial statements.

Pass Key

The omission of one or more notes, when substantially all other disclosures are presented, should be treated in a compilation report like any other departure from the applicable financial reporting framework.

Illustration 1 Compilation Engagement

Jones Retailing, a nonpublic entity, has asked Winters, CPA, to compile financial statements that omit substantially all disclosures required by generally accepted accounting principles (but are otherwise in conformity with GAAP). Winters may compile such financial statements provided the omission is not undertaken to mislead the users of the financial statements and is properly disclosed in the accountant's report.

Pass Key

Compiled financial statements that omit GAAP disclosures are acceptable if the:

- Financial statements are otherwise in conformity with GAAP.
- Reason for omission was not to deceive the user.
- Compilation report warns the user of missing disclosures.

3.4.1 Sample Report: Compilation Report on Financial Statements That Omit Substantially All Disclosures

Management is responsible for the accompanying financial statements of XYZ Partnership, which comprise the *statements of assets, liabilities, and partners' capital tax basis* as of December 31, 20X2 and 20X1, and *the related statements of revenue and expenses tax basis, and changes in partners' capital tax basis* for the years then ended in accordance with the tax basis of accounting, and for *determining that the tax basis of accounting is an acceptable financial reporting framework*. We have performed compilation engagements in accordance with Statements on Standards for Accounting and Review Services promulgated by the Accounting and Review Services Committee of the AICPA. We did not audit or review the financial statements nor were we required to perform any procedures to verify the accuracy or completeness of the information provided by management. Accordingly, we do not express an opinion, a conclusion, nor provide any form of assurance on these financial statements.

The financial statements are prepared in accordance with the tax basis of accounting, which is a basis of accounting other than accounting principles generally accepted in the United States of America.

Management has elected to omit substantially all the disclosures required by [*the applicable financial reporting framework*]. *If the omitted disclosures were included in the financial statements, they might influence the user's conclusions about the company's financial position, results of operations, and cash flows. Accordingly, the financial statements are not designed for those who are not informed about such matters.*

[*Signature of accounting firm or accountant*]

[*Accountant's city and state*]

[*Date*]

3.5 Departures From the Applicable Financial Reporting Framework

Departures from the applicable financial reporting framework should be disclosed in a separate paragraph of the report and should include disclosure of the effects of the departure on the financial statements (if known). If the accountant believes that disclosure in the report would not be adequate to indicate the deficiencies in the financial statements, he or she should withdraw from the engagement and provide no further services with respect to those financial statements.

3.5.1 Sample Report: Compilation Report With Departures From U.S. GAAP

Management is responsible for the accompanying financial statements of XYZ Company, which comprise the balance sheets as of December 31, 20X2 and 20X1, and the related statements of income, changes in stockholders' equity, and cash flows for the years then ended, and the related notes to the financial statements in accordance with accounting principles generally accepted in the United States of America. I (We) have performed compilation engagements in accordance with Statements on Standards for Accounting and Review Services promulgated by the Accounting and Review Services Committee of the AICPA. I (We) did not audit or review the financial statements nor was (were) I (we) required to perform any procedures to verify the accuracy or completeness of the information provided by management. Accordingly, I (we) do not express an opinion, a conclusion, nor provide any form of assurance on these financial statements.

Accounting principles generally accepted in the United States of America require that land be stated at cost. Management has informed me (us) that XYZ Company has stated its land at appraised value and that if accounting principles generally accepted in the United States of America had been followed, the land account and stockholders' equity would have been decreased by $500,000.

[*Signature of accounting firm or accountant*]

[*Accountant's city and state*]

[*Date*]

Pass Key

The accountant should not modify the compilation report to include a statement that the financial statements are not in conformity with the applicable financial reporting framework.

The accountant is precluded from including a statement that the financial statements are not in conformity with the applicable financial reporting framework because such a statement would be tantamount to expressing an adverse opinion on the financial statements as a whole. Such an opinion can be expressed only in the context of an audit engagement.

3.6 Reporting When Not Independent: Disclosure Required

An accountant who is not independent with respect to an entity may compile financial statements for such an entity and issue a report. The last paragraph of the report should disclose this lack of independence. The accountant is permitted, but not required, to disclose the reason(s) for the independence impairment in the report. If the accountant chooses to disclose the reason, all reasons must be included in the disclosure.

3.6.1 Sample Report: Compilation Report Where Accountant Is Not Independent

Management is responsible for the accompanying financial statements of XYZ Company, which comprise the balance sheets as of December 31, 20X2 and 20X1 and the related statements of income, changes in stockholders' equity, and cash flows for the years then ended, and the related notes to the financial statements in accordance with accounting principles generally accepted in the United States of America. I (We) have performed compilation engagements in accordance with Statements on Standards for Accounting and Review Services promulgated by the Accounting and Review Services Committee of the AICPA. I (We) did not audit or review the financial statements nor was (were) I (we) required to perform any procedures to verify the accuracy or completeness of the information provided by management. Accordingly, I (we) do not express an opinion, a conclusion, nor provide any form of assurance on these financial statements.

I am (we are) not independent with respect to XYZ Company.

[*Signature of accounting firm or accountant*]

[*Accountant's city and state*]

[*Date*]

Pass Key

Compilation vs. Preparation

The client's needs determine what kind of engagement (preparation or compilation) the accountant performs.

The type of procedures to be performed are substantially the same. The biggest exception is that compilations require a report while preparation engagements do not. In addition, compilation engagements require the consideration of independence while preparation engagements do not.

No title in compilation report.

restricted use is not required

no analytical procedure required

Question 1	**MCQ-03044**

Which of the following procedures is ordinarily performed by an accountant in a compilation engagement of a nonissuer?

a. Reading the financial statements to consider whether they are free of obvious mistakes in the application of accounting principles.

b. Obtaining written representations from management indicating that the compiled financial statements will not be used to obtain credit.

c. Making inquiries of management concerning actions taken at meetings of the stockholders and the board of directors.

d. Applying analytical procedures designed to corroborate management's assertions that are embodied in the financial statement components.

Question 2	**MCQ-03011**

Financial statements of a nonissuer compiled without audit or review by an accountant should be accompanied by a report stating that:

a. The scope of the accountant's procedures has not been restricted in testing the financial information that is the representation of management.

b. The accountant evaluated the appropriateness of the accounting principles used and the reasonableness of significant accounting estimates made by management.

c. The accountant has not audited or reviewed the financial statements.

d. A compilation primarily includes applying analytical procedures to management's financial data and making inquiries of company management.

NOTES

MODULE

4 Review Engagements

1 Review of Financial Statements

A review is a higher level of service than a preparation or compilation because it results in an expression of limited assurance. The review report states that the accountant is not aware of any material modifications necessary for the statements to conform with the applicable financial reporting framework. Inquiry and analytical procedures provide the accountant with a reasonable basis for this conclusion. The accountant is not required to obtain an understanding of internal control or assess control risk.

1.1 Accountant's Objective and Independence

The objective of the accountant when performing a review of financial statements is to obtain limited assurance as a basis for reporting whether the accountant is aware of any material modifications that should be made to the financial statements for them to be in accordance with the applicable financial reporting framework, primarily through the performance of inquiry and analytical procedures.

The accountant must be independent of the entity when performing a review of financial statements in accordance with SSARS.

1.2 Review Procedures Should Be Tailored

Review procedures should be tailored to the specific engagement. For example, if the accountant becomes aware of significant changes in operations, additional procedures would be considered. The following factors may affect the procedures performed:

- The nature and materiality of financial statement items
- The likelihood of misstatement
- Knowledge from current and previous engagements
- Qualifications of the entity's accounting personnel
- The extent to which an item is affected by management's judgment
- Inadequacies in the entity's underlying financial data

2 Review Requirements

The performance requirements applicable to a review are:

- **Understanding** with client should be established
- **Learn** and/or obtain sufficient knowledge of the entity's business
- **Inquiries** should be addressed to appropriate individuals
- **Analytical** procedures should be performed
- **Review**—other procedures should be performed
- **Client** representation letter should be obtained from management
- **Professional** judgment should be used to evaluate results
- **Accountant** (CPA) should communicate results

2.1 Understanding With the Client Should Be Established

Understanding
Learn client
Inquiries
Analytical
Review—other
Client rep. letter
Prof. judgment
Acct. report

In order to reduce the likelihood of misunderstanding, the accountant should establish an understanding with management and, when appropriate, those charged with governance regarding the services to be performed and should document the understanding in the form of an engagement letter. The understanding should include:

- The objectives of the engagement.
- Management's responsibilities.
- The accountant's responsibilities.
- The limitations of the engagement.
- Identification of the applicable financial reporting framework for the preparation of the financial statements.
- The expected form and content of the accountant's review report and a statement that there may be circumstances in which the report may differ from its expected form and content.

The engagement letter or other suitable form of written agreement should be signed by the accountant or the accountant's firm and management or those charged with governance, as appropriate.

2.1.1 Sample: Review Engagement Letter

[*Appropriate representative of management of ABC Company*]

You have requested that we prepare the financial statements of ABC Company, which comprise the balance sheet as of December 31, 20XX, and the related statements of income, changes in stockholder's equity, and cash flows for the year then ended and the related notes to the financial statements and perform a review with respect to those financial statements. We are pleased to confirm our acceptance and our understanding of this engagement by means of this letter.

(continued)

(continued)

Our Responsibilities

The objective of our engagement is to:

a. prepare financial statements in accordance with accounting principles generally accepted in the United States of America based on information provided by you; and

b. obtain limited assurance as a basis for reporting whether we are aware of any material modifications that should be made to the financial statements in order for the statements to be in accordance with accounting principles generally accepted in the United States of America.

We will conduct our engagement in accordance with Statements on Standards for Accounting and Review Services (SSARS) promulgated by the Accounting and Review Services Committee of the AICPA and comply with the AICPA's Code of Professional Conduct, including the ethical principles of integrity, objectivity, professional competence, and due care.

A review includes primarily applying analytical procedures to your financial data and making inquiries of company management. A review is substantially less in scope than an audit, the objective of which is the expression of an opinion regarding the financial statements as a whole. A review does not contemplate obtaining an understanding of the entity's internal control; assessing fraud risk; tests of accounting records by obtaining sufficient appropriate audit evidence through inspection, observation, confirmation, or the examination of source documents; or other procedures ordinarily performed in an audit. Accordingly, we will not express an opinion regarding the financial statements.

Our engagement cannot be relied upon to identify or disclose any financial statement misstatements, including those caused by error or fraud, or to identify or disclose any wrongdoing within the entity or noncompliance with laws and regulations. However, we will inform the appropriate level of management of any material errors, and of any evidence or information that comes to our attention during the performance of our review procedures that indicates fraud may have occurred. In addition, we will report to you any evidence or information that comes to our attention during the performance of our review procedures regarding noncompliance with laws and regulations that may have occurred, unless they are clearly inconsequential.

Your Responsibilities

The engagement to be performed is conducted on the basis that management acknowledges and understands that our role is to prepare the financial statements in accordance with the accounting principles generally accepted in the United States of America and to obtain limited assurance as a basis for reporting whether we are aware of any material modifications that should be made to the financial statements in order for the statements to be in accordance with accounting principles generally accepted in the United States of America. You will have the following overall responsibilities that are fundamental to our undertaking the engagement in accordance with SSARS:

a. The selection of accounting principles generally accepted in the United States of America as the financial reporting framework to be applied in the preparation of the financial statements.

b. The preparation and fair presentation of financial statements in accordance with accounting principles generally accepted in the United States of America.

c. The design, implementation, and maintenance of internal control relevant to the preparation and fair presentation of the financial statements.

(continued)

(continued)

d. The prevention and detection of fraud.

e. To ensure that the entity complies with the laws and regulations applicable to its activities.

f. To make all financial records and related information available to us.

g. The accuracy and completeness of the records, documents, explanations, and other information, including significant judgments, you provide to us for the engagement to prepare financial statements.

h. To provide us with unrestricted access to persons within the entity of which we determine it necessary to make inquiries.

i. To provide us, at the conclusion of the engagement, with a letter that confirms certain representations during the review.

You are also responsible for all management decisions and responsibilities and for designating an individual with suitable skills, knowledge, and experience to oversee our preparation of your financial statements. You are responsible for evaluating the adequacy and results of services performed and accepting responsibility for such services.

Our Report

We will issue a written report upon completion of our review of ABC Company's financial statements. Our report will be addressed to the board of directors of ABC Company. We cannot provide assurance that an unmodified accountant's review report will be issued. Circumstances may arise in which it is necessary for us to report known departures from accounting principles generally accepted in the United States of America, add an emphasis-of-matter or other-matter paragraph(s), or withdraw from the engagement. If, for any reason, we are unable to complete the review of your financial statements, we will not issue a report on such statements as a result of this engagement.

Other Relevant Information

Our fees for these services ... .

[*The accountant may include language, such as the following, regarding limitation of or other arrangements regarding the liability of the accountant or the entity, such as indemnification to the accountant for liability arising from knowing misrepresentations to the accountant by management (regulators may restrict or prohibit such liability limitation arrangements):*

You agree to hold us harmless and to release, indemnify, and defend us from any liability or costs, including attorney's fees, resulting from management's knowing misrepresentations to us.]

Please sign and return the attached copy of this letter to indicate your acknowledgment of, and agreement with, the arrangements for our engagement to prepare the financial statements described herein and to perform a review of those same financial statements and our respective responsibilities.

Sincerely yours,

____

[*Signature of accountant or accountant's firm*]

Acknowledged and agreed on behalf of ABC Company by:

____

[*Name, title, and date*]

2.2 Learn and/or Obtain Sufficient Knowledge of the Entity's Business

Understanding
Learn client
Inquiries
Analytical
Review—other
Client rep. letter
Prof. judgment
Acct. report

2.2.1 Knowledge of Accounting Principles and Practices of the Industry

As in a compilation, the accountant must be familiar with the accounting principles common to the client's industry. Lack of experience in an industry does not preclude acceptance of an engagement, but the accountant is required to obtain appropriate knowledge.

2.2.2 Understanding of Client's Business

The accountant should possess an understanding of the client's business and the accounting principles and practices used by the client. This would ordinarily involve an understanding of the client's organization, its operating characteristics, and the nature of its assets, liabilities, equity, revenues, and expenses.

2.2.3 Not Required

The accountant is not required to:

- **Test Internal Control:** An understanding of internal control is not required in a review.
- **Perform Audit Tests:** No testing or audit procedures are required in a review.
- **Assess Fraud Risk:** A fraud risk assessment is not required in a review, nor is the accountant required to perform procedures designed to detect material misstatement due to fraud or noncompliance with laws and regulations.

  If, however, an accountant becomes aware that fraud or noncompliance with laws and regulations may have occurred, he or she should consider the effect of the matter on the review report, and should request management to consider the effect on the financial statements.
- **Communicate With the Predecessor Accountant:** The successor accountant may decide (but is not required) to communicate with the predecessor accountant regarding acceptance of the engagement and matters of continuing accounting significance.

2.2.4 Designing Review Procedures

The accountant should design the analytical procedures to be performed and the inquiries of management based on:

1. the accountant's understanding of the industry;
2. the accountant's knowledge of the client; and
3. the risk that the accountant may unknowingly fail to modify the accountant's review report on financial statements that are materially misstated.

The results of the accountant's inquiries and analytical procedures may modify the accountant's risk awareness.

2.3 Inquiries Should Be Addressed to Appropriate Individuals

Understanding
Learn client
Inquiries
Analytical
Review—other
Client rep. letter
Prof. judgment
Acct. report

The accountant's inquiries within the client's organization should be directed to members of management with financial and accounting responsibilities, to assure that adequate responses are obtained. The accountant is generally not required to corroborate management's responses with other evidence. Inquiries should cover the following:

- Accounting principles and practices used, and the method of applying them;
- Procedures for recording, classifying, and summarizing transactions, and for accumulating information for disclosure in footnotes;
- Whether the financial statements have been prepared and fairly presented in conformity with the applicable financial reporting framework;
- Whether there have been changes in the entity's business activities or accounting principles and practices;
- Matters as to which questions have arisen during the course of the review;
- Material subsequent events;
- Unusual or complex situations that may affect the financial statements;
- Significant transactions occurring or recognized during the period, particularly those near the end of the period;
- The status of uncorrected misstatements from previous engagements;
- Material fraud or suspected fraud;
- Significant journal entries and adjustments;
- Communications from regulatory agencies;
- Whether management has disclosed all known instances of noncompliance with laws and regulations;
- Litigation, claims, and assessments;
- Whether management believes that significant assumptions used for accounting estimates are reasonable;
- Actions authorized by the stockholders, board of directors, or other management groups;
- The entity's ability to continue as a going concern (and, if applicable, management's plans to mitigate the going concern issue); and
- Other items, such as the existence of related party transactions that have been discussed with management and would be considered for inclusion in the representation letter.

Pass Key

The inquiries are of internal personnel, not of external people or entities. The examiners frequently have incorrect responses stating, "Make inquiries of outside ... ."

Pass Key

The accountant should consider the reasonableness and consistency of management's responses in light of the results of other review procedures and the accountant's knowledge of the entity's business. However, the accountant is not required to corroborate management's responses with other evidence.

2.4 Analytical Procedures Should Be Performed

Understanding
Learn client
Inquiries
Analytical
Review—other
Client rep. letter
Prof. judgment
Acct. report

Analytical procedures involve developing an expectation (based on plausible relationships) and comparing recorded amounts or ratios based on recorded amounts to that expectation. Although expectations are not as encompassing as those developed during an audit (and corroboration is not required), analytical procedures in a review should still be designed to detect relationships and individual items that appear to be unusual and may indicate material misstatement. These procedures consist of:

- comparing the current financial statements with prior period financial statements, or current ratios with prior period ratios;
- comparing actual financial statements with budgets or forecasts, if available;
- comparing financial and relevant nonfinancial information;
- comparing the entity's ratios and indicators with those of other entities in the industry;
- comparing relationships among elements in the financial statements within the period and with corresponding prior period relationships; and
- comparing disaggregated revenue data.

Analytical procedures may be performed at the financial statement level or at the detailed account level. If the results of analytical procedures identify fluctuations or relationships that are inconsistent with other relevant information or that differ significantly from expected values, the accountant should investigate these differences by inquiring of management and performing other procedures as necessary.

2.5 Review: Other Procedures

Understanding
Learn client
Inquiries
Analytical
Review—other
Client rep. letter
Prof. judgment
Acct. report

During a review, the accountant should also:

- Read the financial statements for conformity with the applicable financial reporting framework.
- Obtain reports of other accountants who have been engaged to audit or review significant components of the reporting entity.
- Obtain evidence that the financial statements agree or reconcile with accounting records.
- If appropriate, request management to consider the effects of any going concern uncertainties or any subsequent events. The accountant should then consider whether management's conclusions are reasonable and whether the client's accounting and disclosures are adequate.

- If during the performance of review procedures the accountant becomes aware of information that is incorrect, incomplete, or otherwise unsatisfactory, the accountant should request that management consider the effect of these matters on the financial statements. The accountant should consider management's assessment of the matter and determine the effect, if any, on the accountant's review report.

2.6 Client Representation Letter From Management Must Be Obtained

The accountant is required to obtain a representation letter from management for all financial statements and periods covered by the review report, even if current management was not present during all such periods. The letter should be dated as of the date of the accountant's report. The letter should be addressed to the accountant and signed by the members of management responsible for and knowledgeable about the matters in the letter (generally the CEO and CFO). Management's failure to provide a representation letter results in an incomplete review (see below).

- Understanding
- Learn client
- Inquiries
- Analytical
- Review—other
- **Client rep. letter**
- Prof. judgment
- Acct. report

Management's representations should include the following information:

- Management has fulfilled its responsibility for the preparation and fair presentation of the financial statements in accordance with the applicable reporting framework.
- Management acknowledges its responsibility for designing, implementing, and maintaining internal control relevant to the preparation and fair presentation of the financial statements, including its responsibility to prevent and detect fraud.
- Management has provided the accountant with all relevant information and access, as agreed upon in the terms of the engagement.
- Management has responded fully and truthfully to all inquiries.
- All transactions have been recorded and are reflected in the financial statements.
- Management has disclosed its knowledge of fraud involving management, employees who have significant roles in internal control, or others, when the fraud could have a material effect on the financial statements.
- Management has disclosed its knowledge of any allegations or suspected fraud affecting the entity's financial statements.
- Management has disclosed all known instances of noncompliance or suspected noncompliance with laws and regulations the effects of which should be considered when preparing financial statements.
- Management has disclosed whether it believes that the effects of uncorrected misstatements are immaterial, individually and in aggregate, to the financial statements as a whole. (A summary of such items should be included in, or attached to, the written representation.)
- Management has disclosed to the accountant all known actual or possible litigation, and has appropriately accounted for and disclosed such litigation and claims in accordance with the applicable financial reporting framework.
- Management has disclosed whether it believes that significant assumptions used by it in making accounting estimates are reasonable.
- Management has disclosed the identity of the entity's related parties and has appropriately accounted for and disclosed such relationships and transactions.

- All events subsequent to the date of the financial statements that require adjustment or disclosure have been adjusted or disclosed.
- Management has disclosed additional representations related to matters specific to the entity's business and industry.

If management does not provide the written representations, or the accountant concludes that there is cause to doubt management's integrity such that the written representations provided are not reliable, the accountant should discuss the matter with management and those charged with governance, as appropriate.

If management does not provide the required representations or the accountant continues to doubt management's integrity, the accountant should withdraw from the engagement.

2.6.1 Sample: Management Representation Letter

Entity Letterhead

[*Date*]

To [*the accountant*]

This representation letter is provided in connection with your review of the [*identification of financial statements*] of [*name of entity*] as of [*dates*] and for the [*periods of review (for example, the years then ended)*] for the purpose of obtaining limited assurance that there were no material modifications that should be made to the financial statements in order for the statements to be in conformity with [*the applicable financial reporting framework (for example, accounting principles generally accepted in the United States of America)*]. We confirm that we are responsible for the fair presentation of the financial statements in accordance with [*the applicable financial accounting framework*] and the selection and application of the accounting policies.

Certain representations in this letter are described as being limited to matters that are material. Items are considered material, regardless of size, if they involve an omission or misstatement of accounting information that, in the light of surrounding circumstances, makes it probable that the judgment of a reasonable person using the information would be changed or influenced by the omission or misstatement.

We represent, to the best of our knowledge and belief, [*as of (date of the accountant's review report)*] the following representations made to you during your review:

Financial Statements

- We acknowledge our responsibility for the preparation and fair presentation of the financial statements in accordance with [*the applicable financial reporting framework (for example, accounting principles generally accepted in the United States of America)*].
- We acknowledge our responsibility and have fulfilled our responsibilities for the design, implementation and maintenance of internal control relevant to the preparation and fair presentation of the financial statements that are free from material misstatement whether due to fraud or error.
- We acknowledge our responsibility for the design, implementation, and maintenance of internal control to prevent and detect fraud.
- Significant assumptions used by us in making accounting estimates, including those measured at fair value, are reasonable.

(continued)

(continued)

- Related party relationships and transactions have been appropriately accounted for and disclosed in accordance with [*the applicable financial reporting framework (for example, accounting principles generally accepted in the United States of America)*].
- Guarantees, whether written or oral, under which the company is contingently liable have been properly accounted for and disclosed in accordance with [*the applicable financial reporting framework (for example, accounting principles generally accepted in the United States of America)*].
- Significant estimates and material concentrations known to management that are required to be disclosed in accordance with FASB ASC 275, *Risks and Uncertainties*, have been properly disclosed in accordance with the requirements of accounting principles generally accepted in the United States of America. [*Significant estimates are estimates at the balance sheet date that could change materially within the next year. Concentrations refer to volumes of business, revenues, available sources of supply, or markets or geographic areas for which events could occur that would significantly disrupt normal finances within the next year.*]
- All events subsequent to the date of the financial statements and for which [*the applicable financial reporting framework (for example, accounting principles generally accepted in the United States of America)*] requires adjustment or disclosure have been adjusted or disclosed.
- The effects of uncorrected misstatements are immaterial, both individually and in the aggregate, to the financial statements as a whole.
- The effects of all known actual or possible litigation and claims have been accounted for and disclosed in accordance with [*the applicable financial reporting framework (for example, accounting principles generally accepted in the United States of America.)*]

Information Provided

- We have responded fully and truthfully to all inquiries made to us by you during your review.
- We have provided you with:
  - Access to all information, of which we are aware, that is relevant to the preparation and fair presentation of the financial statements, such as records, documentation, and other matters;
  - Minutes of meetings of stockholders, directors, and committees of directors or summaries of actions of recent meetings for which minutes have not yet been prepared;
  - Additional information that you have requested from us for the purpose of the review; and
  - Unrestricted access to persons within the entity from which you determined it necessary to obtain review evidence.
- All transactions have been recorded in the accounting records and are reflected in the financial statements.

(continued)

(continued)

- We have no knowledge of any fraud or suspected fraud that affects the entity and involves:
  - management;
  - employees who have significant roles in internal control; or
  - others, when fraud could have a material effect on the financial statements.
- We have no knowledge of any allegations of fraud, or suspected fraud, affecting the entity's financial statements as a whole communicated by employees, former employees, analysts, regulators, or others.
- We have no plans or intentions that may materially affect the carrying amounts or classification of assets and liabilities.
- We have disclosed to you all known instances of noncompliance or suspected noncompliance with laws or regulations the effects of which should be considered when preparing financial statements.
- We have disclosed to you all known actual or possible litigation and claims the effects of which should be considered when preparing the financial statements.
- We have disclosed to you any other material liabilities or gain or loss contingencies that are required to be accrued or disclosed by FASB ASC 450, *Contingencies*.
- We have disclosed to you the identity of the entity's related parties and all the related party relationships and transactions of which we are aware.
- No material losses exist (such as from obsolete inventory or purchase or sale commitments) that have not been properly accrued or disclosed in the financial statements.
- The company has satisfactory title to all owned assets, and no liens or encumbrances on such assets exist, nor has any asset been pledged as collateral, except as disclosed to you and reported on the financial statements.
- We have complied with all aspects of contractual agreements that have a material effect on the financial statements in the event of noncompliance.
- We are in agreement with the adjusting journal entries you have recommended, and they have been posted to the company's accounts (if applicable).

____

[*Name of chief executive officer and title*]

____

[*Name of chief financial officer and title*]

2.7 Professional Judgment to Evaluate Results

- Understanding
- Learn client
- Inquiries
- Analytical
- Review—other
- Client rep. letter
- **Prof. judgment**
- Acct. report

2.7.1 Incomplete Review

Accountants must be able to perform whatever procedures they deem necessary, and if those procedures are not accomplished, the review is incomplete. A review that is incomplete will prevent the issuance of a review report.

In such a situation, the accountant should consider whether the circumstances also prevent issuing a compilation report.

2.7.2 Form and Content of Documentation

Review engagement documentation provides support for the representation that the accountant performed the review in accordance with SSARS and for the conclusion that the accountant is not aware of any material modifications that should be made to the financial statements in order for them to be in conformity with the applicable financial reporting framework.

Documentation should be sufficient to provide a clear understanding of the work performed, including the nature, timing, and extent of review procedures performed, the review evidence obtained and its source, and the engagement conclusions.

- The form and content of documentation in a review should be designed to meet the needs of the particular engagement.
- Written documentation from other types of engagements may be used to support the review report.
- Documentation should include:
  - The engagement letter documenting the understanding with the client.
  - Significant findings, actions taken, and the basis for conclusions reached.
  - Matters about which the accountant has made inquiry and responses thereto.
  - Analytical procedures performed, including expectations and how they were developed, results of comparison to recorded amounts, and procedures performed with respect to significant differences.
  - Communications with management regarding the accountant's expectation to include an emphasis-of-matter or other-matter paragraph in the review report.
  - Communications (oral or written) to management regarding fraud and noncompliance with laws and regulations.
  - Communications with other accountants that have audited or reviewed the financial statements of significant components.
  - The management representation letter.
  - A copy of the reviewed financial statements and the accountant's review report.

Pass Key

The examiners frequently have incorrect responses to questions that suggest that audit test work, including testing of internal controls, is to be performed.

2.8 Accountant (CPA) Communicates Results

Understanding
Learn client
Inquiries
Analytical
Review—other
Client rep. letter
Prof. judgment
Acct. report

The accountant's report in a review engagement should include:

- **Title:** An appropriate title that includes the word "*independent*," such as "*Independent Accountant's Review Report*."
- **Addressee:** The report should be addressed as appropriate.
- **Introductory Paragraph:** The introductory paragraph should:
  - Identify the entity.
  - State that the financial statements have been reviewed.
  - Identify the financial statements.
  - Specify the date or period covered by the financial statements.
  - Include a statement that a review includes primarily applying analytical procedures to management's financial data and making inquiries of company management.
  - Include a statement that a review is substantially less in scope than an audit, the objective of which is the expression of an opinion regarding the financial statements as a whole, and that, accordingly, the accountant does not express such an opinion.
- **Management's Responsibility Paragraph:** This paragraph should state that management is responsible for the preparation and fair presentation of the financial statements in accordance with the applicable financial reporting framework; this responsibility includes the design, implementation, and maintenance of internal control relevant to the preparation and fair presentation of financial statements that are free from material misstatement, whether due to fraud or error.
- **Accountant's Responsibility Paragraph:** This paragraph should:
  - State that the accountant's responsibility is to conduct the review in accordance with SSARS promulgated by the Accounting and Review Services Committee of the AICPA.
  - State that those standards require the accountant to perform procedures to obtain limited assurance as a basis for reporting whether the accountant is aware of any material modifications that should be made to the financial statements for them to be in accordance with the applicable financial reporting framework.
  - State that the accountant believes that the results of the accountant's procedures provide a reasonable basis for the accountant's conclusion.
- **Accountant's Conclusion Paragraph:** This paragraph should state that the accountant is not aware of any material modifications that should be made to the financial statements in order for them to be in accordance with the applicable financial reporting framework, other than those modifications, if any, indicated in the report.
- **Signature of Accountant**
- **City and State:** This may be indicated in the letterhead rather than below the signature of the accountant.
- **Date of the Accountant's Report:** This should be the date of the completion of the review.
- Each page of the statements should be marked, "see Independent Accountant's Review Report."

Question 1 **MCQ-03142**

Which of the following procedures would an accountant least likely perform during an engagement to review the financial statements of a nonissuer?

- **a.** Observing the safeguards over access to and use of assets and records.
- **b.** Comparing the financial statements with anticipated results in budgets and forecasts.
- **c.** Inquiring of management about actions taken at the board of directors' meetings.
- **d.** Studying the relationships of financial statement elements expected to conform to predictable patterns.

Question 2 **MCQ-02976**

Financial statements of a nonissuer that have been reviewed by an accountant should be accompanied by a report stating that a review:

- **a.** Provides only limited assurance that the financial statements are fairly presented.
- **b.** Includes examining, on a test basis, information that is the representation of management.
- **c.** Is substantially less in scope than an audit.
- **d.** Does not contemplate obtaining corroborating evidential matter or applying certain other procedures ordinarily performed during an audit.

MODULE

5 Review Reports

AUD 6

1 Reports on Review Engagements

1.1 Accountant's Independence Required

An accountant must be independent of the client to issue a review report on the financial statements of such a client. Note that any direct ownership of a company, no matter how small, will impair independence.

1.2 Review Report Modifications

Uncertainties and inconsistencies in the application of accounting principles do not require modification of the review report as long as the financial statements include adequate disclosure.

The accountant should modify the review report when the accountant becomes aware that the financial statements do not include:

- A description of the special purpose framework.
- A summary of significant accounting policies.
- An adequate description about how the special purpose framework differs from GAAP. The effects of these differences need not be quantified.
- Informative disclosures similar to those required by GAAP when the financial statements contain items that are the same as, or similar to, those in financial statements prepared in accordance with GAAP.

1.2.1 Sample Report: Standard Review Report

Independent Accountant's Review Report

[*Appropriate addressee*]

We have reviewed the accompanying balance sheet of XYZ Company as of December 31, 20XX, and the related statements of income, retained earnings, and cash flows for the year then ended. A review includes primarily applying analytical procedures to management's financial data and making inquiries of company management. A review is substantially less in scope than an audit, the objective of which is the expression of an opinion regarding the financial statements as a whole. Accordingly, we do not express such an opinion.

(continued)

(continued)

Management's Responsibility for the Financial Statements

Management is responsible for the preparation and fair presentation of the financial statements in accordance with [the applicable financial reporting framework (for example, accounting principles generally accepted in the United States of America)]; and this includes the design, implementation, and maintenance of internal control relevant to the preparation and fair presentation of the financial statements that are free from material misstatement, whether due to fraud or error.

Accountant's Responsibility

Our responsibility is to conduct the review in accordance with Statements on Standards for Accounting and Review Services promulgated by the Accounting and Review Services Committee of the AICPA. Those standards require us to perform procedures to obtain limited assurance as a basis for reporting whether we are aware of material modifications that should be made to the financial statements for them to be in accordance with accounting principles generally accepted in the United States of America. We believe that the results of our procedures provide a reasonable basis for our report.

Accountant's Conclusion

Based on our review, *we are not aware of any material modifications* that should be made to the accompanying financial statements in order for them to be in accordance with [*the applicable financial reporting framework*].

[*Signature of accounting firm or accountant*]

[*Accountant's city and state*]

[*Date*]

1.3 Emphasis-of-Matter Paragraph and Other-Matter Paragraphs

At the accountant's discretion, an emphasis-of-matter paragraph may be added to the report to discuss uncertainties or inconsistencies, or to emphasize any matter already disclosed in the financial statements, such as subsequent events, significant related party transactions, or changes in accounting principle. Emphasis-of-matter paragraphs draw users' attention to a matter appropriately presented or disclosed in the financial statements. The emphasis-of-matter paragraph should include a heading "Emphasis of a Matter" or another appropriate heading and appear immediately after the accountant's conclusion paragraph.

If the accountant considers it necessary to communicate a matter other than those that are presented or disclosed in the financial statements, then the accountant should include a paragraph with the heading "Other Matter" or another appropriate heading. The paragraph should appear immediately after the accountant's conclusion paragraph and any emphasis-of-matter paragraph.

If the accountant expects to include an emphasis-of-matter or other-matter paragraph in the accountant's review report, the accountant should communicate with management regarding this expectation and the proposed wording of this paragraph.

Pass Key

Some emphasis-of-matter paragraphs that may be included at the discretion of the accountant include:

- An uncertainty relating to the future outcome of unusually important litigation or regulatory action.
- A major catastrophe that has had, or continues to have, a significant effect on the entity's financial position.
- Significant transactions with related parties.
- Unusually important subsequent events.

1.4 Reporting on Financial Statements That Are Prepared in Accordance With a Special Purpose Framework

A review report prepared in accordance with a special purpose framework should:

- Make reference to management's responsibility for determining the applicable financial reporting framework.
- Include an emphasis-of-matter paragraph, under an appropriate heading that indicates that the financial statements are prepared in accordance with the applicable special purpose framework, refers to the note to the financial statements that describes the framework, and states that the special purpose framework is a basis of accounting other than GAAP.
- *If prepared using the regulatory or contractual basis of accounting*, include a description of the purpose for which the financial statements are prepared or refer to the appropriate note in the financial statements in the management's responsibility paragraph and include an other-matter paragraph, under an appropriate heading, restricting the use of the accountant's review report.

1.5 Reference to the Work of Other Accountants in an Accountant's Review Report

If the accountant of the reporting entity decides not to assume responsibility for the audit or review performed by other accountants, the accountant may make reference to any or all other accountants who audited or reviewed significant components, as long as the other accountant's report is not restricted. The decision is solely at the discretion and judgment of the accountant of the reporting entity. Reference to other accountants would occur in the accountant's responsibility paragraph and should indicate the portion of the financial statements audited or reviewed by the other accountants.

1.6 Departures From the Applicable Financial Reporting Framework

In a review engagement, an accountant may become aware of a material departure from the applicable financial reporting framework. The accountant should recommend that the financial statements be revised to conform with the framework. If the financial statements are not revised, the accountant must then consider whether to modify the report or to withdraw from the engagement.

1.6.1 Report Modification

When the accountant believes that modification of the report is appropriate, a separate paragraph disclosing the departure should be added to the end of the report.

- The paragraph should appear after the accountant's conclusion paragraph under the heading, "Known Departures From the [*identify the applicable financial reporting framework*]." This paragraph should include the effects of the departure on the financial statements, if known.
- The accountant's conclusion paragraph of the report would refer to the additional paragraph as follows:

> Based on our review, except for the issue noted in the Known Departure From Accounting Principles Generally Accepted in the United States of America paragraph, we are not aware of any material modifications that should be made ... .

- Optional—Depending on the accountant's assessment of the possible dollar magnitude of the departure, the pervasiveness and overall impact of the misstatements, and whether disclosures have been made of the effect of the departures, the accountant may also add another additional separate paragraph discussing the limitations of the financial statements.

1.6.2 Report Modification Not Adequate

If the accountant believes that disclosure in the report would not be adequate to indicate the deficiencies in the financial statements, he or she should withdraw from the engagement and provide no further services.

Pass Key

The accountant should not modify the standard report to include a statement that the financial statements are not in accordance with the applicable financial reporting framework.

An opinion, even qualified or adverse, requires an audit. When an accountant performing a compilation or review becomes aware of a GAAP departure, the report would be modified or the accountant would withdraw. An opinion would not be expressed.

1.7 Consideration of an Entity's Ability to Continue as a Going Concern

The auditor should perform review procedures related to going concern if the applicable financial reporting framework includes requirements for management to evaluate the entity's ability to continue as a going concern or if the accountant becomes aware of conditions that raise substantial doubt about the entity's ability to continue as a going concern. This includes determining whether the going concern basis of accounting is appropriate, reviewing management's evaluation of going concern, inquiring about management's plan to mitigate those matters, and determining the adequacy of those disclosures.

If after considering conditions or events that raise substantial doubt about the entity's ability to continue as a going concern and management's plans, the accountant concludes that:

- Going concern is alleviated—the accountant may, but is not required to, include an emphasis-of-matter paragraph.
- Going concern remains—the accountant should include an emphasis-of-matter paragraph that includes the terms "substantial doubt" and "going concern."

If the accountant determines that the entity's disclosures are inadequate, the accountant should treat the missing disclosures as a departure from the applicable financial reporting framework that exists and follow the appropriate guidance.

Pass Key

An accountant may decide to restrict the use of a compilation or review report to certain specified parties (e.g., when the subject matter of the report is based on criteria other than GAAP or a special purpose framework). Because the accountant cannot control distribution of his or her report after issuance, the report itself should clearly state that it is intended to be used only by the identified parties.

2 Reporting on Comparative Financial Statements

When comparative financial statements are presented, the accountant's report should refer to each period for which financial statements are presented.

2.1 Updating the Report

When reporting on all periods presented, a continuing accountant should update the report on one or more prior periods presented on a comparative basis with those of the current period.

When issuing an updated report, the continuing accountant should consider information that the accountant has become aware of during the engagement for the current period financial statements.

If, during the current engagement, circumstances or events come to the accountant's attention that may affect the prior period financial statements presented, the accountant should consider the effects on the accountant's report.

2.2 Period(s) in Question

2.2.1 All Periods Compiled or Reviewed

When the periods presented in comparative financial statements are either all compiled or all reviewed, a continuing accountant should update the report on the prior period and issue it as part of the current report.

2.2.2 Current Period Reviewed and Prior Period Compiled

When the continuing accountant performs a higher level of service in the current period, the report on the prior period(s) should be updated and issued as the last paragraph of the current period's report.

2.2.3 Current Period Compiled and Prior Period Reviewed

In the event that accountants have reviewed the prior period statements but compiled the current period statements, they can do one of the following:

1. Issue a compilation report and add a paragraph to the report on the current period statements. The added paragraph should describe the responsibility assumed for the prior period statements. This description should include the date of the original report and a statement that no review procedures were performed in connection with the review engagement after the date of the review report.
2. Reissue the prior period review report. The reissued review report may be:
   - combined with the current period compilation report; or
   - presented separately from the current period compilation report.

   If a combined report is used, the report should state:

   > No review procedures were performed in connection with the review engagement after the date of the review report.

2.2.4 Current Period Prepared and Prior Period Compiled or Reviewed

In the event that accountants have compiled or reviewed the prior period statements but prepared the current period statements, there is no requirement to reference the prior period.

2.3 Other Requirements

2.3.1 Columnar Form

Accountants may advise a client to include a clear indication when financial statements that have not been audited, reviewed, or compiled are presented in columnar form with financial statements on which an accountant has compiled the financial statements, so that a user does not inappropriately extend the accountant's compilation report to such financial statements.

2.3.2 Omission of Required Disclosures

Compiled financial statements that omit substantially all of the disclosures required by GAAP are not comparable to financial statements including such disclosures. The accountant should not issue a report on comparative financial statements when statements for one or more, but not all, of the periods presented omit substantially all of the disclosures required by GAAP.

2.3.3 Information Affecting Previous Reports

During the current engagement, an accountant may become aware of information that would have affected the report on the prior periods. In such a situation, a previous modification made to disclose a departure from GAAP (or another applicable financial reporting framework) may no longer be necessary, or a new modification to disclose a departure from GAAP (or another applicable financial reporting framework) may be required.

An other-matter paragraph should be added to the prior period report that states:

1. the date of the original report;
2. that the statements of the prior period have been changed, if applicable; and
3. the reason for the change in the original report.

2.4 Other Accountants Involved in Prior Periods

2.4.1 Predecessor Accountant's Compilation or Review Report Reissued Unchanged

Predecessor accountants are not required to reissue their report on prior periods. If the predecessor accountants decide to reissue their report, they should:

1. Decide if their report is still appropriate:
   - considering the current presentation of statements for the prior period;
   - based on subsequent events; and
   - in light of required modifications that may be necessary in their report.
2. Perform the following procedures:
   - read the statements and the report of the current period;
   - compare the prior period statements with those issued previously and currently; and
   - obtain a letter from the successor accountants stating that they are not aware of any relevant information that might have a material effect on the prior period statements.

If the predecessor accountants become aware of information that may affect the financial statements or their report, they should (i) perform the same procedures they would have performed during the previous engagement; and (ii) perform any additional procedures they deem necessary.

Pass Key

Whenever predecessor accountants are asked to reissue their prior report (audit, review, or compilation), they should read the new financial statements and obtain a representation letter from the new accountant.

2.4.2 Predecessor's Report Not Reissued

When the prior period financial statements have been subject to a compilation or review by a predecessor accountant and the predecessor's report is not presented, the successor is not required to make reference to the compilation or review report on the prior period financial statements. However, the successor accountant may (but is not required to) make reference to the report of the predecessor accountant in the current report or perform that level of service himself or herself.

In making reference to the predecessor accountant's report, the successor accountants may expand the report by including an additional paragraph mentioning the following:

- a statement that the prior periods were compiled or reviewed by other accountants (who are generally not named, unless the predecessor's and successor's practices are combined);
- the date of their report; and
- a description of any modifications contained in the report.

If the predecessor accountant's report was compiled in the prior year, the paragraph should also include a statement that the other accountant(s) did not audit or review the financial statements and, accordingly, did not express an opinion or provide any assurance about whether the financial statements are in accordance with the applicable financial reporting framework.

If the predecessor accountant's report was reviewed in the prior year, then the paragraph should include a statement that, based on his or her review, the other accountant(s) are not aware of any material modifications that should be made to the financial statements in order for them to be in accordance with the applicable financial reporting framework other than those modifications, if any, indicated in the report.

2.4.3 Restated Prior Period Financial Statements

The predecessor or successor accountant may report on changed prior period financial statements, as restated.

Alternatively, the successor accountant may report only on the restatement adjustment, while indicating a predecessor accountant reported on the prior period financial statements before restatement.

2.5 Reporting When One Period Is Audited

When unaudited (i.e., compiled or reviewed) financial statements are presented in comparative form with audited financial statements, the unaudited financial statements should be clearly marked and the accountant should either:

1. reissue the prior period report; or
2. include an other-matter paragraph in the current report describing the responsibility assumed for the prior period's statements.

2.5.1 Current Period Unaudited and Prior Period Audited

When the prior period has been audited, the accountant should issue the current period compilation or review report, and add an other-matter paragraph, which should indicate:

- that prior period statements were audited;
- the date of the previous report(s);
- the opinions expressed, and, if other than unmodified, the reasons for the modification; and
- that no auditing procedures have been performed since the previous report date.

2.5.2 Current Period Audited and Prior Period Unaudited

When the current period statements are audited, the auditor should include an other-matter paragraph in the auditor's report that includes:

- the service (review or compilation) performed in the prior period;
- the date of the prior period report;
- a description of any material modifications described in the report;
- a statement that the service was less in scope than an audit and did not provide the basis for an opinion.

Note: If unaudited financial statements are presented in comparative form with audited financial statements in documents filed with the SEC, such statements should be marked "*unaudited,*" but should not be referred to in the auditor's report.

Pass Key

A great deal of overlap exists in the procedures performed in preparation, compilation, and review engagements. Each level of service requires progressively more procedures. The chart below summarizes the overlap of procedures performed in SSARS engagements.

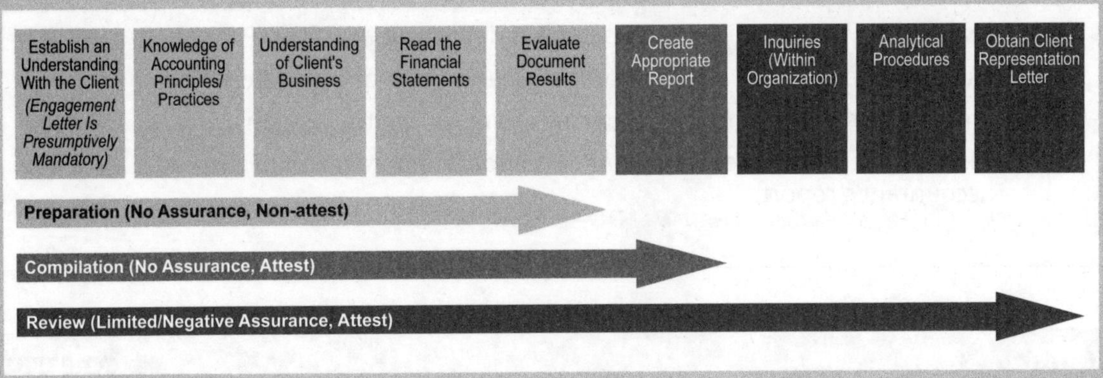

Question 1 **MCQ-04629**

Under which of the following circumstances would an accountant most likely conclude that it is necessary to withdraw from an engagement to review a nonissuer's financial statements?

a. The entity does *not* have reasonable justification for making a change in accounting principle.

b. The entity prepares its financial statements on the income tax basis of accounting.

c. The entity requests the accountant to report only on the balance sheet and *not* on the other financial statements.

d. The entity declines to provide the accountant with a signed representation letter.

Question 2	MCQ-02970

During an engagement to review the financial statements of a nonissuer, an accountant becomes aware that several leases that should be capitalized are not capitalized. The accountant considers these leases to be material to the financial statements. The accountant decides to modify the standard review report because management will not capitalize the leases. Under these circumstances, the accountant should:

- **a.** Issue an adverse opinion because of the departure from GAAP.
- **b.** Express no assurance of any kind on the entity's financial statements.
- **c.** Emphasize that the financial statements are for limited use only.
- **d.** Disclose the departure from GAAP in a separate paragraph of the accountant's report.

Question 3	MCQ-03381

Gole, CPA, is engaged to review the Year 2 financial statements of North Co., a nonissuer. Previously, Gole audited North's Year 1 financial statements and expressed an unmodified opinion. Gole decides to include a separate paragraph in the Year 2 review report because North plans to present comparative financial statements for Year 2 and Year 1. This separate paragraph should indicate that:

- **a.** The Year 2 review report is intended solely for the information of management and the board of directors.
- **b.** The Year 1 auditor's report may no longer be relied on.
- **c.** No auditing procedures were performed after the date of the Year 1 auditor's report.
- **d.** There are justifiable reasons for changing the level of service from an audit to a review.

MODULE 6 Interim Reviews

1 Overview

Interim financial information may be condensed or in the form of complete financial statements, and may cover:

1. a period less than a full year; or
2. a 12-month period ending on a date other than the entity's fiscal year-end.

1.1 Applicability: Nonissuers (SAS)

An auditor may conduct a review of the interim financial information of a nonissuer if:

1. the latest financial statements have been audited;
2. the auditor either has been engaged to audit the entity's current year financial statements, or audited the entity's latest annual financial statements and the appointment of another auditor to audit the current year financial statements is not effective before the beginning of the period covered by the review;
3. the same financial reporting framework is used for the interim financial statements as was used in the annual financial statements; and
4. the interim financial information is condensed information, it conforms with an appropriate financial reporting framework, it includes an explanatory note, and it accompanies the latest audited financial statements (or those statements are made readily available).

   The explanatory note should indicate that the information does not represent complete financial statements, and that it should be read in conjunction with the latest annual financial statements.

1.2 Applicability: Issuers (PCAOB)

1.2.1 Situations Requiring a Review of Interim Financial Information

Certain entities are required by the SEC to file quarterly reports. The SEC requires that an independent auditor review such quarterly information before the quarterly report is filed.

Many entities are required by the SEC to include selected quarterly financial data in their annual reports or in other SEC filings. A review of such quarterly information is also required.

An auditor performing an initial audit of financial statements that include selected quarterly data should also perform a review of that data as part of the overall audit.

1.2.2 Written Report

Although auditing standards do not require a written report on a review of interim financial information, if a client states, in a document filed with a regulatory agency or issued to shareholders or third parties, that an auditor has reviewed the interim financial information included therein, the review report must also be included in that document.

For example, the SEC requires that a review report be filed along with the interim financial information if an entity states, in any filing, that an independent public auditor has reviewed the interim financial statements.

2 Procedures

Auditing standards require the auditor to perform the following procedures, each of which will be covered in greater detail below.

- **Understanding** with the client should be established.
- **Learn** and/or obtain sufficient understanding of the entity, its environment, including internal control.
- **Inquiries** should be addressed to the appropriate individuals.
- **Analytical** procedures should be performed.
- **Review**—other procedures should be performed.
- **Client** representation letter should be obtained from management.
- **Professional** judgment should be used to evaluate results.
- **Auditor** (CPA) should communicate results.

2.1 Understanding With the Client Should Be Established

Understanding
Learn client
Inquiries
Analytical
Review—other
Client rep. letter
Prof. judgment
Acct. report

2.1.1 Pre-acceptance Procedures

Before accepting an engagement to review an entity's interim financial information, the auditor should:

- Determine whether the financial reporting framework used to prepare the interim financial information is acceptable.
- Obtain the agreement of management that it acknowledges and understands its responsibility for:
  - the preparation and fair presentation of the interim financial information;
  - the design, implementation, and maintenance of internal control sufficient to provide a reasonable basis for the preparation and fair presentation of the interim financial information;
  - providing the auditor with access to the information and persons needed to complete the review; and
  - including the auditor's review report in any document containing interim financial information that indicates that the information has been reviewed by the entity's auditor.

2.1.2 Engagement Letter

In order to reduce the likelihood of misunderstanding, the auditor should establish an understanding with the client regarding the services to be performed through the use of an engagement letter. The understanding should include:

- **Objectives and Scope of the Engagement:** The objective of a review of interim financial information is to determine whether material modifications are necessary for the information to be in conformity with the applicable financial reporting framework. Making inquiries and performing analytical procedures provide the support for this type of reporting.
- **Management's Responsibilities:** Management's responsibilities with respect to interim financial information are analogous to its responsibilities for annual financial statements, as covered previously.

- **Auditor's Responsibilities:** The auditor is responsible for conducting the review in accordance with appropriate standards (SAS or PCAOB standards). A review, which consists primarily of analytical procedures and inquiries, is substantially less in scope than an audit, and therefore no opinion should be expressed.
- **Limitations of the Engagement:** A review does not provide a basis for expressing an opinion, does not provide the auditor with a basis for obtaining reasonable assurance that the auditor will become aware of the significant issues and findings that would be identified in an audit, and is not designed to provide assurance regarding internal control. Communication is required if significant deficiencies or material weaknesses in internal control are noted.
- **Financial Reporting Framework:** The engagement letter should identify the applicable financial reporting framework for the preparation of the interim financial information.

2.2 Learn and/or Obtain an Understanding of the Entity and Its Environment, Including Its Internal Control

- Understanding
- **Learn client**
- Inquiries
- Analytical
- Review—other
- Client rep. letter
- Prof. judgment
- Acct. report

2.2.1 Purpose

The auditor needs to have an understanding of the entity and its environment, including its internal control, in order to:

1. Determine what types of material misstatements may occur;
2. Evaluate the likelihood that such misstatements will occur; and
3. Select appropriate inquiries and analytical procedures.

2.2.2 Planning

During planning, the auditor should update this understanding by performing the following procedures:

1. Read the documentation of prior audits and reviews to identify matters that may affect the current period's interim financial information.
2. Read the most recent annual financial information and financial information from recent comparable prior interim periods.
3. Consider the results of any audit procedures performed on the entity's current year financial statements.
4. Inquire of management regarding changes in business activities or internal control.
5. Inquire of management about the identity of and transactions with related parties.

2.2.3 Obtaining Knowledge

In an initial review of interim financial information, the auditor should make inquiries of the predecessor auditor and, if permitted, review the predecessor's documentation. The successor auditor remains solely responsible for the review procedures performed and the conclusions reached.

An auditor who has audited the most recent annual financial statements may already have sufficient knowledge of internal control as it relates to interim financial information. If the auditor has not audited the most recent annual financial statements, he or she should perform procedures to obtain knowledge about the entity's internal control. Internal control over interim financial information may differ from internal control over annual financial statements (e.g., greater use of estimates may require different accounting principles and practices).

Significant deficiencies in internal control may make it impracticable for the auditor to perform a review.

2.3 Inquiries Should Be Addressed to Appropriate Individuals

2.3.1 Required Inquiries

Understanding
Learn client
Inquiries
Analytical
Review—other
Client rep. letter
Prof. judgment
Acct. report

Inquiries should be directed to members of management with responsibility for financial and accounting matters, and should include queries regarding the following items:

- Whether the interim financial information has been prepared in conformity with the applicable financial reporting framework.
- Unusual or complex situations affecting the interim financial information.
- Significant transactions during the last several days of the interim period.
- The status of uncorrected misstatements from previous audits/reviews.
- Subsequent events.
- Fraud, suspected fraud, or allegations of fraud.
- Significant journal entries and adjustments.
- Communications from regulatory agencies.
- Significant deficiencies and material weaknesses in internal control.
- Changes in related parties or significant new related party transactions.
- The entity's ability to continue as a going concern (and, if applicable, management's plans to mitigate the going concern issue).
- Questionable matters noted during other review procedures.

2.3.2 Inquiry of Client's Lawyer

Inquiry of the entity's lawyer regarding litigation, claims, and assessments generally is not required, but may be appropriate in certain circumstances.

2.3.3 Going Concern

Although a review of interim financial information is not designed to provide information regarding an entity's ability (or lack thereof) to continue as a going concern for a reasonable period of time, such condition or events that raise substantial doubt about the entity's ability to continue as a going concern may come to the auditor's attention, or may have existed at the date of prior period financial statements. In such cases, the auditor should make appropriate inquiries and consider the adequacy of disclosure, but is not required to corroborate mitigating factors.

2.4 Analytical Procedures Should Be Performed

Understanding
Learn client
Inquiries
Analytical
Review—other
Client rep. letter
Prof. judgment
Acct. report

The auditor uses his or her understanding of the entity and its environment, including its internal control, to develop appropriate analytical procedures, inquiries, and other procedures.

Analytical procedures are performed to provide a basis for inquiry about unusual items, and should include the following items:

- Comparisons over time of interim financial information:
  - Current interim financial information vs. immediately preceding interim period.
  - Current interim financial information vs. comparable period from prior year.
- Consideration of plausible relationships among both financial and relevant nonfinancial information.
- Comparison of recorded amounts (or related ratios) to the auditor's expectations. Expectations generally will be less precise than those developed during an audit.
- Comparison of disaggregated revenue data (e.g., revenue by month and by product line) for the current interim period with that of comparable prior periods.

2.5 Review: Other Procedures

Understanding
Learn client
Inquiries
Analytical
Review—other
Client rep. letter
Prof. judgment
Acct. report

Other procedures may also be used to address significant accounting and disclosure matters relating to interim financial information. The auditor should:

1. Read minutes of stockholder meetings, directors' meetings, etc., making appropriate inquiries if minutes are unavailable.
2. Obtain reports from any component auditors engaged to review the interim financial information of subsidiaries, investees, etc., making appropriate inquiries if reports have not been issued.
3. Obtain evidence that the interim financial information agrees or reconciles with the accounting records, and inquire of management regarding the reliability of those accounting records.
4. Read the interim financial information for conformity with the applicable financial reporting framework.
5. Read other information in documents containing the interim financial information for material inconsistencies or material misstatements of fact.
6. Extend review procedures to resolve any outstanding questions regarding the interim financial information's conformity with the applicable financial reporting framework.

Review procedures may be performed before or simultaneously with the entity's preparation of the interim financial information. Certain audit procedures related to the annual financial statement audit may be performed concurrently with the review.

2.6 Client Written Representation Letter From Management Should Be Obtained

Understanding
Learn client
Inquiries
Analytical
Review—other
Client rep. letter
Prof. judgment
Acct. report

As is the case with an audit, the auditor should obtain written representations from management related to the financial information, the completeness of information, recognition, measurement, disclosure, and subsequent events.

If management refuses to provide one or more requested written representations or the auditor has concerns about the reliability of the representations, the auditor should:

1. discuss the matter with management and those charged with governance;
2. reevaluate the integrity of management; and
3. consider whether to withdraw from the review engagement and, if applicable, withdraw as the entity's auditor.

2.7 Professional Judgment to Evaluate Results

Understanding
Learn client
Inquiries
Analytical
Review—other
Client rep. letter
Prof. judgment
Acct. report

2.7.1 Misstatements

The auditor should accumulate misstatements identified during the review, including inadequate disclosures, and should evaluate the misstatements individually and in the aggregate to determine whether material modification should be made to the financial information for it to be in accordance with the applicable financial reporting framework.

2.7.2 Scope Limitations

If the auditor is unable to perform necessary procedures or management does not provide appropriate representations, no review report should be issued. The auditor should communicate such matters, as well as known material departures from the applicable financial reporting framework, to management, those charged with governance, etc.

2.8 Auditor Communicates Results

Understanding
Learn client
Inquiries
Analytical
Review—other
Client rep. letter
Prof. judgment
Acct. report

2.8.1 Communications to Management

Prompt communication to management is required if the auditor believes:

- Material modifications should be made to the interim financial information for it to be in accordance with the applicable financial reporting framework.
- An issuer filed quarterly reports with the SEC (Form 10-Q or Form 10-QSB) prior to completion of the review.
- A nonissuer issued the interim financial information prior to completion of the review (in situations that required a review).

If management does not respond appropriately to such communications, the auditor should inform those charged with governance. If those charged with governance do not respond appropriately, the auditor should consider resigning, and may wish to consult legal counsel.

2.8.2 Required Communications With Those Charged With Governance

An auditor conducting a review of interim financial information is subject to communication requirements analogous to those required in an audit. Communications are required with respect to:

- Fraud and noncompliance with laws and regulations.
- Significant deficiencies or material weaknesses in internal control.

If the auditor cannot complete the review, the auditor should communicate to the appropriate level of management and those charged with governance:

1. the reason the review cannot be completed;
2. that an incomplete review does not provide a basis for reporting and, accordingly, that the auditor is precluded from issuing a review report; and
3. any material modifications that the auditor has become aware of during the review that should be made to the interim financial information for it to be in accordance with the applicable financial reporting framework.

Communications to those charged with governance should be made on a timely basis (for issuers, communications should be made before the entity files its interim financial information with a regulatory agency, or as soon as practicable).

2.8.3 Sample Report: Review of Interim Financial Statements (Nonissuer)

Independent Auditor's Review Report

[*Appropriate Addressee*]

Report on the Financial Statements

We have reviewed the accompanying [*describe the interim financial information or statements reviewed*] of ABC Company and subsidiaries as of *September 30, 20X1*, and for the *three-month and nine-month periods* then ended.

Management's Responsibility

The Company's management is responsible for the preparation and fair presentation of the interim financial information in accordance with [*identify the applicable financial reporting framework; for example, accounting principles generally accepted in the United States of America*]; this responsibility includes the design, implementation, and maintenance of internal control sufficient to provide a reasonable basis for the preparation and fair presentation of interim financial information in accordance with [*identify the applicable financial reporting framework; for example, accounting principles generally accepted in the United States of America*].

Auditor's Responsibility

Our responsibility is to conduct our review in accordance with auditing standards generally accepted in the United States of America applicable to reviews of interim financial information. A review of interim financial information consists principally of *applying analytical procedures and making inquiries of persons responsible for financial and accounting matters.* It is *substantially less in scope* than an audit conducted in accordance with auditing standards generally accepted in the United States, the objective of which is the expression of an opinion regarding the financial information. Accordingly, *we do not express such an opinion.*

Conclusion

Based on our review, *we are not aware of any material modifications* that should be made to the accompanying interim financial information for it to be in accordance with [*identify the applicable financial reporting framework; for example, accounting principles generally accepted in the United States of America*].

[*Auditor's Signature*]

[*Auditor's city and state*]

[*Date of the auditor's report*]

Pass Key

Each page of the interim financial information should be clearly marked *unaudited*.

2.8.4 Sample Report: Review of Interim Financial Statements (Issuer)

Report of the Independent Registered Public Accounting Firm

To the shareholders and the board of directors of X Company:

Results of Review of Interim [Financial Information or Statements]

We have reviewed the accompanying [*describe the interim financial statements reviewed*] of X Company (the "Company") and consolidated subsidiaries as of September 30, 20X1, and for the three-month and nine-month periods then ended, and the related notes and schedules (collectively referred to as the "interim financial statements"). Based on our review, we are not aware of any material modifications that should be made to the accompanying interim financial statements for them to be in conformity with accounting principles generally accepted in the United States of America.

Basis for Review Results

These interim financial statements are the responsibility of the Company's management. We are a public accounting firm registered with the Public Company Accounting Oversight Board (United States) (PCAOB) and are required to be independent with respect to the Company in accordance with the U.S. federal securities laws and the applicable rules and regulations of the Securities and Exchange Commission and the PCAOB.

We conducted our review in accordance with the standards of the PCAOB. A review of interim financial information consists principally of applying analytical procedures and making inquiries of persons responsible for financial and accounting matters. It is substantially less in scope than an audit conducted in accordance with the standards of the PCAOB, the objective of which is the expression of an opinion regarding the financial statements taken as a whole. Accordingly, we do not express such an opinion.

[*Signature*]

[*City and state or country*]

[*Date*]

2.8.5 Departures From the Applicable Financial Reporting Framework

The auditor should modify the report if, during the review, the auditor becomes aware of a departure from the applicable framework, such as inadequate disclosure or changes in accounting principle that are not in conformity with the framework. The modification should include a description of the departure and, if determinable, the effects of the departure. If there is inadequate disclosure in the interim information, auditors should also modify the report to include the necessary information, if practicable.

The report is modified by adding a basis for modification paragraph (immediately following the conclusion), and by modifying the conclusion to read:

> Based on our review, with the exception of the matter described in the following paragraph(s), we are not aware of any material modifications ... .

If the auditor believes that modification of the review report is not sufficient to address the deficiencies, the auditor should withdraw from the engagement.

2.8.6 Going Concern

- **For nonissuers:** The auditor should include an emphasis-of-matter paragraph when:
  1. a going concern emphasis-of-matter paragraph was included in the prior year's auditor's report and the conditions that give rise to the substantial doubt still exist and management's plans do not alleviate them; or

2. a going concern emphasis-of-matter paragraph was not included in the prior year's auditor report and management has included a statement that substantial doubt exits in its financial statements.

- **For issuers:** As long as disclosure about going concern is adequate, the auditor is not required to include an explanatory paragraph.
- **For both nonissuers and issuers:** If the auditor determines that the disclosure related to substantial doubt about the entity's ability to continue as a going concern is inadequate, resulting in a departure from the applicable financial reporting framework, the auditor should modify the report.

3 Other Uses of Interim Financial Information

3.1 Interim Financial Information Accompanying Audited Financial Statements

Normally, there is no need to refer to the review in the audit report because interim financial information is not a required part of the financial statements. However, modifications to the audit report are necessary in the following circumstances:

- When interim financial information included in a note to the financial statements is not marked *unaudited,* the auditor would disclaim an opinion on the interim financial information.
- When interim financial information accompanies the audited financial statements, the auditor should include an other-matter paragraph in the auditor's report when all of the following conditions exist:
  - The interim financial information that has been reviewed is included in a document containing audited financial statements.
  - The interim financial information accompanying the audited financial statements does not appear to be presented in accordance with the applicable financial reporting framework.
  - The auditor's separate review report that refers to the departure from the applicable financial reporting framework is not presented with the interim financial information.
- For issuers, when quarterly information required by the SEC has not been reviewed, an explanatory paragraph with an appropriate title should be added to the auditor's report, indicating that the auditor was unable to review such information.
- For issuers, when quarterly information required by the SEC is omitted, an explanatory paragraph with an appropriate title should be added to the auditor's report, indicating that the company has not presented such information.

3.2 Interim Financial Information Presented in a Registration Statement

The Securities Act of 1933 imposes certain responsibilities on an auditor who prepares a report that is used in connection with a registration statement.

If an auditor's review report on interim financial information is presented (or incorporated by reference) in a registration statement, a prospectus that includes a statement about the independent auditor's involvement should clarify that the report is not considered to be a *report* or *part* of the registration statement within this context.

4 Summary of Engagements

	Preparation Engagement	Compilation Engagement	Review Engagement			Audit Engagement
	SSARS	*SSARS*	*SSARS*	*SAS*	*PCAOB*	*SAS/PCAOB*
Level of Assurance	None	None	Limited			Reasonable
Entities	Nonissuers only	Nonissuers only	Nonissuers	Nonissuers: Interim FS	Issuers: Interim FS	Nonissuers/Issuers
Knowledge Required	Knowledge of accounting principles and practices of industry; general understanding of client's business	Knowledge of accounting principles and practices of industry; general understanding of client's business	Same as compilation plus increased knowledge of client's business			Extensive knowledge of economy, industry, and client's business
Inquiry and Analytical Procedures Required	None unless information is questionable	None unless information is questionable	Inquiries of internal personnel Analytical procedures			Inquiries of external parties and internal personnel Analytical procedures Audit procedures
GAAP Disclosure Omitted	May omit, but need to disclose in the financial statement	May omit most without restricting use; warn with ending paragraph	All are required or modify review report			All are required or "qualified/adverse" opinion
GAAP Departures	May depart from GAAP, but need to disclose in the financial statement	Modify report to discuss GAAP departure	Modify report to discuss GAAP departure			Modify report; "qualified/adverse" opinion
Independence	Not required (non-attest engagement)	Not required but disclosure is required	Required			Required
Engagement Letter	Presumptively mandatory	Presumptively mandatory	Presumptively mandatory			Presumptively mandatory
Representation Letter	Not required	Not required	Required			Required
Understanding of Internal Control	Not required	Not required (no test work)	Not required (no test work)	Required	Required	Required
Errors and Irregularities Detection	Only obvious errors	Only obvious errors found when reading financial statements	Only errors discovered through inquiry and analytical procedures			Must be designed to provide reasonable assurance of detection of material misstatements
FS Reported on (BS/IS/RE/CF)	One or more financial statements may be prepared	One or more financial statements allowed to be reported on	One or more financial statements allowed if scope of inquiry and analytical procedures have not been restricted			One or more financial statements allowed if scope of audit is not limited and all necessary procedures are applied
Communication With Predecessor	Not required	Not required	Not required	Required	Required	Required
Subsequent Event Inquiries	Not required	Not required	Required			Required

Engagement Summary						
	Nonissuers				*Issuers*	
	Preparation	*Compilation*	*Review*	*Review*	*Review*	*No Audit or Review*
Service	Prepared	Compiled	Review	Review	Review	Unaudited
Worked on	FS	FS	FS	Financial information	FS	FS
Period	Any date	Any date	Any date	Interim only	Interim only	Any date
Standards	AICPA—SSARS	AICPA—SSARS	AICPA—SSARS	AICPA—SAS	PCAOB	PCAOB
Procedures	Knowledge of industry Understand business Prepare the FS	Knowledge of industry Understand business Read the FS	**Understanding** with client **Learn** entity's business **Inquiry** **Analytical** procedures **Review**—other procedures **Client** rep. letter **Professional** judgment **Accountant** communicates results	**Understanding** with client **Learn** entity's business **Inquiry** **Analytical** procedures **Review**—other procedures **Client** rep. letter **Professional** judgment **Accountant** communicates results	**Understanding** with client **Learn** entity's business **Inquiry** **Analytical** procedures **Review**—other procedures **Client** rep. letter **Professional** judgment **Accountant** communicates results	None—however, CPA must read the financial statements for obvious errors
Findings	No assurance (include legend or disclaimer)	No assurance (disclaimer)	Limited assurance	Limited assurance	Limited assurance	No assurance (disclaimer)

Question 1 **MCQ-03419**

Green, CPA, is aware that Green's name is to be included in the annual report of National Company, a publicly held entity, because Green has audited the annual financial statements included therein. National's quarterly financial statements are also contained in the annual report. Green has not audited but has reviewed these interim financial statements. Green should request that:

I. Green's name not be included in the annual report.

II. The interim financial statements be marked as unaudited.

a. I only.

b. Both I and II.

c. Either I or II.

d. II only.

NOTES

MODULE

7 Letters for Underwriters

1 Comfort Letter

A comfort letter is a letter from the CPA to the named underwriter and/or certain other requesting parties (e.g., selling shareholder, sales agent, broker-dealer, financial intermediary, or buyer/seller) just before the registration of the client's securities. The auditor should not provide a comfort letter to any parties other than these listed requesting parties.

A comfort letter does not update the opinion on previously issued financial statements. It covers the period from the date of the last auditors' report to the effective date of the registration.

Auditors are neither required to accept an engagement to issue a comfort letter nor required to provide comfort on every matter requested when accepting an engagement to issue a comfort letter.

1.1 Due Diligence

The Securities Act of 1933 provides that underwriters, among others, could be held liable for material omissions or misstatements in a registration statement.

A "due diligence defense" may be used by the underwriter (i.e., an underwriter who performs a reasonable investigation will not be held liable). Underwriters request comfort letters from accountants as a part of their process of reasonable investigation.

1.2 Attorney's Opinion or Representation Letter Required

To obtain a comfort letter, the requesting party must provide the auditor with an attorney's opinion or a representation letter, confirming that such party has a due diligence defense.

If a requesting party, other than the underwriter, requests a comfort letter but does not provide a legal opinion or representation letter, the comfort letter provided by the auditor should not provide negative assurance on the financial statements as a whole, or on any specified elements, accounts, or items thereof.

1.3 Restricted Use

A comfort letter must include a statement that the letter is solely for the information of the addressees and to assist the underwriters in conducting and documenting their investigation of the affairs of the company in connection with the offering, and that it is not to be used, circulated, quoted, or otherwise referred to for any other purpose.

2 Auditor Responsibilities

2.1 Agreeing Upon the Scope of Services

The auditor should:

- Obtain an understanding of the specific matters to be addressed in the comfort letter and ask to meet with the requesting party and the client to discuss the procedures to be followed.
- Clearly describe the procedures performed by the auditor.
- Clearly communicate that the auditor cannot provide any assurance regarding the sufficiency of the procedures.
- Provide the requesting party with a draft of the form of the letter the auditor expects to furnish.

2.2 Knowledge of Internal Control

The auditor should obtain an understanding of the entity's internal control over financial reporting for both annual and interim periods when commenting in a comfort letter on:

- Unaudited interim financial information, including unaudited condensed interim financial information
- Capsule financial information
- A financial forecast when historical financial statements provide a basis for one or more significant assumptions for the forecast
- Subsequent changes in specified financial statement items

2.3 Format and Contents of Comfort Letters

The contents of comfort letters vary depending on the extent of the information in the securities offering and the wishes of the requesting party, but will generally include the following:

- **Date:** The date of the letter does not have to be the date of cutoff of procedures. The letter should indicate that no procedures were performed between the cutoff date and the date of the report.
- **Addressee:** The letter should be addressed only to the requesting party, or both the requesting party and the entity, and should not be provided to any other parties.
- **Introductory Paragraph:** The introductory paragraph identifies the financial statements and the securities offering.
- **Auditor's Report:** The auditor should reference the report of the audited financial statements.
- **Representations:** The auditor should refer to the requesting party's representations.
- **Independence:** The auditor should state in the comfort letter that the auditor is independent, or the date through which the auditor was independent, with respect to the entity, and identify the applicable independence rules (positive assurance).

- **SEC Compliance:** If the auditor is requested to include an opinion in the comfort letter on whether the financial statements comply as to form with the pertinent accounting requirements adopted by the SEC, the auditor's opinion should refer to compliance as to form, in all material respects, with the applicable accounting requirements of the 1933 act and the related rules and regulations adopted by the SEC (positive assurance).
- **Information Other Than Audited Financial Statements:** The auditor should describe the procedures performed, the criteria specified by the requesting party, and state that the procedures performed with respect to interim periods may not disclose matters of significance regarding certain matters about which negative assurance is requested (negative assurance).
- **Concluding Paragraph:** The auditor should restrict the use of the comfort letter for the information of the addressees and to assist the requesting parties in connection with the securities offering.

2.4 Positive Assurance

Positive assurance is provided with respect to:

- A CPA's independence.
- Compliance as to form of the financial statements with the SEC Act, assuming that the financial statements are audited. If the financial statements are not audited, negative assurance on compliance as to form is given.

2.5 Negative Assurance

Negative assurance is provided with respect to:

- Unaudited financial statements, unaudited condensed interim financial statements, and capsule financial information, assuming a review of such information has been performed.

  If a review has not been performed, the procedures performed and findings obtained should be listed.
- Changes in selected financial statement items during a period subsequent to the date and period of the latest financial statements included in the registration statement, assuming an audit or review has recently been performed.
- Whether certain nonfinancial statement information included in the registration statement complies as to form in all material respects with Regulation S-K.

  In a comfort letter, no comment should be made regarding compliance of the Management's Discussion and Analysis (MD&A) with SEC rules and regulations. However, accountants may agree to examine or review MD&A.

The auditor may provide negative assurance as long as:

- The information is derived, directly or by analysis or computation, from the accounting records subject to internal control over financial reporting.
- The information is capable of evaluation against reasonable criteria that have been established by the SEC.

The auditor should not express an opinion on conformity with the disclosure requirements of Regulation S-K.

3 Commenting on Other Information

3.1 Pro Forma Financial Information

Negative assurance on pro forma financial information may be provided if the auditor has an appropriate level of knowledge of the accounting and financial reporting practices of the entity and has performed:

- an audit of the annual financial statements; or
- a review of the interim financial information of the entity to which the pro forma adjustments were applied, in accordance with GAAS applicable to reviews of interim financial information.

3.2 Financial Forecasts

When performing procedures agreed to with the requesting party on a financial forecast and commenting thereon in a comfort letter, the auditor should:

- obtain an understanding of the entity's internal control over financial reporting for both annual and interim periods;
- perform procedures required by the attestation standards for reporting on the compilation of a forecast;
- issue a report on the compilation of prospective financial information and attach the report to the comfort letter; and
- perform additional procedures as requested by the requesting party and report the findings in the comfort letter.

The auditor should not provide negative assurance unless the auditor has performed an examination of the financial forecast in accordance with the attestation standards. If a financial forecast that the auditor has not examined is included in the securities offering, the auditor should not issue a comfort letter unless the financial forecast is accompanied by an indication that the auditor has not examined the financial forecast and, therefore, does not express an opinion on it.

3.3 Tables, Statistics, and Other Financial Information

The auditor should not comment unless the information is expressed in dollars (or percentages derived from dollar amounts) and has been obtained from accounting records that are subject to internal control over financial reporting, or has been derived directly from such accounting records by analysis or computation.

The auditor's comments should include a clear identification of the specific information commented on, a description of the procedures performed, and the findings, expressed in terms of agreement between items compared.

3.4 Subsequent Changes

The auditor should base comments regarding subsequent changes in specified financial statement items solely on the limited procedures performed with respect to the change period as determined by the requesting party.

The auditor should provide negative assurance in the comfort letter regarding subsequent changes in specified financial statement items only as of a date less than 135 days from the end of the most recent period for which the auditor has performed an audit or a review.

When the requesting party requests negative assurance regarding subsequent changes in specified financial statement items as of a date 135 days or more from the end of the most recent period for which the auditor has performed an audit or a review, the auditor is limited to reporting procedures performed and findings obtained.

The auditor should note in the comfort letter if there has been a change in the application of the requirements of the applicable financial reporting framework.

The auditor should comment only on the occurrence of subsequent changes in specified financial statement items that are not disclosed in the securities offering.

3.5 The Auditor Should Not Comment or Provide Assurance

The auditor should not comment or provide assurance on:

- Market risk sensitive instruments
- Qualitative disclosures
- Information subject to legal interpretation

Question 1 **MCQ-03424**

Which of the following statements is correct concerning letters for underwriters, commonly referred to as comfort letters?

a. Letters for underwriters are required by the Securities Act of 1933 for the initial public sale of registered securities.

b. Letters for underwriters typically give negative assurance on unaudited interim financial information.

c. Letters for underwriters usually are included in the registration statement accompanying a prospectus.

d. Letters for underwriters ordinarily update auditors' opinions on the prior year's financial statements.

NOTES

MODULE

8 The AICPA Code of Professional Conduct

AUD 6

1 Overview

The AICPA's Code of Professional Conduct governs any service that a member of the AICPA performs. These services include audits, special reports, compilations, reviews, and services performed on financial forecasts and projections, as well as attestation engagements. Members not in public practice are governed by certain requirements of the Code of Professional Conduct as well.

A professional code of conduct is a *distinguishing mark of a profession* that accepts a high degree of responsibility toward the public. It is a voluntary acceptance for the purpose of benefiting society. The AICPA Code of Professional Conduct addresses the question of what is "right" and "just." The code consists of principles and rules as well as *interpretations* and other guidance.

The code utilizes certain terms to enhance the clarity of the interpretations and definitions.

- **Consider:** Used when the member is required to think about several matters.
- **Evaluate:** Used when the member has to assess and weigh the significance of a matter.
- **Determine:** Used when the member has to come to a conclusion and make a decision on a matter.

The code is separated into three parts:

1. Members in public practice
2. Members in business
3. Other members

2 Principles

Principles provide the framework that is the basis for the code of conduct.

- **Responsibilities:** "In carrying out their responsibilities as professionals, members should exercise sensitive professional and moral judgments in all their activities."
- **Public Interest:** "Members should accept the obligation to act in a way that will serve the public interest, honor the public trust, and demonstrate commitment to professionalism." This relates to the profession's acceptance of responsibility to the public.
- **Integrity:** "To maintain and broaden public confidence, members should perform all professional responsibilities with the highest sense of integrity." Integrity addresses the question of what is right and just.
- **Objectivity and Independence:** "A member should maintain objectivity and be free of conflicts of interest in discharging professional responsibilities. A member in public practice should be *independent in fact and appearance* when providing auditing and other attestation services." (Emphasis added.)

Pass Key

For exam purposes, it is key to remember that objectivity applies to all services rendered; but independence applies to attest services only (audits, special reports, examinations, agreed-upon procedures, and reviews).

- **Due Care:** "A member should observe the profession's technical and ethical standards, strive continually to improve competence and the quality of services, and discharge professional responsibility to the best of the member's ability."
- **Scope and Nature of Services:** "A member in public practice should observe the Principles of the Code of Professional Conduct in determining the scope and nature of services to be provided."

This requires members to:

1. Have adequate internal quality control measures to ensure quality work;
2. Determine whether, for audit clients, conflicts of interest arise due to the scope and nature of other services; and
3. Assess whether the firm's activities are consistent with professionalism.

3 Rules

The "rules" portion of the code consists of rules, interpretations, and rulings that govern the specific performance of members. The rules that apply to members are based on whether they are a member in public practice, a member in business, and/or an other member.

Rules by Type of Member

	Member		
Rules	*Member in Public Practice*	*Member in Business*	*Other Member (i.e., retired or unemployed)*
Independence Rule	✓		
Integrity and Objectivity Rule	✓	✓	
General Standards Rule	✓	✓	
Compliance With Standards Rule	✓	✓	
Accounting Principles Rule	✓	✓	
Confidential Client Information Rule	✓		
Contingent Fees Rule	✓		
Acts Discreditable Rule	✓	✓	✓
Advertising and Other Forms of Solicitation Rule	✓		
Commissions and Referral Fees Rule	✓		
Form of Organization and Name Rule	✓		

3.1 Independence Rule

A member in public practice shall be independent in the performance of professional services as required by standards promulgated by bodies designated by the AICPA Council.

- Independence is *not required* for compilations and non-attestation services (e.g., tax services, consulting services).
- Independence must be maintained by "covered members."
- A covered member's spouse and dependents are also generally subject to the Independence Rule.
- A member must have independence of mind and in appearance.

Pass Key

A "covered member" is:

- An individual on the attest engagement team
- An individual in a position to influence the attest engagement
- A partner who provides more than 10 hours of non-attest services to the attest client within any fiscal year
- A partner in the office in which the lead attest engagement partner primarily practices in connection with the attest engagement
- The firm, including the firm's employee benefit plans
- An entity for which operating, financial, or accounting policies can be controlled by any of the individuals or entities described above

3.1.1 Independence Impaired by Financial Interests

- Independence is impaired if a covered member has a direct financial interest (regardless of materiality) or a material indirect financial interest in an attestation client.

Illustration 1 Financial Interests

Direct financial interests are ownership interests held directly in a client. Examples would include:

- Stock ownership, even if owned in a blind trust.
- Financial interest in a client through a partnership and the member is a general partner.
- Financial interest in a trust when the member is the trustee.

An indirect financial interest involves a removed relationship. Examples would include:

- Member owns shares in a mutual fund that invests in the attestation client.
- Member owns a direct financial interest in Company A, and Company A has a direct financial interest in the attestation client.

- Independence is impaired if a covered member or his immediate family (spouse or dependents) has a loan to or from a client.
- Independence is impaired by acceptance of more than a token gift.
- Independence is *not impaired* in a financial institution client by:
  - Fully collateralized car loans with a financial institution client.
  - Cash advance or credit card balances not exceeding $10,000.
  - A bank account that is fully insured by the government.
  - A passbook loan.
- Independence is impaired if a close relative has a financial interest in the attest client that the covered member knows or has reason to believe is material to the close relative or enabled the close relative to exercise significant influence over the attest client.

3.1.2 Independence Impaired by Employment Relationships

Independence may be impaired if a member was previously employed by the attest client, or if a member leaves the audit firm for a position with the client.

- Independence is impaired if an individual who was formerly employed by the client participates on the engagement team or is in a position to influence the engagement when the engagement covers any period of his or her former employment with the client.
- Independence is impaired by an immediate family member or close relative's employment with a client in a *key position* (e.g., independence would be impaired if the spouse was the client's internal auditor).
- Independence is impaired if a partner or professional employee leaves the firm and is employed by the client in a key position unless the individual is no longer in a position to influence or participate in the firm's business decisions and the amounts due to the individual are immaterial to the firm.
  - When the individual joins the client in a key position within one year of disassociating from the firm and has significant interaction with the engagement team, independence will be impaired unless the engagement is reviewed by a qualified professional to determine whether the engagement team members maintained the appropriate level of skepticism when evaluating the representations and work of the former firm member.
- Independence is impaired if an individual who is a member of the engagement team or is in a position to influence the engagement is seeking or discussing potential employment with the client or has been offered employment by the client unless the individual notifies the firm and is removed from the engagement.

3.1.3 Independence Impaired by Business Relationships

Independence is impaired if a member makes management decisions for an attest client.

Illustration 2 Business Relationships

Examples of business relationships with an attestation client that impair independence would include:

- Director, officer, employee, or a position where the member acts in a management capacity
- Promoter, underwriter, broker-dealer, or voting trustee
- Stock transfer or escrow agent
- General counsel
- Trustee for a client's pension or profit-sharing trust

- A firm may perform non-attest services for a client and still be independent as long as the firm does not serve or appear to serve as a member of a client's management (e.g., the firm may not make operational or financial decisions for the client, perform management functions, or report to the board on behalf of management).

Illustration 3 Activities That Impair Independence

Examples of activities with an attestation client that impair independence would include:

- Bookkeeping activities that include authorizing, executing, or consummating a transaction on behalf of a client or preparing source documents or originating data (e.g., purchase orders).
- Having custody of the client's assets.
- Supervising client employees in the performance of normal recurring activities.
- Financial information systems design and implementation.
- Appraisal, valuation, or actuarial services when the results are material to the financial statements and subject to a significant degree of subjectivity.
- Management of internal audit activities.
- Litigation services where the firm serves as a trier of fact, special master, court-appointed expert, or arbitrator.
- Expert witness services.

- Independence is not impaired by being a member of or an honorary trustee for a not-for-profit charitable, civic, or religious group if the position is purely honorary and the member does not participate in any management functions.
- Membership in the same trade association as a client does not impair independence unless the member serves in a management capacity.

3.1.4 Other Reasons Independence May Be Impaired

- A member's independence is impaired with respect to a client who is more than one year overdue in the payment of professional fees. Usually, fees from one year must be paid before the issuance of a report on the following year's work.
- Actual or threatened litigation may impair independence, regardless of who is the plaintiff and who is the defendant.
  - For example, independence is impaired if an auditor sues management for fraud or if the client sues the auditor for audit deficiencies. Even the threat of a suit for audit deficiencies would impair independence if it is likely the suit will be initiated.
  - Independence is *not impaired* by a suit for an immaterial dollar amount for work unrelated to an attestation service.

Pass Key

The most heavily tested area of the Code of Conduct and professional responsibilities is the Independence Rule. Candidates should be very familiar with the rules covered above.

3.2 Integrity and Objectivity Rule

The Code of Conduct states, "In the performance of any professional service, a member shall maintain objectivity and integrity, shall be free of conflicts of interest, and shall not knowingly misrepresent facts or subordinate his or her judgment to others."

A conflict of interest may occur if a member has a significant relationship with a client that could be viewed as impairing the member's objectivity. The service may still be performed if the relationship is disclosed and the consent of the client is obtained. Disclosure and consent cannot eliminate the necessity for independence when it is required.

Members engaged in educational services and client advocacy must act with integrity and objectivity.

3.3 General Standards Rule

A member must comply with the following standards in all engagements:

- **Professional Competence:** Undertake only those professional services that the member or the member's firm can reasonably be expected to complete with professional competence.

  Professional competence includes the technical qualifications of the CPA and of the CPA's staff, the ability to supervise and evaluate work, and the knowledge of technical subject matter or the ability to obtain that knowledge by research or by consulting with others.
- **Due Professional Care:** Exercise due professional care in the performance of professional services.
  - The member must possess the same degree of skill commonly possessed by others in the field.
  - The member must act as a reasonably prudent accountant would.
  - The member must critically review work done by those assisting in the engagement at every level of supervision.

- **Planning and Supervision:** Adequately plan and supervise the performance of professional services.
- **Sufficient Relevant Data:** Obtain sufficient relevant data to afford a reasonable basis for conclusions or recommendations in relation to any professional services performed.

3.4 Compliance With Standards Rule

A member who performs auditing, review, compilation, management consulting, tax, or other professional services must comply with standards promulgated by bodies designated by the AICPA Council.

- Auditing Standards Board and PCAOB (issue statements on auditing standards).
- Management Consulting Services Executive Committee (issues statements on standards for management consulting services).
- Accounting and Review Services Committee (issues statements on standards for accounting and review services).
- Government Accounting Standards Board (issues statements of governmental accounting standards).
- Tax Executive Committee (issues statements on tax services).
- Attestation Standards (issue statements for attestation standards).
- Financial Accounting Standards Board (establishes standards for U.S. financial accounting and reporting).
- International Accounting Standards Board (establishes standards for international financial accounting and reporting).
- Personal Financial Planning Executive Committee (issue standards on personal financial planning).

3.5 Accounting Principles Rule

A member shall not express an opinion or state affirmatively or negatively that financial statements are presented in conformity with generally accepted accounting principles (GAAP) if there is any departure from an accounting principle that has a material effect on the financial statements.

Unusual circumstances may justify a departure from GAAP if compliance would cause the financial statements to be misleading.

- Interpretations of the code specifically recognize *new legislation and new forms of business transactions* as occasions that might justify a departure from GAAP.
- An unusual degree of materiality or the existence of conflicting industry practices would not justify departure from GAAP.
- The departure, when justified, must be described and explained.

3.6 Confidential Client Information Rule

A member in public practice shall not disclose any confidential client information without the specific consent of the client.

3.6.1 Exceptions

A member is obligated to disclose confidential information even without the consent of the client in the following circumstances:

1. A member must disclose confidential client information if necessary to comply with a validly issued subpoena or summons.
   - The member is not required to notify the client that its records have been subpoenaed or that a summons related to the client's records has been issued. The member may wish to consult with legal counsel to determine the validity and enforceability of the subpoena or summons and the specific client information required to be provided. The member may also wish to consult with his or her state board of accountancy.
2. A member must disclose confidential information as a part of a quality review of the member's professional practices authorized by the AICPA (i.e., a request for confidential information by a state CPA society voluntary quality control review panel).
3. A member must disclose confidential client information in response to any inquiry either made by the ethics division or the trial board of the AICPA or by a duly constituted investigative or disciplinary body of a state CPA society, or under authority of state statutes.

Pass Key

The examiners often ask to whom a CPA may disclose client audit documentation without consent of the client. Memorize the above paragraphs and you will have no problem with such a question on your exam.

3.7 Contingent Fees Rule

A contingent fee is established for performing services when:

1. No fee is charged unless a specific finding or result is obtained; or
2. The fee amount is dependent upon the finding or result obtained.

Contingent fees are specifically prohibited for audits and reviews of financial statements or examinations of prospective financial information. In addition, a member in public practice is prohibited from preparing an original or amended tax return or claim for a tax refund for a contingent fee for any client.

Contingent fees are permitted in the following cases:

- Fees are not regarded as being contingent when they are fixed by courts or other public authorities or in tax matters, if they are based on the results of court proceedings or the findings of governmental agencies (e.g., a contingent fee is permitted when representing a client in an examination of a tax return by an IRS agent).
- Contingent fees are permitted for compilations of financial statements expected to be used by third parties only if the member includes a statement that the member is not independent.

3.8 Acts Discreditable Rule

A member shall not commit an act discreditable to the profession.

The following acts are discreditable to the profession:

- Failure to return records to a client after the client makes demand.
- Determination by a court or administrative agency of discrimination or harassment in public practice.
- Failing to follow applicable standards or procedures in government audits unless the member discloses that the standards were not followed and the reasons for noncompliance.
- Negligence in preparing financial statements or records.
- Failing to follow GAAS and other applicable standards of government agencies unless the member discloses that the standards were not followed and the reasons for noncompliance.
- Solicitation or disclosure of CPA Examination questions and answers.
- Failure to timely file a personal or firm tax return or to timely remit payroll or other taxes collected on behalf of others.
- Failure to follow regulatory requirements (where applicable) prohibiting the use of certain types of indemnification and limitation of liability provisions.
- Promotion or marketing of the member's abilities to provide professional services or making claims about the member's experience or qualifications in a manner that is false, misleading, or deceptive. This includes any representation about CPA licensure or any other professional certification or accreditation that is not in compliance with the requirements of the relevant licensing authority or designating body.
- A member whose employment relationship is terminated shall not take or retain (a) originals or copies (in any format) from the firm's client files; or (b) proprietary information without the firm's permission unless the member has a contractual arrangement with the firm allowing such action.
- Disclosure of confidential information obtained from a prospective client or non-client without consent.

3.9 Advertising and Other Forms of Solicitation Rule

A member in public practice shall not seek to obtain clients by advertising or other forms of solicitation in a manner that is false, misleading, or deceptive.

Advertisements and solicitations are misleading or deceptive if they:

- Create false or unjustified expectations of favorable results.
- Imply the ability to influence a court, regulatory agent, or official.
- Intentionally underestimate fees.
- Would mislead or deceive a reasonable person.

3.10 Commissions and Referral Fees Rule

A member in public practice shall not for a commission recommend or refer to a client any product or service when the member or the member's firm also performs for that client:

- An audit or review of financial statements.
- A compilation of financial statements expected to be used by third parties, when the member does not disclose a lack of independence.
- An examination of prospective financial information.

A member performing other services not prohibited above may receive a commission, but the commission must be disclosed to the client.

A member who receives a referral fee for recommending another CPA or pays a referral fee to obtain a client must disclose this to the client.

3.11 Form of Organization and Name Rule

3.11.1 The Use of Misleading Firm Names Is Not Allowed

- A firm may not designate itself as "Members of the American Institute of Certified Public Accountants" unless all of its CPA owners are members of the Institute.
- A firm may not designate itself as "CPAs" unless all of its owners are CPAs.
- The ideal designation following the firm name would be "CPAs, Members AICPA," if all owners were both CPAs and members of the AICPA.
- A firm may continue to use the names of one or more past owners.
- If all partners except one have died or left the firm, the remaining partner may continue to practice under the partnership name for up to two years after becoming a sole practitioner.

3.11.2 Ownership of CPA Firms

- **CPA Ownership:** A majority of the ownership, both in financial interests and in voting rights, must belong to CPAs. Any non-CPA owner must be actively engaged as a firm member in providing services to the firm's clients.

  A CPA must have ultimate responsibility for all services provided by the firm and by each business unit providing attest and compilation services and other services governed by Statements on Auditing Standards (SAS) or Statements on Standards for Accounting and Review Services (SSARS).

- **Non-CPA Owners:** Non-CPA owners can use the title, "principal," "owner," "officer," "member," "shareholder," or any other title permitted by state law, but not hold themselves out to be CPAs.

  Owners shall own their equity in their own right and be the beneficial owners of the equity capital ascribed to them.

3.11.3 Use of CPA Title in Private Industry

A CPA employee in private industry may use the designation CPA in signing a report only if the use of that designation does not imply to readers of the report that the CPA is independent.

It is advisable to indicate one's own employment title within the private firm.

4 Conceptual Framework

4.1 Background

The AICPA Code of Professional Conduct includes principles, rules, and interpretations. The conceptual frameworks are applied when none of the other three components provide adequate guidance or in a situation in which there is a threat or threats to complying with the rules.

Pass Key

The rules and interpretations portion of the AICPA Code of Professional Conduct seek to address many situations; however, they cannot address all relationships or circumstances that may arise. Thus, in the absence of an interpretation that addresses a particular relationship or circumstance, a member should apply the appropriate conceptual framework approach. The conceptual framework cannot be used to override any rules stated in the code.

There are three conceptual frameworks included in the AICPA Code of Professional Conduct:

1. **Conceptual Framework for Members in Public Practice**

   Members in public practice render attest, tax, and management advisory services.

2. **Conceptual Framework for Independence**

   Members in public practice are required to apply the Conceptual Framework Approach for Independence when faced with threats to independence.

3. **Conceptual Framework for Members in Business**

   Members in business are employed or engaged on a contractual or volunteer basis in a(n) executive, staff, governance, advisory, or administrative capacity in such areas as industry, the public sector, education, the not-for-profit sector, and regulatory or professional bodies (e.g., controller). This does not include a member engaged in public practice.

A member may have multiple roles, such as a member in business and a member in public practice. In such circumstances, the member should consult all applicable parts of the code and apply the most restrictive provisions.

The conceptual framework approach requires entities to:

- Identify threats to compliance with the fundamental principles listed above.
- Evaluate the significance of the threat.
- Apply safeguards to eliminate threats or reduce threats to an acceptable level, whenever possible.

  The acceptable level is the level at which a reasonable and informed third party who is aware of the relevant information would be expected to conclude that a member's compliance with the rules is not compromised.

4.2 Threats to Compliance With the Fundamental Principles

Threats to compliance with the fundamental principles may fall into one or more threat categories, as shown in the table below.

(The threat categories are virtually the same among the conceptual frameworks. Generally, the difference in definition is that threats related to members in public practice reference the *client,* threats to members in business reference the *employing organization,* and threats to independence reference the *attest client*. Where slight differences exist, the wording is italicized.)

Conceptual Framework For:			
	Members in Public Practice	*Members in Business*	*Independence*
Adverse Interest threat	The threat that a member will not act with objectivity because the member's interests are opposed to the *client's interests*.	The threat that a member will not act with objectivity because the member's interests are opposed to the interests of the *employing organization*.	The threat that a member will not act with objectivity because the member's interests are in opposition to the interests of an *attest client*.
Advocacy Threat	The threat that a member will promote a *client's* interests or position to the point that his or her *objectivity or independence* is compromised.	The threat that a member will promote an *employing organization's* interests or position to the point that his or her *objectivity* is compromised.	The threat that a member will promote an *attest client's* interests or position to the point that his or her *independence* is compromised.
Familiarity Threat	The threat that, because of a long or close relationship with a *client*, a member will become too sympathetic to the *client's interests* or too accepting of the *client's work* or product.	The threat that, because of a long or close relationship with *a person or an employing organization*, a member will become too sympathetic to their interests or too accepting of the *person's work or employing organization's* product or *service*.	The threat that, because of a long or close relationship with an *attest* client, a member will become too sympathetic to the *attest client's* interests or too accepting of the *attest client's work* or product.
Management Participation Threat	The threat that a member will take on the role of *client* management or otherwise assume management responsibilities; *such may occur during an engagement to provide non-attest services*.	N/A	The threat that a member will take on the role of *attest* client management or otherwise assume management responsibilities for an *attest* client.
Self-Interest Threat	The threat that a member could benefit, financially or otherwise, from an interest in, or relationship with, *a client* or persons associated with the *client*.	The threat that a member could benefit, financially or otherwise, from an interest in, or relationship with, the *employing organization* or persons associated with the *employing organization*.	The threat that a member could benefit, financially or otherwise, from an interest in, or relationship with, an *attest client* or persons associated with the *attest client*.

	Members in Public Practice	*Members in Business*	*Independence*
Self-Review Threat	The threat that a member will not appropriately evaluate the results of a previous judgment made or service performed or supervised by the member or an individual in the *member's firm* and that the member will rely on that service in forming a judgment as part of *another service*.	The threat that a member will not appropriately evaluate the results of a previous judgment made or service performed or supervised by the member, or an individual in the *employing organization* and that the member will rely on that service in forming a judgment as part of *another service*.	The threat that a member will not appropriately evaluate the results of a previous judgment made, or service performed or supervised by the member or an individual in *the member's firm* and that the member will rely on that service in forming a judgment as part of an *attest engagement*.
Undue Influence Threat	The threat that a member will subordinate his or her judgment to an individual associated with *a client* or any relevant third party due to that individual's reputation or expertise, aggressive or dominant personality, or attempts to coerce or exercise excessive influence over the member.	The threat that a member will subordinate his or her judgment to that of an individual associated with *the employing organization* or any relevant third party due to that individual's position, reputation or expertise, aggressive or dominant personality, or attempts to coerce or exercise excessive influence over the member.	The threat that a member will subordinate his or her judgment to that of an individual associated with *an attest client* or any relevant third party due to that individual's reputation or expertise, aggressive or dominant personality, or attempts to coerce or exercise excessive influence over the member.

4.3 Evaluate the Significance of the Threat

In evaluating the significance of an identified threat, the member should determine whether a threat is at an acceptable level. Members should consider both qualitative and quantitative factors when evaluating the significance of a threat, including the extent to which existing safeguards already reduce the threat to an acceptable level.

If the member evaluates the threat and concludes that a reasonable and informed third party who is aware of the relevant information would be expected to conclude that the threat does not compromise a member's compliance with the rules, the threat is at an acceptable level, and the member is not required to evaluate the threat any further under the conceptual framework approach.

4.4 Safeguards That May Eliminate or Reduce Threats

If, in evaluating the significance of an identified threat, the member concludes that the threat is not at an acceptable level, the member should apply safeguards to eliminate the threat or reduce it to an acceptable level, if possible.

Safeguards fall into one of the following categories for the conceptual framework for members in public practice and conceptual framework for independence:

1. Safeguards created by the profession, legislation, or regulation.
2. Safeguards implemented by the client: It is not possible to rely solely on safeguards implemented by the client to eliminate or reduce significant threats to an acceptable level.
3. Safeguards implemented by the firm: This includes policies and procedures to implement professional and regulatory requirements.

Safeguards fall into one of the following categories for the conceptual framework for members in business:

1. Safeguards created by the profession, legislation, or regulation.
2. Safeguards implemented by the employing organization.

Illustration 4 Threats

Example of **adverse interest threat** includes:

- The member or *client/attest client/employing organization* commences litigation against the other or expressing the intent to commence litigation.

Examples of **advocacy threat** include:

- A member endorses a *client's* services or products.
- The member gives or fails to give information that the member knows will unduly influence the conclusions reached by an external service provider or other third party.
- A member promotes the *attest client's* securities as part of an initial public offering.

Examples of **familiarity threat** include:

- A member has a close friend who is employed by the *client/attest client*.
- A member regularly accepts gifts or entertainment from a vendor or customer of the *employing organization*.

Examples of **management participation threat** include:

- A member serves as an officer or a director of the *attest client*.
- A member accepts responsibility for designing, implementing, or maintaining internal controls for the *attest client*.

Examples of **self-interest threat** include:

- A member or his or her firm relies excessively on revenue from a single *client/attest client*.
- A member is eligible for a profit or other performance-related bonus at the *employing organization*, and the value of that bonus is directly affected by the member's decisions.

Examples of **self-review threat** include:

- The member performs bookkeeping services for a *client*.
- When the member performs an internal audit procedure at the *employing organization*, the member reviews work that he or she previously performed in a different position.

Examples of **undue influence threat** include:

- The client indicates that it will not award additional engagements to the firm if the firm continues to disagree with the *client* on an accounting or tax matter.
- A member is pressured to become associated with misleading information.
- The *attest client's* management pressures the member to reduce necessary audit procedures in order to reduce audit fees.

Illustration 5 Safeguards

Examples of safeguards **created by the profession, legislation, or regulation**:

- Education and training requirements on ethics, independence, and/or professional responsibilities.
- Continuing education requirements on independence and/or ethics.
- Professional standards and the threat of discipline.
- Legislation establishing prohibitions and requirements for employees.
- Competency and experience requirements for professional licensure.
- Professional resources, such as hot lines, for consultation on ethical issues.

Examples of safeguards **implemented by the client** that would operate in combination with other safeguards are as follows:

- The client has personnel with suitable skill, knowledge, or experience who make managerial decisions about the delivery of professional services and makes use of third-party resources for consultation as needed.
- The tone at the top emphasizes the client's commitment to fair financial reporting and compliance with the applicable laws, rules, regulations, and corporate governance policies.
- A governance structure, such as an active audit committee, is in place to ensure appropriate decision making, oversight, and communications regarding a firm's services.

Examples of safeguards **implemented by the firm:**

- Documented policies regarding the identification of threats to compliance with the rules, the evaluation of the significance of those threats, and the identification and application of safeguards that can eliminate identified threats or reduce them to an acceptable level.
- Discussion of independence and ethics issues with the audit committee or others responsible for the client's governance.
- The removal of an individual from an attest engagement team when that individual's financial interests or relationships pose a threat to independence or objectivity.
- Client acceptance and continuation policies that are designed to prevent association with clients that pose a threat that is not at an acceptable level to the member's compliance with the rules.
- Policies and procedures that are designed to monitor the firm's, partner's, or partner equivalent's reliance on revenue from a single client and that, if necessary, trigger action to address excessive reliance.

Examples of safeguards **implemented by the employing organization** are as follows:

- A tone at the top emphasizing a commitment to fair financial reporting and compliance with applicable laws, rules, regulations, and corporate governance policies.
- An audit committee charter, including independent audit committee members.
- Internal policies and procedures requiring disclosure of identified interests or relationships among the employing organization, its directors or officers, and vendors, suppliers, or customers.
- Human resource policies and procedures stressing the hiring and retention of technically competent employees.

Question 1	MCQ-01499

According to the standards of the profession, which of the following circumstances will prevent a CPA who is performing audit engagements from being independent?

- **a.** Obtaining a collateralized automobile loan from a financial institution client.
- **b.** Litigation with a client relating to billing for consulting services for which the amount is immaterial.
- **c.** Employment of the CPA's spouse as a client's internal auditor.
- **d.** Acting as an honorary trustee for a not-for-profit organization client.

Question 2	MCQ-01486

According to the ethical standards of the profession, which of the following acts by a CPA is generally prohibited?

- **a.** Purchasing a product from a third party and reselling it to a client.
- **b.** Writing a financial management newsletter promoted and sold by a publishing company.
- **c.** Accepting a commission for recommending a product to an audit client.
- **d.** Accepting engagements obtained through the efforts of third parties.

Question 3	MCQ-05805

Which of the following actions by a CPA most likely violates the profession's ethical standards?

- **a.** Using a records-retention agency to store confidential client records.
- **b.** Retaining client records after the client has demanded their return.
- **c.** Arranging with a financial institution to collect notes issued by a client in payment of fees due.
- **d.** Compiling the financial statements of a client that employed the CPA's spouse as a bookkeeper.

MODULE

9 Ethical Requirements of the SEC and PCAOB

AUD 6

1 The Sarbanes-Oxley Act of 2002

In the wake of the collapse of Enron and WorldCom corporations and the restatement of financial statements of a number of other SEC reporting companies, Congress passed the Sarbanes-Oxley Act (SOX), which created the Public Company Accounting Oversight Board (PCAOB).

1.1 SOX Title I: Public Company Accounting Oversight Board (PCAOB)

Title I of the Sarbanes-Oxley Act provides for a Public Company Accounting Oversight Board composed of five members. Two members must be CPAs and three members cannot be CPAs.

The board is subject to oversight by the SEC and has the duty to:

1. register public accounting firms that prepare audit reports for issuers;
2. establish rules relating to the preparation of audit reports for issuers; and
3. conduct inspections, investigations, and disciplinary proceedings concerning registered public accounting firms.

Pass Key

The PCAOB must conduct annual inspections of registered public accounting firms that regularly provide audit reports for more than 100 issuers. Registered public accounting firms that provide audit reports for 100 or fewer issuers must be inspected at least once every three years.

1.1.1 Registration With PCAOB: Only Registered Firms Can Audit an SEC Issuer

Only a "registered public accounting firm" (i.e., an accounting firm registered with the PCAOB) may prepare audit reports for an SEC issuer.

The application for registration must be updated annually and contain:

1. The names of issuers audited in the preceding and current year, including annual fees received for such audits;
2. A statement of the firm's quality control policies;
3. A list of all firm accountants who will participate in the audits;
4. Legal or disciplinary proceedings pending against the firm; and
5. Disclosures filed by audited issuers concerning accounting disagreements between the issuer and the firm related to audits.

Each registered firm must consent to cooperate with any request from the Oversight Board concerning testimony or production of documents.

1.1.2 Each Registered Firm Must Adhere to the Following Auditing Standards

- Audit documentation must be maintained for seven years (criminal penalties will apply for failure to retain papers for at least seven years);
- Provide a concurring or second partner review of each audit report; and
- Describe in audit reports the scope of the testing of the issuer's internal control structure and procedures.

1.1.3 Quality Control Standards Required of Registered Firms

Registered accounting firms must monitor professional ethics and independence from issuers that they audit and must supervise audit work.

1.1.4 Investigations and Sanctions

The board can conduct investigations of wrongdoing by registered firms or associated persons of those firms. If a firm or associated person is found to have violated the provisions of the Sarbanes-Oxley Act, the rules of the PCAOB, or the provisions of securities laws relating to the preparation and issuance of audit reports, the PCAOB can impose the following sanctions:

- temporary suspension or permanent revocation of PCAOB registration;
- temporary or permanent suspension or bar of a person from associating with a registered firm;
- temporary or permanent limitation on the activities, functions or operations of a firm or person;
- civil monetary penalties of no more than $750,000 for individuals and $15,000,000 for registered firms for intentional or knowing conduct, including reckless conduct, that results in violations or repeated instances of negligent conduct; and penalties of no more than $100,000 for individuals and $2,000,000 for registered firms for other violations;
- censure;
- require professional education or training; and
- any other PCAOB approved sanction.

1.2 SOX Title II: Auditor Independence

1.2.1 Prohibited Services

In order to maintain auditor independence, a registered public accounting firm that performs SEC audits may not provide the following services to the audit client:

- Bookkeeping;
- Financial information systems design and implementation;
- Appraisal and valuation services;
- Actuarial services;
- Management functions or human resources services;
- Internal audit outsourcing services;
- Services as a broker, dealer, investment adviser, or investment banker;
- Legal services; or
- Expert services unrelated to the audit.

Tax services are permissible if preapproved by the audit committee.

1.2.2 Audit Partner Requirements

The lead audit or coordinating partner and the reviewing partner must rotate off the audit every five years. Under new PCAOB rules, auditors of issuers must also disclose the name of the engagement partner.

1.2.3 Registered Firms Must Report to Audit Committees

All auditing services and permitted non-audit services provided by an auditor to an issuer should be preapproved by the audit committee of the issuer.

Registered firms must report the following to the audit committees of audited corporations:

1. The critical accounting policies and practices to be used;
2. Alternative accounting treatments discussed with the corporation's management, the ramifications of the alternatives, and the treatment the firm prefers; and
3. Material written communications between the audit firm and management, including a schedule of unadjusted audit differences and any management letter.

1.2.4 Conflicts of Interest

The audit firm cannot have employed the issuer's CEO, CFO, controller, chief accounting officer, or any person serving in an equivalent position for a one-year period preceding the audit.

1.3 SOX Title III, Section 303: Improper Influence on Conduct of Audits

It is unlawful for any officer or director of an issuer, or any person acting under the direction of an officer or director, to take any action to fraudulently influence, coerce, manipulate, or mislead any independent CPA engaged in the performance of an audit of the financial statements of the issuer for the purpose of rendering such financial statements materially misleading.

2 Independence Requirements of the SEC

Rule 2-01 of the U.S. Securities and Exchange Commission (SEC) Regulation S-X outlines the independence rules that apply to the auditors of SEC registrants. The SOX independence rules have been incorporated into these rules.

2.1 Principles of Independence

When considering whether a circumstance raises independence concerns, the SEC looks to whether a client relationship or a service provided to an audit client:

- Creates a mutual or conflicting interest between the auditor and client.
- Results in the auditor acting as management or an employee of the audit client.
- Places the auditor in a position of auditing his or her own work.
- Places the auditor in a position of being an advocate for the audit client.

2.2 Circumstances That Impair Auditor Independence

Rule 2-01 states that an accountant is not independent with respect to an audit client if the accountant is not, or a reasonable, knowledgeable investor would conclude that the accountant is not, capable of exercising objective and impartial judgment on all issues related to the accountant's engagement. The following is a non-exhaustive list of circumstances that impair auditor independence.

2.2.1 Financial Relationships

- **Investments in Audit Clients:** All direct investments and material indirect investments in audit clients by the firm, any covered person in the firm, or any member of his or her immediate family impair auditor independence. Such investments include:
  - Direct investments in stocks, bonds, notes, options, or other securities of the audit client, including direct investments held through an intermediary.
  - Beneficial ownership of more than 5 percent of an audit client's equity securities.
  - Service as a voting trustee of a trust or executor of an estate containing securities of the audit client, unless there is no authority to make investment decisions for the trust or estate.
  - Material indirect investment in the audit client.

Pass Key

Under SEC rules, covered persons include the audit engagement team; the audit chain of command, which includes all persons who supervise or have direct management responsibility for the audit, all persons who evaluate the performance or recommend the compensation of the audit engagement partner, and all persons who provide quality control or other oversight of the audit; any other partner, principal, shareholder, or managerial employee of the firm who provided 10 or more hours of non-audit services to the audit client or expects to provide 10 or more hours of non-audit services to the client on a recurring basis; and any other partner, principal, or shareholder from an office of the accounting firm in which the lead audit engagement partner primarily practices in connection with the audit.

- **Other Financial Interests in Audit Clients:** The following financial interests in the audit client by the firm, any covered person in the firm, or any member of his or her immediate family impair auditor independence:
  - Loans to or from an audit client, or an audit client's officers, directors, or beneficial owners of more than 10 percent of the audit client's equity securities.
    - —This rule excludes loans obtained from financial institutions under normal lending circumstances, such as automobile loans or leases, loans fully collateralized by the cash surrender value of life insurance, loans fully collateralized by cash deposits at the financial institution, and mortgage loans on a primary residence obtained before the covered person was a covered person.
  - Savings and checking account balances that exceed the amount insured by the FDIC.
  - Broker-dealer accounts if the account includes assets other than cash or securities, or the amount in the account exceeds the insured amount.
  - Futures commission merchant accounts.
  - Credit card balances in excess of $10,000.
  - Insurance products issued by an audit client.
  - Financial interest in an investment company complex that includes an audit client.

- **Exceptions:** Investments or other financial interests in an audit client will not impair independence in the following circumstances:
  - The financial interest is received through an unsolicited gift or inheritance and is disposed of as soon as practicable, no later than 30 days after the person has knowledge of and the right to dispose of the financial interest.
  - In a new audit engagement, any person with a financial interest that would impair auditor independence disposes of the financial interest before the earlier of: 1) the signing of the initial engagement letter or other agreement to provide services; or 2) the commencement of any audit, review, or attestation services.
  - An immediate family member of a covered person has a financial interest that would impair independence as an unavoidable consequence of participation in his or her employer's employee compensation or benefits program and the financial interest is disposed of as soon as practicable, no later than 30 days after the person has knowledge of and the right to dispose of the financial interest.
- **Audit Clients' Financial Interests:** The following financial relationships of the audit client impair auditor independence:
  - Investment by the audit client in the accounting firm.
  - Engagement of the accounting firm by the audit client to act as an underwriter, broker-dealer, market-maker, promoter, or analyst.

2.2.2 Employment Relationships

Employment relationships between the accountant and the audit client during the engagement period that impair auditor independence include:

- Employment of a covered person by the audit client or service on the board of directors or other management or governing body of the audit client.
- Employment of a close family member of a covered person in an accounting or financial reporting role at the audit client.
- Employment at the audit client of a former member of the audit engagement team in an accounting role or a financial oversight role, unless the individual:
  1. does not influence the accounting firm's operations or financial policies;
  2. has no capital balances in the accounting firm; and
  3. has no financial arrangement with the accounting firm, other than one providing for regular payment of a fixed dollar amount (not dependent on the firm's revenues, profits, or earnings) that is either:
     —from a fully funded retirement plan or similar vehicle; or
     —immaterial to the former professional employee (only in the case of a former employee who was not a partner, principal, or shareholder and who has been disassociated from the firm for more than five years).
- Employment at the audit client of a former member of the audit engagement team in a financial oversight role, if the individual was a member of the engagement team during the one-year period preceding the commencement of audit procedures (the "cooling-off" period).
- Employment at the accounting firm of a former employee of the audit client, unless the individual does not participate in and is not in a position to influence, the financial statement audit of the audit client covering any period in which the individual was employed by or associated with the audit client.

Pass Key

SEC and SOX rules prohibit an accounting firm from auditing an issuer's financial statements if certain members of management of the issuer (members in financial oversight roles such as the CEO, CFO, or controller) had been members of the accounting firm's audit engagement team within the one-year period preceding the commencement of audit procedures (the required "cooling-off" period). The audit engagement team includes the lead partner, the concurring partner, and other individuals who provided more than 10 hours of service during the annual audit period.

2.2.3 Business Relationships

Direct or material indirect business relationships between the firm or any covered person in the firm and an audit client or persons participating in decision making for an audit client (officers, directors, substantial stockholders) impair auditor independence.

2.2.4 Non-audit Services

Auditor independence is impaired if any of the following *non-audit services* are provided during the audit and professional engagement period:

- Bookkeeping or other services related to the accounting records or financial statements of the audit client
- Financial information systems design and implementation
- Appraisal or valuation services, fairness opinions, or contribution-in-kind reports
- Actuarial services
- Internal audit outsourcing services
- Management functions or human resources
- Broker or dealer, investment adviser, or investment banking services
- Legal services (including representing an audit client before a tax court, district court, or federal court of claims)
- Expert services unrelated to the audit

2.2.5 Contingent Fees

Independence is impaired by contingent fee or commission arrangements in which the accountant provides any service or product to the audit client for a contingent fee or a commission, or receives a contingent fee or commission from an audit client.

2.2.6 Partner Rotation

Failure of the lead audit partner and the concurring partner on the audit engagement team to rotate off the audit engagement after five years or failure of other audit partners to rotate off the audit engagement after no more than seven years impairs independence. (Other audit partners include partners who have responsibility for decision making on significant auditing, accounting, or reporting matters, or who maintain regular contact with management and the audit committee of the client.)

- **Required "Time-Out" Period:** Lead partners and concurring partners are subject to a five-year "time-out" period before returning to an engagement. Other audit partners are subject to a two-year "time-out" period.

- **Small Firms:** Small accounting firms with fewer than five clients who are issuers and have fewer than 10 partners may be exempted from the partner rotation requirement.

2.2.7 Audit Committee Administration of the Engagement

Auditor independence is impaired when the audit committee fails to administer the engagement. Audit committees are required to preapprove all audit, review, or attest engagements and all permissible non-audit services, including tax compliance, tax planning, and tax advice either on a case-by-case basis or pursuant to preestablished policies and procedures.

- **Preapproval Not Required:** *Preapproval is not required* for non-audit services that do not exceed 5 percent of total revenues from the audit client during the fiscal year when services are provided, as long as the non-audit services are promptly brought to the attention of the audit committee and approved before the completion of the audit.
- **Required Auditor Reporting to the Audit Committee:** The auditor of an issuer's financial statements is required to report certain matters to the issuer's audit committee, including:
  - Critical accounting principles and practices used;
  - Alternative accounting treatments discussed with management, the ramifications of the use of the alternatives, and the treatment preferred by the audit firm;
  - Material written communications between the audit firm and management, including the management letter and the schedule of unadjusted audit differences.

2.2.8 Compensation

Auditor independence is impaired if an audit partner earns or receives compensation based on selling engagements to an audit client for services other than audit, review, and attest services. Audit partners include the lead audit partner, the concurring audit partner, and other audit partners who have responsibility for decision making on significant auditing, accounting, or reporting matters, or who maintain regular contact with management and the audit committee of the client.

3 Independence Requirements of the PCAOB

The PCAOB has adopted Rules 101 (Independence) and 102 (Integrity and Objectivity) from the AICPA Code of Professional Conduct on an interim basis.

3.1 PCAOB Independence Standards

In addition to the interim independence standards, the PCAOB's independence standards include the independence rules outlined in SOX and the SEC independence rules outlined above. The PCAOB has also issued the following independence standards. The collective PCAOB standards apply to all audits of issuers by registered firms.

- **Responsibility Not to Knowingly or Recklessly Contribute to Violations:** A person associated with a registered public accounting firm should not take or omit to take an action knowing, or recklessly not knowing, that the action or omission would contribute to a violation by the registered public accounting firm of the Sarbanes-Oxley Act, the rules of the PCAOB, securities laws, rules of the SEC, or professional standards.
- **Auditor Independence:** A registered public accounting firm and its associated persons must be independent of the firm's audit client throughout the audit and professional engagement period.
- **Contingent Fees:** A registered public accounting firm may not provide services or products for a contingent fee (i.e., those in which the amount of the fee is dependent upon the results of the services performed) or a commission, or receive from the audit client a contingent fee or commission.

- **Tax Transactions:** Registered public accounting firms may not provide to audit clients any tax services related to certain confidential or aggressive tax transactions.
- **Tax Services for Persons in Financial Reporting Oversight Roles:** Registered public accounting firms may not provide any tax services to corporate officers of audit clients or to immediate family members of corporate officers.
- **Audit Committee Preapproval of Certain Tax Services:** Proposed tax services and related fees must be communicated to the audit committee in writing. The potential effects of the services on the firm's independence should also be discussed with the audit committee, and this discussion must be documented.
- **Audit Committee Preapproval of Non-audit Services Related to Internal Control Over Financial Reporting:** Non-audit services related to internal control over financial reporting must be communicated to the audit committee in writing. The potential effects of the services on the firm's independence should also be discussed with the audit committee, and this discussion must be documented.
- **Communication With the Audit Committee Concerning Independence:** Before accepting an initial engagement with an issuer and at least annually for each issuer audit client, a registered public accounting firm must describe in writing to the audit committee of the issuer all relationships that may reasonably be thought to bear on independence, discuss the potential effects of those relationships on the audit firm's independence, and document the discussion. As part of the annual communication, the audit firm must affirm, in writing, that the audit firm is independent as of the date of the communication.

Question 1 **MCQ-06110**

Under the ethical standards of the profession in the United States, which of the following circumstances would impair independence in the audit of an issuer but would not impair independence in the audit of a nonissuer?

both and N **a.** The firm performing the financial statement audit also designed and implemented the client's financial information system.

both and N **b.** The audit firm provided a loan to the client during the prior year.

c. The lead partner has worked on the audit engagement of a client for 10 years. 5 yrs

both and N **d.** The audit firm has an immaterial direct financial interest in the client.

MODULE

10 Ethical Requirements of the GAO and DOL

AUD 6

1 The Government Accountability Office (GAO)

The U.S. Government Accountability Office (GAO), along with issuing Generally Accepted Government Auditing Standards (GAGAS), includes the following ethical principles and general standards:

1.1 Ethical Principles

The ethical principles of GAGAS provide the foundation that influences the application of GAGAS. The ethical principles that guide the work of auditors who conduct audits in accordance with GAGAS are serving the public interest, integrity, objectivity, proper use of governmental information, resources and positions, and professional behavior.

- **Serving the Public Interest:** The public interest is defined as the collective well-being of the community of people and entities served by the auditor.
- **Integrity:** Integrity includes auditors conducting their work with an attitude that is objective, fact-based, nonpartisan, and nonideological with regard to the audited entities and users of the auditors' reports.
- **Objectivity:** Objectivity includes independence of mind and appearance when providing audits, maintaining an attitude of impartiality, having intellectual honesty, and being free of conflicts of interest.
- **Proper Use of Government Information, Resources, and Positions:** The auditor is to use government information, resources, and positions for official purposes and not inappropriately for the auditor's personal gain.
- **Professional Behavior:** Professional behavior includes an auditor's honest effort in the performance of professional services in accordance with the relevant technical and professional standards. The auditor must avoid any conduct that might bring discredit to the auditor's work, including actions that would cause an objective third party to conclude that the auditor's work was professionally deficient.

1.2 General Standards

The general standards provide guidance for performing financial audits, attestation engagements, and performance audits under GAGAS. The general standards address independence, professional judgment, competence, and quality control and assurance.

1.2.1 Independence

Independence includes the concepts of independence of mind and appearance. GAGAS provides a conceptual framework (described in greater detail below) to evaluate and respond to threats to independence.

- **Independence of Mind:** An auditor's state of mind should permit the performance of an audit without being affected by influences that compromise professional judgment.
- **Independence in Appearance:** Auditors should avoid circumstances that would cause a reasonable third party to conclude that independence has been compromised.

1.2.2 Professional Judgment

Auditors must use professional judgment in planning and performing audits and in reporting the results. Professional judgment includes exercising reasonable care and professional skepticism.

1.2.3 Competence

The staff assigned to conduct the audit in accordance with GAGAS must collectively possess:

- The adequate professional competence needed to address the audit objectives and perform the work in accordance with GAGAS.
- The technical knowledge, skills, and experience necessary to be competent for the type of work being performed before beginning work on the audit.

1.2.4 Quality Control and Assurance

Each audit organization performing audits in accordance with GAGAS must:

- Establish and maintain a system of quality control that is designed to provide the audit organization with reasonable assurance that the organization and its personnel comply with professional standards and applicable legal and regulatory requirements.
- Have an external peer review at least once every three years.

2 GAGAS Conceptual Framework for Independence

2.1 Introduction

Similar to the AICPA Code of Conduct, GAGAS independence guidance includes a conceptual framework for making independence determinations. The conceptual framework requires that the auditor:

1. identify threats to independence;
2. evaluate the significance of the threats identified, both individually and in the aggregate; and
3. apply safeguards as necessary to eliminate the threats or reduce them to an acceptable level.

If no safeguards are available to eliminate an unacceptable threat or reduce it to an acceptable level, independence would be considered to be impaired.

2.2 Threats to Independence

The following broad categories of threats to independence are identified by GAGAS:

- **Self-Interest Threat:** Self-interest threat is the threat that a financial or other interest will inappropriately influence an auditor's judgment or behavior.
- **Self-Review Threat:** Self-review threat is the threat that an auditor or audit organization that has provided non-audit services will not appropriately evaluate the results of previous judgments made or services performed as part of the non-audit services when forming a judgment significant to an audit.
- **Bias Threat:** Bias threat is the threat that an auditor will, as a result of political, ideological, social, or other convictions, take a position that is not objective.

- **Familiarity Threat:** Familiarity threat is the threat that aspects of a relationship with management or personnel of an audited entity, such as a close or long relationship or that of an immediate or close family member, will lead an auditor to take a position that is not objective.
- **Undue Influence Threat:** Undue influence threat is the threat that external influences or pressures will impact an auditor's ability to make independent and objective judgments.
- **Management Participation Threat:** Management participation threat is the threat that results from an auditor's taking on the role of management or otherwise performing management functions on behalf of the entity undergoing an audit.
- **Structural Threat:** Structural threat is the threat that an audit organization's placement within a government entity, in combination with the structure of the government entity being audited, will impact the audit organization's ability to perform work and report results objectively.

2.3 Safeguards

Safeguards are controls designed to eliminate or reduce to an acceptable level threats to independence. Under the conceptual framework, the auditor applies safeguards that address the specific facts and circumstances under which threats to independence exist. In some cases, multiple safeguards may be necessary to address a threat. Examples of safeguards include:

- consulting an independent third party, such as a professional organization, a professional regulatory body, or another auditor;
- involving another audit organization to perform or reperform part of the audit;
- having a professional staff member who was not a member of the audit team review the work performed; and
- removing an individual from an audit team when that individual's financial or other interests or relationships pose a threat to independence.

2.4 Evaluation of Non-audit Services

The auditor should determine whether providing such a non-audit service would create a threat to independence, either by itself or in aggregate with other non-audit services provided, with respect to any GAGAS audit it performs.

- A critical component of this determination is consideration of management's ability to effectively oversee the non-audit service to be performed.
  - The auditor should determine:
    - —that the audited entity has designated an individual who possesses suitable skill, knowledge, or experience; and
    - —that the individual understands the services to be performed sufficiently to oversee them.
  - The individual is not required to possess the expertise to perform or reperform the services.
  - The auditor should document consideration of management's ability to effectively oversee non-audit services to be performed.

- Auditors performing non-audit services for entities for which they perform audits should obtain assurance that audited entity management performs the following functions in connection with the non-audit services:
  - Assumes all management responsibilities;
  - Oversees the services, by designating an individual, preferably within senior management, who possesses suitable skill, knowledge, or experience;
  - Evaluates the adequacy and results of the services performed; and
  - Accepts responsibility for the results of the services.

2.5 Management Participation Threat

If an auditor were to assume management responsibilities for an audited entity, the management participation threat created would be so significant that no safeguards could reduce the threat to an acceptable level.

Management responsibilities involve leading and directing an entity, including making decisions regarding the acquisition, deployment and control of human, financial, physical, and intangible resources. Whether an activity is a management responsibility depends on the facts and circumstances. The auditor exercises professional judgment in identifying these activities.

Examples of activities that are considered management responsibilities and would therefore impair independence if performed for an audited entity include:

- setting policies and strategic direction for the audited entity;
- directing and accepting responsibility for the actions of the audited entity's employees in the performance of their routine, recurring activities; and
- having custody of an audited entity's assets.

2.6 Documentation of Independence

The independence standards require the auditor to document:

- Threats to independence that require the application of safeguards, along with the safeguards applied, in accordance with the conceptual framework for independence.
- The safeguards if an audit organization is structurally located within a government entity and is considered independent based on those safeguards.
- Consideration of audited entity management's ability to effectively oversee a non-audit service to be provided by the auditor.
- The auditor's understanding with an audited entity for which the auditor will perform a non-audit service.

Question 1 **MCQ-07267**

Generally accepted government auditing standards specifically include all of the following ethics principles except:

a. Serving the public interest.
b. Integrity.
c. Fraud detection.
d. Proper use of government information.

3 Department of Labor (DOL)

The U.S. Department of Labor (DOL) has established guidelines for determining when a qualified public accountant is independent for the purpose of rendering an opinion on an employee benefit plan under the Employee Retirement Income Security Act of 1974 (ERISA).

3.1 Independence Required

Auditor independence is required when auditing and rendering an opinion on the financial information required to be submitted to the Employee Benefits Security Administration of the DOL.

3.2 Impairment of Independence

The following situations impair independence with respect to an employee benefit plan:

- Any direct financial interest or a material indirect financial interest in the plan or the plan sponsor.

  Labor Department rules would consider independence to be impaired with respect to a plan if an interest is held during the period of the professional engagement, at the date of the opinion, or during the period covered by the financial statements which is more restrictive than the AICPA rules.
- Connection to the plan or the plan sponsor as a promoter, underwriter, investment advisor, voting trustee, director, officer, or employee.
- An accountant or a member of the accounting firm maintains financial records for the employee benefit plan.

3.3 Independence Not Impaired

An accountant's independence is not impaired when:

- A former officer or employee of the plan or plan sponsor is employed by the firm, the individual has completely disassociated from the plan or plan sponsor, and the individual does not participate in auditing the financial statements of the plan covering any period of his or her employment by the plan or plan sponsor.
- The accountant or the accountant's firm was engaged by the plan sponsor during the period of the professional engagement with the employee benefit plan.
- An actuary associated with the accountant or the accountant's firm rendered services to the plan.

4 Summary of Independence Standards

Summary of Independence Standards			
	AICPA	*SOX/ PCAOB/SEC*	*DOL*
	Standards for assurance engagements (issuer and nonissuer)	Standards for audits/reviews of issuers	Standards for audits of employee benefit plans
The following items impair independence:			
Direct financial interest	✓	✓	✓
Material indirect financial Interest	✓	✓	✓
Nonfinancial institution loan to or from client	✓	✓	
Employment at client of a former employee of the firm, unless the former employee cannot influence the firm and amounts owed to the former employee are immaterial	✓	✓	
Employment at client of a former employee of the firm as the client's CEO, CFO, controller, etc., during the one-year period preceding the commencement of audit procedures	Permitted with appropriate safeguards	✓	
Employment at client of immediate/close family member in a key position	✓	✓	
Individual who participates in the engagement is seeking or discussing potential employment with the client or has been offered employment by the client, unless the individual notifies the firm and is removed from the engagement	✓	✓	
Former employee of the client participates on the engagement team when the engagement covers any period of the individual's employment with the client	✓	✓	✓
Non-attest services:			
Bookkeeping	✓	✓	✓
Financial information systems design and implementation	✓	✓	
Appraisal and valuation services	✓	✓	
Actuarial services	✓	✓	
Management (officer, director, or employee in management capacity) or human resources services	✓	✓	✓
Internal audit	✓	✓	
Service as broker, dealer, investment advisor, or investment banker	✓	✓	✓
Legal services	✓	✓	
Expert services	✓	✓	
Overdue in payment of fees	✓	✓	
Actual or threatened litigation	✓	✓	
Contingent fees (audits, reviews, examinations)	✓	✓	
Significant gifts from clients	✓	✓	
Tax services related to confidential or aggressive tax transactions		✓	
Tax services to corporate officers of client or immediate family members		✓	
Partner compensated for selling services other than audit, review, and attestation services		✓	
The following items are required for independence:			
Audit committee preapproval		✓	
Lead and concurring audit partner rotation		✓	
Other audit partner rotation		✓	
Reporting to audit committee/those charged with governance	✓ (covered in SASs)	✓	

Class Question Explanations

AUD

NOTES

AUDITING 1

Auditing 1, Module 1

1. MCQ-02298

Choice "c" is correct. General guidance provided by a Statement on Auditing Standards is the most authoritative of level of auditing guidance for audits of nonissuers. Auditors are required to comply with SASs, and should be prepared to justify any departures therefrom.

Choices "a" and "d" are incorrect. AICPA audit and accounting guides and SAS interpretations are interpretive publications that provide guidance regarding how SASs should be applied in specific situations. They are not as authoritative as SASs.

Choice "b" is incorrect. Journal of Accountancy articles have no authoritative status, but may be helpful to the auditor.

Auditing 1, Module 2

1. MCQ-02820

Choice "c" is correct. The auditor should consider that fraud might occur regardless of any past experience with the entity. An assessment of management's honesty and integrity performed during the previous year would not necessarily be relevant to the current year's audit.

Choice "a" is incorrect. An auditor might apply professional skepticism by performing additional audit procedures designed to improve the reliability of evidence.

Choice "b" is incorrect. Corroborating management's explanations is an example of the application of professional skepticism, because the auditor is obtaining additional support rather than simply accepting the explanation as given.

Choice "d" is incorrect. Using third-party confirmations to provide support for management's representations is an example of the application of professional skepticism, because the auditor is obtaining additional support rather than simply accepting the explanation as given.

Auditing 1, Module 3

1. MCQ-02539

Choice "b" is correct. If the financial statements, including accompanying notes, fail to disclose information that is required by generally accepted accounting principles, the auditor should express a qualified or adverse opinion, depending on pervasiveness.

Choice "a" is incorrect. A disclaimer of opinion is not an appropriate report for inadequate disclosure or a GAAP departure.

Choice "c" is incorrect. Neither a disclaimer of opinion nor an unmodified opinion with an emphasis-of-matter paragraph is appropriate for a client with a material undisclosed item or GAAP departure.

Choice "d" is incorrect. An unmodified opinion with an other-matter paragraph is not appropriate for a client with a material undisclosed item or GAAP departure.

Auditing 1, Module 4

1. MCQ-02764

Choice "a" is correct. When circumstances indicate that a financial presentation in accordance with U.S. GAAP would be misleading, a departure from U.S. GAAP is permissible. In such cases, the auditor should issue an unmodified opinion because the financial statements are not materially misstated.

Choices "b", "c", and "d" are incorrect. The auditor's opinion need not be qualified or adverse because the financial statements are presented fairly.

Auditing 1, Module 5

1. MCQ-02469

Choice "c" is correct. When inadequate disclosure has a material but not pervasive effect on the financial statements, the auditor's opinion should state "In our opinion, except for the omission of the information described in the basis for qualified opinion paragraph . . ."

Choice "a" is incorrect. This language is not used. When inadequate disclosure has a material but not pervasive effect on the financial statements, the auditor's opinion should state "In our opinion, except for the omission of the information described in the basis for qualified opinion paragraph . . ."

Choice "b" is incorrect. This language is not used. When inadequate disclosure has a material but not pervasive effect on the financial statements, the auditor's opinion should state "In our opinion, except for the omission of the information described in the basis for qualified opinion paragraph . . ."

Choice "d" is incorrect. The statement "do not present fairly" would be used in an adverse opinion, not a qualified opinion.

Auditing 1, Module 6

1. MCQ-02452

Choice "b" is correct. A disclaimer of opinion means that the auditor was unable to obtain sufficient appropriate audit evidence to provide a reasonable basis for an opinion, thus no opinion is expressed. An unjustified change in accounting principle could result in a material misstatement of the financial statements that would result in a qualified or adverse opinion, not a disclaimer of opinion.

Choice "a" is incorrect. An inability to determine amounts associated with an employee fraud scheme is a scope limitation that may result in a disclaimer of opinion.

Choice "c" is incorrect. Refusal by the client to permit the auditor to confirm accounts receivable is a scope limitation that may result in a disclaimer of opinion.

Choice "d" is incorrect. Refusal of management to sign a management representation letter casts doubt on the audit evidence gathered and is a scope limitation that would likely result in a disclaimer of opinion.

2. MCQ-02834

Choice "d" is correct. When a qualified opinion results from an inability to obtain sufficient appropriate audit evidence, the situation should be described in a basis for qualified opinion paragraph preceding the opinion paragraph and should be referred to in the opinion paragraph. The scope limitation is not mentioned in the management's responsibility paragraph.

Choices "a", "b", and "c" are incorrect, per the above explanation.

Auditing 1, Module 7

1. MCQ-02787

Choice "d" is correct. If a contingent liability is probable, but not estimable, and it is disclosed in the footnotes, the auditor should issue an unmodified opinion.

Choice "a" is incorrect. When a contingent liability is probable, but not estimable, it should be disclosed in the footnotes. A qualified opinion due to a scope limitation results when the auditor is unable to obtain sufficient appropriate audit evidence and the auditor concludes that the possible effects of any undetected misstatements could be material but not pervasive.

Choice "b" is incorrect. A qualified opinion due to a material misstatement of the financial statements would be issued if the client did not disclose the contingent liability in the footnotes to the financial statements and the resulting misstatement was material but not pervasive.

Choice "c" is incorrect. If a contingent liability is probable, but not estimable, and it is disclosed in the footnotes, the auditor should issue an unmodified opinion. An other-matter paragraph would not be used in this situation, although the auditor could choose to add a emphasis-of-matter paragraph describing the uncertainty.

2. MCQ-02417

Choice "c" is correct. A change in accounting estimate (such as a change in the useful life of a depreciable asset) is accounted for prospectively and does not affect the comparability of financial statements between periods. Because the auditor's unmodified opinion implies that consistency exists, no modification to the report is necessary.

Choices "a", "b", and "d" are incorrect. Assuming the effect is material, a change in accounting principle results in the addition of an emphasis-of-matter paragraph (following the opinion paragraph) in the auditor's report. An emphasis-of-matter paragraph is required even if the previous accounting principle was not GAAP and even if management lacks reasonable justification for the change. (Note: A lack of reasonable justification for the change may also give rise to a report modification based on material misstatement of the financial statements.)

Auditing 1, Module 8

1. MCQ-03040

Choice "a" is correct. If, during the current audit, auditors become aware of circumstances or events that affect the financial statements of a prior period, they should consider such matters when updating the report on the financial statements of the prior period. For example, if auditors have previously qualified their opinion or expressed an adverse opinion on financial statements of a prior period because of a departure from generally accepted accounting principles, and the prior period financial statements are restated in the current period to conform with generally accepted accounting principles, the auditor's updated report on the financial statements of the prior period should indicate that the statements have been restated and should express an unmodified opinion with respect to the restated financial statements.

Choice "b" is incorrect. The predecessor auditor generally would not change a previously issued opinion when reissuing the audit report.

Choice "c" is incorrect. A difference of opinions between periods would not result in the auditor changing the opinion on a previously issued audit report.

Choice "d" is incorrect. Restatement of financial statements following a change in reporting entity affects comparability of the financial statements, but would not result in a change in opinion from the audit report previously issued.

2. MCQ-04614

Choice "c" is correct. When a successor auditor does not present the predecessor auditor's report, the successor should indicate in an other-matter paragraph that the predecessor auditor expressed an unmodified opinion on the prior year's financial statements.

Choice "a" is incorrect. No assurance is provided regarding the fair presentation of the prior year's financial statements.

Choice "b" is incorrect. The auditor does make reference to the prior year's financial statements, indicating in an other-matter paragraph that the predecessor auditor expressed an unmodified opinion on the prior year's financial statements.

Choice "d" is incorrect. There is no requirement that the successor obtain a letter of representation from the predecessor auditor, although the reverse may be true (the predecessor should obtain a letter of representation from the successor if the previous report is to be reissued).

3. MCQ-02544

Choice "d" is correct. When the group auditor decides not to make reference to the audit of a component auditor, the group auditor assumes responsibility for the work of the component auditor and should determine the type of work to be performed on the financial information of the component. If the component is significant, the component should be audited by the group engagement team or the component auditor.

Choice "a" is incorrect. The group auditor may decide not to make reference to the component auditor even when the portion of the group financial statements audited by the component auditor is material. When the group auditor assumes responsibility for the work of a component auditor, no reference to the component auditor is made in the auditor's report.

Choice "b" is incorrect. The group auditor's decision not to assume responsibility for the component auditor's work need not be included in the engagement letter.

Choice "c" is incorrect. The group auditor does not need permission from the component auditor to assume responsibility. Permission is needed only if the group auditor decides to make reference to the component auditor in the auditor's report and would like to refer to the other auditor by name.

Auditing 1, Module 9

1. MCQ-02302

Choice "c" is correct. An audit of a single financial statement is permitted under U.S. GAAS. An audit of a single financial statement can be performed as a separate audit or in conjunction with an audit of the complete set of financial statements.

Choice "a" is incorrect. Compliance with this request would not violate any ethical standards of the profession.

Choice "b" is incorrect. A "piecemeal" opinion, which is prohibited, is one in which different opinions are issued on enough different elements in the same financial statement as to constitute a "major portion" of the financial statements.

Choice "d" is incorrect. An audit of a single financial statement can be performed as a separate audit or in conjunction with an audit of the complete set of financial statements.

Auditing 1, Module 10

1. MCQ-04612

Choice "a" is correct. If the auditor chooses to use the later date for the report, this extends the auditor's responsibility for all subsequent events to this later date.

Choice "b" is incorrect. Dating the report August 27 means that the auditor is taking responsibility for all subsequent events through August 27.

Choice "c" is incorrect. Dating the report August 27 means that the auditor is taking responsibility for all subsequent events through August 27. If the auditor wishes to be responsible for all subsequent events through August 13 and only the one specific event after that date, the auditor would need to dual date the report.

Choice "d" is incorrect. Dating the report August 27 means that the auditor is taking responsibility for all subsequent events through August 27.

Auditing 1, Module 11

1. MCQ-04617

Choice "b" is correct. The auditor should perform limited procedures on required supplementary information accompanying the financial statements. In addition, the auditor's report on the financial statements should include an other-matter paragraph regarding the required supplementary information.

Choice "a" is incorrect. The auditor is not required to audit supplementary information.

Choice "c" is incorrect. The auditor is required to perform certain limited procedures with respect to supplementary information.

Choice "d" is incorrect. The auditor is responsible for performing certain limited procedures on supplementary information and for adding an other-matter paragraph to the audit report.

Auditing 1, Module 12

1. MCQ-02732

Choice "b" is correct. The auditor's report on financial statements prepared in conformity with a comprehensive basis of accounting other than GAAP would include a statement that the basis is a comprehensive basis of accounting other than GAAP. It would not state that the cash receipts and disbursements basis is not a comprehensive basis of accounting.

Choice "a" is incorrect. The auditor's report should include a paragraph that states the basis and refers to the note to the financial statements that describes the basis.

Choice "c" is incorrect. The auditor's report should include a paragraph that expresses the auditor's opinion on whether the financial statements are presented fairly, in all material respects, in conformity with the basis described.

Choice "d" is incorrect. The auditor's report should state that the audit was conducted in accordance with U.S. GAAS.

NOTES

AUDITING 2

Auditing 2, Module 1

1. MCQ-02432

Choice "c" is correct. The AICPA's *Statements on Quality Control Standards* assert that a system of quality control for a firm encompasses the firm's organizational structure and the policies and procedures established by the firm in order to provide reasonable assurance of conforming to professional standards. Toward that end, policies and procedures for human resources, including assigning personnel to engagements, should be established to provide reasonable assurance that the persons assigned will have the technical training and proficiency required to perform their work and progress within the firm.

Choice "a" is incorrect. Compliance with laws and regulations falls under the Code of Professional Conduct.

Choice "b" is incorrect. The use of statistical sampling techniques involves auditing standards, not standards of quality control.

Choice "d" is incorrect. The consideration of audit risk and materiality involves auditing standards, not standards of quality control.

2. MCQ-02418

Choice "c" is correct. A firm's failure to establish or comply with an appropriate system of quality control does not necessarily imply that the firm has failed to follow professional standards on individual engagements.

Choice "a" is incorrect. Quality control standards relate to the conduct of a firm's entire practice, whereas professional standards such as GAAS relate to the conduct of an individual engagement.

Choice "b" is incorrect. The adoption of an effective system of quality control standards is conducive to complying with professional standards on individual engagements.

Choice "d" is incorrect. Deficiencies in or noncompliance with a firm's quality control standards do not necessarily indicate a lack of compliance with professional standards for any one specific engagement.

Auditing 2, Module 2

1. MCQ-02643

Choice "c" is correct. Audit documentation should show that the accounting records agree or reconcile with the financial statements.

Choice "a" is incorrect. Audit documentation may be permitted to serve as a reference source for the client.

Choice "b" is incorrect. Audit documentation may contain critical comments concerning management (e.g., documentation of disagreement with the opinions of management, such as accounts receivable valuation).

Choice "d" is incorrect. Audit documentation is not the support for the financial statements. The client's books and records are the support for the financial statements. Audit documentation should be the principal support for the work the auditor has done to support the opinion provided on the auditor's report.

Auditing 2, Module 3

1. MCQ-04620

Choice "c" is correct. It is not appropriate for the auditor to request a review of the predecessor auditor's engagement letter. This is a business matter between the client and the predecessor auditor that has no impact on the current period audit. Conversely, review of the predecessor auditor's working papers (audit documentation) is appropriate and customary to facilitate the auditor's audit.

Choices "a", "b", and "d" are incorrect, based on the above explanation.

2. MCQ-02673

Choice "a" is correct. An understanding with the client should be established regarding management's responsibilities, which include the preparation and fair presentation of the financial statements in accordance with the applicable financial reporting framework. The understanding should be documented through a written communication, such as an engagement letter.

Choice "b" is incorrect. Judgments about materiality are the auditor's responsibility and would not be included in an engagement letter.

Choice "c" is incorrect. Management would not necessarily be responsible for violations of laws and regulations committed by employees.

Choice "d" is incorrect. The auditor is not responsible for searching for significant internal control deficiencies.

Auditing 2, Module 4

1. MCQ-02675

Choice "c" is correct. Procedures that an auditor may consider in planning the audit include discussing the type, scope, and timing of the audit with the client's management.

Choice "a" is incorrect. Identifying specific internal control activities that are likely to prevent fraud is an audit procedure, but not an initial planning activity.

Choice "b" is incorrect. Evaluating the reasonableness of the client's accounting estimates is not a planning activity. It is part of the evidence gathered later in the audit process.

Choice "d" is incorrect. Inquiring of the client's attorney is not a planning activity. It is part of the evidence gathered later in the audit process.

2. MCQ-03088

Choice "d" is correct. In developing an overall audit strategy, an auditor should consider preliminary evaluations of materiality, audit risk, and internal control.

Choice "a" is incorrect. Evaluation of results from sampling applications would be performed during fieldwork, after the planning process has been completed.

Choice "b" is incorrect. Findings from interim audit testing would be considered during fieldwork, after the planning process has been completed.

Choice "c" is incorrect. Inquiry of a client's attorney and evaluation of the attorney's response is performed during fieldwork, after the planning process has been completed.

Auditing 2, Module 5

1. MCQ-02682

Choice "d" is correct. The independent auditor is solely responsible for reporting on the financial statements. Thus, while he or she may use the work of the entity's internal auditor (both work already performed and work performed as part of the audit), independent auditors may not share any responsibility involving judgments, including the assessment of inherent and control risk. This is true because the internal auditor, even if assessed to be both competent and objective, is not independent.

Choices "a", "b", and "c" are incorrect, based on the above explanation.

Auditing 2, Module 6

1. MCQ-02761

Choice "b" is correct. Materiality levels include an overall level for each statement; however, because the statements are interrelated, and for reasons of efficiency, the auditor ordinarily considers materiality for planning purposes in terms of the smallest aggregate level of misstatements that could be considered material to any one of the financial statements.

Choice "a" is incorrect. The concept of materiality recognizes that some matters, either individually or in the aggregate, are important for the fair presentation of financial statements in conformity with GAAP, while other matters are not important.

Choice "c" is incorrect. Materiality judgments are made in light of the surrounding circumstances and necessarily involve both quantitative and qualitative considerations.

Choice "d" is incorrect. The auditor's consideration of materiality is influenced by his or her perception of the needs of a reasonable person relying on the financial statements.

Auditing 2, Module 7

1. MCQ-02426

Choice "a" is correct. The auditor should obtain an understanding of the entity and its environment sufficient to assess the risk of material misstatement and to design and perform further audit procedures.

Choice "b" is incorrect. Assessing inherent risk is not the primary objective of obtaining an understanding of the entity and its environment.

Choice "c" is incorrect. Obtaining an understanding of the entity and its environment is not a sufficient basis for issuing an audit opinion.

Choice "d" is incorrect. Procedures performed to gain an understanding of the entity and its environment would not ordinarily test the consistency of the application of management's policies. If the auditor intends to rely on a control, its consistency in application would then be tested.

2. MCQ-02799

Choice "a" is correct. The objective of performing analytical procedures during planning is to discover unusual transactions or events that may have an impact on the planning of the financial statement audit.

Choice "b" is incorrect. Analytical procedures are not effective in identifying acts of noncompliance with laws and regulations that went undetected due to internal control weaknesses.

Choice "c" is incorrect. Analytical procedures are not effective in identifying related party transactions.

Choice "d" is incorrect. Analytical procedures are not effective as tests of controls to identify unauthorized transactions.

Auditing 2, Module 8

1. MCQ-02374

Choice "a" is correct. In every audit, the auditor should obtain a sufficient understanding of the design of relevant internal controls pertaining to financial reporting in each of the five internal control components.

Choice "b" is incorrect. The auditor is not required, as a part of obtaining an understanding of the entity and its environment (including its internal control), to determine whether internal controls are operating effectively.

Choice "c" is incorrect. The auditor is not required, as a part of obtaining an understanding of the entity and its environment (including its internal control), to determine the consistency with which a control is applied.

Choice "d" is incorrect. Audit planning does not require an understanding of the controls related to each account balance, transaction class, and disclosure component in the financial statements. For certain items, a primarily substantive approach may be used instead.

2. MCQ-02348

Choice "a" is correct. Knowledge about the design and implementation of relevant internal controls should be used to identify types of misstatements that could occur.

Choice "b" is incorrect. The operating efficiency of a control is not significant to the auditor; the auditor is concerned with operating effectiveness. Also, the auditor is not required to assess operating effectiveness during the planning stage of the audit.

Choice "c" is incorrect. Determining whether a control has been circumvented by collusion is not a normal part of the audit planning process.

Choice "d" is incorrect. Documentation of the assessed level of control risk should be based on the design and implementation (and if applicable, testing) of internal control.

3. MCQ-02372

Choice "c" is correct. Client records documenting the use of EDP programs would be a relevant item for an auditor to examine while determining if internal control is operating as designed.

Choice "a" is incorrect. Industry gross margin information is evidence an auditor would examine while performing analytical procedures. Analytical procedures may be used as substantive tests, because they deal with dollar amounts rather than controls.

Choice "b" is incorrect. Confirmation of receivables is evidence an auditor would examine while performing substantive tests, because they deal with dollar amounts rather than controls.

Choice "d" is incorrect. Budgets and forecasts are evidence an auditor would examine while performing analytical procedures (comparison of expected results to actual). Analytical procedures may be used as substantive tests, because they deal with dollar amounts rather than controls.

Auditing 2, Module 9

1. MCQ-02927

Choice "a" is correct. An integrated test facility uses test data commingled with actual data to test transactions.

Choice "b" is incorrect. An input controls matrix is an input control.

Choice "c" is incorrect. Parallel simulation involves writing a computer program that duplicates the logic of a client's program, using identical data as input, and comparing output.

Choice "d" is incorrect. A data entry monitor is an input control.

2. MCQ-02920

Choice "d" is correct. Parallel simulation is a technique in which the auditor reprocesses the client's data using the auditor's own software. The auditor then compares his or her results to those obtained by the client.

Choice "a" is incorrect. The test data approach uses the auditor's input data on the client's system, off-line.

Choice "b" is incorrect. Reviewing program logic is not a computer-assisted audit technique.

Choice "c" is incorrect. An integrated test facility uses the auditor's input data on the client's system, on-line.

3. MCQ-02924

Choice "a" is correct. One of the primary benefits of using generalized audit software is the ability to access client data stored in computer files without having a detailed understanding of the client's hardware and software features.

Choice "b" is incorrect. The use of generalized audit software would not affect the auditor's decision with respect to using substantive tests of transactions in place of analytical procedures.

Choice "c" is incorrect. Generalized audit software is used to extract and analyze data. Self-checking digits and hash totals are controls embedded in client software applications to ensure accuracy. They are not a part of generalized audit software.

Choice "d" is incorrect. The use of generalized audit software does not reduce the need to perform tests of controls if reliance on controls is planned.

NOTES

AUDITING 3

Auditing 3, Module 1

1. MCQ-02903

Choice "a" is correct. The auditor should design the audit to provide reasonable assurance of detecting material errors and fraud.

Choice "b" is incorrect. The auditor is not "responsible for" detecting all material errors, but is responsible for designing an audit to provide reasonable assurance of detecting material misstatements. Due to the concealment aspects of fraudulent activity, however, even a properly planned and performed audit may not detect a material misstatement resulting from fraud. While auditors provide only reasonable (and not absolute) assurance of detecting fraud (due to such concealment factors), the presence of risk factors may still alert the auditor to the possibility that fraud exists.

Choice "c" is incorrect. The auditor should specifically assess the risk of material misstatement of the financial statements due to fraud and consider that assessment in designing the audit, even if analytical procedures or tests of transactions do not identify specific conditions indicative of potential misstatement.

Choice "d" is incorrect. The auditor does have some responsibility for detecting errors and fraud. The auditor has a responsibility to plan and perform the audit to obtain reasonable assurance about whether the financial statements are free of material misstatement, whether caused by error or fraud.

Auditing 3, Module 2

1. MCQ-02754

Choice "c" is correct. Inherent risk and control risk differ from detection risk in that they exist independently of the audit of financial statements, whereas detection risk is related to the auditor's procedures and can be changed at the auditor's sole discretion.

Choice "a" is incorrect. Inherent risk and control risk exist independently of the audit and do not arise from misapplication of auditing procedures.

Choice "b" is incorrect. Both the risk of material misstatement (including control risk and inherent risk) and detection risk may be assessed in quantitative terms, such as percentages, or in nonquantitative terms that range, for example, from a minimum to a maximum.

Choice "d" is incorrect. The auditor cannot change inherent risk or control risk since they exist independently of the financial statement audit. Only detection risk can be changed at the auditor's discretion.

2. MCQ-02759

Choice "b" is correct. Detection risk is inversely related to the risk of material misstatement. Therefore, an increase in the risk of material misstatement would cause a decrease in allowable detection risk.

Choice "a" is incorrect. The auditor uses the assessed risk of material misstatement (combined assessments of inherent and control risks) to determine the acceptable level of detection risk, which is then used to determine the nature, extent, and timing of substantive tests. An increase in the risk of material misstatement would cause a decrease in allowable detection risk. This is accomplished by increasing substantive testing.

Choice "c" is incorrect. The auditor uses the assessed risk of material misstatement (combined assessments of inherent and control risks) to determine the acceptable level of detection risk, which is then used to determine the nature, extent, and timing of substantive tests. Inherent risk exists independently of the audit and cannot be changed by the auditor.

Choice "d" is incorrect. Materiality is a matter of professional judgment and is influenced by the auditor's perception of the needs of a reasonable person who will rely on the financial statements. Materiality levels would not be affected by a change in the assessed risk of material misstatement.

Auditing 3, Module 3

1. MCQ-05603

Choice "d" is correct. Risk assessment procedures must be performed to assess the risk of material misstatement and to determine whether and to what extent further audit procedures are necessary. In addition, the planning process and the overall review stage of the audit must include application of analytical procedures. Tests of the operating effectiveness of controls, however, are only performed when the auditor's risk assessment is based on the assumption that controls are operating effectively, or when substantive procedures alone are insufficient.

Choices "a", "b", and "c" are incorrect, based on the above explanation.

2. MCQ-02888

Choice "c" is correct. After performing risk assessment procedures, an auditor might decide not to perform tests of controls because it would be inefficient. In other words, the time required to perform tests of controls would be greater than the reduction in time spent on substantive testing.

Choice "a" is incorrect. The auditor might decide not to perform tests of controls if the available audit evidence obtained through those tests would not support a decrease (not increase) in the level of control risk.

Choice "b" is incorrect. A reduction in the assessed level of control risk can only be justified based on tests of controls. If the auditor decides not to perform tests of controls, the assessed level of control risk may not be reduced.

Choice "d" is incorrect. The relationship of inherent risk to control risk does not determine the level of control testing to be performed.

Auditing 3, Module 4

1. MCQ-02536

Choice "c" is correct. Reviewing confirmations of loans receivable and payable is useful for determining the existence of related party transactions because guarantees are commonly provided by or for related parties.

Choice "a" is incorrect. Detection of unreported contingent liabilities is not a procedure that would assist the auditor in identifying related party transactions.

Choice "b" is incorrect. Recurring transactions after year-end are a usual business occurrence. Related party transactions would most likely be nonrecurring.

Choice "d" is incorrect. While financial difficulties may be associated with related party transactions, it is unlikely that analytical procedures would assist the auditor in identifying such transactions.

Auditing 3, Module 5

1. MCQ-02342

Choice "c" is correct. When audit evidence can be obtained from independent sources outside an entity, it provides greater assurance of reliability for the purposes of an independent audit than does evidence secured solely within the entity. While the bank statement was obtained from the client, it is still more persuasive than any of the other three items because it was not prepared by the client.

Choice "a" is incorrect. Prenumbered client purchase orders are client-generated documents; as such, they are not as persuasive as externally generated evidence received through a client.

Choice "b" is incorrect. Client work sheets supporting cost allocations are client-generated documents; as such, they are not as persuasive as externally generated evidence received through a client.

Choice "d" is incorrect. The client representation letter is a client-generated document; as such, it is not as persuasive as externally generated evidence received through a client.

Auditing 3, Module 6

1. MCQ-02334

Choice "c" is correct. Substantive tests are concerned with dollar amounts and consist of tests of details of transactions and balances and analytical procedures. The objective of tests of details of transactions performed as substantive tests is to detect material (dollar) misstatements in the financial statements.

Choice "a" is incorrect. Tests of details of transactions (performed as substantive tests) are used to evaluate management's assertions. While tests of details of transactions do help the auditor comply with GAAS, such compliance is not the primary objective of the tests.

Choice "b" is incorrect. Attaining assurance about the reliability of the information system relevant to financial reporting is an objective of tests of controls rather than of substantive tests.

Choice "d" is incorrect. Evaluation of the operating effectiveness of management controls is an objective of tests of controls rather than of substantive tests.

2. MCQ-02373

Choice "b" is correct. Relationships among income statement accounts tend to be more predictable than balance sheet accounts (accounts receivable, accounts payable) because they represent transactions over a period of time rather than at one point in time. In addition, relationships involving transactions subject to management discretion (travel and entertainment) are less predictable.

Choices "a", "c", and "d" are incorrect, per the above explanation.

3. MCQ-02354

Choice "c" is correct. To determine whether transactions have been recorded (completeness assertion), the auditor should trace from the source documents to the accounting records (general ledger, trial balances, etc.).

Choices "a", "b", and "d" are incorrect. Testing from the accounting records to the source documents provides evidence of existence or occurrence, not completeness.

Auditing 3, Module 7

1. MCQ-04769

Choice "c" is correct. The accounts receivable turnover ratio is calculated as sales (net) / average accounts receivable (net). More aggressive collection policies will result in a decrease in the receivables balance, which in turn causes the turnover ratio to increase.

Choice "a" is incorrect. A deterioration in the aging of receivables implies a greater receivables balance, which would cause the turnover ratio to decline.

Choice "b" is incorrect. Elimination of the company's discount policy would increase both the sales figure and the receivables balance. The net effect on the turnover ratio would depend upon the proportionate impact of each increase.

Choice "d" is incorrect. A decline in sales would cause a decrease in both sales and receivables. The net effect on the turnover ratio would depend upon the proportionate impact of each decrease.

Auditing 3, Module 8

1. MCQ-02588

Choice "b" is correct. Attribute sampling is used to test controls. Inspecting employee time cards for proper approval by supervisors is a test of controls. Controls often relate to authorization, validity, completeness, accuracy, appropriate classification, accounting in conformity with GAAP, and proper period. Look for these terms in identifying which option is a test of controls. Words such as account balance, amount, valuation, presentation, and disclosure are more likely to relate to substantive tests.

Choice "a" is incorrect. Selecting accounts receivable for confirmation of accounts balances is a substantive test.

Choice "c" is incorrect. Making an independent estimate of the amount of a LIFO inventory is a substantive test.

Choice "d" is incorrect. Examining invoices in support of the valuation of fixed asset additions is a substantive test.

2. MCQ-02602

Choice "d" is correct. If the actual deviation rate in the population exceeds the maximum deviation rate based on the sample, control risk will be understated, because the control will be less effective than sample results would indicate.

Choice "a" is incorrect. No comparison should be made between the true deviation rate and the risk of assessing control risk too low.

Choice "b" is incorrect. If the true deviation rate is lower than the deviation rate in the sample, control risk may be assessed at a rate that is too high, potentially leading to audit inefficiencies.

Choice "c" is incorrect. No comparison should be made between the true deviation rate and the risk of assessing control risk too low.

3. MCQ-02620

Choice "c" is correct. Erroneously concluding that an account balance is materially misstated is an example of incorrect rejection.

Choice "a" is incorrect. The assessment of control risk relates to tests of controls, not to tests of details (substantive testing).

Choice "b" is incorrect. The assessment of control risk relates to tests of controls, not to tests of details (substantive testing).

Choice "d" is incorrect. If the auditor had concluded that the account was fairly presented when, in fact, it was not, it would be an example of incorrect acceptance.

4. MCQ-02594

Choice "d" is correct. The auditor will reduce reliance on a control if the upper deviation rate exceeds the tolerable rate. The upper deviation rate consists of the sample deviation rate plus an allowance for sampling risk. Therefore, if the sample deviation rate plus the allowance for sampling risk exceeds the tolerable rate, that is equivalent to the upper deviation rate exceeding the tolerable rate.

Choice "a" is incorrect. If the sample deviation rate plus the allowance for sampling risk equals the tolerable rate, the auditor may still place the planned amount of reliance on the control.

Choice "b" is incorrect. Whether the actual sample deviation rate is less than the expected deviation rate is irrelevant for making decisions about planned reliance levels.

Choice "c" is incorrect. If the tolerable rate less the allowance for sampling risk exceeds the sample rate of deviation, then the upper deviation rate is less than the tolerable rate. This situation supports the planned reliance, and no reduction in planned reliance would be necessary.

Auditing 3, Module 9

1. MCQ-02584

Choice "b" is correct. The sample error of $1,000 ($5,000 – $4,000) is projected to the entire interval through use of a "tainting factor" of 20 percent ($1,000 / $5,000). If this were the only misstatement discovered by the auditor, the projected misstatement of this sample would be 20 percent of $10,000, or $2,000.

Choice "a" is incorrect, as the sample error of $1,000 needs to be projected to the entire interval.

Choices "c" and "d" are incorrect, per the above explanation.

2. MCQ-02607

Choice "b" is correct. The auditor may be able to reduce the required sample size by separating items subject to sampling into relatively homogenous groups on the basis of some characteristic related to the specific audit objective.

Choice "a" is incorrect. While PPS sampling results in a stratified sample, it is a result of the sampling method employed and does not require the auditor to perform stratification because it occurs automatically.

Choice "c" is incorrect. The estimated tolerable misstatement does not affect the decision to stratify.

Choice "d" is incorrect. The standard deviation of the recorded amounts represents the population's variability. Therefore, the auditor would be most likely to stratify when the standard deviation is high, not low.

3. MCQ-02596

Choice "d" is correct. The auditor should consider both the qualitative and the quantitative aspects of deviations in tests of controls. Qualitative aspects might include whether deviations are indicative of an error or fraud. Such an evaluation is important because fraud is intentional, has implications beyond the direct monetary effect, and requires consideration of the implications for other aspects of the audit. Thus, a deviation initially concealed by a forged document is very serious and deserves broader consideration than a deviation of the same dollar amount due to an error.

Choice "a" is incorrect. The fact that a deviation was the only one discovered would have no importance beyond its impact on the computation of the upper deviation rate.

Choice "b" is incorrect. Discovery of a deviation identical to one discovered during the prior year's audit is not necessarily cause for additional concern.

Choice "c" is incorrect. Employee misunderstanding of instructions is an inherent limitation of internal control and is not necessarily cause for concern.

AUDITING 4

Auditing 4, Module 1

1. MCQ-04627

Choice "d" is correct. Blank forms may result in lower response rates because a greater effort is required for response.

Choice "a" is incorrect. Use of the blank form does not necessarily imply that subsequent cash receipts will need to be verified. This is an alternative procedure that might be used to follow up on nonresponses.

Choice "b" is incorrect. The decision regarding whether or not to use statistical sampling is independent of the decision regarding what form of accounts receivable confirmation to use.

Choice "c" is incorrect. Blank forms provide a greater degree of assurance, because the recipient cannot simply sign off without checking the balance. A greater degree of assurance results in a lower assessed level of detection risk.

Auditing 4, Module 2

1. MCQ-02314

Choice "a" is correct. Because the employee is destroying the invoices and related vouchers, the most obvious documentation remaining would be the file of all cash disbursements. The auditor would select items from this file and then attempt to trace from specific cash disbursements to the related invoices and approved vouchers. Missing documentation might be indicative of fraud.

Choices "b" and "d" are incorrect. Because the employee destroys the related invoices and vouchers, selecting items from the file of remaining invoices and vouchers would never identify the fraud.

Choice "c" is incorrect. Selecting items from the file of receiving reports will not identify fraudulent purchases that are shipped directly to the employees' home addresses.

Auditing 4, Module 3

1. MCQ-02574

Choice "a" is correct. The auditor should obtain bank cutoff statements that include transactions for 10 to 15 days after year-end. The outstanding checks and deposits in transit at year-end on the bank reconciliation should agree with the information in the bank cutoff statement.

Choice "b" is incorrect. Companies may have a tendency to overstate their cash balance. A company that is trying to improve its balance sheet will have a tendency to accelerate recording of deposits, so a deposit that wasn't really made until January might be erroneously listed as a deposit in transit at year-end. Tracing deposits from the cutoff statement to the year-end bank reconciliation won't identify this error, because there is no mention in this option of identifying the actual dates the deposits were made.

Choice "c" is incorrect. Checks dated after year-end would not be included in the year-end outstanding checklist.

Choice "d" is incorrect. Deposits recorded in the cash receipts journal after year-end do not affect the cash balance at year-end, and therefore the auditor would not perform audit procedures with respect to those deposits.

Auditing 4, Module 4

1. MCQ-02443

Choice "c" is correct. Tracing from the inventory schedule to the inventory tags and the auditor's recorded count sheets verifies the validity (existence) of the items. Note that the correct term for the directional test for existence is "vouch." However, in practice (and on the CPA Exam), the term trace is sometime used interchangeably with the term vouch.

Choice "a" is incorrect. Tracing from inventory tags to the inventory listing schedule verifies the completeness of the schedule, not the existence (or validity) of the items.

Choice "b" is incorrect. Tracing to receiving reports and to vendors' invoices from the inventory tags might be used to verify completeness of purchases or payables.

Choice "d" is incorrect. Tracing from receiving reports and vendors' invoices to the inventory listing are cutoff procedures used to verify completeness of the inventory listing.

Auditing 4, Module 5

1. MCQ-02500

Choice "b" is correct. The auditor would consider subsequent events and transactions occurring before the completion of the audit, not after. The auditor is not responsible for predicting the future, and would not be expected to evaluate the effect of conditions arising subsequent to the audit, that, if known at the time of the audit, might have affected fair value measurements and disclosures.

Choice "a" is incorrect. The auditor is responsible for understanding relevant controls. Segregation of duties between those committing the entity to certain transactions and those responsible for undertaking the valuations related to those transactions is a relevant control.

Choice "c" is incorrect. The auditor is responsible for understanding the entity's process for determining fair value measurements and disclosures. Considering the role of information technology in determining fair value measurements and disclosures is part of understanding this process.

Choice "d" is incorrect. The auditor should evaluate whether the valuation model is appropriate given the entity's circumstances. As part of this evaluation, the auditor should consider whether the valuation method is appropriate in relation to the business, industry, and environment in which the entity operates.

Auditing 4, Module 6

1. MCQ-02447

Choice "a" is correct. In a search for unrecorded disposals, the auditor would vouch a sample of assets on the property ledger to those on hand in the client's facility.

Choice "b" is incorrect. By touring the facility first, and then comparing assets found to those recorded on the property ledger, the auditor is testing the completeness of the property ledger, a procedure used to search for unrecorded additions.

Choice "c" is incorrect. Analysis of the repair and maintenance account is useful in identifying transactions that should have been capitalized versus expensed (e.g., unrecorded additions).

Choice "d" is incorrect. Analysis of the repair and maintenance account is useful in identifying transactions that should have been capitalized versus expensed (e.g., unrecorded additions).

2. MCQ-02416

Choice "b" is correct. By vouching to time card data, the auditor is testing the occurrence assertion for hours worked.

Choice "a" is incorrect. Vouching to approved clock card data would provide evidence about hours worked, not pay rates. Pay rates would be tested by comparing to personnel records.

Choice "c" is incorrect. Vouching to approved clock card data does not provide evidence about segregation of duties.

Choice "d" is incorrect. Vouching to approved clock card data does not provide evidence about internal controls related to unclaimed paychecks. The auditor would need to observe a payroll distribution to evaluate these controls.

3. MCQ-02478

Choice "c" is correct. Comparing interest expense with the bond payable amount for reasonableness provides evidence that all interest expense was included and that the outstanding balance of the bonds payable is reasonable, as well as providing limited evidence concerning the amortization of bond discounts or premiums.

Choice "a" is incorrect. The auditor would recalculate bond premiums and discounts, rather than use an analytical procedure.

Choice "b" is incorrect. The auditor would normally examine documentation of the bond instruments rather than of assets purchased to determine the existence of any liens on the assets.

Choice "d" is incorrect. The auditor would confirm the outstanding bonds payable balance, not the existence of individual bondholders.

Auditing 4, Module 7

1. MCQ-02529

Choice "c" is correct. The independent auditor's procedures with respect to litigation, claims, and assessments should include discussing with management the controls adopted for identifying, evaluating, and accounting for litigation, claims, and assessments.

Choice "a" is incorrect. The evaluation of going concern issues is the auditor's responsibility.

Choice "b" is incorrect. The auditor should examine documents in the client's possession concerning litigation, claims, and assessments, including correspondence and invoices from lawyers. The auditor does not generally examine documents held by the client's lawyer.

Choice "d" is incorrect. The client's lawyer would only know about matters that he or she has been engaged to handle, which might not include all litigation, claims, and assessments. In addition, it is the auditor's responsibility (not the lawyer's) to determine whether litigation, claims, and assessments have been adequately recorded or disclosed in the financial statements.

2. MCQ-02389

Choice "c" is correct. The auditor has a responsibility to evaluate whether there is substantial doubt about the entity's ability to continue as a going concern for a reasonable period of time. If the auditor concludes that there is substantial doubt, the auditor should include an emphasis-of-matter paragraph following the opinion paragraph that includes the terms "substantial doubt" and "going concern." The time period is not mentioned in the auditor's report.

Choices "a", "b", and "d" are incorrect, as explained above.

Auditing 4, Module 8

1. MCQ-02310

Choice "b" is correct. If control accounts in the general ledger do not reconcile to the subsidiary ledgers, there may be a problem in the way transactions were recorded and posted. Failure to investigate such differences implies that, if such a problem exists, it has not been identified and corrected. The auditor would therefore suspect that material misstatements exist in the client's financial statements.

Choice "a" is incorrect. The assumptions used in developing accounting estimates generally do change as new information becomes available or as situations or conditions change. This would not necessarily indicate that a material misstatement exists.

Choice "c" is incorrect. Because responses to negative confirmations are only received when there are discrepancies, a lower response rate likely would be indicative of fewer problems with accounts receivable. This corresponds to a reduced likelihood of material misstatement.

Choice "d" is incorrect. Management's consultation with another CPA firm about complex accounting matters indicates proactive steps on the part of management to accurately address those matters. Material misstatements with respect to the complex accounting matters therefore would be less likely to exist.

2. MCQ-06812

Choice "d" is correct. The dollar amount of the error is a quantitative standard, not a qualitative standard.

Choice "a" is incorrect. The effect of misclassifications is a qualitative standard that should be considered when evaluating the materiality of an uncorrected misstatement.

Choice "b" is incorrect. The significance of the misstatement relative to the needs of users is a qualitative standard that should be considered when evaluating the materiality of an uncorrected misstatement.

Choice "c" is incorrect. The cost of the correction is a qualitative standard that should be considered when evaluating the materiality of an uncorrected misstatement.

3. MCQ-06701

Choice "a" is correct. The auditor should document the errors in the summary of uncorrected errors, and document the conclusion that the errors do not cause the financial statements to be misstated.

Choice "b" is incorrect. The auditor is required to document both his/her conclusion and summarize uncorrected errors in the working papers.

Choice "c" is incorrect. The auditor is required to summarize the uncorrected errors in the working papers and document whether the errors cause the financial statements to be misstated.

Choice "d" is incorrect. The auditor is required to perform both of these procedures.

Auditing 4, Module 9

1. MCQ-02533

Choice "b" is correct. Specific written representations obtained by the auditor should include a statement that the significant assumptions used by management in making accounting estimates are reasonable.

Choice "a" is incorrect. Communications with those charged with governance are generally not included in the management representation letter, whereas communications from regulatory agencies regarding noncompliance with, or deficiencies in, financial reporting practices would be included.

Choice "c" is incorrect. Management's subsequent plans need not be included in the management representation letter, unless they will affect the carrying value or classification of assets and liabilities.

Choice "d" is incorrect. Management acknowledges its responsibility for the design, implementation, and maintenance of internal control to prevent and detect fraud, but does not acknowledge its responsibility to detect fraud.

Auditing 4, Module 10

1. MCQ-02540

Choice "b" is correct. If those charged with governance are not involved with managing the entity, the auditor should communicate material, corrected misstatements brought to management's attention as a result of the audit.

Choice "a" is incorrect. Certain matters communicated to those charged with governance, such as those related to the competence and integrity of management, might not be appropriate for discussion with management.

Choice "c" is incorrect. The auditor should communicate disagreements with management, whether or not resolved.

Choice "d" is incorrect. Previously communicated significant deficiencies that have not been corrected should be communicated again, in writing, during the current audit.

2. MCQ-02542

Choice "d" is correct. Conditions noted by the auditor that are significant deficiencies or material weaknesses should be reported in writing. Any report issued on such conditions should (1) indicate that the purpose of the audit was to report on the financial statements and not to provide an opinion on internal control; (2) include the definition of a material weakness and, if applicable, significant deficiency; (3) include a restriction on use (e.g., the report is intended solely for the information and use of management, those charged with governance, etc.).

Choice "a" is incorrect. During an audit, the auditor is not required to design tests specifically to detect significant deficiencies or material weaknesses in internal control.

Choice "b" is incorrect. Significant deficiencies in internal control are not generally disclosed in the annual report, and the auditor's letter on internal control matters observed during a financial statement audit is intended solely for the information and use of management, those charged with governance, and others within the organization.

Choice "c" is incorrect. Management does not provide an assessment concerning the effectiveness of internal control as part of a financial statement audit of a nonissuer (but would provide such an assessment in a separate engagement related to internal control).

Auditing 4, Module 11

1. MCQ-06712

Choice "c" is correct. The auditor may conclude that withdrawal is necessary when the client does not take the remedial action that the auditor considers necessary in the circumstances, even when the act of noncompliance with laws and regulations is not material to the financial statements. Factors that should affect the auditor's conclusion include the implications of the failure to take remedial action, which may affect the auditor's ability to rely on management representations, and the effects of continuing association with the client. In reaching a conclusion on such matters, the auditor may wish to consult with his own legal counsel.

Choice "a" is incorrect. Adding an explanatory paragraph emphasizing that certain matters, while not affecting the unmodified opinion, require disclosure is not an option as management has committed an act of noncompliance with laws and regulations and those charged with governance (board of directors) have not taken appropriate action.

Choice "b" incorrect. The auditor does not have a duty to report to parties outside of the entity, with certain exceptions.

Choice "d" is incorrect. Issuing an "except for" qualified opinion or an adverse opinion with a separate paragraph that explains the circumstances is not an option as management has committed an act of noncompliance with laws and regulations and those charged with governance (board of directors) have not taken appropriate action.

AUDITING 5

Auditing 5, Module 1

1. MCQ-05389

Choice "a" is correct. The auditor provides an opinion on the entity's financial statements and on the effectiveness of internal control. The auditor is not required to provide an opinion on the audit committee's oversight (but is required to report to the board when such oversight is ineffective).

Choices "b", "c", and "d" are incorrect, based on the explanation above.

Auditing 5, Module 2

1. MCQ-05391

Choice "b" is correct. In an audit of an issuer, the auditor is required to communicate both significant deficiencies and material weaknesses to management and the audit committee, but only material weaknesses result in an adverse opinion on the effectiveness of internal control.

Choice "a" is incorrect. In an audit of an issuer, significant deficiencies (that do not rise to the level of being material weaknesses) do not result in an adverse opinion on the effectiveness of internal control.

Choice "c" is incorrect. In an audit of an issuer, both significant deficiencies and material weaknesses must be communicated, in writing, to management and the audit committee. In addition, significant deficiencies (that do not rise to the level of being material weaknesses) do not result in an adverse opinion on the effectiveness of internal control.

Choice "d" is incorrect. In an audit of an issuer, the auditor is required to communicate both significant deficiencies and material weaknesses to management and the audit committee.

Auditing 5, Module 3

1. MCQ-02445

Choice "b" is correct. A CPA is required to comply with the provisions of Statements on Standards for Attestation Engagements (SSAE) when engaged to review management's discussion and analysis (MD&A) prepared pursuant to rules and regulations adopted by the SEC.

Choice "a" is incorrect. Attestation standards were created to provide assurance on representations other than historical financial statements and in forms other than the positive opinion. Unless the financial statements in question are something other than historical financial statements (which is not indicated in the question), it is likely that other standards (SAS, SSARS) would be more appropriate for this engagement.

Choice "c" is incorrect. An attest engagement is one in which a CPA is engaged to issue an examination, a review, or an agreed-upon procedures report on subject matter, or on an assertion about the subject matter, that is the responsibility of another party. Providing the client with a financial statement format does not fall under this description.

Choice "d" is incorrect. Statements on Standards for Attestation Engagements (SSAE) do not apply to audits of financial statements. (The CPA would, however, be required to comply with GAAS when engaged to audit financial statements prepared for use in another country.)

Auditing 5, Module 4

1. MCQ-02450

Choice "b" is correct. A report on agreed-upon procedures should include a list of the procedures performed (or reference thereto) and the related findings.

Choice "a" is incorrect. An agreed-upon procedures engagement to evaluate compliance with contractual requirements does not address the fair presentation of financial statements.

Choice "c" is incorrect. A report on agreed-upon procedures should be in the form of procedures and findings. An opinion is not provided.

Choice "d" is incorrect. A report on agreed-upon procedures would indicate that the sufficiency of the procedures is solely the responsibility of the specified parties, who in this case would be the group of royalty recipients (not Mill).

2. MCQ-02514

Choice "c" is correct. Financial projections are hypothetical, "what if" prospective financial statements. Because the user may need to ask the responsible party questions about the underlying assumptions, financial projections are "restricted use" reports, whose use is restricted to the responsible party and those third parties with whom the responsible party is negotiating directly.

Choices "a", "b", and "d" are incorrect. Only financial forecasts (based on expected conditions) are appropriate for general use.

3. MCQ-02436

Choice "b" is correct. When a CPA examines projected financial statements, the standard report should include a statement that the examination "...included such procedures as we considered necessary to evaluate both the assumptions used by management and the preparation and presentation of the projection."

Choice "a" is incorrect. The accountant's report on the examination of projected financial statements would not explain the principal differences between historical and projected financial statements.

Choice "c" is incorrect. The accountant's report on the examination of projected financial statements would not make any reference to the CPA's auditor's report on the historical financial statements.

Choice "d" is incorrect. The accountant's report would not express an opinion on the client's ability to continue as a going concern.

Auditing 5, Module 5

1. MCQ-04739

Choice "c" is correct. In some situations, the controls at a service organization are designed under the assumption that there will be certain complementary controls implemented by user organizations. These complementary controls should be included in the description of controls. The service auditor should obtain an understanding of such situations, in order to evaluate whether the complementary controls are necessary to achieve stated control objectives.

Choice "a" is incorrect. The auditor would need to understand controls before assessing their operating effectiveness.

Choice "b" is incorrect. Substantive procedures are not performed by a service auditor, who is either reporting on controls placed in operation, or on controls placed in operation and their operating effectiveness. Remember that a service auditor's engagement is not the same as an audit of financial statements.

Choice "d" is incorrect. Although a service auditor's engagement differs from an audit of financial statements, it is performed in accordance with the general standards as well as the relevant fieldwork and reporting standards. It is not considered to be an agreed-upon procedures engagement, as the auditor has not been engaged by the service organization to issue a report of findings based on specific, agreed-upon procedures.

Auditing 5, Module 6

1. MCQ-02499

Choice "a" is correct. The practitioner's report on agreed-upon procedures related to management's assertion about the entity's compliance with specified requirements is intended solely for the use of specified parties. Thus, the report should include a statement of limitations on the use of the report.

Choice "b" is incorrect. The report is in the form of procedures and findings. Since the work performed is less in scope than an examination, the accountant disclaims any opinion.

Choice "c" is incorrect. The auditor does not provide any negative assurance relative to assessment of control risk or to compliance with the specified requirements.

Choice "d" is incorrect. The report contains a statement that the sufficiency of the procedures is solely the responsibility of the parties specifying the procedures and a disclaimer of responsibility on the part of the accountant.

Auditing 5, Module 7

1. MCQ-03542

Choice "b" is correct. Auditors should report on the scope of their testing of compliance with laws and regulations and of internal controls.

Choice "a" is incorrect. The auditor would assess whether the entity has reportable measures of economy and efficiency that are valid and reliable as part of an economy and efficiency (performance) audit, not a financial statement audit.

Choice "c" is incorrect. The auditor may report the methods of statistical sampling used as part of a performance audit.

Choice "d" is incorrect. A program audit would determine the extent to which the entity's programs achieve the desired level of results.

Auditing 5, Module 8

1. MCQ-05604

Choice "b" is correct. Under the Single Audit Act, materiality is determined separately for each major federal financial assistance program.

Choice "a" is incorrect. Under a GAAS audit, materiality is determined in relation to the financial statements taken as a whole. Under a GAGAS audit, materiality levels may be lower due to the public accountability of the entity, the various legal requirements, and the visibility and sensitivity of governmental programs, activities, and functions.

Choice "c" is incorrect. Materiality must be determined before risk is assessed.

Choice "d" is incorrect. The Single Audit Act does not require that all balances be tested.

2. MCQ-03517

Choice "b" is correct. The auditor must assess whether management has identified laws and regulations that have a direct and material effect on the determination of amounts in an entity's financial statements and obtain an understanding of the possible effects on the financial statements of such laws and regulations.

Choice "a" is incorrect. The auditor must issue a separate report on the consideration of the entity's internal control, not on the expected benefits and related costs.

Choice "c" is incorrect. *Government Auditing Standards* (the Yellow Book) specify that the auditor should design the audit to provide reasonable assurance that material errors and fraud are detected.

Choice "d" is incorrect. The auditor may be required to express an opinion on whether the entity has complied with the requirements applicable to its major federal financial assistance programs, but not whether it is still eligible to receive assistance.

3. MCQ-03514

Choice "a" is correct. Audits of federal financial assistance under the Single Audit Act require that the auditor determine if the auditee has complied with laws, regulations, and provisions of the contracts or grant agreements.

Choice "b" is incorrect. Materiality in audits of federal financial assistance is set at the program level and is not determined by the government entities that provided the federal financial assistance to the recipient.

Choice "c" is incorrect. An external auditor need not be involved in the internal audit, and no written management representations regarding the internal auditors need be obtained.

Choice "d" is incorrect. In audits of federal financial assistance under the Single Audit Act, the auditor does not express negative assurance on items not tested.

AUDITING 6

Auditing 6, Module 1

1. MCQ-06300

Choice "d" is correct. SSARS apply when an accountant prepares, compiles, or reviews financial statements. Using information in the general ledger to prepare financial statements outside an accounting software system is considered a preparation engagement.

Choice "a" is incorrect. Typing or reproducing client-prepared financial statements, without modification, as an accommodation to a client does not constitute preparation of financial statements because the accountant has not prepared those statements.

Choice "b" is incorrect. Providing a client with a financial statement format does not constitute preparation of financial statements and, therefore, this does not fall within the guidelines of SSARS.

Choice "c" is incorrect. Proposing correcting journal entries does not constitute preparation of financial statements. Even entering general ledger transactions or processing payments (general bookkeeping) in an accounting system does not constitute a preparation engagement because it is considered merely "assisting " in preparing the financial statements (bookkeeping service.)

Auditing 6, Module 3

1. MCQ-03044

Choice "a" is correct. In a compilation engagement, the accountant should read the financial statements for obvious material misstatements.

Choice "b" is incorrect. Compiled financial statements may be used to obtain credit.

Choice "c" is incorrect. As part of a review engagement, an accountant would ask about actions taken at board of directors' meetings that affect the financial statements. Inquiry is not part of a compilation engagement.

Choice "d" is incorrect. Analytical procedures are part of a review engagement, but not necessary for a compilation engagement.

2. MCQ-03011

Choice "c" is correct. Financial statements compiled by an accountant should be accompanied by a report stating that the financial statements have not been audited or reviewed.

Choice "a" is incorrect. There is no discussion of the scope of the accountant's procedures in a compilation report.

Choice "b" is incorrect. This statement is part of the standard audit report, not the accountant's compilation report.

Choice "d" is incorrect. It is a review report, not a compilation report, that states that a review primarily includes applying analytical procedures to management's financial data and making inquiries of company management.

Auditing 6, Module 4

1. MCQ-03142

Choice "a" is correct. Observing safeguards over access to and use of assets and records is part of the study and evaluation of the client's internal control; such an evaluation is not conducted in a review.

Choice "b" is incorrect. As part of a review engagement, the accountant performs analytical procedures to identify relationships and items that appear to be unusual. Analytical procedures consist of comparisons of the financial statements with statements for a comparable prior period, comparisons of the financial statements with anticipated results (budgets and forecasts), and a study of the relationships of the elements of the financial statements that would be expected to conform to a predictable pattern.

Choice "c" is incorrect. As part of a review engagement, the accountant inquires of management about actions taken at the board of directors' meetings.

Choice "d" is incorrect. As part of a review engagement, the accountant performs analytical procedures to identify relationships and items that appear to be unusual. Analytical procedures consist of comparisons of the financial statements with statements for a comparable prior period, comparisons of the financial statements with anticipated results (budgets and forecasts), and a study of the relationships of the elements of the financial statements that would be expected to conform to a predictable pattern.

2. MCQ-02976

Choice "c" is correct. Financial statements reviewed by an accountant should be accompanied by a report stating that a review is substantially less in scope than an audit.

Choice "a" is incorrect. The review report provides limited assurance that the accountant is not aware of any material modifications that need to be made to the accompanying financial statements. The term "presented fairly" is used in the opinion paragraph of the audit report.

Choice "b" is incorrect. Examination of client information is part of an audit engagement, not a review engagement.

Choice "d" is incorrect. Although this statement is true, it is not explicitly stated in the accountant's review report.

Auditing 6, Module 5

1. MCQ-04629

Choice "d" is correct. The accountant is required to obtain a representation letter from management. When the client does not provide such a letter, the review is incomplete and the accountant may not issue the review report.

Choice "a" is incorrect. Lack of a reasonable justification for a change in accounting principle is a departure from GAAP, generally resulting in a modified report. It would not require the accountant to withdraw from the engagement.

Choice "b" is incorrect. The income tax basis is a special purpose framework. It is acceptable for an auditor to review special purpose financial statements, and there would be no need to withdraw.

Choice "c" is incorrect. A review engagement may involve reporting on only one financial statement as long as the scope of the engagement is not limited. There would be no need to withdraw in this circumstance.

2. MCQ-02970

Choice "d" is correct. Failure to properly capitalize leases that the accountant considers material to the financial statements is a departure from GAAP. If management will not capitalize the leases, the accountant should modify the standard review report or withdraw from the engagement. If modification to the report is sufficient to disclose the departure from GAAP, then the accountant may modify the review report.

Choice "a" is incorrect. An opinion is not issued with a review report. Instead, the report may be modified to disclose the departure from GAAP.

Choice "b" is incorrect. The accountant may still provide limited assurance with respect to the entity's financial statements in the review report, as long as the departures from GAAP are disclosed. A paragraph should be added at the end of the review report that should state, "Based on my review, except for the issue noted in the 'known departures from accounting principles generally accepted in the United States of America' paragraph, I am not aware of any material modifications...."

Choice "c" is incorrect. There is no need for the accountant to restrict the use of the financial statements.

3. MCQ-03381

Choice "c" is correct. If the review report on the current period includes a separate paragraph describing the responsibility assumed for the prior period's financial statements, the additional paragraph should explicitly state that no audit procedures were performed subsequent to the previous period's audit.

Choice "a" is incorrect. The review report can be considered a general use report; no restriction on use is necessary.

Choice "b" is incorrect. The previous year's audit report may still be relied upon.

Choice "d" is incorrect. No mention of the reasons for the change in engagement service is necessary.

Auditing 6, Module 6

1. MCQ-03419

Choice "d" is correct. Because the CPA has not audited the interim financial statements of this publicly held entity, the CPA (Green) should request that the first-quarter interim financial statements be marked as unaudited.

Choices "a", "b", and "c" are incorrect. As long as the CPA has completed his or her review, his name may be included in the annual report.

Auditing 6, Module 7

1. MCQ-03424

Choice "b" is correct. Comments concerning the unaudited interim financial information provide negative assurance as to whether any material modifications should be made to the unaudited interim financial information in order for it to be in conformity with GAAP.

Choice "a" is incorrect. Comfort letters are not required by the Securities Act of 1933, and copies are not filed with the SEC.

Choice "c" is incorrect. Comfort letters are addressed to the underwriter and are not included in the registration statement accompanying the prospectus.

Choice "d" is incorrect. The comfort letter does not update the opinion on previous financial statements. Often, underwriters will request that the accountants repeat in the comfort letter their report on the audited financial statements. Because of the special significance of the auditor's report, the auditors should not repeat their report.

Auditing 6, Module 8

1. MCQ-01499

Choice "c" is correct. Independence of a member is impaired if the CPA's spouse is employed by the client in a position which is audit-sensitive. Examples of positions that are audit-sensitive include cashier, internal auditor, accounting supervisor, purchasing agent, or inventory warehouse supervisor.

Choice "a" is incorrect. The following types of loans do not impair independence:

1. Automobile loans
2. Loans of the surrender value under terms of an insurance policy
3. Borrowings fully collateralized by cash deposits at the same financial institution
4. Credit cards and cash advances on checking accounts with an aggregate unpaid balance of $10,000 or less

Choice "b" is incorrect. Litigation not related to the engagement for an immaterial amount does not impair independence.

Choice "d" is incorrect. Acting as an honorary trustee for a not-for-profit company does not impair independence.

2. MCQ-01486

Choice "c" is correct. A CPA may not accept a commission for recommending a product to a client if the CPA audits or reviews that client's financial statements.

Choice "a" is incorrect. A CPA may resell a product to a client.

Choice "b" is incorrect. This is not considered incompatible with a CPA's practice.

Choice "d" is incorrect. A CPA may accept engagements obtained through the efforts of third parties.

3. MCQ-05805

Choice "b" is correct. Failure to return records to a client after the client makes a demand is considered to be an act discreditable to the profession, and as such violates the profession's ethical standards.

Choice "a" is incorrect. There is no prohibition against using a records-retention agency to store confidential client records.

Choice "c" is incorrect. Arranging with a financial institution to collect notes issued by a client in payment of fees due does not violate the profession's ethical standards.

Choice "d" is incorrect. A compilation of financial statements does not require the auditor to be independent (although the lack of independence should be disclosed). Although this engagement poses a familiarity threat, the firm may have implemented appropriate safeguards to bring the threat to an acceptable level.

Auditing 6, Module 9

1. MCQ-06110

Choice "c" is correct. The ethical standards that apply to the audits of issuers (SOX/PCAOB/SEC) require that the lead partner rotate off the audit engagement after five years. The AICPA Code of Professional Conduct, which is followed when auditing nonissuers, does not require audit partner rotation.

Choice "a" is incorrect. All U.S. ethical standards prohibit the performance of financial information systems design and implementation services for audit clients.

Choice "b" is incorrect. Loans to or from clients, other than loans from financial institutions under normal lending policies, are prohibited for audits of issuers and nonissuers under all ethical standards.

Choice "d" is incorrect. Any direct financial interest in a client impairs independence, whether the client is an issuer or a nonissuer.

Auditing 6, Module 10

1. MCQ- 07267

Choice "c" is correct. Generally accepted government auditing standards (GAGAS) ethics do not include a specific reference to fraud detection. Ethics, as defined by GAGAS, address the topics of serving the public interest, integrity, objectivity, proper use of government information, resources and positions, and professional behavior.

Choice "a" is incorrect. Generally accepted government auditing standards (GAGAS) include standards for the following principles of ethics: serving the public interest, integrity, objectivity, proper use of government information, resources and positions, and professional behavior.

Choice "b" is incorrect. Generally accepted government auditing standards (GAGAS) include standards for the following principles of ethics: serving the public interest, integrity, objectivity, proper use of government information, resources and positions, and professional behavior.

Choice "d" is incorrect. Generally accepted government auditing standards (GAGAS) include standards for the following principles of ethics: serving the public interest, integrity, objectivity, proper use of government information, resources and positions, and professional behavior.

NOTES

Summary blueprint

Content area allocation	Weight
I. Ethics, Professional Responsibilities and General Principles	15–25%
II. Assessing Risk and Developing a Planned Response	20–30%
III. Performing Further Procedures and Obtaining Evidence	30–40%
IV. Forming Conclusions and Reporting	15–25%

Skill allocation	Weight
Evaluation	5–15%
Analysis	15–25%
Application	30–40%
Remembering and Understanding	30–40%

Blueprint

AUD

Area I — Ethics, Professional Responsibilities and General Principles (15–25%)

Content group/topic	Skill: Remembering and Understanding	Skill: Application	Skill: Analysis	Skill: Evaluation	Representative task
A. Nature and scope					
1. Nature and scope: audit engagements	✓				Identify the nature, scope and objectives of the different types of audit engagements, including issuer and nonissuer audits.
2. Nature and scope: engagements conducted under Government Accountability Office Government Auditing Standards	✓				Identify the nature, scope and objectives of engagements performed in accordance with Government Accountability Office Government Auditing Standards.
3. Nature and scope: non-audit engagements	✓				Identify the nature, scope and objectives of the different types of non-audit engagements, including engagements conducted in accordance with the attestation standards and the accounting and review services standards.
B. Ethics, independence and professional conduct					
1. AICPA Code of Professional Conduct	✓				Understand the principles, rules and interpretations included in the AICPA Code of Professional Conduct.
	✓				Recognize situations that present threats to compliance with the AICPA Code of Professional Conduct, including threats to independence.
		✓			Apply the principles, rules and interpretations included in the AICPA Code of Professional Conduct to given situations.
		✓			Apply the Conceptual Framework for Members in Public Practice included in the AICPA Code of Professional Conduct to situations that could present threats to compliance with the rules included in the Code.
		✓			Apply the Conceptual Framework for Members in Business included in the AICPA Code of Professional Conduct to situations that could present threats to compliance with the rules included in the Code.
		✓			Apply the Conceptual Framework for Independence included in the AICPA Code of Professional Conduct to situations that could present threats to compliance with the rules included in the Code.

Auditing and Attestation (AUD)

Area I — Ethics, Professional Responsibilities and General Principles (15–25%) (continued)

Content group/topic	Skill: Remembering and Understanding	Application	Analysis	Evaluation	Representative task
B. Ethics, independence and professional conduct (continued)					
2. Requirements of the Securities and the Exchange Commission and the Public Company Accounting Oversight Board	✓				Understand the ethical requirements of the Securities and Exchange Commission and the Public Company Accounting Oversight Board.
	✓				Recognize situations that present threats to compliance with the ethical requirements of the Securities and Exchange Commission and the Public Company Accounting Oversight Board.
		✓			Apply the ethical requirements and independence rules of the Securities and Exchange Commission and the Public Company Accounting Oversight Board to situations that could present threats to compliance during an audit of an issuer.
3. Requirements of the Government Accountability Office and the Department of Labor	✓				Recognize situations that present threats to compliance with the ethical requirements of the Government Accountability Office Government Auditing Standards.
	✓				Recognize situations that present threats to compliance with the ethical requirements of the Department of Labor.
		✓			Apply the ethical requirements and independence rules of the Government Accountability Office Government Auditing Standards to situations that could present threats to compliance during an audit of, or attestation engagement for, a government entity or an entity receiving federal awards.
		✓			Apply the independence rules of the Department of Labor to situations that could present threats to compliance during an audit of employee benefit plans.
4. Professional skepticism and professional judgment	✓				Understand the concepts of professional skepticism and professional judgment.
	✓				Understand personal bias and other impediments to acting with professional skepticism, such as threats, incentives and judgment-making shortcuts.

Area I — Ethics, Professional Responsibilities and General Principles (15–25%) (continued)

Content group/topic	Skill: Remembering and Understanding	Application	Analysis	Evaluation	Representative task
C. Terms of engagement					
1. Preconditions for an engagement	✓				Identify the preconditions needed for accepting or continuing an audit or non-audit engagement.
		✓			Perform procedures to determine whether the preconditions needed for accepting or continuing an audit or non-audit engagement are present.
		✓			Perform procedures to determine whether the financial reporting framework to be applied to an entity's financial statements is acceptable.
		✓			Perform procedures to obtain the agreement of management that it acknowledges and understands its responsibilities for an audit or non-audit engagement.
2. Terms of engagement and engagement letter	✓				Identify the factors affecting the acceptance or continuance of an audit or non-audit engagement.
	✓				Identify the factors to consider when management requests a change in the type of engagement (e.g., from an audit to a review).
		✓			Perform procedures to confirm that a common understanding of the terms of an engagement exist with management and those charged with governance.
		✓			Document the terms of an audit or non-audit engagement in a written engagement letter or other suitable form of written agreement.
D. Requirements for engagement documentation					
	✓				Identify the elements that comprise sufficient appropriate documentation for an audit or non-audit engagement.
	✓				Identify the requirements for the assembly and retention of documentation for an audit or non-audit engagement.

Area I — Ethics, Professional Responsibilities and General Principles (15–25%) (continued)

Content group/topic	Skill: Remembering and Understanding	Skill: Application	Skill: Analysis	Skill: Evaluation	Representative task
D. Requirements for engagement documentation (continued)					
		✓			Prepare documentation that is sufficient to enable an experienced auditor having no previous connection with an audit engagement to understand the nature, timing, extent and results of procedures performed and the significant findings and conclusions reached.
		✓			Prepare documentation that is sufficient to enable an accountant having no previous connection with a non-audit engagement to understand the nature, timing, extent and results of procedures performed and the significant findings and conclusions reached.
E. Communication with management and those charged with governance					
1. Planned scope and timing of an engagement	✓				Identify the matters related to the planned scope and timing of an audit or non-audit engagement that should be communicated to management and those charged with governance.
		✓			Prepare presentation materials and supporting schedules for use in communicating the planned scope and timing of an audit or non-audit engagement to management and those charged with governance.
2. Internal control related matters	✓				Identify the matters related to deficiencies and material weaknesses in internal control that should be communicated to those charged with governance and management for an audit or non-audit engagement and the timing of such communications.
		✓			Prepare written communication materials for use in communicating identified internal control deficiencies and material weaknesses for an audit or non-audit engagement to those charged with governance and management.
3. All other matters	✓				Identify matters, other than those related to the planned scope and timing or deficiencies, and material weaknesses in internal control that should be communicated to management and those charged with governance for an audit or non-audit engagement.

Area I — Ethics, Professional Responsibilities and General Principles (15–25%) (continued)

Content group/topic	Skill: Remembering and Understanding	Skill: Application	Skill: Analysis	Skill: Evaluation	Representative task
F. Communication with component auditors and parties other than management and those charged with governance					
	✓				Identify matters that should be communicated to component auditors in a group audit engagement.
	✓				Identify matters that should be communicated to parties other than management and those charged with governance (e.g., communications required by law or regulation) for an audit or non-audit engagement.
G. A firm's system of quality control, including quality control at the engagement level					
	✓				Recognize a CPA firm's responsibilities for its accounting and auditing practice's system of quality control.
		✓			Apply quality control procedures on an audit or non-audit engagement.

Area II — Assessing Risk and Developing a Planned Response (20–30%)

Content group/topic	Skill: Remembering and Understanding	Skill: Application	Skill: Analysis	Skill: Evaluation	Representative task
A. Planning an engagement					
1. Developing an overall engagement strategy	✓				Explain the purpose and significance of the overall engagement strategy for an audit or non-audit engagement.
2. Developing a detailed engagement plan		✓			Prepare a detailed engagement plan for an audit or non-audit engagement starting with the prior-year engagement plan or with a template.
		✓			Prepare supporting planning related materials (e.g., client assistance request listings, time budgets) for a detailed engagement plan starting with the prior-year engagement plan or with a template.
			✓		Develop or modify a detailed engagement plan for an audit or non-audit engagement based on planning inputs and constraints.
B. Understanding an entity and its environment					
1. External factors, including the applicable financial reporting framework		✓			Identify and document the relevant industry, regulatory and other external factors that impact an entity and/or the inherent risk of material misstatement, including the applicable financial reporting framework.
		✓			Document the procedures that were performed to obtain an understanding of the relevant industry, regulatory and other external factors that impact an entity and/or the inherent risk of material misstatement, including the applicable financial reporting framework.
2. Internal factors, including nature of the entity, ownership and governance structures and risk strategy		✓			Identify and document the relevant factors that define the nature of an entity, including the impact on the risk of material misstatement (e.g., its operations, ownership and governance structure, investment and financing plans, selection of accounting policies and objectives and strategies).
		✓			Document the procedures that were performed to obtain an understanding of the relevant factors that define the nature of an entity, including the impact on the risk of material misstatement (e.g., its operations, ownership and governance structure, investment and financing plans, selection of accounting policies, and objectives and strategies).

Area II — Assessing Risk and Developing a Planned Response (20–30%) (continued)

Content group/topic	Skill: Remembering and Understanding	Skill: Application	Skill: Analysis	Skill: Evaluation	Representative task
C. Understanding an entity's internal control					
1. Control environment and entity-level controls		✓			Identify and document the significant components of an entity's control environment, including its entity-level controls.
2. Flow of transactions and design of internal controls		✓			Perform and document the procedures to obtain an understanding of the significant components of an entity's control environment, including its entity-level controls.
		✓			Perform a walkthrough and document the flow of transactions relevant to an audit of an entity's financial statements, including an audit of an entity's internal controls.
		✓			Perform tests of the design and implementation of internal controls relevant to an audit of an entity's financial statements, including an audit of an entity's internal controls.
			✓		Identify and document the key controls within the flow of an entity's transactions relevant to an audit of an entity's financial statements, including an audit of an entity's internal controls.
				✓	Evaluate whether internal controls relevant to an audit of an entity's financial statements, including an audit of an entity's internal controls, are effectively designed and placed in operation.
3. Implications of an entity using a service organization		✓			Identify and document the purpose and significance of an entity's use of a service organization, including its impact on an audit of an entity's financial statements, including an audit of an entity's internal controls.
		✓			Use a service organization report to determine the nature and extent of testing procedures to be performed in an audit of an entity's financial statements, including an audit of an entity's internal controls.

Area II — Assessing Risk and Developing a Planned Response (20–30%) (continued)

Content group/topic	Skill: Remembering and Understanding	Skill: Application	Skill: Analysis	Skill: Evaluation	Representative task
C. Understanding an entity's internal control (continued)					
4. Information Technology (IT) general and application controls		✓			Identify and document an entity's key IT general and application controls, their impact on the audit of an entity's financial statements, including an audit of an entity's internal controls, and consider the effect of these controls and manual controls on the completeness and reliability of an entity's data.
		✓			Perform and document tests of an entity's key IT general and application controls, their impact on the audit of an entity's financial statements, including an audit of an entity's internal controls, and consider the effect of these controls and manual controls on the completeness and reliability of an entity's data.
5. Limitations of controls and risk of management override	✓				Understand the limitations of internal controls and the potential impact on the risk of material misstatement of an entity's financial statements.
		✓			Identify and document the risks associated with management override of internal controls and the potential impact on the risk of material misstatement of an entity's financial statements.
D. Assessing risks due to fraud, including discussions among the engagement team about the risk of material misstatement due to fraud or error					
			✓		Assess risks of material misstatement of an entity's financial statements due to fraud or error (e.g., during a brainstorming session), leveraging the combined knowledge and understanding of the engagement team.
E. Identifying and assessing the risk of material misstatement, whether due to error or fraud, and planning further procedures responsive to identified risks					
1. Impact of risks at the financial statement level		✓			Identify and document the assessed impact of risks of material misstatement at the financial statement level, taking into account the effect of relevant controls.
			✓		Analyze identified risks to detect those that relate to an entity's financial statements as a whole (as contrasted to the relevant assertion level).

Area II — Assessing Risk and Developing a Planned Response (20–30%) (continued)

Content group/topic	Skill: Remembering and Understanding	Skill: Application	Skill: Analysis	Skill: Evaluation	Representative task
E. Identifying and assessing the risk of material misstatement, whether due to error or fraud, and planning further procedures responsive to identified risks (continued)					
2. Impact of risks for each relevant assertion at the class of transaction, account balance and disclosure levels		✓			Identify and document risks and related controls at the relevant assertion level for significant classes of transactions, account balances and disclosures in an entity's financial statements.
			✓		Analyze the potential impact of identified risks at the relevant assertion level for significant classes of transactions, account balances and disclosures in an entity's financial statements, taking account of the controls the auditor intends to test.
3. Further procedures responsive to identified risks		✓			Develop planned audit procedures that are responsive to identified risks of material misstatement due to fraud or error at the relevant assertion level for significant classes of transactions and account balances.
			✓		Analyze the risk of material misstatement, including the potential impact of individual and cumulative misstatements, to provide a basis for developing planned audit procedures.
			✓		Assess risks of material misstatement using audit data analytic outputs (e.g., reports and visualizations) to determine relationships among variables and interpret results to provide a basis for developing planned audit procedures.
F. Materiality					
1. For the financial statements as a whole	✓				Understand materiality as it relates to the financial statements as a whole.
		✓			Calculate materiality for an entity's financial statements as a whole.
		✓			Calculate the materiality level (or levels) to be applied to classes of transactions, account balances and disclosures in an audit of an issuer or nonissuer.

Area II — Assessing Risk and Developing a Planned Response (20–30%) (continued)

Content group/topic	Skill: Remembering and Understanding	Skill: Application	Skill: Analysis	Skill: Evaluation	Representative task
F. Materiality (continued)					
2. Performance materiality and tolerable misstatement	✓				Understand the use of performance materiality and tolerable misstatement in an audit of an issuer or nonissuer.
		✓			Calculate performance materiality or tolerable misstatement for the purposes of assessing the risk of material misstatement and determining the nature, timing and extent of further audit procedures in an audit of an issuer or nonissuer.
G. Planning for and using the work of others, including group audits, the internal audit function and the work of a specialist					
	✓				Identify the factors to consider in determining the extent to which an engagement team can use the work of the internal audit function in an audit or non-audit engagement.
	✓				Identify the factors to consider in determining the extent to which an engagement team should use the work of a specialist in an audit or non-audit engagement.
	✓				Identify the factors to consider in determining the extent to which an auditor can use the work of a component auditor in a group audit.
		✓			Determine the nature and scope of the work of the internal audit function that can be used in an audit or non-audit engagement.
		✓			Perform procedures to utilize the work of a specialist to obtain evidence in an audit or non-audit engagement.
		✓			Determine the nature and scope of the work of a component auditor, including the identification of significant components that can be used in a group audit.

Area II — Assessing Risk and Developing a Planned Response (20–30%) (continued)

Content group/topic	Skill: Remembering and Understanding	Application	Analysis	Evaluation	Representative task
H. Specific areas of engagement risk					
1. An entity's compliance with laws and regulations, including possible illegal acts	✓				Understand the accountant's responsibilities with respect to laws and regulations that have a direct effect on the determination of material amounts or disclosures in an entity's financial statements for an audit or non-audit engagement.
	✓				Understand the accountant's responsibilities with respect to laws and regulations that are fundamental to an entity's business but do not have a direct effect on the entity's financial statements in an audit or non-audit engagement.
		✓			Perform tests of compliance with laws and regulations that have a direct effect on material amounts or disclosures in an entity's financial statements in an audit or non-audit engagement.
		✓			Perform tests of compliance with laws and regulations that are fundamental to an entity's business, but do not have a direct effect on the entity's financial statements for an audit or non-audit engagement.
2. Accounting estimates, including fair value estimates	✓				Recognize the potential impact of significant accounting estimates on the risk of material misstatement, including the indicators of management bias.
3. Related parties and related party transactions		✓			Perform procedures to identify related party relationships and transactions for an audit or non-audit engagement, including consideration of significant unusual transactions and transactions with executive officers.
			✓		Analyze the potential impact of related party relationships and transactions on the risk of material misstatement for an audit or non-audit engagement, including consideration of significant unusual transactions and transactions with executive officers.

Auditing and Attestation (AUD)

Area III — Performing Further Procedures and Obtaining Evidence (30–40%)

Content group/topic	Skill: Remembering and Understanding	Skill: Application	Skill: Analysis	Skill: Evaluation	Representative task
A. Understanding sufficient appropriate evidence					
			✓		Investigate evidence that either contradicts or corroborates management explanations, expectations and other hypotheses throughout an audit or non-audit engagement.
				✓	Conclude on the sufficiency and appropriateness of evidence obtained during the audit engagement for an issuer or nonissuer.
				✓	Conclude on the sufficiency and appropriateness of evidence obtained during a non-audit engagement based on the objectives and reporting requirements of the engagement.
B. Sampling techniques					
	✓				Understand the purpose and application of sampling techniques in an audit or non-audit engagement.
		✓			Use sampling techniques to extrapolate the characteristics of a population from a sample of items.
C. Performing specific procedures to obtain evidence					
1. Analytical procedures			✓		Determine the suitability of substantive analytical procedures to provide evidence to support an identified assertion.
			✓		Develop an expectation of recorded amounts or ratios when performing analytical procedures in an audit or non-audit engagement and determine whether the expectation is sufficiently precise to identify a misstatement in the entity's financial statements or disclosures.
			✓		Perform analytical procedures during engagement planning for an audit or non-audit engagement.
			✓		Perform analytical procedures near the end of an audit engagement that assist the auditor when forming an overall conclusion about whether the financial statements are consistent with the auditor's understanding of the entity.
			✓		Perform analytical procedures using outputs (e.g., reports and visualizations) from audit data analytic techniques to determine relationships among variables and interpret results in an audit or non-audit engagement.
				✓	Evaluate the reliability of data from which an expectation of recorded amounts or ratios is developed when performing analytical procedures in an audit or non-audit engagement.

Auditing and Attestation (AUD)

Area III — Performing Further Procedures and Obtaining Evidence (30–40%)

Content group/topic	Skill: Remembering and Understanding	Skill: Application	Skill: Analysis	Skill: Evaluation	Representative task
C. Performing specific procedures to obtain evidence (continued)					
1. Analytical procedures (continued)				✓	Evaluate the significance of the differences of recorded amounts from expected values when performing analytical procedures in an audit or non-audit engagement.
2. External confirmations		✓			Prepare external confirmation requests to obtain relevant and reliable evidence in an audit engagement of an issuer or nonissuer, including considerations when using electronic confirmations.
		✓			Use external confirmations to obtain relevant and reliable evidence in an audit engagement of an issuer or nonissuer, including considerations when using electronic confirmations.
			✓		Analyze external confirmation responses in the audit of an issuer or nonissuer to determine the need for follow-up or further investigation.
3. Inquiry of management and others		✓			Inquire of management and others to gather evidence and document the results in an audit or non-audit engagement.
			✓		Analyze responses obtained during structured or informal interviews with management and others, including those in non-financial roles, and ask relevant and effective follow-up questions to understand their perspectives and motivations in an audit or non-audit engagement.
4. Observation and inspection			✓		Perform tests of operating effectiveness of internal controls, including the analysis of exceptions to identify deficiencies in an audit of financial statements or an audit of internal control.
				✓	Evaluate evidence through the use of observation and inspection procedures in an audit or non-audit engagement.
5. Recalculation and reperformance		✓			Use recalculation and reperformance to obtain evidence in an audit or non-audit engagement.
6. All other procedures	✓				Identify other procedures in addition to those set out in professional standards, as necessary, to achieve the audit objectives in an audit of an issuer or a nonissuer.
		✓			Perform other procedures in addition to those set out in professional standards, as necessary, to achieve the audit objectives in an audit of an issuer or nonissuer.

Uniform CPA Examination Blueprints: Auditing and Attestation (AUD)

AUD19

Area III — Performing Further Procedures and Obtaining Evidence (30–40%) (continued)

Content group/topic	Skill: Remembering and Understanding	Skill: Application	Skill: Analysis	Skill: Evaluation	Representative task
C. Performing specific procedures to obtain evidence (continued)					
6. All other procedures (continued)			✓		Modify planned procedures based upon new information, such as inconsistent explanations, new evidence and environmental cues, to achieve audit objectives in an audit of an issuer or a nonissuer.
			✓		Determine the attributes, structure and sources of data needed to complete audit data analytic procedures.
			✓		Use audit data analytic outputs (e.g., reports and visualizations) to determine relationships among variables and interpret results to meet objectives of planned procedures in an audit or non-audit engagement.
D. Specific matters that require special consideration					
1. Opening balances		✓			Test whether prior-period closing balances have been correctly brought forward to the current period or restated in the audit of an issuer or nonissuer, including investigation of differences.
2. Investments in securities and derivative instruments	✓				Identify the considerations relating to the measurement and disclosure of the fair value of investments in securities and derivative instruments in an audit of an issuer or nonissuer.
		✓			Test management's assumptions, conclusions and adjustments related to the valuation of investments in securities and derivative instruments in an audit of an issuer or nonissuer.
3. Inventory and inventory held by others			✓		Analyze management's instructions and procedures for recording and controlling the results of an entity's physical inventory counting in an audit of an issuer or nonissuer.
				✓	Observe the performance of inventory counting procedures, inspect the inventory and perform test counts to verify the ending inventory quantities in an audit of an issuer or nonissuer.

Auditing and Attestation (AUD)

Area III — Performing Further Procedures and Obtaining Evidence (30–40%) (continued)

Content group/topic	Skill: Remembering and Understanding	Skill: Application	Skill: Analysis	Skill: Evaluation	Representative task
D. Specific matters that require special consideration (continued)					
4. Litigation, claims and assessments		✓			Perform appropriate audit procedures, such as inquiring of management and others, reviewing minutes and sending external confirmations, to detect the existence of litigation, claims and assessments in an audit of an issuer or nonissuer.
			✓		Analyze management's estimate of the liability associated with litigation, claims and assessments in an audit of an issuer or nonissuer.
5. An entity's ability to continue as a going concern	✓				Identify the factors that could cause substantial doubt about an entity's ability to continue as a going concern for a reasonable period of time in an audit of an issuer or nonissuer.
		✓			Perform procedures related to the assessment of management's evaluation and conclusion regarding an entity's ability to continue as a going concern in an audit of an issuer or nonissuer.
6. Accounting estimates, including fair value estimates			✓		Perform procedures to analyze an entity's calculations and detailed support for significant accounting estimates in an audit of an issuer or nonissuer, including consideration of information that contradicts assumptions made by management.
				✓	Evaluate the reasonableness of significant accounting estimates in an audit of an issuer or nonissuer.
E. Misstatements and internal control deficiencies					
		✓			Prepare a summary of corrected and uncorrected misstatements.
			✓		Determine the effect of uncorrected misstatements on an entity's financial statements in an audit or non-audit engagement.
			✓		Determine the effect of identified misstatements on the assessment of internal control over financial reporting in an audit of an issuer or nonissuer.
				✓	Evaluate the significance of internal control deficiencies on the risk of material misstatement of financial statements in an audit of an issuer or nonissuer.

Uniform CPA Examination Blueprints: Auditing and Attestation (AUD)

AUD21

Area III — Performing Further Procedures and Obtaining Evidence (30–40%) (continued)

Content group/topic	Skill: Remembering and Understanding	Skill: Application	Skill: Analysis	Skill: Evaluation	Representative task
F. Written representations					
	✓				Identify the written representations that should be obtained from management or those charged with governance in an audit or non-audit engagement.
		✓			Assist in the preparation of required written representations that should be obtained from management or those charged with governance in an audit or non-audit engagement.
G. Subsequent events and subsequently discovered facts					
		✓			Perform procedures to identify subsequent events that could affect an entity's financial statements or the auditor's report, including 1) events that occur between the date of the financial statements and the date of the auditor's report and 2) facts that become known to the auditor after the date of the auditor's report in an audit of an issuer or nonissuer.
		✓			Perform procedures to identify subsequent events that could affect an entity's financial statements or the accountant's report, including 1) events that occur between the date of the financial statements and the date of the report and 2) facts that become known to the accountant after the date of the report in a non-audit engagement.
			✓		Determine whether identified subsequent events are appropriately reflected in an entity's financial statements and disclosures in an audit or non-audit engagement.

Area IV — Forming Conclusions and Reporting (15–25%)

Content group/topic	Skill: Remembering and Understanding	Skill: Application	Skill: Analysis	Skill: Evaluation	Representative task
A. Reports on auditing engagements					
1. Forming an audit opinion, including modification of an auditor's opinion	✓				Identify the factors that an auditor should consider when forming an opinion on an entity's financial statements.
	✓				Identify the type of opinion that an auditor should render on the audit of an issuer or nonissuer's financial statements, including unmodified (or unqualified), qualified, adverse or disclaimer of opinion.
	✓				Identify the factors that an auditor should consider when it is necessary to modify the audit opinion on an issuer or nonissuer's financial statements, including when the financial statements are materially misstated and when the auditor is unable to obtain sufficient appropriate audit evidence.
2. Form and content of an audit report, including the use of emphasis-of-matter and other-matter (explanatory) paragraphs	✓				Identify the appropriate form and content of an auditor's report for an audit of an issuer or nonissuer's financial statements, including the appropriate use of emphasis-of-matter and other-matter (i.e., explanatory) paragraphs.
		✓			Prepare a draft auditor's report starting with a report example (e.g., an illustrative audit report from professional standards) for an audit of an issuer or nonissuer.
3. Audit of internal control integrated with an audit of financial statements	✓				Identify the factors that an auditor should consider when forming an opinion on the effectiveness of internal control in an audit of internal control.
	✓				Identify the appropriate form and content of a report on the audit of internal control, including report modifications and the use of separate or combined reports for the audit of an entity's financial statements and the audit of internal control.
		✓			Prepare a draft report for an audit of internal control integrated with the audit of an entity's financial statements, starting with a report example (e.g., an illustrative report from professional standards).

Area IV — Forming Conclusions and Reporting (15–25%) (continued)

Content group/topic	Skill: Remembering and Understanding	Skill: Application	Skill: Analysis	Skill: Evaluation	Representative task
B. Reports on attestation engagements					
1. General standards for attestation reports	✓				Identify the factors that a practitioner should consider when issuing an examination or review report for an attestation engagement.
		✓			Prepare a draft examination or review report for an attestation engagement starting with a report example (e.g., an illustrative report from professional standards).
2. Agreed-upon procedures reports	✓				Identify the factors that a practitioner should consider when issuing an agreed-upon procedures report for an attestation engagement.
		✓			Prepare a draft agreed-upon procedures report for an attestation engagement starting with a report example (e.g., an illustrative report from professional standards).
3. Reporting on controls at a service organization	✓				Identify the factors that a service auditor should consider when reporting on the examination of controls at a service organization.
		✓			Prepare a draft report for an engagement to report on the examination of controls at a service organization, starting with a report example (e.g., an illustrative report from professional standards).

Area IV — Forming Conclusions and Reporting (15–25%) (continued)

Content group/topic	Skill: Remembering and Understanding	Application	Analysis	Evaluation	Representative task
C. Accounting and review service engagements					
1. Preparation engagements	✓				Identify the factors that an accountant should consider when performing a preparation engagement.
2. Compilation reports	✓				Identify the factors that an accountant should consider when reporting on an engagement to compile an entity's financial statements, including the proper form and content of the compilation report.
		✓			Prepare a draft report for an engagement to compile an entity's financial statements, starting with a report example (e.g., an illustrative report from professional standards).
3. Review reports	✓				Identify the factors that an accountant should consider when reporting on an engagement to review an entity's financial statements, including the proper form and content of the review report.
		✓			Prepare a draft report for an engagement to review an entity's financial statements, starting with a report example (e.g., an illustrative report from professional standards).

Area IV — Forming Conclusions and Reporting (15–25%) (continued)

Content group/topic	Skill: Remembering and Understanding	Skill: Application	Skill: Analysis	Skill: Evaluation	Representative task
D. Reporting on compliance					
	✓				Identify the factors that an auditor should consider when reporting on compliance with aspects of contractual agreements or regulatory requirements in connection with an audit of an entity's financial statements.
	✓				Identify the factors that a practitioner should consider when reporting on an attestation engagement related to an entity's compliance with the requirements of specified laws, regulations, rules, contracts or grants, including reports on the effectiveness of internal controls over compliance with the requirements.
		✓			Prepare a draft compliance report for an attestation engagement to report on an entity's compliance with the requirements of specified laws, regulations, rules, contracts or grants starting with a report example (e.g., an illustrative report from professional standards).
		✓			Prepare a draft compliance report when reporting on compliance with aspects of contractual agreements or regulatory requirements in connection with an audit of an entity's financial statements starting with a report example (e.g., an illustrative report from professional standards).
E. Other reporting considerations					
1. Comparative statements and consistency between periods	✓				Identify the factors that would affect the comparability or consistency of financial statements, including a change in accounting principle, the correction of a material misstatement and a material change in classification.
2. Other information in documents with audited statements	✓				Understand the auditor's responsibilities related to other information included in documents with audited financial statements.
3. Review of interim financial information	✓				Identify the factors an auditor should consider when reporting on an engagement to review interim financial information.

Area IV — Forming Conclusions and Reporting (15–25%) (continued)

Content group/topic	Skill: Remembering and Understanding	Application	Analysis	Evaluation	Representative task
E. Other reporting considerations (continued)					
4. Supplementary information	✓				Identify the factors an auditor should consider when reporting on supplementary information included in or accompanying an entity's financial statements.
5. Single statements	✓				Identify the factors an auditor should consider when reporting on the audit of a single financial statement.
6. Special-purpose and other country frameworks	✓				Identify the factors an auditor should consider when reporting on the audit of financial statements prepared in accordance with a financial reporting framework generally accepted in another country, when the financial statements are intended for use outside of the United States.
	✓				Identify the factors an auditor should consider when reporting on the audit of financial statements prepared in accordance with a special-purpose framework, including cash basis, tax basis, regulatory basis, contractual basis or other basis.
7. Letters for underwriters and filings with the SEC	✓				Identify the factors an auditor should consider when engaged to issue a comfort letter in connection with an entity's financial statements that are included in a securities offering.
	✓				Identify the factors an auditor should consider in connection with audited financial statements of a nonissuer that are included in a registration statement.
8. Alerts that restrict the use of written communication	✓				Identify the factors an auditor should consider when restricting the use of written communication by including an alert when the potential exists for the written communication to be misunderstood or taken out of context.
9. Additional reporting requirements under Government Accountability Office Government Auditing Standards	✓				Identify requirements under Government Accountability Office Government Auditing Standards related to reporting on internal control over financial reporting and compliance with provisions of law, regulations, contracts and grant agreements that have a material effect on the financial statements.

Glossary

AUD

Account Balances: One of three categories of financial statement assertions, relating primarily to assets, liabilities, and equity interests.

Accounting Estimate: An approximation of a financial statement element, item, or account used because data either is not readily available or is dependent upon the outcome of future events.

Accounts Payable Confirmation: A request for independent verification of payables.

Accounts Receivable Confirmation: A request for independent verification of receivables. Note that confirming accounts receivable is a required, generally accepted auditing procedure.

Accuracy: A financial statement assertion in the "transactions and events" category indicating that amounts and other data relating to recorded transactions and events have been recorded properly.

Accuracy and Valuation: A financial statement assertion in the "presentation and disclosure" category indicating that financial and other information are disclosed fairly and at appropriate amounts.

Activity Ratio: A ratio that measures how effectively an enterprise is using its assets.

Adverse Opinion: An auditor's report stating that the financial statements "do not present fairly ... ."

Aging Schedule: A listing of accounts receivable categorized by age (i.e., current, 30 to 60 days, 60 to 90 days, etc.).

Agreed-Upon Procedures: An engagement in which a practitioner is engaged to issue a report of findings based on specific agreed-upon procedures.

AICPA Code of Professional Conduct: Guidelines for the behavior of members of the American Institute of Certified Public Accountants (AICPA) in the conduct of their professional affairs.

Allowance for Sampling Risk: In sampling, a "cushion" for protection against undetected deviations that is added to the sample deviation rate to arrive at the upper deviation rate.

Analytical Procedures: Evaluations of financial information made by a study of plausible relationships among both financial and nonfinancial data.

Applicable Financial Reporting Framework: The financial reporting framework that is acceptable in view of the nature of the entity and the objective of the financial statements, or that is required by law or regulation.

Application Controls: Information processing controls that apply to the processing of individual "applications" (e.g., controls surrounding receivables, controls surrounding payroll, etc.).

Appropriate (Appropriateness of Audit Evidence): The quality of being both reliable (valid, factual, objective, and supportable) and relevant (related to the financial statement assertion under consideration).

Articles of Incorporation: A document filed with the state to create a corporation.

Assertion: A declaration about whether a subject matter is based on or in conformity with selected criteria. *See also* financial statement assertions.

Association With Financial Statements: A relationship that arises when an accountant consents to the use of his or her name in connection with financial statements, or when an accountant has prepared the financial statements.

Assumption of Responsibility: A situation in which the group engagement partner decides to assume responsibility for the work performed by a component auditor, and therefore does not refer to the component auditor in the auditor's report.

Attestation Risk: In an examination or review attest engagement, attestation risk is the risk that the practitioner expresses an inappropriate opinion or conclusion, respectively, when the subject matter or assertion is materially misstated.

Attest Engagements: An engagement in which a practitioner is engaged to issue or does issue an examination, a review, or an agreed-upon procedures report on subject matter, or on an assertion about the subject matter, that is the responsibility of another party.

Attribute Sampling: A statistical sampling method used to estimate the rate of occurrence of a specific characteristic or attribute in a population.

Attributes of Risk: Four characteristics used in analyzing risk: type, significance, likelihood, and pervasiveness.

Audit: A methodical review and objective examination of an enterprise's financial statements.

Audit Adjustment: A proposed correction to the financial statements resulting from the auditor's procedures.

Audit Committee: A committee of the board of directors, generally made up of three to five members of the board who are "outside directors;" responsible for the selection and appointment of the independent external auditor, and for reviewing the nature and scope of the engagement.

Audit Data Analytics: ADAs involve analyzing patterns, identifying anomalies, and extracting other useful information in data underlying or related to the subject matter of an audit through analysis, modeling, and visualization.

Audit Documentation (Working Papers): The principal record of procedures performed, evidence obtained, and conclusions reached; also called "working papers" or "workpapers."

Audit Evidence: The underlying accounting data and corroborating information that must be obtained to support auditor conclusions.

Audit Objectives: Goals of audit testing, developed in light of financial statement assertions.

Audit Plan: A listing of audit procedures necessary to accomplish the objectives of the audit; required for every audit.

Audit Risk: The risk that an auditor may unknowingly fail to modify appropriately the opinion on financial statements that are materially misstated.

Audit Risk of Noncompliance: The risk that the auditor may unknowingly fail to appropriately modify the opinion on compliance in a compliance audit. It comprises the risk of material noncompliance and detection risk of noncompliance.

Audit Sampling: The testing of less than 100 percent of the items within an account balance or class of transactions in order to evaluate some characteristic of the balance or class.

Audit Strategy: An overall plan for the audit, typically used to develop the more detailed audit plan.

Audit Trail: Evidence indicative of the sequential flow of accounting operations.

Auditing Around the Computer: A technique in which the auditor tests the input data, processes the data independently, and then compares his or her independently determined results to the program results.

Auditing Procedures: Tasks performed to accomplish the objectives of the audit.

Bank Confirmation: An independent bank verification of year-end bank balances; also may provide information regarding loans, contingent liabilities, discounted notes, pledged collateral, and guarantees or security agreements.

Bank Reconciliation: A schedule that compares the cash balance reported by the bank with the cash balance reported by the client, and explains any differences.

Bank Transfer Schedule: A schedule that itemizes transfers of cash among banks, including the record date per the client and the transaction date per the bank.

Bias Threat: The threat that an auditor will, as a result of political, ideological, social, or other convictions, take a position that is not objective.

Bill of Lading: A shipping document issued by a carrier evidencing receipt of goods and terms of transport.

Blank Confirmation: A confirmation in which the recipient is requested to fill in the balance.

Block (Cluster) Sampling: In sampling, the selection of groups of adjacent items.

Brainstorming: An open exchange of ideas; required during planning as a means of evaluating the potential for material misstatement due to fraud.

Capsule Financial Information: Unaudited summarized interim information for subsequent periods.

Classification: A financial statement assertion in the "transactions and events" category indicating that transactions and events have been recorded in the proper accounts.

Classification and Understandability: A financial statement assertion in the "transactions and events" category indicating that financial information is appropriately presented and described and disclosures are clearly expressed.

Combined Approach: An audit approach in which both tests of the operating effectiveness of controls and substantive procedures are used. If controls are operating effectively, less assurance will be required from substantive procedures.

Comfort Letter: A letter from the CPA to the named underwriter and/or certain other requesting parties (e.g., client, broker-dealer, financial intermediary, or buyer/seller) just before the registration of the client's securities. It covers the period from the date of the last auditors' report to the "effective date" of the registration.

Common Size Financial Statements: Restated financial statements in which each balance sheet component is expressed as a percentage of total assets, and each income statement component is expressed as a percentage of total revenue.

Compilation: An engagement in which an accountant presents in the form of financial statements information that is the representation of management.

Completeness: A financial statement assertion appearing in all three assertion categories and indicating that all transactions, events, assets, liabilities, and equity interests that should have been recorded have been recorded, and that all disclosures that should have been included in the financial statements have been included.

Compliance Audit: An engagement under GAAS (and sometimes GAGAS) in which the auditor reports on whether the entity complied, in all material respects, with the compliance requirements applicable to its programs. Additional Single Audit Act requirements may apply.

Component: An entity or business activity that prepares financial information that is included in the group financial statements.

Component Auditor: An auditor who performs work on the financial information of a component that will be used as audit evidence for the group audit. A component auditor may be part of the group engagement partner's firm, a network firm, or another firm.

Components of Internal Control: Interrelated elements of internal control used to achieve an entity's objectives; internal control components consist of: control environment, risk assessment, information and communication systems, monitoring, and (existing) control activities.

Computer Assisted Audit Techniques (CAAT): Electronic methods used to test an automated transaction processing system; emphasis is placed on the input and processing stages of transaction processing.

Concurring Approval of Issuance: Approval of the issuance of the engagement report granted by the engagement quality reviewer under PCAOB standards. A firm cannot give an issuer permission to use the engagement report until concurring approval of issuance has been granted.

Condensed Financial Statements: Financial statements that are presented in considerably less detail than complete financial statements and do not include all required disclosures under GAAP.

Confidence Level (also called Reliability): In sampling, a measure of how certain the auditor wants to be that his or her results are accurate. Note that the confidence level plus the risk of being ineffective equals 100 percent.

Confirmation: A direct written response to the auditor from a third party, either in paper form or by electronic or other medium.

Consigned Goods: Goods belonging to one party that are held for sale by another party; the seller does not pay the owner until the goods have been sold.

Consistency: A measure of the comparability of financial statements from one year to the next.

Contingency: An event that may, but is not certain to, occur. A loss contingency that is probable and that can be reasonably estimated should be reflected in the accounts.

Contingent Fee: A fee established for performing services when no fee is charged unless a specific finding or result is obtained, or the fee amount is dependent upon the finding or result obtained.

Continuing Accountant: An accountant with whom the client has an ongoing relationship, as opposed to an accountant hired only to report on the application of accounting principles.

Control Activities: The policies and procedures that help ensure that management directives are carried out and that necessary steps are taken to address risks.

Control Deficiency: A weakness that exists when the design or operation of a control does not allow management or employees, in the normal course of performing their assigned functions, to prevent or detect misstatements on a timely basis.

Control Environment: The tone of an organization, including management attitude, participation of those charged with governance, organizational structure, and human resource policies.

Control Risk: The risk that a material misstatement that could occur in an assertion will not be prevented or detected on a timely basis by the entity's internal control.

Control Risk of Noncompliance: The risk that noncompliance with a compliance requirement that could be material will not be prevented or detected on a timely basis by an entity's internal control.

Controlled Processing: A form of parallel simulation in which the auditor observes an actual processing run and compares the actual results to the expected results based on the auditor's own program.

Controlled Reprocessing: A form of parallel simulation in which the auditor uses an archived copy of the program in question (generally the auditor's control copy) to reprocess transactions. The results are then compared with the results from the normal processing run.

Corroborating Evidence: Support that gives validity to recorded accounting data.

Coverage Ratio: A ratio that measures security for long-term creditors and/or investors.

Credit Approval: A determination by the credit department regarding whether or not a specific customer may receive goods on open account.

Credit Memo: An internal document used to indicate a credit to a particular account, typically accounts receivable.

Critical Audit Matters: Those matters arising from the current period audit of the financial statements that are communicated or required to be communicated to the audit committee and that relate to accounts or disclosures that are material to the financial statements and involve especially challenging, subjective, or complex auditor judgment.

Cross-Foot: To verify the mathematical accuracy of a statement or schedule by adding rows of numbers across, from left to right.

Current File: A collection of audit documentation applicable to the year under audit.

Cutoff: A financial statement assertion in the "transactions and events" category indicating that transactions and events have been recorded in the correct accounting period.

Cutoff Bank Statement: A bank statement sent directly to the auditor, usually shortly after period end.

Cutoff Testing: An examination of transactions occurring several days before and several days after year-end, to ensure that they were recorded in the proper accounting period.

Defalcation (Misappropriation of Assets): Theft of an entity's assets when the effect of the theft causes the financial statements not to be presented in conformity with GAAP.

Detection Risk: The risk that an auditor will not detect a material misstatement that exists in a relevant assertion.

Detection Risk of Noncompliance: The risk that the auditor will not detect material noncompliance that exists.

Deviation Rate: In sampling, the error rate found in a sample, used to estimate the overall error rate in the population.

Difference Estimation: A sampling plan that uses the average difference between the audited (correct) values of items and their book values to project the actual population value.

Directional Testing: Following an audit trail either forward (from source documents to financial records) or backward (from financial records to source documents).

Disclaimer of Opinion: An auditor's report stating that the auditor does not express an opinion on the financial statements.

Discovery Sampling: A special type of attribute sampling appropriate when the auditor believes that the population deviation rate is zero or near zero.

Documentation Completion Date: The end of the period during which the auditor assembles the final audit documentation file. After this date, existing documentation must not be deleted, and additions to the workpapers must be documented as such. Auditing standards define this date as 60 days following the report release date; PCAOB standards define it as 45 days following the report release date.

Dual Purpose Test: An audit procedure in which the auditor uses the same transaction as both a test of controls and a substantive test.

Due Diligence Defense: A legal concept indicating that an underwriter who performs a reasonable investigation will not be held liable for material omissions or misstatements in a registration statement.

Embedded Audit Module: A section of application program code that collects transaction data for the auditor.

Emphasis-of-Matter Paragraph: A paragraph included in the auditor's report when required by GAAS or at the auditor's discretion when referring to a matter that is appropriately presented or disclosed in the financial statements and is of such importance that it is fundamental to the users' understanding of the financial statements. Emphasis-of-matter paragraphs are used by nonissuers only.

Engagement Completion Document: A document identifying all significant audit findings and issues; required by PCAOB standards for audits of issuers.

Engagement Letter: A written communication documenting the understanding between an accountant and a client.

Engagement Partner: The partner responsible for the overall quality of the engagement.

Engagement Quality Review: A review required by PCAOB standards that is performed by a partner who is not otherwise associated with an issuer audit engagement. The engagement quality reviewer evaluates the significant judgments made by the engagement team and the overall conclusion reached on the engagement.

Entity-Level Controls: Controls related to the control environment, management override of controls, the company's risk assessment process, centralized processing, monitoring the results of operations, monitoring other controls, period-end financial reporting, and policies that address significant business controls and risk management practices.

Error: An unintentional misstatement or omission of an amount or disclosure in the financial statements.

Examination: An engagement that provides positive assurance (an opinion) based on procedures such as search, verification, inquiry, and analysis.

Existence: A financial statement assertion in the "account balances" category indicating that assets, liabilities, and equity interests exist.

Expected Deviation Rate: In sampling, the auditor's best estimate of the rate of deviation from a prescribed control procedure.

Explanatory Paragraph: An explanatory paragraph is included in the auditor's report when required by PCAOB auditing standards or at the auditor's discretion whenever the auditor wishes to emphasize a matter regarding the financial statements. Explanatory paragraphs are used for issuers only.

Extent of Testing: The degree to which an audit test is performed; a greater extent of testing is achieved by increasing sample size, performing testing at a more detailed level, or performing more extensive tests.

External Evidence: Information obtained from independent sources outside the enterprise.

Factual Misstatement: Misstatements about which there is no doubt.

Fair Presentation: Accurate representation in the financial statements, within a range of acceptable limits, of a company's financial position, results of its operations, etc.

Fair Presentation Framework: A financial reporting framework that requires compliance with the requirements of the framework, acknowledges explicitly or implicitly that it may be necessary for management to provide disclosures beyond those specifically required by the framework in order to achieve fair presentation of the financial statements, and acknowledges explicitly that it may be necessary for management, in extremely rare circumstances, to depart from a requirement of the framework to achieve fair presentation of the financial statements.

Fair Value: The amount at which an asset could be bought or sold (or the amount at which a liability could be incurred or settled) in a current transaction between willing parties.

Familiarity Threat: The threat that aspects of a relationship with management or personnel of an audited entity, such as a close or long relationship, or that of an immediate or close family member, will lead an auditor to take a position that is not objective.

Financial Forecast: A financial statement that reflects the expected financial results of a future period based on expected conditions and expected courses of action.

Financial Projection: A financial statement that reflects the financial results of a future period based on hypothetical ("what if") assumptions.

Financial Statement Assertions: Claims made implicitly or explicitly by management about the recognition, measurement, presentation, and disclosure of information in the financial statements. Financial statement assertions fall into three categories: transactions and events, account balances, and presentation and disclosure.

Flowchart: A symbolic diagram representing the sequential flow of authority, processes, and documents.

Foot: To verify the mathematical accuracy of a statement or schedule by adding columns of numbers from top to bottom.

Form AP: A form that auditors of issuers are required to file with the PCAOB for each audit report issued and which includes information about the audit.

Fraud: An intentional action that results in misstatement of the financial statements.

Fraud Risk Factors: Three conditions that generally are present when fraud occurs: incentives/pressures (a reason to commit fraud); opportunity (a lack of effective controls); and rationalization/attitude (an attempt to justify fraudulent behavior).

Fraudulent Financial Reporting: Intentional misstatements or omissions of amounts or disclosures in the financial statements that are designed to deceive financial statement users.

General Controls: Information processing controls that apply broadly throughout the company (e.g., access controls, controls related to software/hardware acquisition and maintenance, and controls over data center/network operations).

Generalized Audit Software Package (GASP): Software that is used to interrogate files, extract and analyze data, and allow performance of tests directly on the client's system.

Generally Accepted Accounting Principles (GAAP): The set of accounting rules established by the Financial Accounting Standards Board.

Generally Accepted Auditing Standards (GAAS): Qualitative standards that provide a measure of audit quality and of the objectives to be achieved in an audit.

Generally Accepted Government Auditing Standards (GAGAS): Standards for audits of government organizations, and audits of government assistance received by nongovernmental and government organizations.

General Purpose Framework: A financial reporting framework designed to meet the needs of a wide range of users, such as U.S. GAAP or IFRS.

General Use Report: A report that is not restricted to specified parties.

Going Concern Assumption: The belief that an entity will continue to operate into the foreseeable future.

Government Audit: An engagement that provides an opinion on financial statements as well as testing and reporting on compliance with the laws and regulations that authorize the spending of public funds.

Group Engagement Partner: The partner or other person in the firm who is responsible for the group audit engagement and for the auditor's report on the group financial statements.

Group Engagement Team: The team, which includes the group engagement partner, other partners, and staff, that establishes the overall audit strategy, communicates with component auditors, performs work on the consolidation process, and evaluates the conclusions drawn from the audit evidence as the basis for forming an opinion on the group financial statements.

Group Financial Statements: Financial statements that include the financial information of more than one component.

Hypothetical Transaction: A transaction not involving the facts or circumstances of a specific entity.

Implemented: A control that has been implemented exists and is being used.

Inconsequential: Clearly immaterial, as determined by a "reasonable person" standard.

Independence: The quality of being without bias and free from any obligation to or interest in the client, its management, or its owners.

Information and Communication Systems: A component of internal control that deals with the identification, capture, and exchange of information in a timely and useful manner (information) and with an understanding of individual roles and responsibilities (communication).

Information Technology (IT): Automated means of originating, processing, storing, and communicating information.

Inherent Limitations of an Audit: The provision that the auditor is unable to obtain absolute assurance that the financial statements are free from material misstatement because of the nature of financial reporting, the nature of audit procedures, the timeliness of financial reporting, and the balance between cost and benefit.

Inherent Limitations of Internal Control: The provision of only reasonable (as opposed to absolute) assurance regarding the achievement of internal control objectives. Inherent limitations arise due to human error, deliberate circumvention of controls by collusion, management override, and the difficulty of achieving appropriate segregation of duties in smaller entities.

Inherent Limitations Paragraph: A paragraph included in a report on an entity's internal control indicating that undetected misstatements may occur, and that projections of the evaluation to future periods are subject to the risk that conditions may change.

Inherent Risk: The susceptibility of a relevant assertion to a material misstatement, assuming that there are no related controls.

Inherent Risk of Noncompliance: The susceptibility of a compliance requirement to noncompliance that could be material, assuming that there are no related controls.

Initial Audit: An engagement in which the financial statements of the prior period were not audited or were audited by a predecessor auditor.

Integrated Audit: A concurrent audit of both the financial statements and internal control over financial reporting. PCAOB standards require an integrated audit for all issuers. Integrated audits can also be performed for nonissuers under the SSAE.

Integrated Test Facility (ITF): A computer assisted audit technique in which client personnel unknowingly process a set of test data, the proper results of which are already known.

Interim Audit Work: The performance of auditing procedures before year-end.

Interim Financial Information: Financial information covering a period less than a full year or a 12-month period ending on a date other than the entity's fiscal year-end.

Internal Auditor: A company employee who performs auditing functions for use by management and the board of directors.

Internal Control: A process effected by those charged with governance and management, and other personnel, designed to provide reasonable assurance about the achievement of the entity's objectives.

Internal Control Questionnaire: A list of questions, typically answered by a yes or no response, addressing relevant control procedures.

Internal Evidence: Information generated within the enterprise.

Inventory Tags: Tags that are attached to inventory items to aid in the counting of inventory.

Investor Ratio: A ratio that provides information of interest to investors.

Issuers: Entities subject to the rules of the PCAOB (primarily public companies).

Judgmental Misstatements: Differences that arise from the judgments of management concerning accounting estimates that the auditor considers unreasonable, or the selection and application of accounting policies that the auditor considers inappropriate.

Kiting: A scheme whereby a check drawn on one bank is deposited in another bank, but the disbursement is not recorded on a timely basis, resulting in an overstatement of cash.

Lapping: A scheme whereby a current receipt of cash (or a check) is stolen. To prevent detection, a subsequent receipt is applied to the previously unrecorded customer account.

Letter of Audit Inquiry: A direct letter sent to the client's attorney detailing any pending or threatened litigation matters and requesting the attorney to provide his or her evaluation directly to the independent auditor.

Limited Use Report: A report that is intended only for specified parties.

Liquidity Ratio: A ratio that measures a firm's short-term ability to pay maturing obligations.

Lock Box: A system in which customers send their payments directly to the bank, preventing access by company employees.

Major Programs: Generally speaking, programs that expend $750,000 or more in federal financial assistance (specific guidelines are based on formulas prescribed in federal regulations and the Single Audit Act).

Management Override of Controls: The circumvention of established controls by executives of a company.

Management Participation Threat: The threat that results from an auditor's taking on the role of management or otherwise performing management functions on behalf of the entity undergoing an audit.

Management Representation Letter: A letter the auditor is required to obtain from management at the conclusion of fieldwork, confirming representations explicitly or implicitly given to the auditor, indicating and documenting the continuing appropriateness of such representations, and reducing the possibility of misunderstanding regarding the representations.

Management's Discussion and Analysis (MD&A): The section of a public company's annual report that comprises management's comments regarding performance during the most recent period, background information on the company, etc. The requirements for MD&A are established by the SEC.

Material Concentrations: Volumes of business, revenues, available sources of supply, or markets or geographic areas for which events could occur that would significantly disrupt normal finances within the next year.

Material Weakness: A deficiency, or a combination of deficiencies, in internal control, such that there is a reasonable possibility that a material misstatement of the entity's financial statements will not be prevented, or detected and corrected, on a timely basis.

Materiality: Misstatements, including omissions, are considered material if there is a substantial likelihood that, individually or in the aggregate, they would influence the judgment made by a reasonable user based on the financial statements.

Mean-Per-Unit (MPU) Estimation: A sampling plan that uses the average value of the items in the sample to estimate the true population value.

Misappropriation of Assets (Defalcation): Theft of an entity's assets, when the effect of that theft causes the financial statements not to be presented in conformity with GAAP.

Modified Opinion: An auditor's opinion issued when the auditor concludes that the financial statements are materially misstated or the auditor is unable to obtain sufficient appropriate audit evidence to conclude that the financial statements are free from material misstatement. The three types of modified opinions are the qualified opinion, the adverse opinion, and the disclaimer of opinion.

Monitoring: The process of assessing the quality of internal control performance over time.

More Than Remote Likelihood: At least reasonably possible to occur.

Narrative: A written version of a flowchart describing the auditor's understanding of the system of internal control.

Nature (of an Audit Test): The quality of an audit test as measured in terms of the relevance and reliability of the evidence it provides. The nature of an audit procedure includes both its purpose and its type.

Negative Assurance: A statement indicating that, as a result of performing certain procedures, nothing came to the accountant's attention indicating that the subject matter in question did not meet a specified standard.

Negative Confirmations: A confirmation in which a response is requested only if the amount stated is incorrect.

Nonissuers: Entities that are not subject to the rules of the PCAOB (generally nonpublic companies).

Nonrecognized Subsequent Event: A subsequent event that relates to conditions existing after the balance sheet date that generally requires footnote disclosure, but rarely requires an adjustment to the financial statements.

Nonsampling Risk: All aspects of audit risk that are not due to sampling (e.g., selecting inappropriate audit procedures, failing to recognize a misstatement in documents examined, etc.)

Nonstatistical Sampling: A method of sampling in which auditors use their judgment (rather than mathematical formulae) to estimate risk, determine sample size, and evaluate sample results.

Objectives of an Entity: An entity's goals, often categorized as reliability of financial reporting, effectiveness and efficiency of operations, and compliance with applicable laws and regulations.

Observation: A method of obtaining audit evidence that provides the auditor with direct personal knowledge (e.g., viewing tangible assets, reviewing a process or operating procedure, etc.).

OCBOA (Other Comprehensive Basis of Accounting) Financial Statements: Financial data presented in accordance with a comprehensive basis of accounting other than GAAP.

Occurrence: A financial statement assertion in the "transactions and events" category indicating that transactions and events that have been recorded have occurred and pertain to the entity.

Occurrence and Rights and Obligations: A financial statement assertion in the "presentation and disclosure" category indicating that disclosed events and transactions have occurred and pertain to the entity.

Operating Effectiveness of Controls: A measure of the extent to which controls achieve their stated goals; evaluated by using tests of controls to address how, by whom, and with what level of consistency control policies and procedures have been applied.

Other Auditor: An auditor who examines a portion of the financial statements, but is not deemed to be the principal auditor.

Other-Matter Paragraph: A paragraph included in the auditor's report, when required by GAAS or at the auditor's discretion, that refers to matters other than those presented or disclosed in the financial statements that are relevant to the users' understanding of the audit, the auditor's responsibilities, or the auditor's report. Other-matter paragraphs are used by nonissuers only.

Outside Directors: Members of the board of directors who are neither employees nor part of management and who do not have a material financial interest in the company.

Parallel Simulation (Reperformance Test): A technique by which the auditor reprocesses some or all of the client's live data (using the auditor's own software) and then compares the results with the client's files.

Partial Presentation: A presentation of prospective financial information that excludes one of the following essential elements: sales, gross profit (or cost of sales), unusual or infrequent items, income tax expense, discontinued operations, income from continuing operations, net income, earnings per share, or significant changes in financial position.

Payroll Register: An accounting journal containing a record for each employee, with each record including data such as name, identification number, gross pay (regular and overtime), income taxes withheld, other deductions, and net pay.

Performance Audits: A range of engagements with specific governing standards from the Yellow Book that may embrace one of four objectives: effectiveness, economy, and efficiency; internal control; compliance; or prospective analysis.

Performance Materiality: The amount or amounts set by the auditor at less than materiality for the financial statements as a whole to reduce to an appropriately low level the probability that the aggregate of uncorrected and undetected misstatements exceeds materiality for the financial statements as a whole.

Permanent File: A collection of audit documentation that has a continuing interest from year to year.

Pervasive: Effects on the financial statements that, in the auditor's professional judgment, are not confined to specific elements, accounts, or items of the financial statements, or, if so confined, represent a substantial portion of the financial statements, or are disclosures fundamental to the users' understanding of the financial statements.

Physical Controls: Controls used to safeguard assets (e.g., security devices, limited access to restricted areas, periodic counting and comparison, etc.).

Piecemeal Opinions: Expressions of opinion as to certain identified line items in the financial statements, when those items constitute a major portion of the financial statements.

Planning: The development of an overall strategy for the audit.

Point Estimate: In sampling, an approximation of the true balance of an account, determined by applying the projected misstatement to the recorded balance.

Population: In sampling, the entire group under consideration; a sample is used to estimate population characteristics.

Positive Assurance: An affirmative statement or opinion given by the auditor, generally based on a high level of work performed.

Positive Confirmations: A confirmation in which the recipient is requested to respond regardless of whether the information included (if any) is accurate.

Practicable: Information can be reasonably obtained from management's accounts and records, and providing that the information in the auditor's report does not require the auditor to assume the position of a preparer of financial information.

Precision Interval: In sampling, an allowance for sampling risk that is added to a point estimate to provide a range within which the true population value is expected to fall.

Preconditions for an Audit: Requirements that must be met before an audit can be accepted, including determining that the financial reporting framework used by the client is acceptable and obtaining an agreement from management that it acknowledges and understands certain responsibilities.

Predecessor Auditor: An auditor who has reported (or who was engaged to report) on the most recent financial statements.

Presentation and Disclosure: One of three categories of financial statement assertions, relating primarily to disclosure in the financial statements.

Probability-Proportional-to-Size (PPS) Sampling: A sampling technique in which the sampling unit is defined as an individual dollar in a population. Once a dollar is selected, the entire account (containing that dollar) is audited.

Professional Skepticism: The maintenance of an objective attitude throughout the audit, including a questioning mind and a critical assessment of evidence. The auditor neither presumes management dishonesty nor presumes unquestioned management honesty.

Profitability Ratio: A ratio that measures the success or failure of an enterprise over a given period.

Pro Forma Financial Statements: Financial statements used to demonstrate the effect of a proposed transaction or event by showing how it might have affected the historical financial statements, if it had occurred during the period covered by those statements.

Program-Specific Audit: A governmental audit used in situations when no overall opinion is rendered on the financial statements. A program-specific audit must follow specialized rules designed for the particular type of program involved.

Projected Misstatement: In sampling, an estimate of the total error in a population, determined by finding the error in a sample and adding an adjustment for sampling risk.

Prospective Financial Statements: Financial statements that attempt to reflect a company's expected financial position and expected results of operations. *See also* financial forecast *and* financial projection.

Public Company Accounting Oversight Board (PCAOB): A regulatory body created pursuant to the Sarbanes-Oxley Act of 2002. The PCAOB establishes auditing and related professional practice standards to be used in the preparation and issuance of audit reports for "issuers."

Purchase Order: A document or form generated by a customer (typically within the customer's purchasing department), identifying goods or services to be purchased.

Purchase Requisition: A document or form generated by a user group, requesting goods or services; serves as a request for the purchasing department to prepare a purchase order.

Qualified Opinion: An auditor's report stating that "except for" the effects of the matter(s) to which the qualification relates, the financial statements are presented fairly, in all material respects.

Quality Control System: A system designed to ensure that services are competently delivered and adequately supervised. A firm's quality control system is composed of five elements: acceptance and continuance of clients and engagements; independence, integrity, and objectivity; monitoring; personnel management; and engagement performance.

Questioned Costs: Expenditures deemed to be non-allowable, undocumented, or unreasonable for reimbursement under a grant.

Random Sample: A sample selected in such a way that every item in the population has an equal chance of being included in the sample.

Ratio: A financial indicator that distills relevant information about a business entity by quantifying the relationships among selected items in the financial statements.

Ratio Analysis: The comparison of financial ratios developed from recorded amounts to expected ratios developed by the auditor, as a means of distilling relevant information about a business entity.

Ratio Estimation: A sampling plan that uses the ratio of the audited (correct) values of items to their book values, to project the true population value.

Reasonable Assurance: The high, but not absolute, level of assurance that is intended to be obtained by an auditor.

Receiving Report: A document or form used to indicate that purchased goods have been received and inspected.

Recognized Subsequent Event: A subsequent event that relates to a condition existing on or before the balance sheet date and generally requires adjustment to the financial statements.

Reconciliation: The process of comparing financial amounts from two independent sources for agreement.

Registration Statement: An informational document filed with the SEC to register securities for public offering.

Reissued Report: A report that is issued subsequent to the date of the original report, but which bears the same date as the original report, indicating that no additional work has been performed since that date.

Related Parties: A reporting entity's affiliates, principal owners, and management; also, any members of their immediate families.

Relevant Assertion: An assertion that has a meaningful bearing on whether an account is fairly stated.

Report on Management's Description of the Service Organization's System and the Suitability of the Design of Controls: A report on the design and implementation of a service organization's controls. It does not provide assurance on the operating effectiveness of controls. *See also* Type 1 Report.

Report on Management's Description of the Service Organization's System and the Suitability of the Design and Operating Effectiveness of Controls: A report on the design, implementation, and operating effectiveness of a service organization's controls. *See also* Type 2 Report.

Report Release Date: The date on which the auditor grants the client permission to use the report.

Reporting Accountant: An accountant in public practice who prepares a written report (or provides oral advice) on the application of accounting principles or on the type of opinion that may be rendered.

Representative Sample: A sample whose characteristics are comparable to the characteristics of the population from which the sample was drawn.

Responsible Party: A person who is accountable for a specific subject matter or, if no such person exists, a person who has a reasonable basis for making a written assertion about the subject matter.

Restricted Use Report: A report that is intended only for specified parties.

Restrictively Endorsed: An endorsement limiting future actions on an item (e.g., "for deposit only" marked on the back of a check).

Retention Period: The period for which audit documentation must be kept. Auditing standards define this period as five years from the report release date; PCAOB standards define it as seven years from the report release date.

Review: An engagement in which an accountant performs inquiry and analytical procedures as a basis for providing limited assurance that there are no material modifications that should be made to the financial statements in order for them to be in conformity with generally accepted accounting principles.

Rights and Obligations: A financial statement assertion in the "account balances" category indicating that the entity holds or controls the rights to assets, and that liabilities are the obligations of the entity.

Risk Assessment (performed by the auditor): The process by which an auditor obtains an understanding of an entity and its environment, including its internal control, in order to evaluate the likelihood of material misstatement.

Risk Assessment (performed by the entity): An entity's identification and analysis of risks to the achievement of its objectives.

Risk of Assessing Control Risk Too High: In sampling, the risk that the assessed level of control risk based on the sample is greater than the true risk based on the actual operating effectiveness of the control (i.e., sample results indicate a greater deviation rate than actually exists in the population). Note that this risk relates to tests of controls and to audit efficiency.

Risk of Assessing Control Risk Too Low: In sampling, the risk that the assessed level of control risk based on the sample is less than the true risk based on the actual operating effectiveness of the control (i.e., sample results indicate a lower deviation rate than actually exists in the population). Note that this risk relates to tests of controls and to audit effectiveness.

Risk of Incorrect Acceptance: In sampling, the risk that the sample supports the conclusion that the recorded account balance is not materially misstated when in fact it is materially misstated (i.e., sample results fail to identify an existing material misstatement). Note that this risk relates to substantive testing and to audit effectiveness.

Risk of Incorrect Rejection: In sampling, the risk that the sample supports the conclusion that the recorded account balance is materially misstated when in fact it is not materially misstated (i.e., sample results mistakenly indicate a material misstatement). Note that this risk relates to substantive testing and to audit efficiency.

Risk of Material Misstatement: The susceptibility of the financial statements to error. The risk of material misstatement is composed of inherent risk and control risk.

Risk of Material Noncompliance: The risk that material noncompliance exists, composed of the inherent risk of noncompliance and control risk of noncompliance.

Safeguards: Controls designed to eliminate or reduce to an acceptable level threats to independence.

Sales Invoice: A bill sent to a customer indicating goods and services sold, prices applied, payment terms, etc.

Sales Order: A form or document prepared upon receipt of a customer purchase order indicating goods or services to be provided to that customer.

Sampling Interval: In PPS sampling, a range of dollars from which each sampling unit will be selected (e.g., in a population of $500,000 with a sampling interval of $5,000, there would be 100 sampling intervals; the sample would consist of 100 items, with one item being selected from each of the 100 intervals).

Sampling Risk: In sampling, the risk that the sample is not representative of the population, and that the auditor's conclusion therefore will be different from the conclusion that would have been reached had the tests been applied to all items in the population.

Sampling Unit: In sampling, an item selected from the population for testing.

Sarbanes-Oxley Act of 2002: Legislation that amended federal securities laws after a series of corporate financial scandals exposed serious weaknesses in the self-regulating system that had been intended to provide reliable company financial statements.

Scope Limitation: A restriction on an engagement that occurs when the accountant is unable to fully complete necessary procedures.

Search for Unrecorded Liabilities: Audit procedures that aid the auditor in identifying obligations that should have been recorded at the balance sheet date, but were not.

Securities and Exchange Commission (SEC): A governmental commission of the United States given the authority to set guidelines for publicly traded companies.

Segment Information: Information about certain portions of an enterprise, presented in the annual financial statements of public companies (e.g., information about products and services, about geographic areas, or about major customers).

Segregation of Duties: The separation of the authorization, record keeping, and custodial functions to ensure that individuals do not perform incompatible duties.

Selected Financial Data: Additional financial information presented by management that is not a required part of the basic financial statements.

Self-Review Threat: The threat than an auditor or audit organization that has provided non-audit services will not appropriately evaluate the results of previous judgments made or services performed as part of the non-audit services when forming a judgment significant to an audit.

Service Auditor: The auditor of a service organization.

Service Organization: An outside organization hired to process some portion of another company's accounting transactions (e.g., a payroll processing company such as ADP).

Significant Audit Findings: Findings that should be included in the audit documentation because they are related to the selection and application of accounting principles or to possible material misstatements in the financial statements; or because they cause significant difficulty in, or indicate the need for significant revision of, necessary audit procedures; or because they may result in modification to the auditor's standard report.

Significant Component: A component that is of individual financial significance to the group or that is likely to include significant risks of material misstatement of the group financial statements.

Significant Deficiency: A deficiency, or a combination of deficiencies, in internal control that is less severe than a material weakness, yet important enough to merit attention by those charged with governance.

Significant Engagement Deficiency: Exists when the engagement team fails to obtain sufficient appropriate evidence, the engagement team reaches an inappropriate overall conclusion, the engagement report is not appropriate for the circumstances, or the firm is not independent of the client. The existence of a significant engagement deficiency prevents the engagement quality reviewer from providing concurring approval of issuance.

Significant Estimates: Estimates at the balance sheet date that could change materially within the next year.

Significant Risk: A risk which, in the auditor's judgment, requires special audit consideration.

Single Audit: An audit of entities expending federal assistance and that has two main components: an audit of the entity's financial statements and separate schedule of expenditures of federal awards, and a compliance audit of major federal awards.

Single Audit Act: A federal act requiring entities that expend federal assistance equal to or in excess of $750,000 annually to have a program-specific or entity-wide audit that complies with the act.

Specialist: A person or firm with special skills in a field other than accounting or auditing (e.g., actuaries, appraisers, attorneys, engineers, etc.).

Special Purpose: A financial reporting framework other than GAAP that is one of the following bases of accounting: cash basis, tax basis, regulatory basis, contractual basis, or any other basis of accounting that uses a definite set of logical, reasonable criteria that is applied to all material items appearing in the financial statements. Standard Deviation: A mathematical measure of population variability.

Statements on Auditing Standards (SAS): Standards issued by the Auditing Standards Board (ASB) of the AICPA.

Statements on Standards for Accounting and Review Services (SSARS): Standards established by the AICPA to regulate the provision of services to privately held companies not seeking audited statements.

Statements on Standards for Attestation Engagements (SSAE): Standards issued by senior technical bodies of the AICPA regarding attest engagements, including engagements with respect to agreed-upon procedures; financial forecasts and projections; pro forma financial statements; internal control over financial reporting; compliance; and management's discussion and analysis.

Statistical Sampling: A method of sampling in which auditors use mathematical formulae (rather than simply using judgment) to quantify risk, determine sample size, and evaluate sample results.

Stock Certificate Book: A collection of the documents used to evidence ownership of shares in a corporation.

Stock Transfer Agent: A person hired to maintain records with respect to the transfer (i.e., purchase, sale, etc.) of corporate securities.

Stop-or-Go Sampling (Sequential Sampling): In sampling, a method designed to avoid oversampling for attributes by allowing the auditor to stop an audit test before completing all steps, if the results have become clear.

Stratification: In sampling, the separation of the total population into several relatively homogeneous groups, with each group then treated as a separate population.

Structural Threat: The threat that an audit organization's placement within a government entity, in combination with the structure of the government entity being audited, will affect the audit organization's ability to perform work and report results objectively.

Submission (of Financial Statements): Presentation of financial statements prepared by the accountant to a client or third party.

Subsequent Events: Events or transactions that occur after the balance sheet date, but before the financial statements are issued.

Subsequent Events Review: Procedures the auditor is required to perform for the period after the balance sheet date up to the date of the auditor's report.

Subsequent Period: The period between the date of the financial statements and the date of the auditor's report.

Substantive Approach: An audit approach in which only substantive procedures will be performed, either because controls are nonexistent or because it would be inefficient to test controls.

Substantive Procedures: Tests of details of transactions and balances and analytical review procedures designed to substantiate the account balances shown in the financial statements.

Sufficient (Sufficiency of Audit Evidence): An amount and type of audit evidence that is considered adequate to support an opinion on the financial statements or on a component thereof.

Supplementary Information: Information outside the basic financial statements that is nevertheless required because it is considered an essential part of the financial reporting for that specific entity.

Systematic Selection: In sampling, a method of sample selection whereby every nth item in the population is chosen as part of the sample.

Test Count: An auditor's tally of a specific inventory item, which is later compared with the physical inventory report as a means of testing that report.

Test Data (Test Deck): A computer assisted audit technique in which the auditor uses the client's application program to process, off-line, a set of test data for which the proper results are already known.

Tests of Controls: Audit tests used to obtain evidence about the operating effectiveness of a control by determining how, by whom, and with what level of consistency controls have been applied. Tests of controls include inquiry, inspection, observation, and reperformance, and they are performed when the auditor's risk assessment is based on the assumption that controls are operating effectively.

Tests of Details: Substantive audit procedures that are applied to transaction classes, account balances, and disclosure items in order to substantiate the amounts and disclosures reflected in the financial statements.

Those Charged With Governance: Those who bear responsibility to oversee the obligations and strategic direction of an entity.

Tickmark: A symbol indicating that a specific audit procedure has been performed.

Tolerable Deviation Rate: In sampling, the maximum rate of deviation from a prescribed procedure that the auditor will tolerate without modifying planned reliance on internal control.

Tolerable Misstatement: In sampling, the maximum monetary misstatement in an account balance or class of transactions that may exist without causing the financial statements to be materially misstated. Tolerable misstatement is the application of performance materiality to a particular sampling procedure.

Top-Down Approach: Approach used when selecting controls to test in an integrated audit in which the auditor evaluates overall risks at the financial statement level, considers controls at the entity level, and then focuses on accounts, disclosures, and assertions for which there is a reasonable possibility of material misstatement.

Tracing: Directional testing that starts with source documents and traces forward to provide assurance that an event is being given proper recognition in the financial statements (i.e., testing completeness). Note that the term "tracing" is sometimes used generically to mean comparing one item to another, without indication of direction.

Transaction Tagging: A technique used by the auditor to electronically mark (or "tag") specific transactions and follow them through the client's system.

Transactions and Events: One of three categories of financial statement assertions, relating primarily to the recording of items affecting the financial statements.

Treasury Stock: Stock issued by a company that is subsequently reacquired from shareholders, so that it is no longer considered "outstanding."

Type 1 Report: A report on the design and implementation of a service organization's controls. It does not provide assurance on the operating effectiveness of controls.

Type 2 Report: A report on the design, implementation, and operating effectiveness of a service organization's controls.

Uncertainty: A matter for which conclusive evidential matter concerning its outcome is not currently available and will not be available until sometime in the future.

Underlying Accounting Data: The books and records of a company.

Understanding of Internal Control: Knowledge of the design of relevant controls and whether they have been implemented. The auditor's understanding of internal control is used to assess the risk of material misstatement and to design further audit procedures.

Underwriter: A company that buys an issue of shares from a corporation and arranges for their resale to the public.

Undue Influence Threat: The threat that external influences or pressures will affect an auditor's ability to make independent and objective judgments.

Unmodified Opinion: An auditor's report for a nonissuer stating that the financial statements are presented fairly in all material respects in accordance with the applicable financial reporting framework.

Unqualified Opinion: An auditor's report for an issuer stating that the financial statements are presented fairly in all material respects in accordance with the applicable financial reporting framework.

Updated Report: A report on previously issued financial statements that takes into consideration information that the accountant has become aware of during the current engagement, and includes any necessary revisions to the original report.

Upper (Maximum) Deviation Rate: In sampling, the sum of the sample deviation rate and the allowance for sampling risk.

User Auditor: The auditor of a company that makes use of an outside service organization.

Valuation and Allocation: A financial statement assertion in the "account balances" category indicating that assets, liabilities, and equity interests are included in the financial statements at appropriate amounts and any resulting valuation or allocation adjustments are appropriately recorded.

Variables Sampling: A statistical sampling method used to estimate the numerical measurement of a population, such as a dollar value (e.g., accounts receivable balance).

Vendor Invoice: A bill for goods or services purchased.

Voucher Packets: A group of matched documents related to a particular purchase (i.e., a requisition, purchase order, receiving report, and vendor invoice).

Vouching: Directional testing in which the auditor examines support for what has been recorded, going from the financial statements back to supporting documentation (i.e., testing existence). Note that the term "vouching" is sometimes used generically to mean comparing one item to another, without indication of direction.

Walk-Throughs: The process of tracing transactions relevant to financial reporting through the accounting system from inception through recording in the general ledger and presentation in the financial statements.

Working Papers (Audit Documentation): The principal record of procedures performed, evidence obtained, and conclusions reached; also called "workpapers" or "audit documentation."

Yellow Book: A publication of the U.S. Government Accountability Office (GAO), entitled "Government Auditing Standards," which represents the source of GAGAS.

NOTES

Index

AUD

A

B

C

D

E

F

G

I

J

K

L

M

S

NOTES